FOUR COLOR FEAR

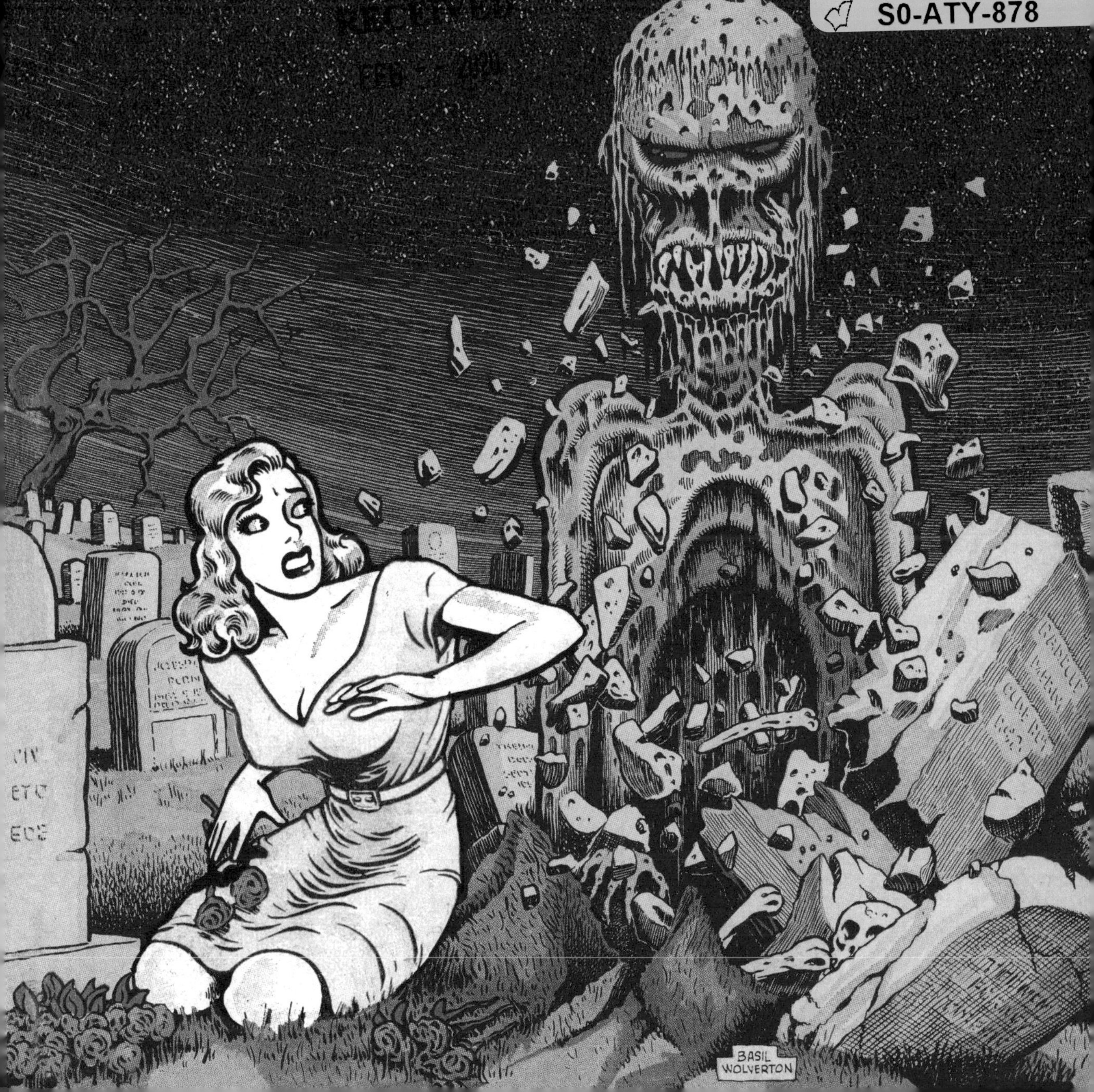
BASIL
WOLVERTON

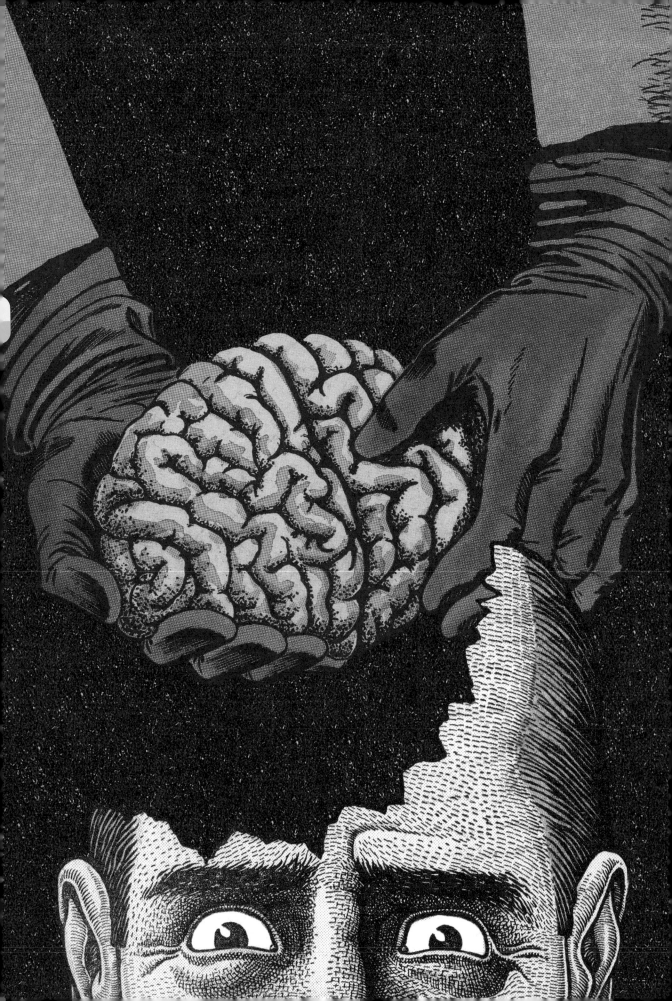

FOUR COLOR FEAR

FORGOTTEN HORROR COMICS OF THE 1950S

Edited and Designed by Greg Sadowski

Introduction by John Benson

Fantagraphics Books

SEATTLE, WASHINGTON

FANTAGRAPHICS BOOKS
7563 Lake City Way NE
Seattle, WA 98115

Publisher: Gary Groth
Associate Publisher: Eric Reynolds
Cover Design: Tony Ong
Editorial Consultant: John Benson
Editor/Design and Production: Greg Sadowski

Thanks: Jim Amash, Michael Anderson, Jill Armus, Paul Baresh, John Benson, Sean Burns, Craig Carlson, Mike Carroll, Sumner Crane, Jay Disbrow, Julia Gorton, Ron Goulart, Rudolph Grey, Todd Hignite, Jef Hinds, John Hitchcock, Erika Olsson, David Pardee, John Petty, Bud Plant, Seth Powell, Ken Quattro, Bill Schelly, Bill Spicer, the late Bhob Stewart, Paul Tomlinson, Roy Thomas, the late Kim Thompson, Jim Vadeboncoeur Jr., Kristy Valenti, Dick Voll, Hames Ware, Monte Wolverton, and Zak Woodruff.

The photos on page 298 originally appeared in *Alter Ego* no. 89, Oct. 2009.

Typeset in Robert Slimbach's Brioso Pro and Paul Renner's Futura

Third Fantagraphics Books edition: January 2017
ISBN 978-1-60699-343-9
Printed in China

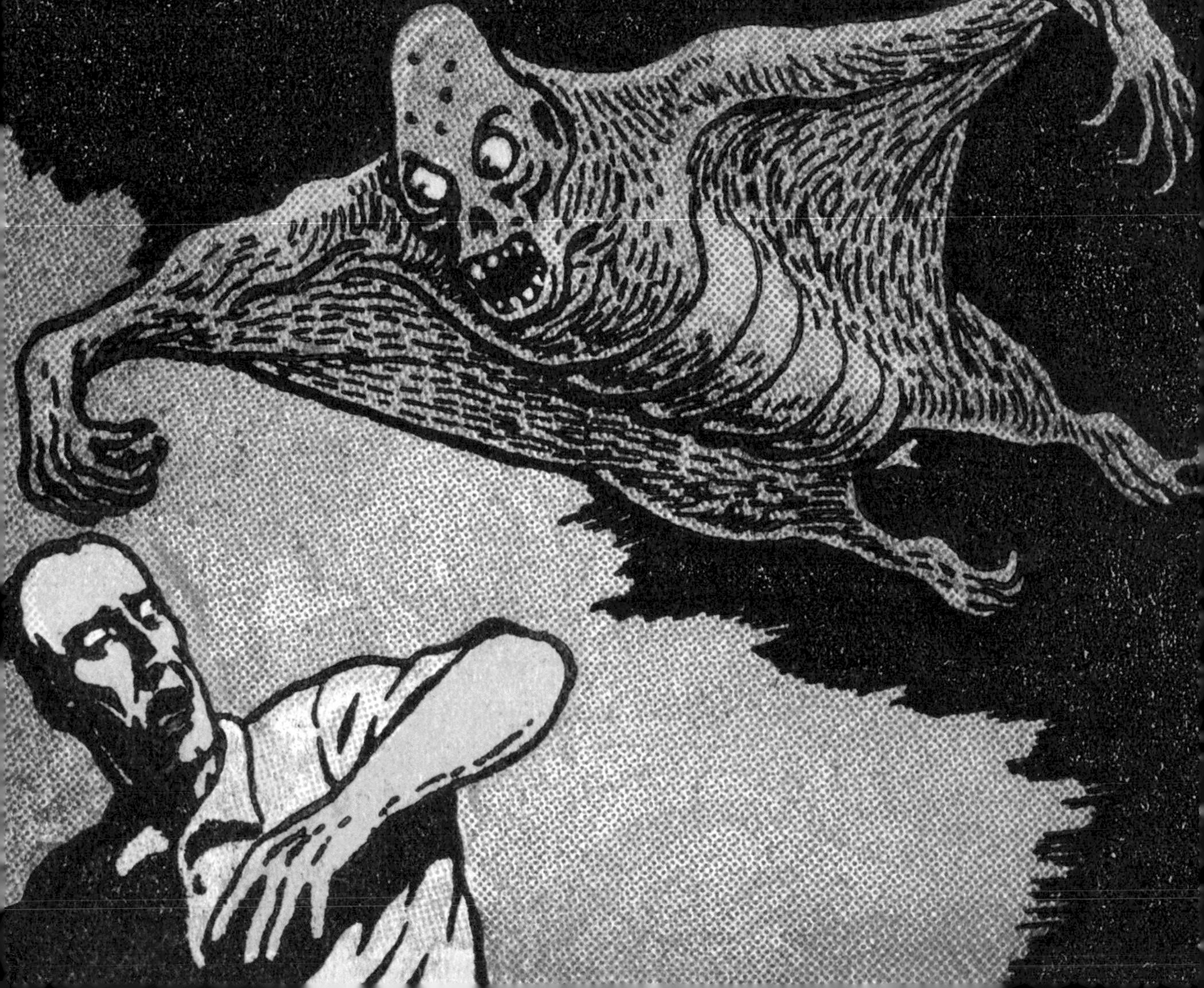

*Attribution not certain

Introduction

THOSE WONDERFUL, TERRIBLE horror comics of the 1950s are still so embedded in our popular culture that it's hard to realize that those who actually remember reading them when they came out are now in their late sixties or early seventies. That these old comics still seem contemporary is largely due to the Entertaining Comics (EC) titles *Tales from the Crypt, Vault of Horror* and *Haunt of Fear,* which have been made into several feature films and a popular HBO series, and have been in print continuously for over forty years in a variety of formats (they've even been adapted in text form for younger readers). Horror masters Stephen King and George Romero have readily acknowledged an indebtedness to EC comics, which alone would be enough to prove their relevance to current entertainment tastes, but many others have also been influenced, directly or indirectly.

Undeniably, EC created a whole new style of horror. Rather than relying on traditional supernatural elements, EC typically focused on events that could actually happen, such as someone being boiled in oil or hacked to pieces. Realistic situations would build to "trick" endings that might be better described as ingenious rather than truly imaginative. When there *was* a fantastic element, it was often in the form of traditional vampires and werewolves entering a modern real-world setting. A vital EC element was its three "GhouLunatics," the hosts whose sardonic and often humorous patter was integral to the horrific proceedings, but EC's most important component was publisher Bill Gaines, who co-plotted most of the stories, loved the material he published, and encouraged his artists to do their best. Gaines brought a rare consistency to EC, though that consistency came at the expense of an increasingly narrow range as the series progressed.

Yet the EC titles represented a mere seven per cent of the total 1950s horror comics output. What about the rest? Is it really possible that they were all so inconsequential that none merit a second look, even though they held 93 per cent of the genre? Truth to tell, many *were* pretty bad. About thirty companies published horror comics, and some were tiny, sometimes one-man outfits that cared little for content. Typical of these was Comic Media, which promised on a cover blurb "SHRUNKEN SKULLS, DECAPITATIONS, CEMETERIES, MURDERS" and featured a rising sales chart as its logo.

But larger companies like Avon, Fawcett, Harvey, Quality, St. John and Standard also published horror comics, often exhibiting high standards and using excellent artists and writers, with a wide range of pictorial and narrative styles. None of the stories in this volume (with one intentional exception) would have been likely to appear in an EC comic, though several of the artists also worked for EC. Here you'll find a panorama of horror themes, not only traditional ones (animated skeletons, rotting flesh, vampires, voodoo, pacts with the devil, old curiosity shops) but a surprising number of disturbing original concepts. In addition to being a selection of the best, this book strives to present many kinds of stories, from the droll put-on of "I, Vampire," the sinister whimsy of "Here Today...," the nightmare intensity of "Valley of Horror," the off-the-wall strangeness of "Nightmare World" and "Servants of the Tomb," to the unsettling think-piece "Experiment in Terror."

Comics writers in the 1950s toiled anonymously for the most part, one factor that has led collectors and enthusiasts to concentrate on the art to the exclusion of the writing. But comics are a narrative medium – they tell stories! The original buyers of these comics didn't just look at the pictures, they read them avidly. So this book isn't intended as merely a collection of horrific images or a portfolio of art by great comics artists, though it should well satisfy those criteria. These stories are also entertaining as *stories.* In the best of these, the art and the narrative complement each other in subtle and sophisticated ways.

Rather than being grouped by artist, publisher, subject matter or chronologically, these stories have been arranged "aesthetically" to provide maximum variety and change of pace when the book is read straight through. So, relax, curl up in a cozy chair, set aside a block of time, and imagine yourself as a kid in the 1950s, reading these stories slowly to savor every chilling moment.

John Benson

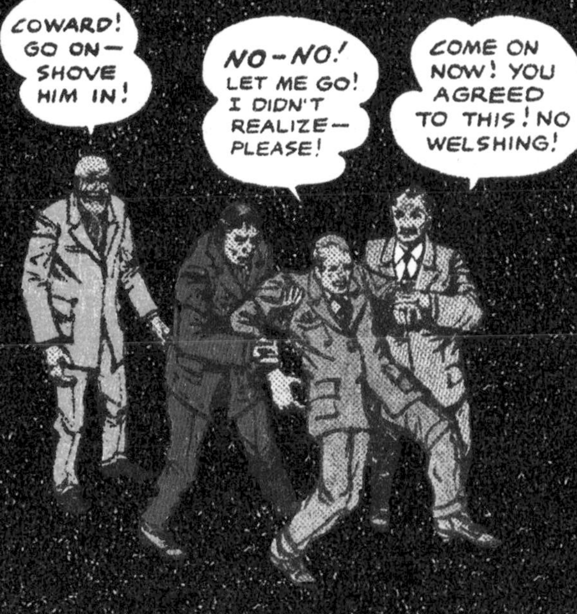
COWARD! GO ON— SHOVE HIM IN!
NO-NO! LET ME GO! I DIDN'T REALIZE— PLEASE!
COME ON NOW! YOU AGREED TO THIS! NO WELSHING!

The BEST in Supernatural THRILLS and CHILLS!
STRANGE FANTASY
HAUNTED THRILLS
THE MAGAZINES THAT ARE READ BY MILLIONS!
VOODOO
FANTASTIC FEARS
ON SALE EVERYWHERE!

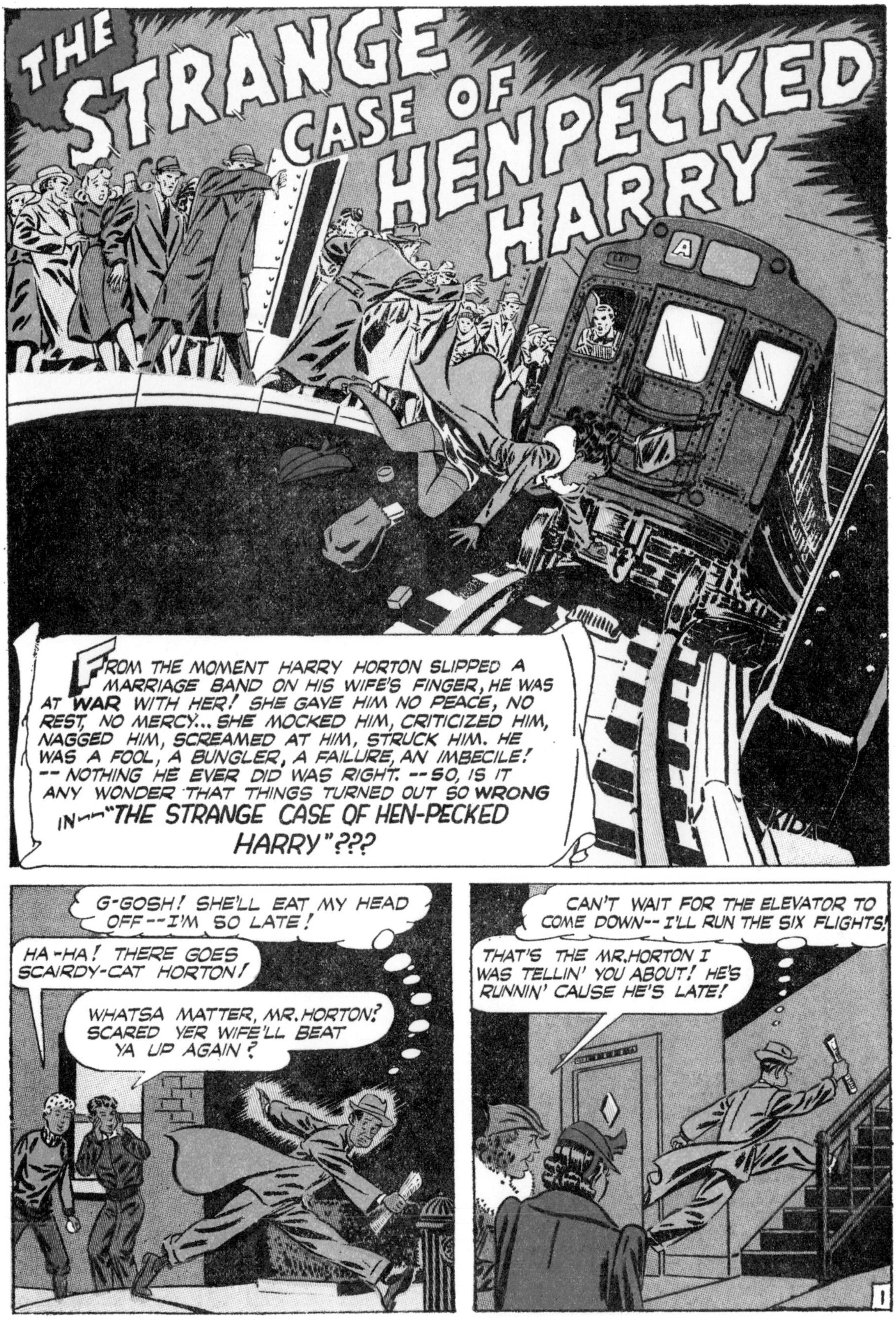
THE STRANGE CASE OF HENPECKED HARRY
FROM THE MOMENT HARRY HORTON SLIPPED A MARRIAGE BAND ON HIS WIFE'S FINGER, HE WAS AT WAR WITH HER! SHE GAVE HIM NO PEACE, NO REST, NO MERCY... SHE MOCKED HIM, CRITICIZED HIM, NAGGED HIM, SCREAMED AT HIM, STRUCK HIM. HE WAS A FOOL, A BUNGLER, A FAILURE, AN IMBECILE! -- NOTHING HE EVER DID WAS RIGHT. --SO, IS IT ANY WONDER THAT THINGS TURNED OUT SO WRONG IN--"THE STRANGE CASE OF HEN-PECKED HARRY"???
KIDA
G-GOSH! SHE'LL EAT MY HEAD OFF--I'M SO LATE!
HA-HA! THERE GOES SCAIRDY-CAT HORTON!
WHATSA MATTER, MR. HORTON? SCARED YER WIFE'LL BEAT YA UP AGAIN?
CAN'T WAIT FOR THE ELEVATOR TO COME DOWN-- I'LL RUN THE SIX FLIGHTS!
THAT'S THE MR. HORTON I WAS TELLIN' YOU ABOUT! HE'S RUNNIN' CAUSE HE'S LATE!
1

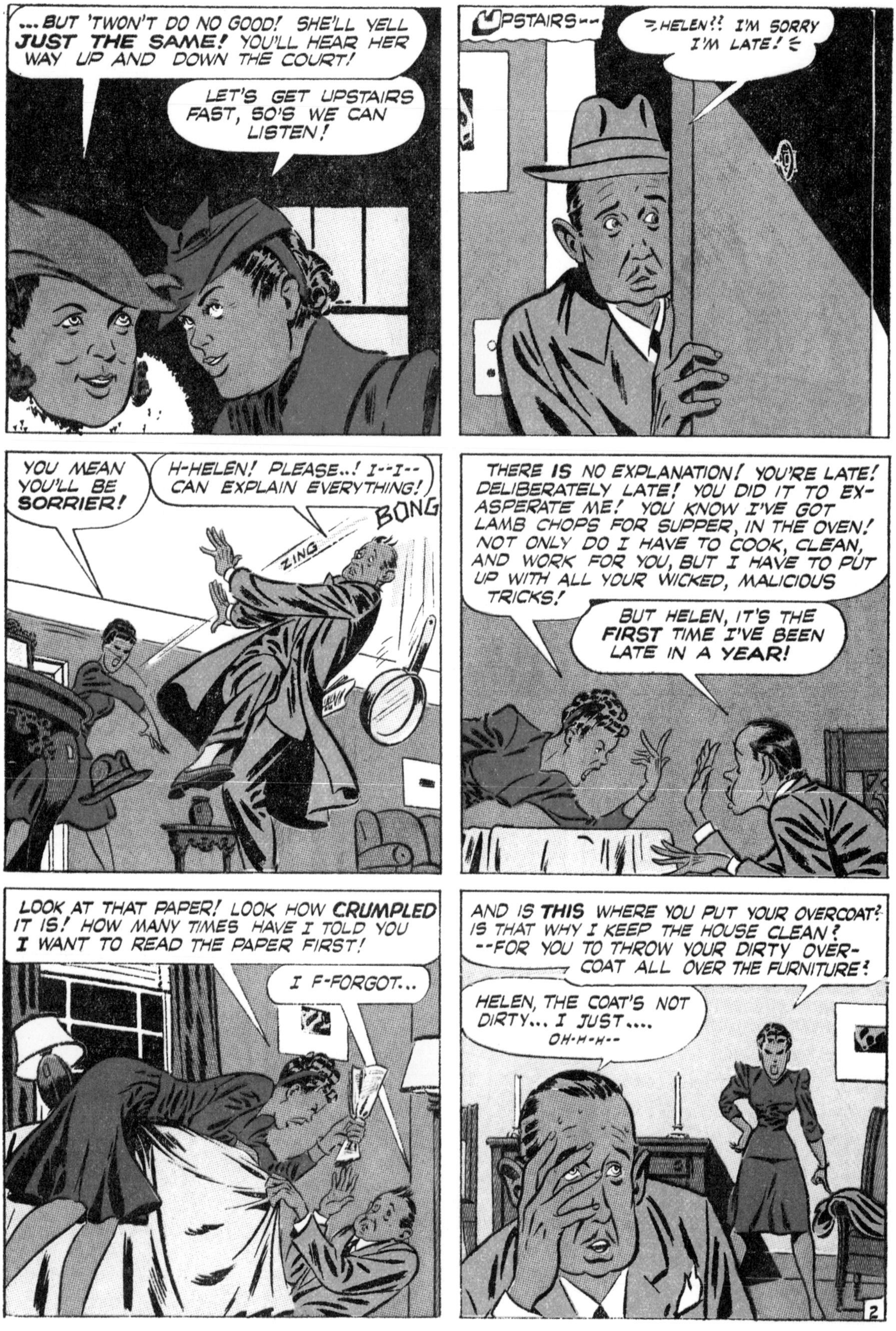
...BUT 'TWON'T DO NO GOOD! SHE'LL YELL JUST THE SAME! YOU'LL HEAR HER WAY UP AND DOWN THE COURT!
LET'S GET UPSTAIRS FAST, SO'S WE CAN LISTEN!
UPSTAIRS--
HELEN?! I'M SORRY I'M LATE!
YOU MEAN YOU'LL BE SORRIER!
H-HELEN! PLEASE..! I--I-- CAN EXPLAIN EVERYTHING!
BONG
ZING
THERE IS NO EXPLANATION! YOU'RE LATE! DELIBERATELY LATE! YOU DID IT TO EXASPERATE ME! YOU KNOW I'VE GOT LAMB CHOPS FOR SUPPER, IN THE OVEN! NOT ONLY DO I HAVE TO COOK, CLEAN, AND WORK FOR YOU, BUT I HAVE TO PUT UP WITH ALL YOUR WICKED, MALICIOUS TRICKS!
BUT HELEN, IT'S THE FIRST TIME I'VE BEEN LATE IN A YEAR!
LOOK AT THAT PAPER! LOOK HOW CRUMPLED IT IS! HOW MANY TIMES HAVE I TOLD YOU I WANT TO READ THE PAPER FIRST!
I F-FORGOT...
AND IS THIS WHERE YOU PUT YOUR OVERCOAT? IS THAT WHY I KEEP THE HOUSE CLEAN? --FOR YOU TO THROW YOUR DIRTY OVERCOAT ALL OVER THE FURNITURE?
HELEN, THE COAT'S NOT DIRTY... I JUST.... OH-H-H--
2

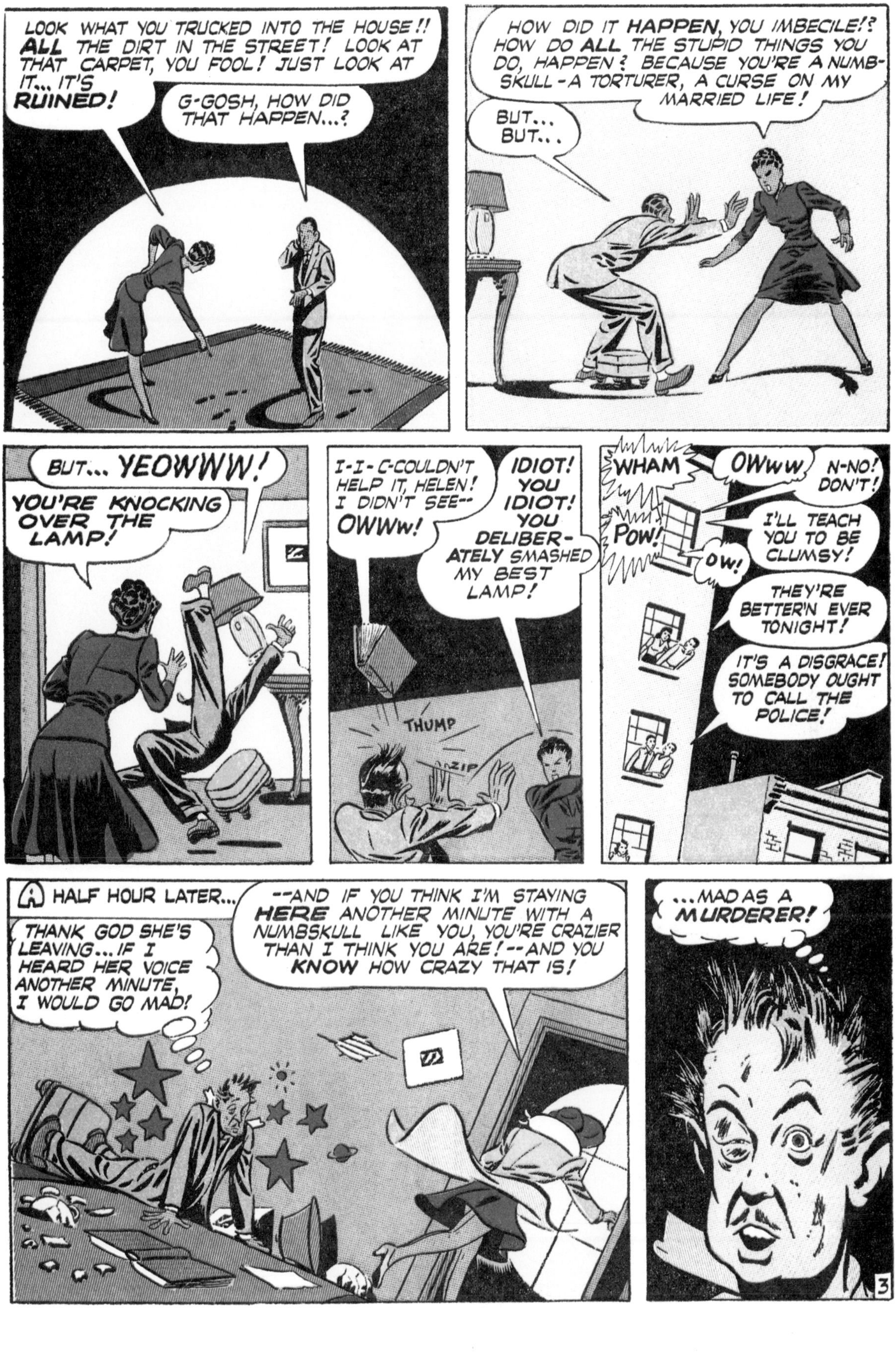

LOOK WHAT YOU TRUCKED INTO THE HOUSE!! ALL THE DIRT IN THE STREET! LOOK AT THAT CARPET, YOU FOOL! JUST LOOK AT IT... IT'S RUINED!
G-GOSH, HOW DID THAT HAPPEN...?
HOW DID IT HAPPEN, YOU IMBECILE!? HOW DO ALL THE STUPID THINGS YOU DO, HAPPEN? BECAUSE YOU'RE A NUMBSKULL - A TORTURER, A CURSE ON MY MARRIED LIFE!
BUT... BUT...
BUT... YEOWWW!
YOU'RE KNOCKING OVER THE LAMP!
I-I-C-COULDN'T HELP IT, HELEN! I DIDN'T SEE-- OWWw!
IDIOT! YOU IDIOT! YOU DELIBERATELY SMASHED MY BEST LAMP!
THUMP
ZIP
WHAM
OWww
N-NO! DON'T!
POW!
I'LL TEACH YOU TO BE CLUMSY!
OW!
THEY'RE BETTER'N EVER TONIGHT!
IT'S A DISGRACE! SOMEBODY OUGHT TO CALL THE POLICE!
A HALF HOUR LATER...
THANK GOD SHE'S LEAVING... IF I HEARD HER VOICE ANOTHER MINUTE, I WOULD GO MAD!
--AND IF YOU THINK I'M STAYING HERE ANOTHER MINUTE WITH A NUMBSKULL LIKE YOU, YOU'RE CRAZIER THAN I THINK YOU ARE! --AND YOU KNOW HOW CRAZY THAT IS!
...MAD AS A MURDERER!
3

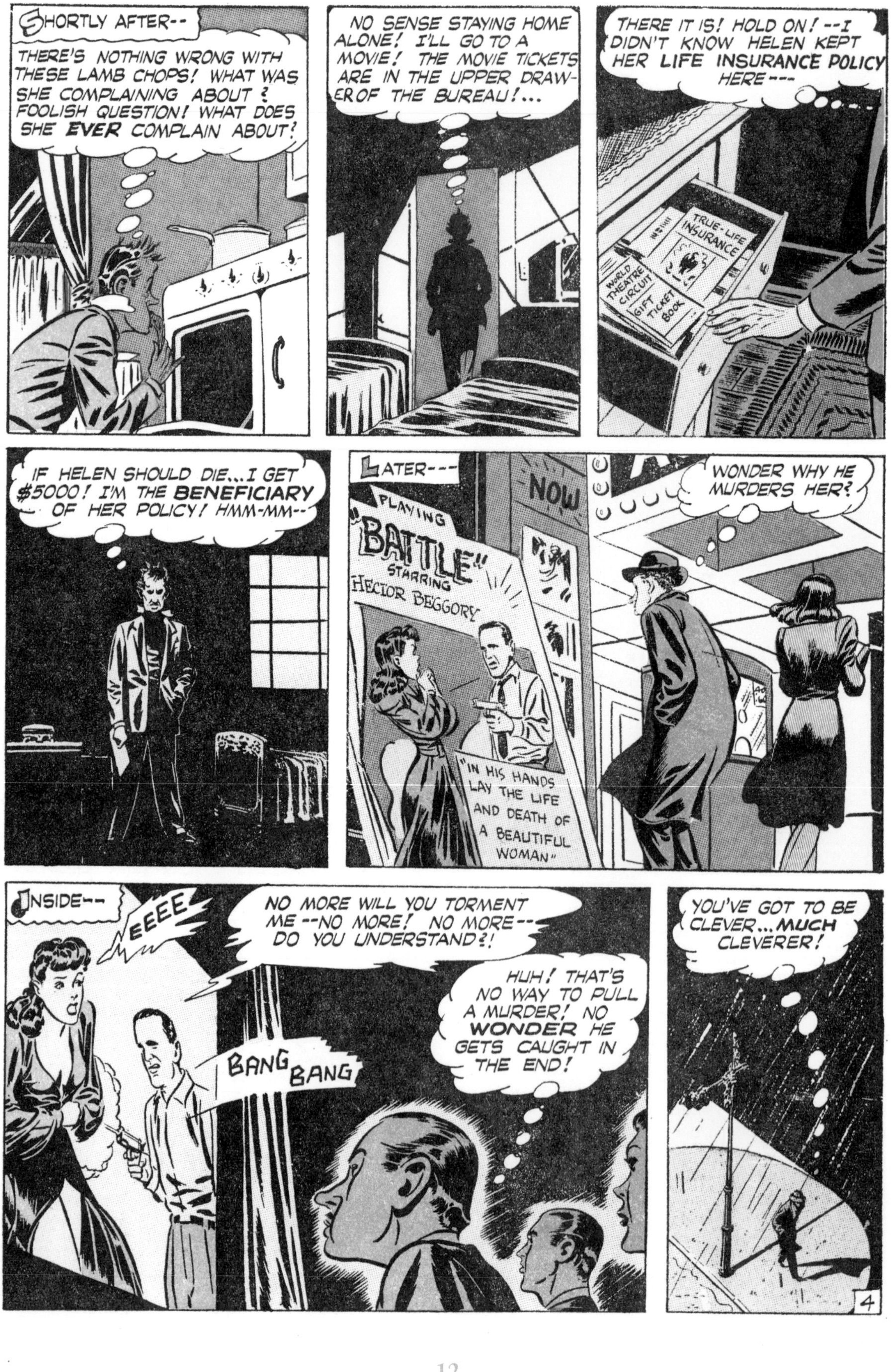
SHORTLY AFTER--
THERE'S NOTHING WRONG WITH THESE LAMB CHOPS! WHAT WAS SHE COMPLAINING ABOUT? FOOLISH QUESTION! WHAT DOES SHE EVER COMPLAIN ABOUT?
NO SENSE STAYING HOME ALONE! I'LL GO TO A MOVIE! THE MOVIE TICKETS ARE IN THE UPPER DRAWER OF THE BUREAU!...
THERE IT IS! HOLD ON! --I DIDN'T KNOW HELEN KEPT HER LIFE INSURANCE POLICY HERE---
TRUE-LIFE INSURANCE
WORLD THEATRE CIRCUIT GIFT TICKET BOOK
IF HELEN SHOULD DIE...I GET $5000! I'M THE BENEFICIARY OF HER POLICY! HMM-MM--
LATER---
NOW
PLAYING "BATTLE" STARRING HECTOR BEGGORY
"IN HIS HANDS LAY THE LIFE AND DEATH OF A BEAUTIFUL WOMAN"
WONDER WHY HE MURDERS HER?
INSIDE--
EEEE
NO MORE WILL YOU TORMENT ME --NO MORE! NO MORE-- DO YOU UNDERSTAND?!
BANG BANG
HUH! THAT'S NO WAY TO PULL A MURDER! NO WONDER HE GETS CAUGHT IN THE END!
YOU'VE GOT TO BE CLEVER...MUCH CLEVERER!
4

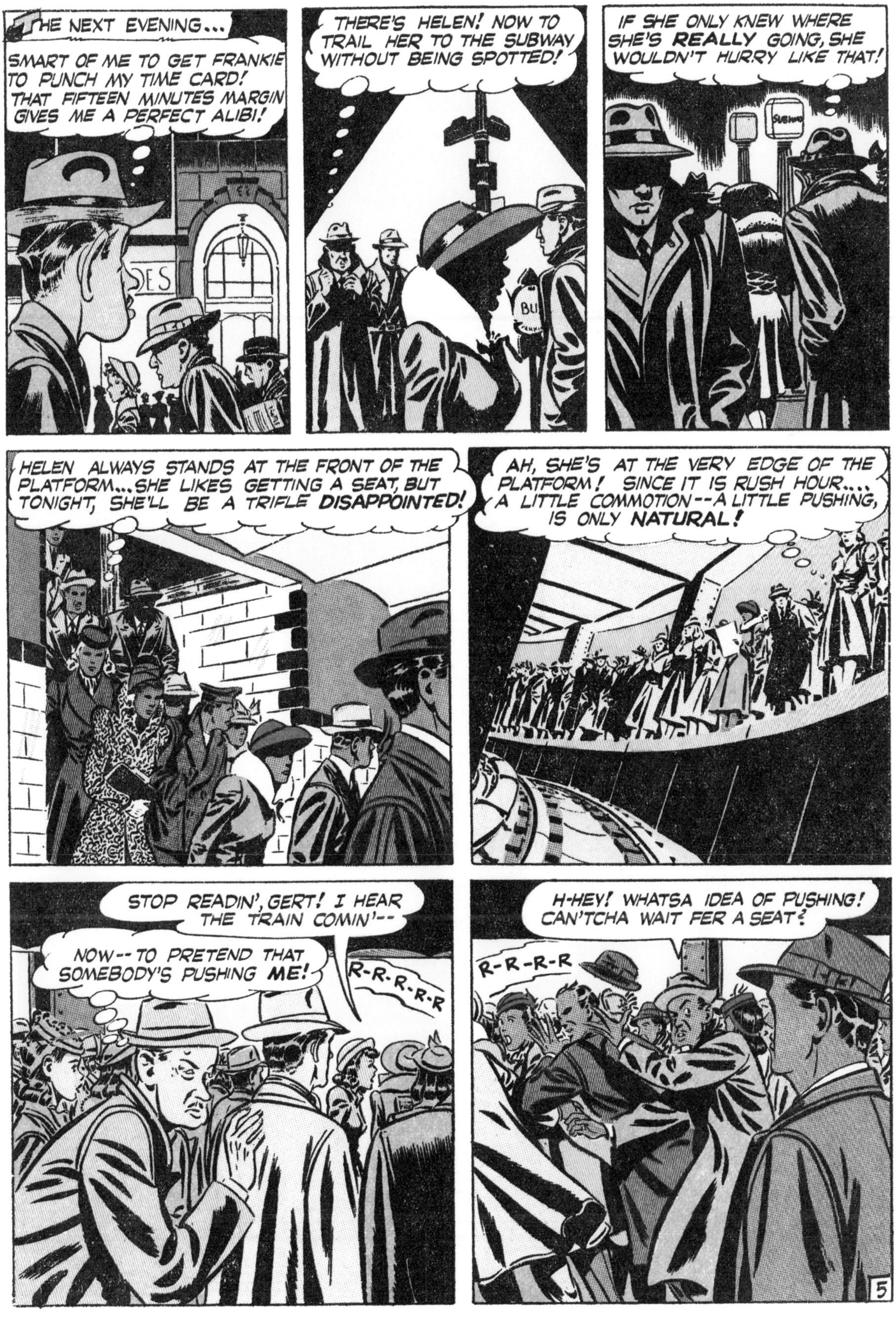
THE NEXT EVENING...
SMART OF ME TO GET FRANKIE TO PUNCH MY TIME CARD! THAT FIFTEEN MINUTES MARGIN GIVES ME A PERFECT ALIBI!
THERE'S HELEN! NOW TO TRAIL HER TO THE SUBWAY WITHOUT BEING SPOTTED!
IF SHE ONLY KNEW WHERE SHE'S REALLY GOING, SHE WOULDN'T HURRY LIKE THAT!
SUBWAY
HELEN ALWAYS STANDS AT THE FRONT OF THE PLATFORM...SHE LIKES GETTING A SEAT, BUT TONIGHT, SHE'LL BE A TRIFLE DISAPPOINTED!
AH, SHE'S AT THE VERY EDGE OF THE PLATFORM! SINCE IT IS RUSH HOUR.... A LITTLE COMMOTION--A LITTLE PUSHING, IS ONLY NATURAL!
STOP READIN', GERT! I HEAR THE TRAIN COMIN'--
NOW--TO PRETEND THAT SOMEBODY'S PUSHING ME!
R-R-R-R-R
H-HEY! WHATSA IDEA OF PUSHING! CAN'TCHA WAIT FER A SEAT?
R-R-R-R
5

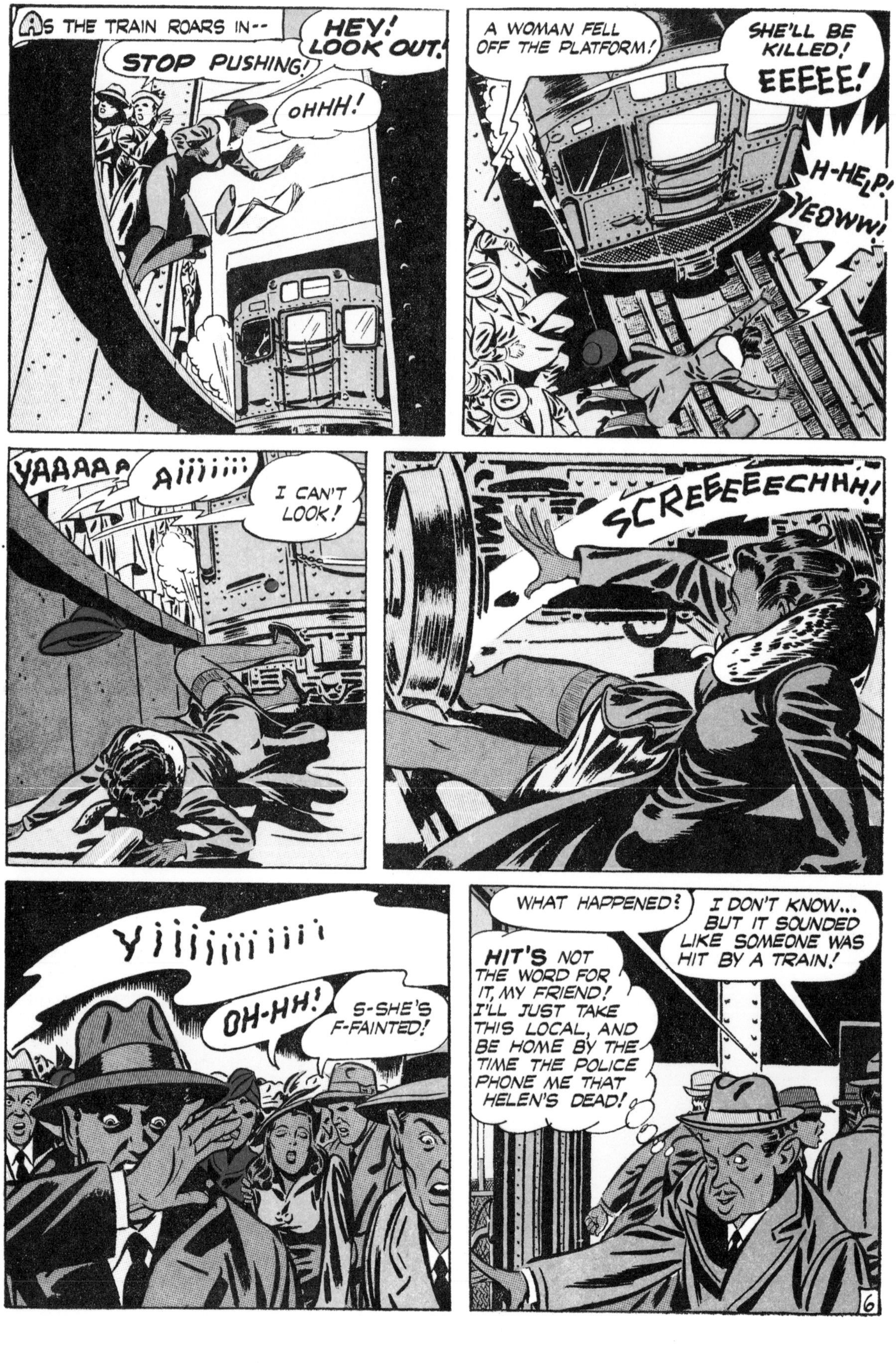
AS THE TRAIN ROARS IN--
HEY! LOOK OUT!
STOP PUSHING!
OHHH!
A WOMAN FELL OFF THE PLATFORM!
SHE'LL BE KILLED! EEEEE!
H-HELP!
YEOWW!
YAAAAA
Aiiiiiii
I CAN'T LOOK!
SCREEEEECHHH!
Yiiiiiiiiii
OH-HH!
S-SHE'S F-FAINTED!
WHAT HAPPENED?
I DON'T KNOW... BUT IT SOUNDED LIKE SOMEONE WAS HIT BY A TRAIN!
HIT'S NOT THE WORD FOR IT, MY FRIEND! I'LL JUST TAKE THIS LOCAL, AND BE HOME BY THE TIME THE POLICE PHONE ME THAT HELEN'S DEAD!
6

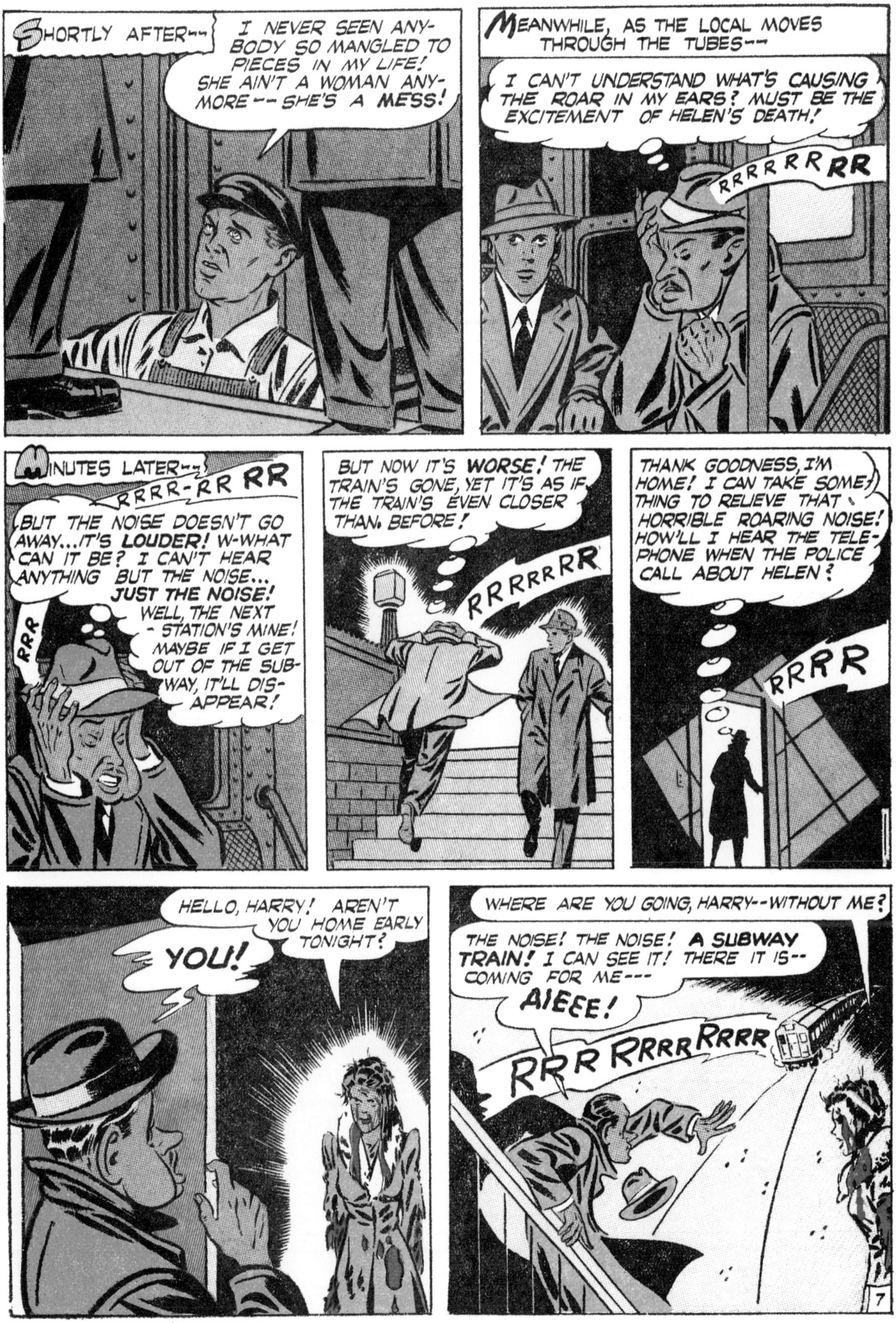
SHORTLY AFTER--
I NEVER SEEN ANYBODY SO MANGLED TO PIECES IN MY LIFE! SHE AIN'T A WOMAN ANYMORE -- SHE'S A MESS!
MEANWHILE, AS THE LOCAL MOVES THROUGH THE TUBES--
I CAN'T UNDERSTAND WHAT'S CAUSING THE ROAR IN MY EARS? MUST BE THE EXCITEMENT OF HELEN'S DEATH!
RRRRRRRR
MINUTES LATER--
RRRR-RR RR
BUT THE NOISE DOESN'T GO AWAY...IT'S LOUDER! W-WHAT CAN IT BE? I CAN'T HEAR ANYTHING BUT THE NOISE... JUST THE NOISE!
WELL, THE NEXT STATION'S MINE! MAYBE IF I GET OUT OF THE SUBWAY, IT'LL DISAPPEAR!
RRR
BUT NOW IT'S WORSE! THE TRAIN'S GONE, YET IT'S AS IF THE TRAIN'S EVEN CLOSER THAN BEFORE!
RRRRRRR
THANK GOODNESS, I'M HOME! I CAN TAKE SOMETHING TO RELIEVE THAT HORRIBLE ROARING NOISE! HOW'LL I HEAR THE TELEPHONE WHEN THE POLICE CALL ABOUT HELEN?
RRRR
HELLO, HARRY! AREN'T YOU HOME EARLY TONIGHT?
YOU!
WHERE ARE YOU GOING, HARRY--WITHOUT ME?
THE NOISE! THE NOISE! A SUBWAY TRAIN! I CAN SEE IT! THERE IT IS-- COMING FOR ME---
AIEEE!
RRR RRRR RRRR
7

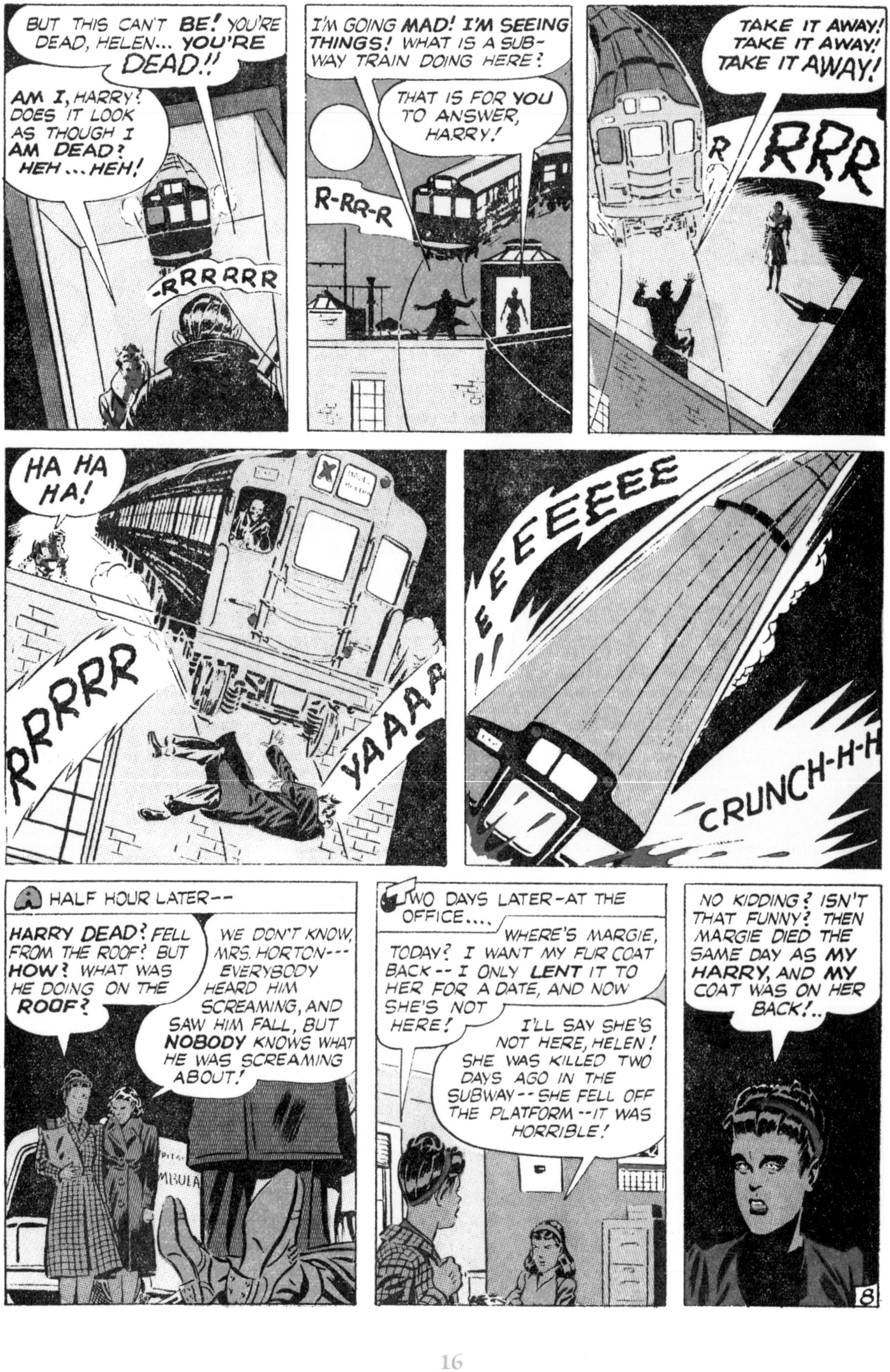
BUT THIS CAN'T BE! YOU'RE DEAD, HELEN... YOU'RE DEAD!!
AM I, HARRY? DOES IT LOOK AS THOUGH I AM DEAD? HEH...HEH!
-RRRRRR
I'M GOING MAD! I'M SEEING THINGS! WHAT IS A SUB-WAY TRAIN DOING HERE?
THAT IS FOR YOU TO ANSWER, HARRY!
R-RR-R
TAKE IT AWAY! TAKE IT AWAY! TAKE IT AWAY!
R RRR
HA HA HA!
RRRRR
YAAAA
EEEEEEEE
CRUNCH-H-H
HALF HOUR LATER--
HARRY DEAD? FELL FROM THE ROOF? BUT HOW? WHAT WAS HE DOING ON THE ROOF?
WE DON'T KNOW, MRS. HORTON--- EVERYBODY HEARD HIM SCREAMING, AND SAW HIM FALL, BUT NOBODY KNOWS WHAT HE WAS SCREAMING ABOUT!
TWO DAYS LATER-AT THE OFFICE....
WHERE'S MARGIE, TODAY? I WANT MY FUR COAT BACK-- I ONLY LENT IT TO HER FOR A DATE, AND NOW SHE'S NOT HERE!
I'LL SAY SHE'S NOT HERE, HELEN! SHE WAS KILLED TWO DAYS AGO IN THE SUBWAY-- SHE FELL OFF THE PLATFORM--IT WAS HORRIBLE!
NO KIDDING? ISN'T THAT FUNNY? THEN MARGIE DIED THE SAME DAY AS MY HARRY, AND MY COAT WAS ON HER BACK!..
8

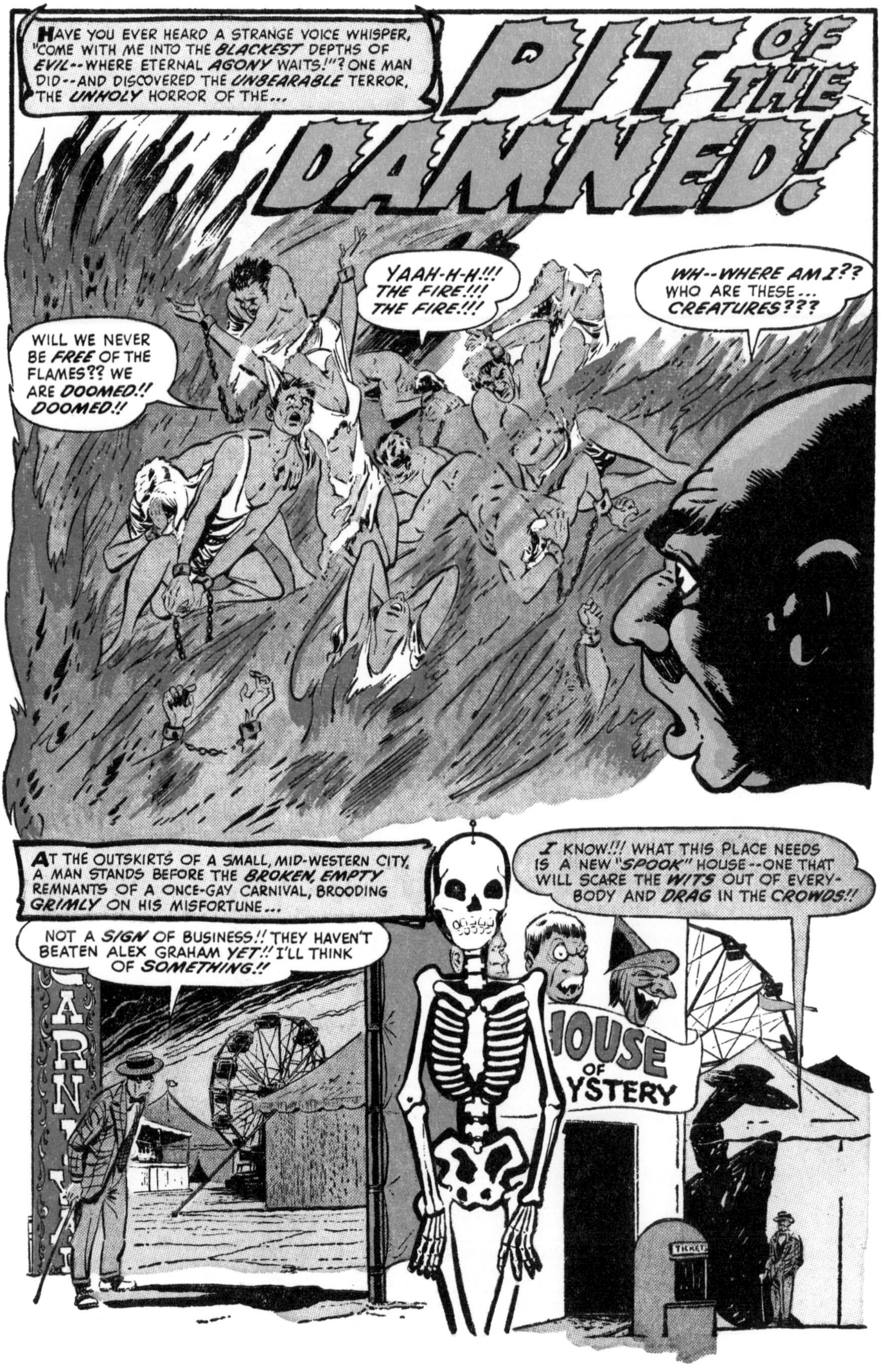
HAVE YOU EVER HEARD A STRANGE VOICE WHISPER, "COME WITH ME INTO THE BLACKEST DEPTHS OF EVIL--WHERE ETERNAL AGONY WAITS!"? ONE MAN DID--AND DISCOVERED THE UNBEARABLE TERROR, THE UNHOLY HORROR OF THE...
PIT OF THE DAMNED!
WILL WE NEVER BE FREE OF THE FLAMES?? WE ARE DOOMED!! DOOMED!!
YAAH-H-H!!! THE FIRE!!! THE FIRE!!!
WH--WHERE AM I?? WHO ARE THESE... CREATURES???
AT THE OUTSKIRTS OF A SMALL, MID-WESTERN CITY, A MAN STANDS BEFORE THE BROKEN, EMPTY REMNANTS OF A ONCE-GAY CARNIVAL, BROODING GRIMLY ON HIS MISFORTUNE...
NOT A SIGN OF BUSINESS!! THEY HAVEN'T BEATEN ALEX GRAHAM YET!! I'LL THINK OF SOMETHING!!
I KNOW!!! WHAT THIS PLACE NEEDS IS A NEW "SPOOK" HOUSE--ONE THAT WILL SCARE THE WITS OUT OF EVERY-BODY AND DRAG IN THE CROWDS!!
HOUSE OF YSTERY

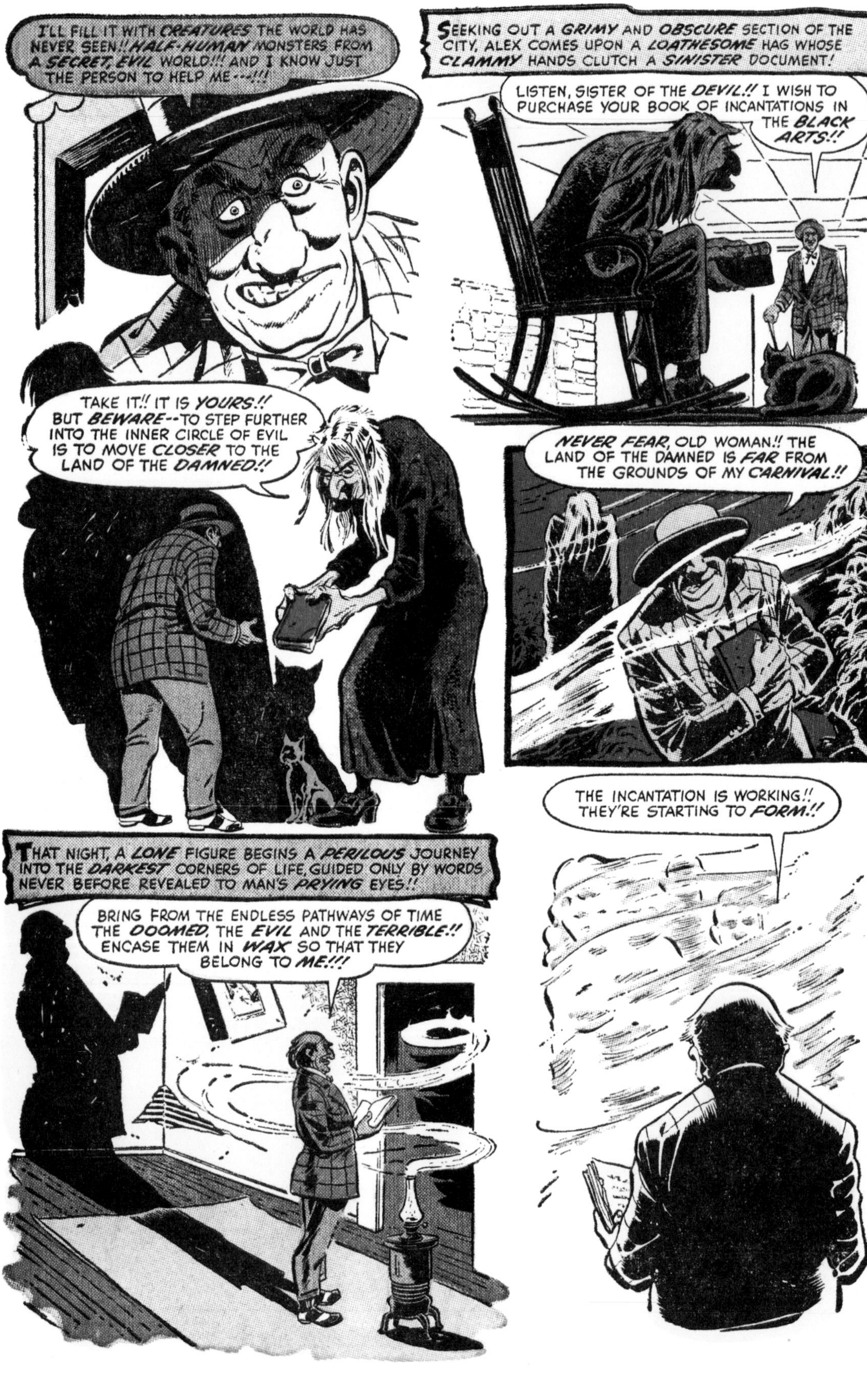
I'LL FILL IT WITH CREATURES THE WORLD HAS NEVER SEEN!! HALF-HUMAN MONSTERS FROM A SECRET, EVIL WORLD!!! AND I KNOW JUST THE PERSON TO HELP ME--!!!
SEEKING OUT A GRIMY AND OBSCURE SECTION OF THE CITY, ALEX COMES UPON A LOATHESOME HAG WHOSE CLAMMY HANDS CLUTCH A SINISTER DOCUMENT!
LISTEN, SISTER OF THE DEVIL!! I WISH TO PURCHASE YOUR BOOK OF INCANTATIONS IN THE BLACK ARTS!!
TAKE IT!! IT IS YOURS!! BUT BEWARE--TO STEP FURTHER INTO THE INNER CIRCLE OF EVIL IS TO MOVE CLOSER TO THE LAND OF THE DAMNED!!
NEVER FEAR, OLD WOMAN!! THE LAND OF THE DAMNED IS FAR FROM THE GROUNDS OF MY CARNIVAL!!
THAT NIGHT, A LONE FIGURE BEGINS A PERILOUS JOURNEY INTO THE DARKEST CORNERS OF LIFE, GUIDED ONLY BY WORDS NEVER BEFORE REVEALED TO MAN'S PRYING EYES!!
BRING FROM THE ENDLESS PATHWAYS OF TIME THE DOOMED, THE EVIL AND THE TERRIBLE!! ENCASE THEM IN WAX SO THAT THEY BELONG TO ME!!!
THE INCANTATION IS WORKING!! THEY'RE STARTING TO FORM!!

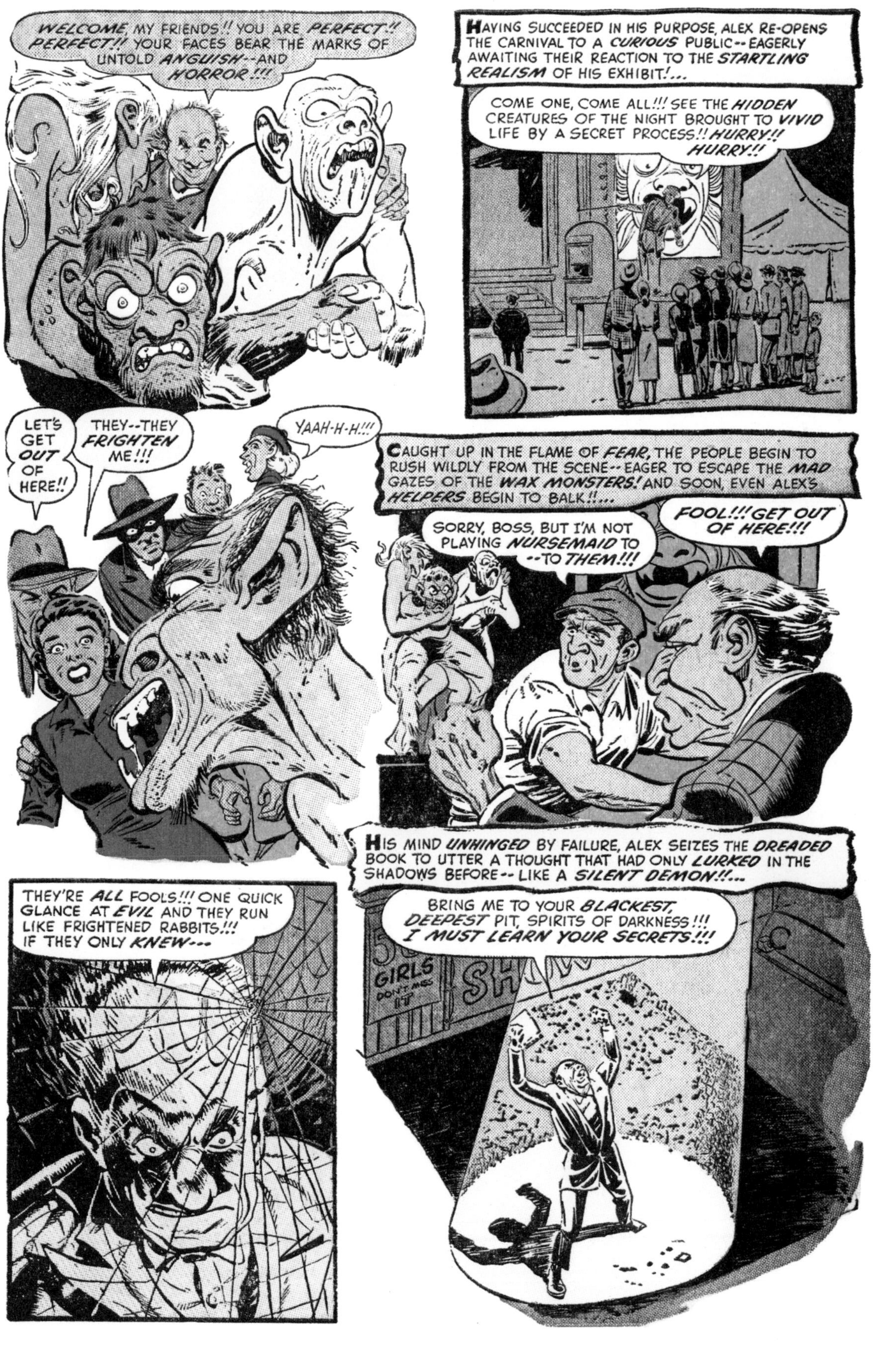

WELCOME MY FRIENDS!! YOU ARE PERFECT!! PERFECT!! YOUR FACES BEAR THE MARKS OF UNTOLD ANGUISH--AND HORROR!!!
HAVING SUCCEEDED IN HIS PURPOSE, ALEX RE-OPENS THE CARNIVAL TO A CURIOUS PUBLIC--EAGERLY AWAITING THEIR REACTION TO THE STARTLING REALISM OF HIS EXHIBIT!...
COME ONE, COME ALL!!! SEE THE HIDDEN CREATURES OF THE NIGHT BROUGHT TO VIVID LIFE BY A SECRET PROCESS!! HURRY!! HURRY!!
LET'S GET OUT OF HERE!!
THEY--THEY FRIGHTEN ME!!!
YAAH-H-H!!!
CAUGHT UP IN THE FLAME OF FEAR, THE PEOPLE BEGIN TO RUSH WILDLY FROM THE SCENE--EAGER TO ESCAPE THE MAD GAZES OF THE WAX MONSTERS! AND SOON, EVEN ALEX'S HELPERS BEGIN TO BALK!!...
SORRY, BOSS, BUT I'M NOT PLAYING NURSEMAID TO --TO THEM!!!
FOOL!!! GET OUT OF HERE!!!
HIS MIND UNHINGED BY FAILURE, ALEX SEIZES THE DREADED BOOK TO UTTER A THOUGHT THAT HAD ONLY LURKED IN THE SHADOWS BEFORE--LIKE A SILENT DEMON!!...
THEY'RE ALL FOOLS!!! ONE QUICK GLANCE AT EVIL AND THEY RUN LIKE FRIGHTENED RABBITS!!! IF THEY ONLY KNEW--
BRING ME TO YOUR BLACKEST, DEEPEST PIT, SPIRITS OF DARKNESS!!! I MUST LEARN YOUR SECRETS!!!
GIRLS
DON'T MISS IT
SHOW

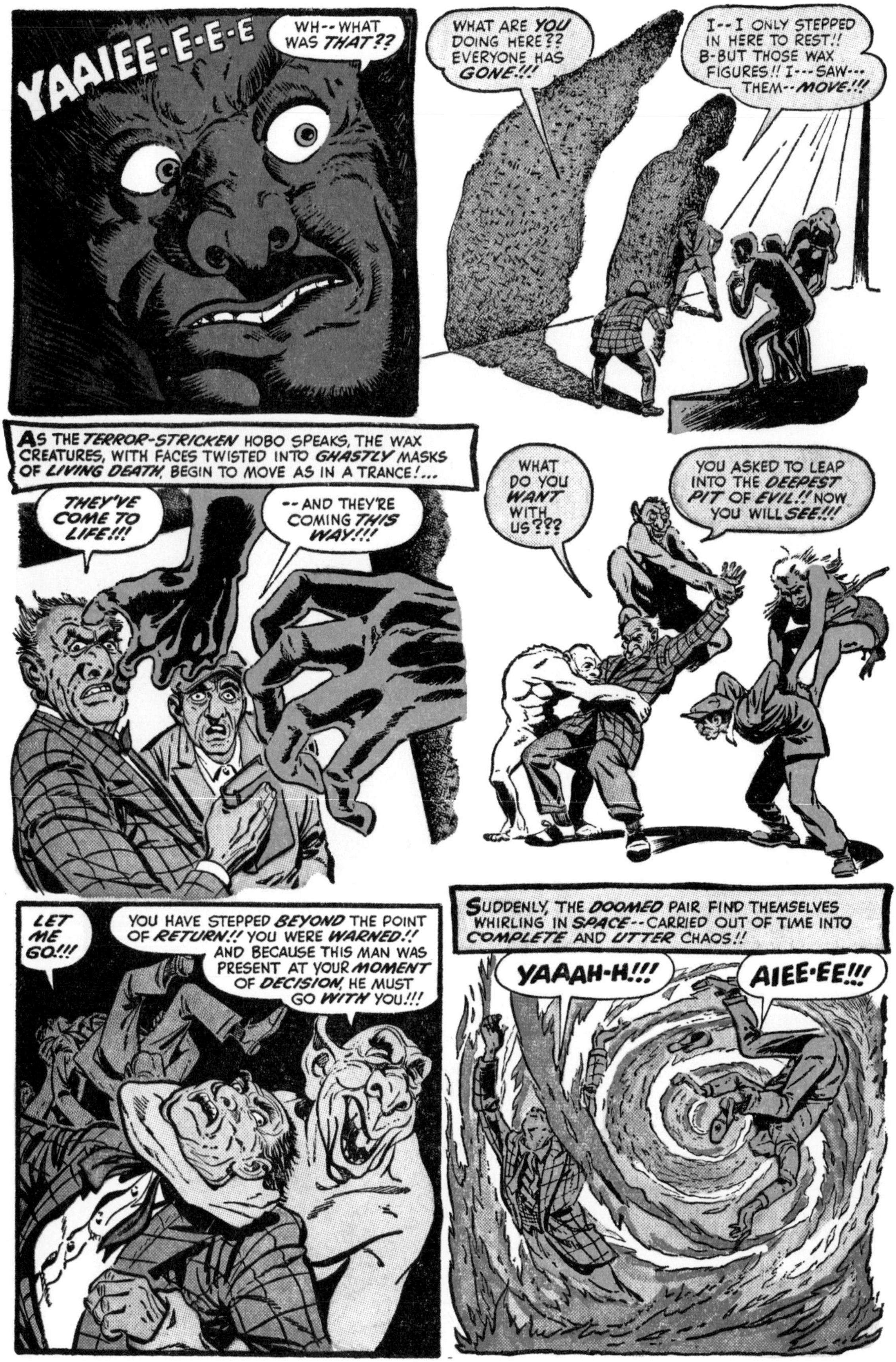
YAAIEE-E-E-E
WH--WHAT WAS THAT??
WHAT ARE YOU DOING HERE?? EVERYONE HAS GONE!!!
I--I ONLY STEPPED IN HERE TO REST!! B-BUT THOSE WAX FIGURES!! I---SAW---THEM--MOVE!!!
AS THE TERROR-STRICKEN HOBO SPEAKS, THE WAX CREATURES, WITH FACES TWISTED INTO GHASTLY MASKS OF LIVING DEATH, BEGIN TO MOVE AS IN A TRANCE!...
THEY'VE COME TO LIFE!!!
--AND THEY'RE COMING THIS WAY!!!
WHAT DO YOU WANT WITH US???
YOU ASKED TO LEAP INTO THE DEEPEST PIT OF EVIL!! NOW YOU WILL SEE!!!
LET ME GO!!!
YOU HAVE STEPPED BEYOND THE POINT OF RETURN!! YOU WERE WARNED!! AND BECAUSE THIS MAN WAS PRESENT AT YOUR MOMENT OF DECISION, HE MUST GO WITH YOU!!!
SUDDENLY, THE DOOMED PAIR FIND THEMSELVES WHIRLING IN SPACE--CARRIED OUT OF TIME INTO COMPLETE AND UTTER CHAOS!!
YAAAH-H!!!
AIEE-EE!!!

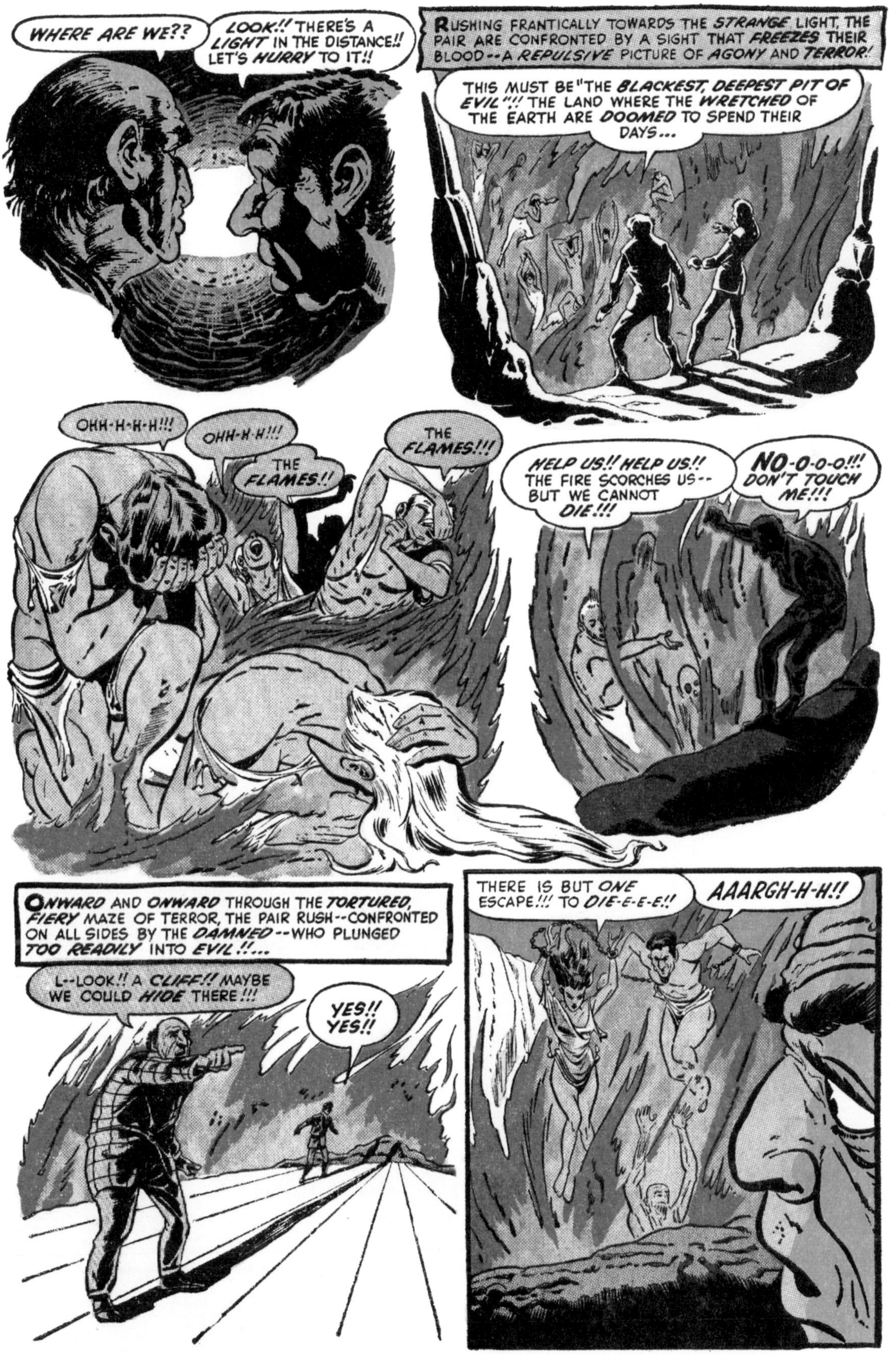
WHERE ARE WE??
LOOK!! THERE'S A LIGHT IN THE DISTANCE!! LET'S HURRY TO IT!!
RUSHING FRANTICALLY TOWARDS THE STRANGE LIGHT, THE PAIR ARE CONFRONTED BY A SIGHT THAT FREEZES THEIR BLOOD--A REPULSIVE PICTURE OF AGONY AND TERROR!
THIS MUST BE "THE BLACKEST, DEEPEST PIT OF EVIL"!! THE LAND WHERE THE WRETCHED OF THE EARTH ARE DOOMED TO SPEND THEIR DAYS...
OHH-H-H-H!!!
OHH-H-H!!!
THE FLAMES!!
THE FLAMES!!!
HELP US!! HELP US!! THE FIRE SCORCHES US--BUT WE CANNOT DIE!!!
NO-O-O-O!!! DON'T TOUCH ME!!!
ONWARD AND ONWARD THROUGH THE TORTURED, FIERY MAZE OF TERROR, THE PAIR RUSH--CONFRONTED ON ALL SIDES BY THE DAMNED--WHO PLUNGED TOO READILY INTO EVIL!!...
L--LOOK!! A CLIFF!! MAYBE WE COULD HIDE THERE!!!
YES!! YES!!
THERE IS BUT ONE ESCAPE!!! TO DIE-E-E-E!!
AAARGH-H-H!!

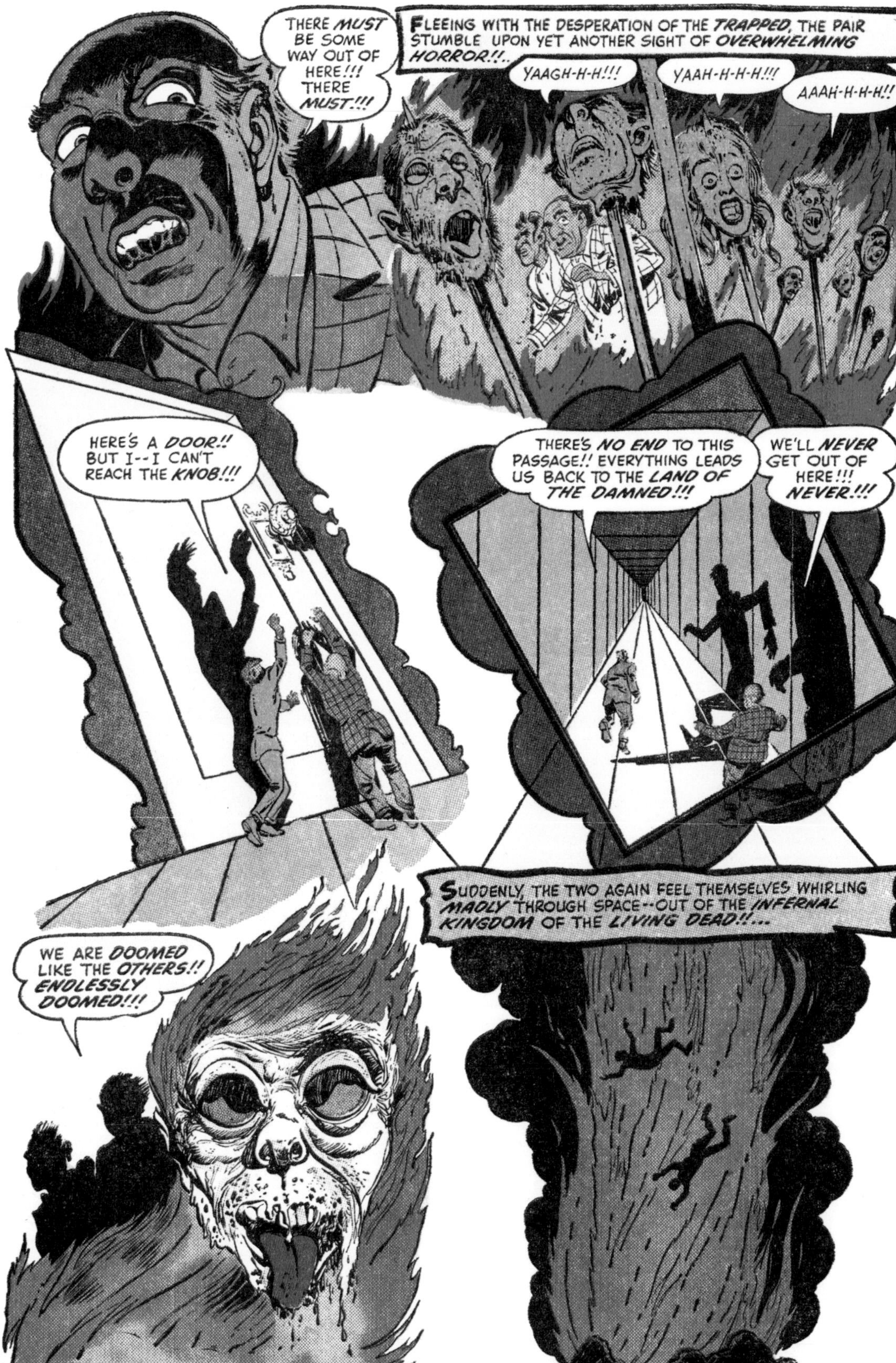
THERE MUST BE SOME WAY OUT OF HERE!!! THERE MUST!!!
FLEEING WITH THE DESPERATION OF THE TRAPPED, THE PAIR STUMBLE UPON YET ANOTHER SIGHT OF OVERWHELMING HORROR!!..
YAAGH-H-H!!!
YAAH-H-H-H!!!
AAAH-H-H-H!!
HERE'S A DOOR!! BUT I--I CAN'T REACH THE KNOB!!!
THERE'S NO END TO THIS PASSAGE!! EVERYTHING LEADS US BACK TO THE LAND OF THE DAMNED!!!
WE'LL NEVER GET OUT OF HERE!!! NEVER!!!
WE ARE DOOMED LIKE THE OTHERS!! ENDLESSLY DOOMED!!!
SUDDENLY, THE TWO AGAIN FEEL THEMSELVES WHIRLING MADLY THROUGH SPACE--OUT OF THE INFERNAL KINGDOM OF THE LIVING DEAD!!...

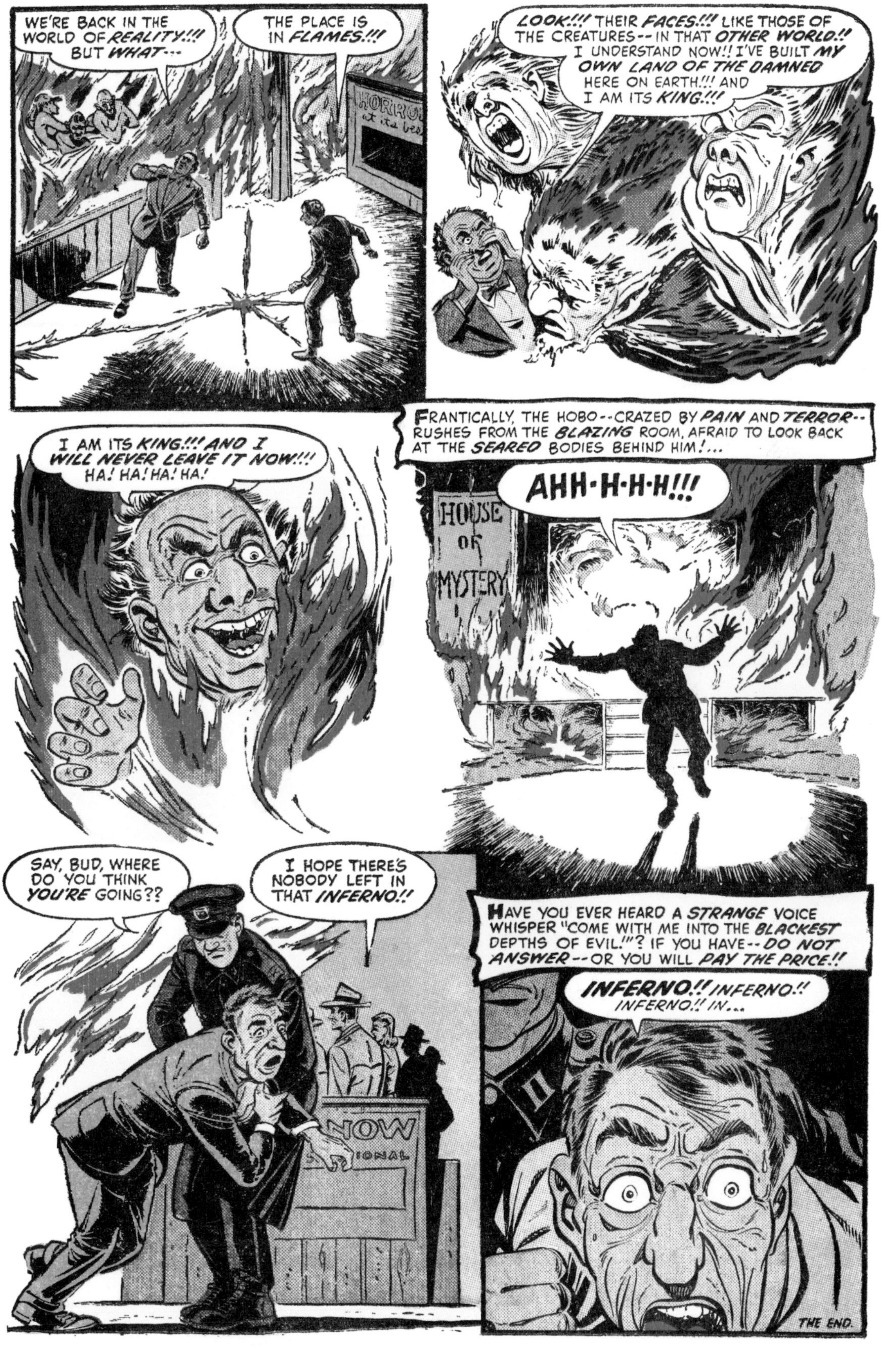
WE'RE BACK IN THE WORLD OF REALITY!!! BUT WHAT---
THE PLACE IS IN FLAMES!!!
HORROR at its best
LOOK!!! THEIR FACES!!! LIKE THOSE OF THE CREATURES--IN THAT OTHER WORLD!! I UNDERSTAND NOW!! I'VE BUILT MY OWN LAND OF THE DAMNED HERE ON EARTH!!! AND I AM ITS KING!!!
I AM ITS KING!!! AND I WILL NEVER LEAVE IT NOW!!! HA! HA! HA! HA!
FRANTICALLY, THE HOBO--CRAZED BY PAIN AND TERROR--RUSHES FROM THE BLAZING ROOM, AFRAID TO LOOK BACK AT THE SEARED BODIES BEHIND HIM!...
AHH-H-H-H!!!
HOUSE OF MYSTERY
SAY, BUD, WHERE DO YOU THINK YOU'RE GOING??
I HOPE THERE'S NOBODY LEFT IN THAT INFERNO!!
NOW
HAVE YOU EVER HEARD A STRANGE VOICE WHISPER "COME WITH ME INTO THE BLACKEST DEPTHS OF EVIL!"? IF YOU HAVE--DO NOT ANSWER--OR YOU WILL PAY THE PRICE!!
INFERNO!! INFERNO!! INFERNO!! IN...
THE END.

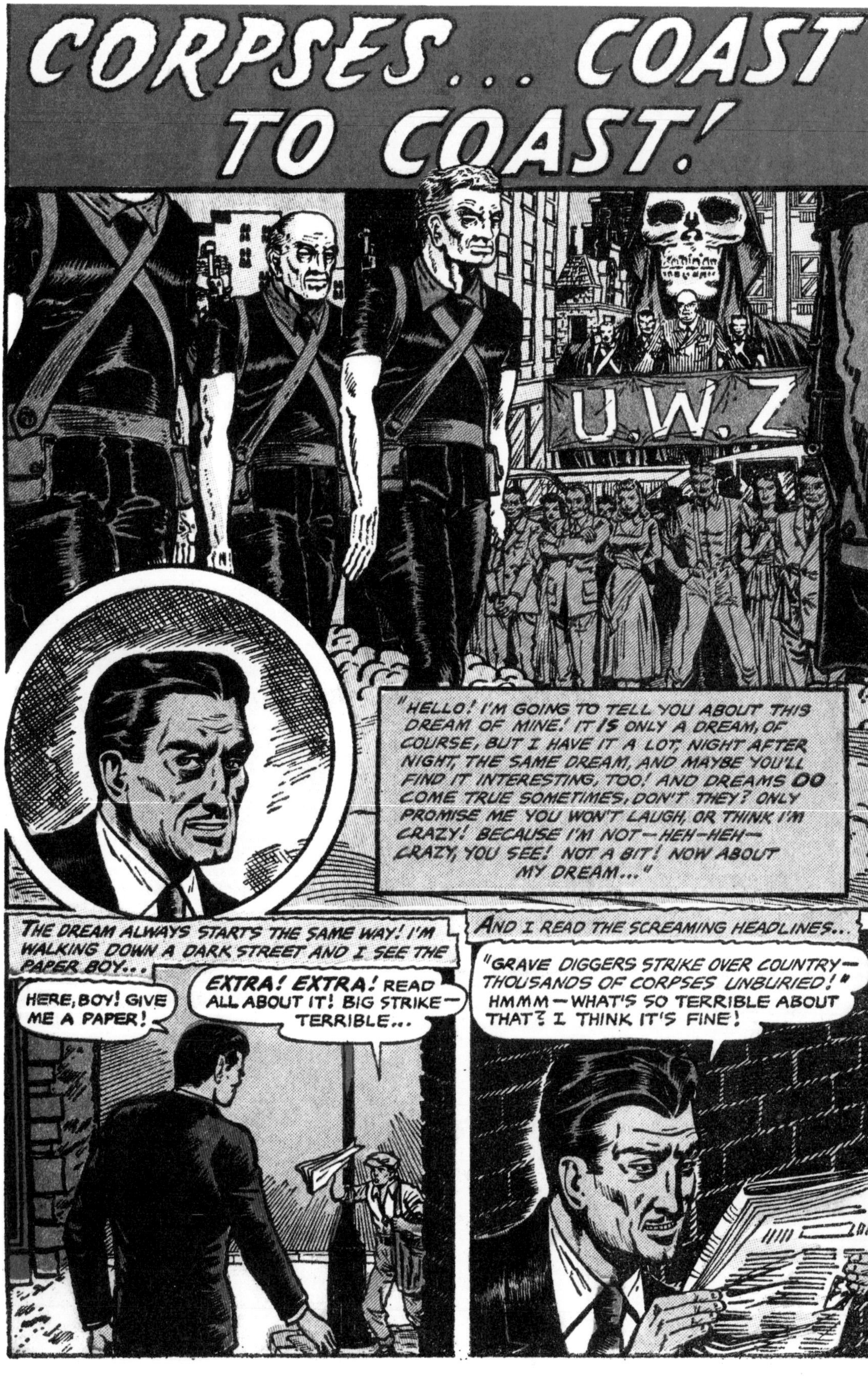
CORPSES... COAST TO COAST!
U.W.Z
"HELLO! I'M GOING TO TELL YOU ABOUT THIS DREAM OF MINE! IT IS ONLY A DREAM, OF COURSE, BUT I HAVE IT A LOT, NIGHT AFTER NIGHT, THE SAME DREAM, AND MAYBE YOU'LL FIND IT INTERESTING, TOO! AND DREAMS DO COME TRUE SOMETIMES, DON'T THEY? ONLY PROMISE ME YOU WON'T LAUGH, OR THINK I'M CRAZY! BECAUSE I'M NOT—HEH-HEH—CRAZY, YOU SEE! NOT A BIT! NOW ABOUT MY DREAM..."
THE DREAM ALWAYS STARTS THE SAME WAY! I'M WALKING DOWN A DARK STREET AND I SEE THE PAPER BOY...
HERE, BOY! GIVE ME A PAPER!
EXTRA! EXTRA! READ ALL ABOUT IT! BIG STRIKE—TERRIBLE...
AND I READ THE SCREAMING HEADLINES...
"GRAVE DIGGERS STRIKE OVER COUNTRY—THOUSANDS OF CORPSES UNBURIED!" HMMM—WHAT'S SO TERRIBLE ABOUT THAT? I THINK IT'S FINE!

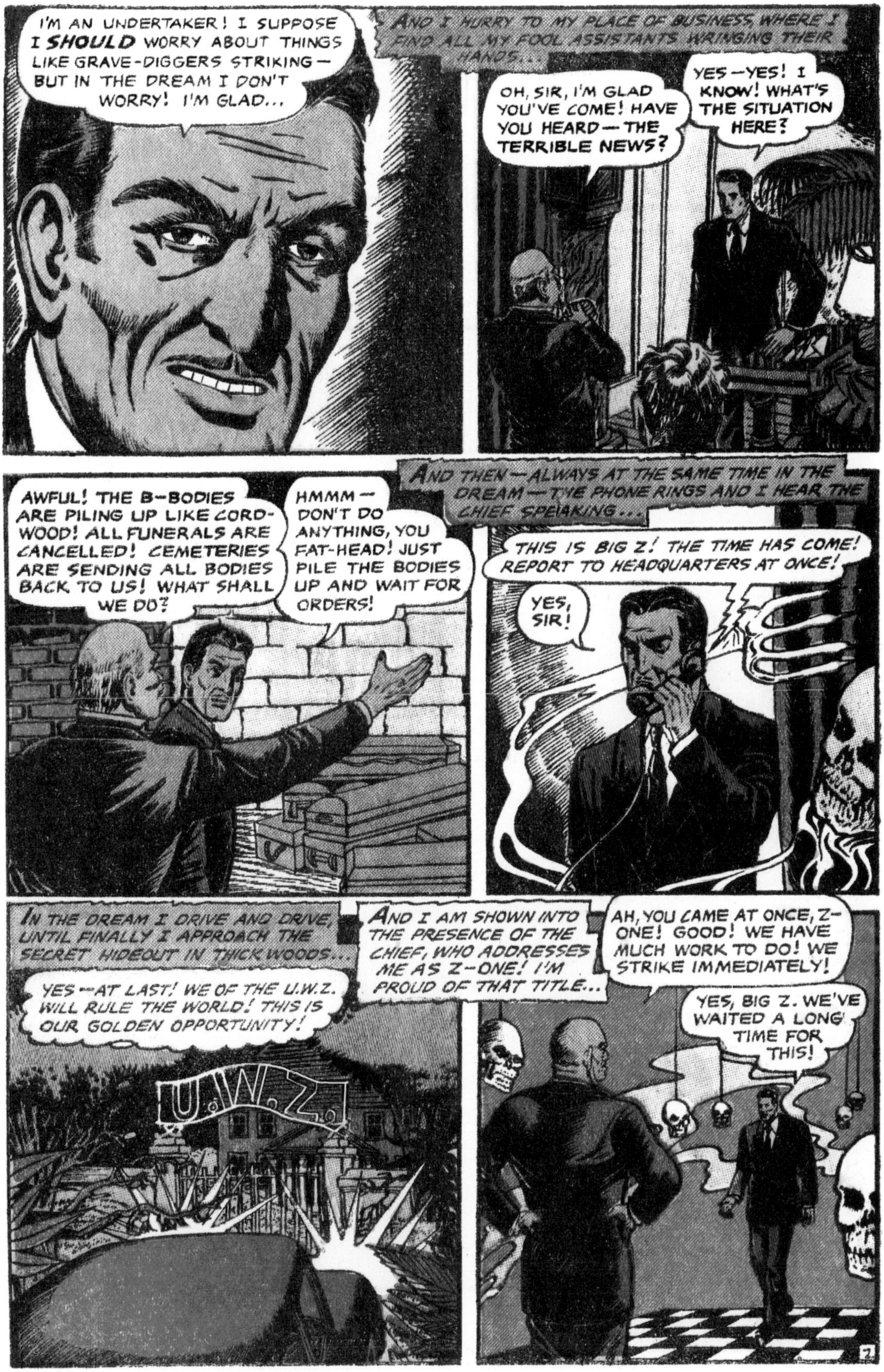
I'M AN UNDERTAKER! I SUPPOSE I SHOULD WORRY ABOUT THINGS LIKE GRAVE-DIGGERS STRIKING— BUT IN THE DREAM I DON'T WORRY! I'M GLAD...
AND I HURRY TO MY PLACE OF BUSINESS WHERE I FIND ALL MY FOOL ASSISTANTS WRINGING THEIR HANDS...
OH, SIR, I'M GLAD YOU'VE COME! HAVE YOU HEARD—THE TERRIBLE NEWS?
YES—YES! I KNOW! WHAT'S THE SITUATION HERE?
AWFUL! THE B-BODIES ARE PILING UP LIKE CORD-WOOD! ALL FUNERALS ARE CANCELLED! CEMETERIES ARE SENDING ALL BODIES BACK TO US! WHAT SHALL WE DO?
HMMM— DON'T DO ANYTHING, YOU FAT-HEAD! JUST PILE THE BODIES UP AND WAIT FOR ORDERS!
AND THEN—ALWAYS AT THE SAME TIME IN THE DREAM—TYE PHONE RINGS AND I HEAR THE CHIEF SPEAKING...
THIS IS BIG Z! THE TIME HAS COME! REPORT TO HEADQUARTERS AT ONCE!
YES, SIR!
IN THE DREAM I DRIVE AND DRIVE, UNTIL FINALLY I APPROACH THE SECRET HIDEOUT IN THICK WOODS...
YES—AT LAST! WE OF THE U.W.Z. WILL RULE THE WORLD! THIS IS OUR GOLDEN OPPORTUNITY!
U.W.Z.
AND I AM SHOWN INTO THE PRESENCE OF THE CHIEF, WHO ADDRESSES ME AS Z-ONE! I'M PROUD OF THAT TITLE...
AH, YOU CAME AT ONCE, Z-ONE! GOOD! WE HAVE MUCH WORK TO DO! WE STRIKE IMMEDIATELY!
YES, BIG Z. WE'VE WAITED A LONG TIME FOR THIS!
7

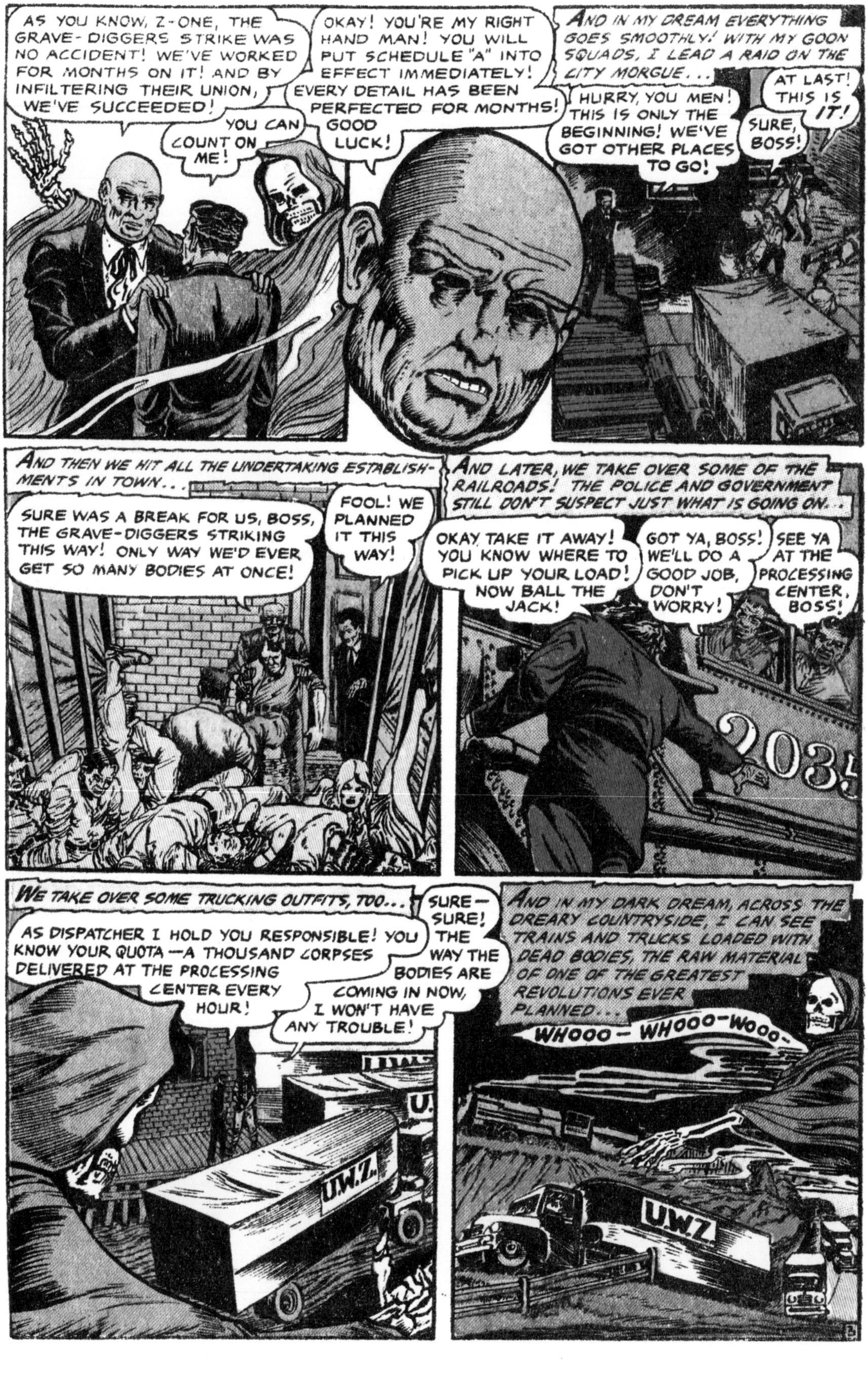
AS YOU KNOW, Z-ONE, THE GRAVE-DIGGERS STRIKE WAS NO ACCIDENT! WE'VE WORKED FOR MONTHS ON IT! AND BY INFILTERING THEIR UNION, WE'VE SUCCEEDED!
OKAY! YOU'RE MY RIGHT HAND MAN! YOU WILL PUT SCHEDULE "A" INTO EFFECT IMMEDIATELY!
EVERY DETAIL HAS BEEN PERFECTED FOR MONTHS!
YOU CAN COUNT ON ME!
GOOD LUCK!
AND IN MY DREAM EVERYTHING GOES SMOOTHLY! WITH MY GOON SQUADS, I LEAD A RAID ON THE CITY MORGUE...
HURRY, YOU MEN! THIS IS ONLY THE BEGINNING! WE'VE GOT OTHER PLACES TO GO!
AT LAST! THIS IS IT!
SURE, BOSS!
AND THEN WE HIT ALL THE UNDERTAKING ESTABLISHMENTS IN TOWN...
SURE WAS A BREAK FOR US, BOSS, THE GRAVE-DIGGERS STRIKING THIS WAY! ONLY WAY WE'D EVER GET SO MANY BODIES AT ONCE!
FOOL! WE PLANNED IT THIS WAY!
AND LATER, WE TAKE OVER SOME OF THE RAILROADS! THE POLICE AND GOVERNMENT STILL DON'T SUSPECT JUST WHAT IS GOING ON...
OKAY, TAKE IT AWAY! YOU KNOW WHERE TO PICK UP YOUR LOAD! NOW BALL THE JACK!
GOT YA, BOSS! WE'LL DO A GOOD JOB, DON'T WORRY!
SEE YA AT THE PROCESSING CENTER, BOSS!
2035
WE TAKE OVER SOME TRUCKING OUTFITS, TOO...
AS DISPATCHER I HOLD YOU RESPONSIBLE! YOU KNOW YOUR QUOTA—A THOUSAND CORPSES DELIVERED AT THE PROCESSING CENTER EVERY HOUR!
SURE—SURE! THE WAY THE BODIES ARE COMING IN NOW, I WON'T HAVE ANY TROUBLE!
U.W.Z.
AND IN MY DARK DREAM, ACROSS THE DREARY COUNTRYSIDE, I CAN SEE TRAINS AND TRUCKS LOADED WITH DEAD BODIES, THE RAW MATERIAL OF ONE OF THE GREATEST REVOLUTIONS EVER PLANNED...
WHOOO-WHOOO-WOOO-
U.W.Z.

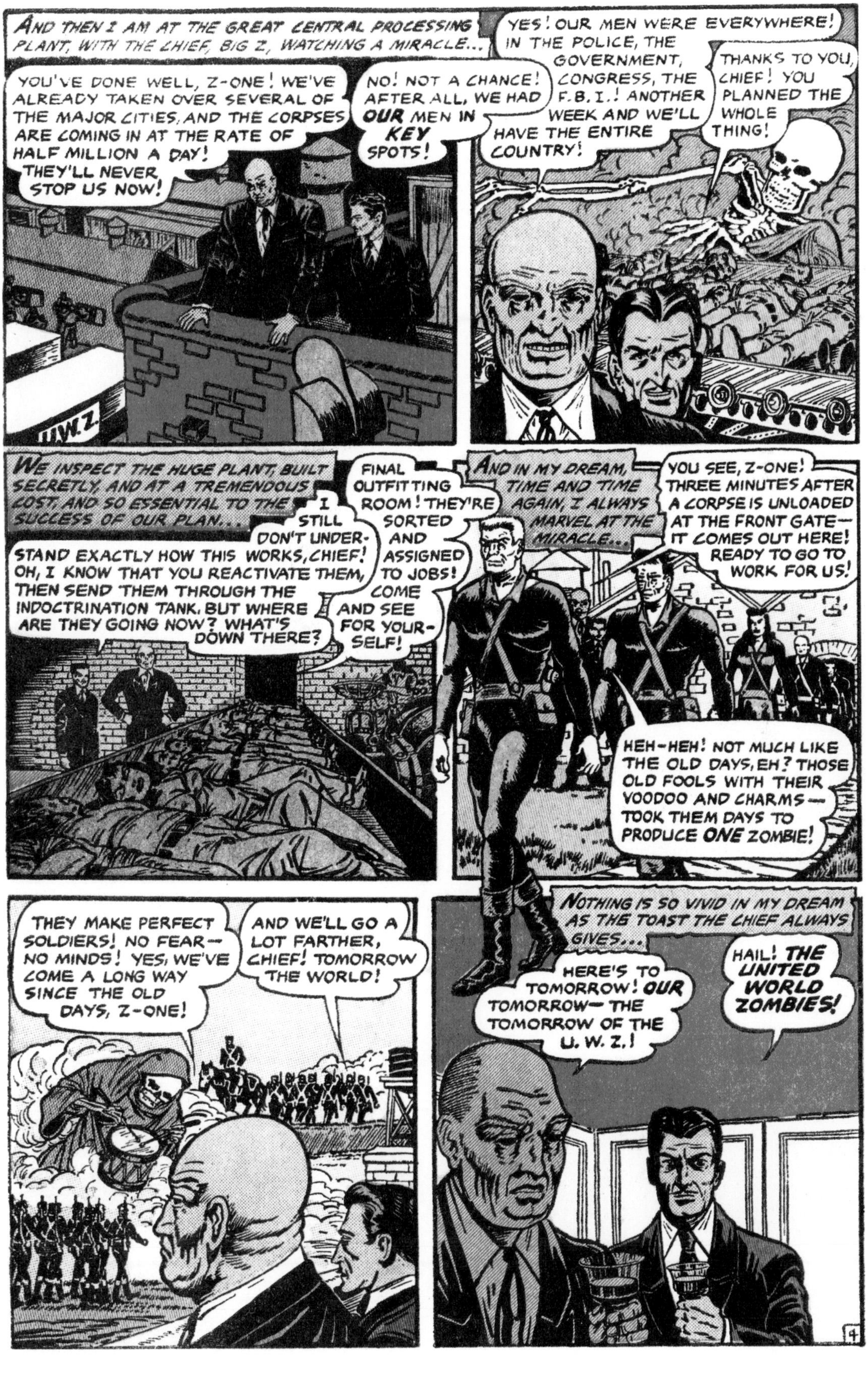

AND THEN I AM AT THE GREAT CENTRAL PROCESSING PLANT, WITH THE CHIEF, BIG Z, WATCHING A MIRACLE...
YOU'VE DONE WELL, Z-ONE! WE'VE ALREADY TAKEN OVER SEVERAL OF THE MAJOR CITIES, AND THE CORPSES ARE COMING IN AT THE RATE OF HALF MILLION A DAY! THEY'LL NEVER STOP US NOW!
NO! NOT A CHANCE! AFTER ALL, WE HAD OUR MEN IN KEY SPOTS!
U.W.Z.
YES! OUR MEN WERE EVERYWHERE! IN THE POLICE, THE GOVERNMENT, CONGRESS, THE F.B.I.! ANOTHER WEEK AND WE'LL HAVE THE ENTIRE COUNTRY!
THANKS TO YOU, CHIEF! YOU PLANNED THE WHOLE THING!
WE INSPECT THE HUGE PLANT, BUILT SECRETLY, AND AT A TREMENDOUS COST, AND SO ESSENTIAL TO THE SUCCESS OF OUR PLAN...
I STILL DON'T UNDERSTAND EXACTLY HOW THIS WORKS, CHIEF! OH, I KNOW THAT YOU REACTIVATE THEM, THEN SEND THEM THROUGH THE INDOCTRINATION TANK. BUT WHERE ARE THEY GOING NOW? WHAT'S DOWN THERE?
FINAL OUTFITTING ROOM! THEY'RE SORTED AND ASSIGNED TO JOBS! COME AND SEE FOR YOURSELF!
AND IN MY DREAM, TIME AND TIME AGAIN, I ALWAYS MARVEL AT THE MIRACLE...
YOU SEE, Z-ONE! THREE MINUTES AFTER A CORPSE IS UNLOADED AT THE FRONT GATE— IT COMES OUT HERE! READY TO GO TO WORK FOR US!
HEH-HEH! NOT MUCH LIKE THE OLD DAYS, EH? THOSE OLD FOOLS WITH THEIR VOODOO AND CHARMS— TOOK THEM DAYS TO PRODUCE ONE ZOMBIE!
THEY MAKE PERFECT SOLDIERS! NO FEAR— NO MINDS! YES, WE'VE COME A LONG WAY SINCE THE OLD DAYS, Z-ONE!
AND WE'LL GO A LOT FARTHER, CHIEF! TOMORROW THE WORLD!
NOTHING IS SO VIVID IN MY DREAM AS THE TOAST THE CHIEF ALWAYS GIVES...
HERE'S TO TOMORROW! OUR TOMORROW— THE TOMORROW OF THE U. W. Z.!
HAIL! THE UNITED WORLD ZOMBIES!
4

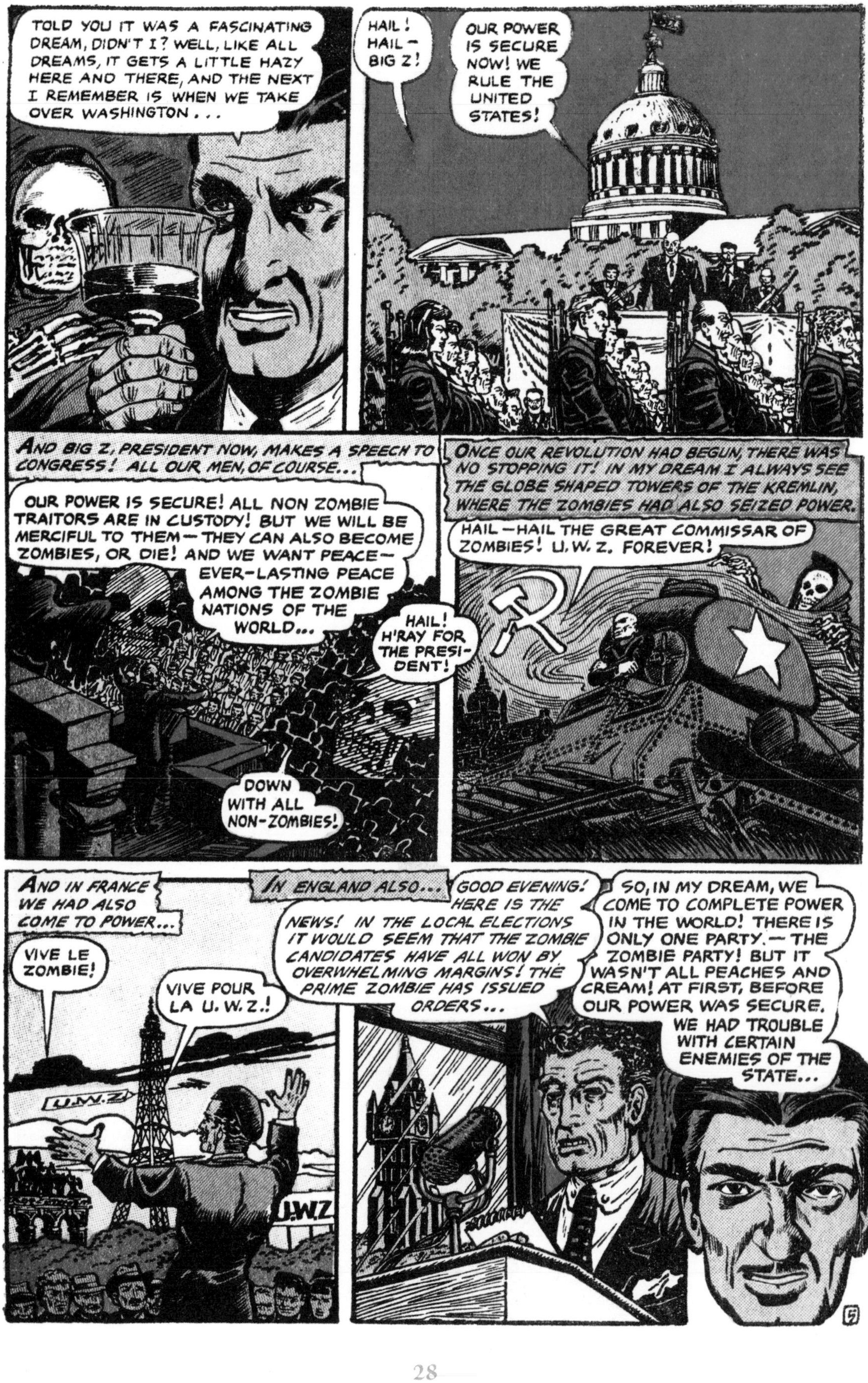
TOLD YOU IT WAS A FASCINATING DREAM, DIDN'T I? WELL, LIKE ALL DREAMS, IT GETS A LITTLE HAZY HERE AND THERE, AND THE NEXT I REMEMBER IS WHEN WE TAKE OVER WASHINGTON . . .
HAIL! HAIL— BIG Z!
OUR POWER IS SECURE NOW! WE RULE THE UNITED STATES!
AND BIG Z, PRESIDENT NOW, MAKES A SPEECH TO CONGRESS! ALL OUR MEN, OF COURSE...
OUR POWER IS SECURE! ALL NON ZOMBIE TRAITORS ARE IN CUSTODY! BUT WE WILL BE MERCIFUL TO THEM—THEY CAN ALSO BECOME ZOMBIES, OR DIE! AND WE WANT PEACE— EVER-LASTING PEACE AMONG THE ZOMBIE NATIONS OF THE WORLD...
HAIL! H'RAY FOR THE PRESI-DENT!
DOWN WITH ALL NON-ZOMBIES!
ONCE OUR REVOLUTION HAD BEGUN, THERE WAS NO STOPPING IT! IN MY DREAM I ALWAYS SEE THE GLOBE SHAPED TOWERS OF THE KREMLIN, WHERE THE ZOMBIES HAD ALSO SEIZED POWER.
HAIL—HAIL THE GREAT COMMISSAR OF ZOMBIES! U.W.Z. FOREVER!
AND IN FRANCE WE HAD ALSO COME TO POWER...
VIVE LE ZOMBIE!
VIVE POUR LA U.W.Z.!
U.W.Z.
U.W.Z
IN ENGLAND ALSO...
GOOD EVENING! HERE IS THE NEWS! IN THE LOCAL ELECTIONS IT WOULD SEEM THAT THE ZOMBIE CANDIDATES HAVE ALL WON BY OVERWHELMING MARGINS! THE PRIME ZOMBIE HAS ISSUED ORDERS...
SO, IN MY DREAM, WE COME TO COMPLETE POWER IN THE WORLD! THERE IS ONLY ONE PARTY.—THE ZOMBIE PARTY! BUT IT WASN'T ALL PEACHES AND CREAM! AT FIRST, BEFORE OUR POWER WAS SECURE. WE HAD TROUBLE WITH CERTAIN ENEMIES OF THE STATE...
5

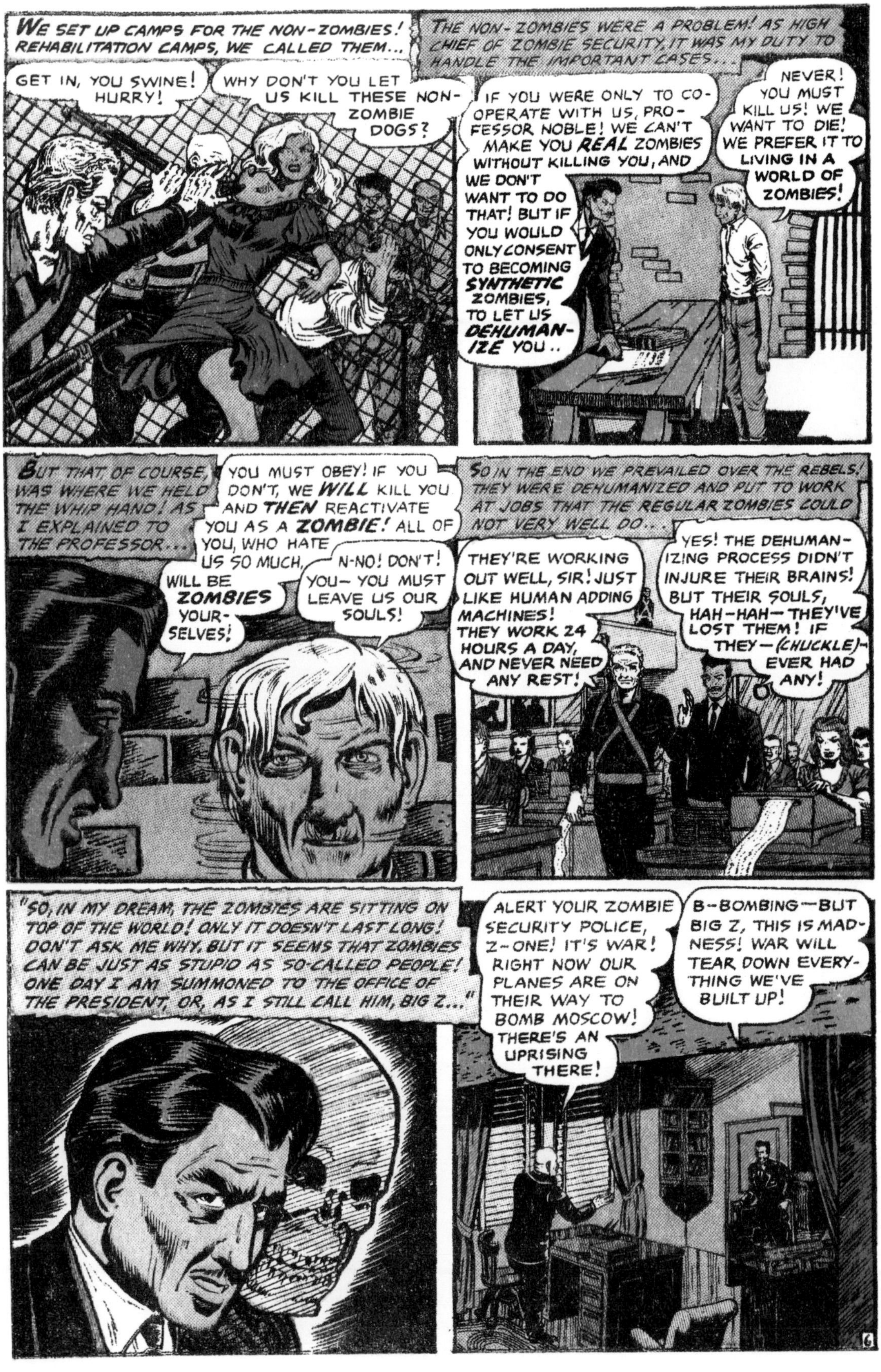
WE SET UP CAMPS FOR THE NON-ZOMBIES! REHABILITATION CAMPS, WE CALLED THEM...
GET IN, YOU SWINE! HURRY!
WHY DON'T YOU LET US KILL THESE NON-ZOMBIE DOGS?
THE NON-ZOMBIES WERE A PROBLEM! AS HIGH CHIEF OF ZOMBIE SECURITY, IT WAS MY DUTY TO HANDLE THE IMPORTANT CASES...
IF YOU WERE ONLY TO CO-OPERATE WITH US, PROFESSOR NOBLE! WE CAN'T MAKE YOU REAL ZOMBIES WITHOUT KILLING YOU, AND WE DON'T WANT TO DO THAT! BUT IF YOU WOULD ONLY CONSENT TO BECOMING SYNTHETIC ZOMBIES, TO LET US DEHUMANIZE YOU..
NEVER! YOU MUST KILL US! WE WANT TO DIE! WE PREFER IT TO LIVING IN A WORLD OF ZOMBIES!
BUT THAT, OF COURSE, WAS WHERE WE HELD THE WHIP HAND! AS I EXPLAINED TO THE PROFESSOR...
YOU MUST OBEY! IF YOU DON'T, WE WILL KILL YOU AND THEN REACTIVATE YOU AS A ZOMBIE! ALL OF YOU, WHO HATE US SO MUCH, WILL BE ZOMBIES YOURSELVES!
N-NO! DON'T! YOU-- YOU MUST LEAVE US OUR SOULS!
SO IN THE END WE PREVAILED OVER THE REBELS! THEY WERE DEHUMANIZED AND PUT TO WORK AT JOBS THAT THE REGULAR ZOMBIES COULD NOT VERY WELL DO...
THEY'RE WORKING OUT WELL, SIR! JUST LIKE HUMAN ADDING MACHINES! THEY WORK 24 HOURS A DAY, AND NEVER NEED ANY REST!
YES! THE DEHUMANIZING PROCESS DIDN'T INJURE THEIR BRAINS! BUT THEIR SOULS, HAH-HAH-- THEY'VE LOST THEM! IF THEY--(CHUCKLE)-- EVER HAD ANY!
"SO, IN MY DREAM, THE ZOMBIES ARE SITTING ON TOP OF THE WORLD! ONLY IT DOESN'T LAST LONG! DON'T ASK ME WHY. BUT IT SEEMS THAT ZOMBIES CAN BE JUST AS STUPID AS SO-CALLED PEOPLE! ONE DAY I AM SUMMONED TO THE OFFICE OF THE PRESIDENT, OR, AS I STILL CALL HIM, BIG Z..."
ALERT YOUR ZOMBIE SECURITY POLICE, Z-ONE! IT'S WAR! RIGHT NOW OUR PLANES ARE ON THEIR WAY TO BOMB MOSCOW! THERE'S AN UPRISING THERE!
B--BOMBING--BUT BIG Z, THIS IS MADNESS! WAR WILL TEAR DOWN EVERYTHING WE'VE BUILT UP!
6

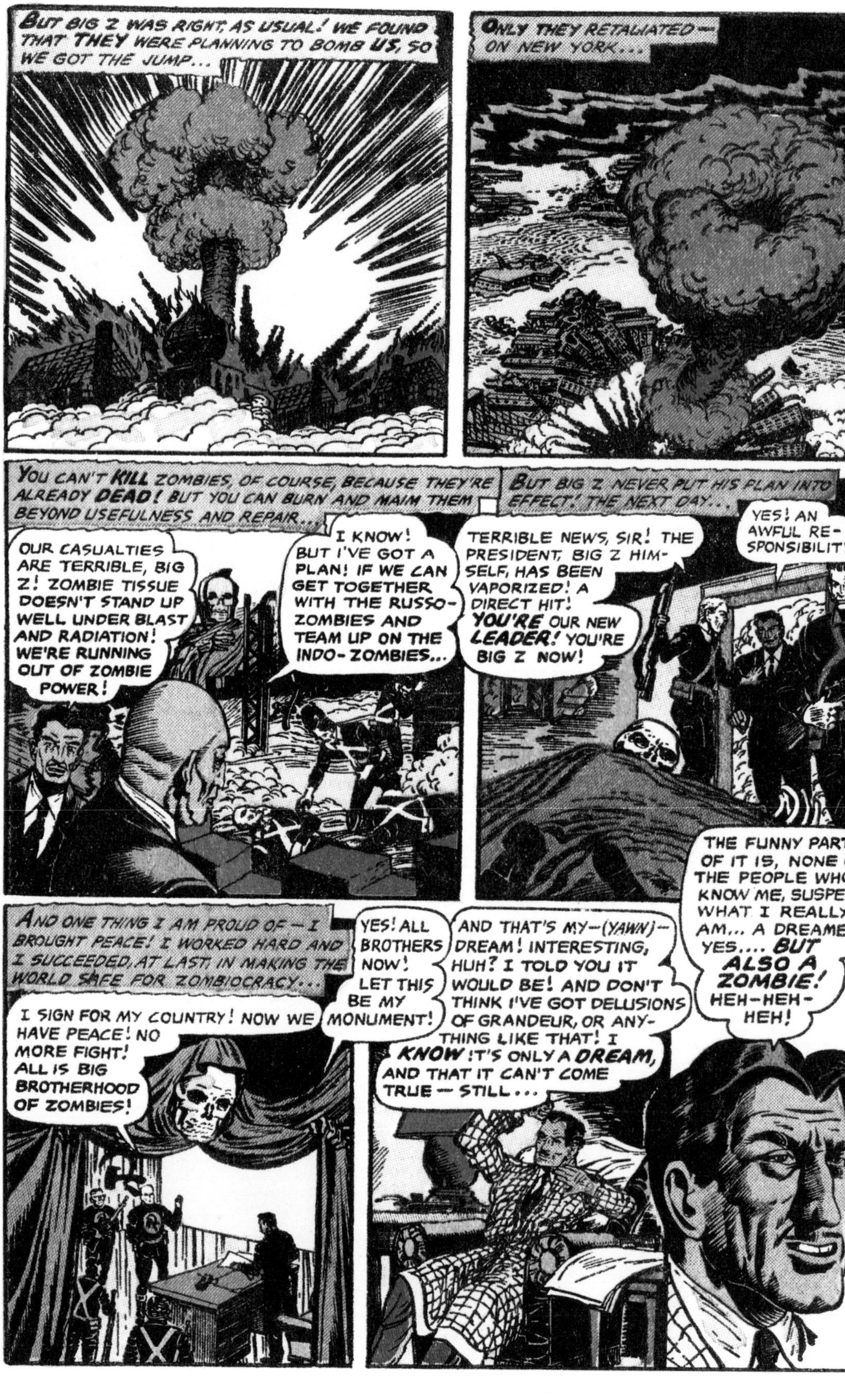
BUT BIG Z WAS RIGHT, AS USUAL! WE FOUND THAT THEY WERE PLANNING TO BOMB US, SO WE GOT THE JUMP...
ONLY THEY RETALIATED— ON NEW YORK...
YOU CAN'T KILL ZOMBIES, OF COURSE, BECAUSE THEY'RE ALREADY DEAD! BUT YOU CAN BURN AND MAIM THEM BEYOND USEFULNESS AND REPAIR...
OUR CASUALTIES ARE TERRIBLE, BIG Z! ZOMBIE TISSUE DOESN'T STAND UP WELL UNDER BLAST AND RADIATION! WE'RE RUNNING OUT OF ZOMBIE POWER!
I KNOW! BUT I'VE GOT A PLAN! IF WE CAN GET TOGETHER WITH THE RUSSO-ZOMBIES AND TEAM UP ON THE INDO-ZOMBIES...
BUT BIG Z NEVER PUT HIS PLAN INTO EFFECT! THE NEXT DAY...
TERRIBLE NEWS, SIR! THE PRESIDENT, BIG Z HIMSELF, HAS BEEN VAPORIZED! A DIRECT HIT! YOU'RE OUR NEW LEADER! YOU'RE BIG Z NOW!
YES! AN AWFUL RESPONSIBILITY!
AND ONE THING I AM PROUD OF— I BROUGHT PEACE! I WORKED HARD AND I SUCCEEDED, AT LAST, IN MAKING THE WORLD SAFE FOR ZOMBIOCRACY...
I SIGN FOR MY COUNTRY! NOW WE HAVE PEACE! NO MORE FIGHT! ALL IS BIG BROTHERHOOD OF ZOMBIES!
YES! ALL BROTHERS NOW! LET THIS BE MY MONUMENT!
AND THAT'S MY—(YAWN)— DREAM! INTERESTING, HUH? I TOLD YOU IT WOULD BE! AND DON'T THINK I'VE GOT DELUSIONS OF GRANDEUR, OR ANYTHING LIKE THAT! I KNOW IT'S ONLY A DREAM, AND THAT IT CAN'T COME TRUE— STILL...
THE FUNNY PART OF IT IS, NONE OF THE PEOPLE WHO KNOW ME, SUSPECT WHAT I REALLY AM... A DREAMER, YES.... BUT ALSO A ZOMBIE! HEH-HEH-HEH!

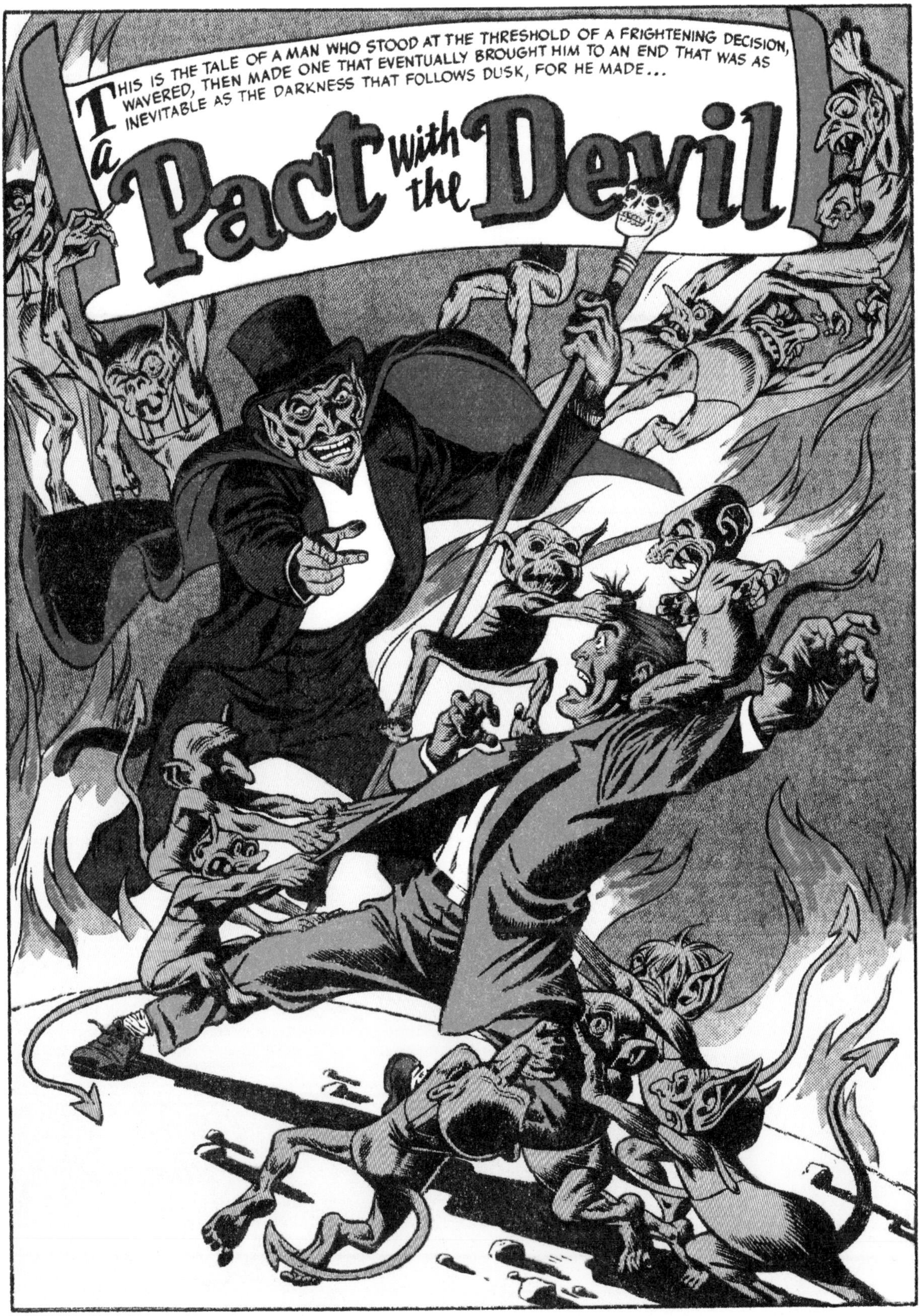
THIS IS THE TALE OF A MAN WHO STOOD AT THE THRESHOLD OF A FRIGHTENING DECISION, WAVERED, THEN MADE ONE THAT EVENTUALLY BROUGHT HIM TO AN END THAT WAS AS INEVITABLE AS THE DARKNESS THAT FOLLOWS DUSK, FOR HE MADE...
a Pact with the Devil

AH! TIME TO VENTURE OUT AGAIN! I HAVE APPOINTMENTS TO KEEP THIS NIGHT--AND I NEVER LIKE TO BE LATE!

I AM A DEALER IN... A DEALER IN PEOPLE... A DEALER IN LIFE AND DEATH!

BUT I CAN'T TARRY ANY LONGER! MY FIRST APPOINTMENT IS WITH A MR. NILES DUNCAN, AT A PAWN SHOP--AND THE PAWN SHOP SHALL CLOSE SOON! SO, OFF I GO...HA,HA,HA!

POP!

JUST A MINUTE! I'LL GO BACK AND SEE HOW MUCH I CAN GIVE YOU ON THE RING!

HA! SO YOU'RE PAWNING YOUR OWN MOTHER'S RING! YOU'RE BROKE AND DOWN AND OUT! DON'T BE A FOOL! HIT THE OLD MAN! ROB THE REGISTER!

HMMM... I JUST GOT AN IDEA... THE REGISTER... QUICK CASH!

SURE! WHY SETTLE FOR THE PRICE OF A RING! HUH! HE PULLED AN EMERGENCY ALARM SWITCH!

YOU'VE HIT HIM! GOOD! NOW GET THE MONEY--AND RUN! RUN! RUN!

CLANG! CLANG! CLANG!

ALARM

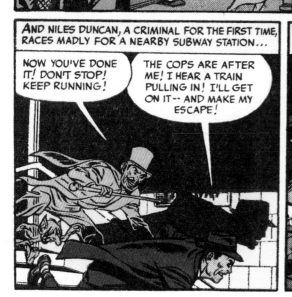

AND NILES DUNCAN, A CRIMINAL FOR THE FIRST TIME, RACES MADLY FOR A NEARBY SUBWAY STATION...

NOW YOU'VE DONE IT! DON'T STOP! KEEP RUNNING!

THE COPS ARE AFTER ME! I HEAR A TRAIN PULLING IN! I'LL GET ON IT-- AND MAKE MY ESCAPE!

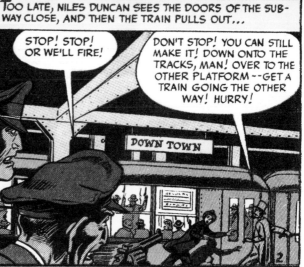

TOO LATE, NILES DUNCAN SEES THE DOORS OF THE SUB-WAY CLOSE, AND THEN THE TRAIN PULLS OUT...

STOP! STOP! OR WE'LL FIRE!

DON'T STOP! YOU CAN STILL MAKE IT! DOWN ONTO THE TRACKS, MAN! OVER TO THE OTHER PLATFORM--GET A TRAIN GOING THE OTHER WAY! HURRY!

DOWN TOWN

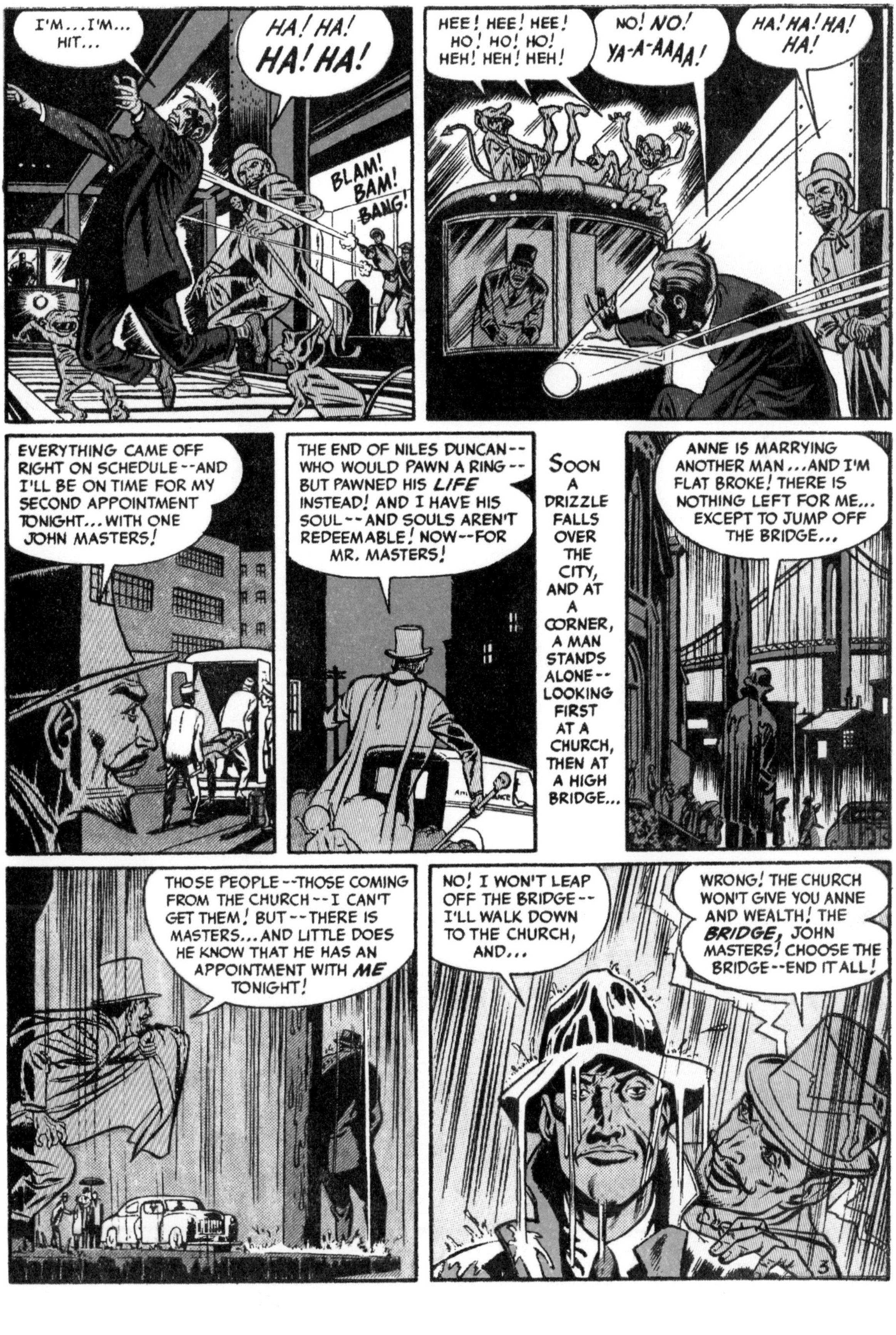
I'M...I'M... HIT...
HA! HA! HA! HA!
BLAM! BAM! BANG!
HEE! HEE! HEE! HO! HO! HO! HEH! HEH! HEH!
NO! NO! YA-A-AAAA!
HA! HA! HA! HA!
EVERYTHING CAME OFF RIGHT ON SCHEDULE--AND I'LL BE ON TIME FOR MY SECOND APPOINTMENT TONIGHT...WITH ONE JOHN MASTERS!
THE END OF NILES DUNCAN--WHO WOULD PAWN A RING--BUT PAWNED HIS LIFE INSTEAD! AND I HAVE HIS SOUL--AND SOULS AREN'T REDEEMABLE! NOW--FOR MR. MASTERS!
SOON A DRIZZLE FALLS OVER THE CITY, AND AT A CORNER, A MAN STANDS ALONE--LOOKING FIRST AT A CHURCH, THEN AT A HIGH BRIDGE...
ANNE IS MARRYING ANOTHER MAN...AND I'M FLAT BROKE! THERE IS NOTHING LEFT FOR ME... EXCEPT TO JUMP OFF THE BRIDGE...
THOSE PEOPLE--THOSE COMING FROM THE CHURCH--I CAN'T GET THEM! BUT--THERE IS MASTERS...AND LITTLE DOES HE KNOW THAT HE HAS AN APPOINTMENT WITH ME TONIGHT!
NO! I WON'T LEAP OFF THE BRIDGE--I'LL WALK DOWN TO THE CHURCH, AND...
WRONG! THE CHURCH WON'T GIVE YOU ANNE AND WEALTH! THE BRIDGE, JOHN MASTERS! CHOOSE THE BRIDGE--END IT ALL!
3

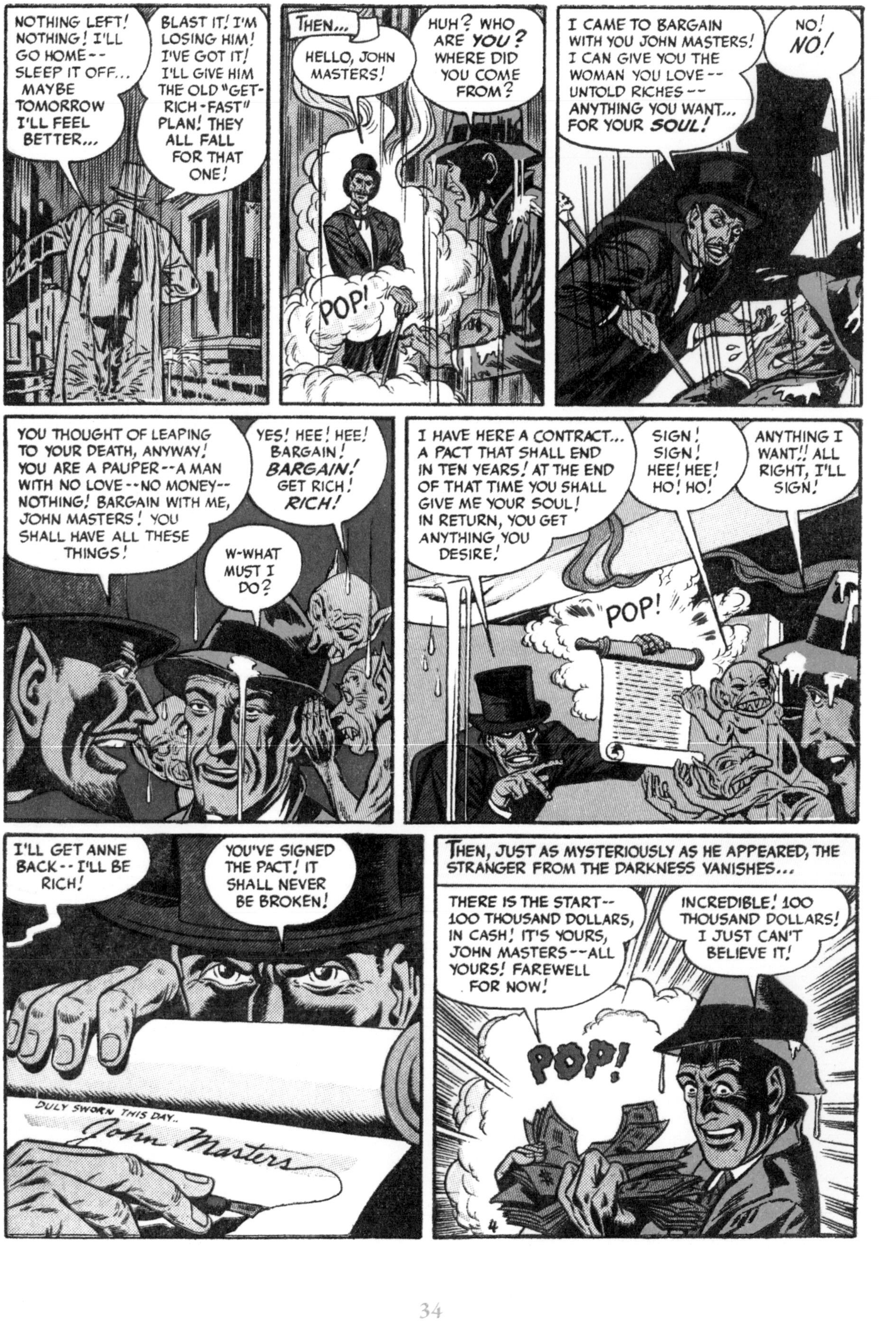
NOTHING LEFT! NOTHING! I'LL GO HOME-- SLEEP IT OFF... MAYBE TOMORROW I'LL FEEL BETTER...
BLAST IT! I'M LOSING HIM! I'VE GOT IT! I'LL GIVE HIM THE OLD "GET-RICH-FAST" PLAN! THEY ALL FALL FOR THAT ONE!
THEN...
HELLO, JOHN MASTERS!
HUH? WHO ARE YOU? WHERE DID YOU COME FROM?
POP!
I CAME TO BARGAIN WITH YOU JOHN MASTERS! I CAN GIVE YOU THE WOMAN YOU LOVE-- UNTOLD RICHES-- ANYTHING YOU WANT... FOR YOUR SOUL!
NO! NO!
YOU THOUGHT OF LEAPING TO YOUR DEATH, ANYWAY! YOU ARE A PAUPER--A MAN WITH NO LOVE--NO MONEY-- NOTHING! BARGAIN WITH ME, JOHN MASTERS! YOU SHALL HAVE ALL THESE THINGS!
YES! HEE! HEE! BARGAIN! BARGAIN! GET RICH! RICH!
W-WHAT MUST I DO?
I HAVE HERE A CONTRACT... A PACT THAT SHALL END IN TEN YEARS! AT THE END OF THAT TIME YOU SHALL GIVE ME YOUR SOUL! IN RETURN, YOU GET ANYTHING YOU DESIRE!
SIGN! SIGN! HEE! HEE! HO! HO!
ANYTHING I WANT!! ALL RIGHT, I'LL SIGN!
POP!
I'LL GET ANNE BACK-- I'LL BE RICH!
YOU'VE SIGNED THE PACT! IT SHALL NEVER BE BROKEN!
DULY SWORN THIS DAY..
John Masters
THEN, JUST AS MYSTERIOUSLY AS HE APPEARED, THE STRANGER FROM THE DARKNESS VANISHES...
THERE IS THE START-- 100 THOUSAND DOLLARS, IN CASH! IT'S YOURS, JOHN MASTERS--ALL YOURS! FAREWELL FOR NOW!
INCREDIBLE! 100 THOUSAND DOLLARS! I JUST CAN'T BELIEVE IT!
POP!

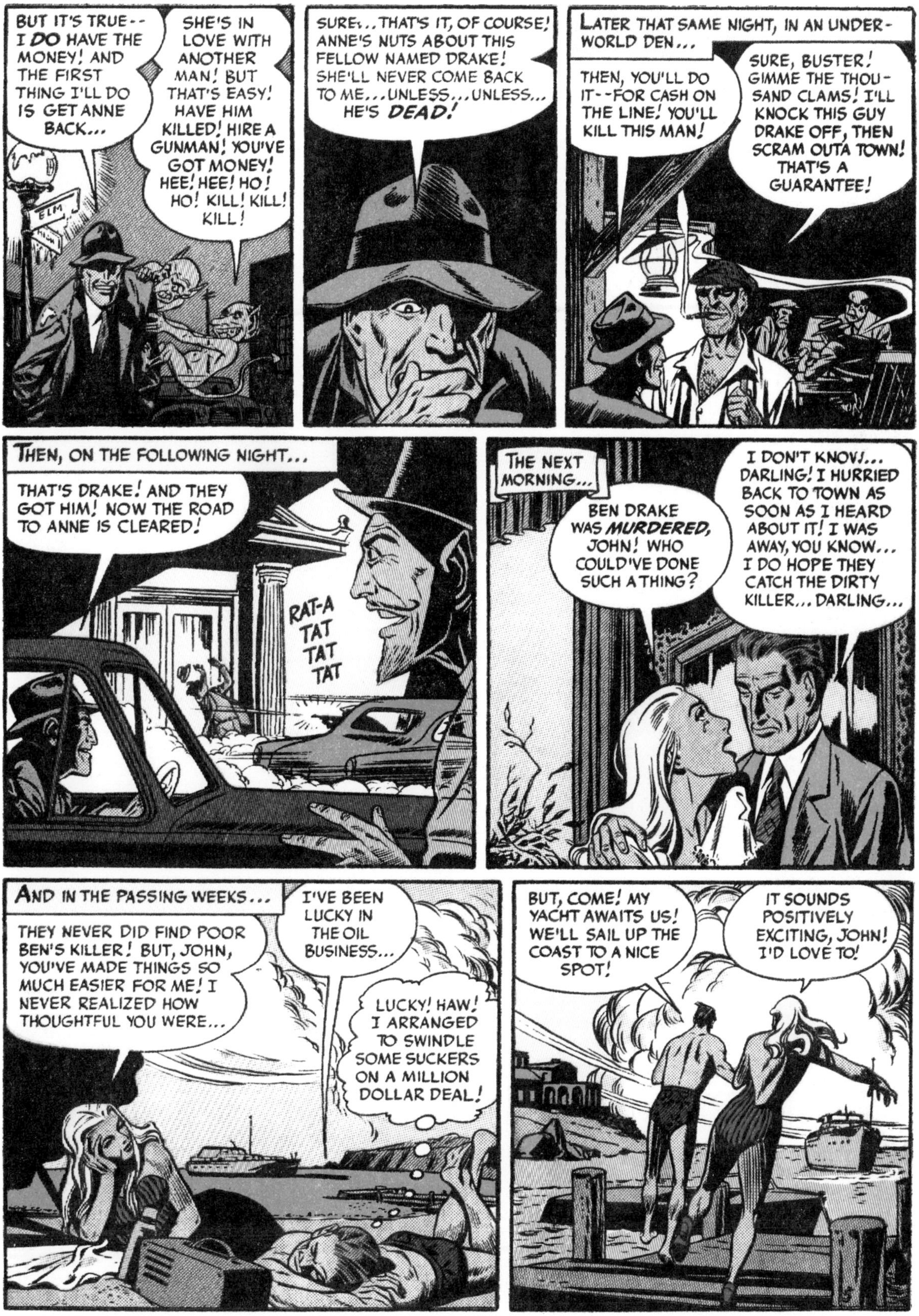
BUT IT'S TRUE-- I DO HAVE THE MONEY! AND THE FIRST THING I'LL DO IS GET ANNE BACK...
SHE'S IN LOVE WITH ANOTHER MAN! BUT THAT'S EASY! HAVE HIM KILLED! HIRE A GUNMAN! YOU'VE GOT MONEY! HEE! HEE! HO! HO! KILL! KILL! KILL!
ELM
SURE...THAT'S IT, OF COURSE! ANNE'S NUTS ABOUT THIS FELLOW NAMED DRAKE! SHE'LL NEVER COME BACK TO ME...UNLESS...UNLESS... HE'S DEAD!
LATER THAT SAME NIGHT, IN AN UNDERWORLD DEN...
THEN, YOU'LL DO IT--FOR CASH ON THE LINE! YOU'LL KILL THIS MAN!
SURE, BUSTER! GIMME THE THOUSAND CLAMS! I'LL KNOCK THIS GUY DRAKE OFF, THEN SCRAM OUTA TOWN! THAT'S A GUARANTEE!
THEN, ON THE FOLLOWING NIGHT...
THAT'S DRAKE! AND THEY GOT HIM! NOW THE ROAD TO ANNE IS CLEARED!
RAT-A TAT TAT TAT
THE NEXT MORNING...
BEN DRAKE WAS MURDERED, JOHN! WHO COULD'VE DONE SUCH A THING?
I DON'T KNOW... DARLING! I HURRIED BACK TO TOWN AS SOON AS I HEARD ABOUT IT! I WAS AWAY, YOU KNOW... I DO HOPE THEY CATCH THE DIRTY KILLER... DARLING...
AND IN THE PASSING WEEKS...
THEY NEVER DID FIND POOR BEN'S KILLER! BUT, JOHN, YOU'VE MADE THINGS SO MUCH EASIER FOR ME! I NEVER REALIZED HOW THOUGHTFUL YOU WERE...
I'VE BEEN LUCKY IN THE OIL BUSINESS...
LUCKY! HAW! I ARRANGED TO SWINDLE SOME SUCKERS ON A MILLION DOLLAR DEAL!
BUT, COME! MY YACHT AWAITS US! WE'LL SAIL UP THE COAST TO A NICE SPOT!
IT SOUNDS POSITIVELY EXCITING, JOHN! I'D LOVE TO!

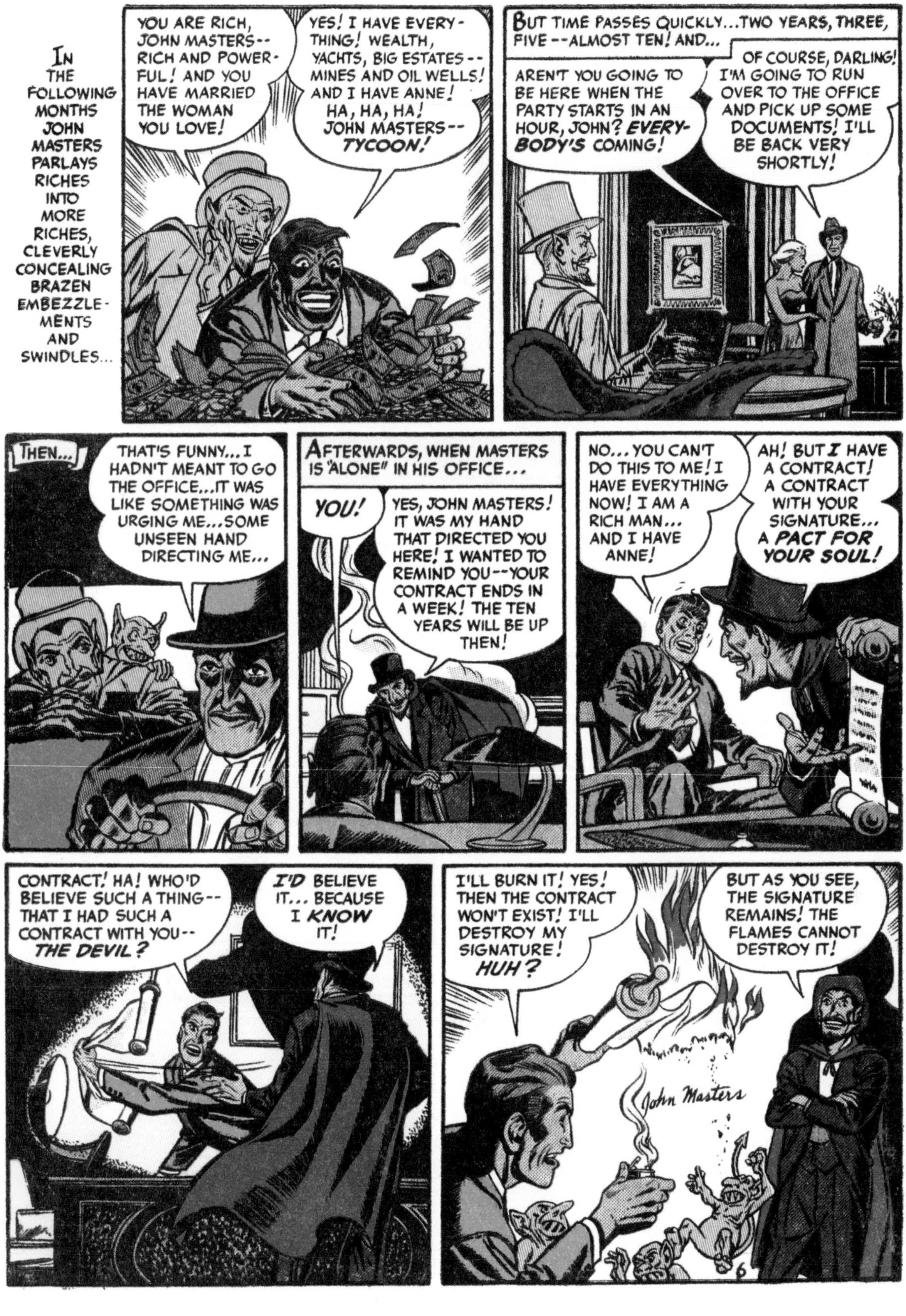
IN THE FOLLOWING MONTHS JOHN MASTERS PARLAYS RICHES INTO MORE RICHES, CLEVERLY CONCEALING BRAZEN EMBEZZLE-MENTS AND SWINDLES...
YOU ARE RICH, JOHN MASTERS-- RICH AND POWER-FUL! AND YOU HAVE MARRIED THE WOMAN YOU LOVE!
YES! I HAVE EVERY-THING! WEALTH, YACHTS, BIG ESTATES -- MINES AND OIL WELLS! AND I HAVE ANNE! HA, HA, HA! JOHN MASTERS -- TYCOON!
BUT TIME PASSES QUICKLY...TWO YEARS, THREE, FIVE --ALMOST TEN! AND...
AREN'T YOU GOING TO BE HERE WHEN THE PARTY STARTS IN AN HOUR, JOHN? EVERY-BODY'S COMING!
OF COURSE, DARLING! I'M GOING TO RUN OVER TO THE OFFICE AND PICK UP SOME DOCUMENTS! I'LL BE BACK VERY SHORTLY!
THEN...
THAT'S FUNNY...I HADN'T MEANT TO GO THE OFFICE...IT WAS LIKE SOMETHING WAS URGING ME...SOME UNSEEN HAND DIRECTING ME...
AFTERWARDS, WHEN MASTERS IS "ALONE" IN HIS OFFICE...
YOU!
YES, JOHN MASTERS! IT WAS MY HAND THAT DIRECTED YOU HERE! I WANTED TO REMIND YOU--YOUR CONTRACT ENDS IN A WEEK! THE TEN YEARS WILL BE UP THEN!
NO... YOU CAN'T DO THIS TO ME! I HAVE EVERYTHING NOW! I AM A RICH MAN... AND I HAVE ANNE!
AH! BUT I HAVE A CONTRACT! A CONTRACT WITH YOUR SIGNATURE... A PACT FOR YOUR SOUL!
CONTRACT! HA! WHO'D BELIEVE SUCH A THING-- THAT I HAD SUCH A CONTRACT WITH YOU-- THE DEVIL?
I'D BELIEVE IT... BECAUSE I KNOW IT!
I'LL BURN IT! YES! THEN THE CONTRACT WON'T EXIST! I'LL DESTROY MY SIGNATURE! HUH?
BUT AS YOU SEE, THE SIGNATURE REMAINS! THE FLAMES CANNOT DESTROY IT!
John Masters
6

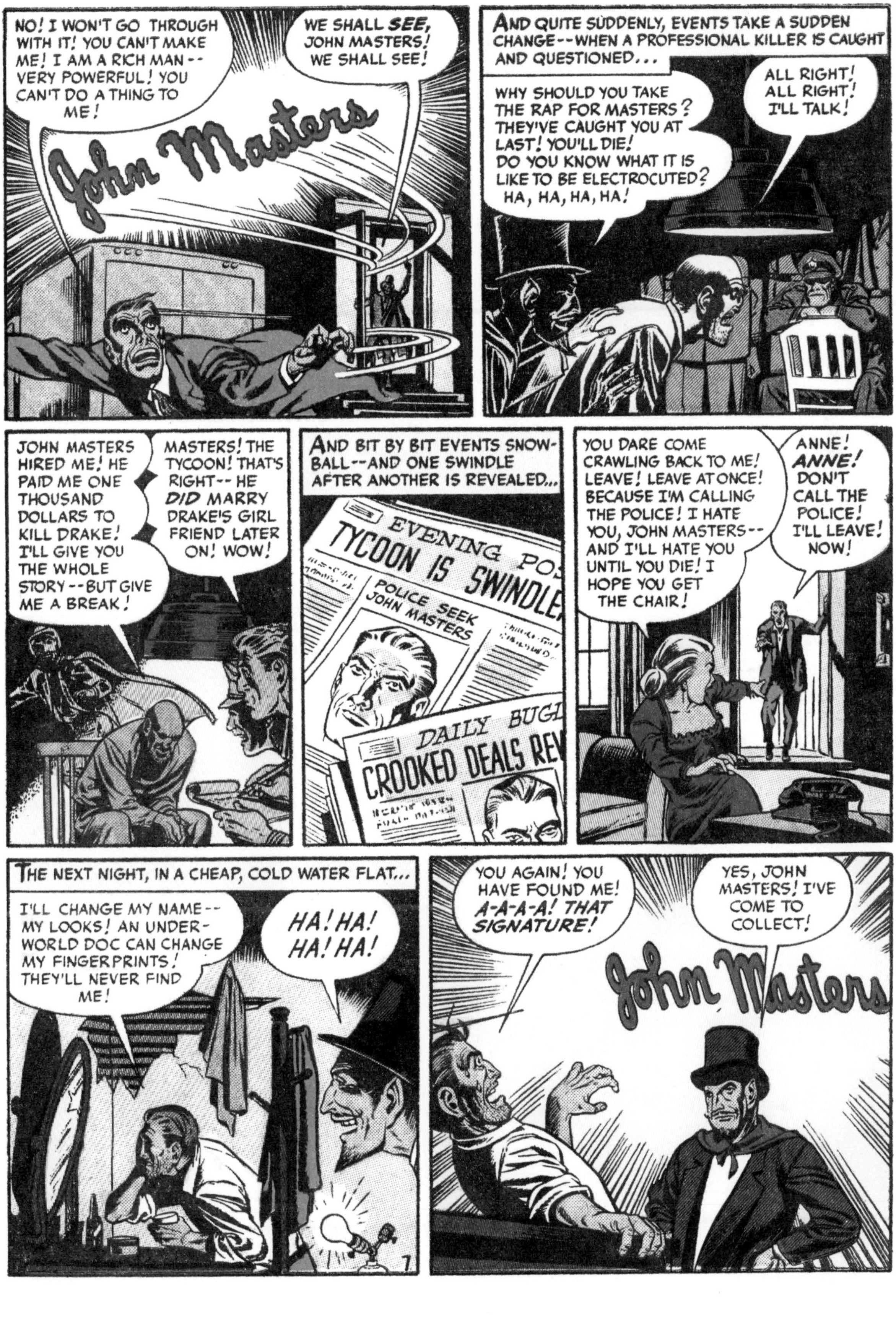

NO! I WON'T GO THROUGH WITH IT! YOU CAN'T MAKE ME! I AM A RICH MAN -- VERY POWERFUL! YOU CAN'T DO A THING TO ME!
WE SHALL SEE, JOHN MASTERS! WE SHALL SEE!
John Masters
AND QUITE SUDDENLY, EVENTS TAKE A SUDDEN CHANGE--WHEN A PROFESSIONAL KILLER IS CAUGHT AND QUESTIONED...
WHY SHOULD YOU TAKE THE RAP FOR MASTERS? THEY'VE CAUGHT YOU AT LAST! YOU'LL DIE! DO YOU KNOW WHAT IT IS LIKE TO BE ELECTROCUTED? HA, HA, HA, HA!
ALL RIGHT! ALL RIGHT! I'LL TALK!
JOHN MASTERS HIRED ME! HE PAID ME ONE THOUSAND DOLLARS TO KILL DRAKE! I'LL GIVE YOU THE WHOLE STORY--BUT GIVE ME A BREAK!
MASTERS! THE TYCOON! THAT'S RIGHT-- HE DID MARRY DRAKE'S GIRL FRIEND LATER ON! WOW!
AND BIT BY BIT EVENTS SNOWBALL--AND ONE SWINDLE AFTER ANOTHER IS REVEALED...
EVENING POS
TYCOON IS SWINDLE
POLICE SEEK JOHN MASTERS
DAILY BUGL
CROOKED DEALS REV
YOU DARE COME CRAWLING BACK TO ME! LEAVE! LEAVE AT ONCE! BECAUSE I'M CALLING THE POLICE! I HATE YOU, JOHN MASTERS-- AND I'LL HATE YOU UNTIL YOU DIE! I HOPE YOU GET THE CHAIR!
ANNE! ANNE! DON'T CALL THE POLICE! I'LL LEAVE! NOW!
THE NEXT NIGHT, IN A CHEAP, COLD WATER FLAT...
I'LL CHANGE MY NAME-- MY LOOKS! AN UNDERWORLD DOC CAN CHANGE MY FINGERPRINTS! THEY'LL NEVER FIND ME!
HA! HA! HA! HA!
YOU AGAIN! YOU HAVE FOUND ME! A-A-A-A! THAT SIGNATURE!
YES, JOHN MASTERS! I'VE COME TO COLLECT!
John Masters

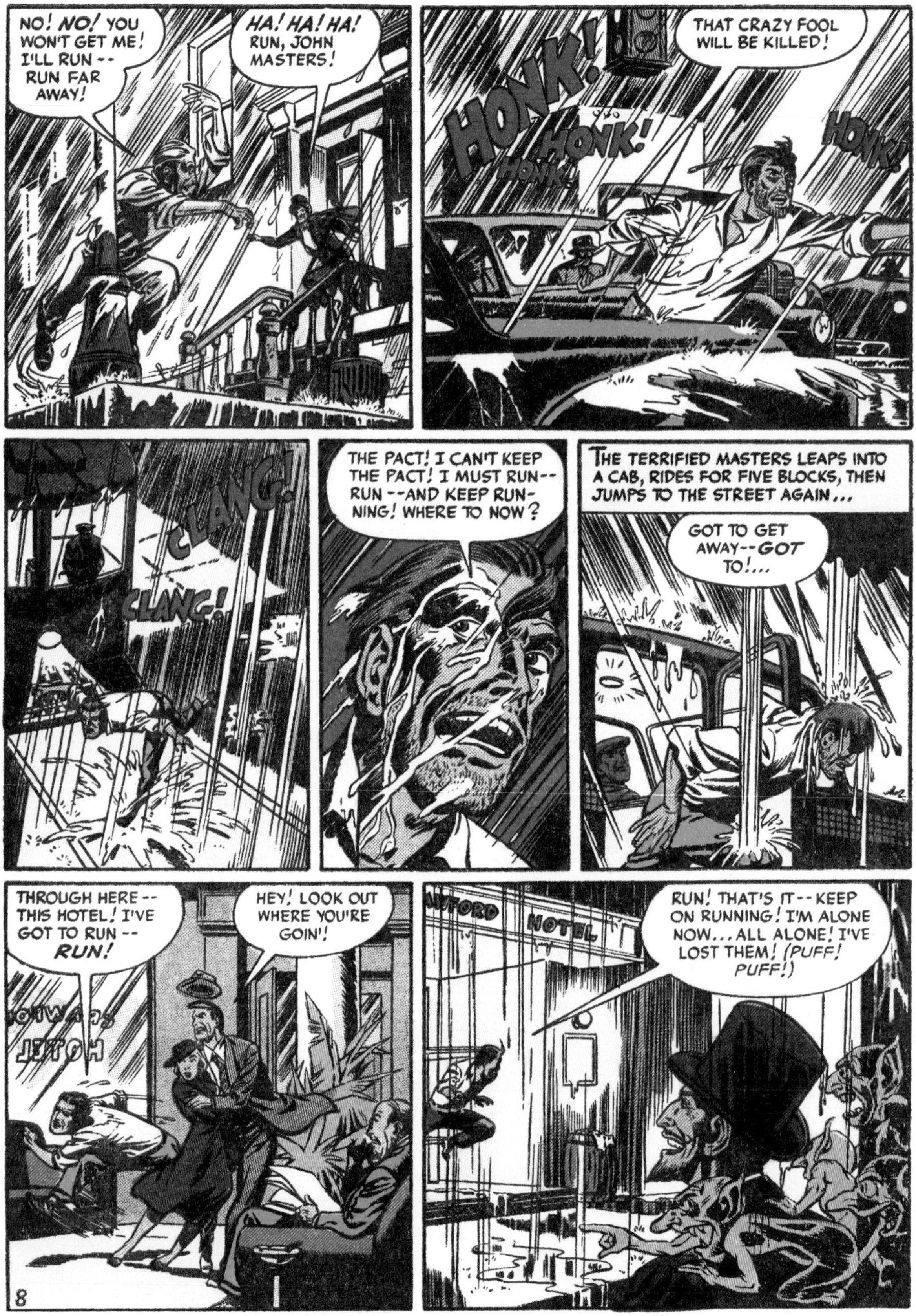
NO! NO! YOU WON'T GET ME! I'LL RUN -- RUN FAR AWAY!
HA! HA! HA! RUN, JOHN MASTERS!
THAT CRAZY FOOL WILL BE KILLED!
HONK! HONK! HONK! HONK!
CLANG! CLANG!
THE PACT! I CAN'T KEEP THE PACT! I MUST RUN-- RUN --AND KEEP RUNNING! WHERE TO NOW?
THE TERRIFIED MASTERS LEAPS INTO A CAB, RIDES FOR FIVE BLOCKS, THEN JUMPS TO THE STREET AGAIN...
GOT TO GET AWAY--GOT TO!...
THROUGH HERE -- THIS HOTEL! I'VE GOT TO RUN -- RUN!
HEY! LOOK OUT WHERE YOU'RE GOIN'!
HOTEL
RUN! THAT'S IT-- KEEP ON RUNNING! I'M ALONE NOW... ALL ALONE! I'VE LOST THEM! (PUFF! PUFF!)
8

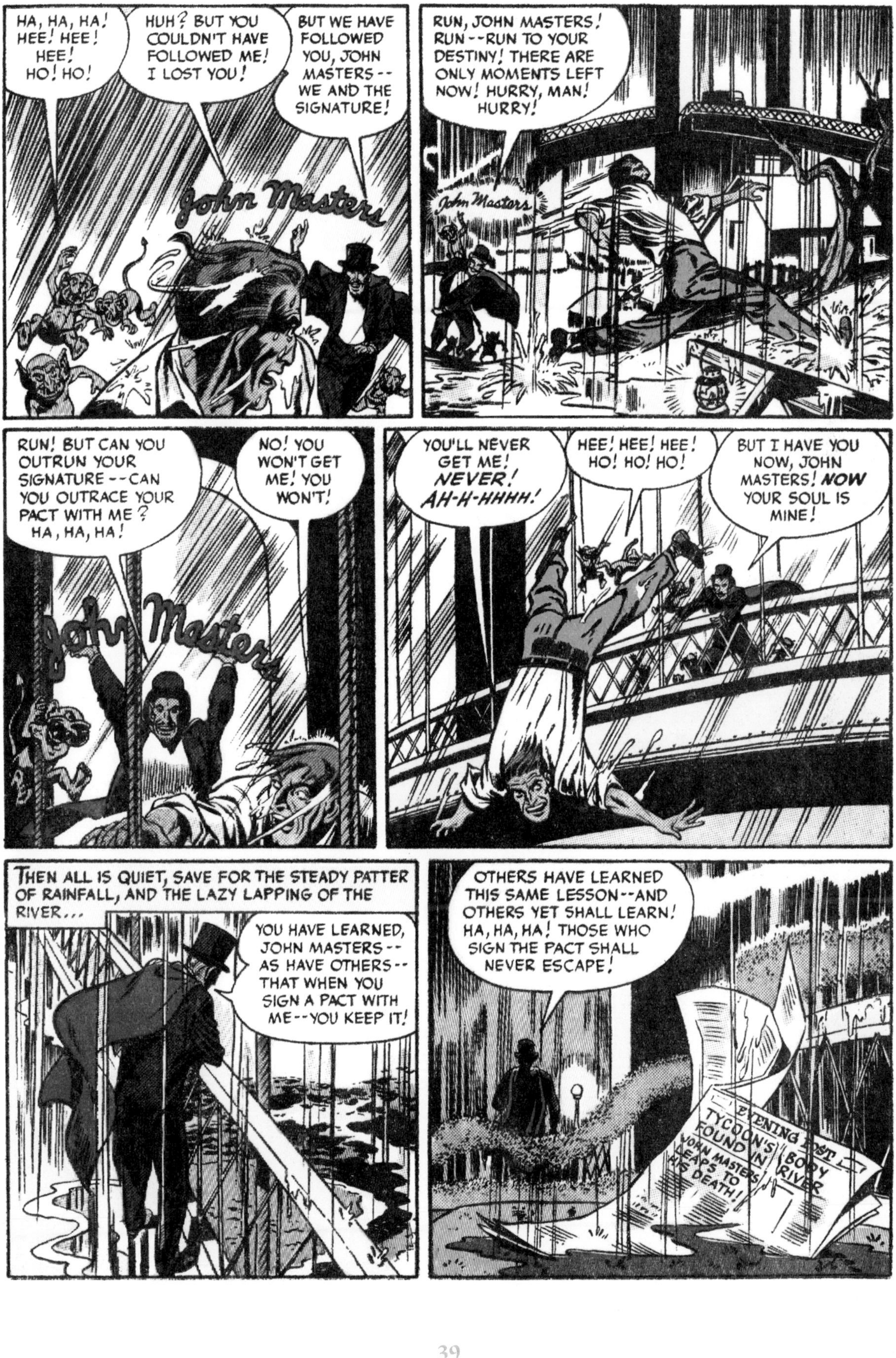
HA, HA, HA! HEE! HEE! HEE! HO! HO!
HUH? BUT YOU COULDN'T HAVE FOLLOWED ME! I LOST YOU!
BUT WE HAVE FOLLOWED YOU, JOHN MASTERS -- WE AND THE SIGNATURE!
John Masters
RUN, JOHN MASTERS! RUN -- RUN TO YOUR DESTINY! THERE ARE ONLY MOMENTS LEFT NOW! HURRY, MAN! HURRY!
John Masters
RUN! BUT CAN YOU OUTRUN YOUR SIGNATURE -- CAN YOU OUTRACE YOUR PACT WITH ME? HA, HA, HA!
NO! YOU WON'T GET ME! YOU WON'T!
John Masters
YOU'LL NEVER GET ME! NEVER! AH-H-HHHH!
HEE! HEE! HEE! HO! HO! HO!
BUT I HAVE YOU NOW, JOHN MASTERS! NOW YOUR SOUL IS MINE!
THEN ALL IS QUIET, SAVE FOR THE STEADY PATTER OF RAINFALL, AND THE LAZY LAPPING OF THE RIVER...
YOU HAVE LEARNED, JOHN MASTERS -- AS HAVE OTHERS -- THAT WHEN YOU SIGN A PACT WITH ME -- YOU KEEP IT!
OTHERS HAVE LEARNED THIS SAME LESSON -- AND OTHERS YET SHALL LEARN! HA, HA, HA! THOSE WHO SIGN THE PACT SHALL NEVER ESCAPE!
EVENING POST
TYCOON'S BODY FOUND IN RIVER
JOHN MASTERS LEAPS TO HIS DEATH!

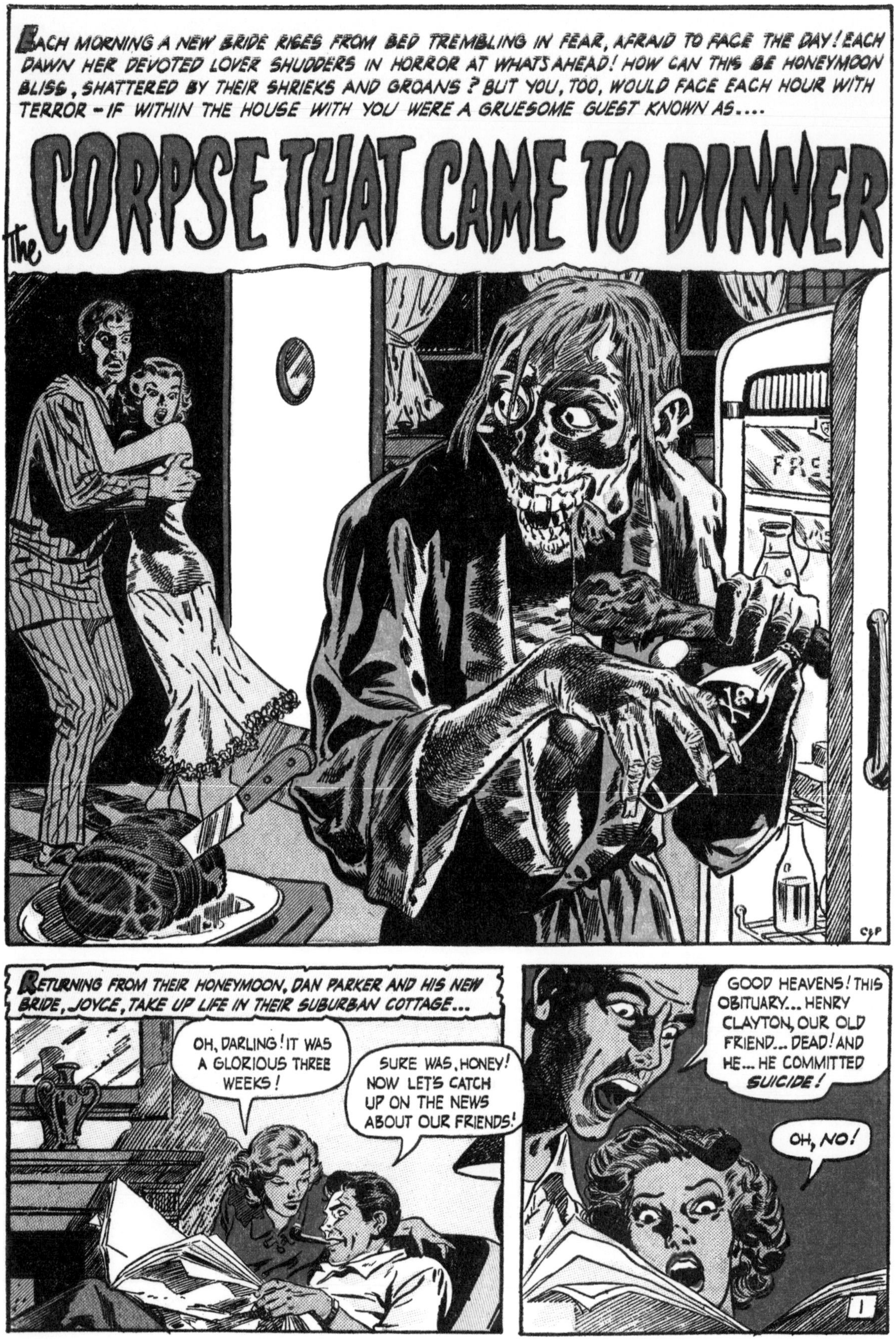

EACH MORNING A NEW BRIDE RISES FROM BED TREMBLING IN FEAR, AFRAID TO FACE THE DAY! EACH DAWN HER DEVOTED LOVER SHUDDERS IN HORROR AT WHAT'S AHEAD! HOW CAN THIS BE HONEYMOON BLISS, SHATTERED BY THEIR SHRIEKS AND GROANS? BUT YOU, TOO, WOULD FACE EACH HOUR WITH TERROR - IF WITHIN THE HOUSE WITH YOU WERE A GRUESOME GUEST KNOWN AS....
The CORPSE THAT CAME TO DINNER
RETURNING FROM THEIR HONEYMOON, DAN PARKER AND HIS NEW BRIDE, JOYCE, TAKE UP LIFE IN THEIR SUBURBAN COTTAGE...
OH, DARLING! IT WAS A GLORIOUS THREE WEEKS!
SURE WAS, HONEY! NOW LET'S CATCH UP ON THE NEWS ABOUT OUR FRIENDS!
GOOD HEAVENS! THIS OBITUARY... HENRY CLAYTON, OUR OLD FRIEND... DEAD! AND HE... HE COMMITTED SUICIDE!
OH, NO!
1

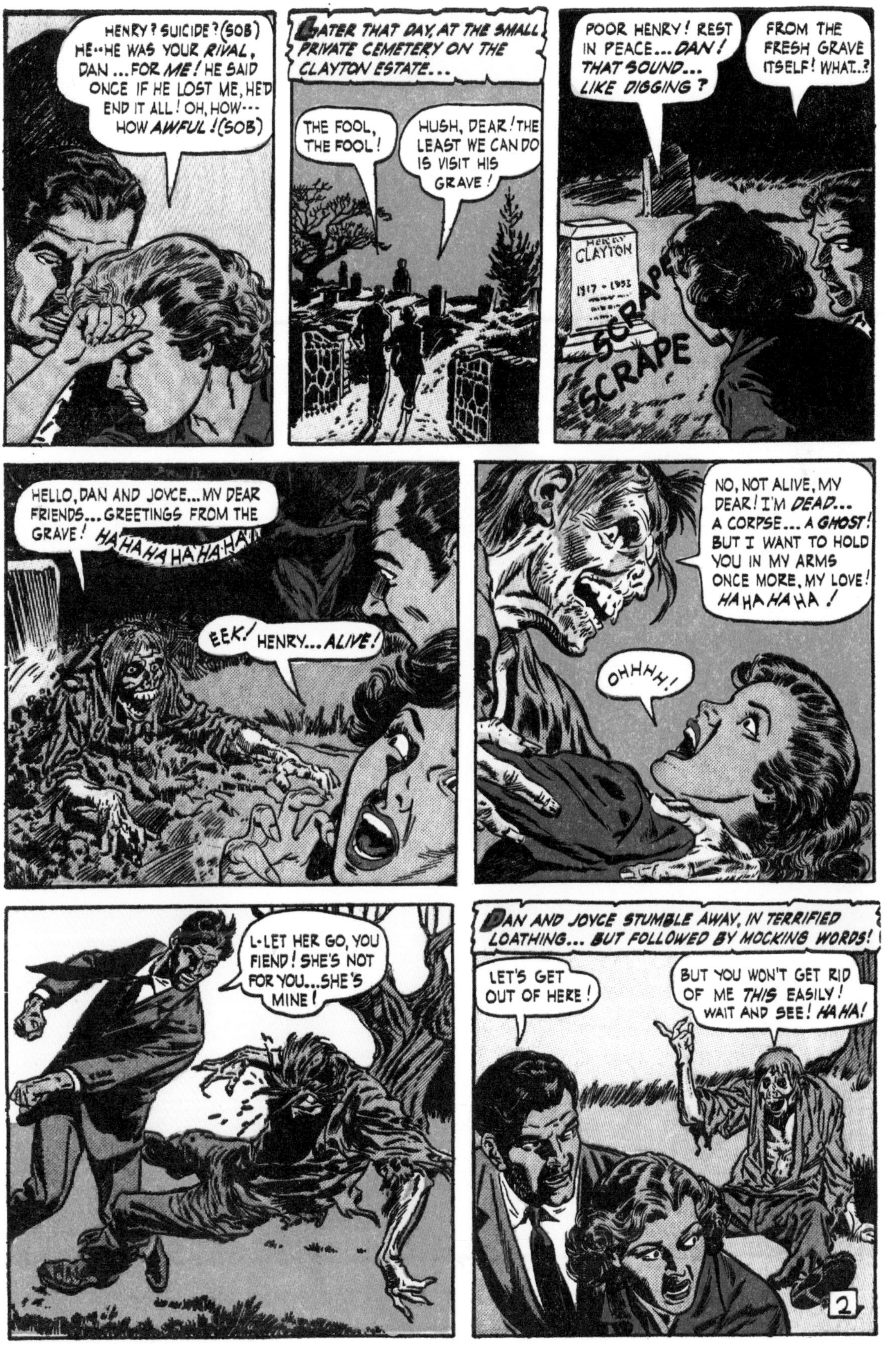
HENRY? SUICIDE? (SOB) HE--HE WAS YOUR RIVAL, DAN ...FOR ME! HE SAID ONCE IF HE LOST ME, HE'D END IT ALL! OH, HOW--- HOW AWFUL! (SOB)
LATER THAT DAY, AT THE SMALL PRIVATE CEMETERY ON THE CLAYTON ESTATE...
THE FOOL, THE FOOL!
HUSH, DEAR! THE LEAST WE CAN DO IS VISIT HIS GRAVE!
POOR HENRY! REST IN PEACE... DAN! THAT SOUND... LIKE DIGGING?
FROM THE FRESH GRAVE ITSELF! WHAT..?
CLAYTON
SCRAPE
SCRAPE
HELLO, DAN AND JOYCE... MY DEAR FRIENDS... GREETINGS FROM THE GRAVE! HA HA HA HA HA HA HA HA
EEK! HENRY... ALIVE!
NO, NOT ALIVE, MY DEAR! I'M DEAD... A CORPSE... A GHOST! BUT I WANT TO HOLD YOU IN MY ARMS ONCE MORE, MY LOVE! HA HA HA HA!
OHHHH!
L-LET HER GO, YOU FIEND! SHE'S NOT FOR YOU...SHE'S MINE!
DAN AND JOYCE STUMBLE AWAY, IN TERRIFIED LOATHING... BUT FOLLOWED BY MOCKING WORDS!
LET'S GET OUT OF HERE!
BUT YOU WON'T GET RID OF ME THIS EASILY! WAIT AND SEE! HA HA!
2

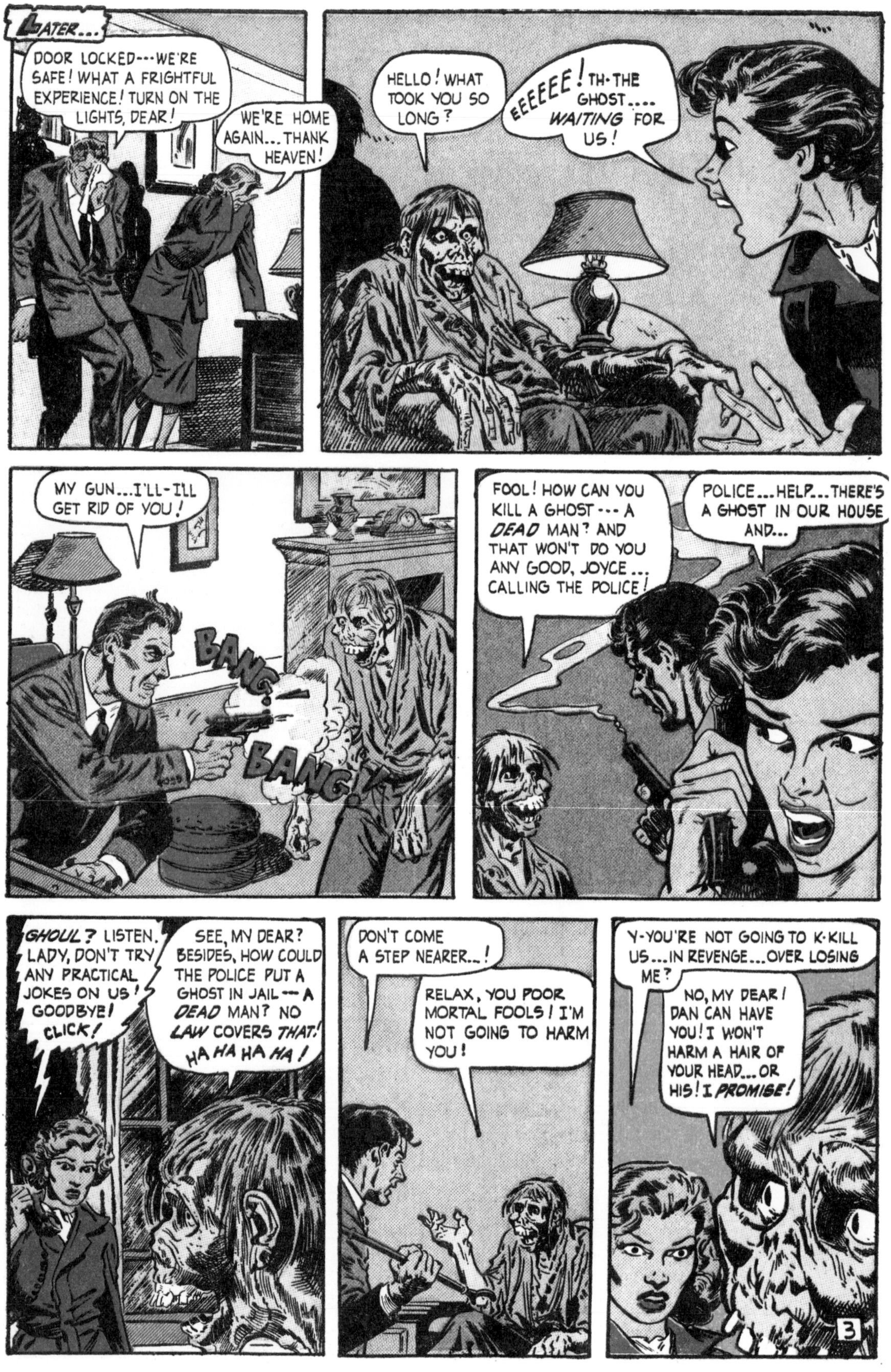
LATER...
DOOR LOCKED---WE'RE SAFE! WHAT A FRIGHTFUL EXPERIENCE! TURN ON THE LIGHTS, DEAR!
WE'RE HOME AGAIN...THANK HEAVEN!
HELLO! WHAT TOOK YOU SO LONG?
EEEEEE! TH-THE GHOST.... WAITING FOR US!
MY GUN...I'LL-I'LL GET RID OF YOU!
BANG! BANG!
FOOL! HOW CAN YOU KILL A GHOST--- A DEAD MAN? AND THAT WON'T DO YOU ANY GOOD, JOYCE... CALLING THE POLICE!
POLICE...HELP...THERE'S A GHOST IN OUR HOUSE AND...
GHOUL? LISTEN. LADY, DON'T TRY ANY PRACTICAL JOKES ON US! GOODBYE! CLICK!
SEE, MY DEAR? BESIDES, HOW COULD THE POLICE PUT A GHOST IN JAIL--- A DEAD MAN? NO LAW COVERS THAT! HA HA HA HA!
DON'T COME A STEP NEARER...!
RELAX, YOU POOR MORTAL FOOLS! I'M NOT GOING TO HARM YOU!
Y-YOU'RE NOT GOING TO K-KILL US...IN REVENGE...OVER LOSING ME?
NO, MY DEAR! DAN CAN HAVE YOU! I WON'T HARM A HAIR OF YOUR HEAD...OR HIS! I PROMISE!
3

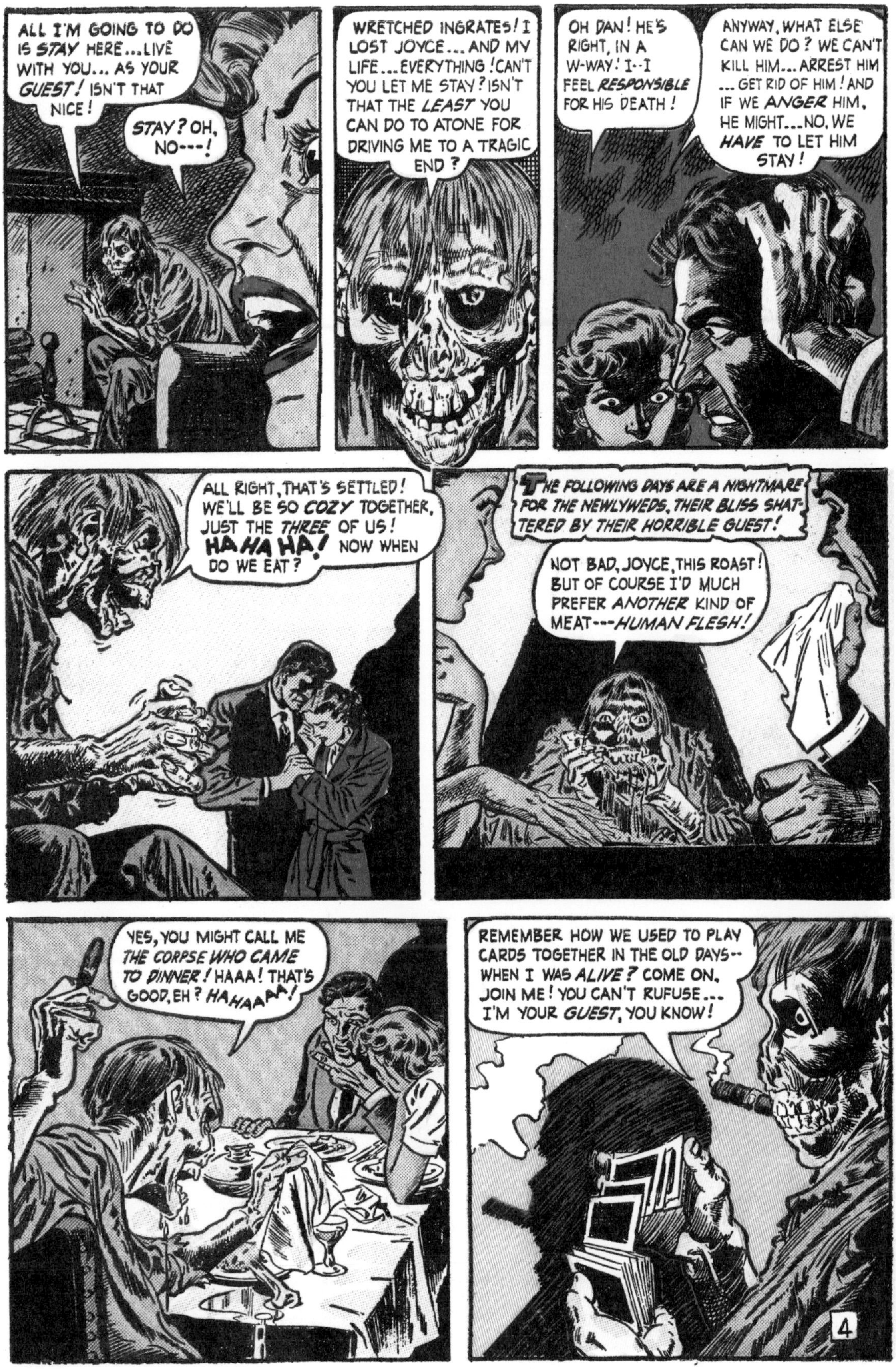
ALL I'M GOING TO DO IS STAY HERE...LIVE WITH YOU... AS YOUR GUEST! ISN'T THAT NICE!
STAY? OH, NO---!
WRETCHED INGRATES! I LOST JOYCE... AND MY LIFE... EVERYTHING! CAN'T YOU LET ME STAY? ISN'T THAT THE LEAST YOU CAN DO TO ATONE FOR DRIVING ME TO A TRAGIC END?
OH DAN! HE'S RIGHT, IN A W-WAY! I--I FEEL RESPONSIBLE FOR HIS DEATH!
ANYWAY, WHAT ELSE CAN WE DO? WE CAN'T KILL HIM... ARREST HIM ... GET RID OF HIM! AND IF WE ANGER HIM, HE MIGHT...NO, WE HAVE TO LET HIM STAY!
ALL RIGHT, THAT'S SETTLED! WE'LL BE SO COZY TOGETHER, JUST THE THREE OF US! HA HA HA! NOW WHEN DO WE EAT?
THE FOLLOWING DAYS ARE A NIGHTMARE FOR THE NEWLYWEDS, THEIR BLISS SHATTERED BY THEIR HORRIBLE GUEST!
NOT BAD, JOYCE, THIS ROAST! BUT OF COURSE I'D MUCH PREFER ANOTHER KIND OF MEAT---HUMAN FLESH!
YES, YOU MIGHT CALL ME THE CORPSE WHO CAME TO DINNER! HAAA! THAT'S GOOD, EH? HAHAAAA!
REMEMBER HOW WE USED TO PLAY CARDS TOGETHER IN THE OLD DAYS-- WHEN I WAS ALIVE? COME ON. JOIN ME! YOU CAN'T RUFUSE... I'M YOUR GUEST, YOU KNOW!
4

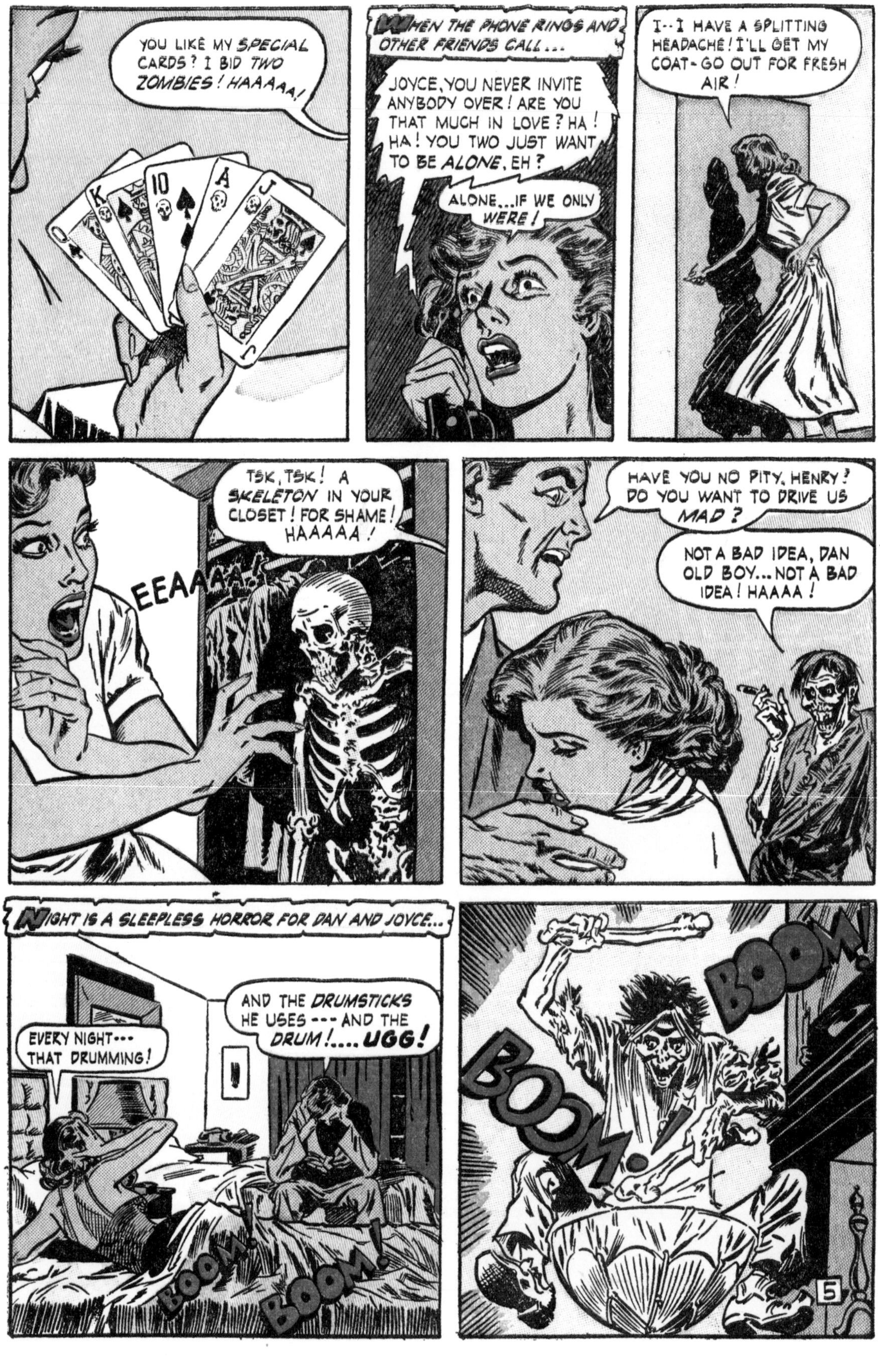

YOU LIKE MY SPECIAL CARDS? I BID TWO ZOMBIES! HAAAAAA!
WHEN THE PHONE RINGS AND OTHER FRIENDS CALL...
JOYCE, YOU NEVER INVITE ANYBODY OVER! ARE YOU THAT MUCH IN LOVE? HA! HA! YOU TWO JUST WANT TO BE ALONE, EH?
ALONE...IF WE ONLY WERE!
I--I HAVE A SPLITTING HEADACHE! I'LL GET MY COAT- GO OUT FOR FRESH AIR!
TSK, TSK! A SKELETON IN YOUR CLOSET! FOR SHAME! HAAAAA!
EEAAAAA!
HAVE YOU NO PITY, HENRY? DO YOU WANT TO DRIVE US MAD?
NOT A BAD IDEA, DAN OLD BOY...NOT A BAD IDEA! HAAAA!
NIGHT IS A SLEEPLESS HORROR FOR DAN AND JOYCE...
EVERY NIGHT--- THAT DRUMMING!
AND THE DRUMSTICKS HE USES --- AND THE DRUM!.... UGG!
BOOM! BOOM!
BOOM! BOOM!
5

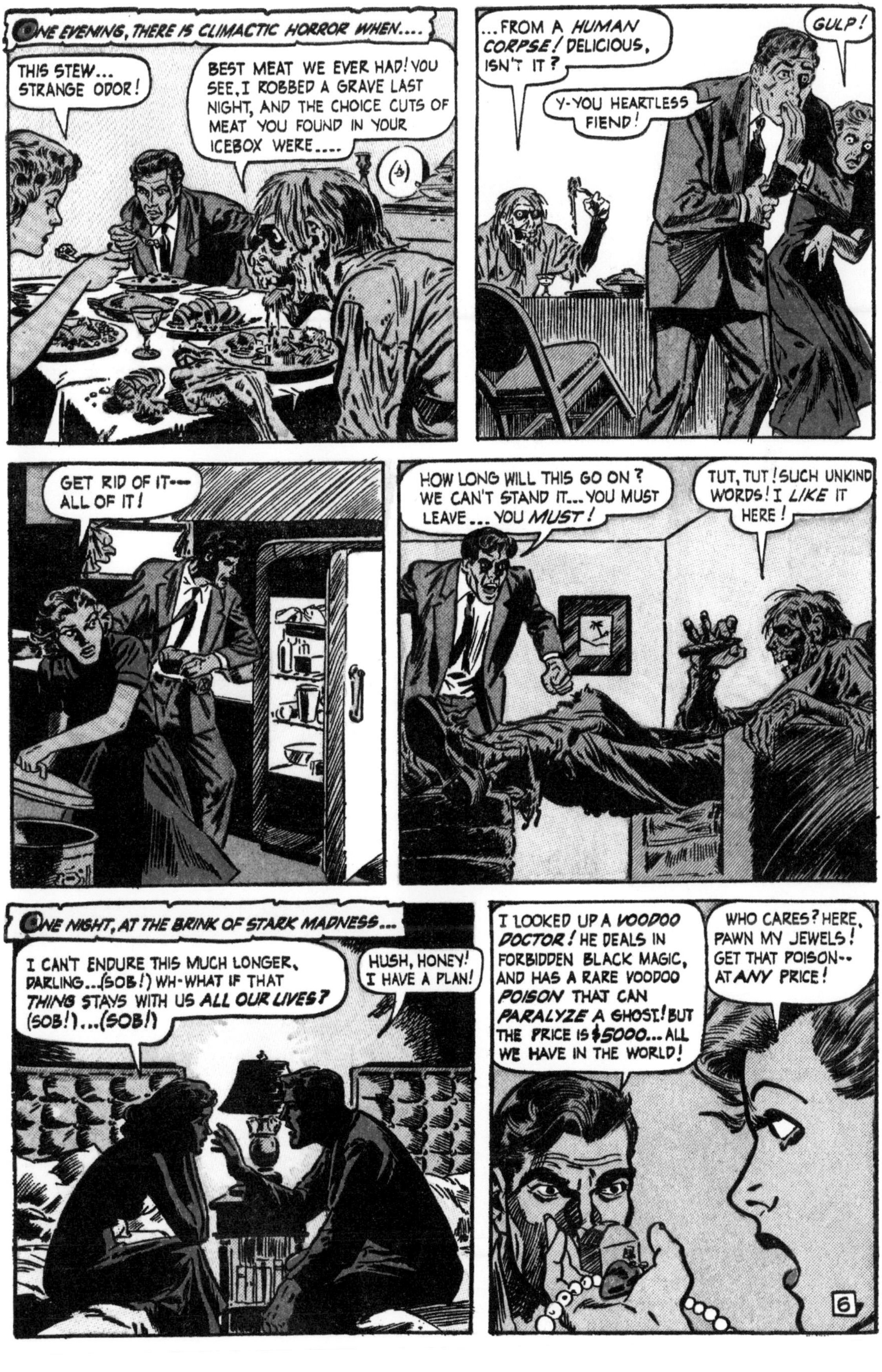
ONE EVENING, THERE IS CLIMACTIC HORROR WHEN....
THIS STEW... STRANGE ODOR!
BEST MEAT WE EVER HAD! YOU SEE, I ROBBED A GRAVE LAST NIGHT, AND THE CHOICE CUTS OF MEAT YOU FOUND IN YOUR ICEBOX WERE....
...FROM A HUMAN CORPSE! DELICIOUS, ISN'T IT?
GULP!
Y-YOU HEARTLESS FIEND!
GET RID OF IT--- ALL OF IT!
HOW LONG WILL THIS GO ON? WE CAN'T STAND IT... YOU MUST LEAVE... YOU MUST!
TUT, TUT! SUCH UNKIND WORDS! I LIKE IT HERE!
ONE NIGHT, AT THE BRINK OF STARK MADNESS...
I CAN'T ENDURE THIS MUCH LONGER, DARLING...(SOB!) WH-WHAT IF THAT THING STAYS WITH US ALL OUR LIVES? (SOB!)...(SOB!)
HUSH, HONEY! I HAVE A PLAN!
I LOOKED UP A VOODOO DOCTOR! HE DEALS IN FORBIDDEN BLACK MAGIC, AND HAS A RARE VOODOO POISON THAT CAN PARALYZE A GHOST! BUT THE PRICE IS $5000... ALL WE HAVE IN THE WORLD!
WHO CARES? HERE, PAWN MY JEWELS! GET THAT POISON-- AT ANY PRICE!
6

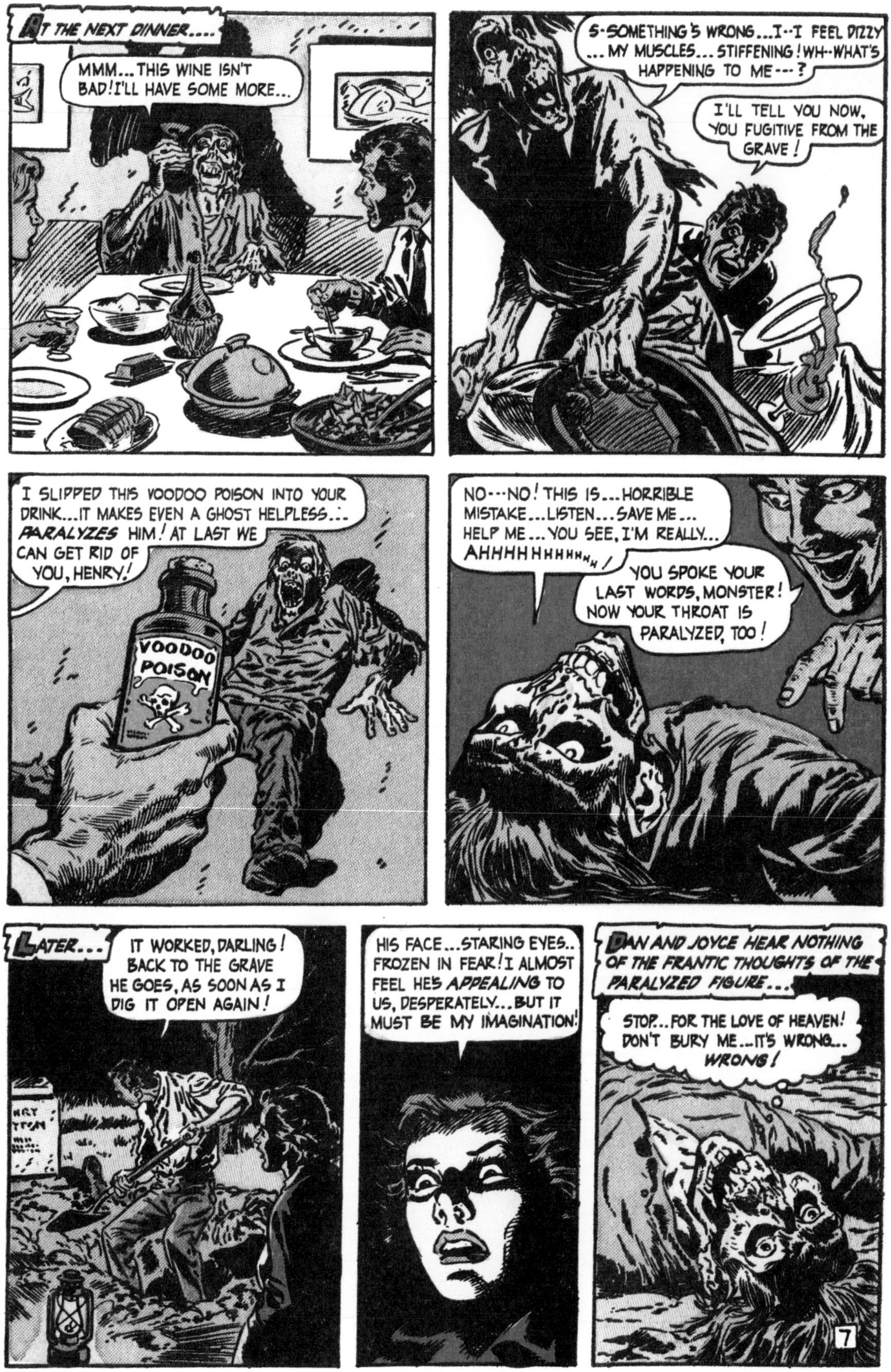
AT THE NEXT DINNER....
MMM...THIS WINE ISN'T BAD! I'LL HAVE SOME MORE...
S-SOMETHING'S WRONG...I--I FEEL DIZZY ...MY MUSCLES... STIFFENING! WH--WHAT'S HAPPENING TO ME---?
I'LL TELL YOU NOW, YOU FUGITIVE FROM THE GRAVE!
I SLIPPED THIS VOODOO POISON INTO YOUR DRINK...IT MAKES EVEN A GHOST HELPLESS... PARALYZES HIM! AT LAST WE CAN GET RID OF YOU, HENRY!
VOODOO POISON
NO---NO! THIS IS...HORRIBLE MISTAKE...LISTEN...SAVE ME... HELP ME...YOU SEE, I'M REALLY... AHHHHHHHHHH!
YOU SPOKE YOUR LAST WORDS, MONSTER! NOW YOUR THROAT IS PARALYZED, TOO!
LATER...
IT WORKED, DARLING! BACK TO THE GRAVE HE GOES, AS SOON AS I DIG IT OPEN AGAIN!
HIS FACE...STARING EYES.. FROZEN IN FEAR! I ALMOST FEEL HE'S APPEALING TO US, DESPERATELY...BUT IT MUST BE MY IMAGINATION!
DAN AND JOYCE HEAR NOTHING OF THE FRANTIC THOUGHTS OF THE PARALYZED FIGURE...
STOP...FOR THE LOVE OF HEAVEN! DON'T BURY ME...IT'S WRONG... WRONG!
7

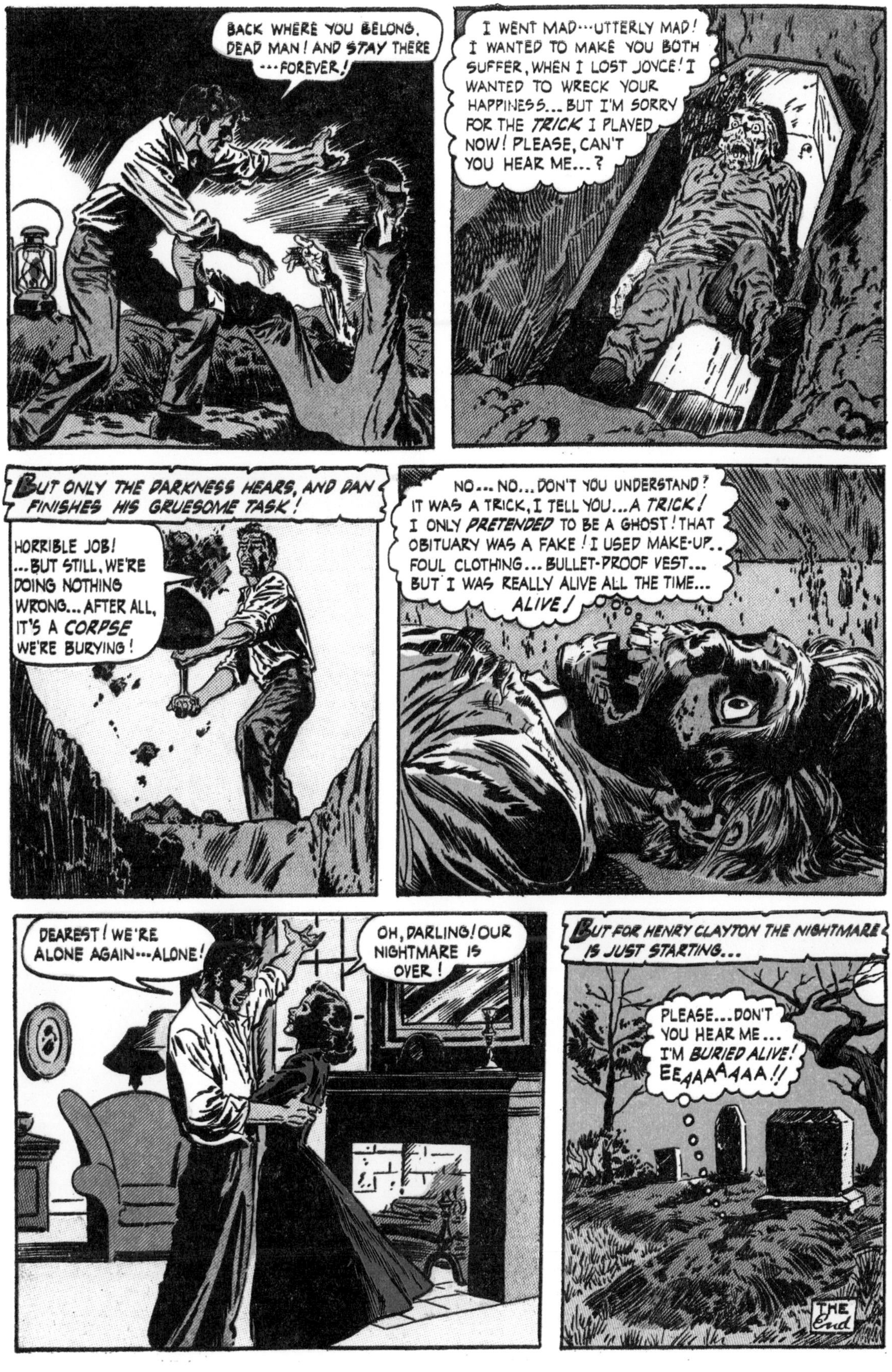
BACK WHERE YOU BELONG, DEAD MAN! AND STAY THERE ...FOREVER!
I WENT MAD...UTTERLY MAD! I WANTED TO MAKE YOU BOTH SUFFER, WHEN I LOST JOYCE! I WANTED TO WRECK YOUR HAPPINESS... BUT I'M SORRY FOR THE TRICK I PLAYED NOW! PLEASE, CAN'T YOU HEAR ME...?
BUT ONLY THE DARKNESS HEARS, AND DAN FINISHES HIS GRUESOME TASK!
HORRIBLE JOB! ...BUT STILL, WE'RE DOING NOTHING WRONG... AFTER ALL, IT'S A CORPSE WE'RE BURYING!
NO... NO... DON'T YOU UNDERSTAND? IT WAS A TRICK, I TELL YOU... A TRICK! I ONLY PRETENDED TO BE A GHOST! THAT OBITUARY WAS A FAKE! I USED MAKE-UP.. FOUL CLOTHING... BULLET-PROOF VEST... BUT I WAS REALLY ALIVE ALL THE TIME... ALIVE!
DEAREST! WE'RE ALONE AGAIN...ALONE!
OH, DARLING! OUR NIGHTMARE IS OVER!
BUT FOR HENRY CLAYTON THE NIGHTMARE IS JUST STARTING...
PLEASE...DON'T YOU HEAR ME... I'M BURIED ALIVE! EEAAAAAAA!!
THE End

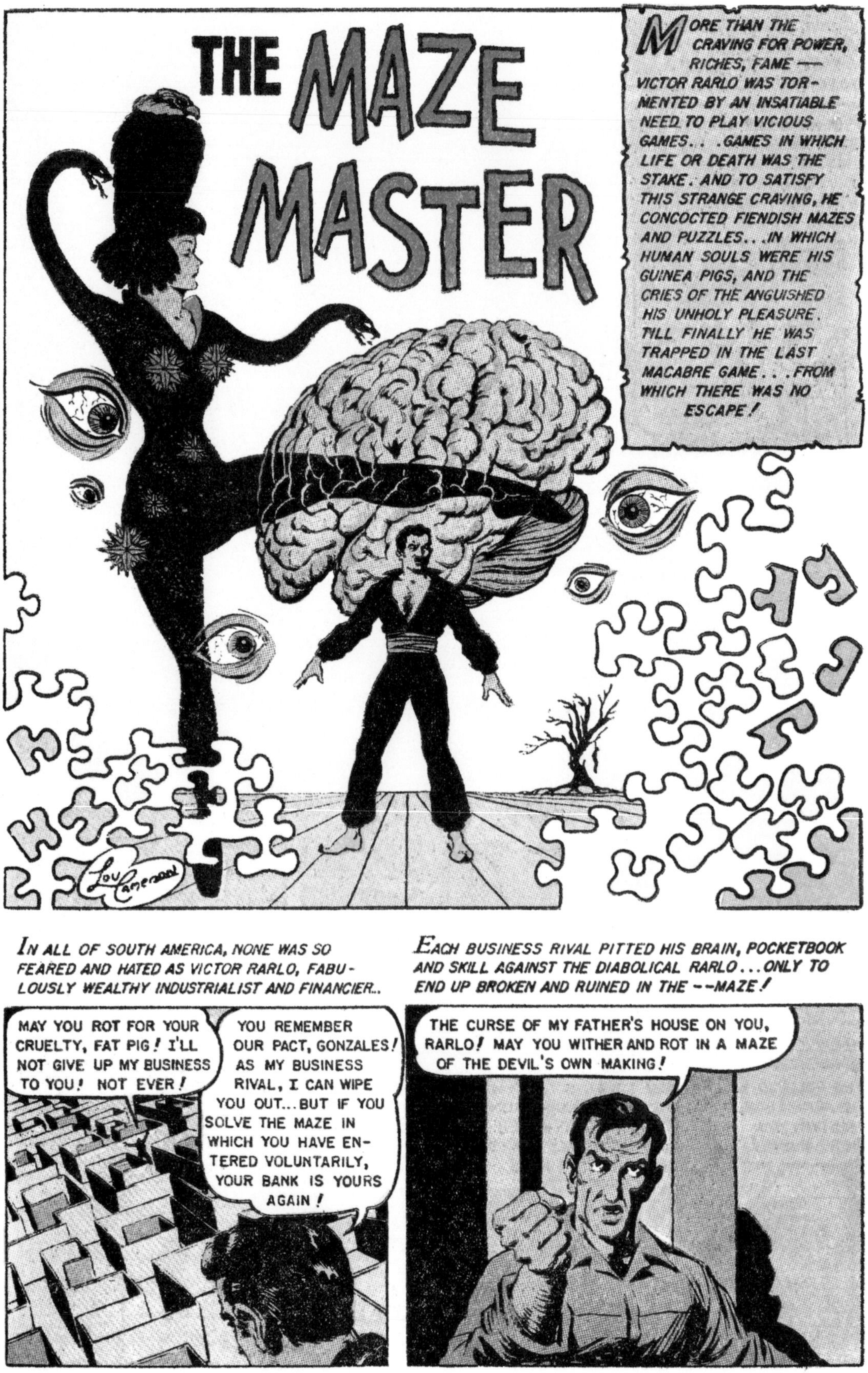
THE MAZE MASTER
MORE THAN THE CRAVING FOR POWER, RICHES, FAME — VICTOR RARLO WAS TORMENTED BY AN INSATIABLE NEED TO PLAY VICIOUS GAMES. . .GAMES IN WHICH LIFE OR DEATH WAS THE STAKE. AND TO SATISFY THIS STRANGE CRAVING, HE CONCOCTED FIENDISH MAZES AND PUZZLES. . .IN WHICH HUMAN SOULS WERE HIS GUINEA PIGS, AND THE CRIES OF THE ANGUISHED HIS UNHOLY PLEASURE. TILL FINALLY HE WAS TRAPPED IN THE LAST MACABRE GAME. . .FROM WHICH THERE WAS NO ESCAPE!
Lou Cameron
IN ALL OF SOUTH AMERICA, NONE WAS SO FEARED AND HATED AS VICTOR RARLO, FABULOUSLY WEALTHY INDUSTRIALIST AND FINANCIER..
MAY YOU ROT FOR YOUR CRUELTY, FAT PIG! I'LL NOT GIVE UP MY BUSINESS TO YOU! NOT EVER!
YOU REMEMBER OUR PACT, GONZALES! AS MY BUSINESS RIVAL, I CAN WIPE YOU OUT...BUT IF YOU SOLVE THE MAZE IN WHICH YOU HAVE ENTERED VOLUNTARILY, YOUR BANK IS YOURS AGAIN!
EACH BUSINESS RIVAL PITTED HIS BRAIN, POCKETBOOK AND SKILL AGAINST THE DIABOLICAL RARLO...ONLY TO END UP BROKEN AND RUINED IN THE --MAZE!
THE CURSE OF MY FATHER'S HOUSE ON YOU, RARLO! MAY YOU WITHER AND ROT IN A MAZE OF THE DEVIL'S OWN MAKING!

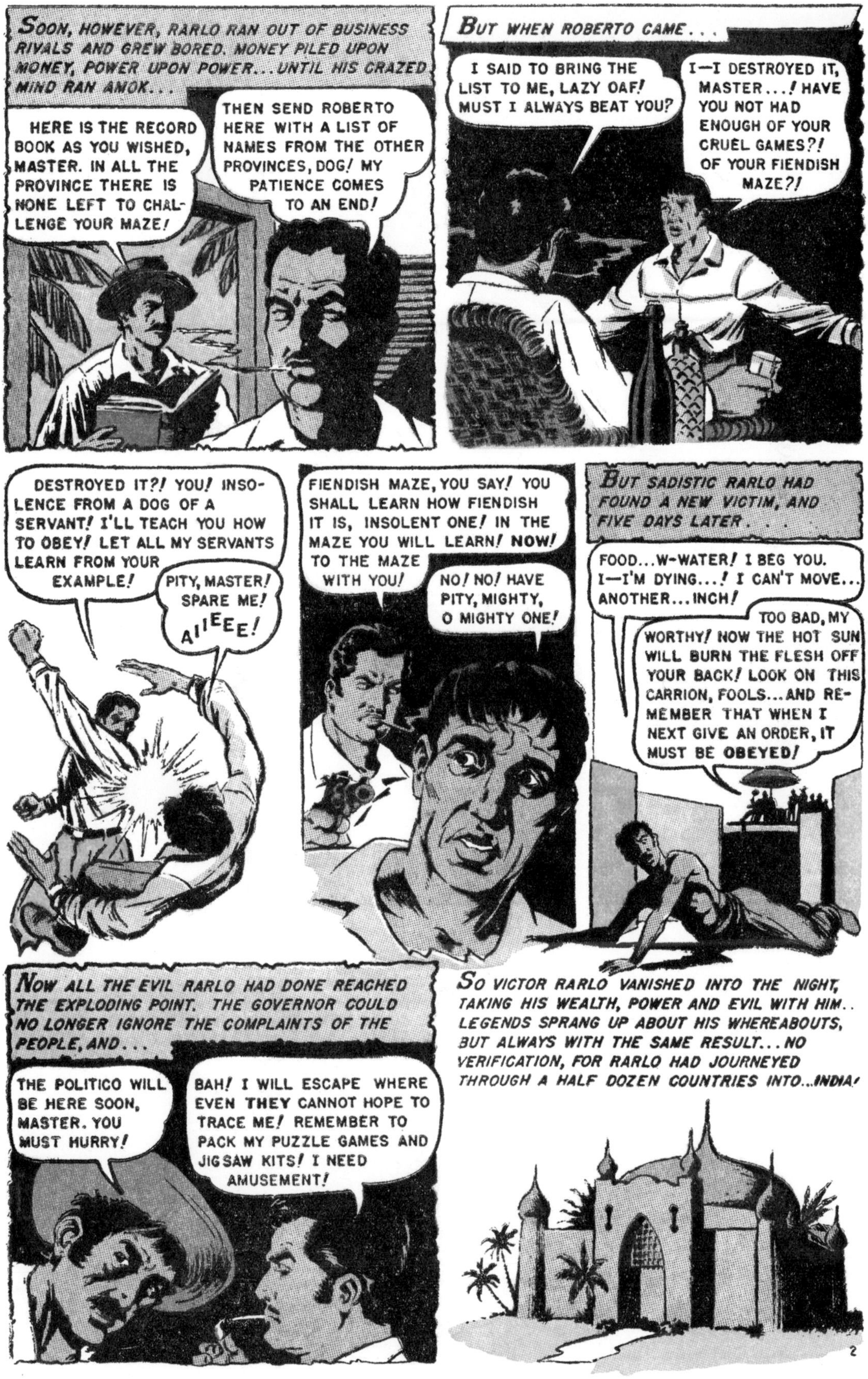
SOON, HOWEVER, RARLO RAN OUT OF BUSINESS RIVALS AND GREW BORED. MONEY PILED UPON MONEY, POWER UPON POWER... UNTIL HIS CRAZED MIND RAN AMOK...
HERE IS THE RECORD BOOK AS YOU WISHED, MASTER. IN ALL THE PROVINCE THERE IS NONE LEFT TO CHALLENGE YOUR MAZE!
THEN SEND ROBERTO HERE WITH A LIST OF NAMES FROM THE OTHER PROVINCES, DOG! MY PATIENCE COMES TO AN END!
BUT WHEN ROBERTO CAME...
I SAID TO BRING THE LIST TO ME, LAZY OAF! MUST I ALWAYS BEAT YOU?
I—I DESTROYED IT, MASTER...! HAVE YOU NOT HAD ENOUGH OF YOUR CRUEL GAMES?! OF YOUR FIENDISH MAZE?!
DESTROYED IT?! YOU! INSOLENCE FROM A DOG OF A SERVANT! I'LL TEACH YOU HOW TO OBEY! LET ALL MY SERVANTS LEARN FROM YOUR EXAMPLE!
PITY, MASTER! SPARE ME! AIIEEE!
FIENDISH MAZE, YOU SAY! YOU SHALL LEARN HOW FIENDISH IT IS, INSOLENT ONE! IN THE MAZE YOU WILL LEARN! NOW! TO THE MAZE WITH YOU!
NO! NO! HAVE PITY, MIGHTY, O MIGHTY ONE!
BUT SADISTIC RARLO HAD FOUND A NEW VICTIM, AND FIVE DAYS LATER...
FOOD...W-WATER! I BEG YOU. I—I'M DYING...! I CAN'T MOVE... ANOTHER...INCH!
TOO BAD, MY WORTHY! NOW THE HOT SUN WILL BURN THE FLESH OFF YOUR BACK! LOOK ON THIS CARRION, FOOLS...AND REMEMBER THAT WHEN I NEXT GIVE AN ORDER, IT MUST BE OBEYED!
NOW ALL THE EVIL RARLO HAD DONE REACHED THE EXPLODING POINT. THE GOVERNOR COULD NO LONGER IGNORE THE COMPLAINTS OF THE PEOPLE, AND...
THE POLITICO WILL BE HERE SOON, MASTER. YOU MUST HURRY!
BAH! I WILL ESCAPE WHERE EVEN THEY CANNOT HOPE TO TRACE ME! REMEMBER TO PACK MY PUZZLE GAMES AND JIGSAW KITS! I NEED AMUSEMENT!
SO VICTOR RARLO VANISHED INTO THE NIGHT, TAKING HIS WEALTH, POWER AND EVIL WITH HIM.. LEGENDS SPRANG UP ABOUT HIS WHEREABOUTS, BUT ALWAYS WITH THE SAME RESULT... NO VERIFICATION, FOR RARLO HAD JOURNEYED THROUGH A HALF DOZEN COUNTRIES INTO...INDIA!
2

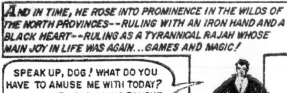

AND IN TIME, HE ROSE INTO PROMINENCE IN THE WILDS OF THE NORTH PROVINCES--RULING WITH AN IRON HAND AND A BLACK HEART--RULING AS A TYRANNICAL RAJAH WHOSE MAIN JOY IN LIFE WAS AGAIN...GAMES AND MAGIC!

SPEAK UP, DOG! WHAT DO YOU HAVE TO AMUSE ME WITH TODAY? I WILL HAVE YOUR LYING TONGUE CUT OUT IF YOU BRING ME SILLY TRICKS!

OH GREAT RAJAH ...I OFFER YOU THE GIFT OF THE GENII! YOU WILL INDEED BE SUPREME!

BEHOLD...YOU SHALL HAVE THE MAGIC POWER OF COMMANDING THE DEAD!

BAH! I ASKED YOU FOR PUZZLES...FOR GAMES THAT KNOW NO COMPARISON... AND YOU OFFER ME MORBID PURSUITS!

GET RID OF THIS DOG AND FIND ME SOMEONE WHO CAN BRIGHTEN UP THE WAKING MOMENTS OF MY LIFE!

AIIEE....! NO, GREAT RAJAH! LET ME LIVE! I—I CAN SHOW YOU THE SECRETS OF THE BEYOND!

THUS MAGICIANS, SORCERERS, SOOTHSAYERS AND OTHER CONJURORS FLOCKED TO RARLO'S DOMAIN... NOW MECCA FOR ALL WEIRD AND EERIE RITES. THEN ONE NIGHT AT DINNER...

WHAT WOULD YOU SAY, OH GREAT ONE... IF YOU COULD PENETRATE THE VEIL OF TIME AND SPACE AND SOLVE THE MAZES OF ANOTHER WORLD SET BEFORE THEE?

I WOULD REWARD YOU WITH MUCH WEALTH, MYSTIC ...IF YOU SUCCEED IN OFFERING ME A WORTHY CHALLENGE! LET US HEAR FURTHER!

TAKE HEED, MIGHTY RARLO! NONE HAS OVERCOME THE MAZES OF THIS MYSTIC! YOUR SOUL MAY BE FOREVER FORFEIT!

SILENCE, FOOLS! I AM TIRED OF STUPID PUZZLES I CAN EASILY SOLVE. I CRAVE A CHALLENGE WORTHY OF ME!

WHILE YOUR BODY REMAINS HERE IN SAFETY, YOUR MIND SHALL TRAVEL TO A DESTINATION ONLY I WILL KNOW. YOUR TASK...TO SOLVE THE MAZE OF YOUR DESTINATION AND RETURN. I WARN THEE AGAIN. IT IS DANGEROUS!

BAH! I FEAR NOTHING! I CAN SOLVE ANY MAZE DEVISED BY MAN!

BUT THE STRANGE MYSTIC HAD ALREADY GONE INTO A TRANCE... AND NOW, AS THE OMINOUS WORDS OF AN EERIE SPELL POURED FORTH FROM HIS LIPS, A VAPOUR TOOK HOLD OF VICTOR RARLO... A VAPOUR THAT SENT HIM REELING INTO THE MISTS OF THE BEYOND!

RARLO...RARLO...COME! COME! COME STRAIGHT INTO THE WEB! HA HA HA HA HA!

FEEL SO NUMB ...SO STRANGE...

3

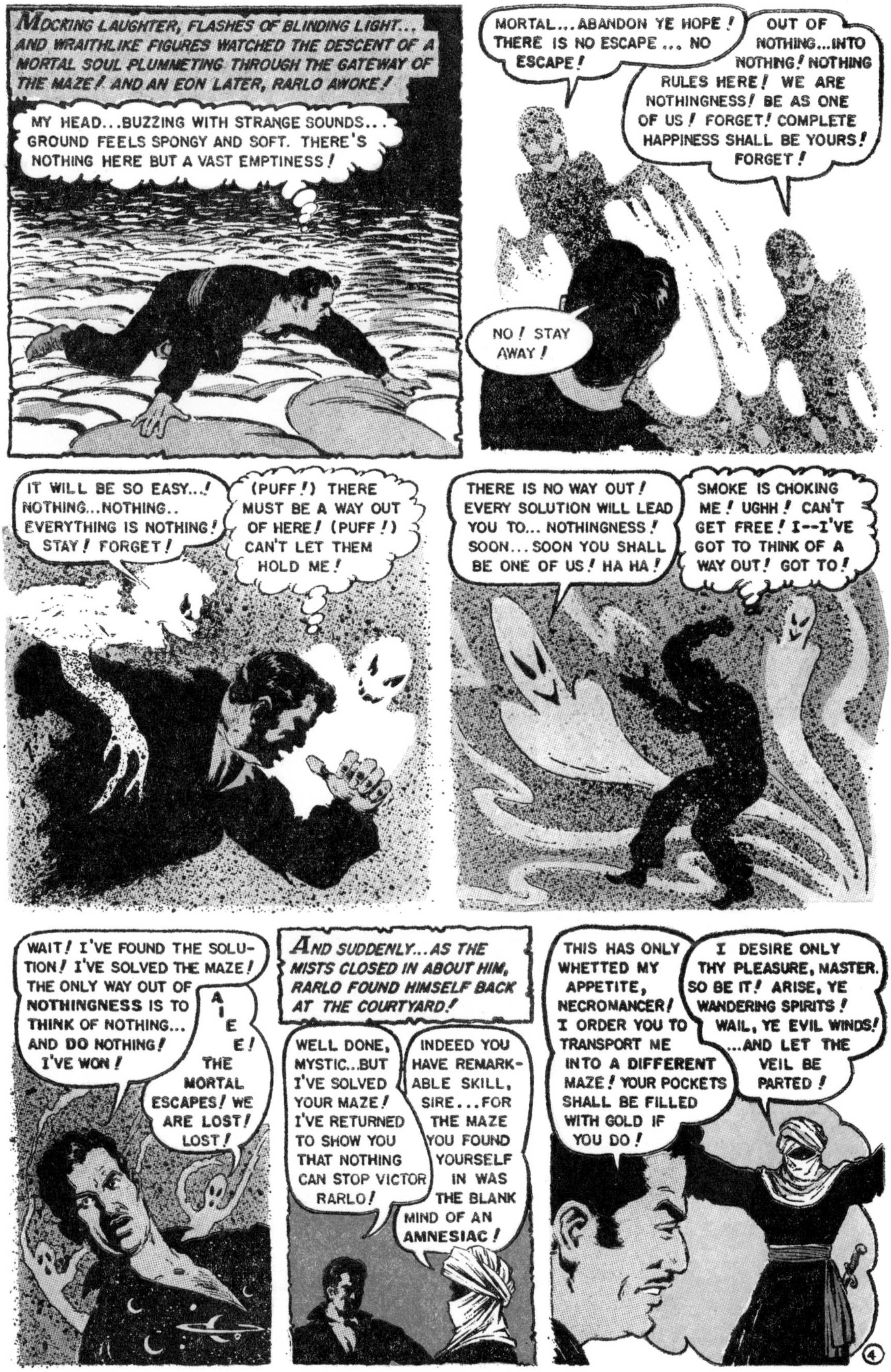
MOCKING LAUGHTER, FLASHES OF BLINDING LIGHT... AND WRAITHLIKE FIGURES WATCHED THE DESCENT OF A MORTAL SOUL PLUMMETING THROUGH THE GATEWAY OF THE MAZE! AND AN EON LATER, RARLO AWOKE!
MY HEAD...BUZZING WITH STRANGE SOUNDS... GROUND FEELS SPONGY AND SOFT. THERE'S NOTHING HERE BUT A VAST EMPTINESS!
MORTAL...ABANDON YE HOPE! THERE IS NO ESCAPE... NO ESCAPE!
OUT OF NOTHING...INTO NOTHING! NOTHING RULES HERE! WE ARE NOTHINGNESS! BE AS ONE OF US! FORGET! COMPLETE HAPPINESS SHALL BE YOURS! FORGET!
NO! STAY AWAY!
IT WILL BE SO EASY...! NOTHING...NOTHING.. EVERYTHING IS NOTHING! STAY! FORGET!
(PUFF!) THERE MUST BE A WAY OUT OF HERE! (PUFF!) CAN'T LET THEM HOLD ME!
THERE IS NO WAY OUT! EVERY SOLUTION WILL LEAD YOU TO... NOTHINGNESS! SOON... SOON YOU SHALL BE ONE OF US! HA HA!
SMOKE IS CHOKING ME! UGHH! CAN'T GET FREE! I--I'VE GOT TO THINK OF A WAY OUT! GOT TO!
WAIT! I'VE FOUND THE SOLUTION! I'VE SOLVED THE MAZE! THE ONLY WAY OUT OF NOTHINGNESS IS TO THINK OF NOTHING... AND DO NOTHING! I'VE WON!
AIEE!
THE MORTAL ESCAPES! WE ARE LOST! LOST!
AND SUDDENLY...AS THE MISTS CLOSED IN ABOUT HIM, RARLO FOUND HIMSELF BACK AT THE COURTYARD!
WELL DONE, MYSTIC...BUT I'VE SOLVED YOUR MAZE! I'VE RETURNED TO SHOW YOU THAT NOTHING CAN STOP VICTOR RARLO!
INDEED YOU HAVE REMARKABLE SKILL, SIRE...FOR THE MAZE YOU FOUND YOURSELF IN WAS THE BLANK MIND OF AN AMNESIAC!
THIS HAS ONLY WHETTED MY APPETITE, NECROMANCER! I ORDER YOU TO TRANSPORT ME INTO A DIFFERENT MAZE! YOUR POCKETS SHALL BE FILLED WITH GOLD IF YOU DO!
I DESIRE ONLY THY PLEASURE, MASTER. SO BE IT! ARISE, YE WANDERING SPIRITS! WAIL, YE EVIL WINDS! ...AND LET THE VEIL BE PARTED!
4

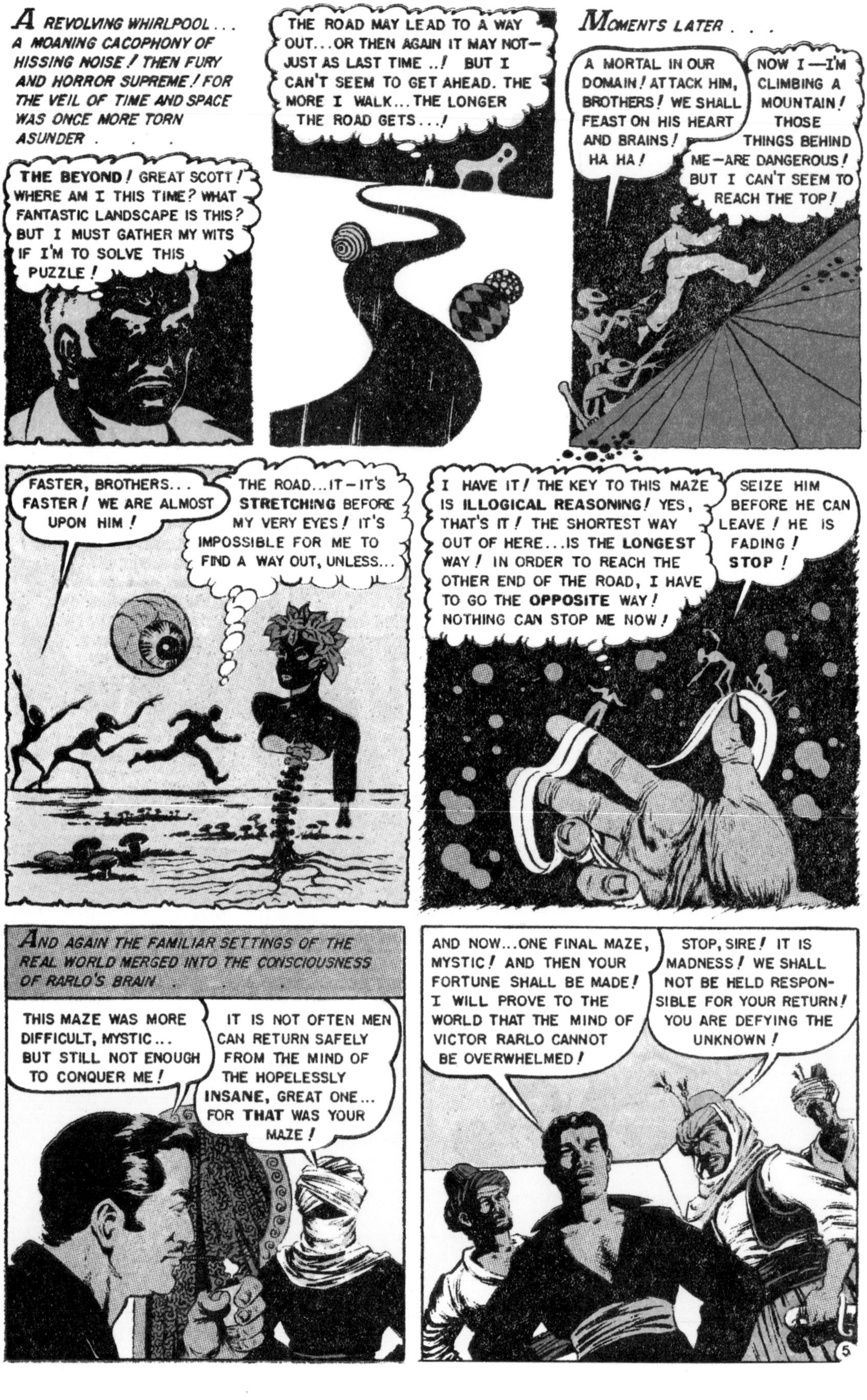
A REVOLVING WHIRLPOOL . . . A MOANING CACOPHONY OF HISSING NOISE! THEN FURY AND HORROR SUPREME! FOR THE VEIL OF TIME AND SPACE WAS ONCE MORE TORN ASUNDER . . .
THE BEYOND! GREAT SCOTT! WHERE AM I THIS TIME? WHAT FANTASTIC LANDSCAPE IS THIS? BUT I MUST GATHER MY WITS IF I'M TO SOLVE THIS PUZZLE!
THE ROAD MAY LEAD TO A WAY OUT...OR THEN AGAIN IT MAY NOT—JUST AS LAST TIME ..! BUT I CAN'T SEEM TO GET AHEAD. THE MORE I WALK... THE LONGER THE ROAD GETS...!
MOMENTS LATER . . .
A MORTAL IN OUR DOMAIN! ATTACK HIM, BROTHERS! WE SHALL FEAST ON HIS HEART AND BRAINS! HA HA!
NOW I—I'M CLIMBING A MOUNTAIN! THOSE THINGS BEHIND ME—ARE DANGEROUS! BUT I CAN'T SEEM TO REACH THE TOP!
FASTER, BROTHERS... FASTER! WE ARE ALMOST UPON HIM!
THE ROAD...IT—IT'S STRETCHING BEFORE MY VERY EYES! IT'S IMPOSSIBLE FOR ME TO FIND A WAY OUT, UNLESS...
I HAVE IT! THE KEY TO THIS MAZE IS ILLOGICAL REASONING! YES, THAT'S IT! THE SHORTEST WAY OUT OF HERE...IS THE LONGEST WAY! IN ORDER TO REACH THE OTHER END OF THE ROAD, I HAVE TO GO THE OPPOSITE WAY! NOTHING CAN STOP ME NOW!
SEIZE HIM BEFORE HE CAN LEAVE! HE IS FADING! STOP!
AND AGAIN THE FAMILIAR SETTINGS OF THE REAL WORLD MERGED INTO THE CONSCIOUSNESS OF RARLO'S BRAIN . . .
THIS MAZE WAS MORE DIFFICULT, MYSTIC... BUT STILL NOT ENOUGH TO CONQUER ME!
IT IS NOT OFTEN MEN CAN RETURN SAFELY FROM THE MIND OF THE HOPELESSLY INSANE, GREAT ONE... FOR THAT WAS YOUR MAZE!
AND NOW...ONE FINAL MAZE, MYSTIC! AND THEN YOUR FORTUNE SHALL BE MADE! I WILL PROVE TO THE WORLD THAT THE MIND OF VICTOR RARLO CANNOT BE OVERWHELMED!
STOP, SIRE! IT IS MADNESS! WE SHALL NOT BE HELD RESPONSIBLE FOR YOUR RETURN! YOU ARE DEFYING THE UNKNOWN!
5

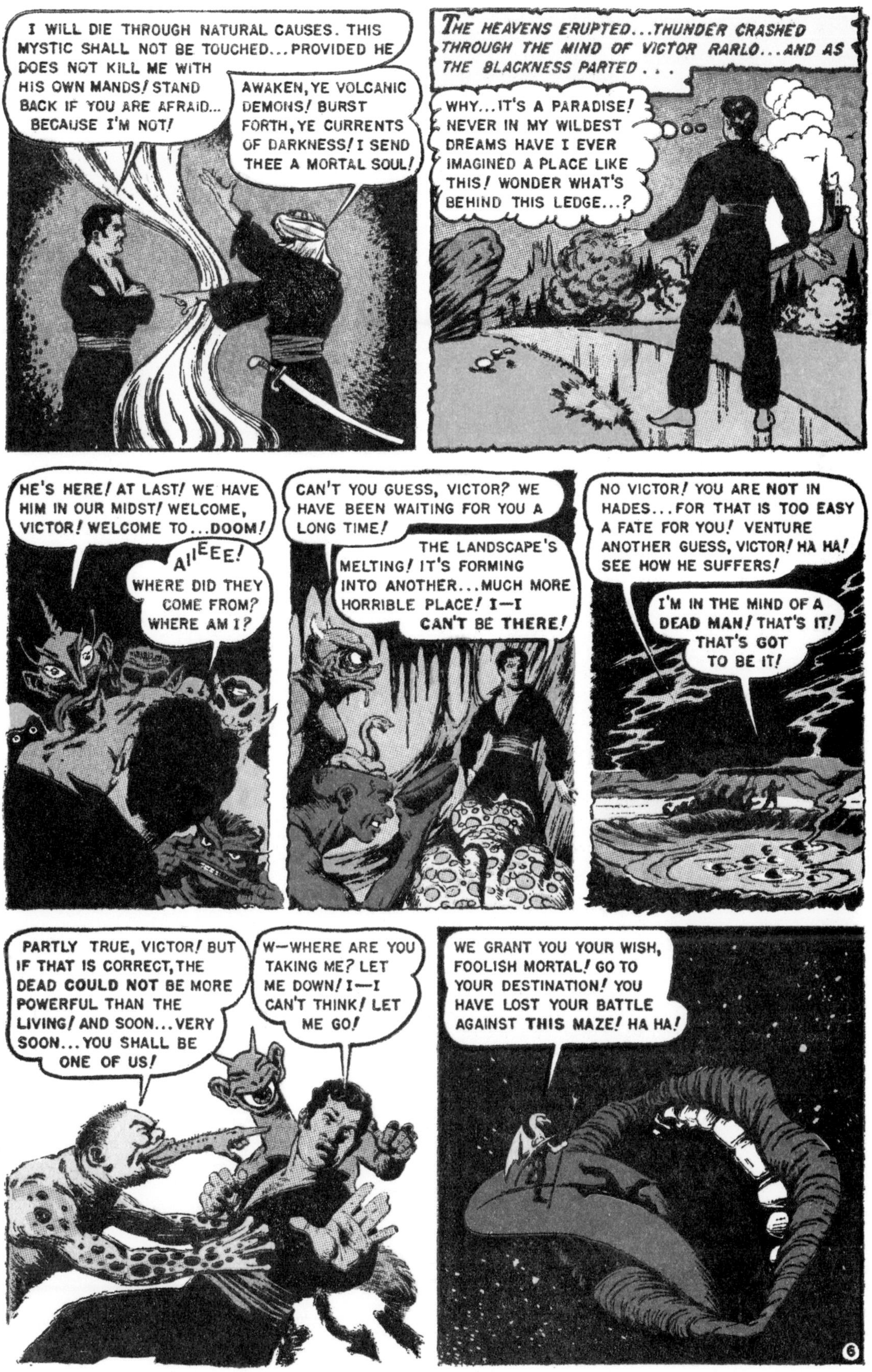
I WILL DIE THROUGH NATURAL CAUSES. THIS MYSTIC SHALL NOT BE TOUCHED... PROVIDED HE DOES NOT KILL ME WITH HIS OWN HANDS! STAND BACK IF YOU ARE AFRAID... BECAUSE I'M NOT!
AWAKEN, YE VOLCANIC DEMONS! BURST FORTH, YE CURRENTS OF DARKNESS! I SEND THEE A MORTAL SOUL!
THE HEAVENS ERUPTED... THUNDER CRASHED THROUGH THE MIND OF VICTOR RARLO... AND AS THE BLACKNESS PARTED . . .
WHY... IT'S A PARADISE! NEVER IN MY WILDEST DREAMS HAVE I EVER IMAGINED A PLACE LIKE THIS! WONDER WHAT'S BEHIND THIS LEDGE...?
HE'S HERE! AT LAST! WE HAVE HIM IN OUR MIDST! WELCOME, VICTOR! WELCOME TO... DOOM!
AIIEEE! WHERE DID THEY COME FROM? WHERE AM I?
CAN'T YOU GUESS, VICTOR? WE HAVE BEEN WAITING FOR YOU A LONG TIME!
THE LANDSCAPE'S MELTING! IT'S FORMING INTO ANOTHER... MUCH MORE HORRIBLE PLACE! I—I CAN'T BE THERE!
NO VICTOR! YOU ARE NOT IN HADES... FOR THAT IS TOO EASY A FATE FOR YOU! VENTURE ANOTHER GUESS, VICTOR! HA HA! SEE HOW HE SUFFERS!
I'M IN THE MIND OF A DEAD MAN! THAT'S IT! THAT'S GOT TO BE IT!
PARTLY TRUE, VICTOR! BUT IF THAT IS CORRECT, THE DEAD COULD NOT BE MORE POWERFUL THAN THE LIVING! AND SOON... VERY SOON... YOU SHALL BE ONE OF US!
W—WHERE ARE YOU TAKING ME? LET ME DOWN! I—I CAN'T THINK! LET ME GO!
WE GRANT YOU YOUR WISH, FOOLISH MORTAL! GO TO YOUR DESTINATION! YOU HAVE LOST YOUR BATTLE AGAINST THIS MAZE! HA HA!
6

SECONDS AFTERWARDS, IN THE COURTYARD OF VICTOR RARLO...

THE GREAT ONE DOES NOT MOVE! HE IS DEAD...AND THIS STRANGE MYSTIC HAS KILLED HIM! OFF WITH HIS HEAD!

STAY YOUR HANDS! I HAVE CARRIED OUT MY PART OF THE BARGAIN TO THE LETTER. NOT ONCE HAVE YOU SEEN ME PLACE A HAND UPON HIM! YOU CONJURORS AND OTHER MYSTICS ...YOU MUST BEAR ME OUT!

YEA! THAT IS INDEED TRUE! HE HAS KEPT HIS WORD! HE IS INNOCENT!

THIS THIRD AND LAST MAZE THE RAJAH SAHIB WAS NOT ABLE TO SOLVE, FOR IT WAS THE MAZE OF HIS OWN MIND! I KNOW NOT OF HIS DEEDS UPON THIS EARTH... BUT A MAN'S MIND IS THE PRISON OF HIS SOUL!

BUT IS HE REALLY DEAD? SURELY YOU CAN CAST ANOTHER SPELL AND DRAW HIM BACK TO THE WORLD OF THE LIVING!

HE IS NOT DEAD --BUT HE WILL NEVER BE SUMMONED BACK HERE AGAIN THOUGH I CAST A HUNDRED SPELLS! THAT IS THE FATE OF THOSE WHO WOULD CHALLENGE THE MAZE OF THEIR OWN MINDS! TAKE YE THE GOLD! MY REWARD HAS BEEN GIVEN ME! I BID THEE FAREWELL!

SLOWLY, A MAN WALKS DOWN A FOREST ROAD. SLOWLY, HE UNWINDS A TURBAN FROM HIS HEAD-- AND HERE AND THERE ARE PATCHES OF WHITE SKIN SHOWING WHERE THE MASK ON HIS FACE HAS RUBBED OFF THE PAINT . . . .

IT IS TIME TO STAND REVEALED. FIVE YEARS OF PURSUIT ARE OVER! MY OCCULT STUDIES HAVE NOT BEEN IN VAIN!

REST WELL, MY ROBERTO. YOUR OWN BROTHER HAS AVENGED YOU. VICTOR RARLO IS NO MORE... FOR HE IS TRAPPED FOREVER IN THE MAZE OF HIS OWN EGOTISTICAL CONSCIENCE...A MAZE OF INCREDIBLE EVIL AND SELF-TORTURE FROM WHICH THE ONLY ESCAPE CAN BE DEATH!

THE END

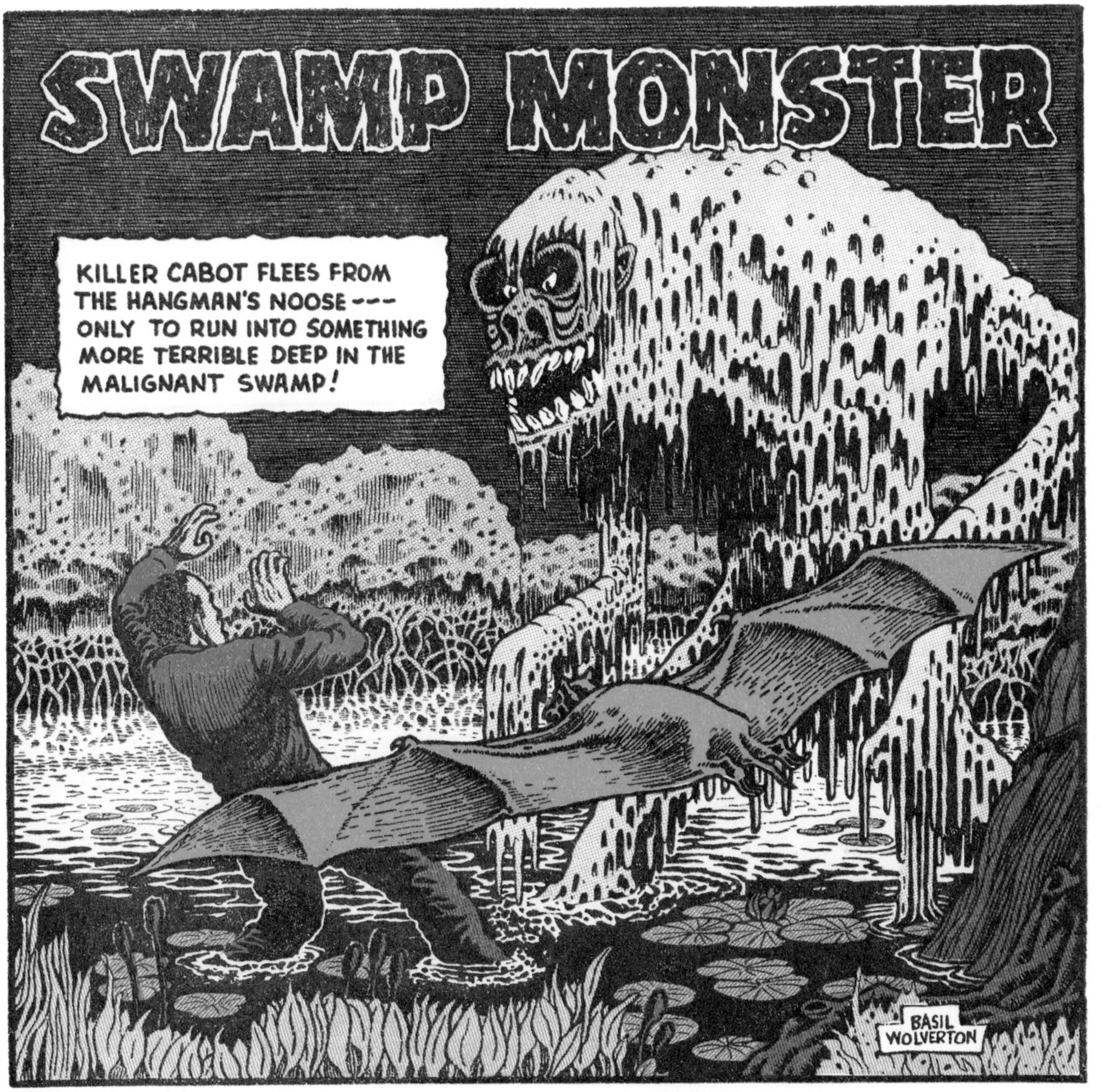
SWAMP MONSTER
KILLER CABOT FLEES FROM THE HANGMAN'S NOOSE--- ONLY TO RUN INTO SOMETHING MORE TERRIBLE DEEP IN THE MALIGNANT SWAMP!
BASIL WOLVERTON

YOU'VE MANAGED TO BREAK JAIL ONLY HOURS BEFORE YOU'RE TO HANG FOR MURDER, JACK CABOT! YOU'VE PLAYED IT SMART---YOU THINK....

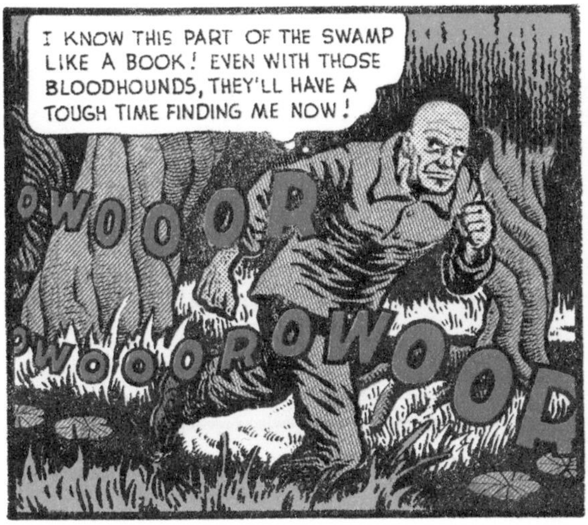
I KNOW THIS PART OF THE SWAMP LIKE A BOOK! EVEN WITH THOSE BLOODHOUNDS, THEY'LL HAVE A TOUGH TIME FINDING ME NOW!

YOU JOG STEADILY INTO THE DISMAL MARSH, TAKING ADVANTAGE OF HIDDEN PATHS YOU KNOW SO WELL.....

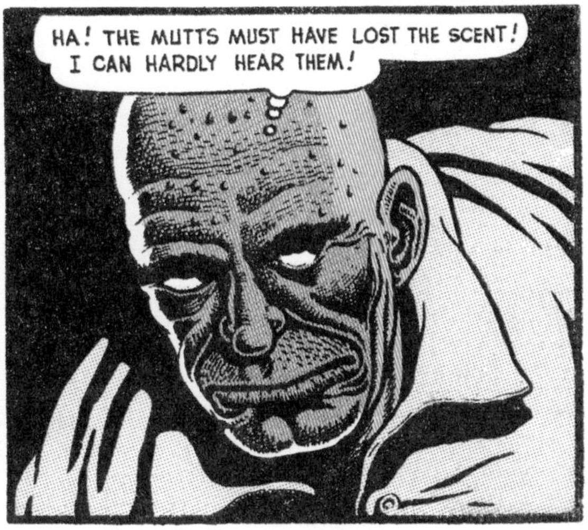
HA! THE MUTTS MUST HAVE LOST THE SCENT! I CAN HARDLY HEAR THEM!

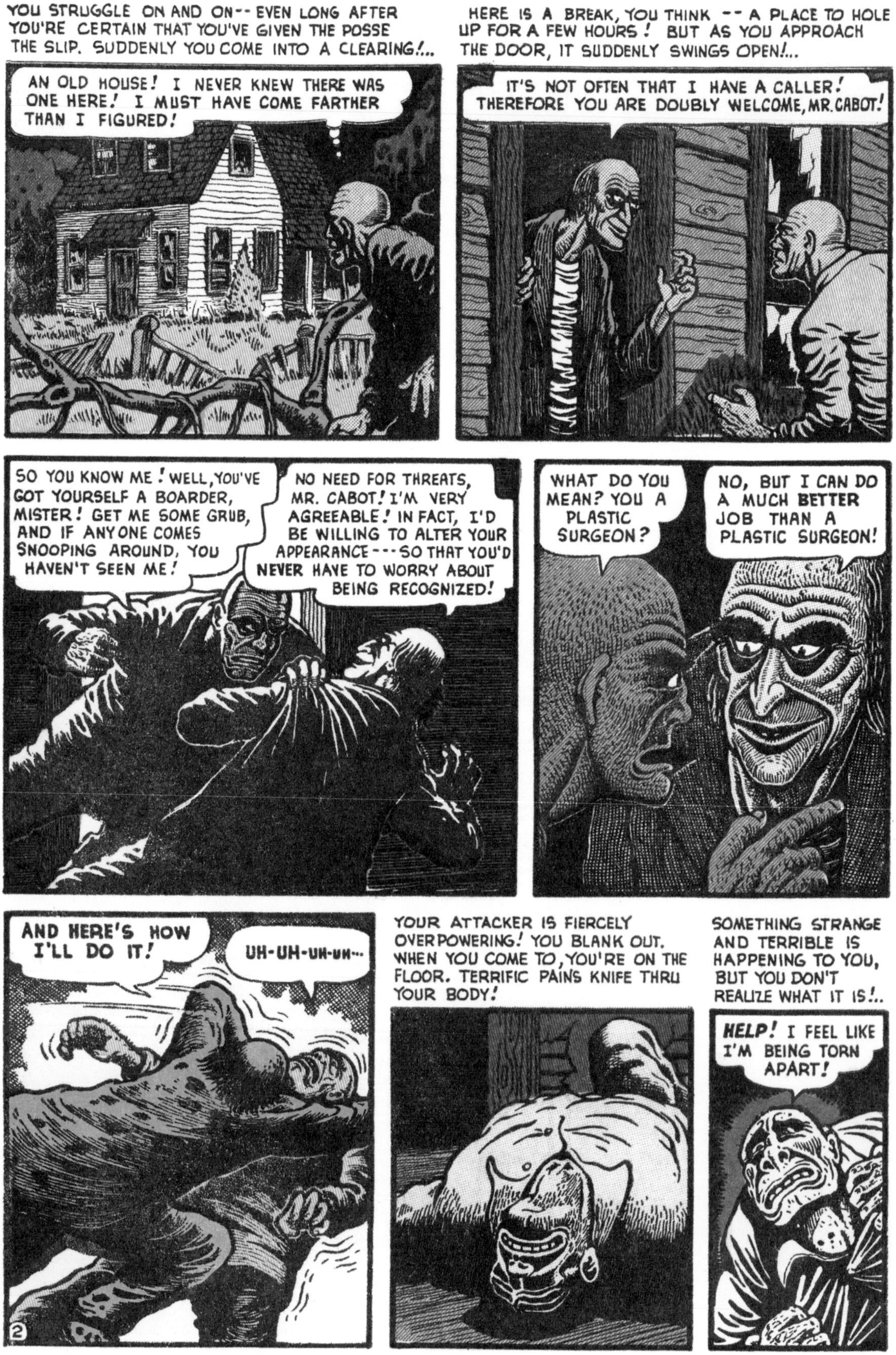
YOU STRUGGLE ON AND ON-- EVEN LONG AFTER YOU'RE CERTAIN THAT YOU'VE GIVEN THE POSSE THE SLIP. SUDDENLY YOU COME INTO A CLEARING!...
AN OLD HOUSE! I NEVER KNEW THERE WAS ONE HERE! I MUST HAVE COME FARTHER THAN I FIGURED!
HERE IS A BREAK, YOU THINK -- A PLACE TO HOLE UP FOR A FEW HOURS! BUT AS YOU APPROACH THE DOOR, IT SUDDENLY SWINGS OPEN!...
IT'S NOT OFTEN THAT I HAVE A CALLER! THEREFORE YOU ARE DOUBLY WELCOME, MR. CABOT!
SO YOU KNOW ME! WELL, YOU'VE GOT YOURSELF A BOARDER, MISTER! GET ME SOME GRUB, AND IF ANYONE COMES SNOOPING AROUND, YOU HAVEN'T SEEN ME!
NO NEED FOR THREATS, MR. CABOT! I'M VERY AGREEABLE! IN FACT, I'D BE WILLING TO ALTER YOUR APPEARANCE--- SO THAT YOU'D NEVER HAVE TO WORRY ABOUT BEING RECOGNIZED!
WHAT DO YOU MEAN? YOU A PLASTIC SURGEON?
NO, BUT I CAN DO A MUCH BETTER JOB THAN A PLASTIC SURGEON!
AND HERE'S HOW I'LL DO IT!
UH-UH-UH-UH...
2
YOUR ATTACKER IS FIERCELY OVERPOWERING! YOU BLANK OUT. WHEN YOU COME TO, YOU'RE ON THE FLOOR. TERRIFIC PAINS KNIFE THRU YOUR BODY!
SOMETHING STRANGE AND TERRIBLE IS HAPPENING TO YOU, BUT YOU DON'T REALIZE WHAT IT IS!...
HELP! I FEEL LIKE I'M BEING TORN APART!

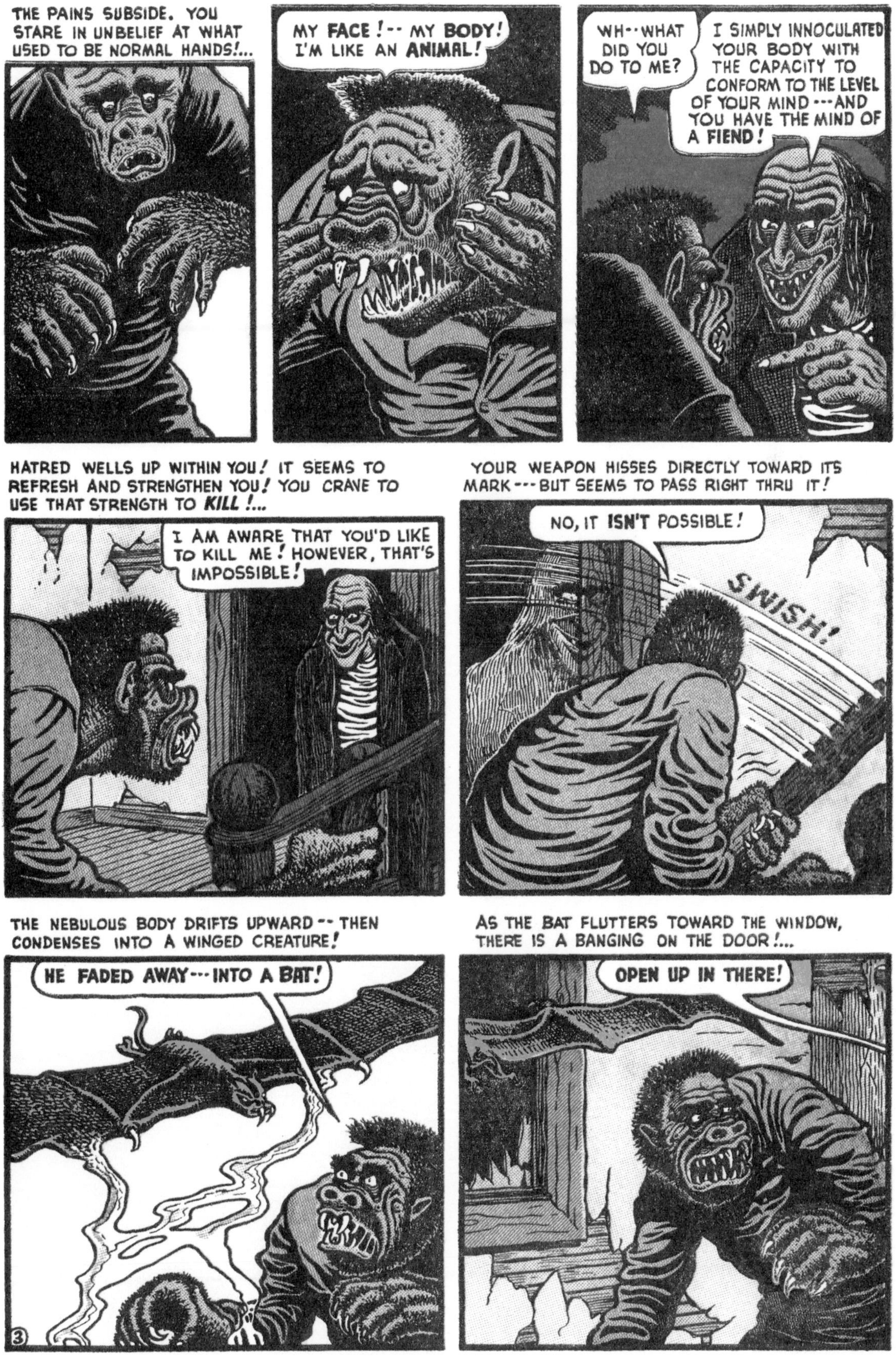
THE PAINS SUBSIDE. YOU STARE IN UNBELIEF AT WHAT USED TO BE NORMAL HANDS!...
MY FACE!-- MY BODY! I'M LIKE AN ANIMAL!
WH--WHAT DID YOU DO TO ME?
I SIMPLY INNOCULATED YOUR BODY WITH THE CAPACITY TO CONFORM TO THE LEVEL OF YOUR MIND---AND YOU HAVE THE MIND OF A FIEND!
HATRED WELLS UP WITHIN YOU! IT SEEMS TO REFRESH AND STRENGTHEN YOU! YOU CRAVE TO USE THAT STRENGTH TO KILL!...
I AM AWARE THAT YOU'D LIKE TO KILL ME! HOWEVER, THAT'S IMPOSSIBLE!
YOUR WEAPON HISSES DIRECTLY TOWARD ITS MARK---BUT SEEMS TO PASS RIGHT THRU IT!
NO, IT ISN'T POSSIBLE!
SWISH!
THE NEBULOUS BODY DRIFTS UPWARD-- THEN CONDENSES INTO A WINGED CREATURE!
HE FADED AWAY---INTO A BAT!
AS THE BAT FLUTTERS TOWARD THE WINDOW, THERE IS A BANGING ON THE DOOR!...
OPEN UP IN THERE!

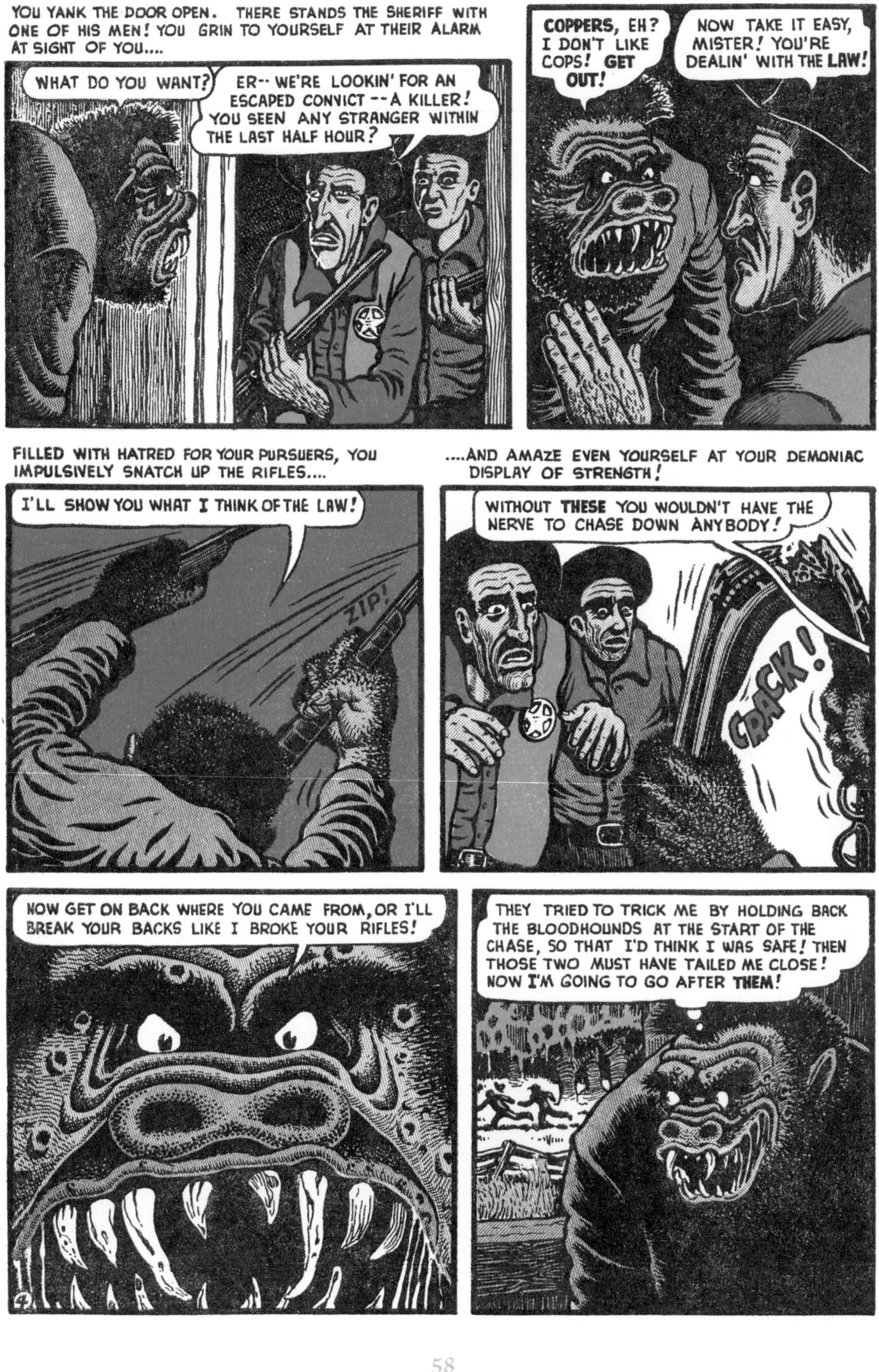
YOU YANK THE DOOR OPEN. THERE STANDS THE SHERIFF WITH ONE OF HIS MEN! YOU GRIN TO YOURSELF AT THEIR ALARM AT SIGHT OF YOU....
WHAT DO YOU WANT?
ER-- WE'RE LOOKIN' FOR AN ESCAPED CONVICT --A KILLER! YOU SEEN ANY STRANGER WITHIN THE LAST HALF HOUR?
COPPERS, EH? I DON'T LIKE COPS! GET OUT!
NOW TAKE IT EASY, MISTER! YOU'RE DEALIN' WITH THE LAW!
FILLED WITH HATRED FOR YOUR PURSUERS, YOU IMPULSIVELY SNATCH UP THE RIFLES....
I'LL SHOW YOU WHAT I THINK OF THE LAW!
ZIP!
....AND AMAZE EVEN YOURSELF AT YOUR DEMONIAC DISPLAY OF STRENGTH!
WITHOUT THESE YOU WOULDN'T HAVE THE NERVE TO CHASE DOWN ANYBODY!
CRACK!
NOW GET ON BACK WHERE YOU CAME FROM, OR I'LL BREAK YOUR BACKS LIKE I BROKE YOUR RIFLES!
THEY TRIED TO TRICK ME BY HOLDING BACK THE BLOODHOUNDS AT THE START OF THE CHASE, SO THAT I'D THINK I WAS SAFE! THEN THOSE TWO MUST HAVE TAILED ME CLOSE! NOW I'M GOING TO GO AFTER THEM!

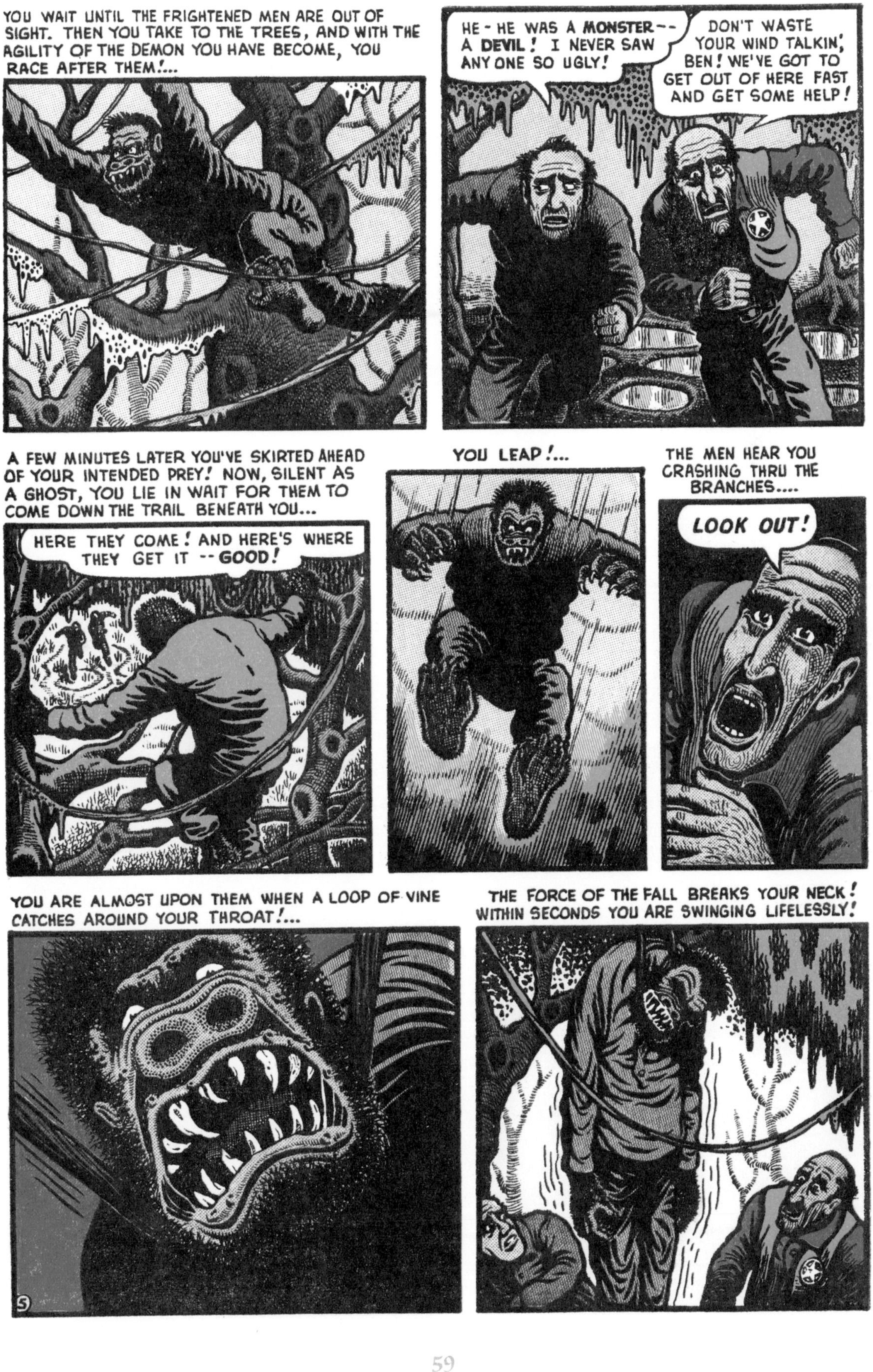
YOU WAIT UNTIL THE FRIGHTENED MEN ARE OUT OF SIGHT. THEN YOU TAKE TO THE TREES, AND WITH THE AGILITY OF THE DEMON YOU HAVE BECOME, YOU RACE AFTER THEM!...
HE - HE WAS A MONSTER-- A DEVIL! I NEVER SAW ANY ONE SO UGLY!
DON'T WASTE YOUR WIND TALKIN', BEN! WE'VE GOT TO GET OUT OF HERE FAST AND GET SOME HELP!
A FEW MINUTES LATER YOU'VE SKIRTED AHEAD OF YOUR INTENDED PREY! NOW, SILENT AS A GHOST, YOU LIE IN WAIT FOR THEM TO COME DOWN THE TRAIL BENEATH YOU...
HERE THEY COME! AND HERE'S WHERE THEY GET IT -- GOOD!
YOU LEAP!...
THE MEN HEAR YOU CRASHING THRU THE BRANCHES....
LOOK OUT!
YOU ARE ALMOST UPON THEM WHEN A LOOP OF VINE CATCHES AROUND YOUR THROAT!...
THE FORCE OF THE FALL BREAKS YOUR NECK! WITHIN SECONDS YOU ARE SWINGING LIFELESSLY!

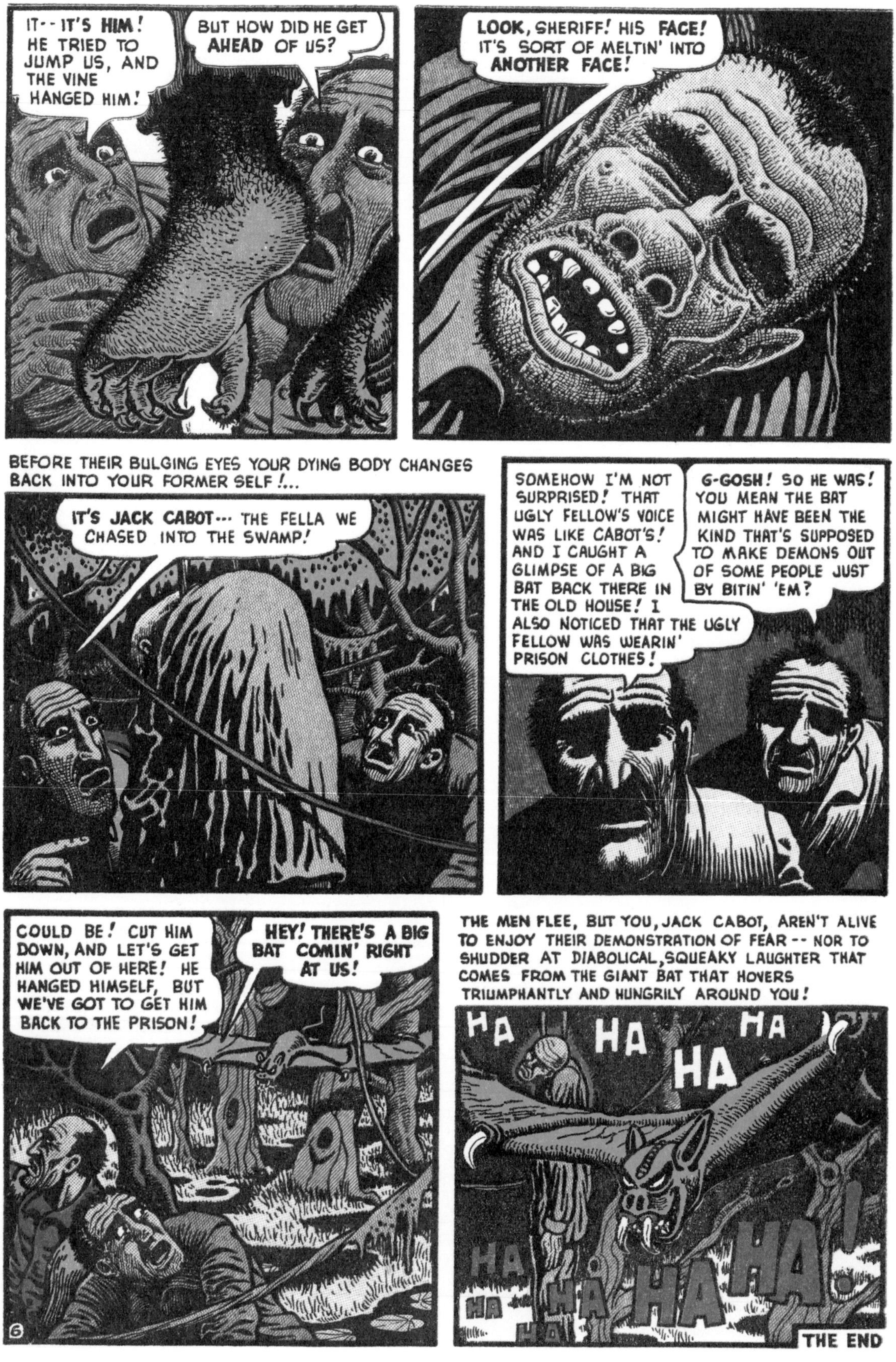

IT-- IT'S HIM! HE TRIED TO JUMP US, AND THE VINE HANGED HIM!
BUT HOW DID HE GET AHEAD OF US?
LOOK, SHERIFF! HIS FACE! IT'S SORT OF MELTIN' INTO ANOTHER FACE!
BEFORE THEIR BULGING EYES YOUR DYING BODY CHANGES BACK INTO YOUR FORMER SELF!...
IT'S JACK CABOT--- THE FELLA WE CHASED INTO THE SWAMP!
SOMEHOW I'M NOT SURPRISED! THAT UGLY FELLOW'S VOICE WAS LIKE CABOT'S! AND I CAUGHT A GLIMPSE OF A BIG BAT BACK THERE IN THE OLD HOUSE! I ALSO NOTICED THAT THE UGLY FELLOW WAS WEARIN' PRISON CLOTHES!
G-GOSH! SO HE WAS! YOU MEAN THE BAT MIGHT HAVE BEEN THE KIND THAT'S SUPPOSED TO MAKE DEMONS OUT OF SOME PEOPLE JUST BY BITIN' 'EM?
COULD BE! CUT HIM DOWN, AND LET'S GET HIM OUT OF HERE! HE HANGED HIMSELF, BUT WE'VE GOT TO GET HIM BACK TO THE PRISON!
HEY! THERE'S A BIG BAT COMIN' RIGHT AT US!
6
THE MEN FLEE, BUT YOU, JACK CABOT, AREN'T ALIVE TO ENJOY THEIR DEMONSTRATION OF FEAR -- NOR TO SHUDDER AT DIABOLICAL, SQUEAKY LAUGHTER THAT COMES FROM THE GIANT BAT THAT HOVERS TRIUMPHANTLY AND HUNGRILY AROUND YOU!
HA HA HA HA
HA HA HA HA HA HA HA!
THE END

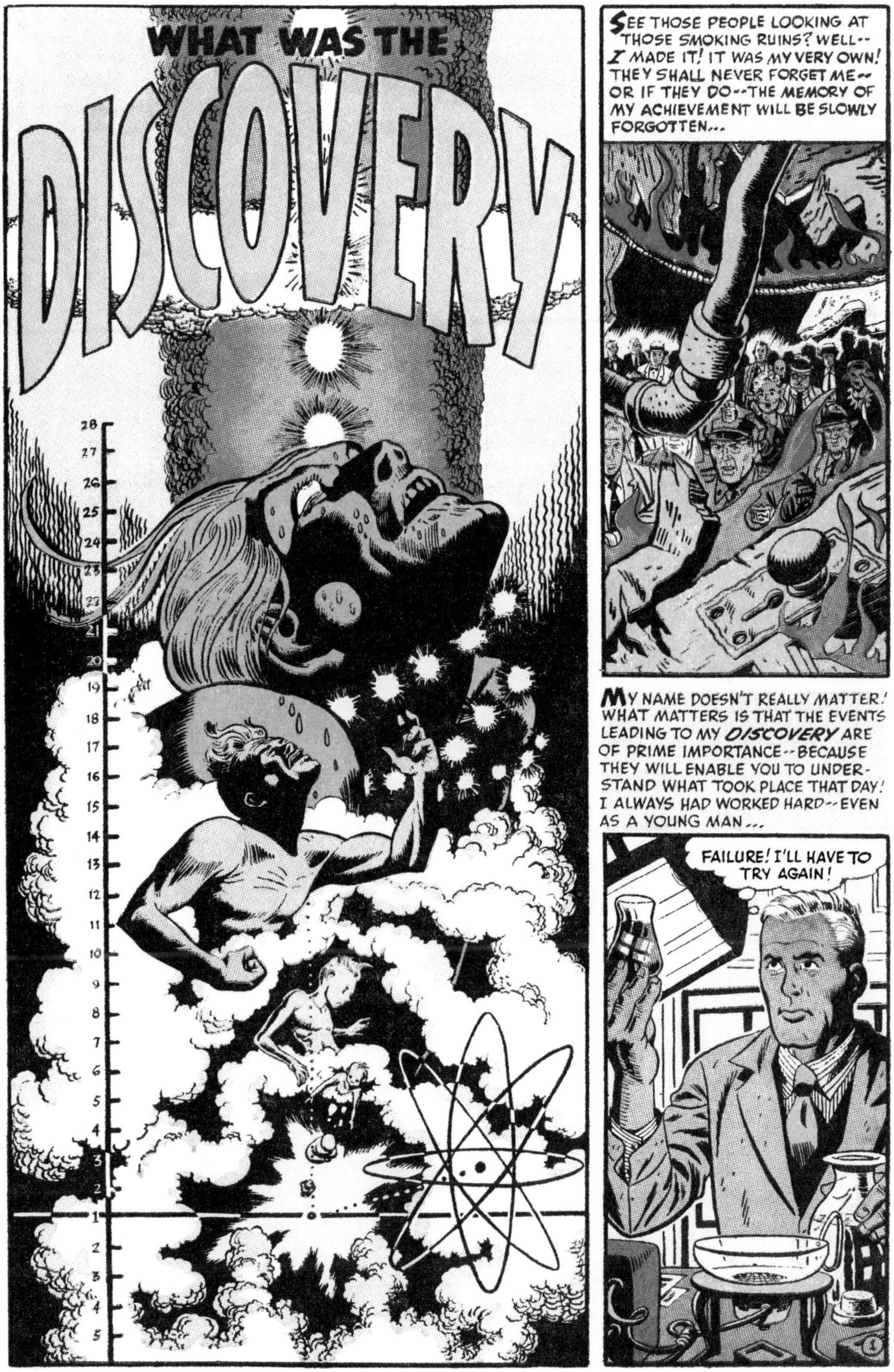
WHAT WAS THE
DISCOVERY
SEE THOSE PEOPLE LOOKING AT THOSE SMOKING RUINS? WELL-- I MADE IT! IT WAS MY VERY OWN! THEY SHALL NEVER FORGET ME-- OR IF THEY DO--THE MEMORY OF MY ACHIEVEMENT WILL BE SLOWLY FORGOTTEN...
MY NAME DOESN'T REALLY MATTER! WHAT MATTERS IS THAT THE EVENTS LEADING TO MY DISCOVERY ARE OF PRIME IMPORTANCE--BECAUSE THEY WILL ENABLE YOU TO UNDERSTAND WHAT TOOK PLACE THAT DAY! I ALWAYS HAD WORKED HARD--EVEN AS A YOUNG MAN...
FAILURE! I'LL HAVE TO TRY AGAIN!

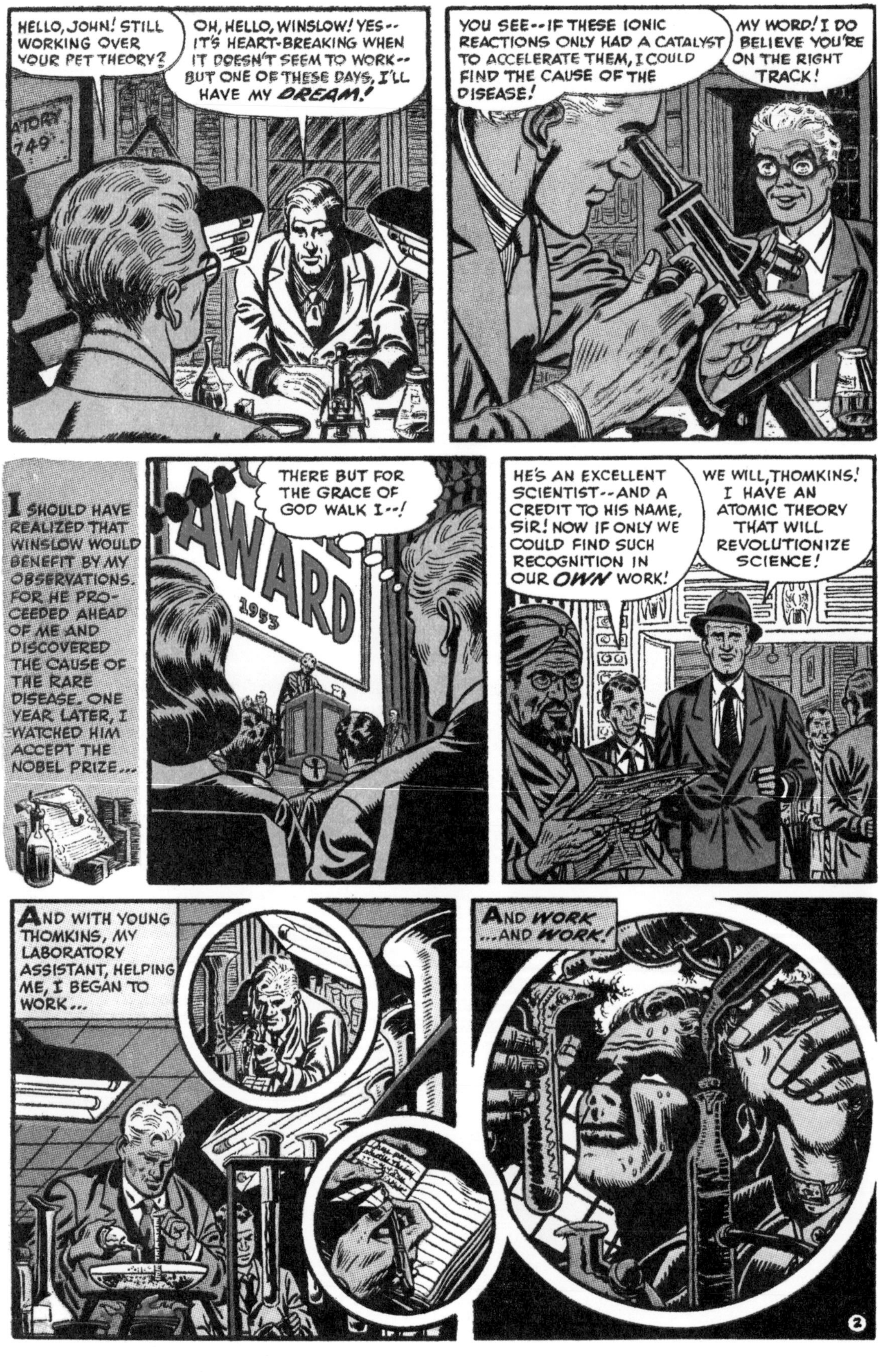

HELLO, JOHN! STILL WORKING OVER YOUR PET THEORY?
OH, HELLO, WINSLOW! YES-- IT'S HEART-BREAKING WHEN IT DOESN'T SEEM TO WORK-- BUT ONE OF THESE DAYS, I'LL HAVE MY DREAM!
YOU SEE--IF THESE IONIC REACTIONS ONLY HAD A CATALYST TO ACCELERATE THEM, I COULD FIND THE CAUSE OF THE DISEASE!
MY WORD! I DO BELIEVE YOU'RE ON THE RIGHT TRACK!
I SHOULD HAVE REALIZED THAT WINSLOW WOULD BENEFIT BY MY OBSERVATIONS. FOR HE PROCEEDED AHEAD OF ME AND DISCOVERED THE CAUSE OF THE RARE DISEASE. ONE YEAR LATER, I WATCHED HIM ACCEPT THE NOBEL PRIZE...
AWARD
1953
THERE BUT FOR THE GRACE OF GOD WALK I--!
HE'S AN EXCELLENT SCIENTIST--AND A CREDIT TO HIS NAME, SIR! NOW IF ONLY WE COULD FIND SUCH RECOGNITION IN OUR OWN WORK!
WE WILL, THOMKINS! I HAVE AN ATOMIC THEORY THAT WILL REVOLUTIONIZE SCIENCE!
AND WITH YOUNG THOMKINS, MY LABORATORY ASSISTANT, HELPING ME, I BEGAN TO WORK...
AND WORK ...AND WORK!
2

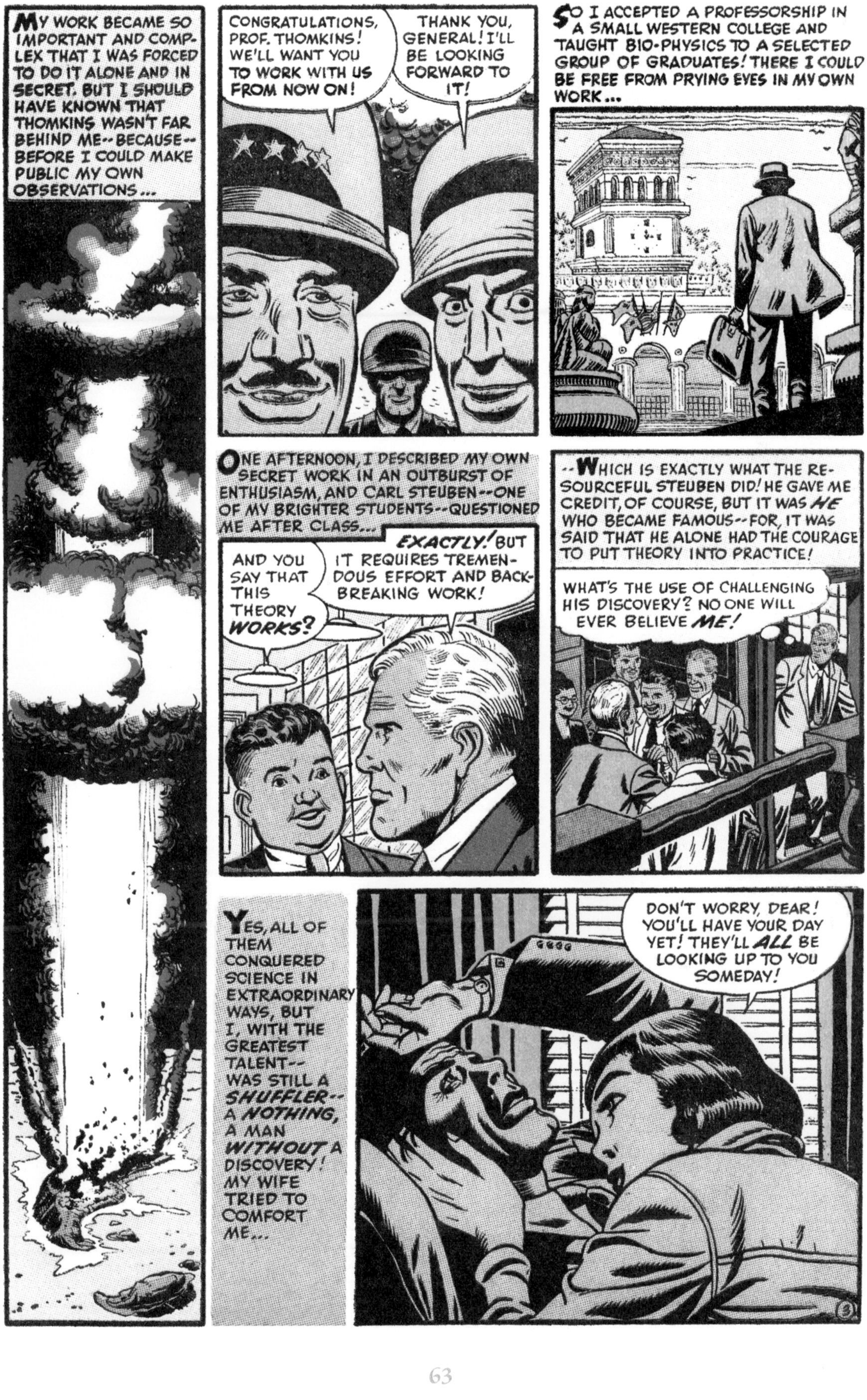
MY WORK BECAME SO IMPORTANT AND COMPLEX THAT I WAS FORCED TO DO IT ALONE AND IN SECRET. BUT I SHOULD HAVE KNOWN THAT THOMKINS WASN'T FAR BEHIND ME--BECAUSE--BEFORE I COULD MAKE PUBLIC MY OWN OBSERVATIONS...
CONGRATULATIONS, PROF. THOMKINS! WE'LL WANT YOU TO WORK WITH US FROM NOW ON!
THANK YOU, GENERAL! I'LL BE LOOKING FORWARD TO IT!
SO I ACCEPTED A PROFESSORSHIP IN A SMALL WESTERN COLLEGE AND TAUGHT BIO-PHYSICS TO A SELECTED GROUP OF GRADUATES! THERE I COULD BE FREE FROM PRYING EYES IN MY OWN WORK...
ONE AFTERNOON, I DESCRIBED MY OWN SECRET WORK IN AN OUTBURST OF ENTHUSIASM, AND CARL STEUBEN--ONE OF MY BRIGHTER STUDENTS--QUESTIONED ME AFTER CLASS...
AND YOU SAY THAT THIS THEORY WORKS?
EXACTLY! BUT IT REQUIRES TREMENDOUS EFFORT AND BACK-BREAKING WORK!
--WHICH IS EXACTLY WHAT THE RESOURCEFUL STEUBEN DID! HE GAVE ME CREDIT, OF COURSE, BUT IT WAS HE WHO BECAME FAMOUS--FOR, IT WAS SAID THAT HE ALONE HAD THE COURAGE TO PUT THEORY INTO PRACTICE!
WHAT'S THE USE OF CHALLENGING HIS DISCOVERY? NO ONE WILL EVER BELIEVE ME!
YES, ALL OF THEM CONQUERED SCIENCE IN EXTRAORDINARY WAYS, BUT I, WITH THE GREATEST TALENT--WAS STILL A SHUFFLER--A NOTHING, A MAN WITHOUT A DISCOVERY! MY WIFE TRIED TO COMFORT ME...
DON'T WORRY, DEAR! YOU'LL HAVE YOUR DAY YET! THEY'LL ALL BE LOOKING UP TO YOU SOMEDAY!

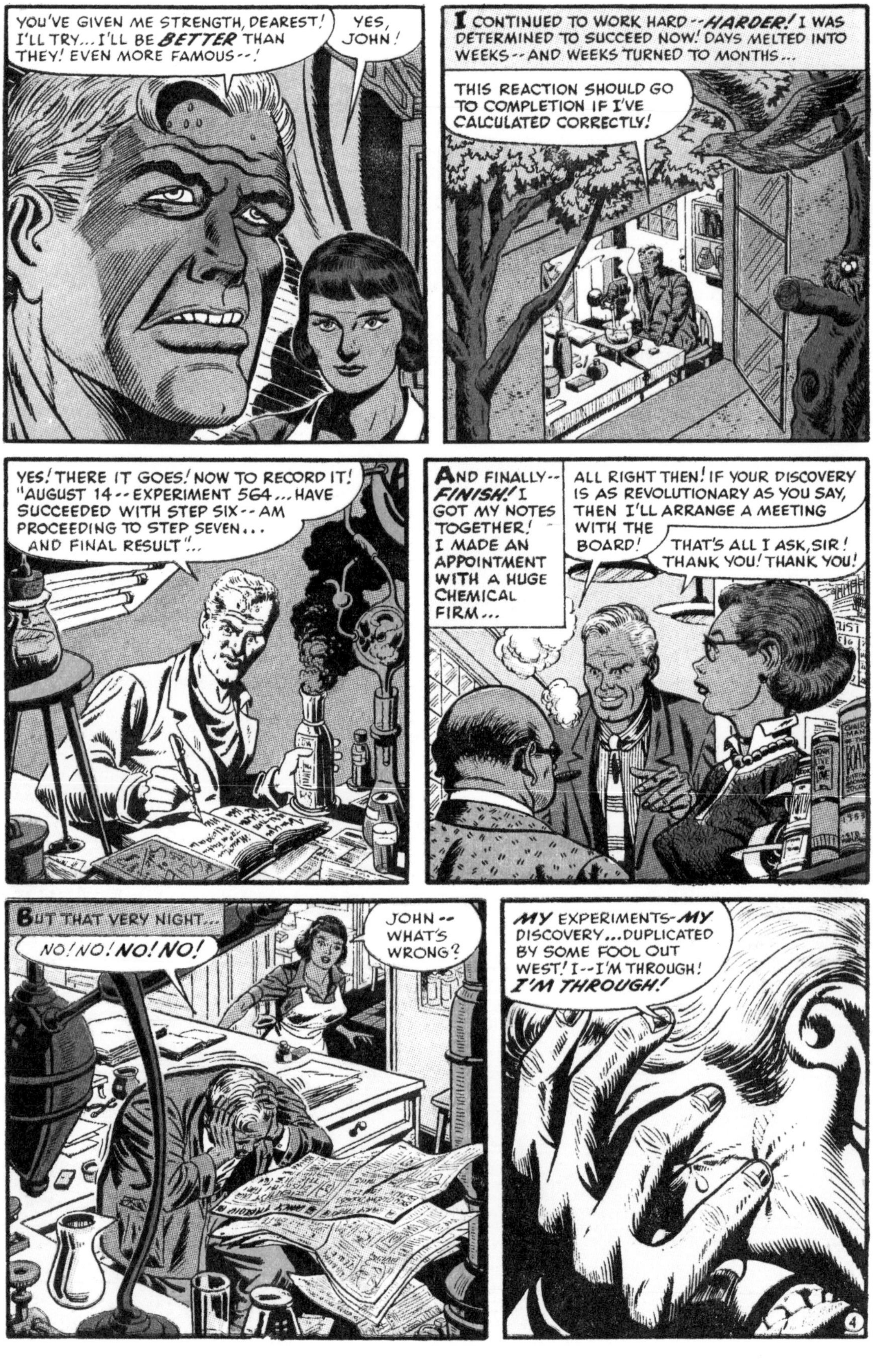
YOU'VE GIVEN ME STRENGTH, DEAREST! I'LL TRY... I'LL BE BETTER THAN THEY! EVEN MORE FAMOUS--!
YES, JOHN!
I CONTINUED TO WORK HARD--HARDER! I WAS DETERMINED TO SUCCEED NOW! DAYS MELTED INTO WEEKS--AND WEEKS TURNED TO MONTHS...
THIS REACTION SHOULD GO TO COMPLETION IF I'VE CALCULATED CORRECTLY!
YES! THERE IT GOES! NOW TO RECORD IT! "AUGUST 14--EXPERIMENT 564...HAVE SUCCEEDED WITH STEP SIX--AM PROCEEDING TO STEP SEVEN... AND FINAL RESULT"...
AND FINALLY--FINISH! I GOT MY NOTES TOGETHER! I MADE AN APPOINTMENT WITH A HUGE CHEMICAL FIRM...
ALL RIGHT THEN! IF YOUR DISCOVERY IS AS REVOLUTIONARY AS YOU SAY, THEN I'LL ARRANGE A MEETING WITH THE BOARD!
THAT'S ALL I ASK, SIR! THANK YOU! THANK YOU!
BUT THAT VERY NIGHT...
NO! NO! NO! NO!
JOHN--WHAT'S WRONG?
MY EXPERIMENTS--MY DISCOVERY...DUPLICATED BY SOME FOOL OUT WEST! I--I'M THROUGH! I'M THROUGH!
4

NO, DARLING! THIS ONLY PROVES YOU *CAN* DO IT! YOU'RE ON THE RIGHT TRACK! I'M SURE YOU'LL HAVE FAME ALL TO YOURSELF... NEXT TIME!

NEXT TIME -- NEXT TIME...

NEXT TIME I WOULDN'T WAIT SO LONG TO FINISH MY WORK! NEXT TIME I WOULD BE PREPARED -- *DOUBLE PREPARED!* I RE-ENTERED MY SILENT LABORATORY DAYS LATER! I SHOOK MY FIST AT THE INSTRUMENTS ...

I'LL CONQUER YOU IF I MUST WORK AROUND THE CLOCK!

I'M GOING TO MAKE MY DISCOVERY! I'M GOING TO DRAW OUT THE HIDDEN SECRETS OF THE UNKNOWN IF--I--MUST--PULL--THEM--OUT ONE BY ONE!

CRASH!

MY ANGER GREW TO FURY! I HATED EVERY TEST-TUBE IN THE LAB! I TWISTED EVERY DIAL I COULD LAY MY HANDS ON! MY CHEMICALS I HURLED FROM THEIR BEAKERS...

I'LL HAVE MY DISCOVERY! DO YOU HEAR ME? *I'M GOING TO BE FAMOUS!*

THEN IN A CHAIN REACTION OF HORROR ...AN EXPLOSION OF FURY, I MADE THE *GREATEST* OF ALL DISCOVERIES! I FOUND OUT THE MEANING OF...

BLOOOOMM

DEATH!

THE END

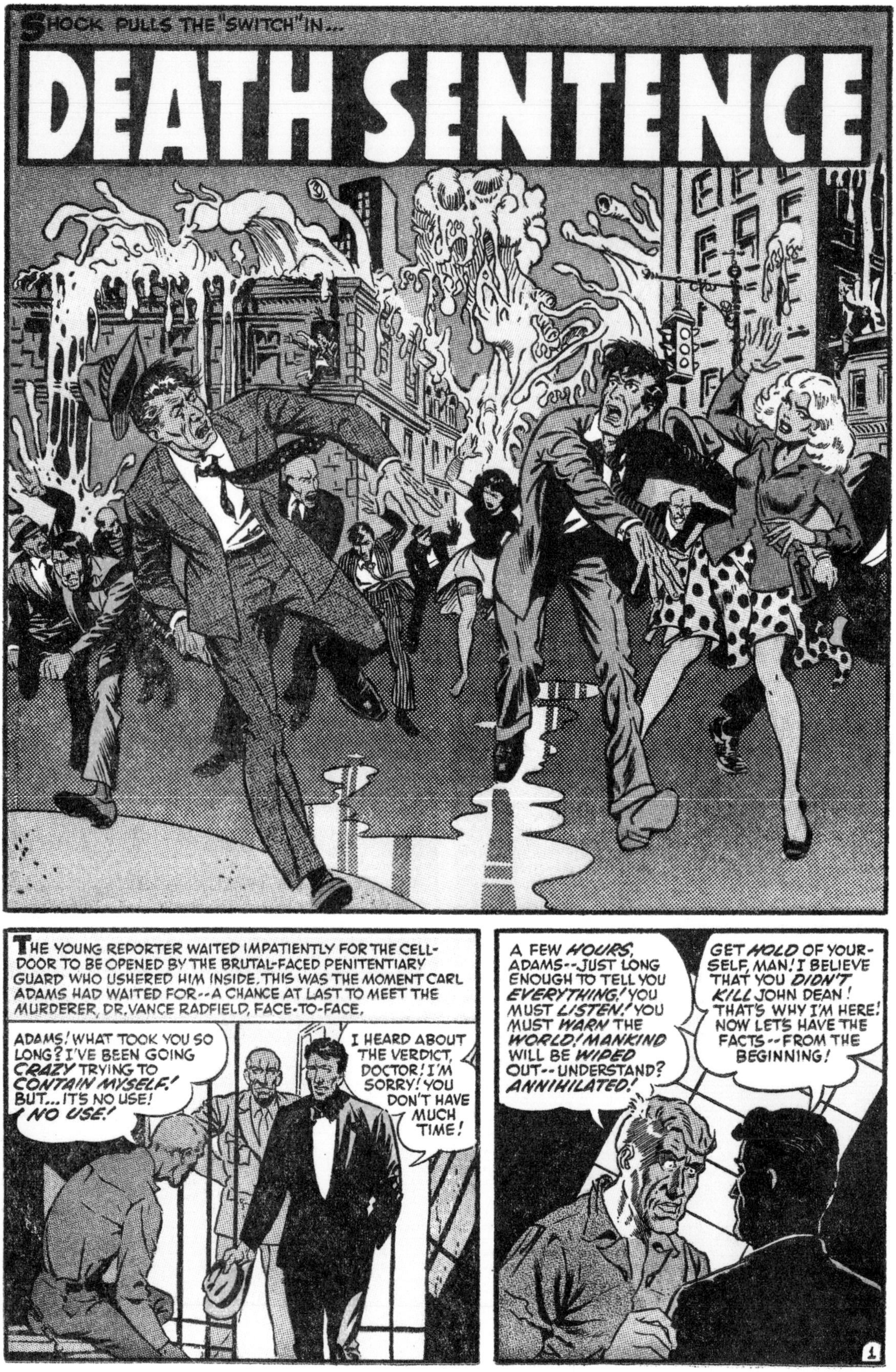
SHOCK PULLS THE "SWITCH" IN...
DEATH SENTENCE
THE YOUNG REPORTER WAITED IMPATIENTLY FOR THE CELL-DOOR TO BE OPENED BY THE BRUTAL-FACED PENITENTIARY GUARD WHO USHERED HIM INSIDE. THIS WAS THE MOMENT CARL ADAMS HAD WAITED FOR--A CHANCE AT LAST TO MEET THE MURDERER, DR. VANCE RADFIELD, FACE-TO-FACE.
ADAMS! WHAT TOOK YOU SO LONG? I'VE BEEN GOING CRAZY TRYING TO CONTAIN MYSELF! BUT... IT'S NO USE! NO USE!
I HEARD ABOUT THE VERDICT, DOCTOR! I'M SORRY! YOU DON'T HAVE MUCH TIME!
A FEW HOURS, ADAMS--JUST LONG ENOUGH TO TELL YOU EVERYTHING! YOU MUST LISTEN! YOU MUST WARN THE WORLD! MANKIND WILL BE WIPED OUT--UNDERSTAND? ANNIHILATED!
GET HOLD OF YOURSELF, MAN! I BELIEVE THAT YOU DIDN'T KILL JOHN DEAN! THAT'S WHY I'M HERE! NOW LET'S HAVE THE FACTS--FROM THE BEGINNING!
1

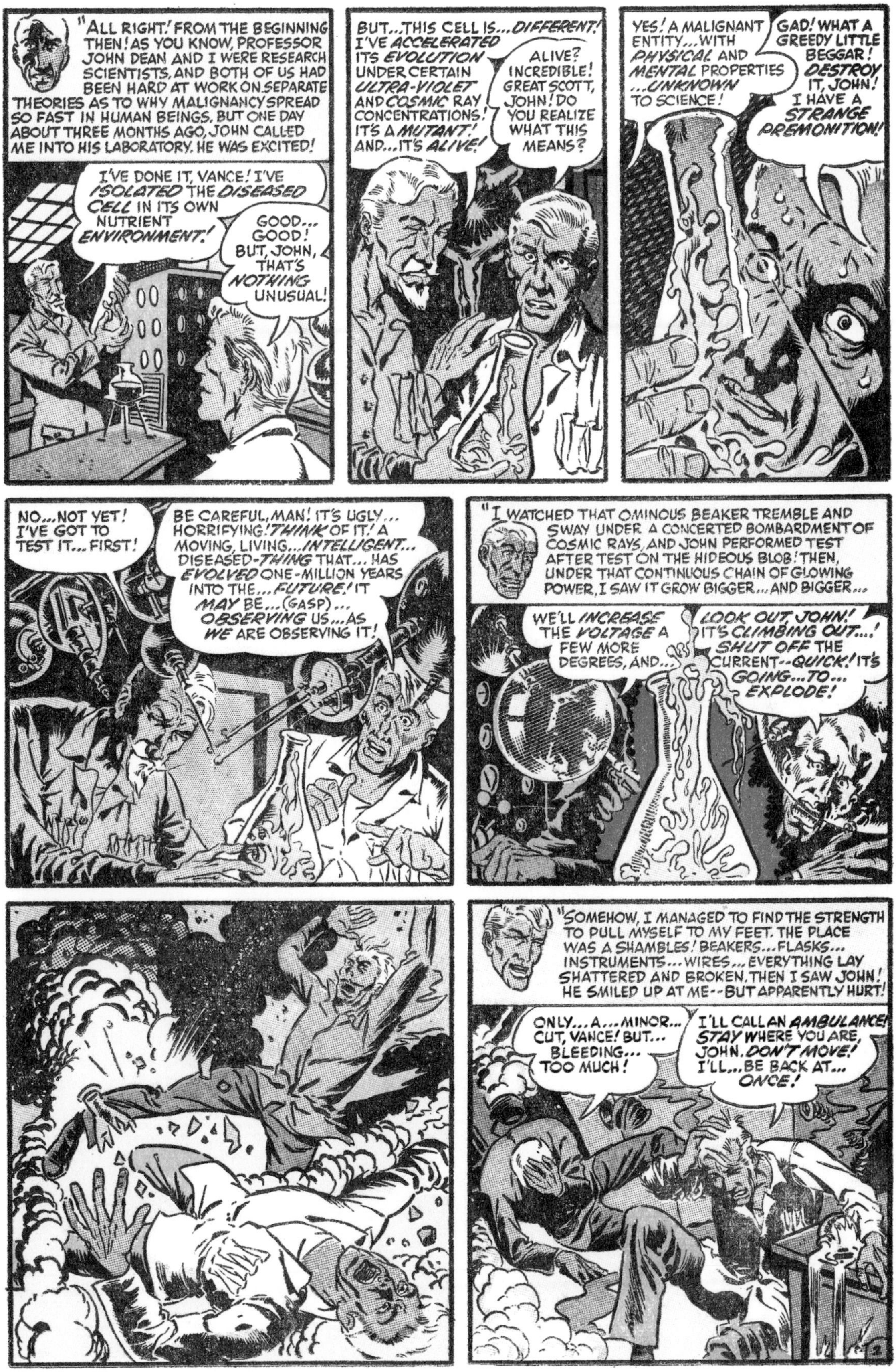
"ALL RIGHT! FROM THE BEGINNING THEN! AS YOU KNOW, PROFESSOR JOHN DEAN AND I WERE RESEARCH SCIENTISTS, AND BOTH OF US HAD BEEN HARD AT WORK ON SEPARATE THEORIES AS TO WHY MALIGNANCY SPREAD SO FAST IN HUMAN BEINGS. BUT ONE DAY ABOUT THREE MONTHS AGO, JOHN CALLED ME INTO HIS LABORATORY. HE WAS EXCITED!
I'VE DONE IT, VANCE! I'VE ISOLATED THE DISEASED CELL IN ITS OWN NUTRIENT ENVIRONMENT!
GOOD... GOOD! BUT, JOHN, THAT'S NOTHING UNUSUAL!
BUT... THIS CELL IS... DIFFERENT! I'VE ACCELERATED ITS EVOLUTION UNDER CERTAIN ULTRA-VIOLET AND COSMIC RAY CONCENTRATIONS! IT'S A MUTANT! AND... IT'S ALIVE!
ALIVE? INCREDIBLE! GREAT SCOTT, JOHN! DO YOU REALIZE WHAT THIS MEANS?
YES! A MALIGNANT ENTITY... WITH PHYSICAL AND MENTAL PROPERTIES ...UNKNOWN TO SCIENCE!
GAD! WHAT A GREEDY LITTLE BEGGAR! DESTROY IT, JOHN! I HAVE A STRANGE PREMONITION!
NO... NOT YET! I'VE GOT TO TEST IT... FIRST!
BE CAREFUL, MAN! IT'S UGLY... HORRIFYING! THINK OF IT! A MOVING, LIVING... INTELLIGENT... DISEASED-THING THAT... HAS EVOLVED ONE-MILLION YEARS INTO THE... FUTURE! IT MAY BE... (GASP)... OBSERVING US... AS WE ARE OBSERVING IT!
"I WATCHED THAT OMINOUS BEAKER TREMBLE AND SWAY UNDER A CONCERTED BOMBARDMENT OF COSMIC RAYS, AND JOHN PERFORMED TEST AFTER TEST ON THE HIDEOUS BLOB! THEN, UNDER THAT CONTINUOUS CHAIN OF GLOWING POWER, I SAW IT GROW BIGGER... AND BIGGER...
WE'LL INCREASE THE VOLTAGE A FEW MORE DEGREES, AND...
LOOK OUT, JOHN! IT'S CLIMBING OUT...! SHUT OFF THE CURRENT--QUICK! IT'S GOING... TO... EXPLODE!
"SOMEHOW, I MANAGED TO FIND THE STRENGTH TO PULL MYSELF TO MY FEET. THE PLACE WAS A SHAMBLES! BEAKERS... FLASKS... INSTRUMENTS... WIRES... EVERYTHING LAY SHATTERED AND BROKEN. THEN I SAW JOHN! HE SMILED UP AT ME--BUT APPARENTLY HURT!
ONLY... A... MINOR... CUT, VANCE! BUT... BLEEDING... TOO MUCH!
I'LL CALL AN AMBULANCE! STAY WHERE YOU ARE, JOHN. DON'T MOVE! I'LL... BE BACK AT... ONCE!

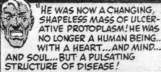
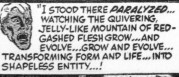

"SUDDENLY JOHN SHRIEKED. IT WAS A HORRIBLE SCREAM! I TURNED FROM THE PHONE... TO SEE HIM! BUT... HE WAS NOT 'HIM' ANY LONGER! HE WAS NOW...IT!

"HE WAS NOW A CHANGING, SHAPELESS MASS OF ULCERATIVE PROTOPLASM! HE WAS NO LONGER A HUMAN BEING... WITH A HEART...AND MIND... AND SOUL...BUT A PULSATING STRUCTURE OF DISEASE!

"I STOOD THERE *PARALYZED*... WATCHING THE QUIVERING, JELLY-LIKE MOUNTAIN OF RED-GASHED FLESH GROW....AND EVOLVE...GROW AND EVOLVE.... TRANSFORMING FORM AND LIFE...INTO SHAPELESS ENTITY...!

VANCE! CELL GOT... INTO MY...CUT! I ... *YAA-A-A-H!*

"REALITY BECAME A NIGHTMARE! UTTERING A HALF-HUMAN WHINE OF SHEER FEROCITY, THE ENTITY SHUFFLED SLOWLY TOWARDS ME-- I SUDDENLY CAME TO MY SENSES WITH DEATH THREATENING ME NOT MORE THAN SIX FEET AWAY...

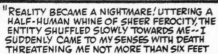

RETREAT FROM IT... SLOWLY... SLOWLY...!

"I KNEW IT WAS JUST A MATTER OF TIME BEFORE IT WOULD MAKE ITS ATTACK ON ME! SO... I TOOK THE INITIATIVE...AND RAMMED IT WITH AN IRON BAR! I HEARD A SQUISH...LIKE SQUEEZING A HUGE, SOPPING-WET SPONGE...BUT...

IT *SPLIT!* OH, LORD... *BINARY FISSION!* THAT MEANS... IT WILL *DIVIDE AGAIN*...AND *AGAIN!*

"AND THEN...JUST AS I SUSPECTED, IT HAPPENED...

LORD...OH, LORD! I CAN'T LET IT SPREAD! IT'S GOT TO REMAIN HERE...WITH ME...!

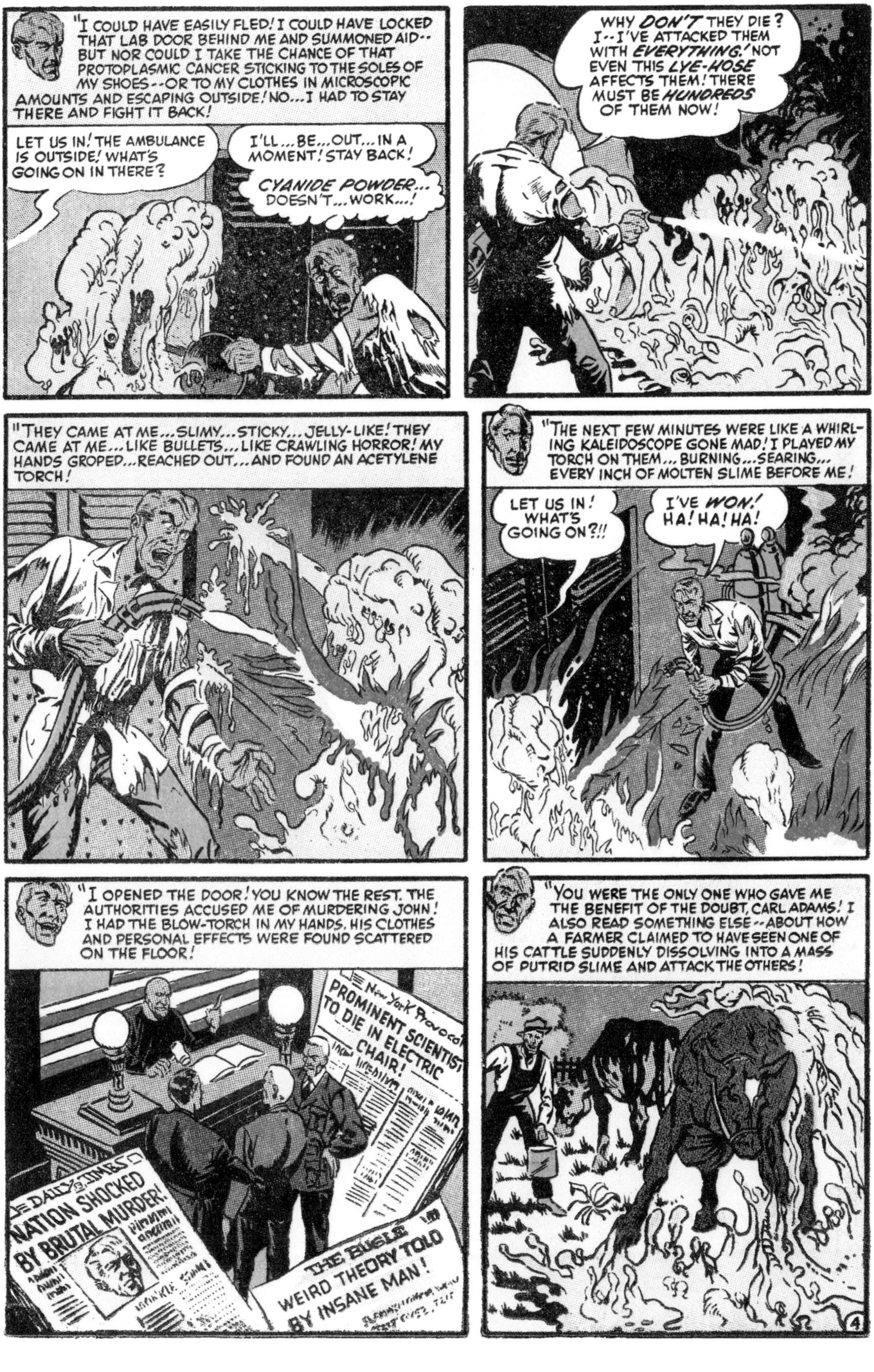
"I COULD HAVE EASILY FLED! I COULD HAVE LOCKED THAT LAB DOOR BEHIND ME AND SUMMONED AID-- BUT NOR COULD I TAKE THE CHANCE OF THAT PROTOPLASMIC CANCER STICKING TO THE SOLES OF MY SHOES--OR TO MY CLOTHES IN MICROSCOPIC AMOUNTS AND ESCAPING OUTSIDE! NO...I HAD TO STAY THERE AND FIGHT IT BACK!
LET US IN! THE AMBULANCE IS OUTSIDE! WHAT'S GOING ON IN THERE?
I'LL...BE...OUT...IN A MOMENT! STAY BACK!
CYANIDE POWDER... DOESN'T...WORK...!
WHY DON'T THEY DIE? I--I'VE ATTACKED THEM WITH EVERYTHING! NOT EVEN THIS LYE-HOSE AFFECTS THEM! THERE MUST BE HUNDREDS OF THEM NOW!
"THEY CAME AT ME...SLIMY...STICKY...JELLY-LIKE! THEY CAME AT ME...LIKE BULLETS...LIKE CRAWLING HORROR! MY HANDS GROPED...REACHED OUT...AND FOUND AN ACETYLENE TORCH!
"THE NEXT FEW MINUTES WERE LIKE A WHIRLING KALEIDOSCOPE GONE MAD! I PLAYED MY TORCH ON THEM...BURNING...SEARING... EVERY INCH OF MOLTEN SLIME BEFORE ME!
LET US IN! WHAT'S GOING ON?!!
I'VE WON! HA! HA! HA!
"I OPENED THE DOOR! YOU KNOW THE REST. THE AUTHORITIES ACCUSED ME OF MURDERING JOHN! I HAD THE BLOW-TORCH IN MY HANDS. HIS CLOTHES AND PERSONAL EFFECTS WERE FOUND SCATTERED ON THE FLOOR!
New York Provocat
PROMINENT SCIENTIST TO DIE IN ELECTRIC CHAIR!
DAILY TIMES
NATION SHOCKED BY BRUTAL MURDER!
THE BUGLE
WEIRD THEORY TOLD BY INSANE MAN!
"YOU WERE THE ONLY ONE WHO GAVE ME THE BENEFIT OF THE DOUBT, CARL ADAMS! I ALSO READ SOMETHING ELSE--ABOUT HOW A FARMER CLAIMED TO HAVE SEEN ONE OF HIS CATTLE SUDDENLY DISSOLVING INTO A MASS OF PUTRID SLIME AND ATTACK THE OTHERS!
4

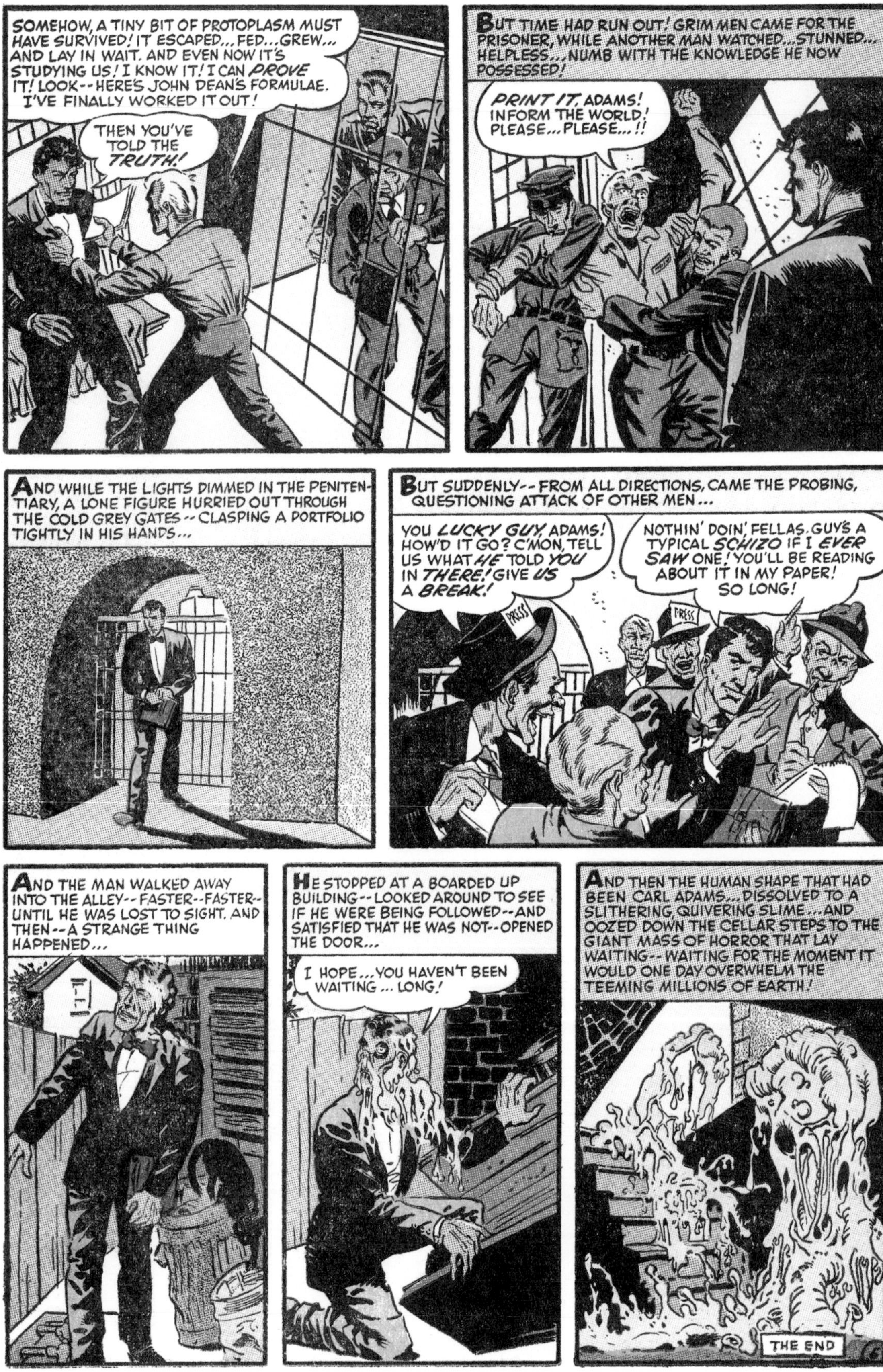

SOMEHOW, A TINY BIT OF PROTOPLASM MUST HAVE SURVIVED! IT ESCAPED... FED... GREW... AND LAY IN WAIT. AND EVEN NOW IT'S STUDYING US! I KNOW IT! I CAN PROVE IT! LOOK -- HERE'S JOHN DEAN'S FORMULAE. I'VE FINALLY WORKED IT OUT!
THEN YOU'VE TOLD THE TRUTH!
BUT TIME HAD RUN OUT! GRIM MEN CAME FOR THE PRISONER, WHILE ANOTHER MAN WATCHED... STUNNED... HELPLESS... NUMB WITH THE KNOWLEDGE HE NOW POSSESSED!
PRINT IT, ADAMS! INFORM THE WORLD! PLEASE... PLEASE...!!
AND WHILE THE LIGHTS DIMMED IN THE PENITENTIARY, A LONE FIGURE HURRIED OUT THROUGH THE COLD GREY GATES -- CLASPING A PORTFOLIO TIGHTLY IN HIS HANDS...
BUT SUDDENLY -- FROM ALL DIRECTIONS, CAME THE PROBING, QUESTIONING ATTACK OF OTHER MEN...
YOU LUCKY GUY, ADAMS! HOW'D IT GO? C'MON, TELL US WHAT HE TOLD YOU IN THERE! GIVE US A BREAK!
NOTHIN' DOIN', FELLAS. GUY'S A TYPICAL SCHIZO IF I EVER SAW ONE! YOU'LL BE READING ABOUT IT IN MY PAPER! SO LONG!
PRESS
PRESS
AND THE MAN WALKED AWAY INTO THE ALLEY -- FASTER -- FASTER -- UNTIL HE WAS LOST TO SIGHT. AND THEN -- A STRANGE THING HAPPENED...
HE STOPPED AT A BOARDED UP BUILDING -- LOOKED AROUND TO SEE IF HE WERE BEING FOLLOWED -- AND SATISFIED THAT HE WAS NOT -- OPENED THE DOOR...
I HOPE... YOU HAVEN'T BEEN WAITING... LONG!
AND THEN THE HUMAN SHAPE THAT HAD BEEN CARL ADAMS... DISSOLVED TO A SLITHERING, QUIVERING SLIME... AND OOZED DOWN THE CELLAR STEPS TO THE GIANT MASS OF HORROR THAT LAY WAITING -- WAITING FOR THE MOMENT IT WOULD ONE DAY OVERWHELM THE TEEMING MILLIONS OF EARTH!
THE END

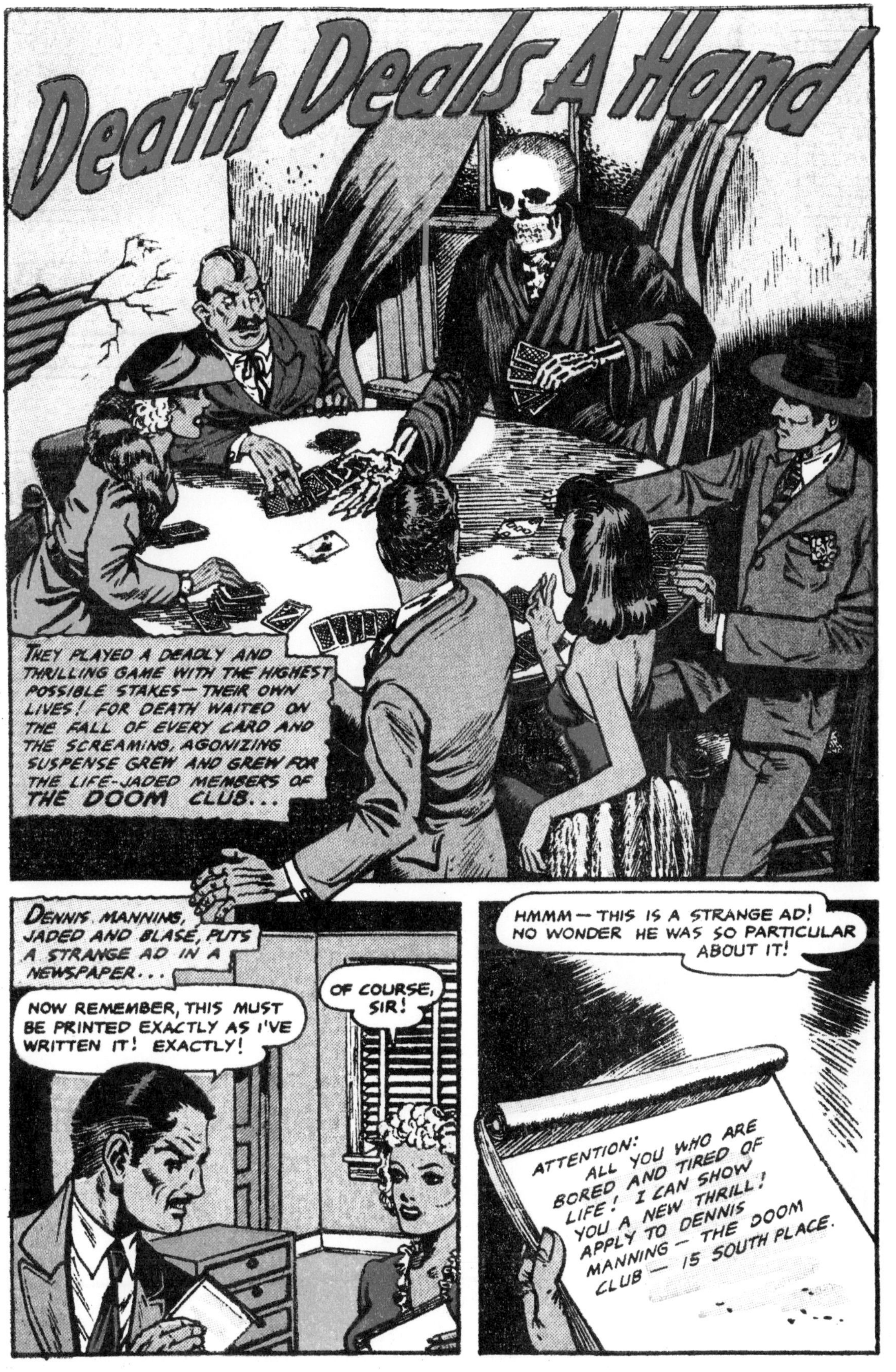
Death Deals A Hand!
THEY PLAYED A DEADLY AND THRILLING GAME WITH THE HIGHEST POSSIBLE STAKES— THEIR OWN LIVES! FOR DEATH WAITED ON THE FALL OF EVERY CARD AND THE SCREAMING, AGONIZING SUSPENSE GREW AND GREW FOR THE LIFE-JADED MEMBERS OF THE DOOM CLUB...
DENNIS MANNING, JADED AND BLASE, PUTS A STRANGE AD IN A NEWSPAPER...
NOW REMEMBER, THIS MUST BE PRINTED EXACTLY AS I'VE WRITTEN IT! EXACTLY!
OF COURSE, SIR!
HMMM — THIS IS A STRANGE AD! NO WONDER HE WAS SO PARTICULAR ABOUT IT!
ATTENTION: ALL YOU WHO ARE BORED AND TIRED OF LIFE! I CAN SHOW YOU A NEW THRILL! APPLY TO DENNIS MANNING — THE DOOM CLUB — 15 SOUTH PLACE.

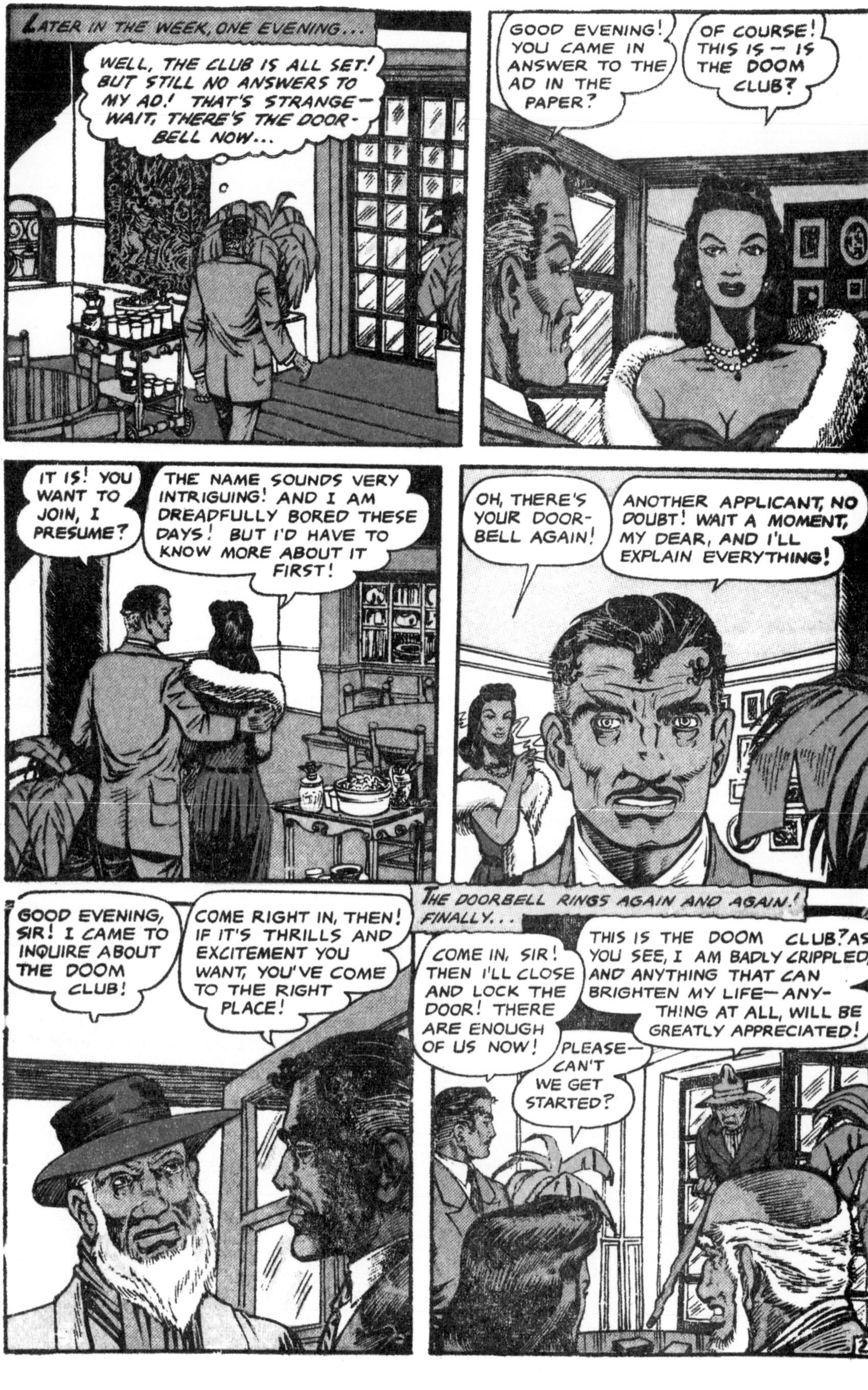
LATER IN THE WEEK, ONE EVENING...
WELL, THE CLUB IS ALL SET! BUT STILL NO ANSWERS TO MY AD! THAT'S STRANGE— WAIT, THERE'S THE DOORBELL NOW...
GOOD EVENING! YOU CAME IN ANSWER TO THE AD IN THE PAPER?
OF COURSE! THIS IS — IS THE DOOM CLUB?
IT IS! YOU WANT TO JOIN, I PRESUME?
THE NAME SOUNDS VERY INTRIGUING! AND I AM DREADFULLY BORED THESE DAYS! BUT I'D HAVE TO KNOW MORE ABOUT IT FIRST!
OH, THERE'S YOUR DOORBELL AGAIN!
ANOTHER APPLICANT, NO DOUBT! WAIT A MOMENT, MY DEAR, AND I'LL EXPLAIN EVERYTHING!
GOOD EVENING, SIR! I CAME TO INQUIRE ABOUT THE DOOM CLUB!
COME RIGHT IN, THEN! IF IT'S THRILLS AND EXCITEMENT YOU WANT, YOU'VE COME TO THE RIGHT PLACE!
THE DOORBELL RINGS AGAIN AND AGAIN! FINALLY...
COME IN, SIR! THEN I'LL CLOSE AND LOCK THE DOOR! THERE ARE ENOUGH OF US NOW!
THIS IS THE DOOM CLUB? AS YOU SEE, I AM BADLY CRIPPLED, AND ANYTHING THAT CAN BRIGHTEN MY LIFE—ANYTHING AT ALL, WILL BE GREATLY APPRECIATED!
PLEASE— CAN'T WE GET STARTED?
2

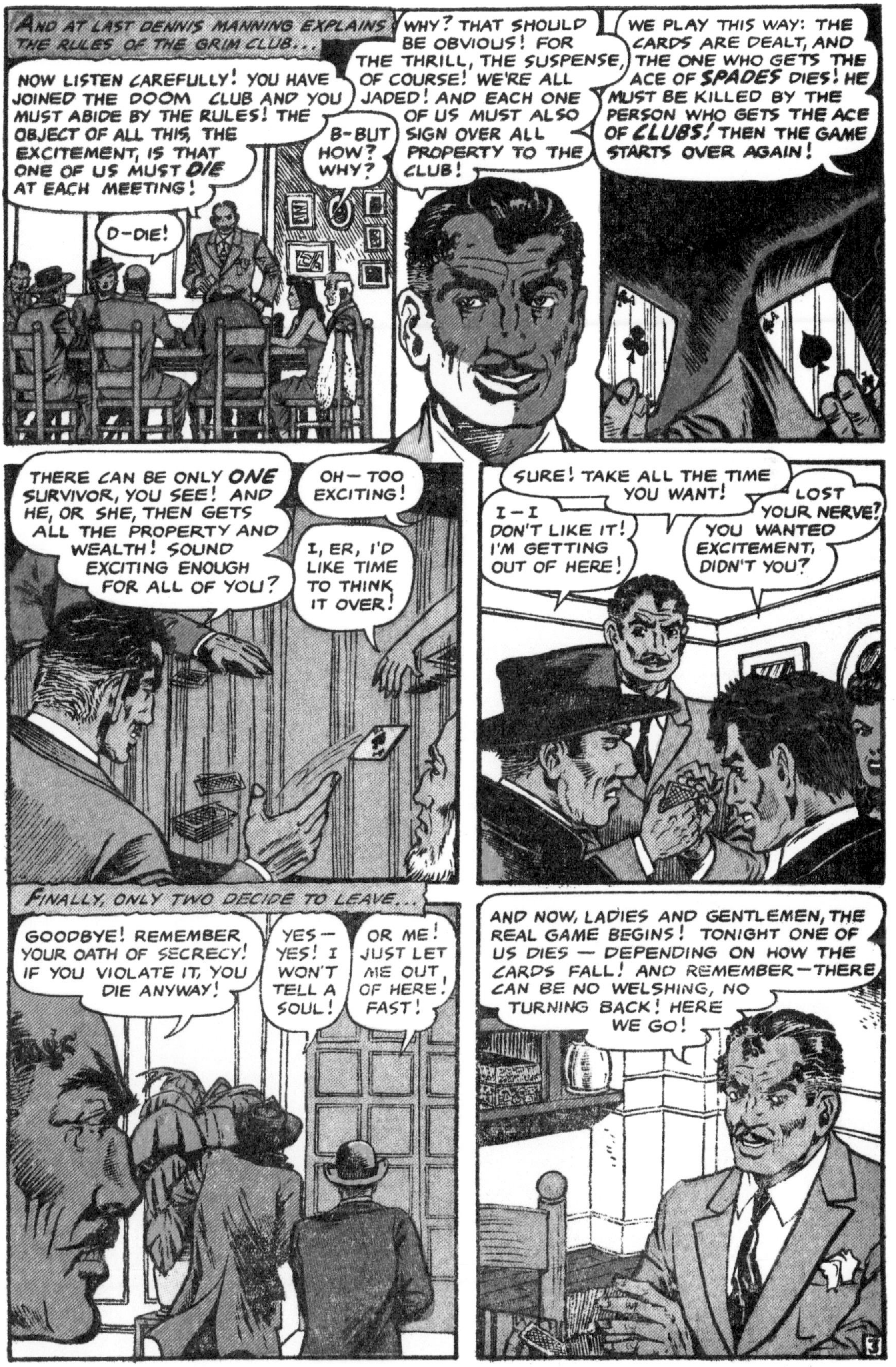
AND AT LAST DENNIS MANNING EXPLAINS THE RULES OF THE GRIM CLUB...
NOW LISTEN CAREFULLY! YOU HAVE JOINED THE DOOM CLUB AND YOU MUST ABIDE BY THE RULES! THE OBJECT OF ALL THIS, THE EXCITEMENT, IS THAT ONE OF US MUST DIE AT EACH MEETING!
D-DIE!
B-BUT HOW? WHY?
WHY? THAT SHOULD BE OBVIOUS! FOR THE THRILL, THE SUSPENSE, OF COURSE! WE'RE ALL JADED! AND EACH ONE OF US MUST ALSO SIGN OVER ALL PROPERTY TO THE CLUB!
WE PLAY THIS WAY: THE CARDS ARE DEALT, AND THE ONE WHO GETS THE ACE OF SPADES DIES! HE MUST BE KILLED BY THE PERSON WHO GETS THE ACE OF CLUBS! THEN THE GAME STARTS OVER AGAIN!
THERE CAN BE ONLY ONE SURVIVOR, YOU SEE! AND HE, OR SHE, THEN GETS ALL THE PROPERTY AND WEALTH! SOUND EXCITING ENOUGH FOR ALL OF YOU?
OH—TOO EXCITING!
I, ER, I'D LIKE TIME TO THINK IT OVER!
I-I DON'T LIKE IT! I'M GETTING OUT OF HERE!
SURE! TAKE ALL THE TIME YOU WANT!
LOST YOUR NERVE? YOU WANTED EXCITEMENT, DIDN'T YOU?
FINALLY, ONLY TWO DECIDE TO LEAVE...
GOODBYE! REMEMBER YOUR OATH OF SECRECY! IF YOU VIOLATE IT, YOU DIE ANYWAY!
YES—YES! I WON'T TELL A SOUL!
OR ME! JUST LET ME OUT OF HERE! FAST!
AND NOW, LADIES AND GENTLEMEN, THE REAL GAME BEGINS! TONIGHT ONE OF US DIES — DEPENDING ON HOW THE CARDS FALL! AND REMEMBER—THERE CAN BE NO WELSHING, NO TURNING BACK! HERE WE GO!
3

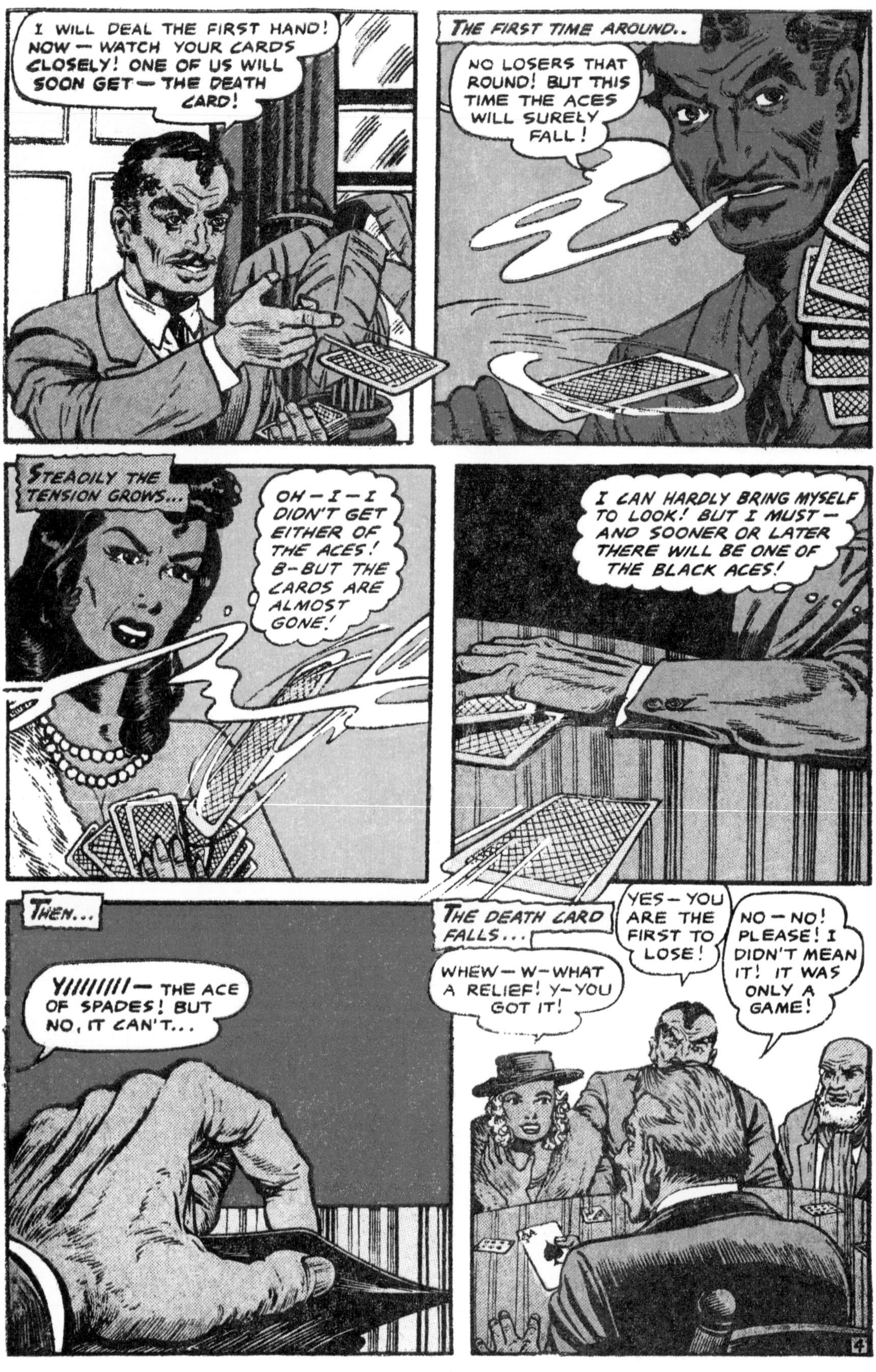
I WILL DEAL THE FIRST HAND! NOW — WATCH YOUR CARDS CLOSELY! ONE OF US WILL SOON GET — THE DEATH CARD!
THE FIRST TIME AROUND..
NO LOSERS THAT ROUND! BUT THIS TIME THE ACES WILL SURELY FALL!
STEADILY THE TENSION GROWS...
OH — I — I DIDN'T GET EITHER OF THE ACES! B-BUT THE CARDS ARE ALMOST GONE!
I CAN HARDLY BRING MYSELF TO LOOK! BUT I MUST — AND SOONER OR LATER THERE WILL BE ONE OF THE BLACK ACES!
THEN...
YIIIIIII — THE ACE OF SPADES! BUT NO, IT CAN'T...
THE DEATH CARD FALLS...
WHEW — W-WHAT A RELIEF! Y-YOU GOT IT!
YES — YOU ARE THE FIRST TO LOSE!
NO — NO! PLEASE! I DIDN'T MEAN IT! IT WAS ONLY A GAME!
4

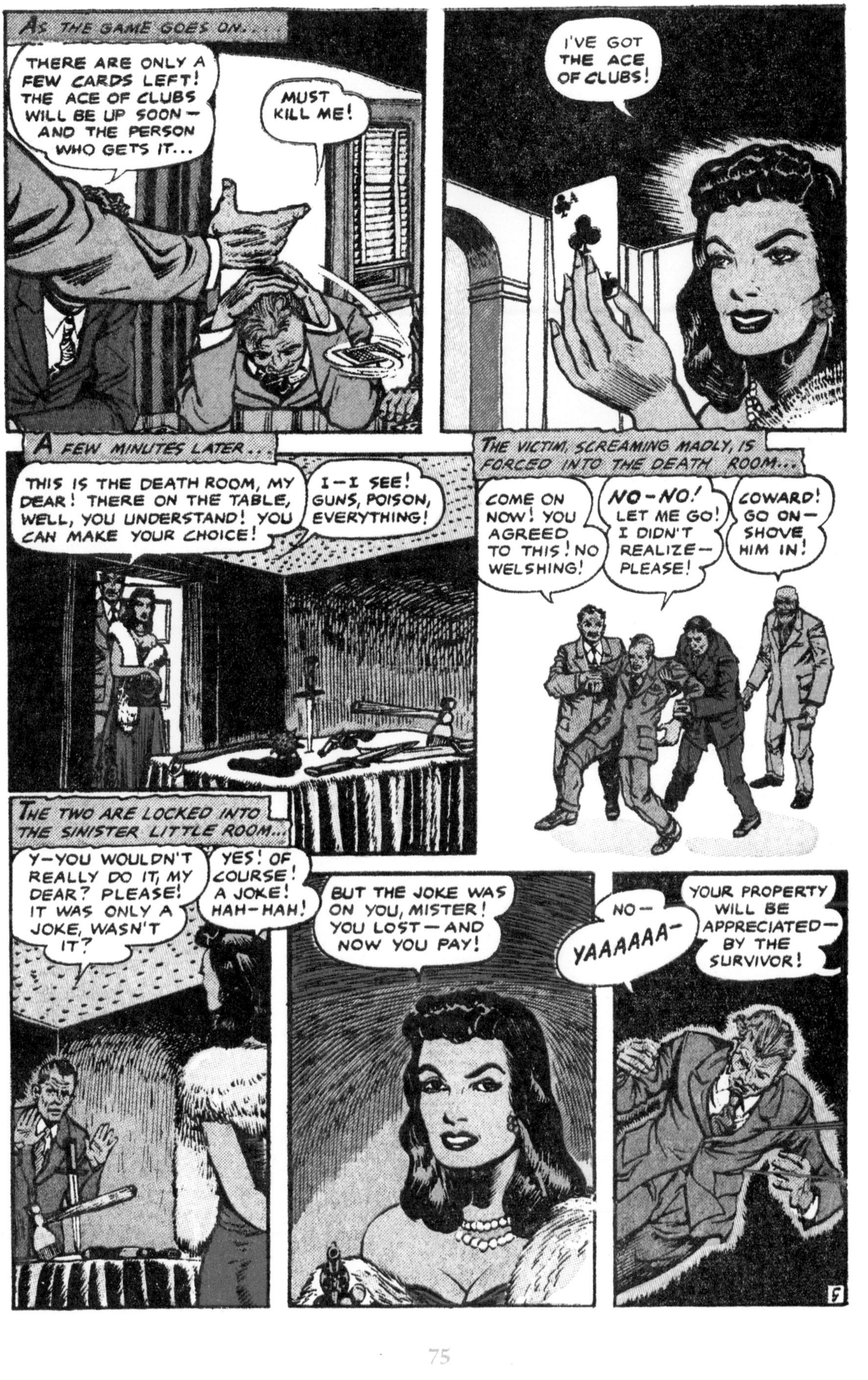
AS THE GAME GOES ON....
THERE ARE ONLY A FEW CARDS LEFT! THE ACE OF CLUBS WILL BE UP SOON — AND THE PERSON WHO GETS IT...
MUST KILL ME!
I'VE GOT THE ACE OF CLUBS!
A FEW MINUTES LATER...
THIS IS THE DEATH ROOM, MY DEAR! THERE ON THE TABLE, WELL, YOU UNDERSTAND! YOU CAN MAKE YOUR CHOICE!
I—I SEE! GUNS, POISON, EVERYTHING!
THE VICTIM, SCREAMING MADLY, IS FORCED INTO THE DEATH ROOM...
COME ON NOW! YOU AGREED TO THIS! NO WELSHING!
NO-NO! LET ME GO! I DIDN'T REALIZE— PLEASE!
COWARD! GO ON— SHOVE HIM IN!
THE TWO ARE LOCKED INTO THE SINISTER LITTLE ROOM...
Y-YOU WOULDN'T REALLY DO IT, MY DEAR? PLEASE! IT WAS ONLY A JOKE, WASN'T IT?
YES! OF COURSE! A JOKE! HAH-HAH!
BUT THE JOKE WAS ON YOU, MISTER! YOU LOST — AND NOW YOU PAY!
NO— YAAAAAA-
YOUR PROPERTY WILL BE APPRECIATED— BY THE SURVIVOR!
F

THE NEXT NIGHT THE CLUB CONVENES ONCE MORE...

WELL, MY FRIENDS, HERE WE ARE AGAIN! ALL READY TO STAKE OUR LIVES AND FORTUNES ON THE TURN OF A CARD!

YES—YES! GET ON WITH IT!

THIS SUSPENSE— AWFUL! BUT SO EXCITING!

BUT...

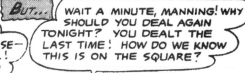

WAIT A MINUTE, MANNING! WHY SHOULD YOU DEAL AGAIN TONIGHT? YOU DEALT THE LAST TIME! HOW DO WE KNOW THIS IS ON THE SQUARE?

A GOOD QUESTION! FAIR ENOUGH! HERE— YOU DEAL THE CARDS!

THAT'S MORE LIKE IT!

HURRY— HURRY, WILL YOU! I CAN'T STAND THIS!

HERE THEY COME! AT LEAST NOW WE KNOW EVERYTHING IS ON THE LEVEL!

BUT THE VERY FIRST TIME AROUND...

YOWWWW— I DEALT MYSELF THE ACE OF SPADES!

AND DENNIS MANNING GETS THE OTHER DEADLY CARD...

PERHAPS YOU SHOULD HAVE LET ME DEAL AFTER ALL! SEE— I HAVE THE HONOR OF KILLING YOU!

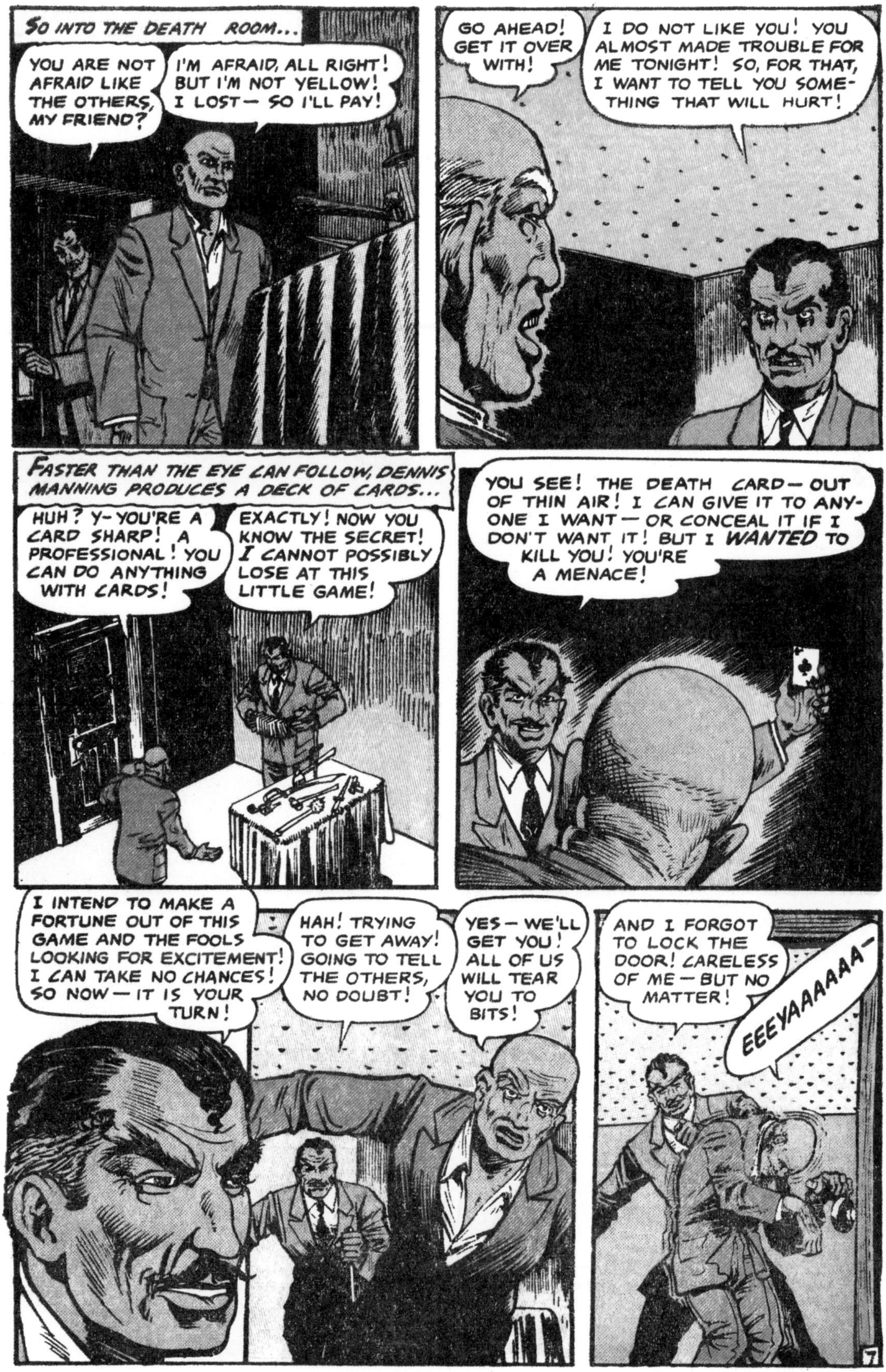
SO INTO THE DEATH ROOM...
YOU ARE NOT AFRAID LIKE THE OTHERS, MY FRIEND?
I'M AFRAID, ALL RIGHT! BUT I'M NOT YELLOW! I LOST— SO I'LL PAY!
GO AHEAD! GET IT OVER WITH!
I DO NOT LIKE YOU! YOU ALMOST MADE TROUBLE FOR ME TONIGHT! SO, FOR THAT, I WANT TO TELL YOU SOMETHING THAT WILL HURT!
FASTER THAN THE EYE CAN FOLLOW, DENNIS MANNING PRODUCES A DECK OF CARDS...
HUH? Y-YOU'RE A CARD SHARP! A PROFESSIONAL! YOU CAN DO ANYTHING WITH CARDS!
EXACTLY! NOW YOU KNOW THE SECRET! I CANNOT POSSIBLY LOSE AT THIS LITTLE GAME!
YOU SEE! THE DEATH CARD— OUT OF THIN AIR! I CAN GIVE IT TO ANYONE I WANT— OR CONCEAL IT IF I DON'T WANT IT! BUT I WANTED TO KILL YOU! YOU'RE A MENACE!
I INTEND TO MAKE A FORTUNE OUT OF THIS GAME AND THE FOOLS LOOKING FOR EXCITEMENT! I CAN TAKE NO CHANCES! SO NOW— IT IS YOUR TURN!
HAH! TRYING TO GET AWAY! GOING TO TELL THE OTHERS, NO DOUBT!
YES— WE'LL GET YOU! ALL OF US WILL TEAR YOU TO BITS!
AND I FORGOT TO LOCK THE DOOR! CARELESS OF ME— BUT NO MATTER!
EEEYAAAAAA-
7

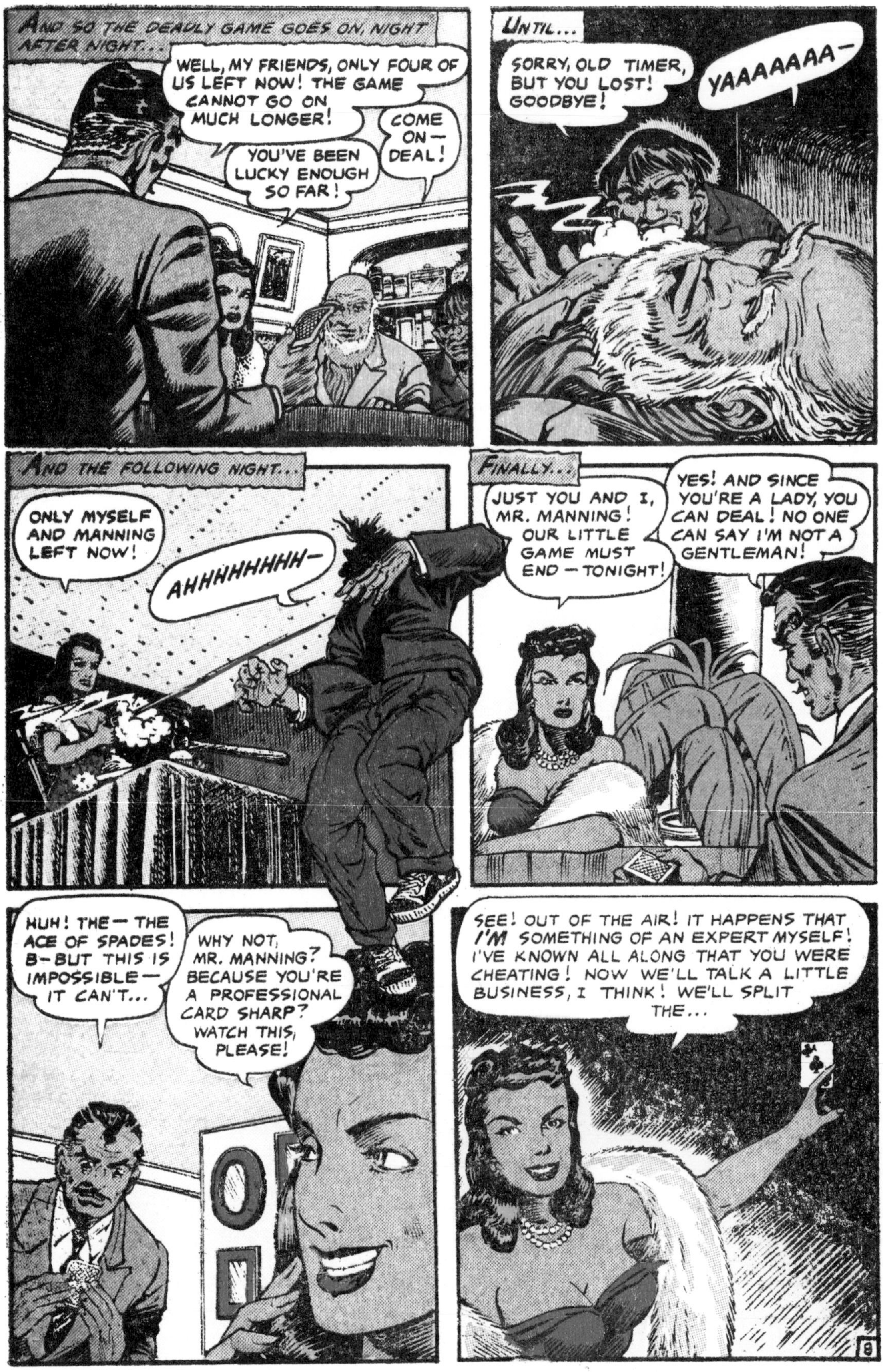
AND SO THE DEADLY GAME GOES ON, NIGHT AFTER NIGHT...
WELL, MY FRIENDS, ONLY FOUR OF US LEFT NOW! THE GAME CANNOT GO ON MUCH LONGER!
COME ON— DEAL!
YOU'VE BEEN LUCKY ENOUGH SO FAR!
UNTIL...
SORRY, OLD TIMER, BUT YOU LOST! GOODBYE!
YAAAAAAA—
AND THE FOLLOWING NIGHT...
ONLY MYSELF AND MANNING LEFT NOW!
AHHHHHHHH—
FINALLY...
JUST YOU AND I, MR. MANNING! OUR LITTLE GAME MUST END—TONIGHT!
YES! AND SINCE YOU'RE A LADY, YOU CAN DEAL! NO ONE CAN SAY I'M NOT A GENTLEMAN!
HUH! THE—THE ACE OF SPADES! B-BUT THIS IS IMPOSSIBLE— IT CAN'T...
WHY NOT, MR. MANNING? BECAUSE YOU'RE A PROFESSIONAL CARD SHARP? WATCH THIS, PLEASE!
SEE! OUT OF THE AIR! IT HAPPENS THAT I'M SOMETHING OF AN EXPERT MYSELF! I'VE KNOWN ALL ALONG THAT YOU WERE CHEATING! NOW WE'LL TALK A LITTLE BUSINESS, I THINK! WE'LL SPLIT THE...
8

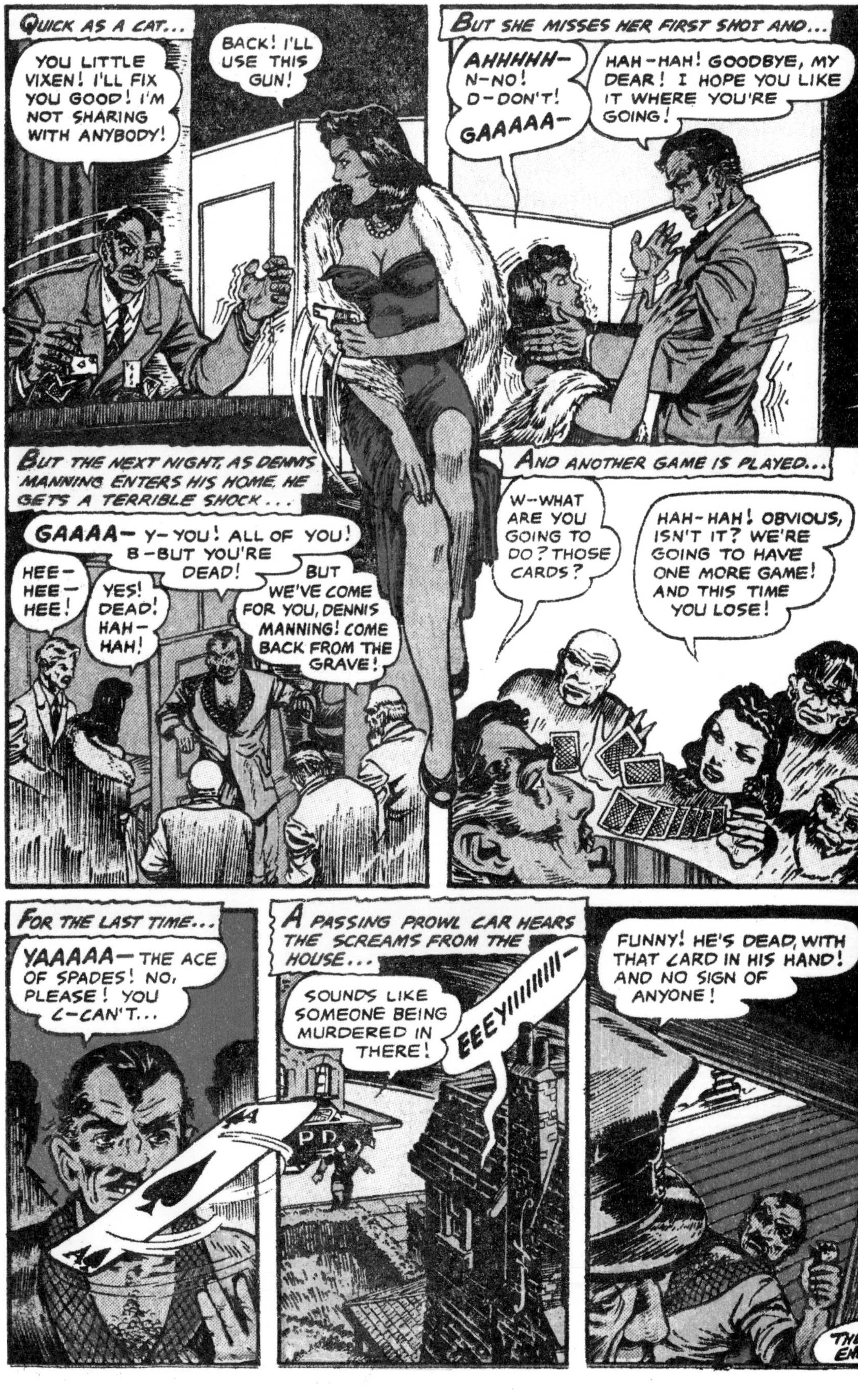
QUICK AS A CAT...
YOU LITTLE VIXEN! I'LL FIX YOU GOOD! I'M NOT SHARING WITH ANYBODY!
BACK! I'LL USE THIS GUN!
BUT SHE MISSES HER FIRST SHOT AND...
AHHHHH— N-NO! D-DON'T! GAAAAA—
HAH-HAH! GOODBYE, MY DEAR! I HOPE YOU LIKE IT WHERE YOU'RE GOING!
BUT THE NEXT NIGHT, AS DENNIS MANNING ENTERS HIS HOME, HE GETS A TERRIBLE SHOCK...
GAAAA— Y-YOU! ALL OF YOU! B-BUT YOU'RE DEAD!
HEE-HEE-HEE!
YES! DEAD! HAH-HAH!
BUT WE'VE COME FOR YOU, DENNIS MANNING! COME BACK FROM THE GRAVE!
AND ANOTHER GAME IS PLAYED...
W-WHAT ARE YOU GOING TO DO? THOSE CARDS?
HAH-HAH! OBVIOUS, ISN'T IT? WE'RE GOING TO HAVE ONE MORE GAME! AND THIS TIME YOU LOSE!
FOR THE LAST TIME...
YAAAAA— THE ACE OF SPADES! NO, PLEASE! YOU C-CAN'T...
A PASSING PROWL CAR HEARS THE SCREAMS FROM THE HOUSE...
SOUNDS LIKE SOMEONE BEING MURDERED IN THERE!
EEEYIIIIIIIII—
FUNNY! HE'S DEAD, WITH THAT CARD IN HIS HAND! AND NO SIGN OF ANYONE!
THE END

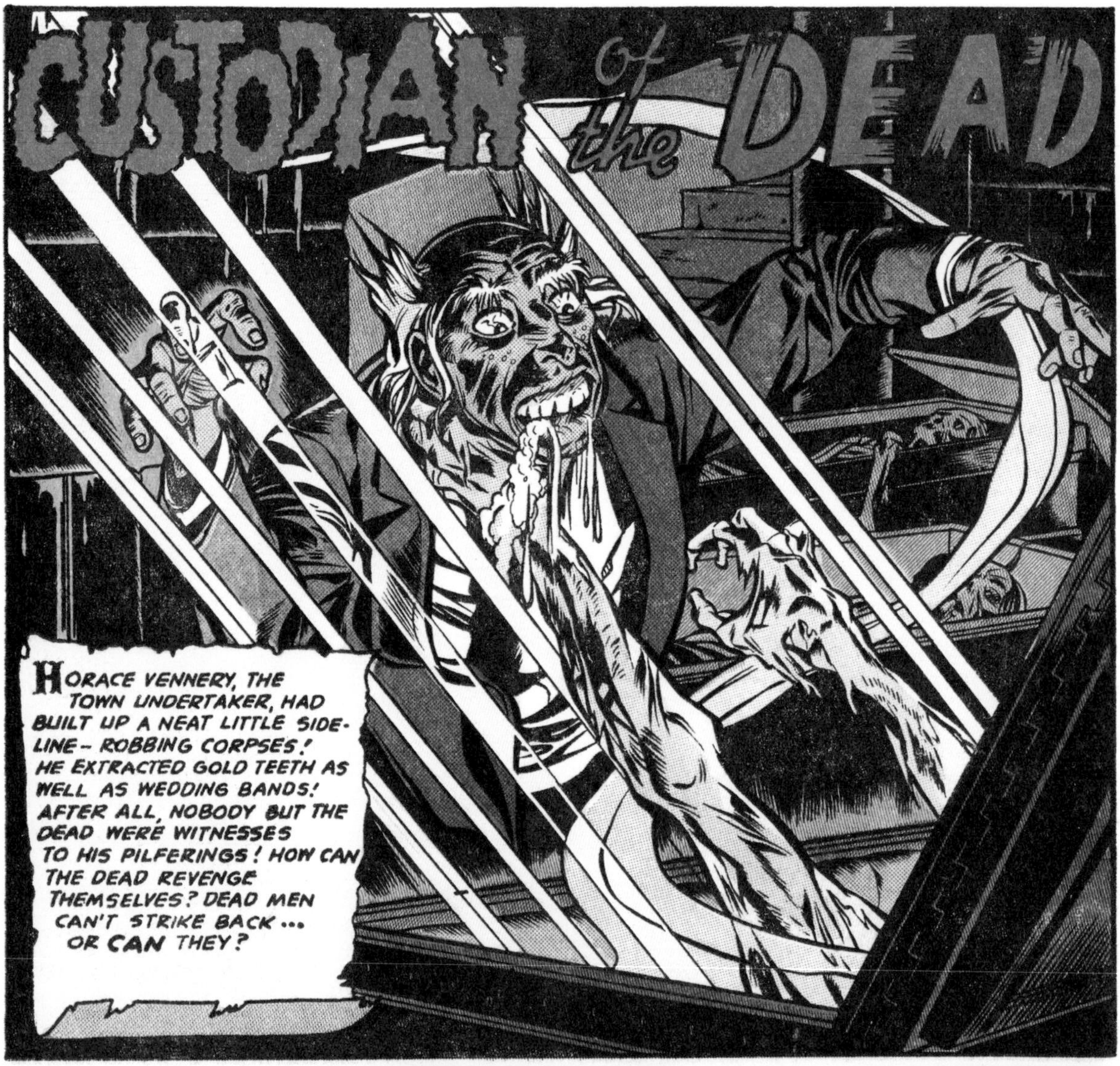
CUSTODIAN of the DEAD
HORACE VENNERY, THE TOWN UNDERTAKER, HAD BUILT UP A NEAT LITTLE SIDE-LINE – ROBBING CORPSES! HE EXTRACTED GOLD TEETH AS WELL AS WEDDING BANDS! AFTER ALL, NOBODY BUT THE DEAD WERE WITNESSES TO HIS PILFERINGS! HOW CAN THE DEAD REVENGE THEMSELVES? DEAD MEN CAN'T STRIKE BACK... OR CAN THEY?

HORACE DID HIS WORK ON FOGGY NIGHTS, WHEN NOBODY WAS ABROAD BUT THE BATS AND THE RATS... THE CEMETERY RATS WHOM HORACE HATED WITH A FANATICAL HATRED!

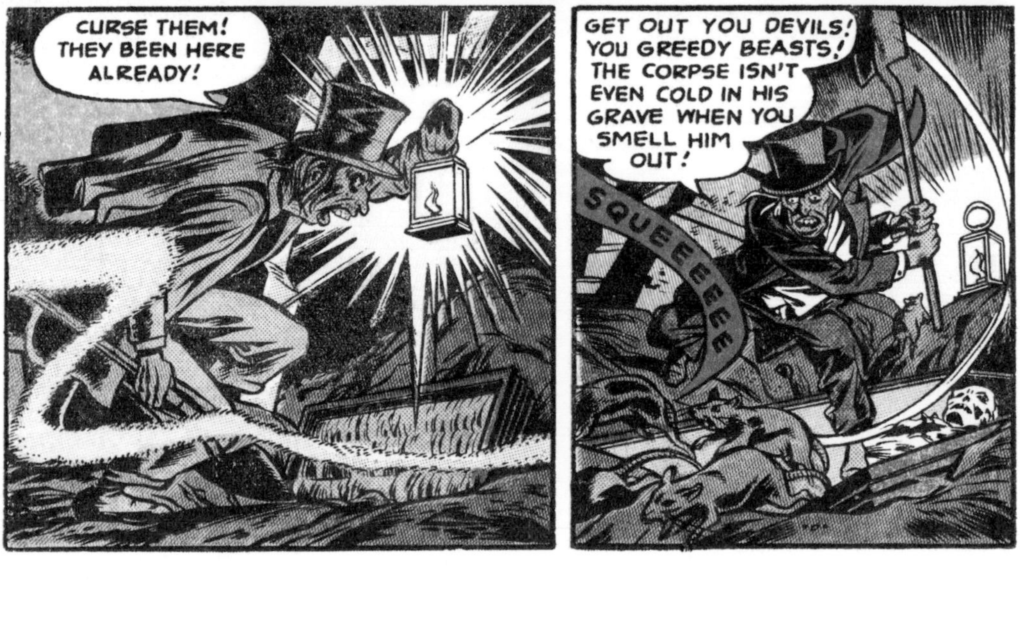
CURSE THEM! THEY BEEN HERE ALREADY!
GET OUT YOU DEVILS! YOU GREEDY BEASTS! THE CORPSE ISN'T EVEN COLD IN HIS GRAVE WHEN YOU SMELL HIM OUT!
SQUEEEEEEE

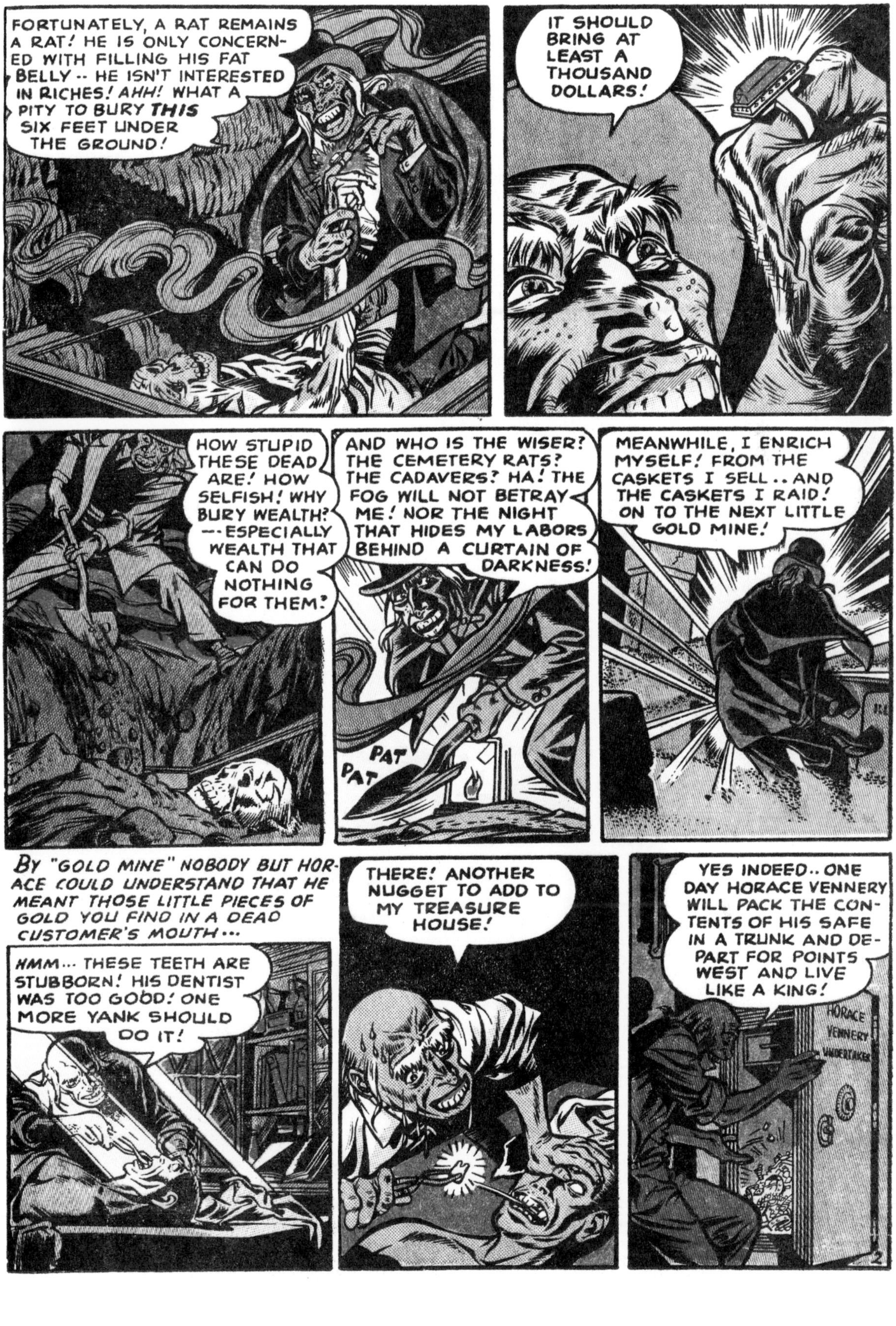

FORTUNATELY, A RAT REMAINS A RAT! HE IS ONLY CONCERNED WITH FILLING HIS FAT BELLY -- HE ISN'T INTERESTED IN RICHES! AHH! WHAT A PITY TO BURY THIS SIX FEET UNDER THE GROUND!
IT SHOULD BRING AT LEAST A THOUSAND DOLLARS!
HOW STUPID THESE DEAD ARE! HOW SELFISH! WHY BURY WEALTH? --- ESPECIALLY WEALTH THAT CAN DO NOTHING FOR THEM?
AND WHO IS THE WISER? THE CEMETERY RATS? THE CADAVERS? HA! THE FOG WILL NOT BETRAY ME! NOR THE NIGHT THAT HIDES MY LABORS BEHIND A CURTAIN OF DARKNESS!
PAT PAT
MEANWHILE, I ENRICH MYSELF! FROM THE CASKETS I SELL .. AND THE CASKETS I RAID! ON TO THE NEXT LITTLE GOLD MINE!
BY "GOLD MINE" NOBODY BUT HORACE COULD UNDERSTAND THAT HE MEANT THOSE LITTLE PIECES OF GOLD YOU FIND IN A DEAD CUSTOMER'S MOUTH ...
HMM ... THESE TEETH ARE STUBBORN! HIS DENTIST WAS TOO GOOD! ONE MORE YANK SHOULD DO IT!
THERE! ANOTHER NUGGET TO ADD TO MY TREASURE HOUSE!
YES INDEED .. ONE DAY HORACE VENNERY WILL PACK THE CONTENTS OF HIS SAFE IN A TRUNK AND DEPART FOR POINTS WEST AND LIVE LIKE A KING!
HORACE VENNERY UNDERTAKER

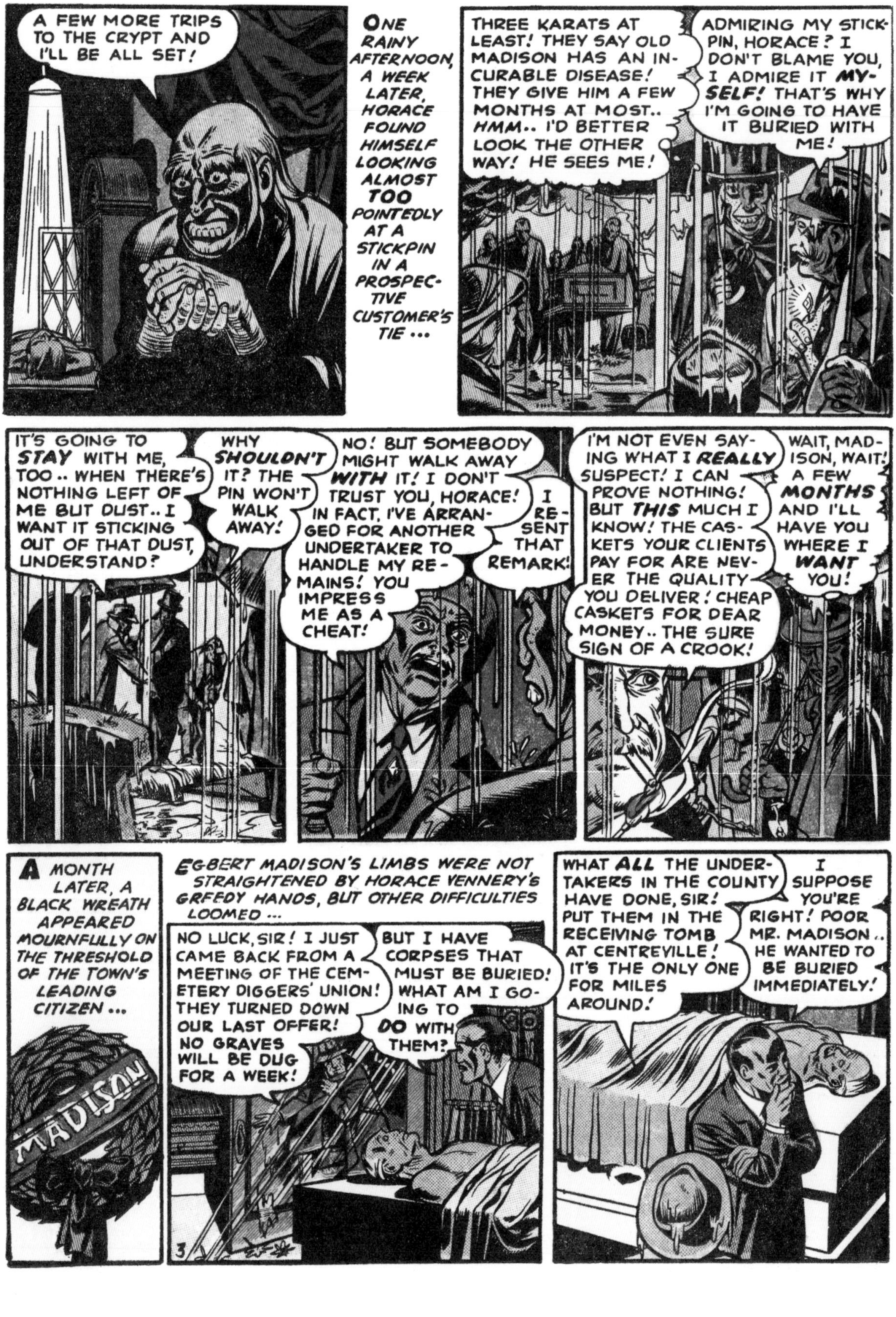
A FEW MORE TRIPS TO THE CRYPT AND I'LL BE ALL SET!
ONE RAINY AFTERNOON, A WEEK LATER, HORACE FOUND HIMSELF LOOKING ALMOST TOO POINTEDLY AT A STICKPIN IN A PROSPECTIVE CUSTOMER'S TIE...
THREE KARATS AT LEAST! THEY SAY OLD MADISON HAS AN INCURABLE DISEASE! THEY GIVE HIM A FEW MONTHS AT MOST.. HMM.. I'D BETTER LOOK THE OTHER WAY! HE SEES ME!
ADMIRING MY STICKPIN, HORACE? I DON'T BLAME YOU, I ADMIRE IT MYSELF! THAT'S WHY I'M GOING TO HAVE IT BURIED WITH ME!
IT'S GOING TO STAY WITH ME, TOO.. WHEN THERE'S NOTHING LEFT OF ME BUT DUST.. I WANT IT STICKING OUT OF THAT DUST, UNDERSTAND?
WHY SHOULDN'T IT? THE PIN WON'T WALK AWAY!
NO! BUT SOMEBODY MIGHT WALK AWAY WITH IT! I DON'T TRUST YOU, HORACE! IN FACT, I'VE ARRANGED FOR ANOTHER UNDERTAKER TO HANDLE MY REMAINS! YOU IMPRESS ME AS A CHEAT!
I RESENT THAT REMARK!
I'M NOT EVEN SAYING WHAT I REALLY SUSPECT! I CAN PROVE NOTHING! BUT THIS MUCH I KNOW! THE CASKETS YOUR CLIENTS PAY FOR ARE NEVER THE QUALITY YOU DELIVER! CHEAP CASKETS FOR DEAR MONEY.. THE SURE SIGN OF A CROOK!
WAIT, MADISON, WAIT! A FEW MONTHS AND I'LL HAVE YOU WHERE I WANT YOU!
A MONTH LATER, A BLACK WREATH APPEARED MOURNFULLY ON THE THRESHOLD OF THE TOWN'S LEADING CITIZEN...
MADISON
EGBERT MADISON'S LIMBS WERE NOT STRAIGHTENED BY HORACE VENNERY'S GREEDY HANDS, BUT OTHER DIFFICULTIES LOOMED...
NO LUCK, SIR! I JUST CAME BACK FROM A MEETING OF THE CEMETERY DIGGERS' UNION! THEY TURNED DOWN OUR LAST OFFER! NO GRAVES WILL BE DUG FOR A WEEK!
BUT I HAVE CORPSES THAT MUST BE BURIED! WHAT AM I GOING TO DO WITH THEM?
WHAT ALL THE UNDERTAKERS IN THE COUNTY HAVE DONE, SIR! PUT THEM IN THE RECEIVING TOMB AT CENTREVILLE! IT'S THE ONLY ONE FOR MILES AROUND!
I SUPPOSE YOU'RE RIGHT! POOR MR. MADISON.. HE WANTED TO BE BURIED IMMEDIATELY!

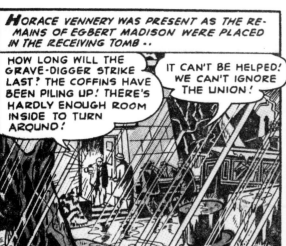

HORACE VENNERY WAS PRESENT AS THE REMAINS OF EGBERT MADISON WERE PLACED IN THE RECEIVING TOMB..

HOW LONG WILL THE GRAVE-DIGGER STRIKE LAST? THE COFFINS HAVE BEEN PILING UP! THERE'S HARDLY ENOUGH ROOM INSIDE TO TURN AROUND!

IT CAN'T BE HELPED! WE CAN'T IGNORE THE UNION!

TECHNICALITIES! NOTHING BUT TECHNICALITIES! A MAN CAN'T EVEN BE BURIED DECENTLY IN THIS COMPLEX SOCIETY OF OURS!

LUCKILY FOR ME! HEH! HEH! I WON'T HAVE TO DIG UP OLD MADISON AFTER ALL!!-- JUST SNEAK INTO THE RECEIVING TOMB TONIGHT AND PRY OPEN THE COFFIN LID!

THAT NIGHT, AS A STORM RAGED...

HMM.. THE CARETAKER IS GETTING READY FOR BED! WHY NOT? WHO SHOULD DISTURB HIS SLEEP? THE DEAD WON'T COME KNOCKING ON HIS DOOR!

FUNNY... MADISON SUSPECTING MY LITTLE SIDELINE! BUT WHAT CAN HE DO ABOUT IT NOW? HE LIES IN A COFFIN, ON A SLAB... DEFENSELESS!

I'LL ALSO HAVE A LOOK INSIDE THE OTHER COFFINS! I'M IN NO RUSH! I'VE GOT ALL NIGHT!

AHH! THERE THEY ARE, MY VICTIMS! I COULD STEAL THE EYEBALLS OUT OF THEIR HEADS AND THEY COULDN'T STOP ME!

WE'LL SAVE OLD MADISON FOR LAST! LET'S SEE... WHAT HAVE WE HERE? MRS. RUPERTS AND HER STRING OF PEARLS!

YOU WON'T NEED THESE ANY MORE MRS. RUPERTS!

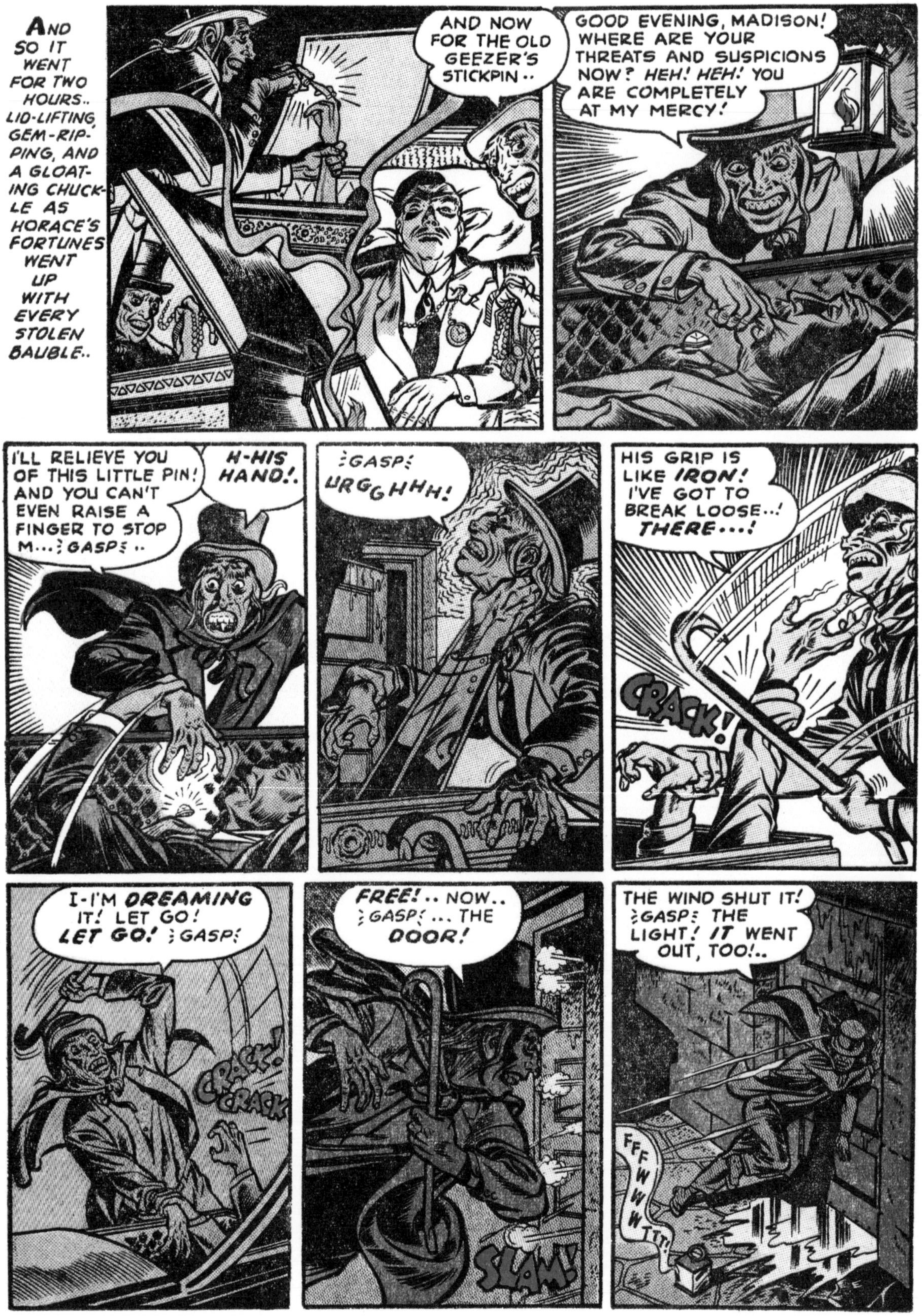
And so it went for two hours.. lid-lifting, gem-ripping, and a gloating chuckle as Horace's fortunes went up with every stolen bauble..
AND NOW FOR THE OLD GEEZER'S STICKPIN ..
GOOD EVENING, MADISON! WHERE ARE YOUR THREATS AND SUSPICIONS NOW? HEH! HEH! YOU ARE COMPLETELY AT MY MERCY!
I'LL RELIEVE YOU OF THIS LITTLE PIN! AND YOU CAN'T EVEN RAISE A FINGER TO STOP M... GASP ..
H-HIS HAND!.
GASP
URGGHHH!
HIS GRIP IS LIKE IRON! I'VE GOT TO BREAK LOOSE..! THERE...!
CRACK!
I-I'M DREAMING IT! LET GO! LET GO! GASP
CRACK! CRACK
FREE! .. NOW.. GASP ... THE DOOR!
SLAM!
THE WIND SHUT IT! GASP THE LIGHT! IT WENT OUT, TOO!..

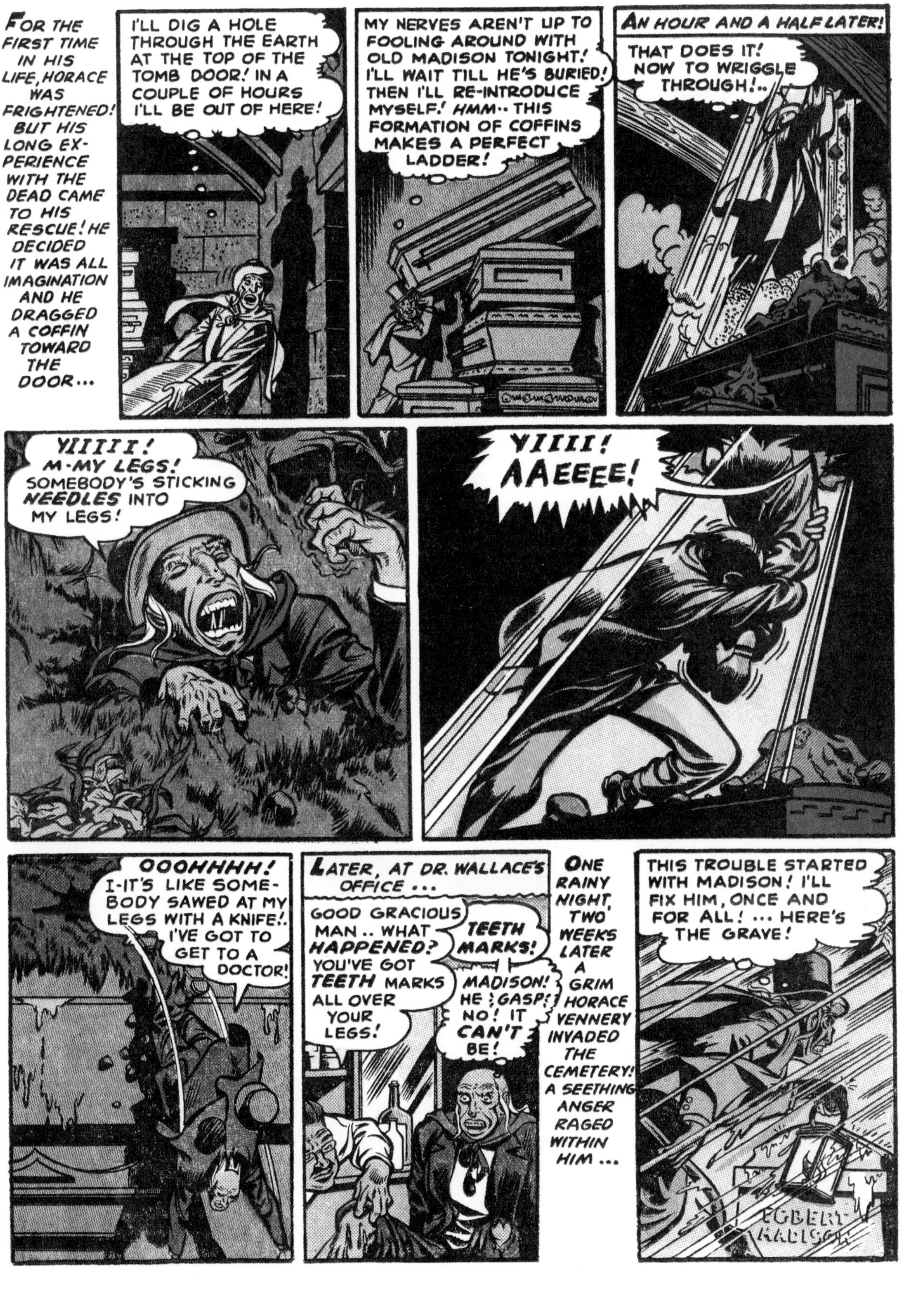
FOR THE FIRST TIME IN HIS LIFE, HORACE WAS FRIGHTENED! BUT HIS LONG EXPERIENCE WITH THE DEAD CAME TO HIS RESCUE! HE DECIDED IT WAS ALL IMAGINATION AND HE DRAGGED A COFFIN TOWARD THE DOOR...
I'LL DIG A HOLE THROUGH THE EARTH AT THE TOP OF THE TOMB DOOR! IN A COUPLE OF HOURS I'LL BE OUT OF HERE!
MY NERVES AREN'T UP TO FOOLING AROUND WITH OLD MADISON TONIGHT! I'LL WAIT TILL HE'S BURIED! THEN I'LL RE-INTRODUCE MYSELF! HMM.. THIS FORMATION OF COFFINS MAKES A PERFECT LADDER!
AN HOUR AND A HALF LATER!
THAT DOES IT! NOW TO WRIGGLE THROUGH!..
YIIIII! M-MY LEGS! SOMEBODY'S STICKING NEEDLES INTO MY LEGS!
YIIIII! AAEEEE!
OOOHHHH! I-IT'S LIKE SOMEBODY SAWED AT MY LEGS WITH A KNIFE!. I'VE GOT TO GET TO A DOCTOR!
LATER, AT DR. WALLACE'S OFFICE ...
GOOD GRACIOUS MAN .. WHAT HAPPENED? YOU'VE GOT TEETH MARKS ALL OVER YOUR LEGS!
TEETH MARKS!
MADISON! HE GASP! NO! IT CAN'T BE!
ONE RAINY NIGHT, TWO WEEKS LATER A GRIM HORACE VENNERY INVADED THE CEMETERY! A SEETHING ANGER RAGED WITHIN HIM...
THIS TROUBLE STARTED WITH MADISON! I'LL FIX HIM, ONCE AND FOR ALL! ... HERE'S THE GRAVE!

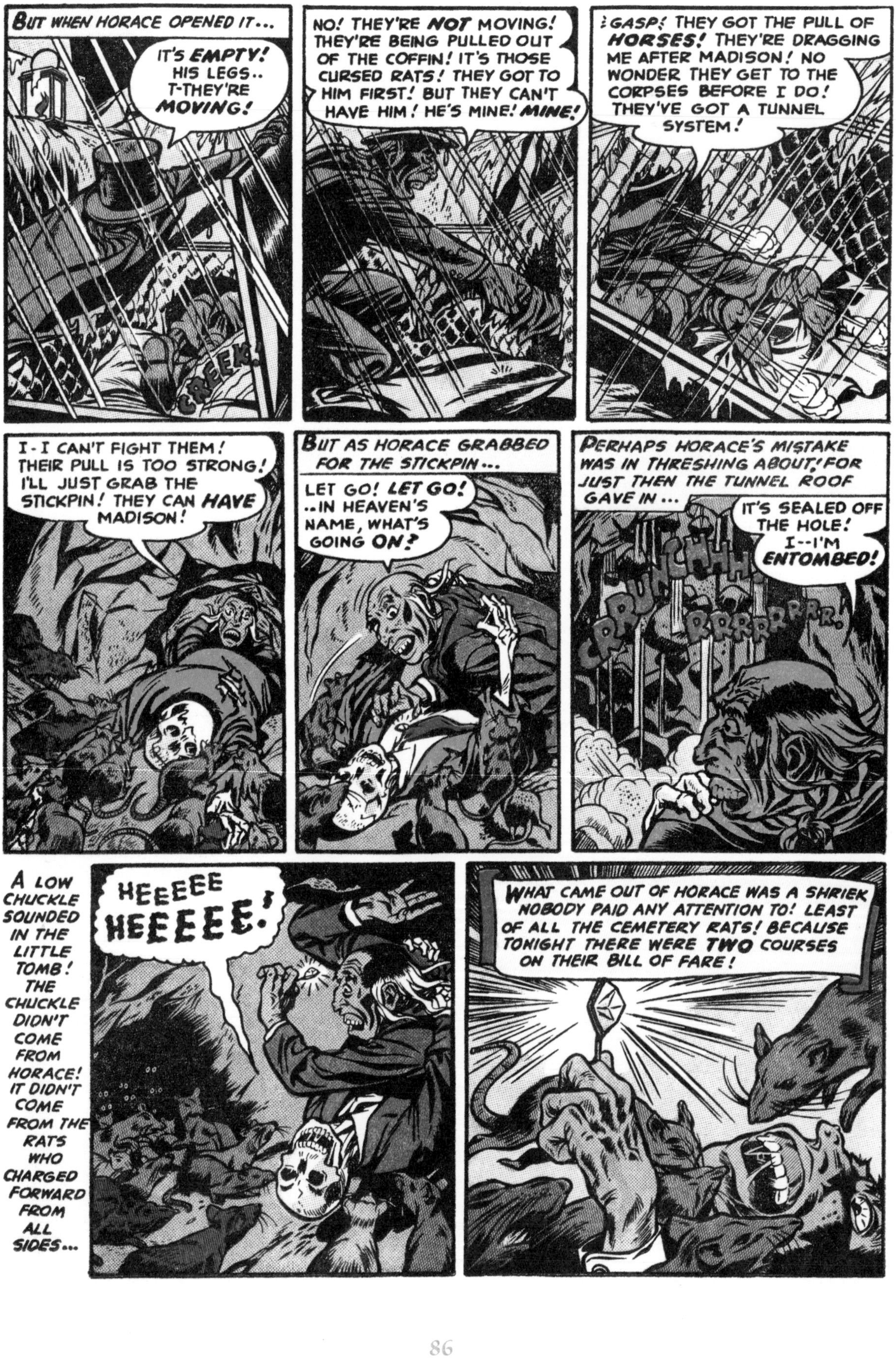
BUT WHEN HORACE OPENED IT...
IT'S EMPTY! HIS LEGS.. T-THEY'RE MOVING!
CREEK!
NO! THEY'RE NOT MOVING! THEY'RE BEING PULLED OUT OF THE COFFIN! IT'S THOSE CURSED RATS! THEY GOT TO HIM FIRST! BUT THEY CAN'T HAVE HIM! HE'S MINE! MINE!
GASP! THEY GOT THE PULL OF HORSES! THEY'RE DRAGGING ME AFTER MADISON! NO WONDER THEY GET TO THE CORPSES BEFORE I DO! THEY'VE GOT A TUNNEL SYSTEM!
I-I CAN'T FIGHT THEM! THEIR PULL IS TOO STRONG! I'LL JUST GRAB THE STICKPIN! THEY CAN HAVE MADISON!
BUT AS HORACE GRABBED FOR THE STICKPIN...
LET GO! LET GO! ..IN HEAVEN'S NAME, WHAT'S GOING ON?
PERHAPS HORACE'S MISTAKE WAS IN THRESHING ABOUT! FOR JUST THEN THE TUNNEL ROOF GAVE IN...
IT'S SEALED OFF THE HOLE! I--I'M ENTOMBED!
CRUNCHHH!
RRRRRRRR!
A LOW CHUCKLE SOUNDED IN THE LITTLE TOMB! THE CHUCKLE DIDN'T COME FROM HORACE! IT DIDN'T COME FROM THE RATS WHO CHARGED FORWARD FROM ALL SIDES...
HEEEEE HEEEEEE!
WHAT CAME OUT OF HORACE WAS A SHRIEK NOBODY PAID ANY ATTENTION TO! LEAST OF ALL THE CEMETERY RATS! BECAUSE TONIGHT THERE WERE TWO COURSES ON THEIR BILL OF FARE!

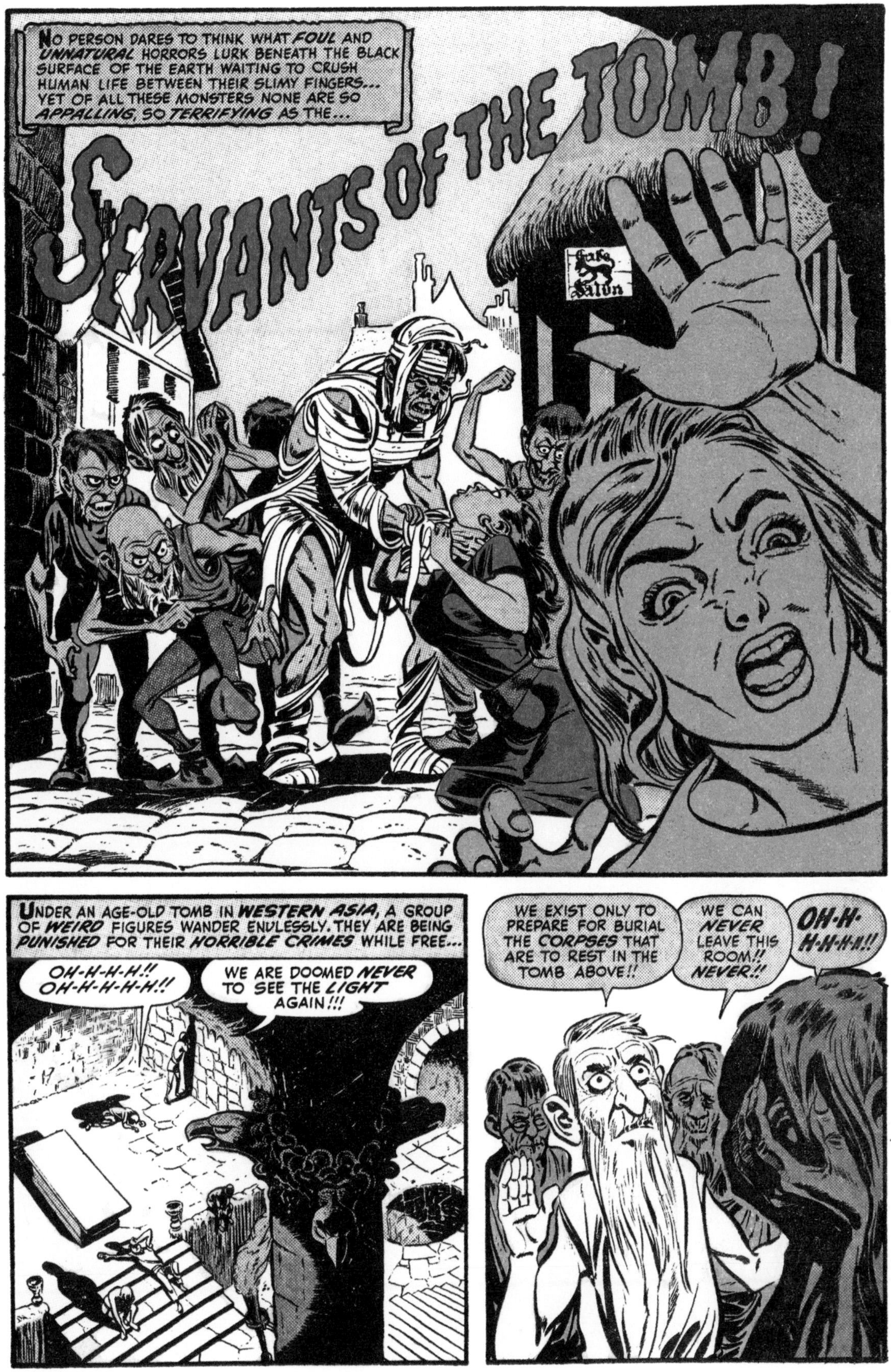

NO PERSON DARES TO THINK WHAT FOUL AND UNNATURAL HORRORS LURK BENEATH THE BLACK SURFACE OF THE EARTH WAITING TO CRUSH HUMAN LIFE BETWEEN THEIR SLIMY FINGERS... YET OF ALL THESE MONSTERS NONE ARE SO APPALLING, SO TERRIFYING AS THE...
SERVANTS OF THE TOMB!
UNDER AN AGE-OLD TOMB IN WESTERN ASIA, A GROUP OF WEIRD FIGURES WANDER ENDLESSLY. THEY ARE BEING PUNISHED FOR THEIR HORRIBLE CRIMES WHILE FREE...
OH-H-H-H!! OH-H-H-H-H!!
WE ARE DOOMED NEVER TO SEE THE LIGHT AGAIN!!!
WE EXIST ONLY TO PREPARE FOR BURIAL THE CORPSES THAT ARE TO REST IN THE TOMB ABOVE!!
WE CAN NEVER LEAVE THIS ROOM!! NEVER!!
OH-H-H-H-H-H!!

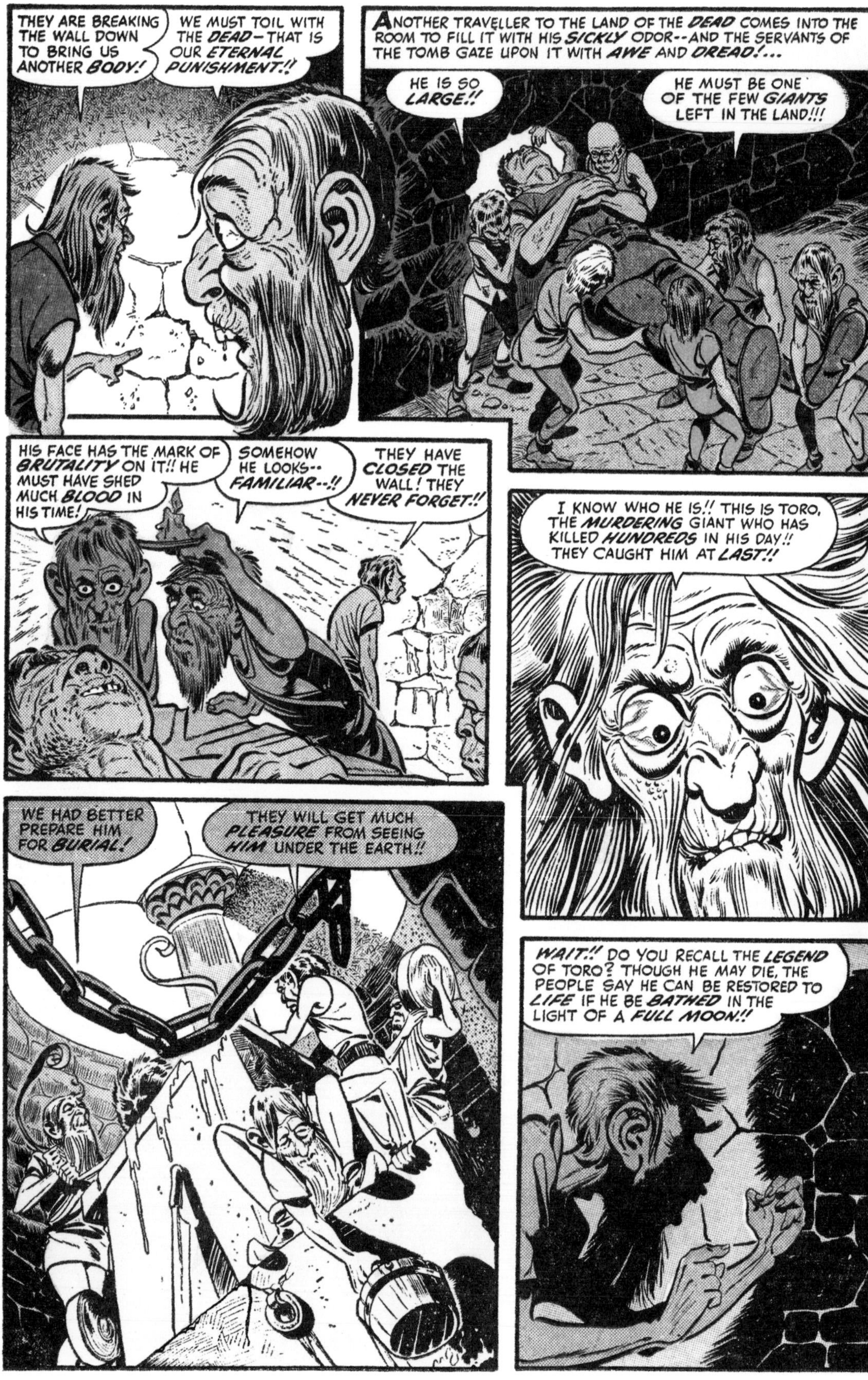
THEY ARE BREAKING THE WALL DOWN TO BRING US ANOTHER BODY!
WE MUST TOIL WITH THE DEAD—THAT IS OUR ETERNAL PUNISHMENT!!
ANOTHER TRAVELLER TO THE LAND OF THE DEAD COMES INTO THE ROOM TO FILL IT WITH HIS SICKLY ODOR--AND THE SERVANTS OF THE TOMB GAZE UPON IT WITH AWE AND DREAD!...
HE IS SO LARGE!!
HE MUST BE ONE OF THE FEW GIANTS LEFT IN THE LAND!!!
HIS FACE HAS THE MARK OF BRUTALITY ON IT!! HE MUST HAVE SHED MUCH BLOOD IN HIS TIME!
SOMEHOW HE LOOKS-- FAMILIAR--!!
THEY HAVE CLOSED THE WALL! THEY NEVER FORGET!!
I KNOW WHO HE IS!! THIS IS TORO, THE MURDERING GIANT WHO HAS KILLED HUNDREDS IN HIS DAY!! THEY CAUGHT HIM AT LAST!!
WE HAD BETTER PREPARE HIM FOR BURIAL!
THEY WILL GET MUCH PLEASURE FROM SEEING HIM UNDER THE EARTH!!
WAIT!! DO YOU RECALL THE LEGEND OF TORO? THOUGH HE MAY DIE, THE PEOPLE SAY HE CAN BE RESTORED TO LIFE IF HE BE BATHED IN THE LIGHT OF A FULL MOON!!

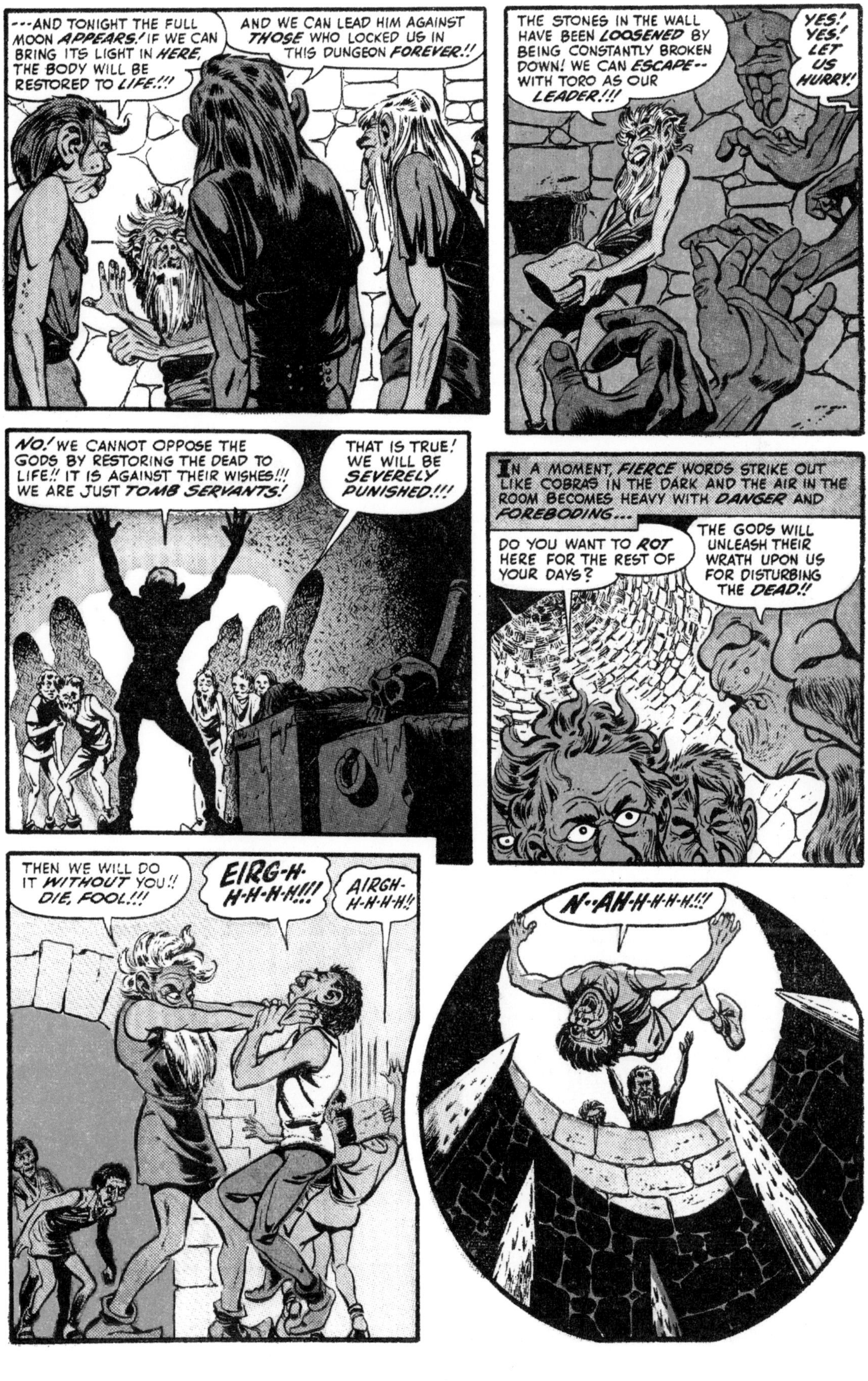
---AND TONIGHT THE FULL MOON APPEARS! IF WE CAN BRING ITS LIGHT IN HERE, THE BODY WILL BE RESTORED TO LIFE!!!
AND WE CAN LEAD HIM AGAINST THOSE WHO LOCKED US IN THIS DUNGEON FOREVER!!
THE STONES IN THE WALL HAVE BEEN LOOSENED BY BEING CONSTANTLY BROKEN DOWN! WE CAN ESCAPE-- WITH TORO AS OUR LEADER!!!
YES! YES! LET US HURRY!
NO! WE CANNOT OPPOSE THE GODS BY RESTORING THE DEAD TO LIFE!! IT IS AGAINST THEIR WISHES!!! WE ARE JUST TOMB SERVANTS!
THAT IS TRUE! WE WILL BE SEVERELY PUNISHED!!!
IN A MOMENT, FIERCE WORDS STRIKE OUT LIKE COBRAS IN THE DARK AND THE AIR IN THE ROOM BECOMES HEAVY WITH DANGER AND FOREBODING...
DO YOU WANT TO ROT HERE FOR THE REST OF YOUR DAYS?
THE GODS WILL UNLEASH THEIR WRATH UPON US FOR DISTURBING THE DEAD!!
THEN WE WILL DO IT WITHOUT YOU!! DIE, FOOL!!!
EIRG-H-H-H-H-H!!!
AIRGH-H-H-H-H!!
N-AN-H-H-H-H!!!

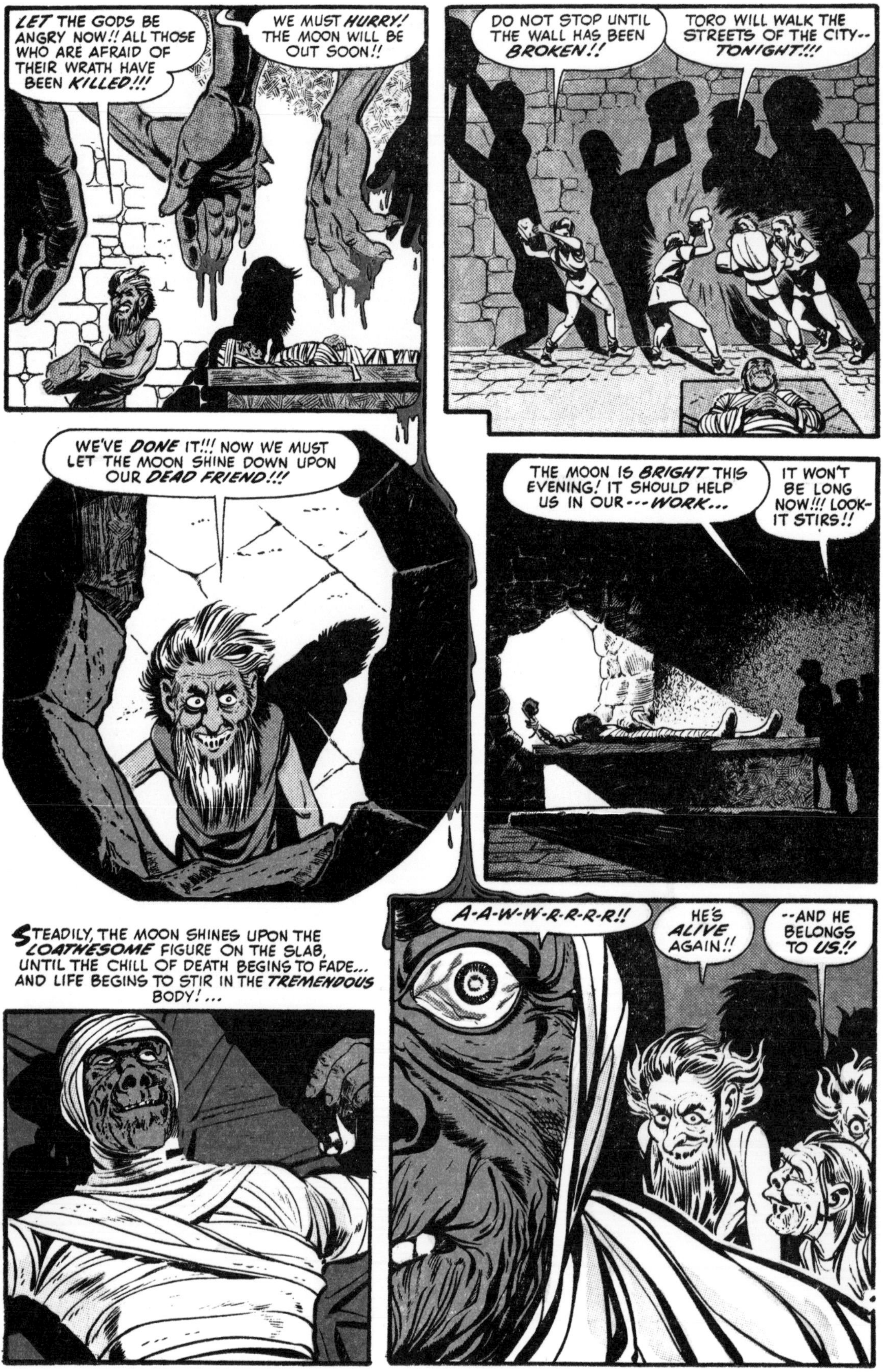
LET THE GODS BE ANGRY NOW!! ALL THOSE WHO ARE AFRAID OF THEIR WRATH HAVE BEEN KILLED!!!
WE MUST HURRY! THE MOON WILL BE OUT SOON!!
DO NOT STOP UNTIL THE WALL HAS BEEN BROKEN!!
TORO WILL WALK THE STREETS OF THE CITY-- TONIGHT!!!
WE'VE DONE IT!!! NOW WE MUST LET THE MOON SHINE DOWN UPON OUR DEAD FRIEND!!!
THE MOON IS BRIGHT THIS EVENING! IT SHOULD HELP US IN OUR---WORK...
IT WON'T BE LONG NOW!!! LOOK-IT STIRS!!
STEADILY, THE MOON SHINES UPON THE LOATHESOME FIGURE ON THE SLAB, UNTIL THE CHILL OF DEATH BEGINS TO FADE... AND LIFE BEGINS TO STIR IN THE TREMENDOUS BODY!...
A-A-W-W-R-R-R-R!!
HE'S ALIVE AGAIN!!
--AND HE BELONGS TO US!!

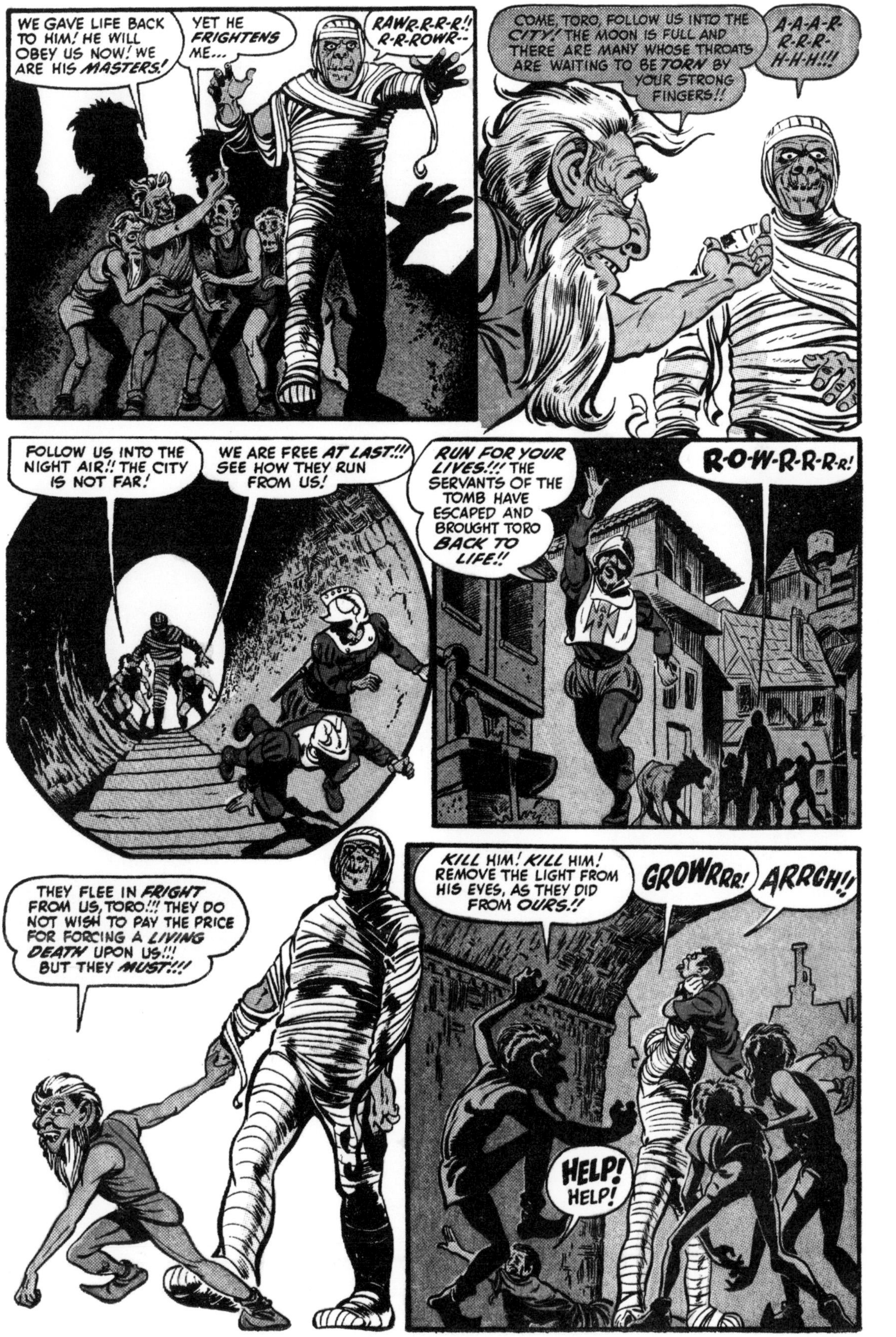
WE GAVE LIFE BACK TO HIM! HE WILL OBEY US NOW! WE ARE HIS MASTERS!
YET HE FRIGHTENS ME...
RAWR-R-R-R!! R-R-ROWR--
COME, TORO, FOLLOW US INTO THE CITY! THE MOON IS FULL AND THERE ARE MANY WHOSE THROATS ARE WAITING TO BE TORN BY YOUR STRONG FINGERS!!
A-A-A-R R-R-R- H-H-H!!!
FOLLOW US INTO THE NIGHT AIR!! THE CITY IS NOT FAR!
WE ARE FREE AT LAST!!! SEE HOW THEY RUN FROM US!
RUN FOR YOUR LIVES!!! THE SERVANTS OF THE TOMB HAVE ESCAPED AND BROUGHT TORO BACK TO LIFE!!
R-O-W-R-R-R-R!
THEY FLEE IN FRIGHT FROM US, TORO!!! THEY DO NOT WISH TO PAY THE PRICE FOR FORCING A LIVING DEATH UPON US!!! BUT THEY MUST!!!
KILL HIM! KILL HIM! REMOVE THE LIGHT FROM HIS EYES, AS THEY DID FROM OURS!!
GROWRRR!
ARRGH!!
HELP! HELP!

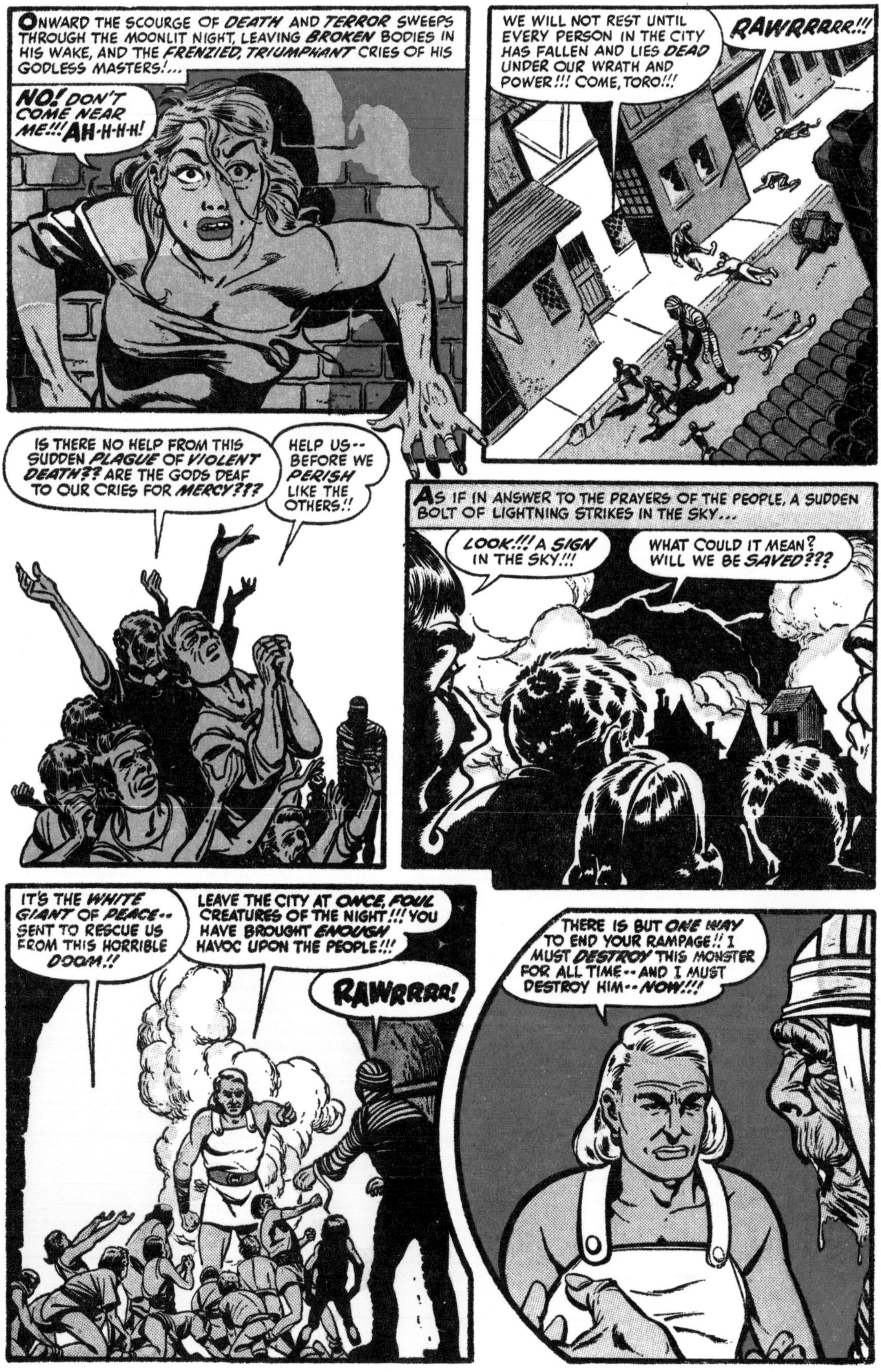

ONWARD THE SCOURGE OF DEATH AND TERROR SWEEPS THROUGH THE MOONLIT NIGHT, LEAVING BROKEN BODIES IN HIS WAKE, AND THE FRENZIED, TRIUMPHANT CRIES OF HIS GODLESS MASTERS!...
NO! DON'T COME NEAR ME!!! AH-H-H-H!
WE WILL NOT REST UNTIL EVERY PERSON IN THE CITY HAS FALLEN AND LIES DEAD UNDER OUR WRATH AND POWER!!! COME, TORO!!!
RAWRRRRR!!!
IS THERE NO HELP FROM THIS SUDDEN PLAGUE OF VIOLENT DEATH?? ARE THE GODS DEAF TO OUR CRIES FOR MERCY???
HELP US-- BEFORE WE PERISH LIKE THE OTHERS!!
AS IF IN ANSWER TO THE PRAYERS OF THE PEOPLE, A SUDDEN BOLT OF LIGHTNING STRIKES IN THE SKY...
LOOK!!! A SIGN IN THE SKY!!!
WHAT COULD IT MEAN? WILL WE BE SAVED???
IT'S THE WHITE GIANT OF PEACE-- SENT TO RESCUE US FROM THIS HORRIBLE DOOM!!
LEAVE THE CITY AT ONCE, FOUL CREATURES OF THE NIGHT!!! YOU HAVE BROUGHT ENOUGH HAVOC UPON THE PEOPLE!!!
RAWRRRR!
THERE IS BUT ONE WAY TO END YOUR RAMPAGE!! I MUST DESTROY THIS MONSTER FOR ALL TIME-- AND I MUST DESTROY HIM--NOW!!!

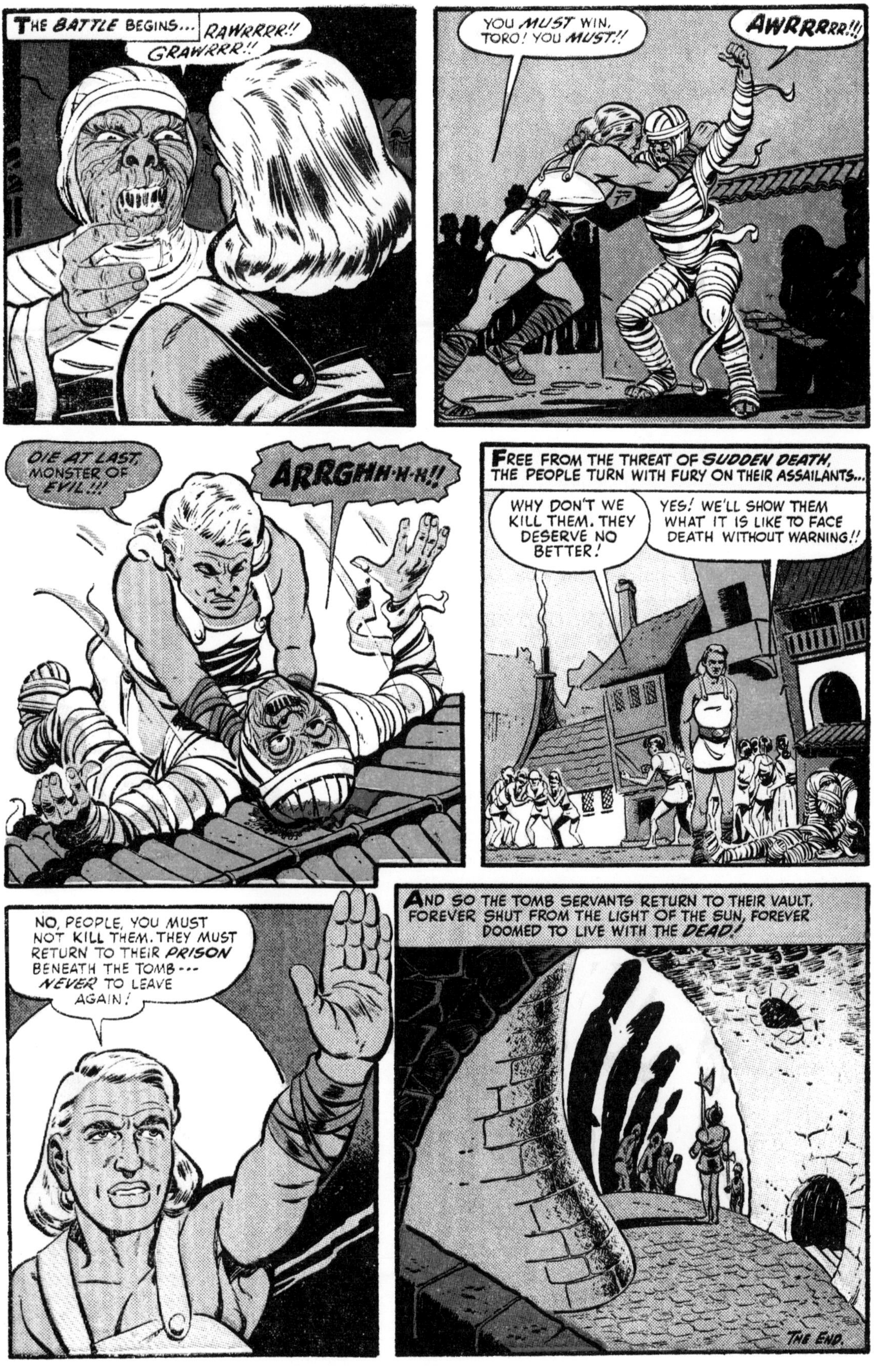
THE BATTLE BEGINS...
RAWRRRR!! GRAWRRR!!
YOU MUST WIN, TORO! YOU MUST!!
AWRRRRR!!!
DIE AT LAST, MONSTER OF EVIL!!!
ARRGHH-H-H!!
FREE FROM THE THREAT OF SUDDEN DEATH, THE PEOPLE TURN WITH FURY ON THEIR ASSAILANTS...
WHY DON'T WE KILL THEM. THEY DESERVE NO BETTER!
YES! WE'LL SHOW THEM WHAT IT IS LIKE TO FACE DEATH WITHOUT WARNING!!
NO, PEOPLE, YOU MUST NOT KILL THEM. THEY MUST RETURN TO THEIR PRISON BENEATH THE TOMB--- NEVER TO LEAVE AGAIN!
AND SO THE TOMB SERVANTS RETURN TO THEIR VAULT, FOREVER SHUT FROM THE LIGHT OF THE SUN, FOREVER DOOMED TO LIVE WITH THE DEAD!
THE END.

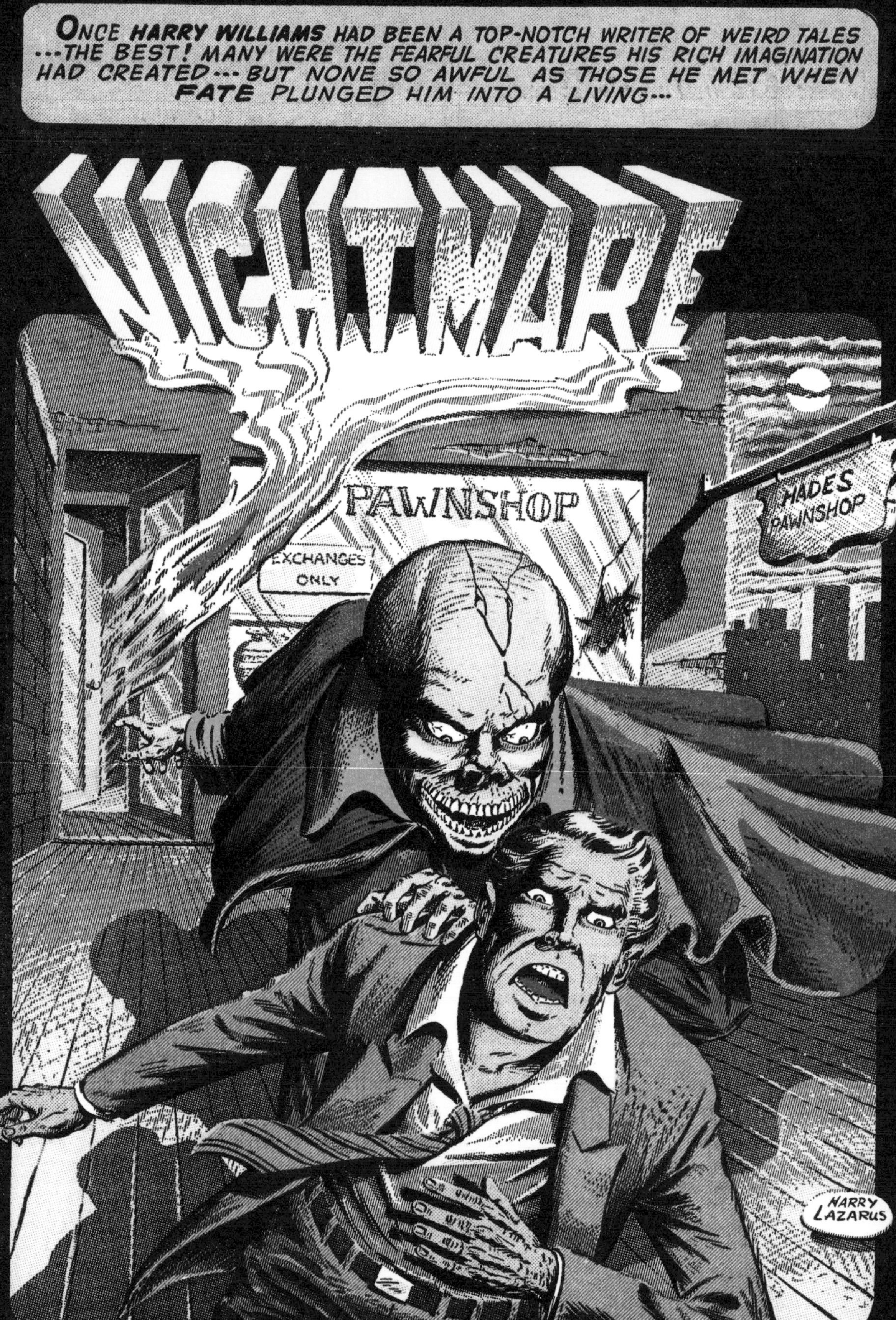
ONCE HARRY WILLIAMS HAD BEEN A TOP-NOTCH WRITER OF WEIRD TALES ---THE BEST! MANY WERE THE FEARFUL CREATURES HIS RICH IMAGINATION HAD CREATED--- BUT NONE SO AWFUL AS THOSE HE MET WHEN FATE PLUNGED HIM INTO A LIVING---
NIGHTMARE
PAWNSHOP
EXCHANGES ONLY
HADES PAWNSHOP
HARRY LAZARUS

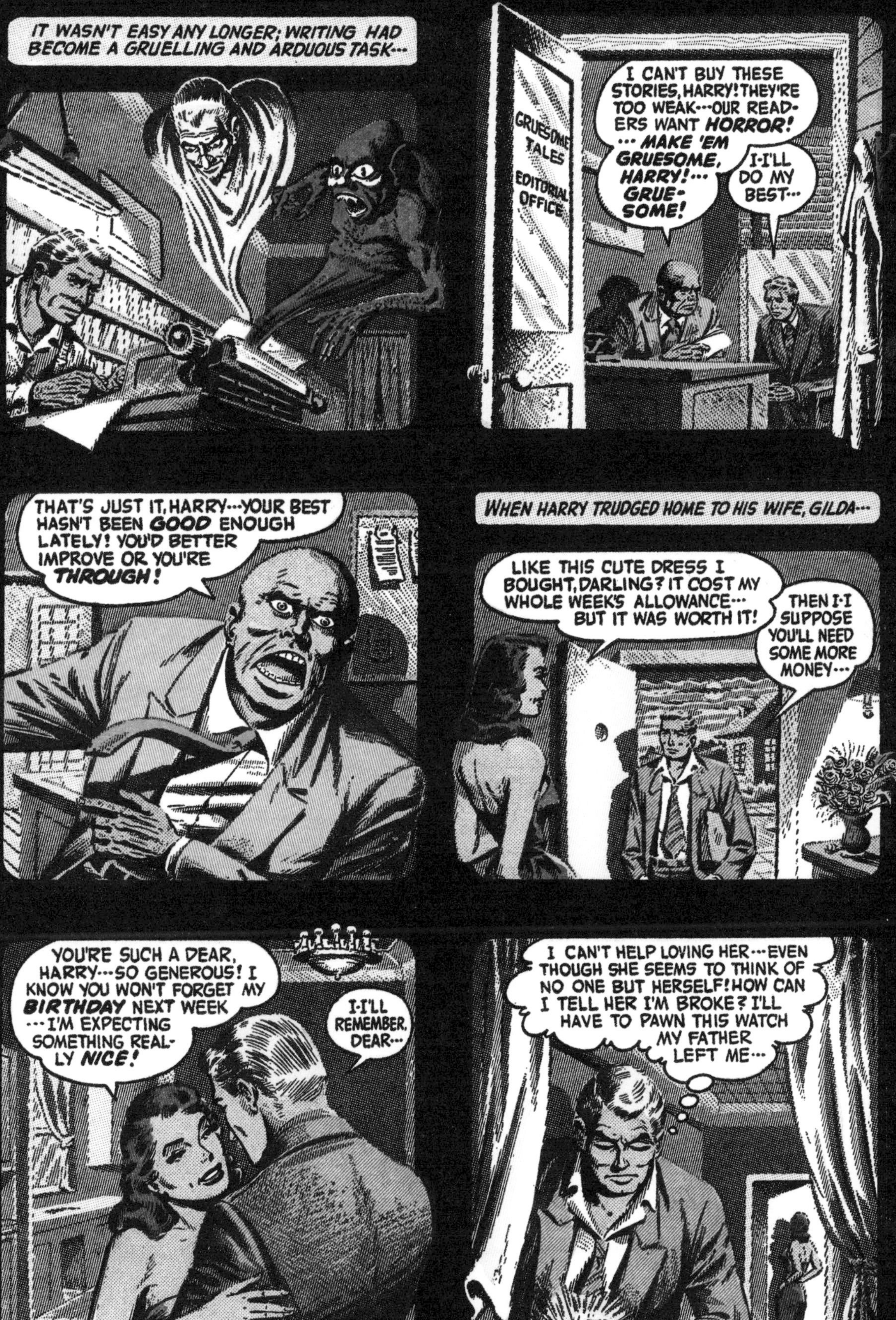
IT WASN'T EASY ANY LONGER; WRITING HAD BECOME A GRUELLING AND ARDUOUS TASK---
GRUESOME TALES EDITORIAL OFFICE
I CAN'T BUY THESE STORIES, HARRY! THEY'RE TOO WEAK---OUR READERS WANT HORROR! ---MAKE 'EM GRUESOME, HARRY!--- GRUESOME!
I-I'LL DO MY BEST---
THAT'S JUST IT, HARRY---YOUR BEST HASN'T BEEN GOOD ENOUGH LATELY! YOU'D BETTER IMPROVE OR YOU'RE THROUGH!
WHEN HARRY TRUDGED HOME TO HIS WIFE, GILDA---
LIKE THIS CUTE DRESS I BOUGHT, DARLING? IT COST MY WHOLE WEEK'S ALLOWANCE--- BUT IT WAS WORTH IT!
THEN I-I SUPPOSE YOU'LL NEED SOME MORE MONEY---
YOU'RE SUCH A DEAR, HARRY---SO GENEROUS! I KNOW YOU WON'T FORGET MY BIRTHDAY NEXT WEEK ---I'M EXPECTING SOMETHING REALLY NICE!
I-I'LL REMEMBER, DEAR---
I CAN'T HELP LOVING HER---EVEN THOUGH SHE SEEMS TO THINK OF NO ONE BUT HERSELF! HOW CAN I TELL HER I'M BROKE? I'LL HAVE TO PAWN THIS WATCH MY FATHER LEFT ME---

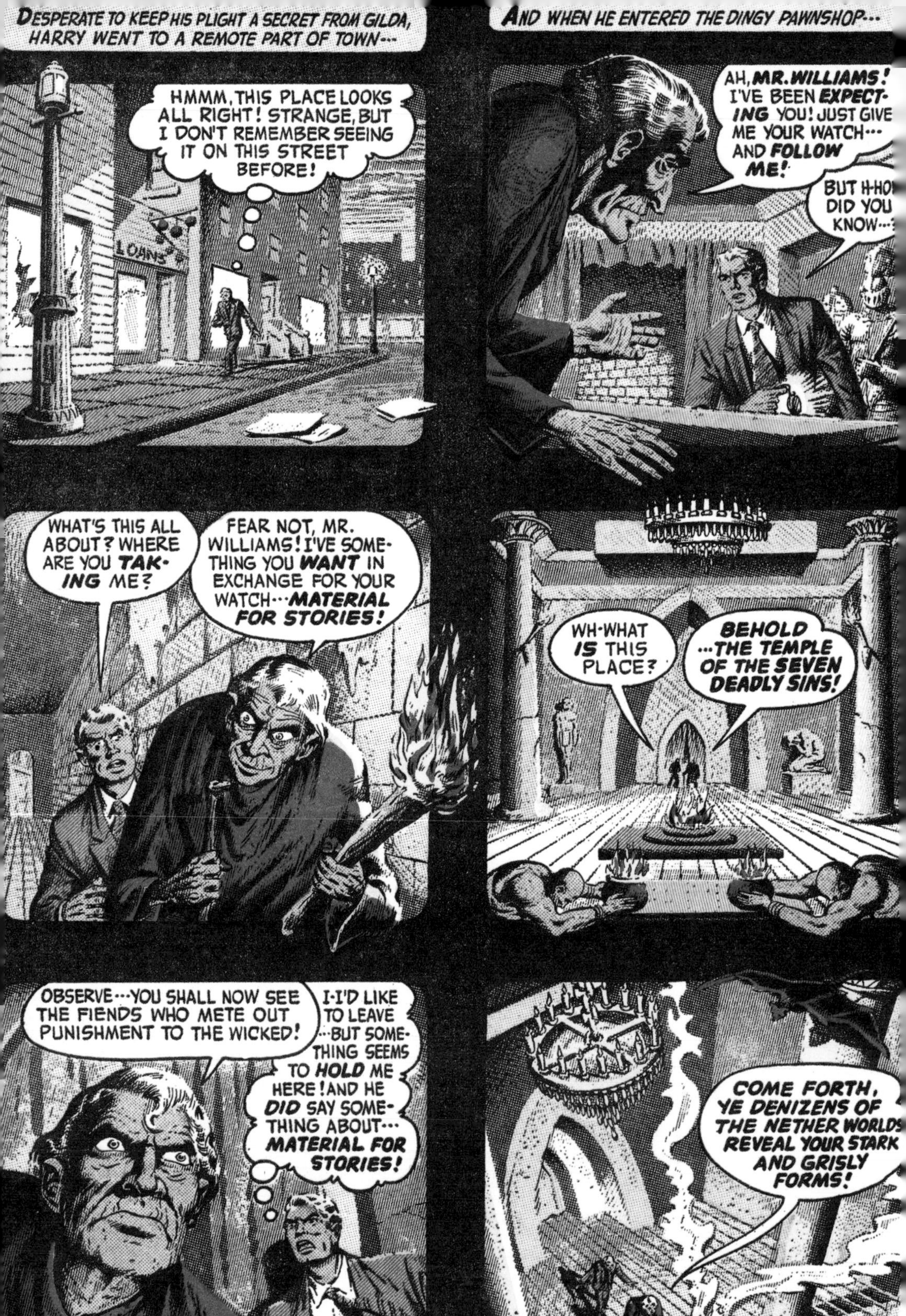
DESPERATE TO KEEP HIS PLIGHT A SECRET FROM GILDA, HARRY WENT TO A REMOTE PART OF TOWN---
HMMM, THIS PLACE LOOKS ALL RIGHT! STRANGE, BUT I DON'T REMEMBER SEEING IT ON THIS STREET BEFORE!
LOANS
AND WHEN HE ENTERED THE DINGY PAWNSHOP---
AH, MR. WILLIAMS! I'VE BEEN EXPECTING YOU! JUST GIVE ME YOUR WATCH--- AND FOLLOW ME!
BUT H-HOW DID YOU KNOW---?
WHAT'S THIS ALL ABOUT? WHERE ARE YOU TAKING ME?
FEAR NOT, MR. WILLIAMS! I'VE SOMETHING YOU WANT IN EXCHANGE FOR YOUR WATCH--- MATERIAL FOR STORIES!
WH-WHAT IS THIS PLACE?
BEHOLD ...THE TEMPLE OF THE SEVEN DEADLY SINS!
OBSERVE--- YOU SHALL NOW SEE THE FIENDS WHO METE OUT PUNISHMENT TO THE WICKED!
I-I'D LIKE TO LEAVE ...BUT SOMETHING SEEMS TO HOLD ME HERE! AND HE DID SAY SOMETHING ABOUT--- MATERIAL FOR STORIES!
COME FORTH, YE DENIZENS OF THE NETHER WORLDS REVEAL YOUR STARK AND GRISLY FORMS!

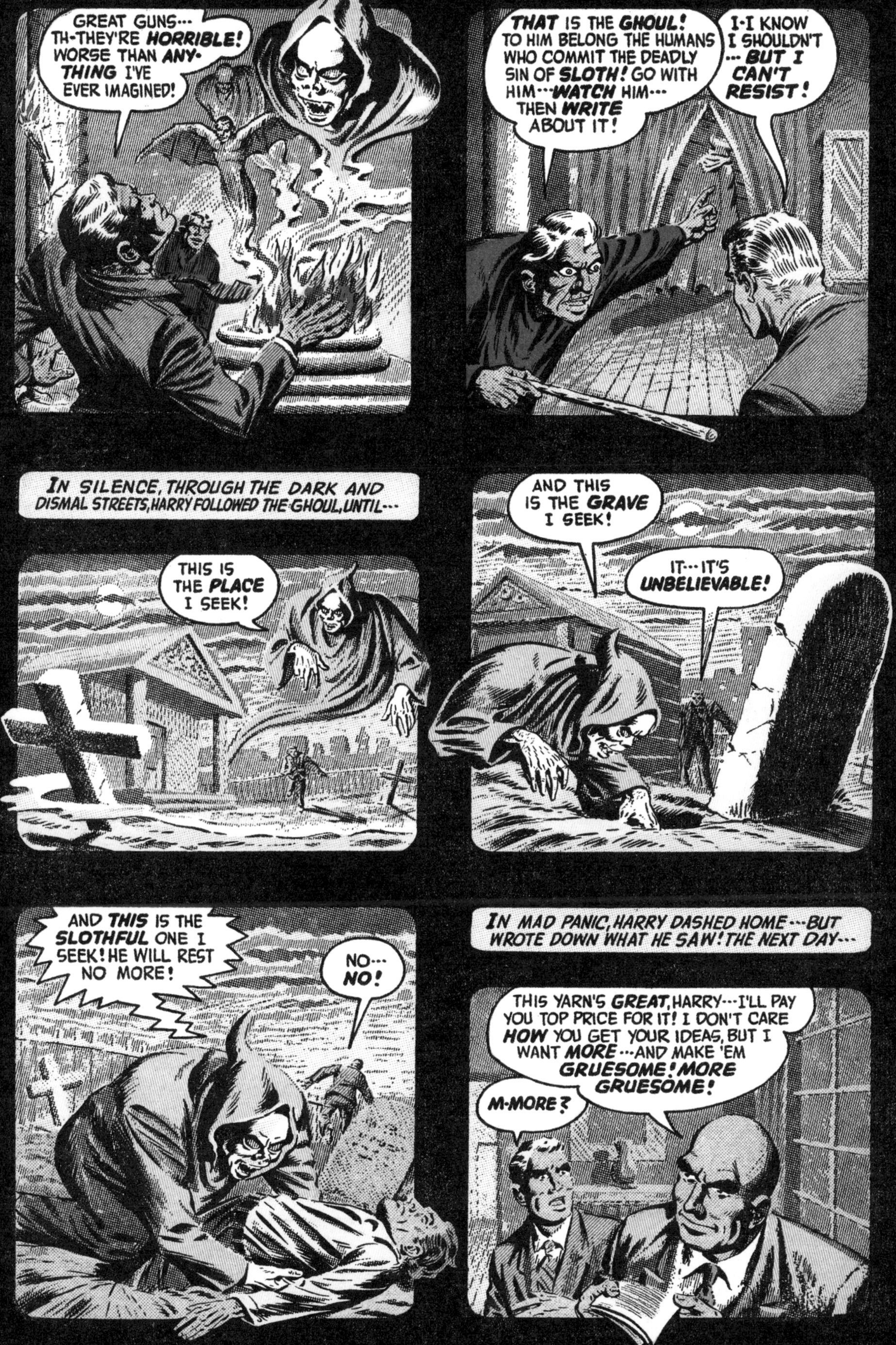
GREAT GUNS... TH-THEY'RE HORRIBLE! WORSE THAN ANYTHING I'VE EVER IMAGINED!
THAT IS THE GHOUL! TO HIM BELONG THE HUMANS WHO COMMIT THE DEADLY SIN OF SLOTH! GO WITH HIM...WATCH HIM... THEN WRITE ABOUT IT!
I-I KNOW I SHOULDN'T ...BUT I CAN'T RESIST!
IN SILENCE, THROUGH THE DARK AND DISMAL STREETS, HARRY FOLLOWED THE GHOUL, UNTIL...
THIS IS THE PLACE I SEEK!
AND THIS IS THE GRAVE I SEEK!
IT...IT'S UNBELIEVABLE!
AND THIS IS THE SLOTHFUL ONE I SEEK! HE WILL REST NO MORE!
NO... NO!
IN MAD PANIC, HARRY DASHED HOME...BUT WROTE DOWN WHAT HE SAW! THE NEXT DAY...
THIS YARN'S GREAT, HARRY...I'LL PAY YOU TOP PRICE FOR IT! I DON'T CARE HOW YOU GET YOUR IDEAS, BUT I WANT MORE...AND MAKE 'EM GRUESOME! MORE GRUESOME!
M-MORE?

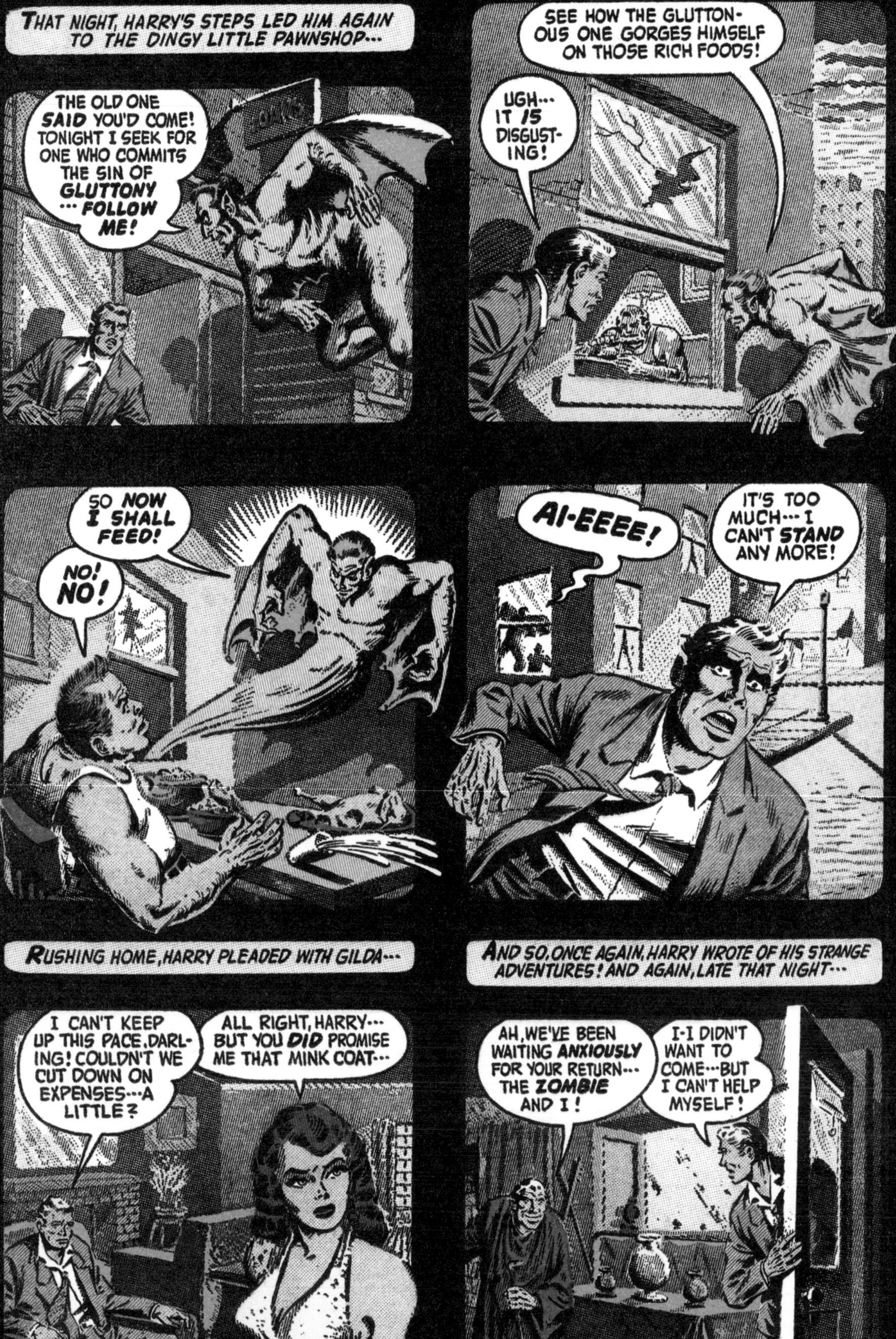
THAT NIGHT, HARRY'S STEPS LED HIM AGAIN TO THE DINGY LITTLE PAWNSHOP...
THE OLD ONE SAID YOU'D COME! TONIGHT I SEEK FOR ONE WHO COMMITS THE SIN OF GLUTTONY ... FOLLOW ME!
SEE HOW THE GLUTTON-OUS ONE GORGES HIMSELF ON THOSE RICH FOODS!
UGH... IT IS DISGUST-ING!
SO NOW I SHALL FEED!
NO! NO!
AI-EEEE!
IT'S TOO MUCH... I CAN'T STAND ANY MORE!
RUSHING HOME, HARRY PLEADED WITH GILDA...
I CAN'T KEEP UP THIS PACE, DARL-ING! COULDN'T WE CUT DOWN ON EXPENSES...A LITTLE?
ALL RIGHT, HARRY... BUT YOU DID PROMISE ME THAT MINK COAT...
AND SO, ONCE AGAIN, HARRY WROTE OF HIS STRANGE ADVENTURES! AND AGAIN, LATE THAT NIGHT...
AH, WE'VE BEEN WAITING ANXIOUSLY FOR YOUR RETURN... THE ZOMBIE AND I!
I-I DIDN'T WANT TO COME...BUT I CAN'T HELP MYSELF!

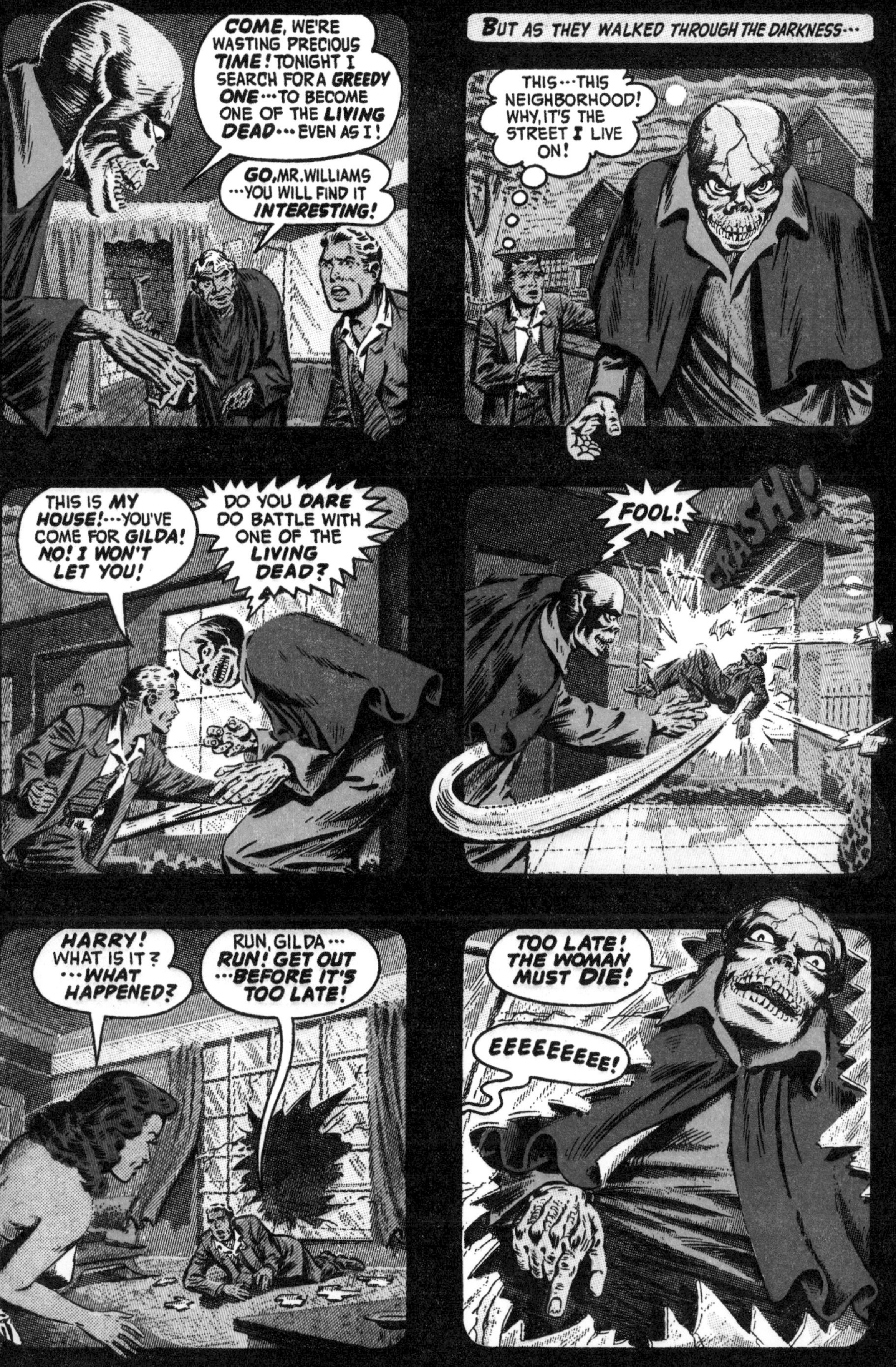
COME, WE'RE WASTING PRECIOUS TIME! TONIGHT I SEARCH FOR A GREEDY ONE···TO BECOME ONE OF THE LIVING DEAD···EVEN AS I!
GO, MR. WILLIAMS ···YOU WILL FIND IT INTERESTING!
BUT AS THEY WALKED THROUGH THE DARKNESS···
THIS···THIS NEIGHBORHOOD! WHY, IT'S THE STREET I LIVE ON!
THIS IS MY HOUSE!···YOU'VE COME FOR GILDA! NO! I WON'T LET YOU!
DO YOU DARE DO BATTLE WITH ONE OF THE LIVING DEAD?
FOOL!
CRASH!
HARRY! WHAT IS IT? ···WHAT HAPPENED?
RUN, GILDA··· RUN! GET OUT ···BEFORE IT'S TOO LATE!
TOO LATE! THE WOMAN MUST DIE!
EEEEEEEEE!

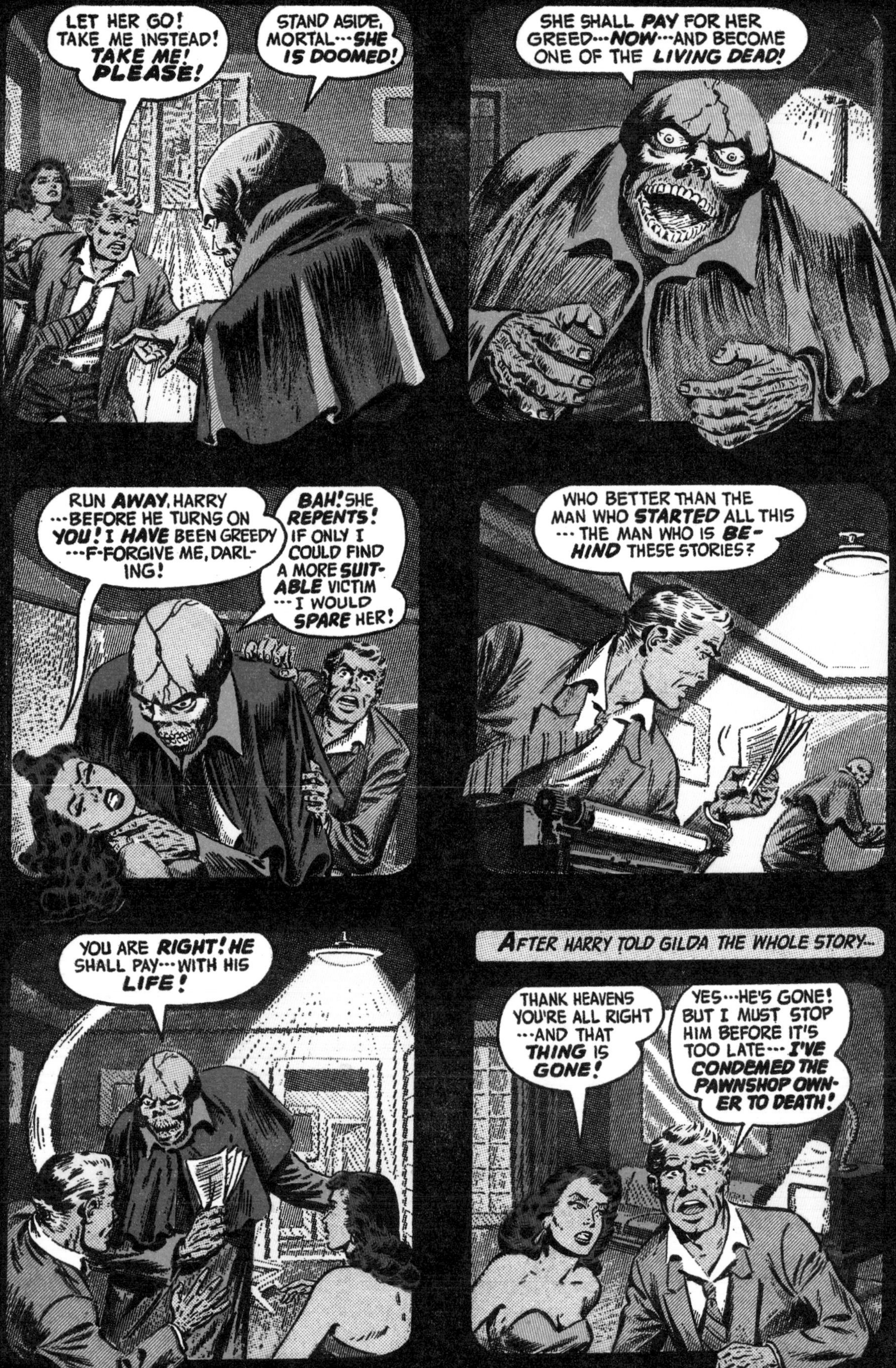
LET HER GO! TAKE ME INSTEAD! TAKE ME! PLEASE!
STAND ASIDE, MORTAL--- SHE IS DOOMED!
SHE SHALL PAY FOR HER GREED---NOW---AND BECOME ONE OF THE LIVING DEAD!
RUN AWAY, HARRY ---BEFORE HE TURNS ON YOU! I HAVE BEEN GREEDY ---F-FORGIVE ME, DARLING!
BAH! SHE REPENTS! IF ONLY I COULD FIND A MORE SUITABLE VICTIM --- I WOULD SPARE HER!
WHO BETTER THAN THE MAN WHO STARTED ALL THIS --- THE MAN WHO IS BEHIND THESE STORIES?
YOU ARE RIGHT! HE SHALL PAY--- WITH HIS LIFE!
AFTER HARRY TOLD GILDA THE WHOLE STORY..
THANK HEAVENS YOU'RE ALL RIGHT ---AND THAT THING IS GONE!
YES---HE'S GONE! BUT I MUST STOP HIM BEFORE IT'S TOO LATE--- I'VE CONDEMED THE PAWNSHOP OWNER TO DEATH!

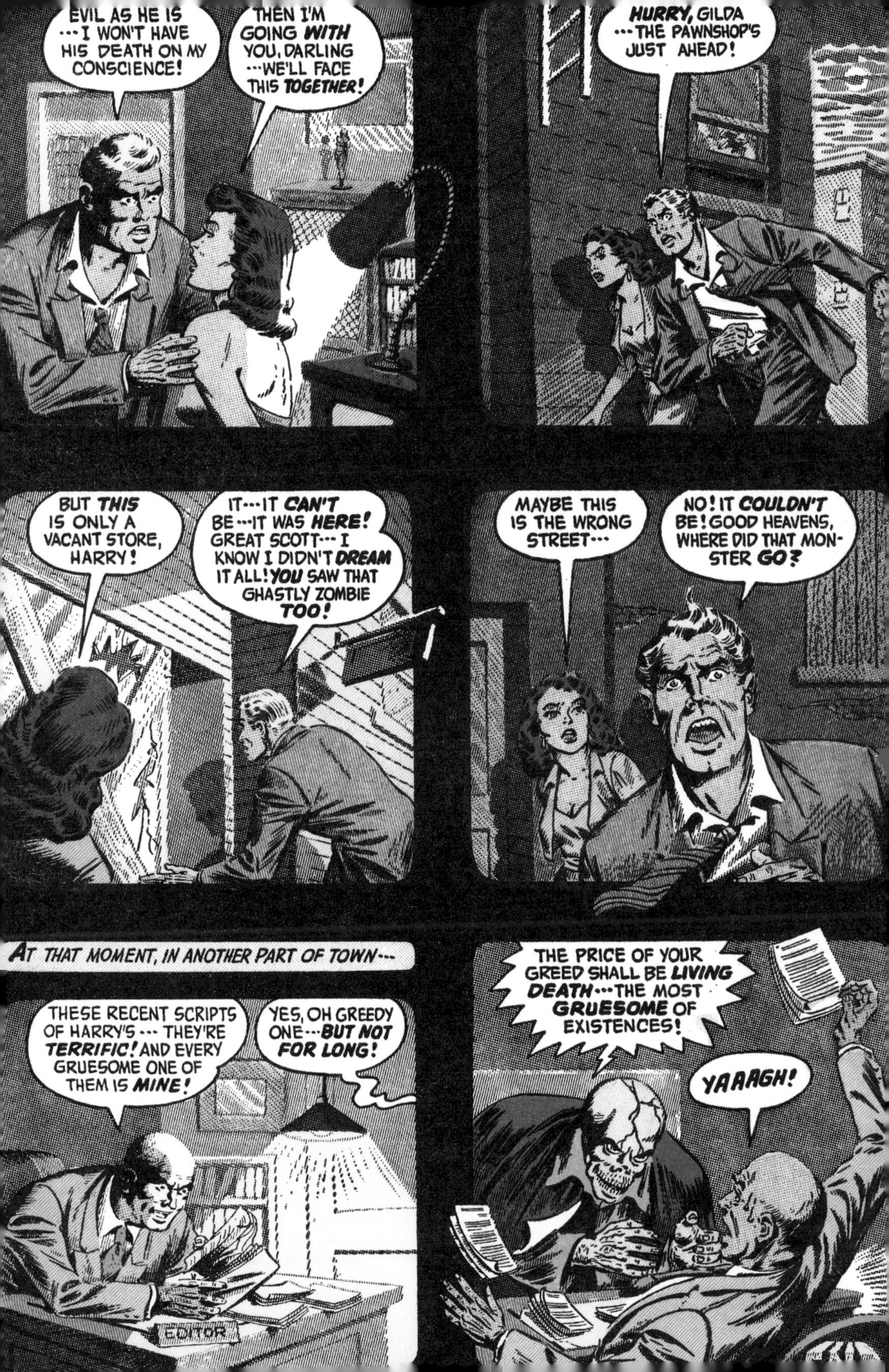
EVIL AS HE IS ···I WON'T HAVE HIS DEATH ON MY CONSCIENCE!
THEN I'M GOING **WITH** YOU, DARLING ···WE'LL FACE THIS **TOGETHER!**
HURRY, GILDA ···THE PAWNSHOP'S JUST AHEAD!
BUT **THIS** IS ONLY A VACANT STORE, HARRY!
IT···IT **CAN'T** BE···IT WAS **HERE!** GREAT SCOTT··· I KNOW I DIDN'T **DREAM** IT ALL! **YOU** SAW THAT GHASTLY ZOMBIE **TOO!**
MAYBE THIS IS THE WRONG STREET···
NO! IT **COULDN'T** BE! GOOD HEAVENS, WHERE DID THAT MONSTER **GO?**
AT THAT MOMENT, IN ANOTHER PART OF TOWN---
THESE RECENT SCRIPTS OF HARRY'S --- THEY'RE **TERRIFIC!** AND EVERY GRUESOME ONE OF THEM IS **MINE!**
YES, OH GREEDY ONE···**BUT NOT FOR LONG!**
EDITOR
THE PRICE OF YOUR GREED SHALL BE **LIVING DEATH**···THE MOST **GRUESOME** OF EXISTENCES!
YAAAGH!

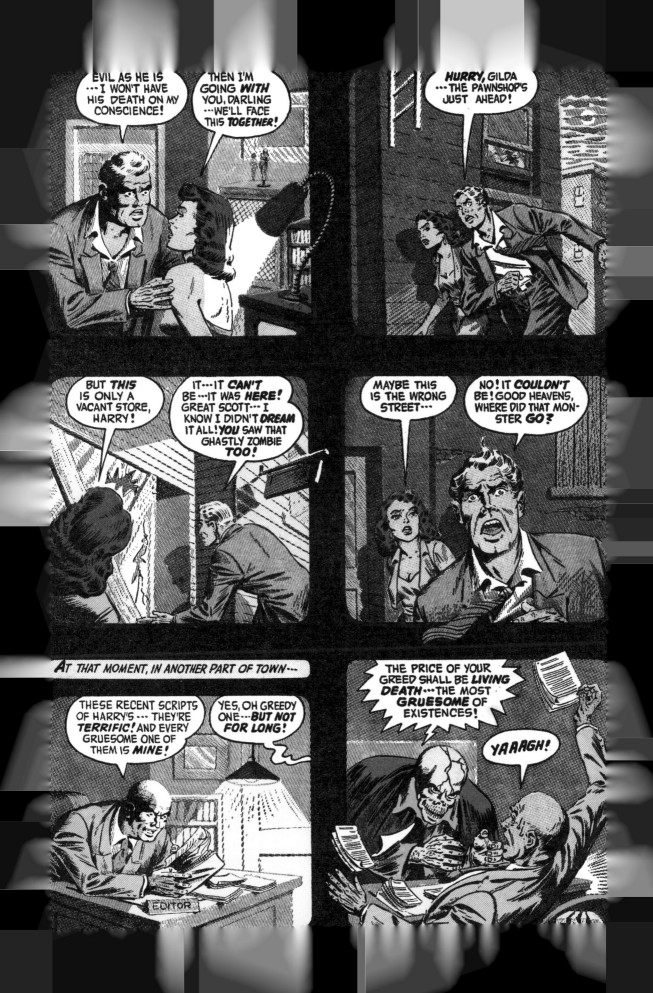

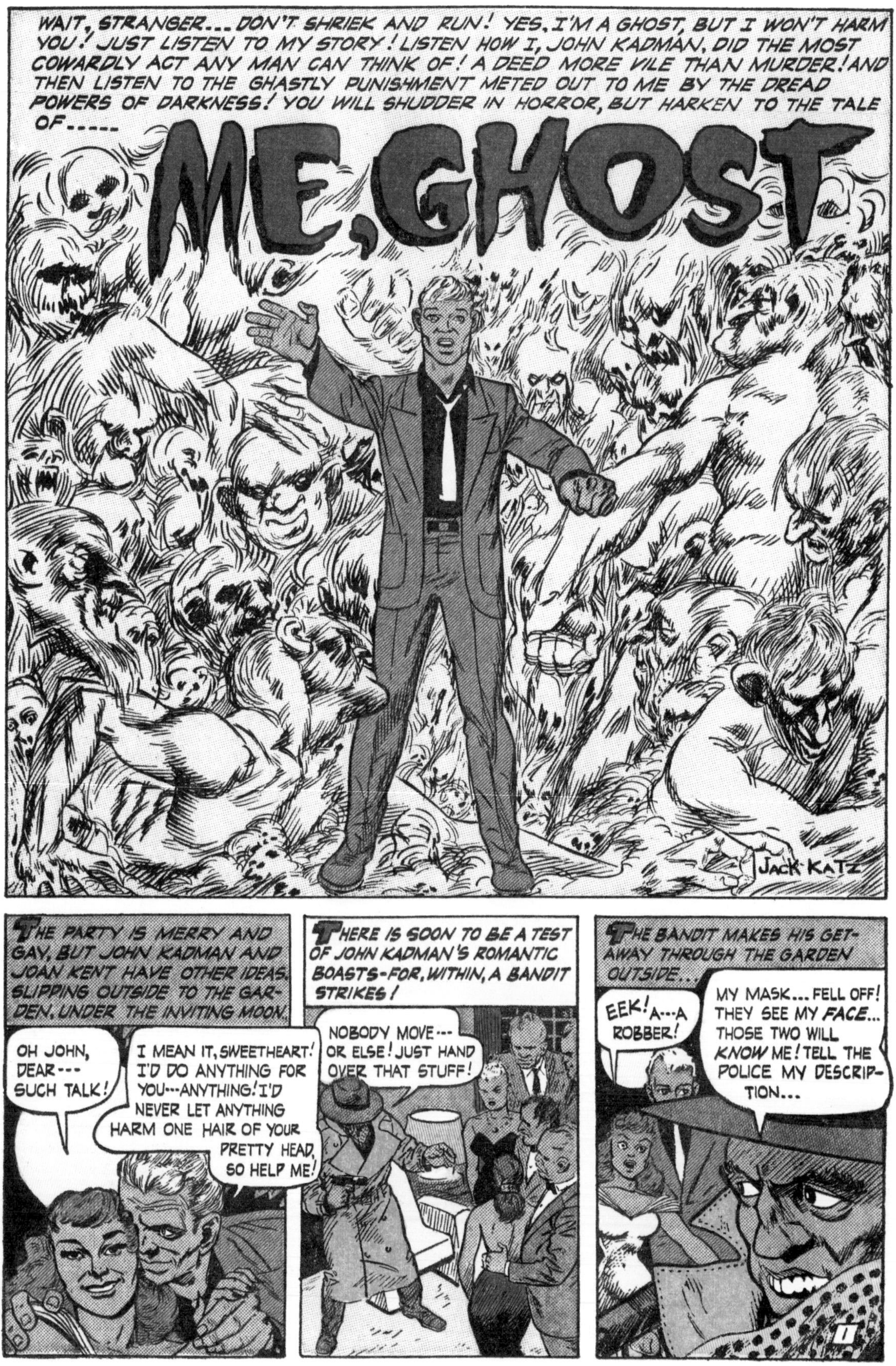
WAIT, STRANGER... DON'T SHRIEK AND RUN! YES, I'M A GHOST, BUT I WON'T HARM YOU! JUST LISTEN TO MY STORY! LISTEN HOW I, JOHN KADMAN, DID THE MOST COWARDLY ACT ANY MAN CAN THINK OF! A DEED MORE VILE THAN MURDER! AND THEN LISTEN TO THE GHASTLY PUNISHMENT METED OUT TO ME BY THE DREAD POWERS OF DARKNESS! YOU WILL SHUDDER IN HORROR, BUT HARKEN TO THE TALE OF-----
ME, GHOST
JACK KATZ
THE PARTY IS MERRY AND GAY, BUT JOHN KADMAN AND JOAN KENT HAVE OTHER IDEAS, SLIPPING OUTSIDE TO THE GARDEN, UNDER THE INVITING MOON.
OH JOHN, DEAR--- SUCH TALK!
I MEAN IT, SWEETHEART! I'D DO ANYTHING FOR YOU---ANYTHING! I'D NEVER LET ANYTHING HARM ONE HAIR OF YOUR PRETTY HEAD, SO HELP ME!
THERE IS SOON TO BE A TEST OF JOHN KADMAN'S ROMANTIC BOASTS-FOR, WITHIN, A BANDIT STRIKES!
NOBODY MOVE--- OR ELSE! JUST HAND OVER THAT STUFF!
THE BANDIT MAKES HIS GET-AWAY THROUGH THE GARDEN OUTSIDE...
EEK! A---A ROBBER!
MY MASK... FELL OFF! THEY SEE MY FACE... THOSE TWO WILL KNOW ME! TELL THE POLICE MY DESCRIPTION...
1

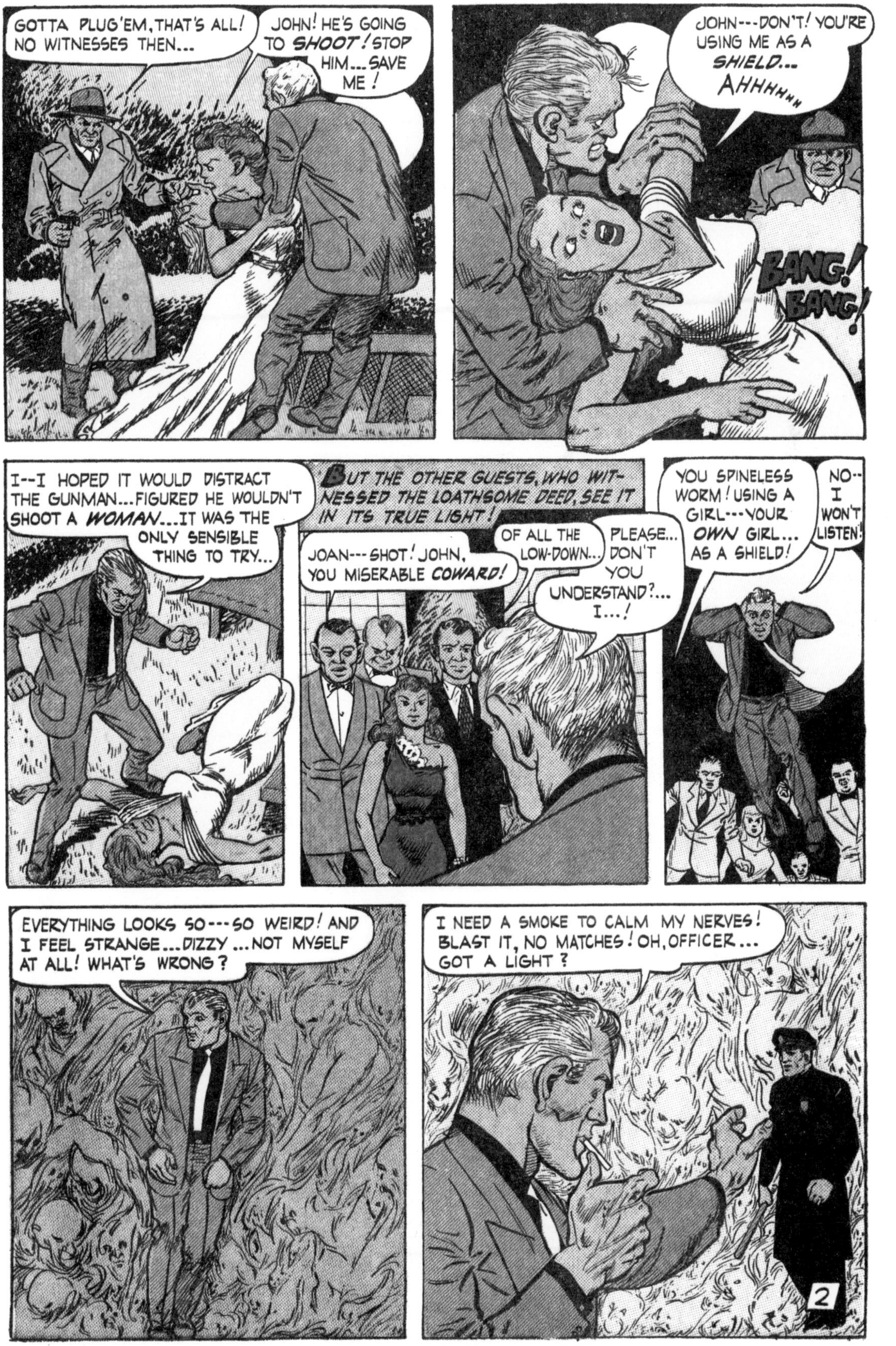
GOTTA PLUG'EM, THAT'S ALL! NO WITNESSES THEN...
JOHN! HE'S GOING TO SHOOT! STOP HIM... SAVE ME!
JOHN---DON'T! YOU'RE USING ME AS A SHIELD... AHHHHHH
BANG! BANG!
I--I HOPED IT WOULD DISTRACT THE GUNMAN...FIGURED HE WOULDN'T SHOOT A WOMAN...IT WAS THE ONLY SENSIBLE THING TO TRY...
BUT THE OTHER GUESTS, WHO WITNESSED THE LOATHSOME DEED, SEE IT IN ITS TRUE LIGHT!
JOAN---SHOT! JOHN, YOU MISERABLE COWARD!
OF ALL THE LOW-DOWN...
PLEASE... DON'T YOU UNDERSTAND?... I...!
YOU SPINELESS WORM! USING A GIRL---YOUR OWN GIRL... AS A SHIELD!
NO-- I WON'T LISTEN!
EVERYTHING LOOKS SO---SO WEIRD! AND I FEEL STRANGE...DIZZY...NOT MYSELF AT ALL! WHAT'S WRONG?
I NEED A SMOKE TO CALM MY NERVES! BLAST IT, NO MATCHES! OH, OFFICER... GOT A LIGHT?
2

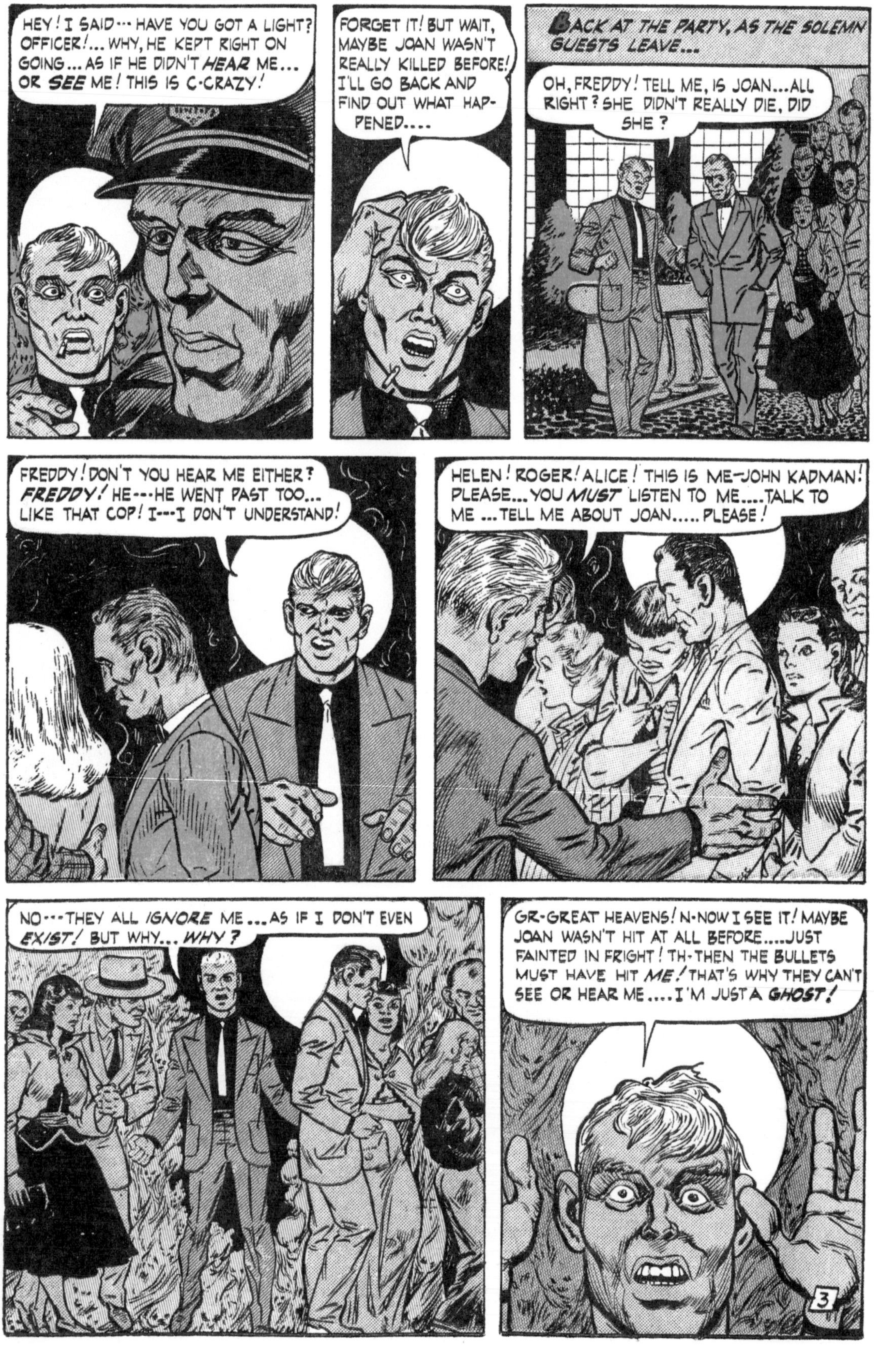
HEY! I SAID··· HAVE YOU GOT A LIGHT? OFFICER!... WHY, HE KEPT RIGHT ON GOING... AS IF HE DIDN'T HEAR ME... OR SEE ME! THIS IS C-CRAZY!
FORGET IT! BUT WAIT, MAYBE JOAN WASN'T REALLY KILLED BEFORE! I'LL GO BACK AND FIND OUT WHAT HAPPENED....
BACK AT THE PARTY, AS THE SOLEMN GUESTS LEAVE...
OH, FREDDY! TELL ME, IS JOAN... ALL RIGHT? SHE DIDN'T REALLY DIE, DID SHE?
FREDDY! DON'T YOU HEAR ME EITHER? FREDDY! HE---HE WENT PAST TOO... LIKE THAT COP! I---I DON'T UNDERSTAND!
HELEN! ROGER! ALICE! THIS IS ME—JOHN KADMAN! PLEASE... YOU MUST LISTEN TO ME.... TALK TO ME ...TELL ME ABOUT JOAN..... PLEASE!
NO---THEY ALL IGNORE ME ... AS IF I DON'T EVEN EXIST! BUT WHY... WHY?
GR-GREAT HEAVENS! N-NOW I SEE IT! MAYBE JOAN WASN'T HIT AT ALL BEFORE....JUST FAINTED IN FRIGHT! TH-THEN THE BULLETS MUST HAVE HIT ME! THAT'S WHY THEY CAN'T SEE OR HEAR ME.... I'M JUST A GHOST!
3

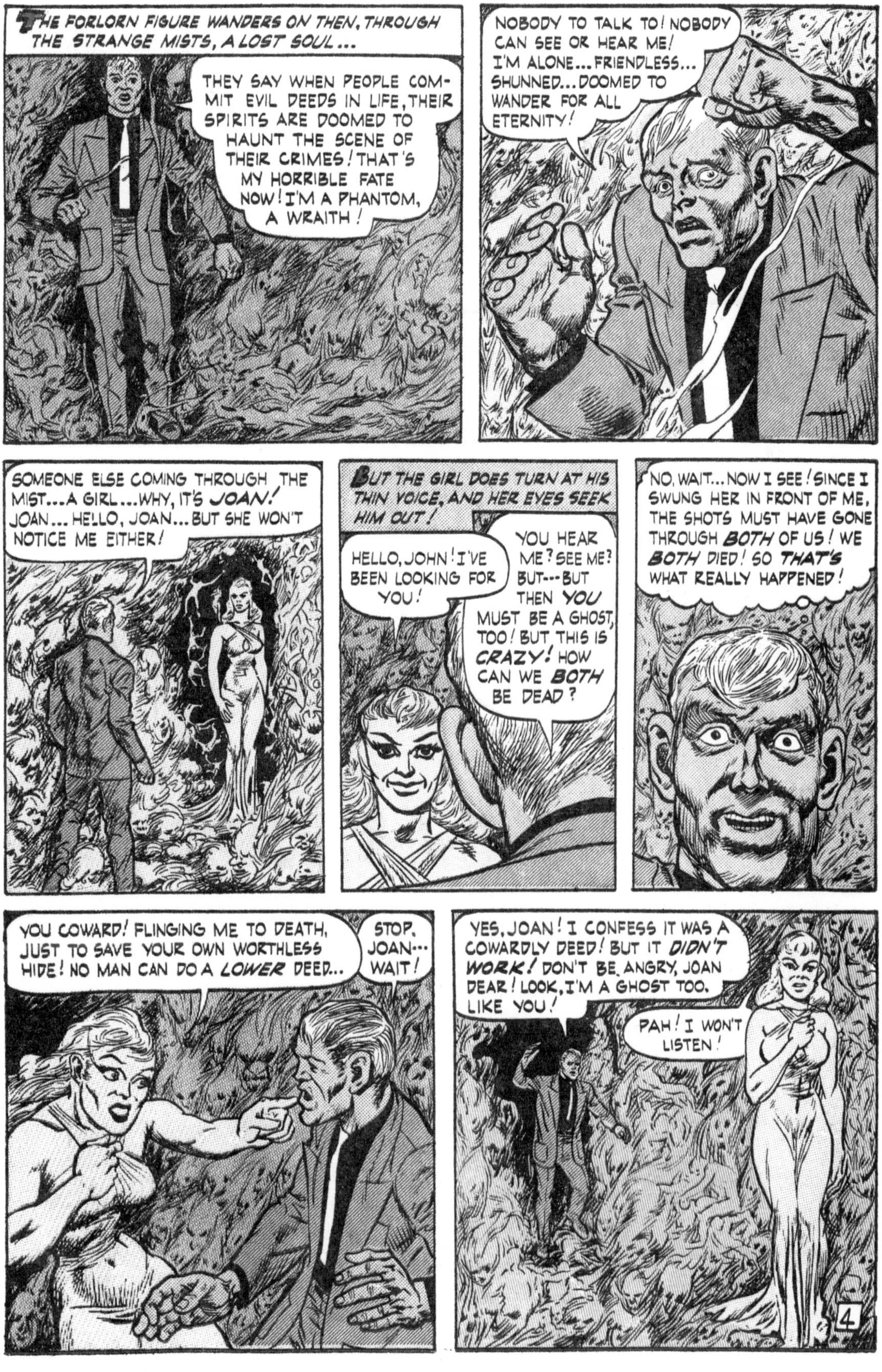
THE FORLORN FIGURE WANDERS ON THEN, THROUGH THE STRANGE MISTS, A LOST SOUL...
THEY SAY WHEN PEOPLE COMMIT EVIL DEEDS IN LIFE, THEIR SPIRITS ARE DOOMED TO HAUNT THE SCENE OF THEIR CRIMES! THAT'S MY HORRIBLE FATE NOW! I'M A PHANTOM, A WRAITH!
NOBODY TO TALK TO! NOBODY CAN SEE OR HEAR ME! I'M ALONE... FRIENDLESS... SHUNNED... DOOMED TO WANDER FOR ALL ETERNITY!
SOMEONE ELSE COMING THROUGH THE MIST... A GIRL... WHY, IT'S JOAN! JOAN... HELLO, JOAN... BUT SHE WON'T NOTICE ME EITHER!
BUT THE GIRL DOES TURN AT HIS THIN VOICE, AND HER EYES SEEK HIM OUT!
HELLO, JOHN! I'VE BEEN LOOKING FOR YOU!
YOU HEAR ME? SEE ME? BUT---BUT THEN YOU MUST BE A GHOST, TOO! BUT THIS IS CRAZY! HOW CAN WE BOTH BE DEAD?
NO, WAIT... NOW I SEE! SINCE I SWUNG HER IN FRONT OF ME, THE SHOTS MUST HAVE GONE THROUGH BOTH OF US! WE BOTH DIED! SO THAT'S WHAT REALLY HAPPENED!
YOU COWARD! FLINGING ME TO DEATH, JUST TO SAVE YOUR OWN WORTHLESS HIDE! NO MAN CAN DO A LOWER DEED...
STOP, JOAN... WAIT!
YES, JOAN! I CONFESS IT WAS A COWARDLY DEED! BUT IT DIDN'T WORK! DON'T BE ANGRY, JOAN DEAR! LOOK, I'M A GHOST TOO. LIKE YOU!
PAH! I WON'T LISTEN!
4

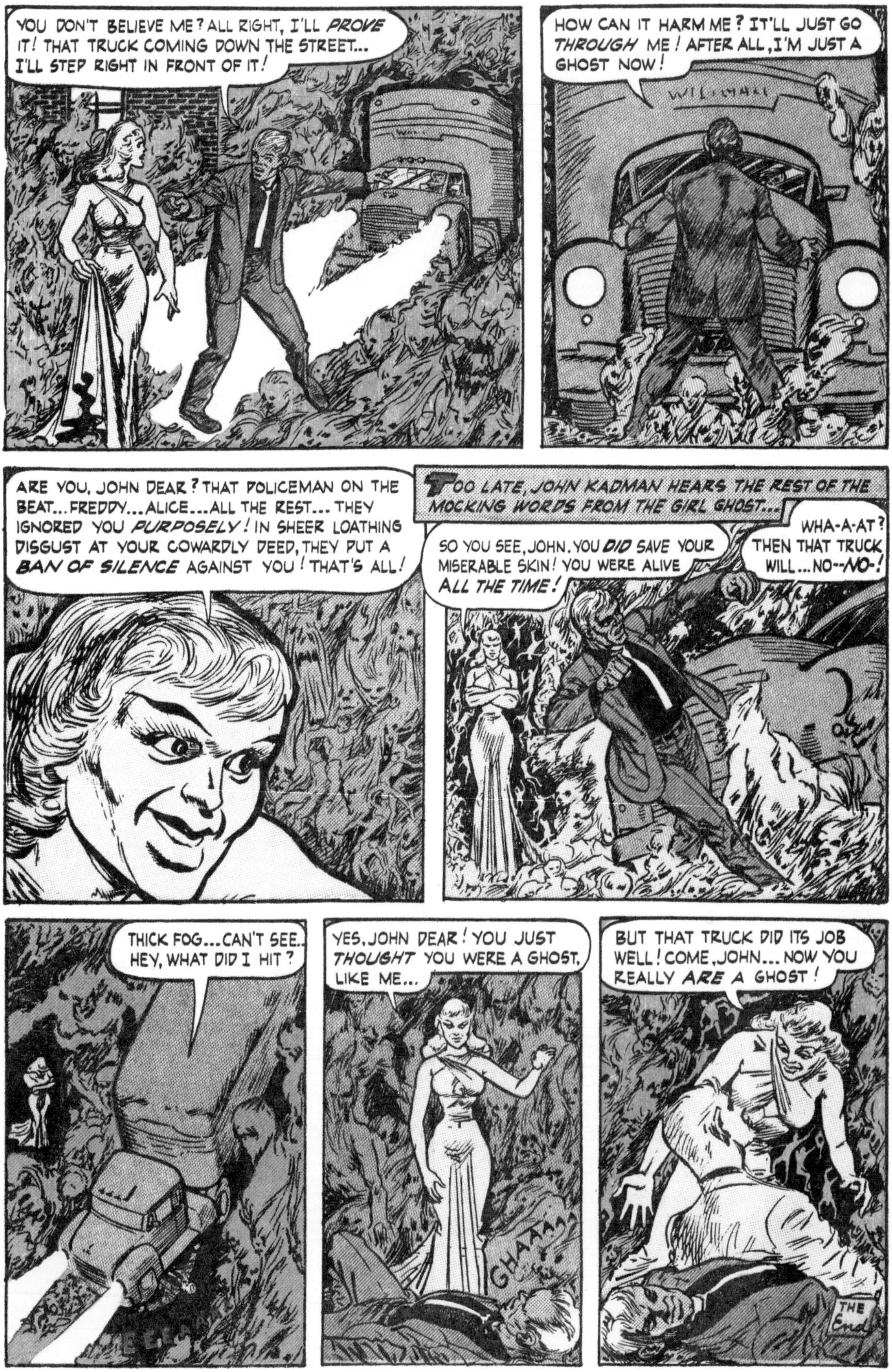

YOU DON'T BELIEVE ME? ALL RIGHT, I'LL PROVE IT! THAT TRUCK COMING DOWN THE STREET... I'LL STEP RIGHT IN FRONT OF IT!
HOW CAN IT HARM ME? IT'LL JUST GO THROUGH ME! AFTER ALL, I'M JUST A GHOST NOW!
ARE YOU, JOHN DEAR? THAT POLICEMAN ON THE BEAT... FREDDY... ALICE... ALL THE REST... THEY IGNORED YOU PURPOSELY! IN SHEER LOATHING DISGUST AT YOUR COWARDLY DEED, THEY PUT A BAN OF SILENCE AGAINST YOU! THAT'S ALL!
TOO LATE, JOHN KADMAN HEARS THE REST OF THE MOCKING WORDS FROM THE GIRL GHOST...
SO YOU SEE, JOHN. YOU DID SAVE YOUR MISERABLE SKIN! YOU WERE ALIVE ALL THE TIME!
WHA-A-AT? THEN THAT TRUCK WILL... NO--NO-!
THICK FOG... CAN'T SEE.. HEY, WHAT DID I HIT?
YES, JOHN DEAR! YOU JUST THOUGHT YOU WERE A GHOST, LIKE ME...
BUT THAT TRUCK DID ITS JOB WELL! COME, JOHN... NOW YOU REALLY ARE A GHOST!
THE End

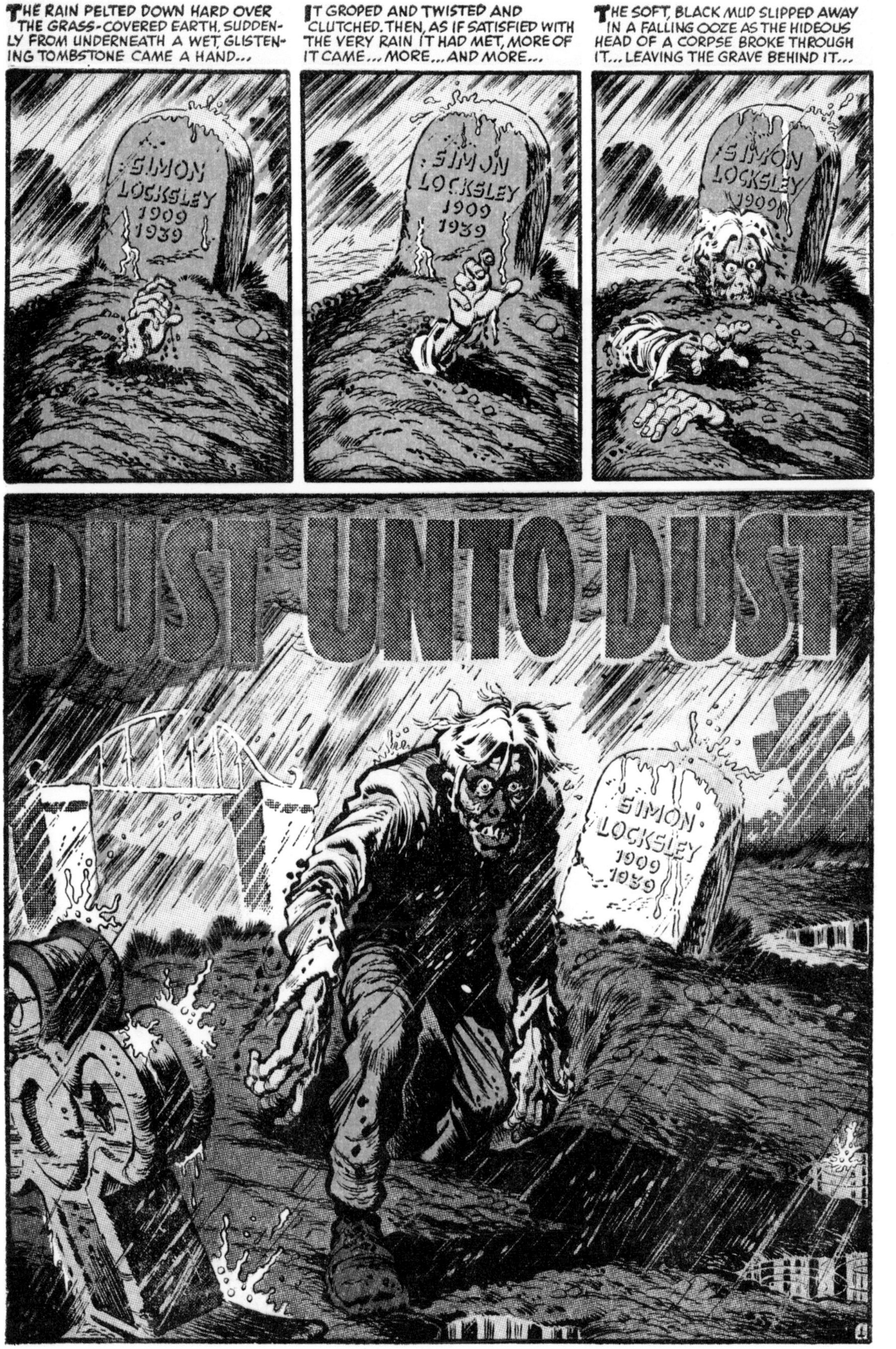
THE RAIN PELTED DOWN HARD OVER THE GRASS-COVERED EARTH. SUDDENLY FROM UNDERNEATH A WET, GLISTENING TOMBSTONE CAME A HAND...
SIMON LOCKSLEY 1909 1939
IT GROPED AND TWISTED AND CLUTCHED. THEN, AS IF SATISFIED WITH THE VERY RAIN IT HAD MET, MORE OF IT CAME... MORE... AND MORE...
SIMON LOCKSLEY 1909 1939
THE SOFT, BLACK MUD SLIPPED AWAY IN A FALLING OOZE AS THE HIDEOUS HEAD OF A CORPSE BROKE THROUGH IT... LEAVING THE GRAVE BEHIND IT...
SIMON LOCKSLEY 1909
DUST UNTO DUST
SIMON LOCKSLEY 1909 1939

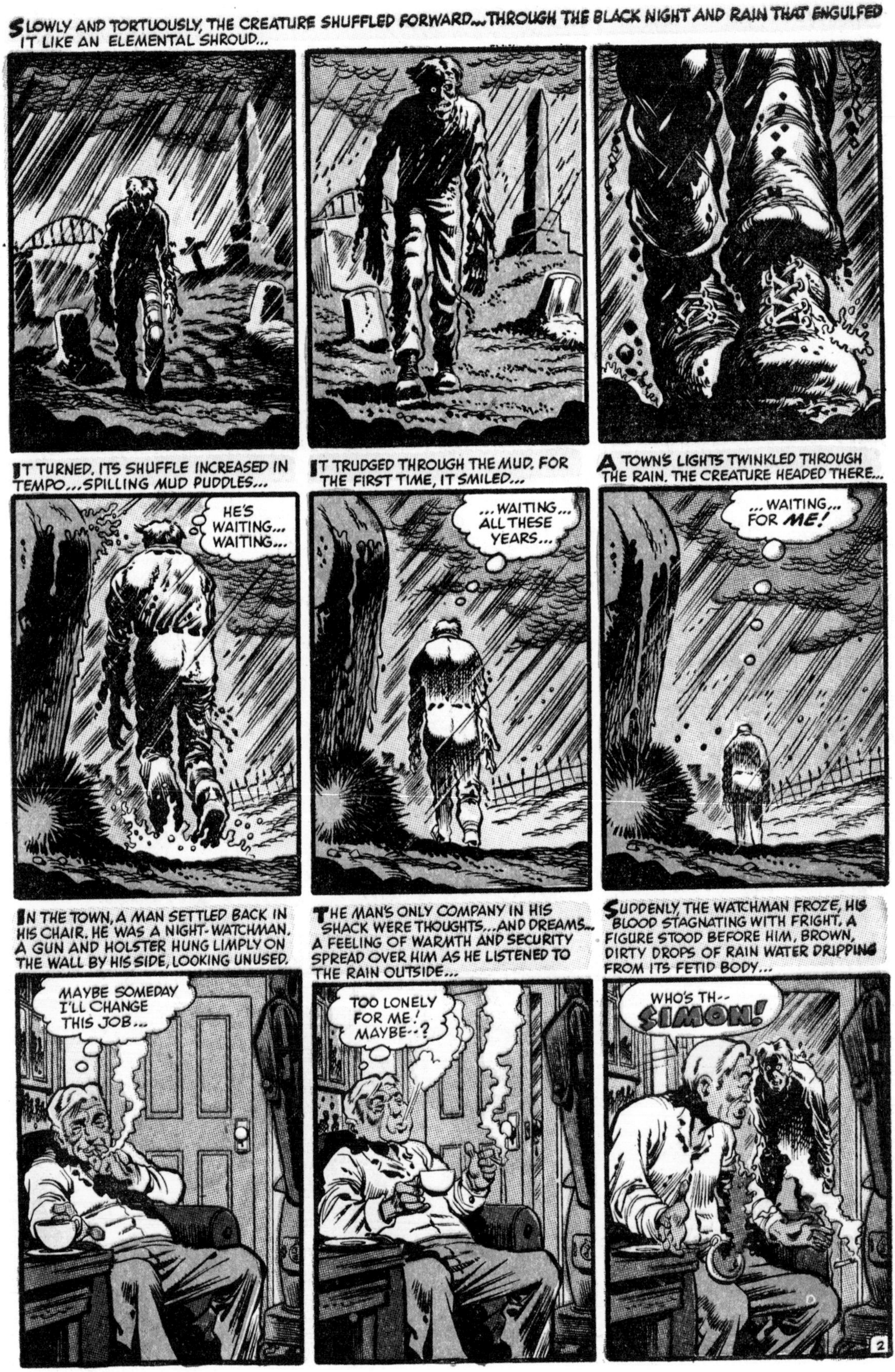
SLOWLY AND TORTUOUSLY, THE CREATURE SHUFFLED FORWARD...THROUGH THE BLACK NIGHT AND RAIN THAT ENGULFED IT LIKE AN ELEMENTAL SHROUD...
IT TURNED. ITS SHUFFLE INCREASED IN TEMPO...SPILLING MUD PUDDLES...
HE'S WAITING... WAITING...
IT TRUDGED THROUGH THE MUD. FOR THE FIRST TIME, IT SMILED...
...WAITING... ALL THESE YEARS...
A TOWN'S LIGHTS TWINKLED THROUGH THE RAIN. THE CREATURE HEADED THERE...
...WAITING... FOR ME!
IN THE TOWN, A MAN SETTLED BACK IN HIS CHAIR. HE WAS A NIGHT-WATCHMAN. A GUN AND HOLSTER HUNG LIMPLY ON THE WALL BY HIS SIDE, LOOKING UNUSED.
MAYBE SOMEDAY I'LL CHANGE THIS JOB...
THE MAN'S ONLY COMPANY IN HIS SHACK WERE THOUGHTS...AND DREAMS... A FEELING OF WARMTH AND SECURITY SPREAD OVER HIM AS HE LISTENED TO THE RAIN OUTSIDE...
TOO LONELY FOR ME! MAYBE--?
SUDDENLY, THE WATCHMAN FROZE, HIS BLOOD STAGNATING WITH FRIGHT. A FIGURE STOOD BEFORE HIM, BROWN, DIRTY DROPS OF RAIN WATER DRIPPING FROM ITS FETID BODY...
WHO'S TH--
SIMON!
2

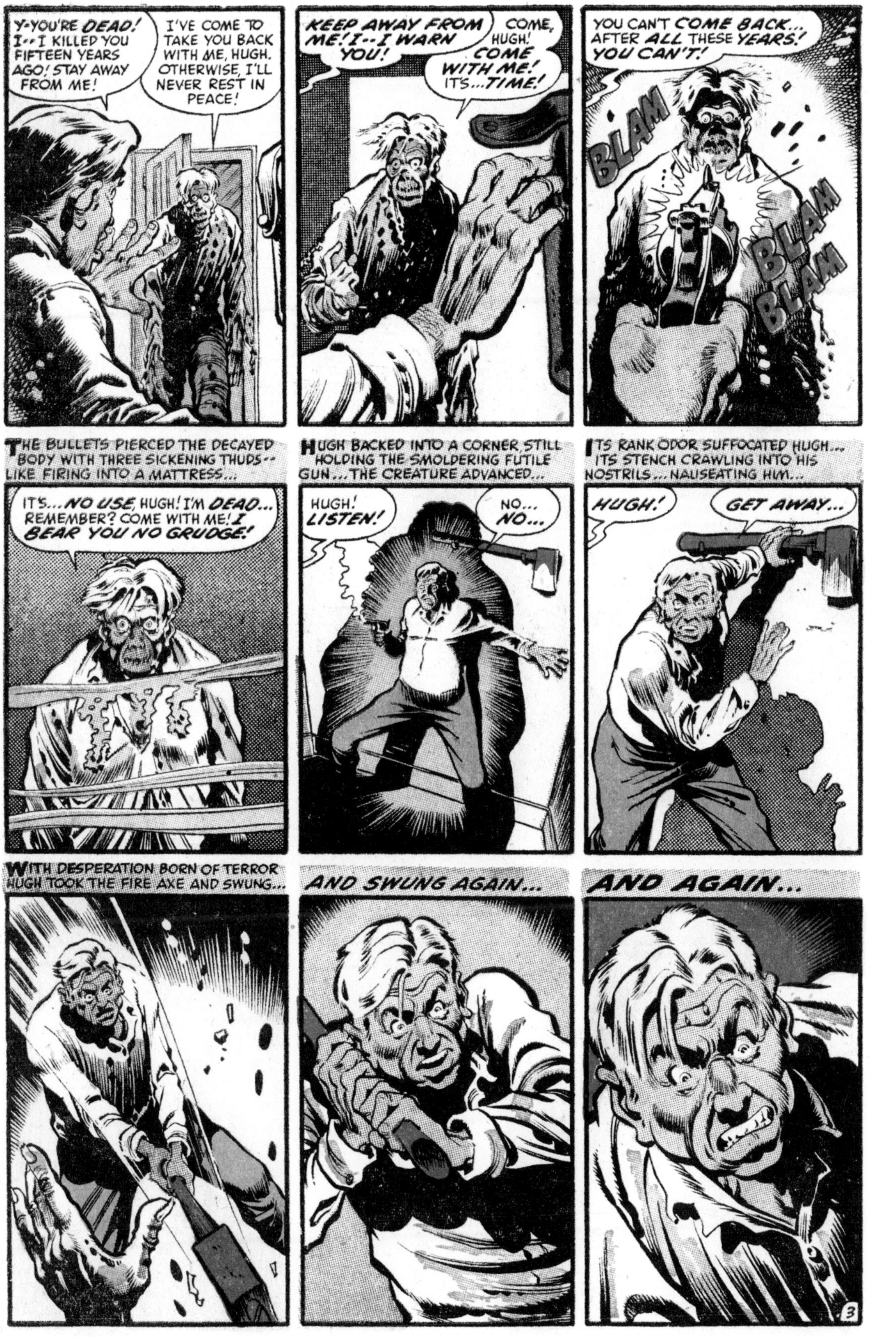
Y-YOU'RE DEAD! I--I KILLED YOU FIFTEEN YEARS AGO! STAY AWAY FROM ME!
I'VE COME TO TAKE YOU BACK WITH ME, HUGH. OTHERWISE, I'LL NEVER REST IN PEACE!
KEEP AWAY FROM ME! I--I WARN YOU!
COME, HUGH! COME WITH ME! IT'S...TIME!
YOU CAN'T COME BACK... AFTER ALL THESE YEARS! YOU CAN'T!
BLAM
BLAM
BLAM
BLAM
THE BULLETS PIERCED THE DECAYED BODY WITH THREE SICKENING THUDS--LIKE FIRING INTO A MATTRESS...
HUGH BACKED INTO A CORNER, STILL HOLDING THE SMOLDERING FUTILE GUN... THE CREATURE ADVANCED...
ITS RANK ODOR SUFFOCATED HUGH... ITS STENCH CRAWLING INTO HIS NOSTRILS... NAUSEATING HIM...
IT'S... NO USE, HUGH! I'M DEAD... REMEMBER? COME WITH ME! I BEAR YOU NO GRUDGE!
HUGH! LISTEN!
NO... NO...
HUGH!
GET AWAY...
WITH DESPERATION BORN OF TERROR HUGH TOOK THE FIRE AXE AND SWUNG...
AND SWUNG AGAIN...
AND AGAIN...
3

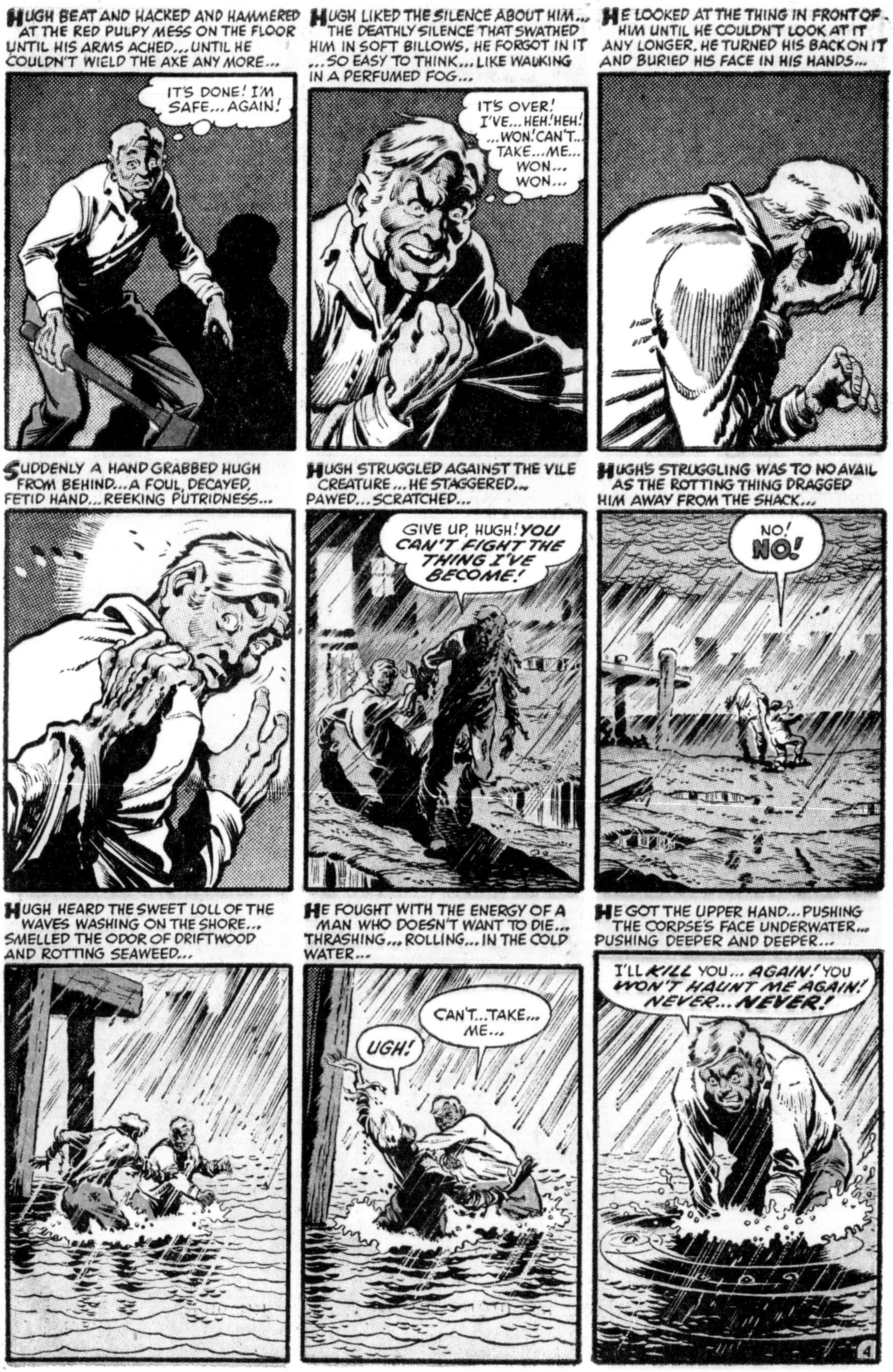
HUGH BEAT AND HACKED AND HAMMERED AT THE RED PULPY MESS ON THE FLOOR UNTIL HIS ARMS ACHED... UNTIL HE COULDN'T WIELD THE AXE ANY MORE...
IT'S DONE! I'M SAFE... AGAIN!
HUGH LIKED THE SILENCE ABOUT HIM... THE DEATHLY SILENCE THAT SWATHED HIM IN SOFT BILLOWS. HE FORGOT IN IT ...SO EASY TO THINK... LIKE WALKING IN A PERFUMED FOG...
IT'S OVER! I'VE... HEH! HEH! ...WON! CAN'T... TAKE... ME... WON... WON...
HE LOOKED AT THE THING IN FRONT OF HIM UNTIL HE COULDN'T LOOK AT IT ANY LONGER. HE TURNED HIS BACK ON IT AND BURIED HIS FACE IN HIS HANDS...
SUDDENLY A HAND GRABBED HUGH FROM BEHIND... A FOUL, DECAYED, FETID HAND... REEKING PUTRIDNESS...
HUGH STRUGGLED AGAINST THE VILE CREATURE... HE STAGGERED... PAWED... SCRATCHED...
GIVE UP, HUGH! YOU CAN'T FIGHT THE THING I'VE BECOME!
HUGH'S STRUGGLING WAS TO NO AVAIL AS THE ROTTING THING DRAGGED HIM AWAY FROM THE SHACK...
NO! NO!
HUGH HEARD THE SWEET LOLL OF THE WAVES WASHING ON THE SHORE... SMELLED THE ODOR OF DRIFTWOOD AND ROTTING SEAWEED...
HE FOUGHT WITH THE ENERGY OF A MAN WHO DOESN'T WANT TO DIE... THRASHING... ROLLING... IN THE COLD WATER...
UGH!
CAN'T... TAKE... ME...
HE GOT THE UPPER HAND... PUSHING THE CORPSE'S FACE UNDERWATER... PUSHING DEEPER AND DEEPER...
I'LL KILL YOU... AGAIN! YOU WON'T HAUNT ME AGAIN! NEVER... NEVER!
4

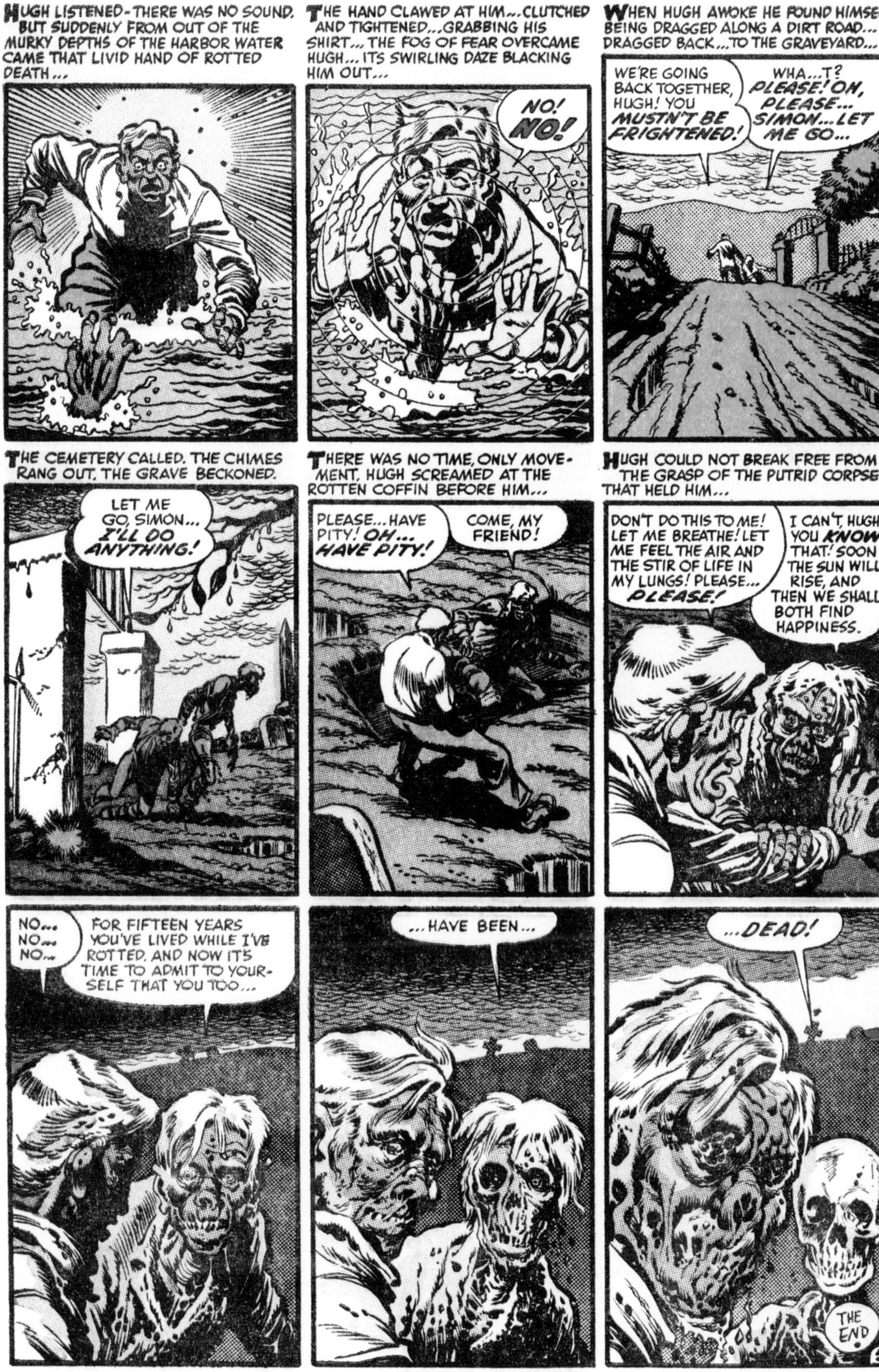
HUGH LISTENED - THERE WAS NO SOUND. BUT SUDDENLY FROM OUT OF THE MURKY DEPTHS OF THE HARBOR WATER CAME THAT LIVID HAND OF ROTTED DEATH...
THE HAND CLAWED AT HIM...CLUTCHED AND TIGHTENED...GRABBING HIS SHIRT... THE FOG OF FEAR OVERCAME HUGH... ITS SWIRLING DAZE BLACKING HIM OUT...
NO! NO!
WHEN HUGH AWOKE HE FOUND HIMSELF BEING DRAGGED ALONG A DIRT ROAD... DRAGGED BACK...TO THE GRAVEYARD...
WE'RE GOING BACK TOGETHER, HUGH! YOU MUSTN'T BE FRIGHTENED!
WHA...T? PLEASE! OH, PLEASE... SIMON...LET ME GO...
THE CEMETERY CALLED. THE CHIMES RANG OUT. THE GRAVE BECKONED.
LET ME GO, SIMON... I'LL DO ANYTHING!
THERE WAS NO TIME, ONLY MOVEMENT. HUGH SCREAMED AT THE ROTTEN COFFIN BEFORE HIM...
PLEASE...HAVE PITY! OH... HAVE PITY!
COME, MY FRIEND!
HUGH COULD NOT BREAK FREE FROM THE GRASP OF THE PUTRID CORPSE THAT HELD HIM...
DON'T DO THIS TO ME! LET ME BREATHE! LET ME FEEL THE AIR AND THE STIR OF LIFE IN MY LUNGS! PLEASE... PLEASE!
I CAN'T, HUGH. YOU KNOW THAT! SOON THE SUN WILL RISE, AND THEN WE SHALL BOTH FIND HAPPINESS.
NO... NO... NO...
FOR FIFTEEN YEARS YOU'VE LIVED WHILE I'VE ROTTED, AND NOW IT'S TIME TO ADMIT TO YOURSELF THAT YOU TOO...
...HAVE BEEN...
...DEAD!
THE END
5

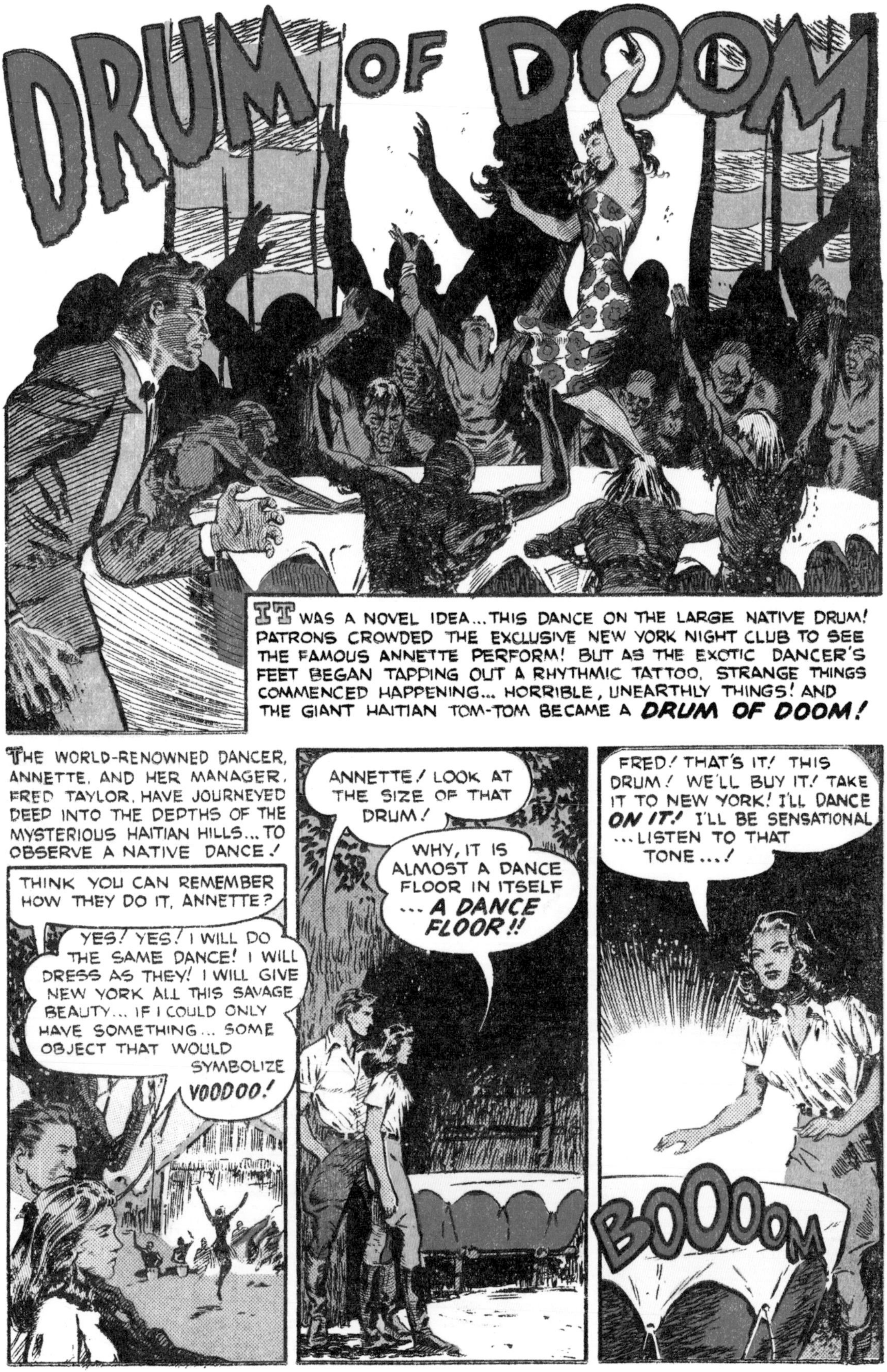
DRUM OF DOOM
IT WAS A NOVEL IDEA... THIS DANCE ON THE LARGE NATIVE DRUM! PATRONS CROWDED THE EXCLUSIVE NEW YORK NIGHT CLUB TO SEE THE FAMOUS ANNETTE PERFORM! BUT AS THE EXOTIC DANCER'S FEET BEGAN TAPPING OUT A RHYTHMIC TATTOO, STRANGE THINGS COMMENCED HAPPENING... HORRIBLE, UNEARTHLY THINGS! AND THE GIANT HAITIAN TOM-TOM BECAME A DRUM OF DOOM!
THE WORLD-RENOWNED DANCER, ANNETTE, AND HER MANAGER, FRED TAYLOR, HAVE JOURNEYED DEEP INTO THE DEPTHS OF THE MYSTERIOUS HAITIAN HILLS... TO OBSERVE A NATIVE DANCE!
THINK YOU CAN REMEMBER HOW THEY DO IT, ANNETTE?
YES! YES! I WILL DO THE SAME DANCE! I WILL DRESS AS THEY! I WILL GIVE NEW YORK ALL THIS SAVAGE BEAUTY... IF I COULD ONLY HAVE SOMETHING... SOME OBJECT THAT WOULD SYMBOLIZE VOODOO!
ANNETTE! LOOK AT THE SIZE OF THAT DRUM!
WHY, IT IS ALMOST A DANCE FLOOR IN ITSELF ... A DANCE FLOOR!!
FRED! THAT'S IT! THIS DRUM! WE'LL BUY IT! TAKE IT TO NEW YORK! I'LL DANCE ON IT! I'LL BE SENSATIONAL ... LISTEN TO THAT TONE...!
BOOOOOM

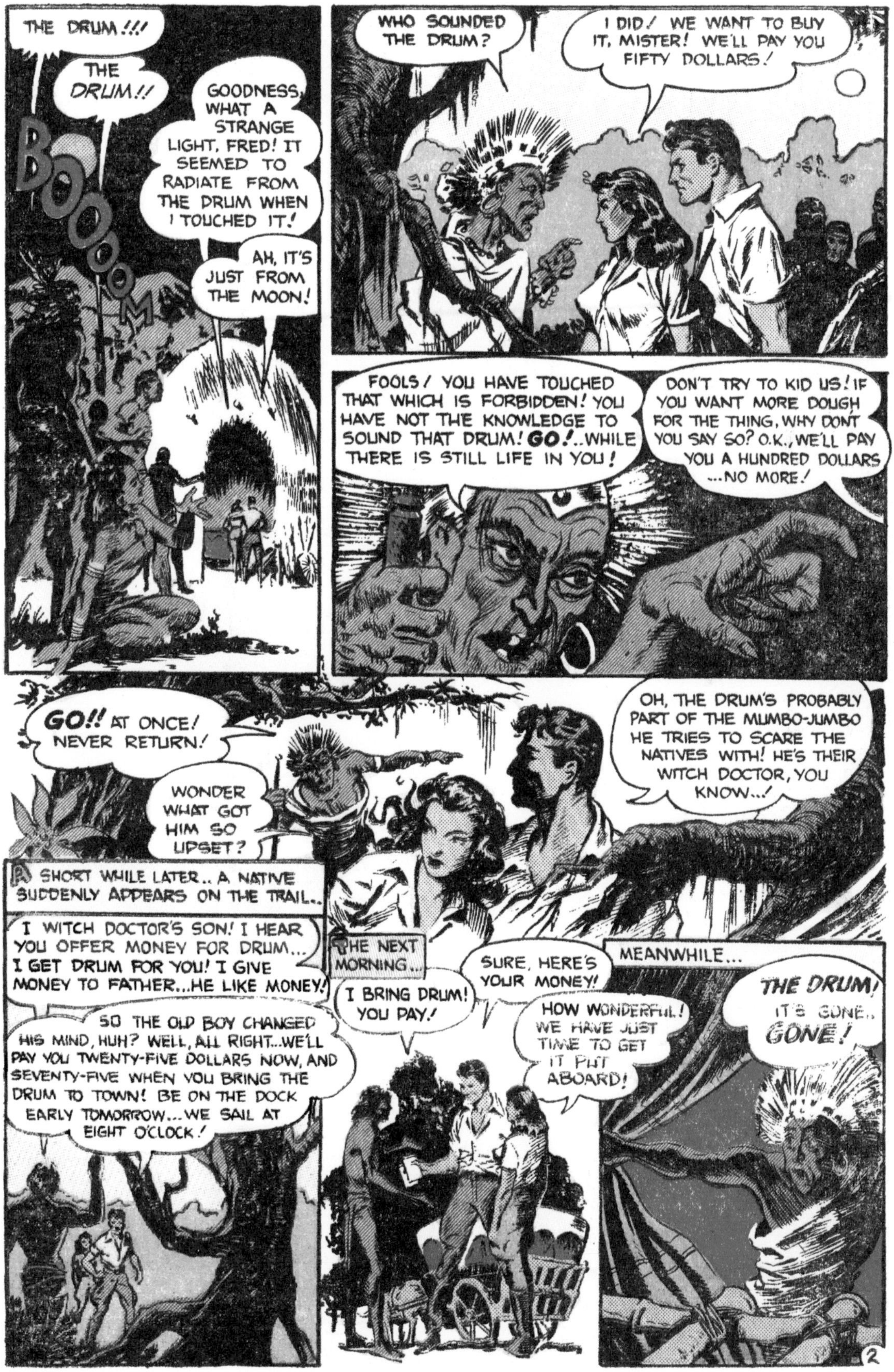

THE DRUM!!!
THE DRUM!!
GOODNESS, WHAT A STRANGE LIGHT, FRED! IT SEEMED TO RADIATE FROM THE DRUM WHEN I TOUCHED IT!
AH, IT'S JUST FROM THE MOON!
BOOOOOM
WHO SOUNDED THE DRUM?
I DID! WE WANT TO BUY IT, MISTER! WE'LL PAY YOU FIFTY DOLLARS!
FOOLS! YOU HAVE TOUCHED THAT WHICH IS FORBIDDEN! YOU HAVE NOT THE KNOWLEDGE TO SOUND THAT DRUM! GO!..WHILE THERE IS STILL LIFE IN YOU!
DON'T TRY TO KID US! IF YOU WANT MORE DOUGH FOR THE THING, WHY DONT YOU SAY SO? O.K., WE'LL PAY YOU A HUNDRED DOLLARS ...NO MORE!
GO!! AT ONCE! NEVER RETURN!
WONDER WHAT GOT HIM SO UPSET?
OH, THE DRUM'S PROBABLY PART OF THE MUMBO-JUMBO HE TRIES TO SCARE THE NATIVES WITH! HE'S THEIR WITCH DOCTOR, YOU KNOW...!
A SHORT WHILE LATER.. A NATIVE SUDDENLY APPEARS ON THE TRAIL..
I WITCH DOCTOR'S SON! I HEAR YOU OFFER MONEY FOR DRUM... I GET DRUM FOR YOU! I GIVE MONEY TO FATHER...HE LIKE MONEY!
SO THE OLD BOY CHANGED HIS MIND, HUH? WELL, ALL RIGHT...WE'LL PAY YOU TWENTY-FIVE DOLLARS NOW, AND SEVENTY-FIVE WHEN YOU BRING THE DRUM TO TOWN! BE ON THE DOCK EARLY TOMORROW...WE SAIL AT EIGHT O'CLOCK!
THE NEXT MORNING...
I BRING DRUM! YOU PAY!
SURE, HERE'S YOUR MONEY!
HOW WONDERFUL! WE HAVE JUST TIME TO GET IT PUT ABOARD!
MEANWHILE...
THE DRUM! IT'S GONE.. GONE!
2

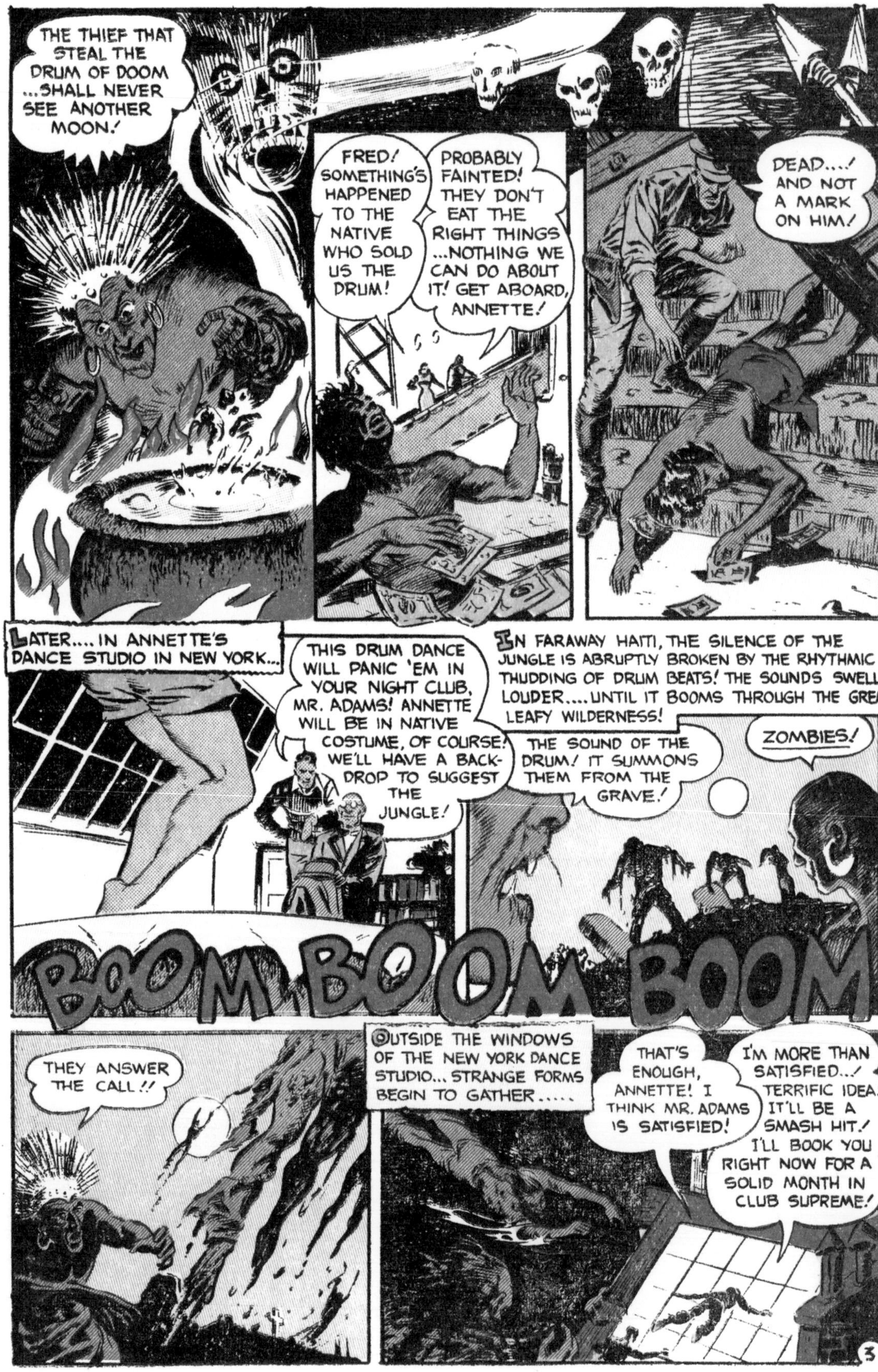
THE THIEF THAT STEAL THE DRUM OF DOOM ...SHALL NEVER SEE ANOTHER MOON!
FRED! SOMETHING'S HAPPENED TO THE NATIVE WHO SOLD US THE DRUM!
PROBABLY FAINTED! THEY DON'T EAT THE RIGHT THINGS ...NOTHING WE CAN DO ABOUT IT! GET ABOARD, ANNETTE!
DEAD....! AND NOT A MARK ON HIM!
LATER.... IN ANNETTE'S DANCE STUDIO IN NEW YORK...
THIS DRUM DANCE WILL PANIC 'EM IN YOUR NIGHT CLUB, MR. ADAMS! ANNETTE WILL BE IN NATIVE COSTUME, OF COURSE! WE'LL HAVE A BACK-DROP TO SUGGEST THE JUNGLE!
IN FARAWAY HAITI, THE SILENCE OF THE JUNGLE IS ABRUPTLY BROKEN BY THE RHYTHMIC THUDDING OF DRUM BEATS! THE SOUNDS SWELL LOUDER.... UNTIL IT BOOMS THROUGH THE GREAT LEAFY WILDERNESS!
THE SOUND OF THE DRUM! IT SUMMONS THEM FROM THE GRAVE!
ZOMBIES!
BOOM BOOM BOOM
THEY ANSWER THE CALL!!
OUTSIDE THE WINDOWS OF THE NEW YORK DANCE STUDIO... STRANGE FORMS BEGIN TO GATHER.....
THAT'S ENOUGH, ANNETTE! I THINK MR. ADAMS IS SATISFIED!
I'M MORE THAN SATISFIED...! TERRIFIC IDEA! IT'LL BE A SMASH HIT! I'LL BOOK YOU RIGHT NOW FOR A SOLID MONTH IN CLUB SUPREME!
3

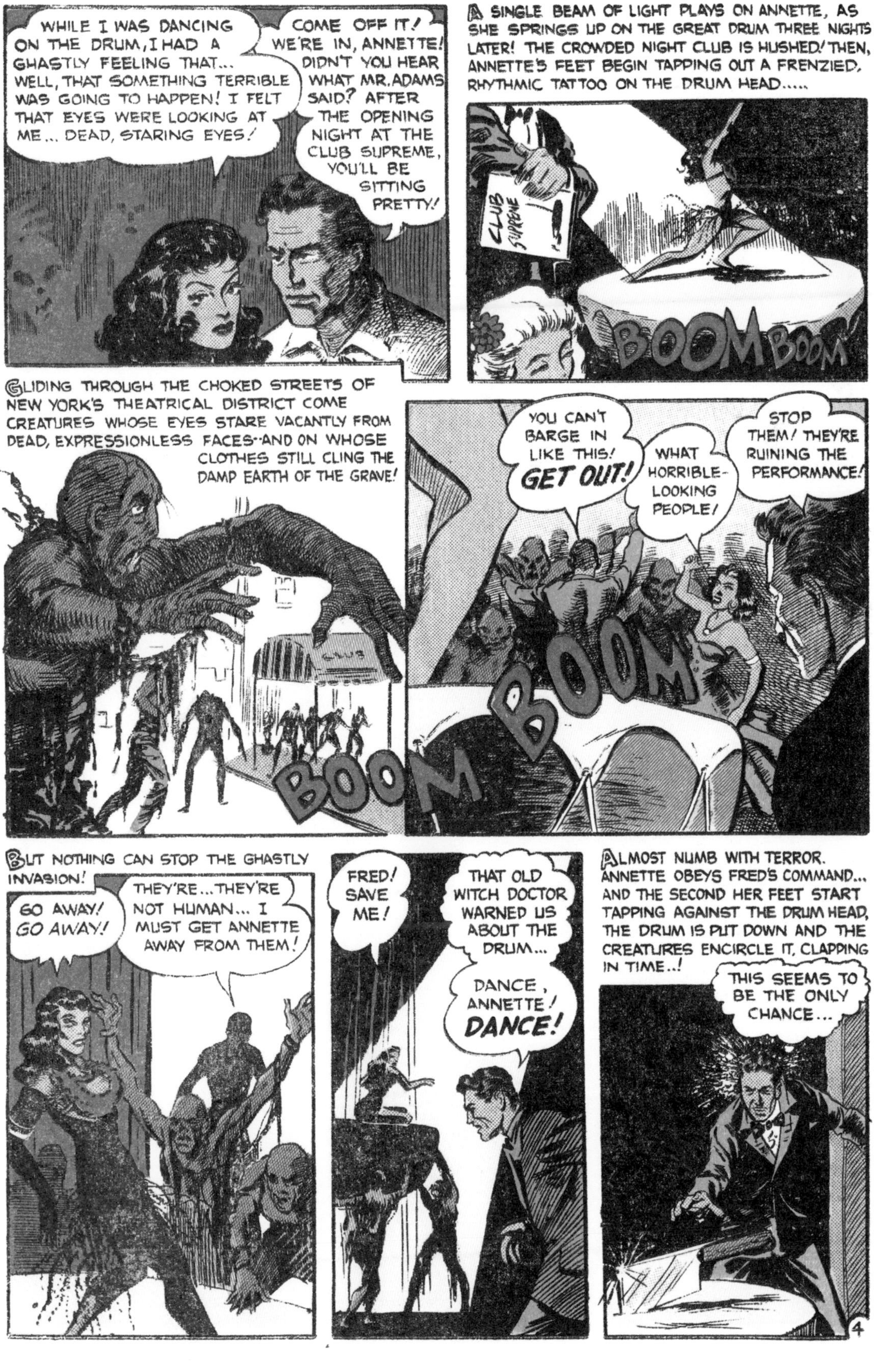
WHILE I WAS DANCING ON THE DRUM, I HAD A GHASTLY FEELING THAT... WELL, THAT SOMETHING TERRIBLE WAS GOING TO HAPPEN! I FELT THAT EYES WERE LOOKING AT ME... DEAD, STARING EYES!
COME OFF IT! WE'RE IN, ANNETTE! DIDN'T YOU HEAR WHAT MR. ADAMS SAID? AFTER THE OPENING NIGHT AT THE CLUB SUPREME, YOU'LL BE SITTING PRETTY!
A SINGLE BEAM OF LIGHT PLAYS ON ANNETTE, AS SHE SPRINGS UP ON THE GREAT DRUM THREE NIGHTS LATER! THE CROWDED NIGHT CLUB IS HUSHED! THEN, ANNETTE'S FEET BEGIN TAPPING OUT A FRENZIED, RHYTHMIC TATTOO ON THE DRUM HEAD.....
CLUB SUPREME
BOOM BOOM
GLIDING THROUGH THE CHOKED STREETS OF NEW YORK'S THEATRICAL DISTRICT COME CREATURES WHOSE EYES STARE VACANTLY FROM DEAD, EXPRESSIONLESS FACES--AND ON WHOSE CLOTHES STILL CLING THE DAMP EARTH OF THE GRAVE!
CLUB
BOOM
YOU CAN'T BARGE IN LIKE THIS! GET OUT!
WHAT HORRIBLE-LOOKING PEOPLE!
STOP THEM! THEY'RE RUINING THE PERFORMANCE!
BOOM
BUT NOTHING CAN STOP THE GHASTLY INVASION!
GO AWAY! GO AWAY!
THEY'RE... THEY'RE NOT HUMAN... I MUST GET ANNETTE AWAY FROM THEM!
FRED! SAVE ME!
THAT OLD WITCH DOCTOR WARNED US ABOUT THE DRUM...
DANCE, ANNETTE! DANCE!
ALMOST NUMB WITH TERROR, ANNETTE OBEYS FRED'S COMMAND... AND THE SECOND HER FEET START TAPPING AGAINST THE DRUM HEAD, THE DRUM IS PUT DOWN AND THE CREATURES ENCIRCLE IT, CLAPPING IN TIME..!
THIS SEEMS TO BE THE ONLY CHANCE...
4

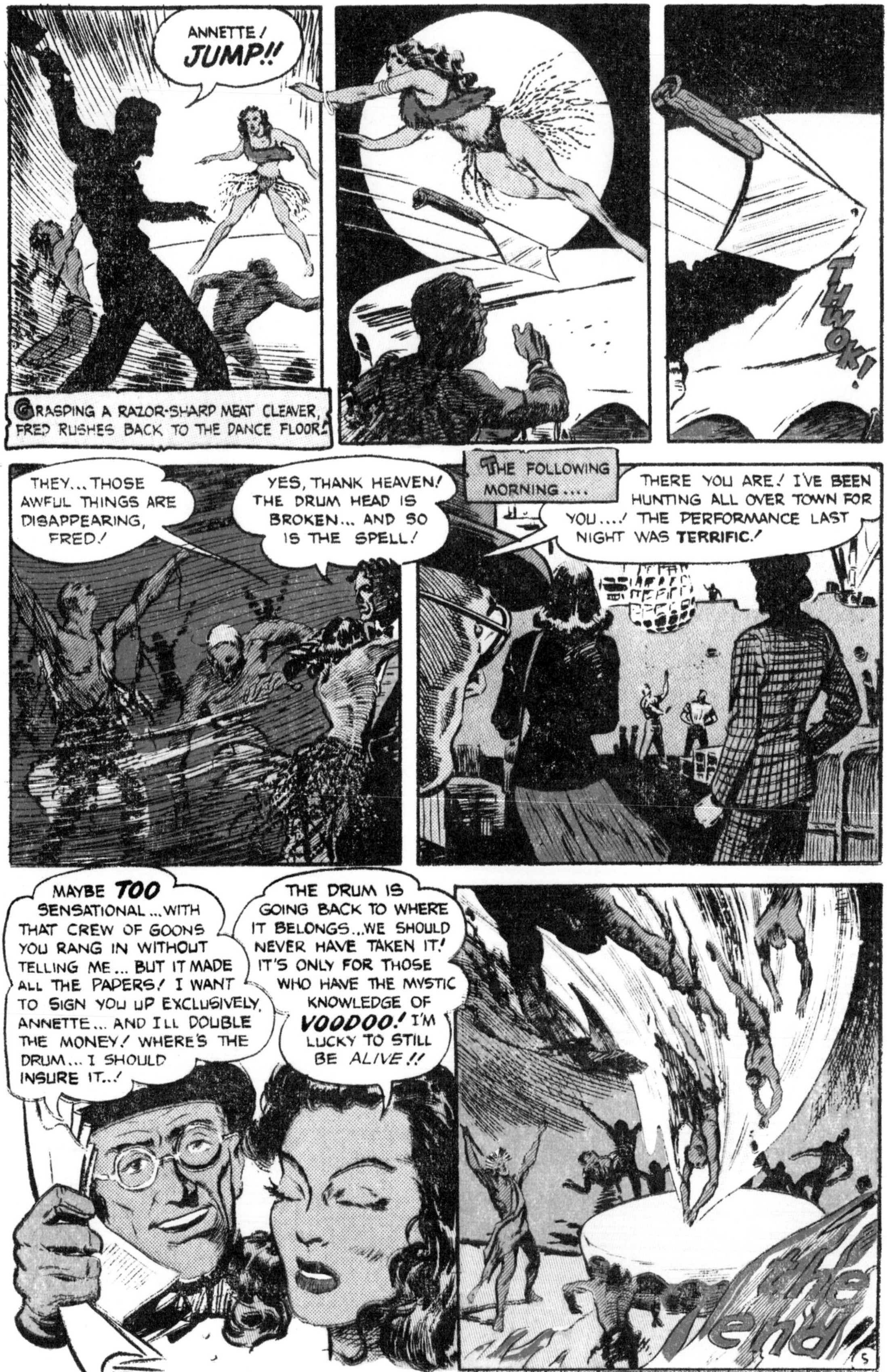
ANNETTE! JUMP!!
GRASPING A RAZOR-SHARP MEAT CLEAVER, FRED RUSHES BACK TO THE DANCE FLOOR!
THWOK!
THEY... THOSE AWFUL THINGS ARE DISAPPEARING, FRED!
YES, THANK HEAVEN! THE DRUM HEAD IS BROKEN... AND SO IS THE SPELL!
THE FOLLOWING MORNING....
THERE YOU ARE! I'VE BEEN HUNTING ALL OVER TOWN FOR YOU....! THE PERFORMANCE LAST NIGHT WAS TERRIFIC!
MAYBE TOO SENSATIONAL... WITH THAT CREW OF GOONS YOU RANG IN WITHOUT TELLING ME... BUT IT MADE ALL THE PAPERS! I WANT TO SIGN YOU UP EXCLUSIVELY, ANNETTE... AND I'LL DOUBLE THE MONEY! WHERE'S THE DRUM... I SHOULD INSURE IT...!
THE DRUM IS GOING BACK TO WHERE IT BELONGS... WE SHOULD NEVER HAVE TAKEN IT! IT'S ONLY FOR THOSE WHO HAVE THE MYSTIC KNOWLEDGE OF VOODOO! I'M LUCKY TO STILL BE ALIVE!!
the end
5

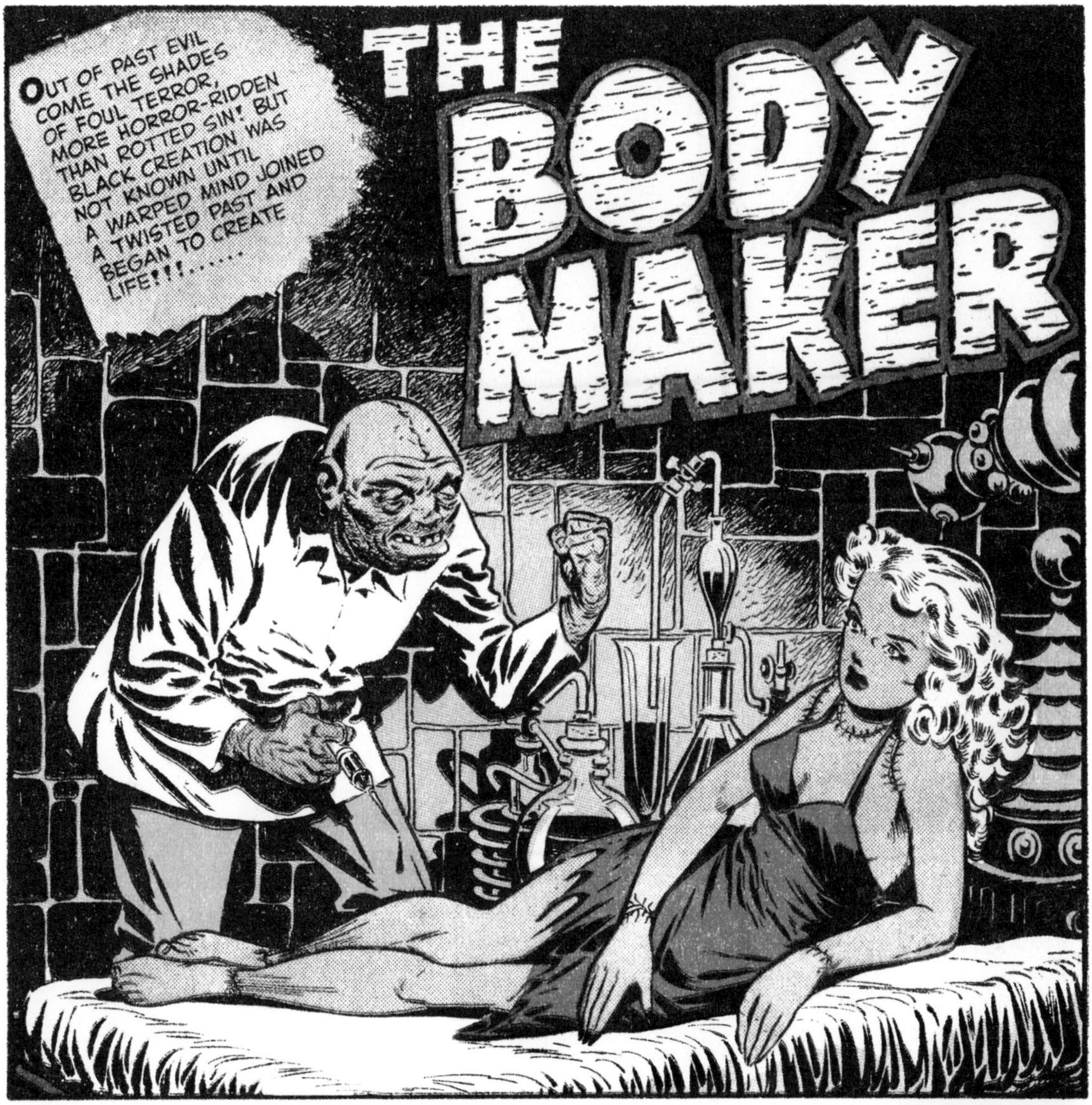
OUT OF PAST EVIL COME THE SHADES OF FOUL TERROR, MORE HORROR-RIDDEN THAN ROTTED SIN! BUT BLACK CREATION WAS NOT KNOWN UNTIL A WARPED MIND JOINED A TWISTED PAST AND BEGAN TO CREATE LIFE!!!......
THE BODY MAKER

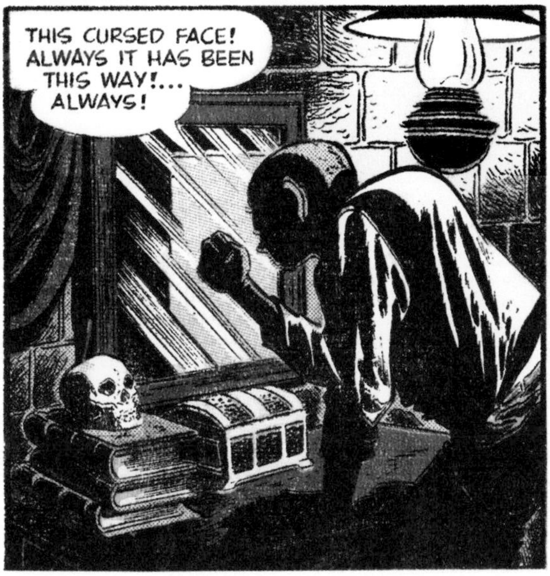
THIS CURSED FACE! ALWAYS IT HAS BEEN THIS WAY!... ALWAYS!

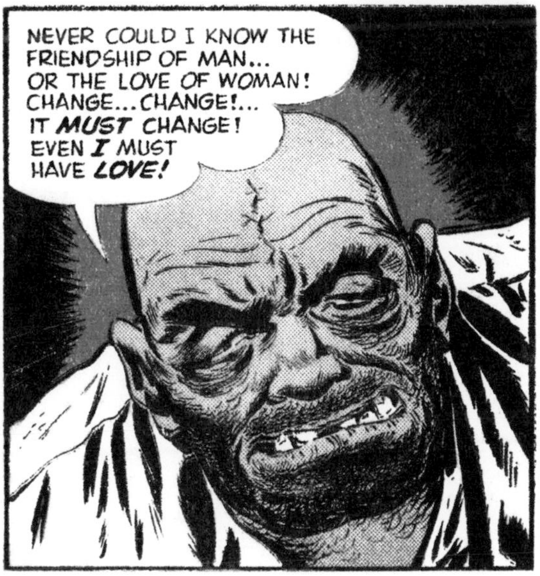
NEVER COULD I KNOW THE FRIENDSHIP OF MAN... OR THE LOVE OF WOMAN! CHANGE... CHANGE!... IT MUST CHANGE! EVEN I MUST HAVE LOVE!

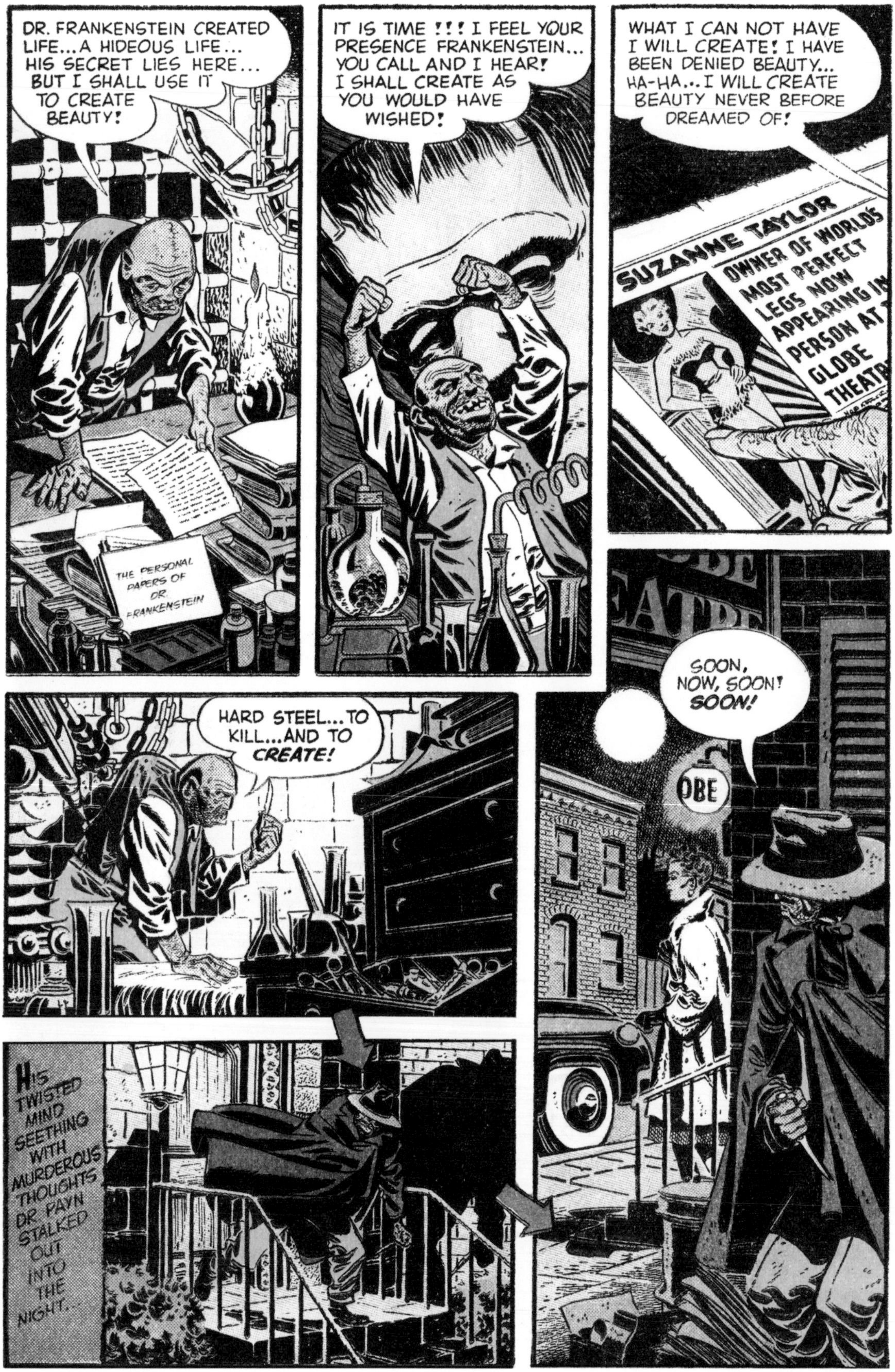
DR. FRANKENSTEIN CREATED LIFE...A HIDEOUS LIFE... HIS SECRET LIES HERE... BUT I SHALL USE IT TO CREATE BEAUTY!
THE PERSONAL PAPERS OF DR. FRANKENSTEIN
IT IS TIME !!! I FEEL YOUR PRESENCE FRANKENSTEIN... YOU CALL AND I HEAR! I SHALL CREATE AS YOU WOULD HAVE WISHED!
WHAT I CAN NOT HAVE I WILL CREATE! I HAVE BEEN DENIED BEAUTY... HA-HA..I WILL CREATE BEAUTY NEVER BEFORE DREAMED OF!
SUZANNE TAYLOR
OWNER OF WORLD'S MOST PERFECT LEGS NOW APPEARING IN PERSON AT THE GLOBE THEATRE
HARD STEEL...TO KILL...AND TO CREATE!
HIS TWISTED MIND SEETHING WITH MURDEROUS THOUGHTS DR PAYN STALKED OUT INTO THE NIGHT...
SOON, NOW, SOON! SOON!

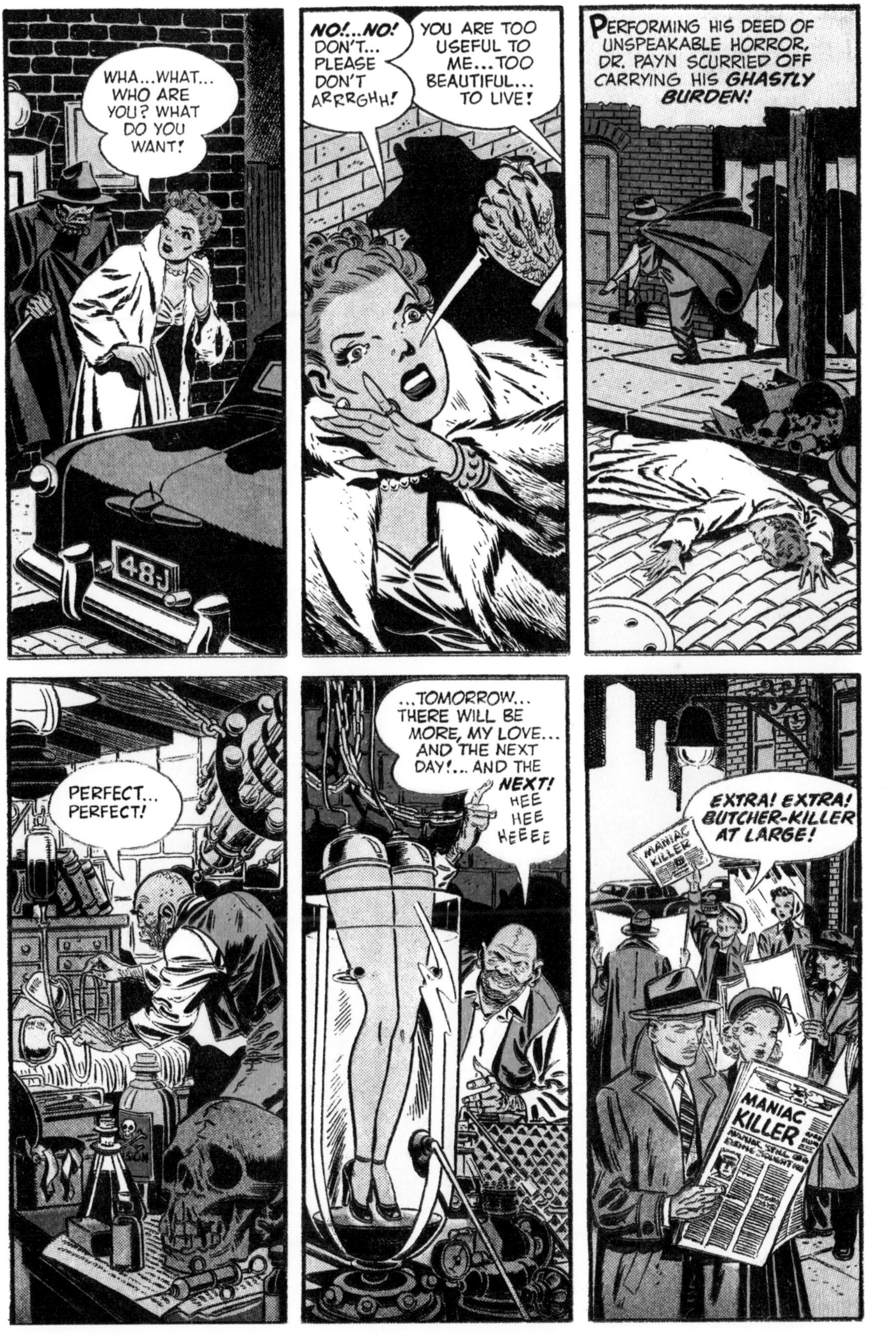
WHA...WHAT... WHO ARE YOU? WHAT DO YOU WANT!
NO!...NO! DON'T... PLEASE DON'T ARRRGHH!
YOU ARE TOO USEFUL TO ME...TOO BEAUTIFUL... TO LIVE!
PERFORMING HIS DEED OF UNSPEAKABLE HORROR, DR. PAYN SCURRIED OFF CARRYING HIS GHASTLY BURDEN!
48-J
PERFECT... PERFECT!
...TOMORROW... THERE WILL BE MORE, MY LOVE... AND THE NEXT DAY!... AND THE NEXT! HEE HEE HEEEE
EXTRA! EXTRA! BUTCHER-KILLER AT LARGE!
MANIAC KILLER
MANIAC KILLER

GET THAT MANIAC...OR WHATEVER HE IS... BEFORE THIS CITY IS THROWN INTO A **COMPLETE PANIC!**

WHEW! GET HIM, HE SAID! BUT **WHO** IS THE KILLER...WHAT IS HE?

POLICE COMMISSIONER

DETERMINED TO CREATE THE PERFECT WOMAN WHO WOULD LOVE HIM ALONE, DR. PAYN, WENT ON A MAD RAMPAGE OF MURDER!

HARDWA

MURDERER STILL AT LARGE

I'M WORRIED... MY OWN WIFE MAY BE NEXT...NO BEAUTIFUL WOMAN IS SAFE!

THAT FIEND IS STILL LOOSE, HONEY! YOU'VE GOT TO BE CAREFUL! WHATEVER HE IS, HE MAY STRIKE ANYWHERE!

DON'T WORRY SO, DARLING! I'LL ONLY BE OUT FOR A MOMENT, TONIGHT! I RECEIVED ANOTHER MODELING JOB FROM A HAND LOTION CONCERN.

MANIAC KILLER

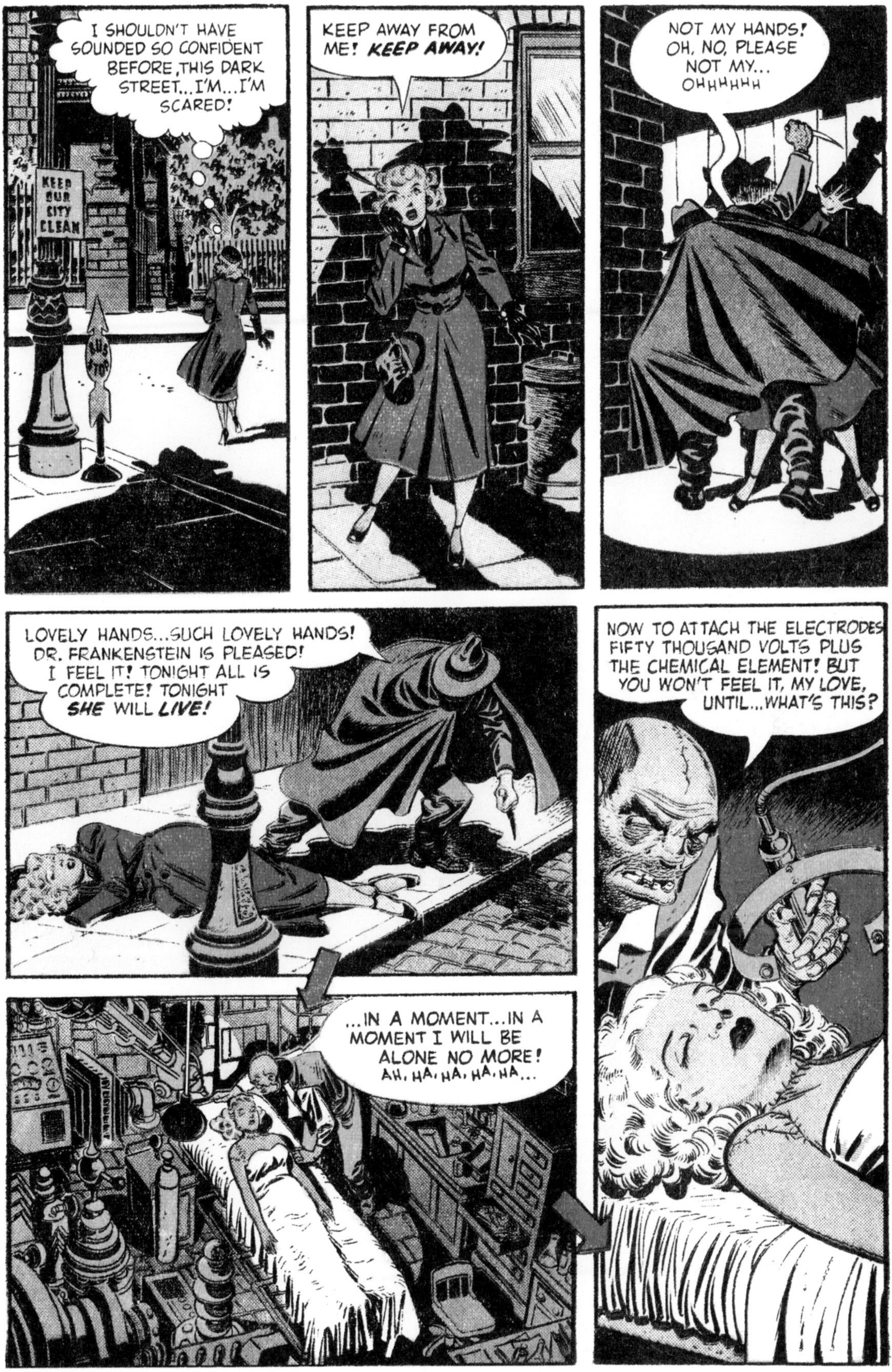
I SHOULDN'T HAVE SOUNDED SO CONFIDENT BEFORE, THIS DARK STREET... I'M... I'M SCARED!
KEEP OUT OUR CITY CLEAN
BUS STOP
KEEP AWAY FROM ME! KEEP AWAY!
NOT MY HANDS! OH, NO, PLEASE NOT MY... OHHHHHH
LOVELY HANDS... SUCH LOVELY HANDS! DR. FRANKENSTEIN IS PLEASED! I FEEL IT! TONIGHT ALL IS COMPLETE! TONIGHT SHE WILL LIVE!
NOW TO ATTACH THE ELECTRODES FIFTY THOUSAND VOLTS PLUS THE CHEMICAL ELEMENT! BUT YOU WON'T FEEL IT, MY LOVE, UNTIL... WHAT'S THIS?
...IN A MOMENT... IN A MOMENT I WILL BE ALONE NO MORE! AH, HA, HA, HA, HA...

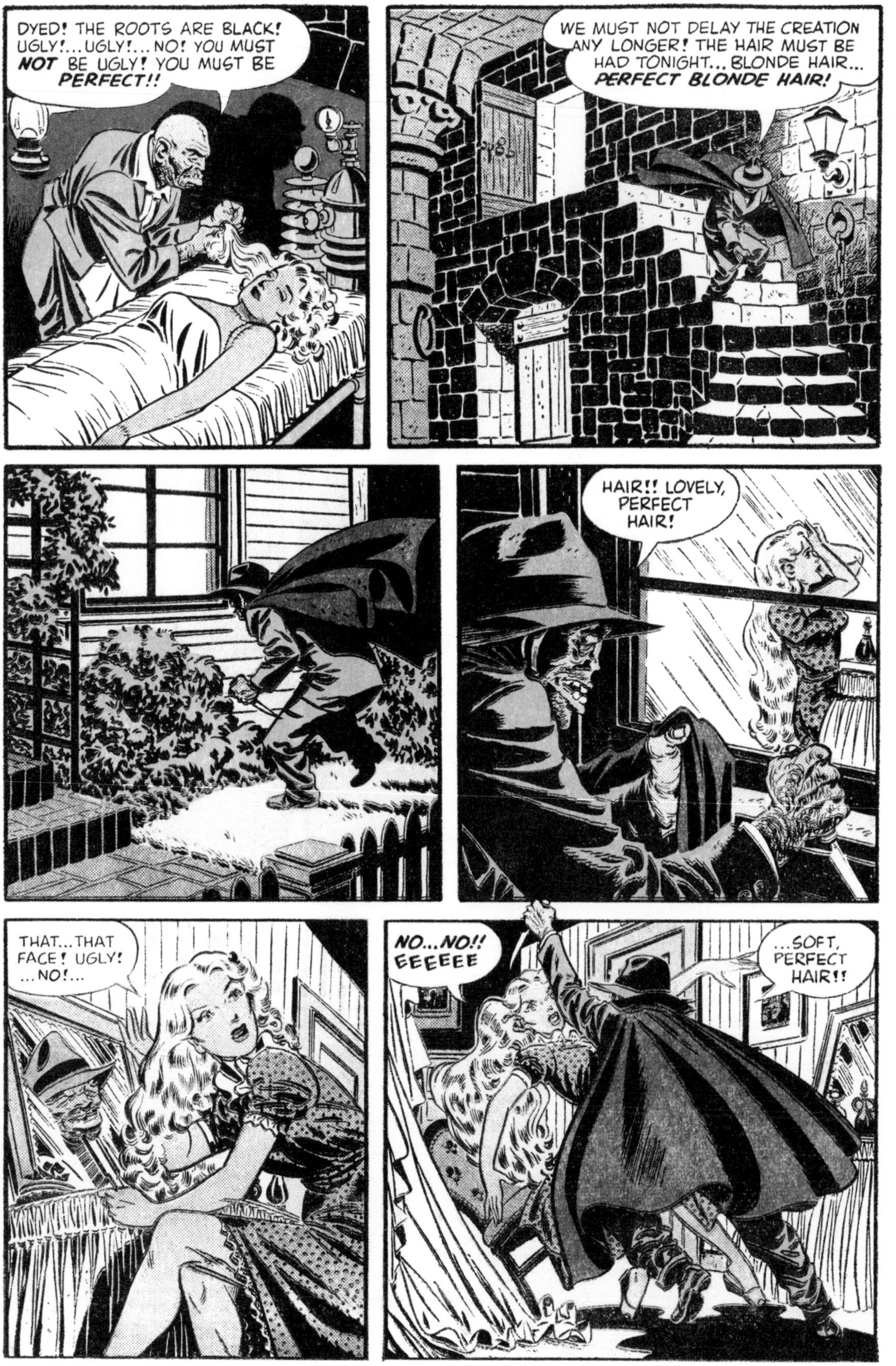
DYED! THE ROOTS ARE BLACK! UGLY!...UGLY!...NO! YOU MUST NOT BE UGLY! YOU MUST BE PERFECT!!
WE MUST NOT DELAY THE CREATION ANY LONGER! THE HAIR MUST BE HAD TONIGHT... BLONDE HAIR... PERFECT BLONDE HAIR!
HAIR!! LOVELY, PERFECT HAIR!
THAT...THAT FACE! UGLY! ...NO!...
NO...NO!! EEEEEE
...SOFT, PERFECT HAIR!!

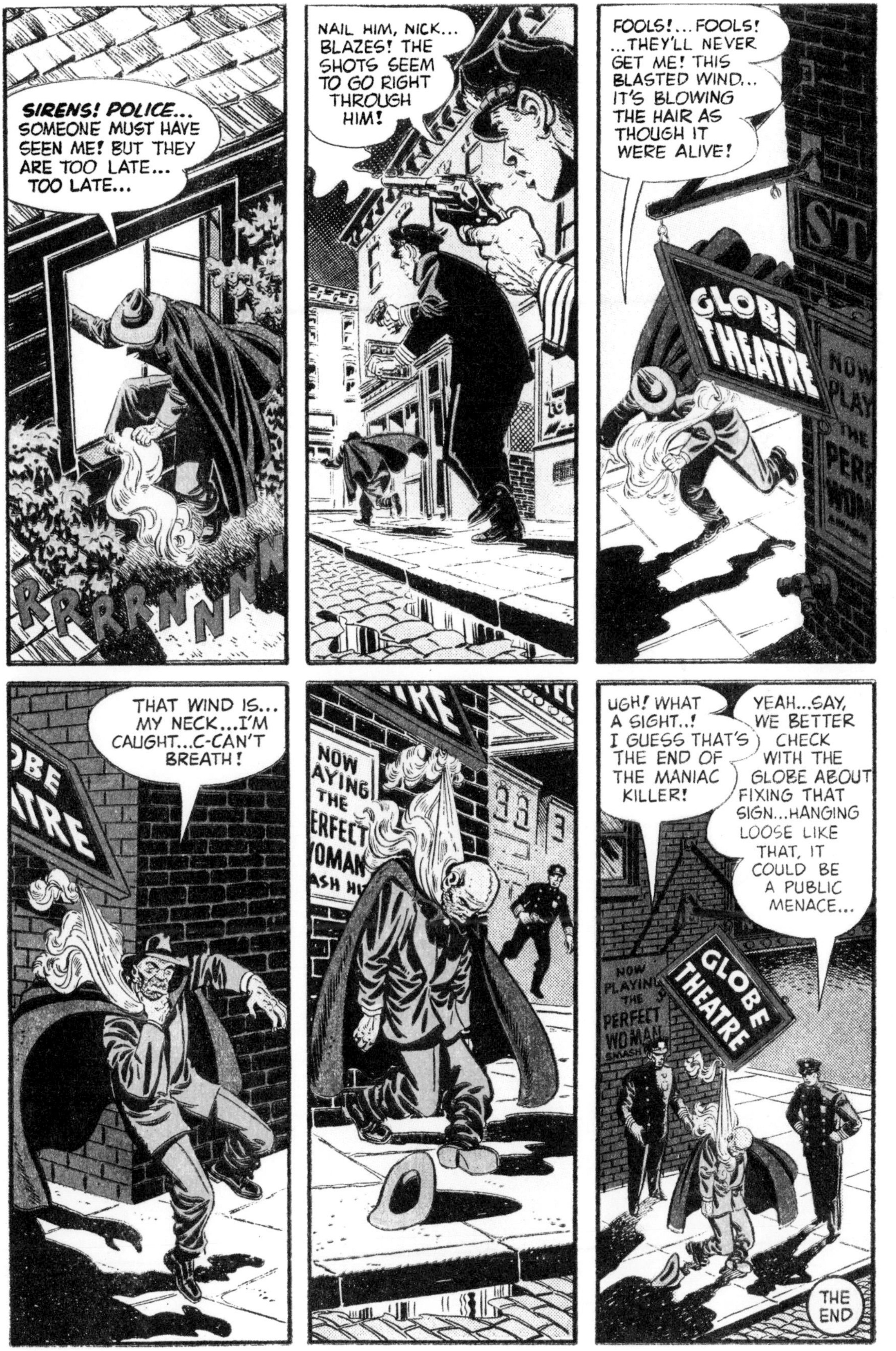
SIRENS! POLICE... SOMEONE MUST HAVE SEEN ME! BUT THEY ARE TOO LATE... TOO LATE...
RRRRNNNNN
NAIL HIM, NICK... BLAZES! THE SHOTS SEEM TO GO RIGHT THROUGH HIM!
FOOLS!... FOOLS! ...THEY'LL NEVER GET ME! THIS BLASTED WIND... IT'S BLOWING THE HAIR AS THOUGH IT WERE ALIVE!
GLOBE THEATRE
THAT WIND IS... MY NECK...I'M CAUGHT...C-CAN'T BREATH!
NOW PLAYING THE PERFECT WOMAN
UGH! WHAT A SIGHT..! I GUESS THAT'S THE END OF THE MANIAC KILLER!
YEAH...SAY, WE BETTER CHECK WITH THE GLOBE ABOUT FIXING THAT SIGN...HANGING LOOSE LIKE THAT, IT COULD BE A PUBLIC MENACE...
GLOBE THEATRE
NOW PLAYING THE PERFECT WOMAN
THE END

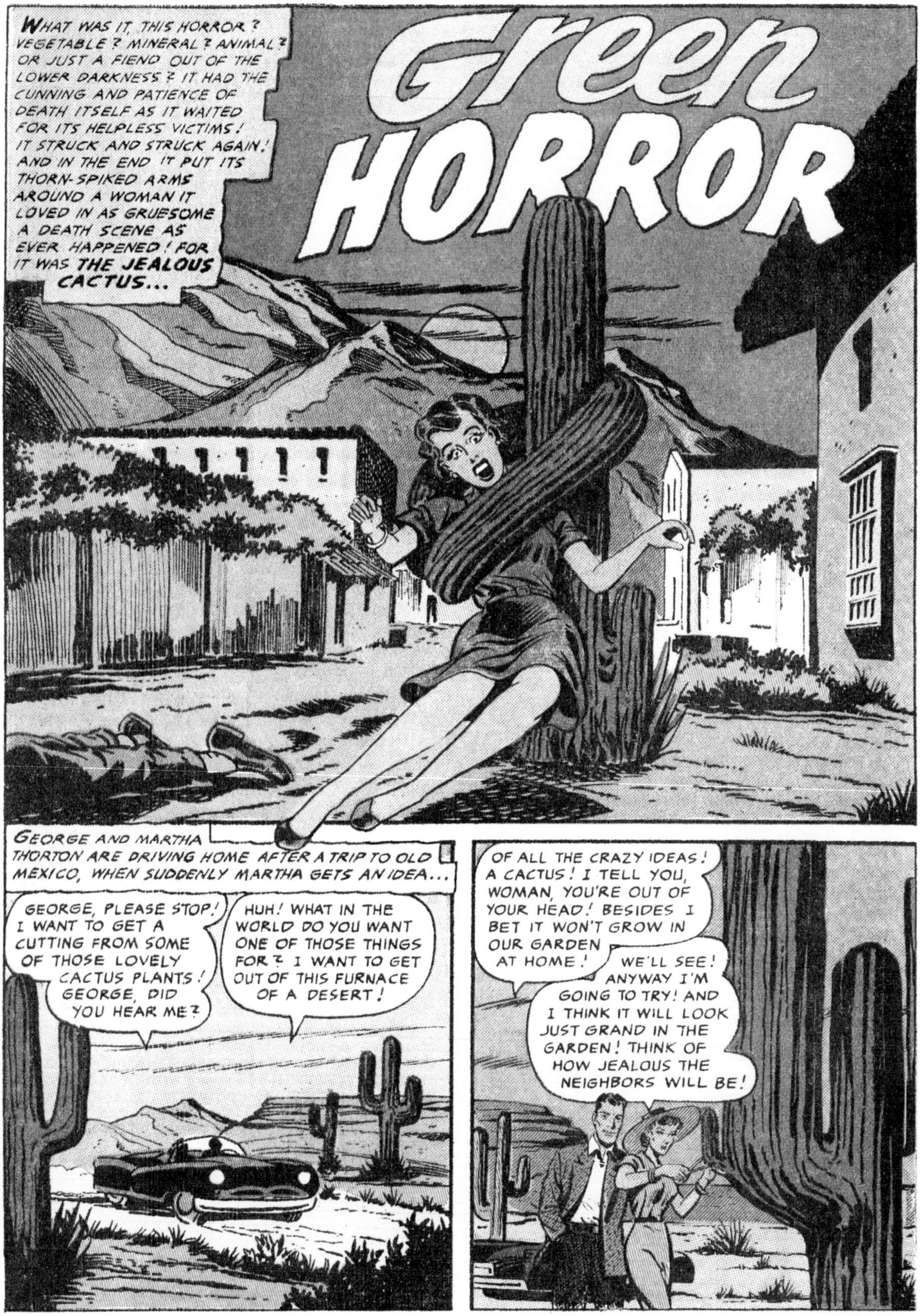
WHAT WAS IT, THIS HORROR? VEGETABLE? MINERAL? ANIMAL? OR JUST A FIEND OUT OF THE LOWER DARKNESS? IT HAD THE CUNNING AND PATIENCE OF DEATH ITSELF AS IT WAITED FOR ITS HELPLESS VICTIMS! IT STRUCK AND STRUCK AGAIN! AND IN THE END IT PUT ITS THORN-SPIKED ARMS AROUND A WOMAN IT LOVED IN AS GRUESOME A DEATH SCENE AS EVER HAPPENED! FOR IT WAS THE JEALOUS CACTUS...
Green HORROR
GEORGE AND MARTHA THORTON ARE DRIVING HOME AFTER A TRIP TO OLD MEXICO, WHEN SUDDENLY MARTHA GETS AN IDEA...
GEORGE, PLEASE STOP! I WANT TO GET A CUTTING FROM SOME OF THOSE LOVELY CACTUS PLANTS! GEORGE, DID YOU HEAR ME?
HUH! WHAT IN THE WORLD DO YOU WANT ONE OF THOSE THINGS FOR? I WANT TO GET OUT OF THIS FURNACE OF A DESERT!
OF ALL THE CRAZY IDEAS! A CACTUS! I TELL YOU, WOMAN, YOU'RE OUT OF YOUR HEAD! BESIDES I BET IT WON'T GROW IN OUR GARDEN AT HOME!
WE'LL SEE! ANYWAY I'M GOING TO TRY! AND I THINK IT WILL LOOK JUST GRAND IN THE GARDEN! THINK OF HOW JEALOUS THE NEIGHBORS WILL BE!

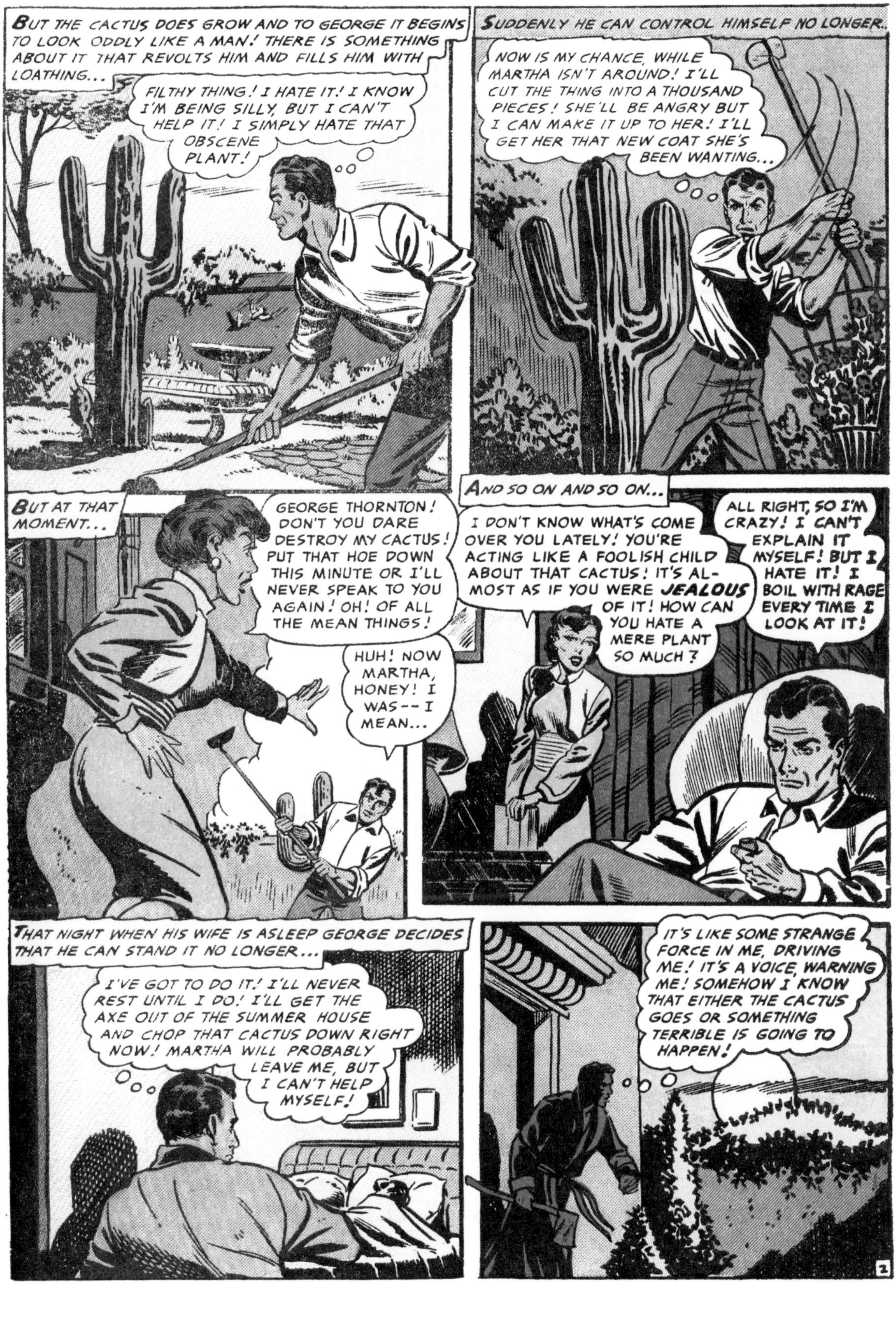
BUT THE CACTUS DOES GROW AND TO GEORGE IT BEGINS TO LOOK ODDLY LIKE A MAN! THERE IS SOMETHING ABOUT IT THAT REVOLTS HIM AND FILLS HIM WITH LOATHING...
FILTHY THING! I HATE IT! I KNOW I'M BEING SILLY, BUT I CAN'T HELP IT! I SIMPLY HATE THAT OBSCENE PLANT!
SUDDENLY HE CAN CONTROL HIMSELF NO LONGER...
NOW IS MY CHANCE, WHILE MARTHA ISN'T AROUND! I'LL CUT THE THING INTO A THOUSAND PIECES! SHE'LL BE ANGRY BUT I CAN MAKE IT UP TO HER! I'LL GET HER THAT NEW COAT SHE'S BEEN WANTING...
BUT AT THAT MOMENT...
GEORGE THORNTON! DON'T YOU DARE DESTROY MY CACTUS! PUT THAT HOE DOWN THIS MINUTE OR I'LL NEVER SPEAK TO YOU AGAIN! OH! OF ALL THE MEAN THINGS!
HUH! NOW MARTHA, HONEY! I WAS-- I MEAN...
AND SO ON AND SO ON...
I DON'T KNOW WHAT'S COME OVER YOU LATELY! YOU'RE ACTING LIKE A FOOLISH CHILD ABOUT THAT CACTUS! IT'S ALMOST AS IF YOU WERE JEALOUS OF IT! HOW CAN YOU HATE A MERE PLANT SO MUCH?
ALL RIGHT, SO I'M CRAZY! I CAN'T EXPLAIN IT MYSELF! BUT I HATE IT! I BOIL WITH RAGE EVERY TIME I LOOK AT IT!
THAT NIGHT WHEN HIS WIFE IS ASLEEP GEORGE DECIDES THAT HE CAN STAND IT NO LONGER...
I'VE GOT TO DO IT! I'LL NEVER REST UNTIL I DO! I'LL GET THE AXE OUT OF THE SUMMER HOUSE AND CHOP THAT CACTUS DOWN RIGHT NOW! MARTHA WILL PROBABLY LEAVE ME, BUT I CAN'T HELP MYSELF!
IT'S LIKE SOME STRANGE FORCE IN ME, DRIVING ME! IT'S A VOICE, WARNING ME! SOMEHOW I KNOW THAT EITHER THE CACTUS GOES OR SOMETHING TERRIBLE IS GOING TO HAPPEN!
2

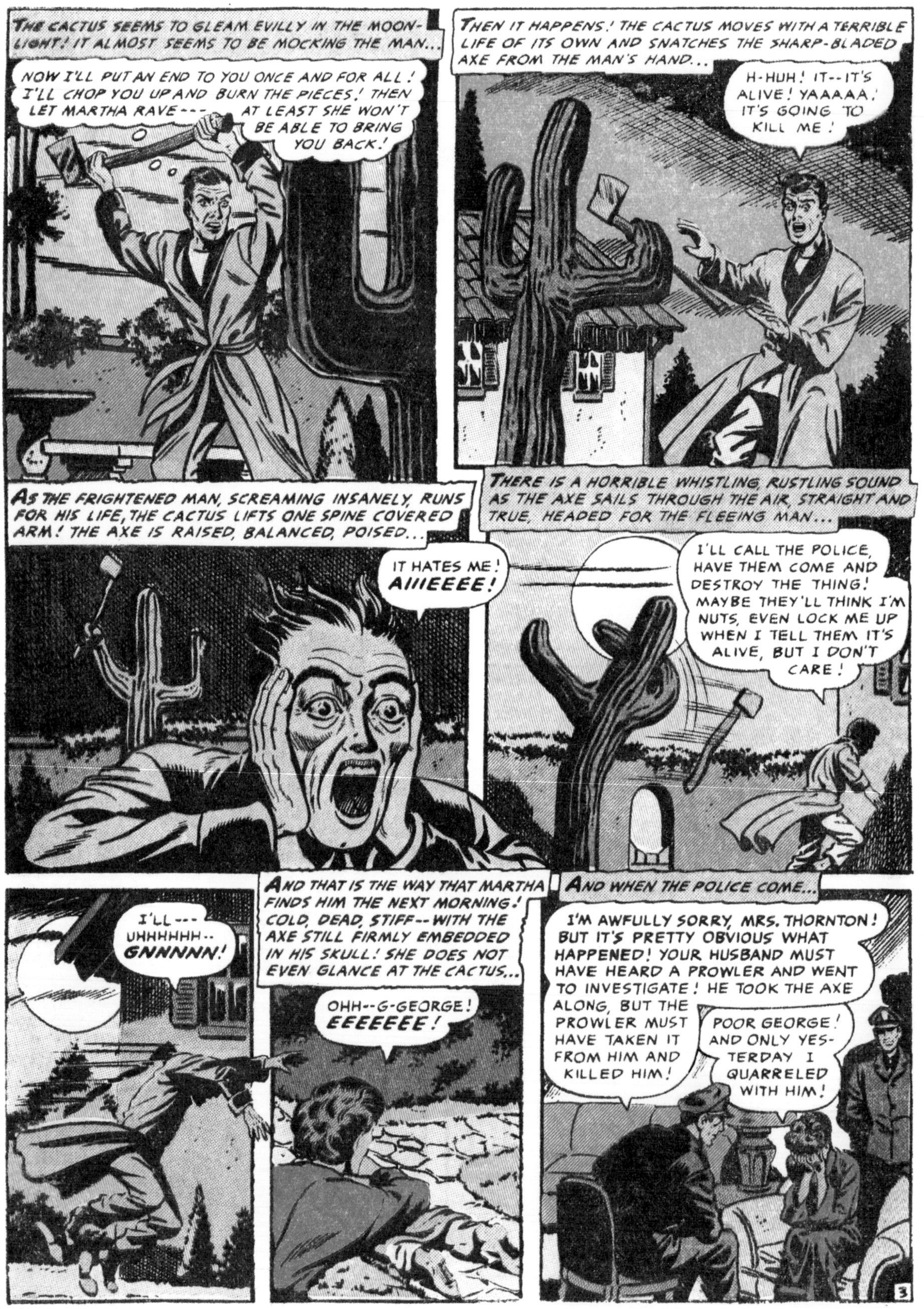
THE CACTUS SEEMS TO GLEAM EVILLY IN THE MOON-LIGHT! IT ALMOST SEEMS TO BE MOCKING THE MAN...
NOW I'LL PUT AN END TO YOU ONCE AND FOR ALL! I'LL CHOP YOU UP AND BURN THE PIECES! THEN LET MARTHA RAVE--- AT LEAST SHE WON'T BE ABLE TO BRING YOU BACK!
THEN IT HAPPENS! THE CACTUS MOVES WITH A TERRIBLE LIFE OF ITS OWN AND SNATCHES THE SHARP-BLADED AXE FROM THE MAN'S HAND...
H-HUH! IT--IT'S ALIVE! YAAAAA! IT'S GOING TO KILL ME!
AS THE FRIGHTENED MAN, SCREAMING INSANELY, RUNS FOR HIS LIFE, THE CACTUS LIFTS ONE SPINE COVERED ARM! THE AXE IS RAISED, BALANCED, POISED...
IT HATES ME! AIIEEEE!
THERE IS A HORRIBLE WHISTLING, RUSTLING SOUND AS THE AXE SAILS THROUGH THE AIR, STRAIGHT AND TRUE, HEADED FOR THE FLEEING MAN...
I'LL CALL THE POLICE, HAVE THEM COME AND DESTROY THE THING! MAYBE THEY'LL THINK I'M NUTS, EVEN LOCK ME UP WHEN I TELL THEM IT'S ALIVE, BUT I DON'T CARE!
I'LL--- UHHHHHH.. GNNNNN!
AND THAT IS THE WAY THAT MARTHA FINDS HIM THE NEXT MORNING! COLD, DEAD, STIFF--WITH THE AXE STILL FIRMLY EMBEDDED IN HIS SKULL! SHE DOES NOT EVEN GLANCE AT THE CACTUS...
OHH--G-GEORGE! EEEEEEE!
AND WHEN THE POLICE COME...
I'M AWFULLY SORRY, MRS. THORNTON! BUT IT'S PRETTY OBVIOUS WHAT HAPPENED! YOUR HUSBAND MUST HAVE HEARD A PROWLER AND WENT TO INVESTIGATE! HE TOOK THE AXE ALONG, BUT THE PROWLER MUST HAVE TAKEN IT FROM HIM AND KILLED HIM!
POOR GEORGE! AND ONLY YES-TERDAY I QUARRELED WITH HIM!
3

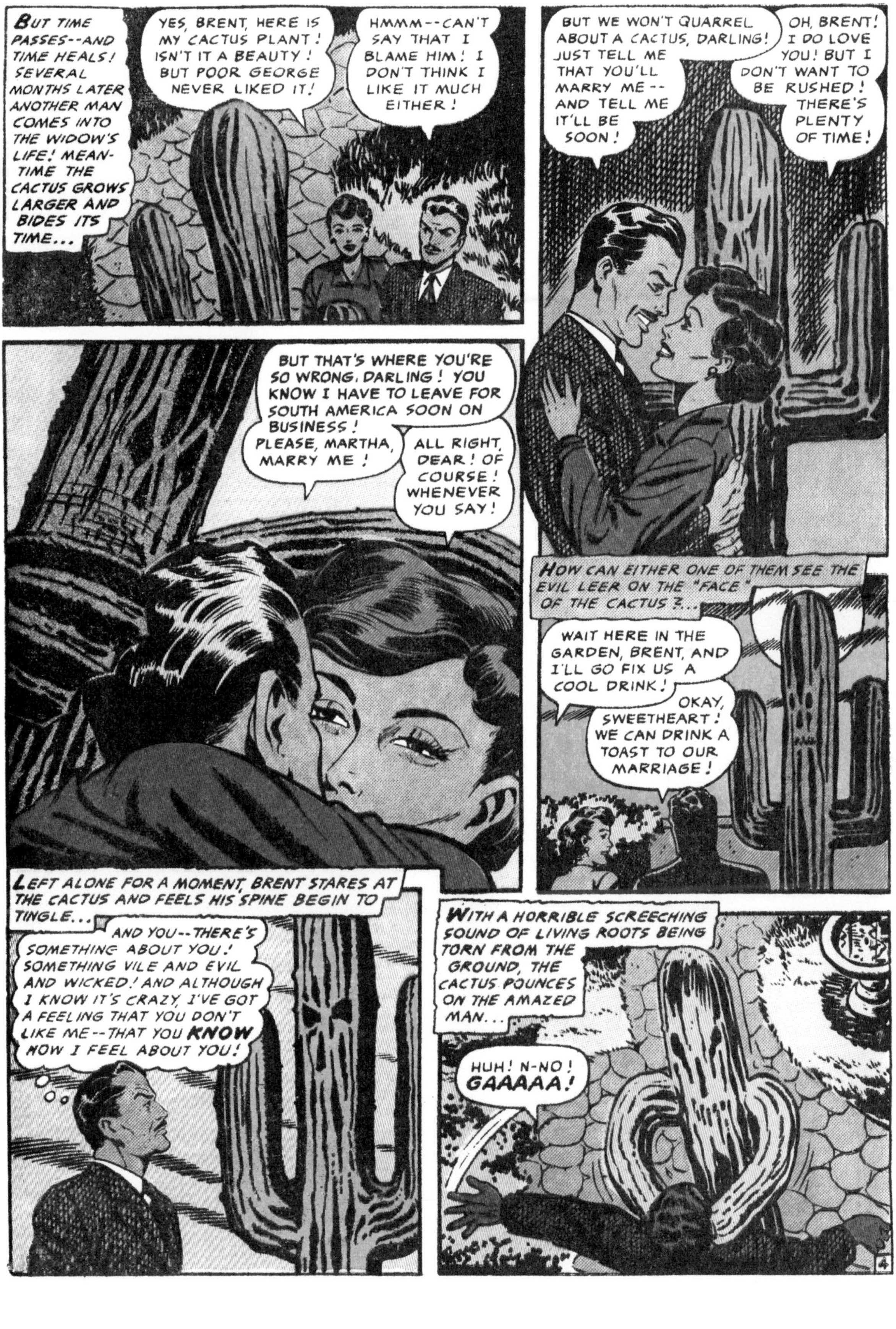
BUT TIME PASSES--AND TIME HEALS! SEVERAL MONTHS LATER ANOTHER MAN COMES INTO THE WIDOW'S LIFE! MEANTIME THE CACTUS GROWS LARGER AND BIDES ITS TIME...
YES, BRENT, HERE IS MY CACTUS PLANT! ISN'T IT A BEAUTY! BUT POOR GEORGE NEVER LIKED IT!
HMMM--CAN'T SAY THAT I BLAME HIM! I DON'T THINK I LIKE IT MUCH EITHER!
BUT WE WON'T QUARREL ABOUT A CACTUS, DARLING! JUST TELL ME THAT YOU'LL MARRY ME--AND TELL ME IT'LL BE SOON!
OH, BRENT! I DO LOVE YOU! BUT I DON'T WANT TO BE RUSHED! THERE'S PLENTY OF TIME!
BUT THAT'S WHERE YOU'RE SO WRONG, DARLING! YOU KNOW I HAVE TO LEAVE FOR SOUTH AMERICA SOON ON BUSINESS! PLEASE, MARTHA, MARRY ME!
ALL RIGHT, DEAR! OF COURSE! WHENEVER YOU SAY!
HOW CAN EITHER ONE OF THEM SEE THE EVIL LEER ON THE "FACE" OF THE CACTUS?...
WAIT HERE IN THE GARDEN, BRENT, AND I'LL GO FIX US A COOL DRINK!
OKAY, SWEETHEART! WE CAN DRINK A TOAST TO OUR MARRIAGE!
LEFT ALONE FOR A MOMENT, BRENT STARES AT THE CACTUS AND FEELS HIS SPINE BEGIN TO TINGLE...
AND YOU--THERE'S SOMETHING ABOUT YOU! SOMETHING VILE AND EVIL AND WICKED! AND ALTHOUGH I KNOW IT'S CRAZY, I'VE GOT A FEELING THAT YOU DON'T LIKE ME--THAT YOU KNOW HOW I FEEL ABOUT YOU!
WITH A HORRIBLE SCREECHING SOUND OF LIVING ROOTS BEING TORN FROM THE GROUND, THE CACTUS POUNCES ON THE AMAZED MAN...
HUH! N-NO! GAAAAA!
4

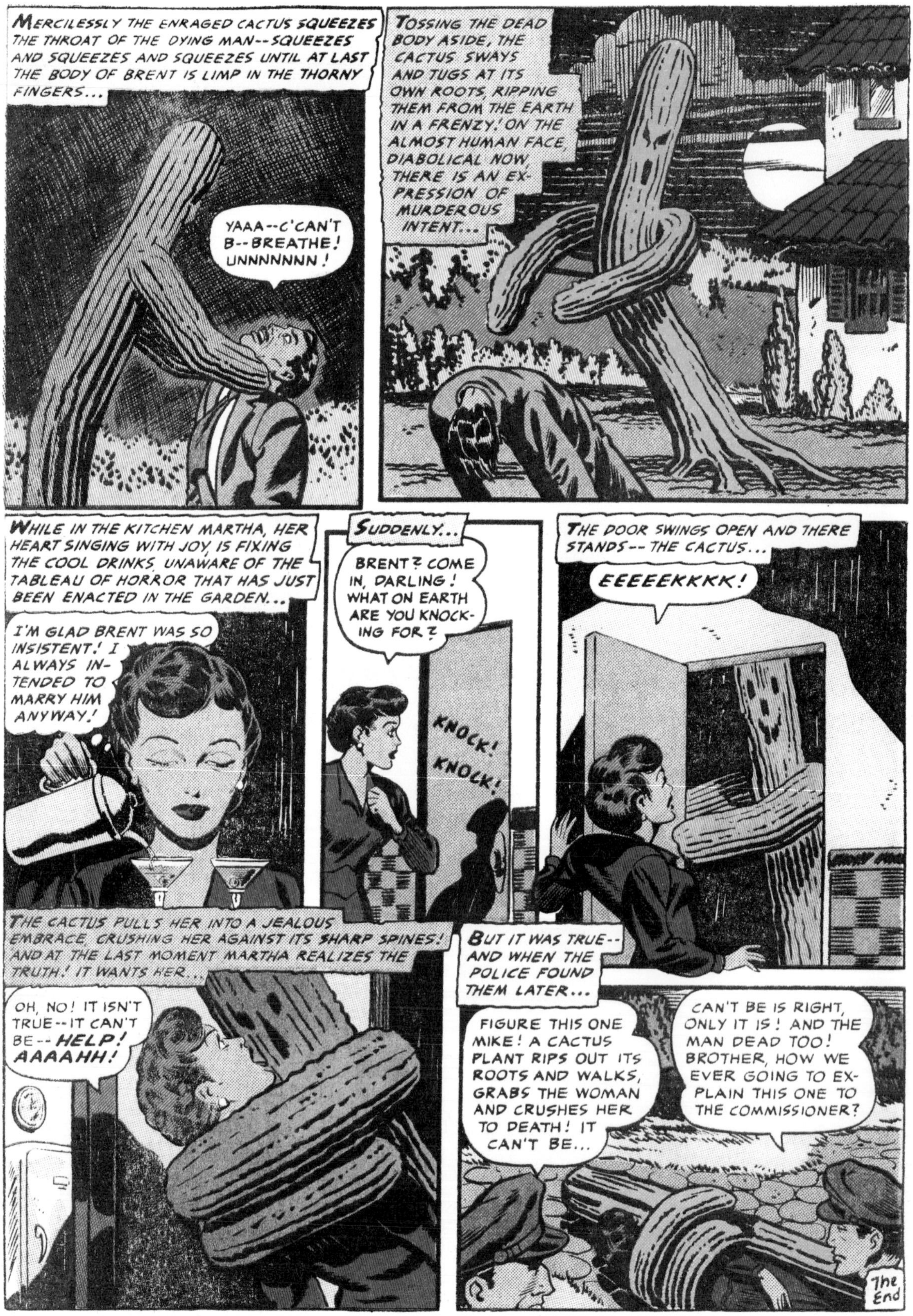
MERCILESSLY THE ENRAGED CACTUS SQUEEZES THE THROAT OF THE DYING MAN--SQUEEZES AND SQUEEZES AND SQUEEZES UNTIL AT LAST THE BODY OF BRENT IS LIMP IN THE THORNY FINGERS...
YAAA--C'CAN'T B--BREATHE! UNNNNNNN!
TOSSING THE DEAD BODY ASIDE, THE CACTUS SWAYS AND TUGS AT ITS OWN ROOTS, RIPPING THEM FROM THE EARTH IN A FRENZY! ON THE ALMOST HUMAN FACE DIABOLICAL NOW, THERE IS AN EXPRESSION OF MURDEROUS INTENT...
WHILE IN THE KITCHEN MARTHA, HER HEART SINGING WITH JOY, IS FIXING THE COOL DRINKS, UNAWARE OF THE TABLEAU OF HORROR THAT HAS JUST BEEN ENACTED IN THE GARDEN...
I'M GLAD BRENT WAS SO INSISTENT! I ALWAYS INTENDED TO MARRY HIM ANYWAY!
SUDDENLY...
BRENT? COME IN, DARLING! WHAT ON EARTH ARE YOU KNOCKING FOR?
KNOCK! KNOCK!
THE DOOR SWINGS OPEN AND THERE STANDS-- THE CACTUS...
EEEEEKKKK!
THE CACTUS PULLS HER INTO A JEALOUS EMBRACE, CRUSHING HER AGAINST ITS SHARP SPINES! AND AT THE LAST MOMENT MARTHA REALIZES THE TRUTH! IT WANTS HER...
OH, NO! IT ISN'T TRUE--IT CAN'T BE--HELP! AAAAHH!
BUT IT WAS TRUE--AND WHEN THE POLICE FOUND THEM LATER...
FIGURE THIS ONE MIKE! A CACTUS PLANT RIPS OUT ITS ROOTS AND WALKS, GRABS THE WOMAN AND CRUSHES HER TO DEATH! IT CAN'T BE...
CAN'T BE IS RIGHT, ONLY IT IS! AND THE MAN DEAD TOO! BROTHER, HOW WE EVER GOING TO EXPLAIN THIS ONE TO THE COMMISSIONER?
The End

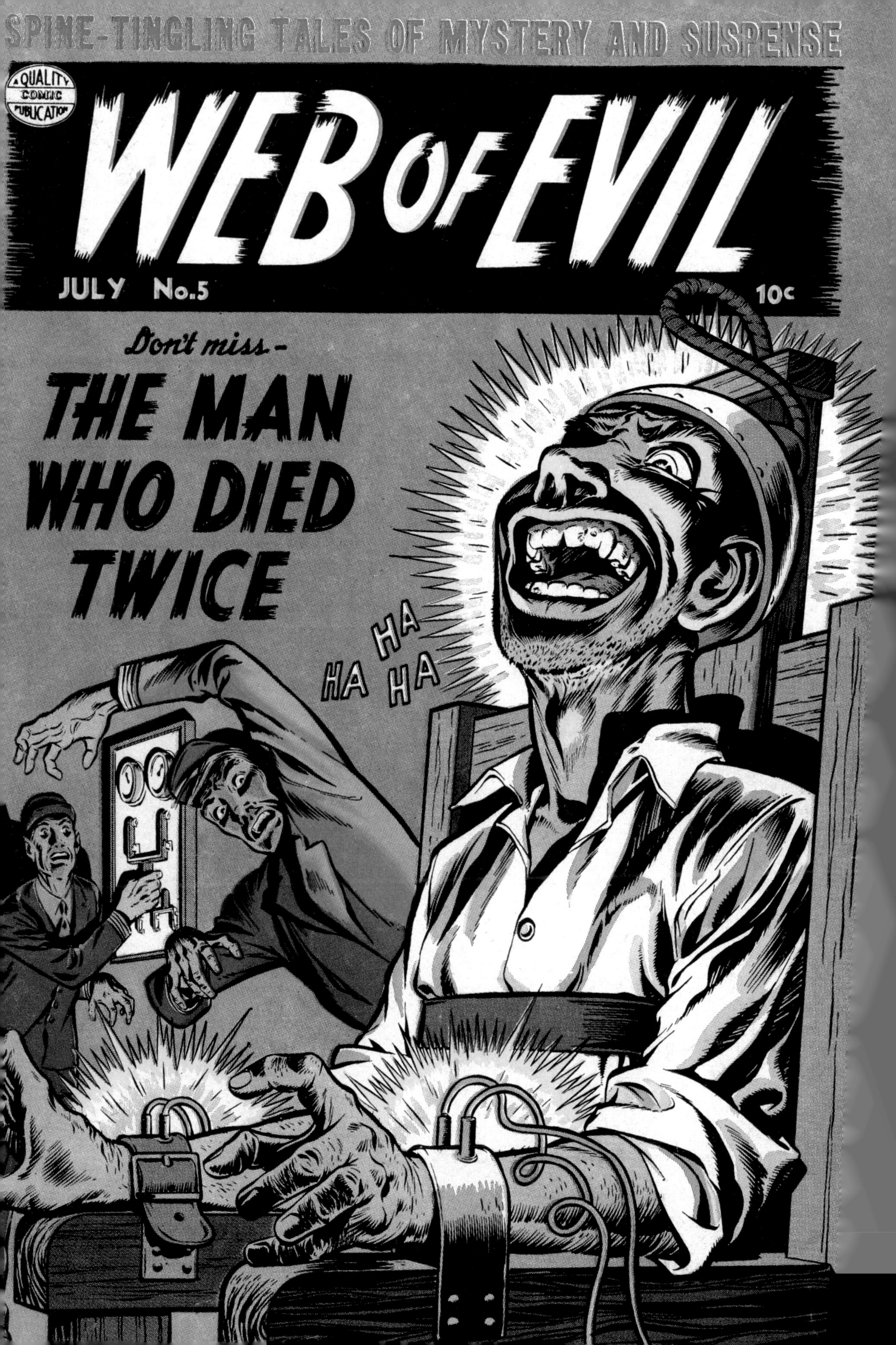

SPINE-TINGLING TALES OF MYSTERY AND SUSPENSE
A QUALITY COMIC PUBLICATION
WEB OF EVIL
JULY No.5
10¢
Don't miss -
THE MAN WHO DIED TWICE
HA HA HA HA

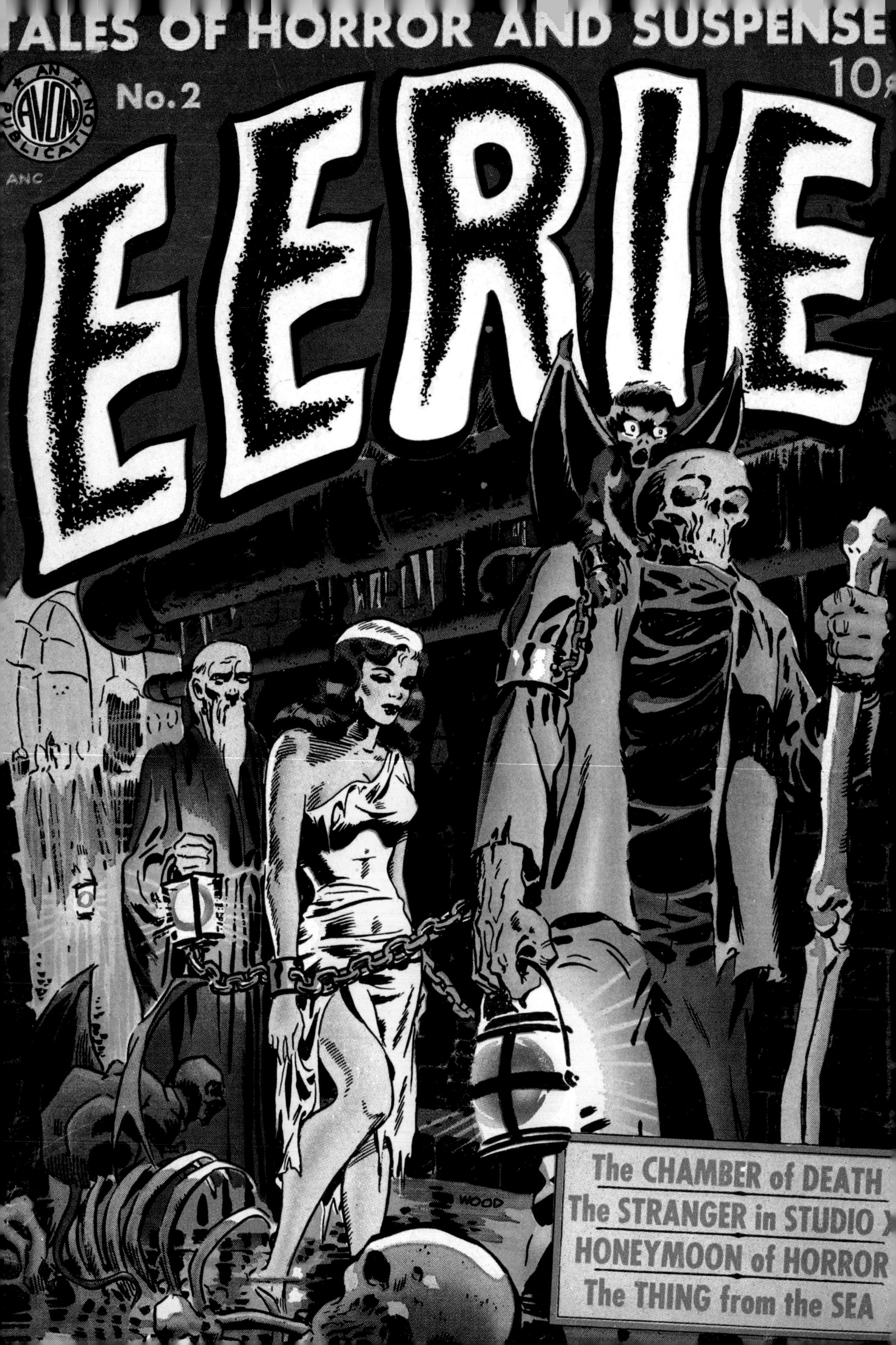

TALES OF HORROR AND SUSPENSE
AN AVON PUBLICATION
No. 2
10¢
ANC
EERIE
WOOD
The CHAMBER of DEATH
The STRANGER in STUDIO X
HONEYMOON of HORROR
The THING from the SEA

WITCHES TALES
WE DARE YOU TO READ THESE EERIE TALES OF SUPERNATURAL HORROR!
No. 25 JUNE 10c
WITCHES TALES
WEIRD YARNS OF UNSEEN TERRORS
WHAT HAPPENS AT 8:30 P.M.?

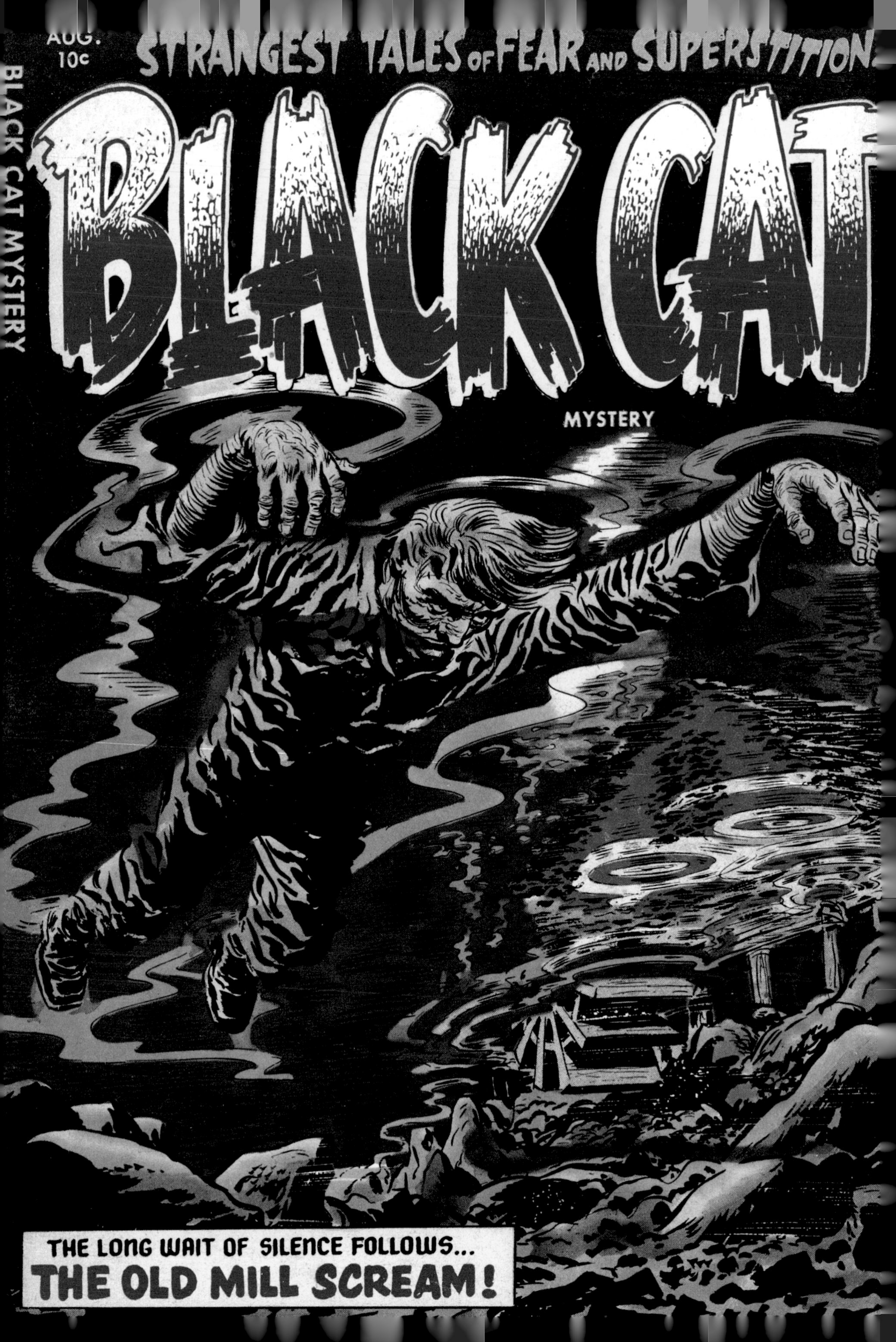
AUG.
10¢
STRANGEST TALES OF FEAR AND SUPERSTITION
BLACK CAT
MYSTERY
BLACK CAT MYSTERY
THE LONG WAIT OF SILENCE FOLLOWS...
THE OLD MILL SCREAM!

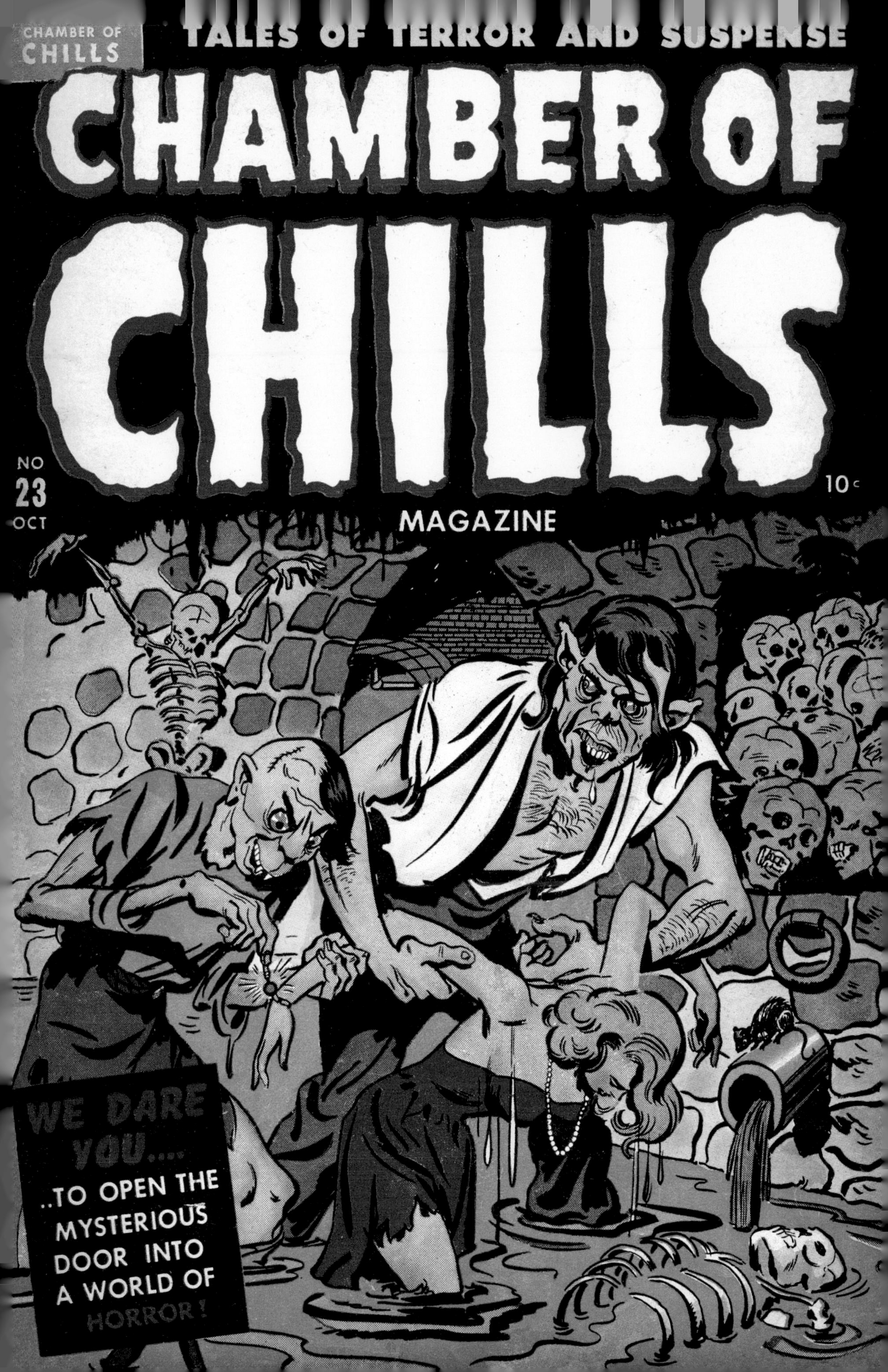
CHAMBER OF CHILLS
TALES OF TERROR AND SUSPENSE
CHAMBER OF CHILLS
NO 23 OCT
10¢
MAGAZINE
WE DARE YOU....
..TO OPEN THE MYSTERIOUS DOOR INTO A WORLD OF HORROR!

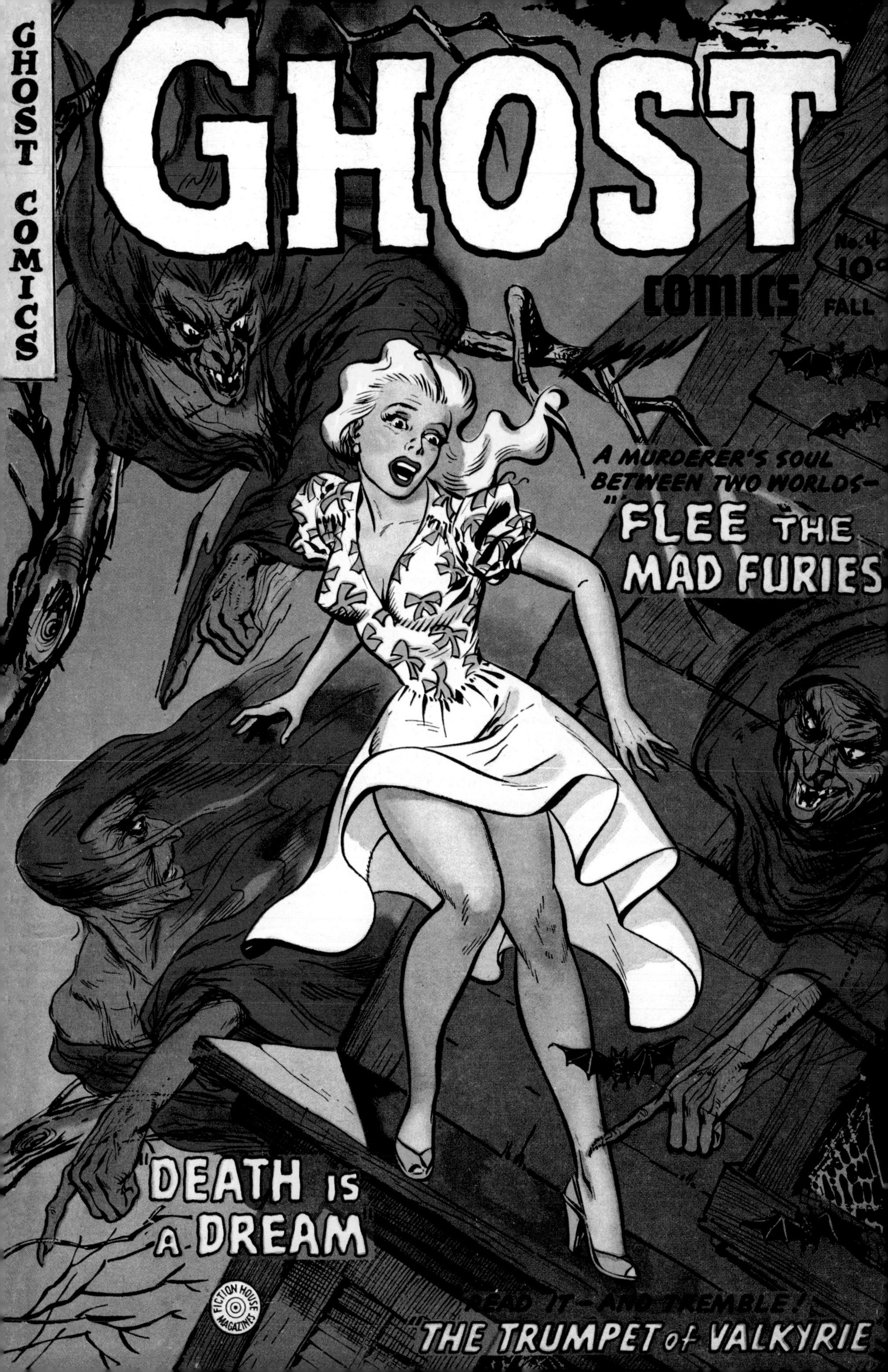
GHOST COMICS
GHOST
COMICS
No.4
10¢
FALL
A MURDERER'S SOUL BETWEEN TWO WORLDS—
"FLEE THE MAD FURIES"
"DEATH IS A DREAM"
FICTION HOUSE MAGAZINES
READ IT—AND TREMBLE!
"THE TRUMPET of VALKYRIE"

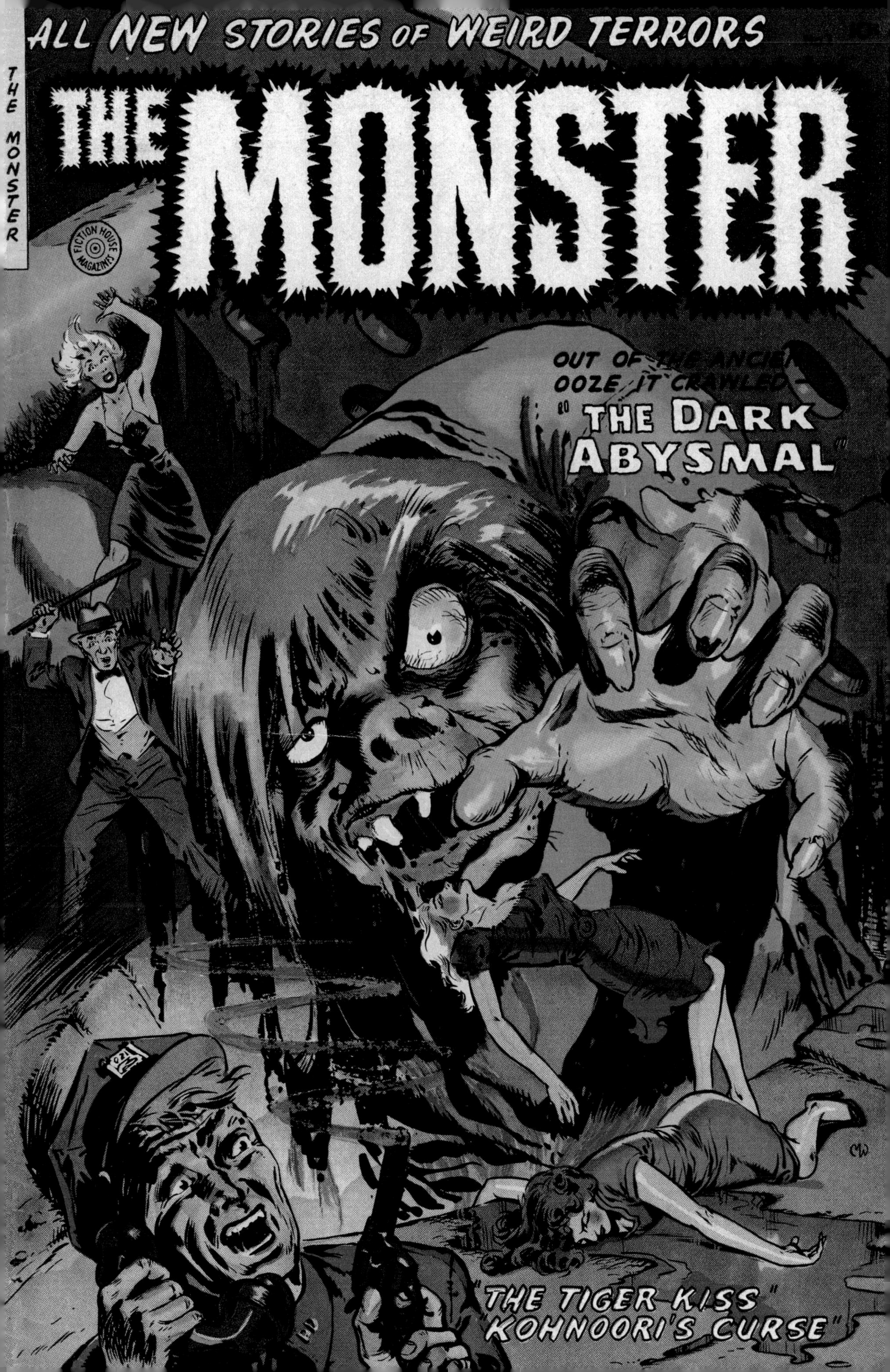
ALL NEW STORIES OF WEIRD TERRORS
THE MONSTER
THE MONSTER
FICTION HOUSE MAGAZINES
OUT OF THE ANCIE
OOZE IT CRAWLED
"THE DARK ABYSMAL"
"THE TIGER KISS"
KOHNOORI'S CURSE"

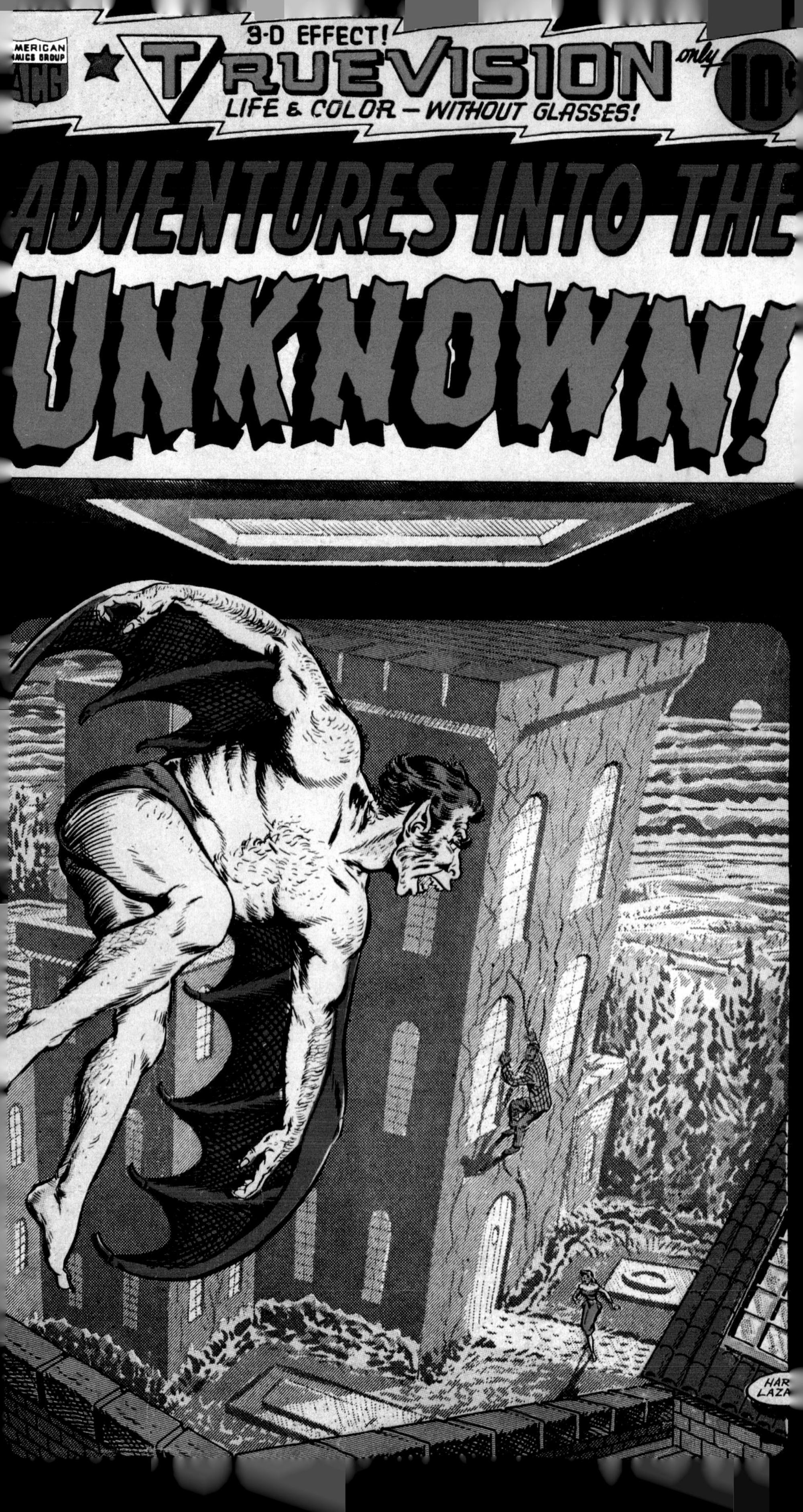
AMERICAN COMICS GROUP
3-D EFFECT!
TRUEVISION
LIFE & COLOR—WITHOUT GLASSES!
only 10¢
ADVENTURES INTO THE
UNKNOWN!
HAR
LAZA

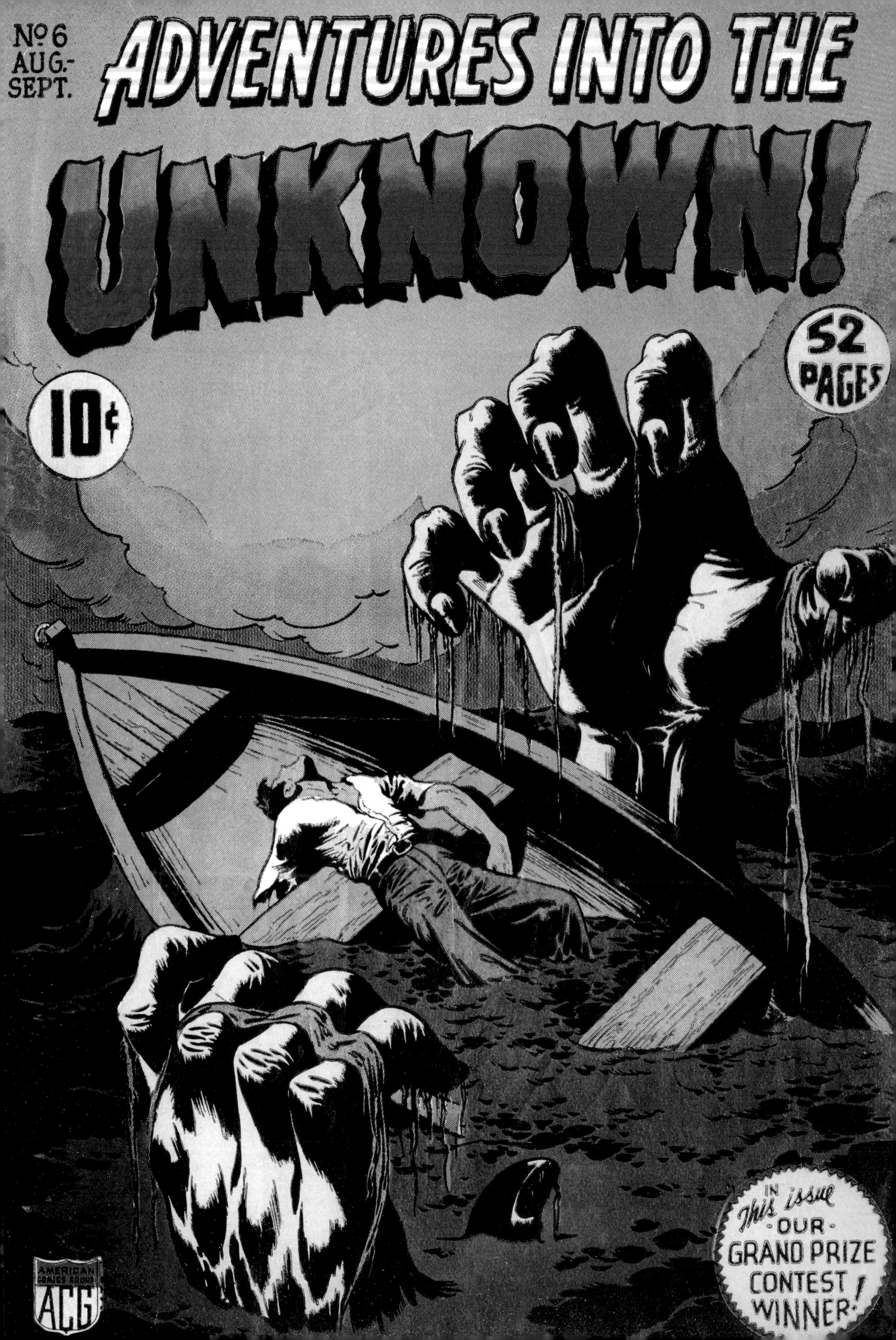
No 6
AUG.-
SEPT.
ADVENTURES INTO THE
UNKNOWN!
10¢
52
PAGES
AMERICAN
COMICS GROUP
ACG
IN
This issue
-OUR-
GRAND PRIZE
CONTEST
WINNER!

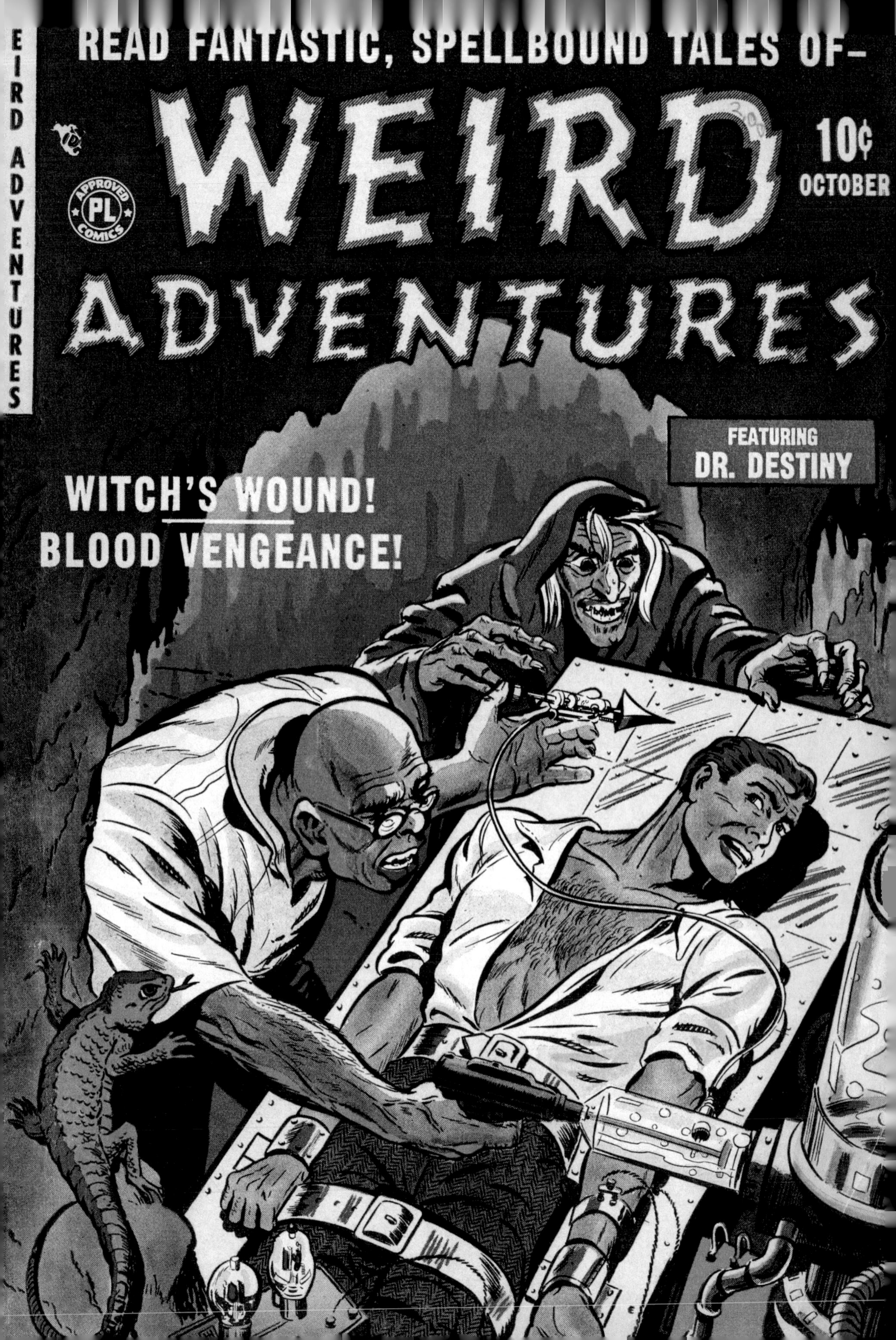
READ FANTASTIC, SPELLBOUND TALES OF–
WEIRD ADVENTURES
10¢
OCTOBER
APPROVED PL COMICS
EIRD ADVENTURES
FEATURING DR. DESTINY
WITCH'S WOUND!
BLOOD VENGEANCE!

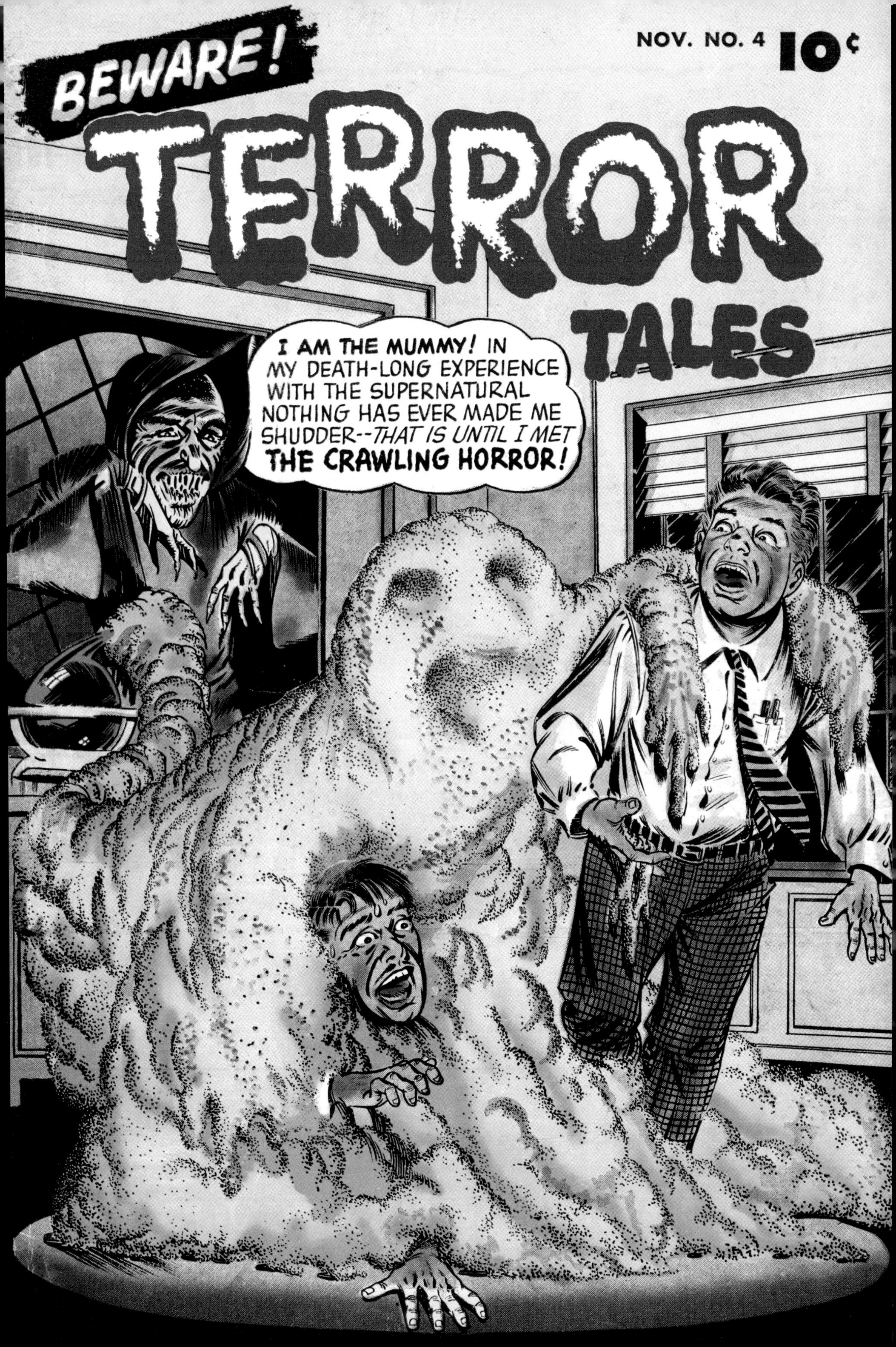

NOV. NO. 4 10¢
BEWARE! TERROR TALES
I AM THE MUMMY! IN MY DEATH-LONG EXPERIENCE WITH THE SUPERNATURAL NOTHING HAS EVER MADE ME SHUDDER--THAT IS UNTIL I MET THE CRAWLING HORROR!

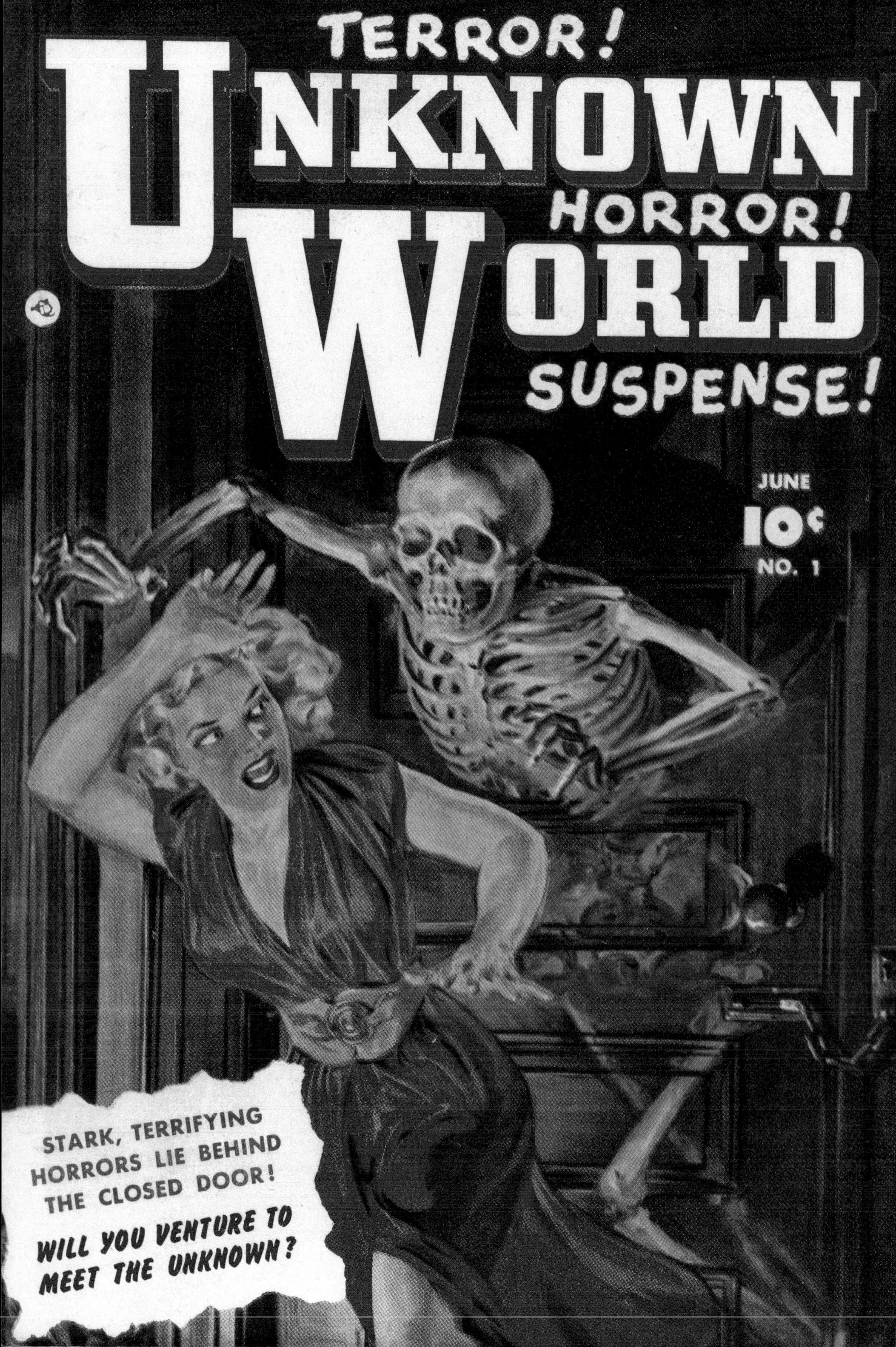
TERROR!
UNKNOWN
HORROR!
WORLD
SUSPENSE!
JUNE
10¢
NO. 1
STARK, TERRIFYING HORRORS LIE BEHIND THE CLOSED DOOR!
WILL YOU VENTURE TO MEET THE UNKNOWN?

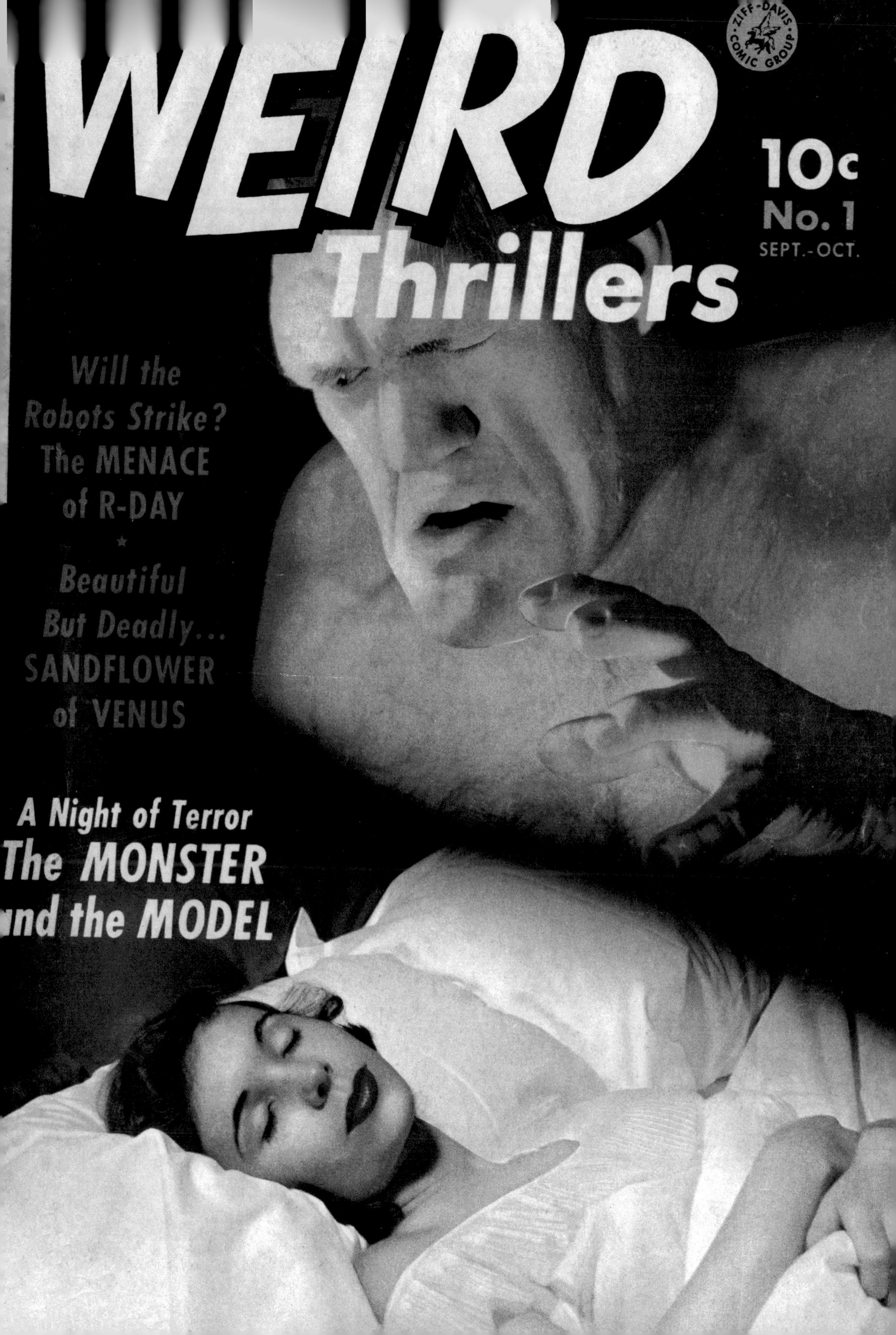
ZIFF-DAVIS COMIC GROUP
WEIRD Thrillers
10c
No. 1
SEPT.-OCT.
Will the Robots Strike? The MENACE of R-DAY
Beautiful But Deadly... SANDFLOWER of VENUS
A Night of Terror
The MONSTER and the MODEL

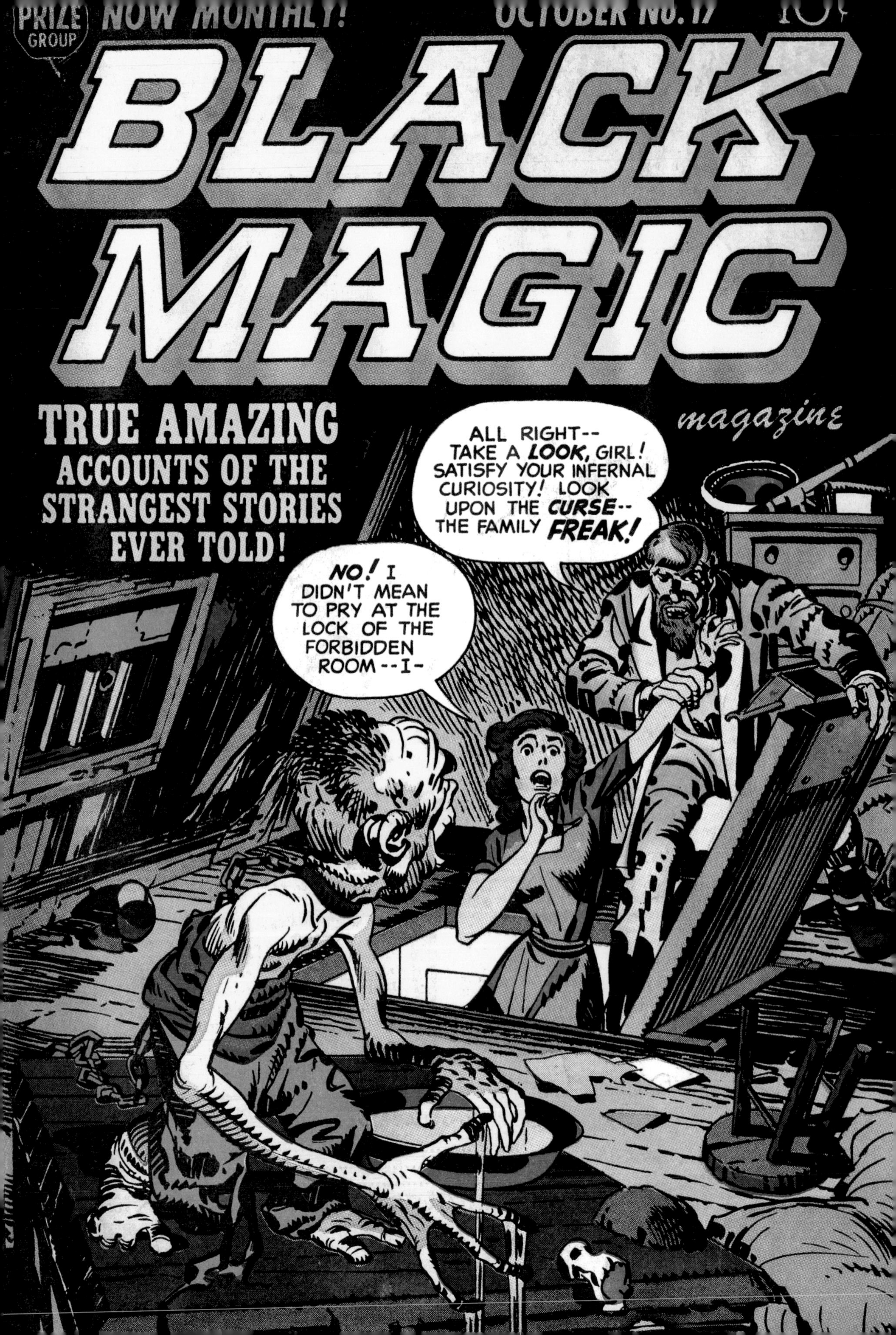
PRIZE GROUP
NOW MONTHLY!
OCTOBER No. 17
10¢
BLACK MAGIC
magazine
TRUE AMAZING ACCOUNTS OF THE STRANGEST STORIES EVER TOLD!
ALL RIGHT-- TAKE A LOOK, GIRL! SATISFY YOUR INFERNAL CURIOSITY! LOOK UPON THE CURSE-- THE FAMILY FREAK!
NO! I DIDN'T MEAN TO PRY AT THE LOCK OF THE FORBIDDEN ROOM --I-

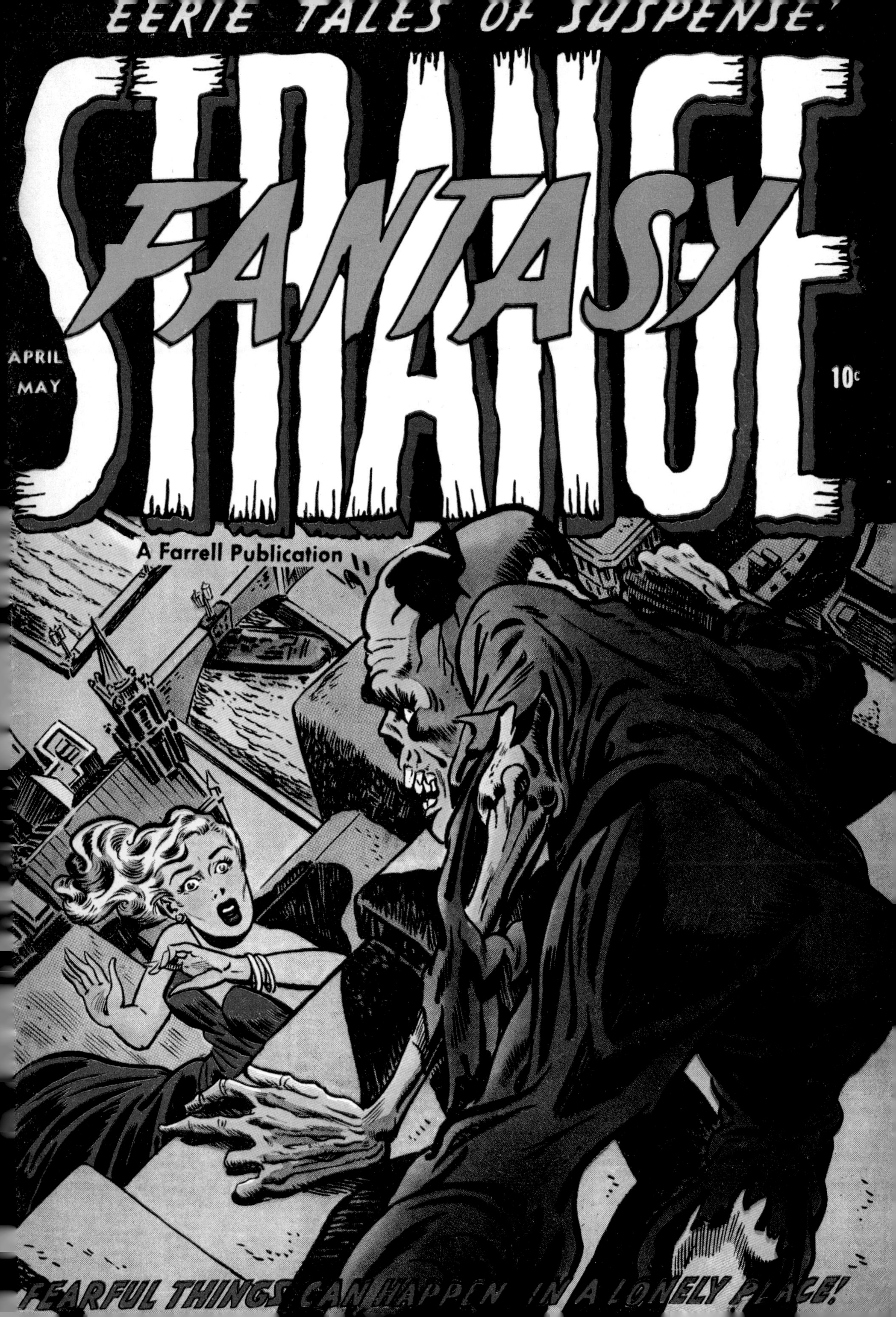
EERIE TALES OF SUSPENSE!
STRANGE FANTASY
APRIL MAY
10¢
A Farrell Publication
FEARFUL THINGS CAN HAPPEN IN A LONELY PLACE!

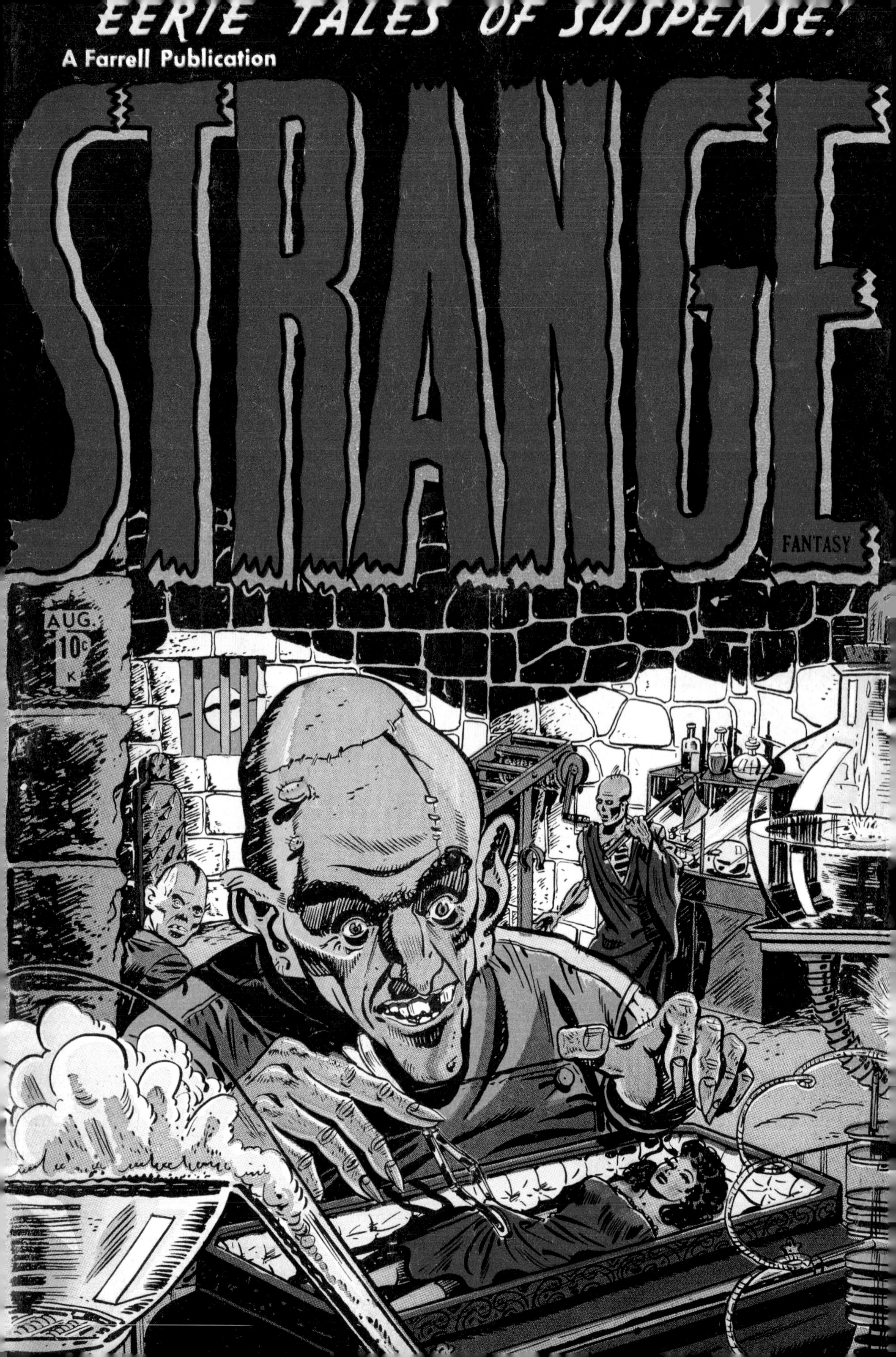
EERIE TALES OF SUSPENSE!
A Farrell Publication
STRANGE
FANTASY
AUG.
10¢
K

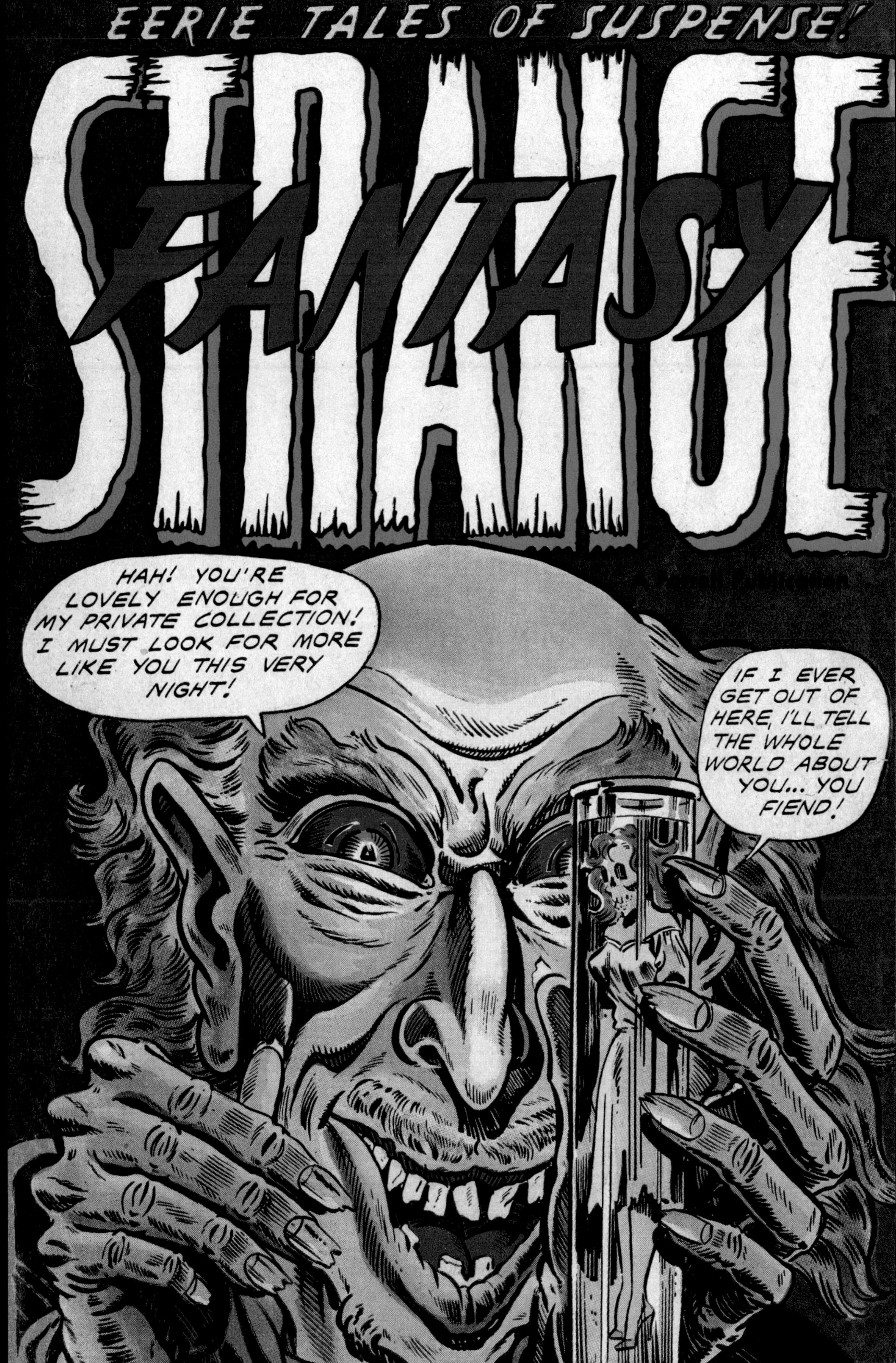
EERIE TALES OF SUSPENSE!
STRANGE
FANTASY
HAH! YOU'RE LOVELY ENOUGH FOR MY PRIVATE COLLECTION! I MUST LOOK FOR MORE LIKE YOU THIS VERY NIGHT!
IF I EVER GET OUT OF HERE, I'LL TELL THE WHOLE WORLD ABOUT YOU... YOU FIEND!

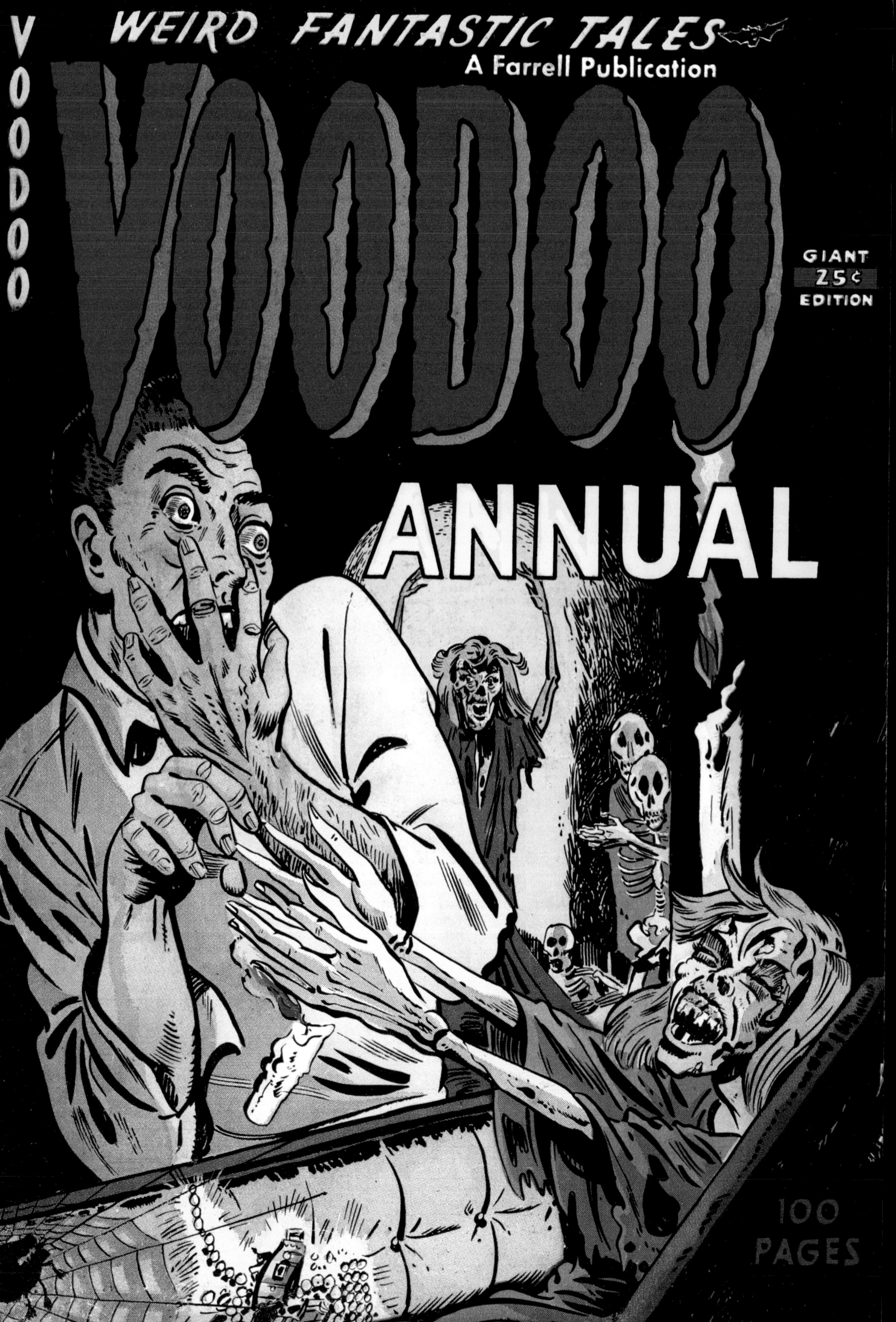
WEIRD FANTASTIC TALES
A Farrell Publication
VOODOO
VOODOO
GIANT 25¢ EDITION
ANNUAL
100 PAGES

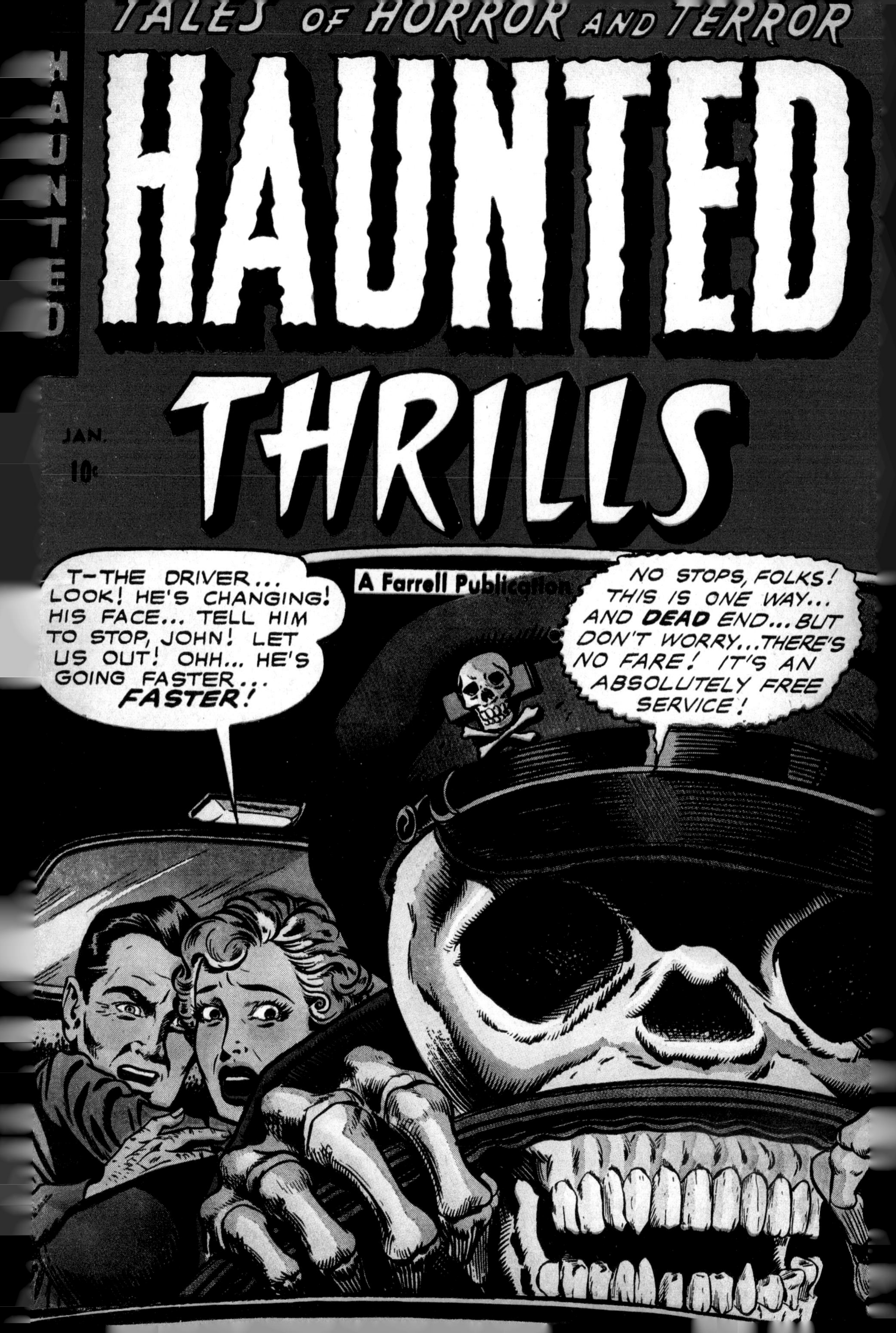
TALES OF HORROR AND TERROR
HAUNTED
HAUNTED THRILLS
JAN.
10¢
A Farrell Publication
T-THE DRIVER... LOOK! HE'S CHANGING! HIS FACE... TELL HIM TO STOP, JOHN! LET US OUT! OHH... HE'S GOING FASTER... FASTER!
NO STOPS, FOLKS! THIS IS ONE WAY... AND DEAD END... BUT DON'T WORRY...THERE'S NO FARE! IT'S AN ABSOLUTELY FREE SERVICE!

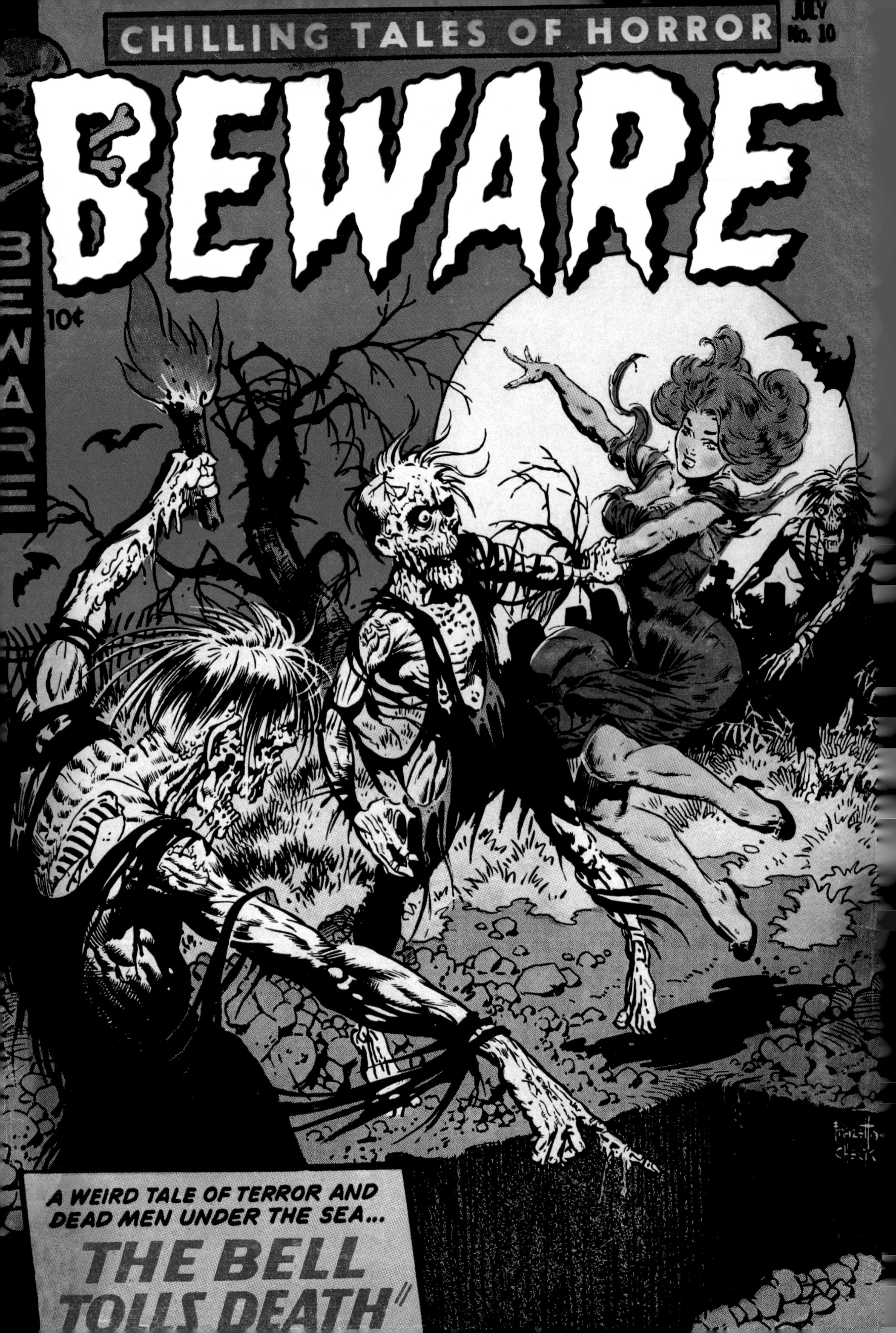
CHILLING TALES OF HORROR
JULY
No. 10
BEWARE
10¢
BEWARE
A WEIRD TALE OF TERROR AND DEAD MEN UNDER THE SEA...
"THE BELL TOLLS DEATH"

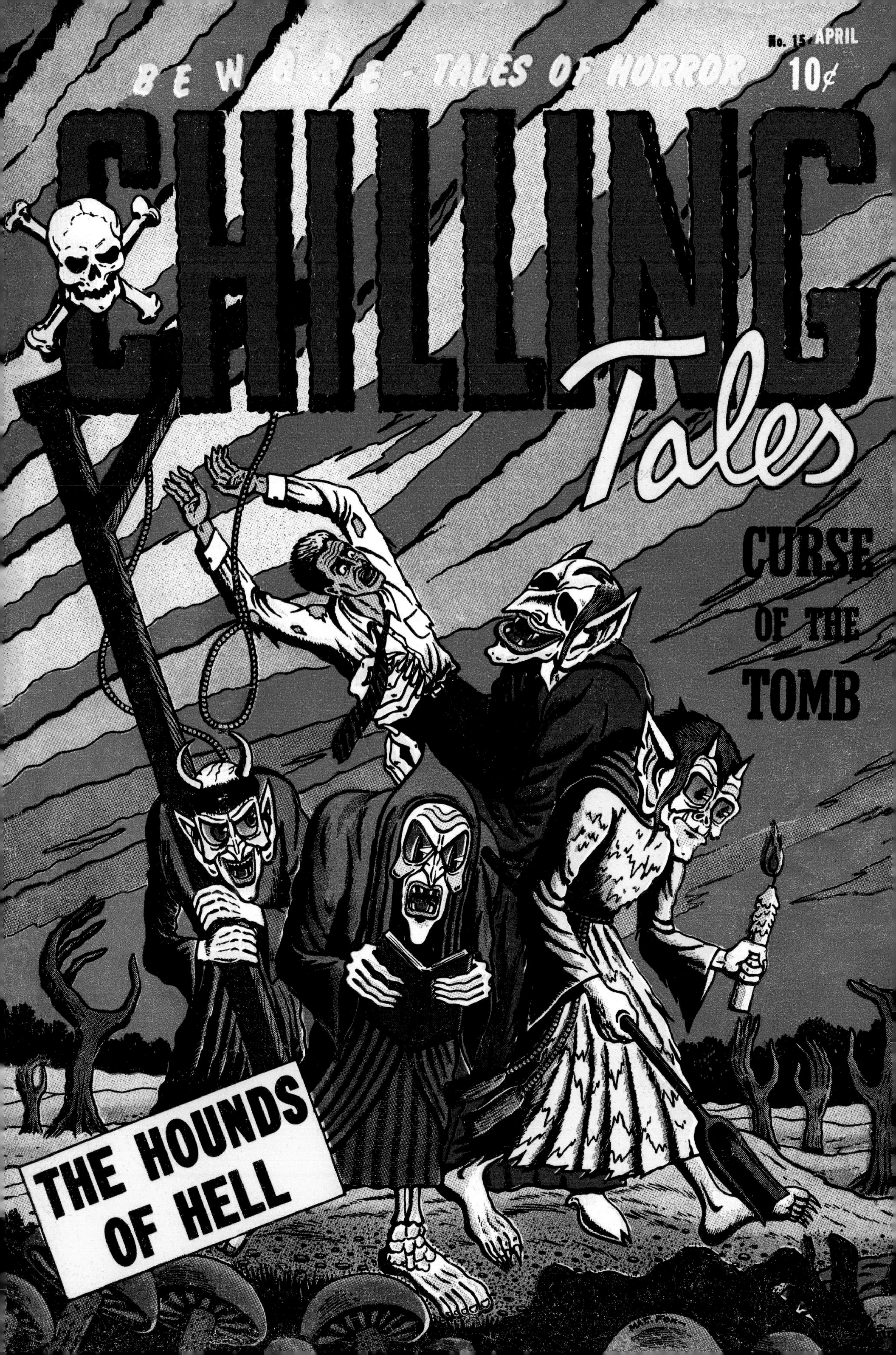
No. 15 APRIL
BEWARE - TALES OF HORROR
10¢
CHILLING Tales
CURSE OF THE TOMB
THE HOUNDS OF HELL

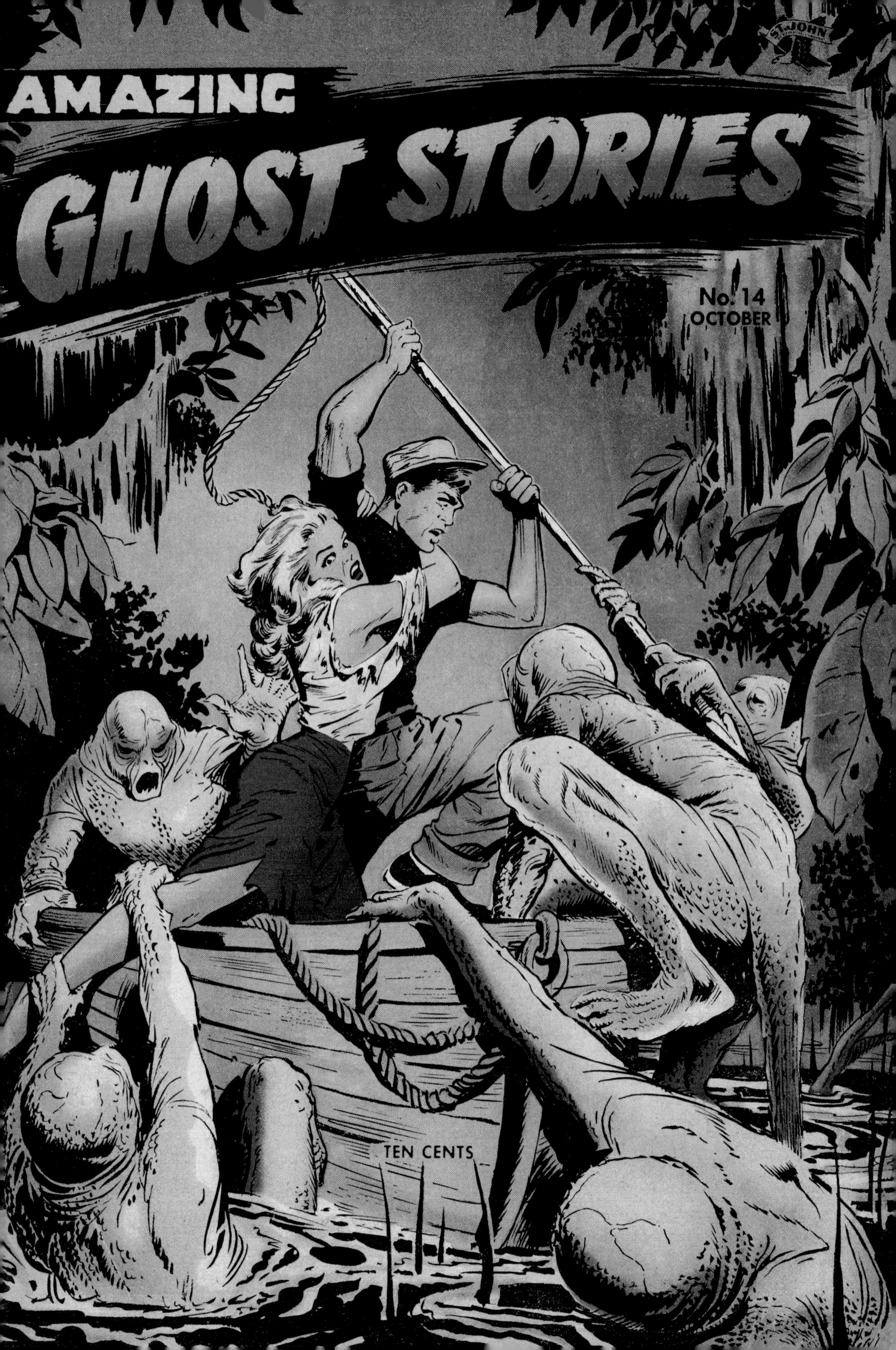

ST. JOHN
AMAZING
GHOST STORIES
No. 14
OCTOBER
TEN CENTS

CONQUEST OF THE UNEARTHLY POWERS

STRANGE TERRORS

St. JOHN

UNSHACKLED FLIGHT INTO NOWHERE

SUPERNATURAL KNIFE OF VENGEANCE

No. 2   TEN CENTS

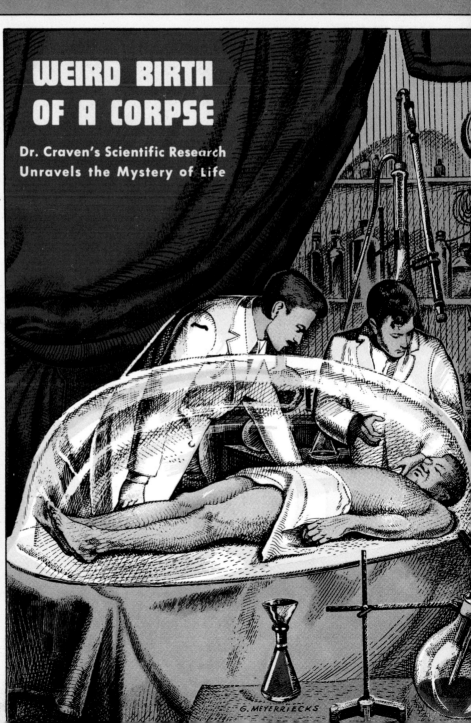

WEIRD BIRTH OF A CORPSE

Dr. Craven's Scientific Research Unravels the Mystery of Life

G. MEYERRIECKS

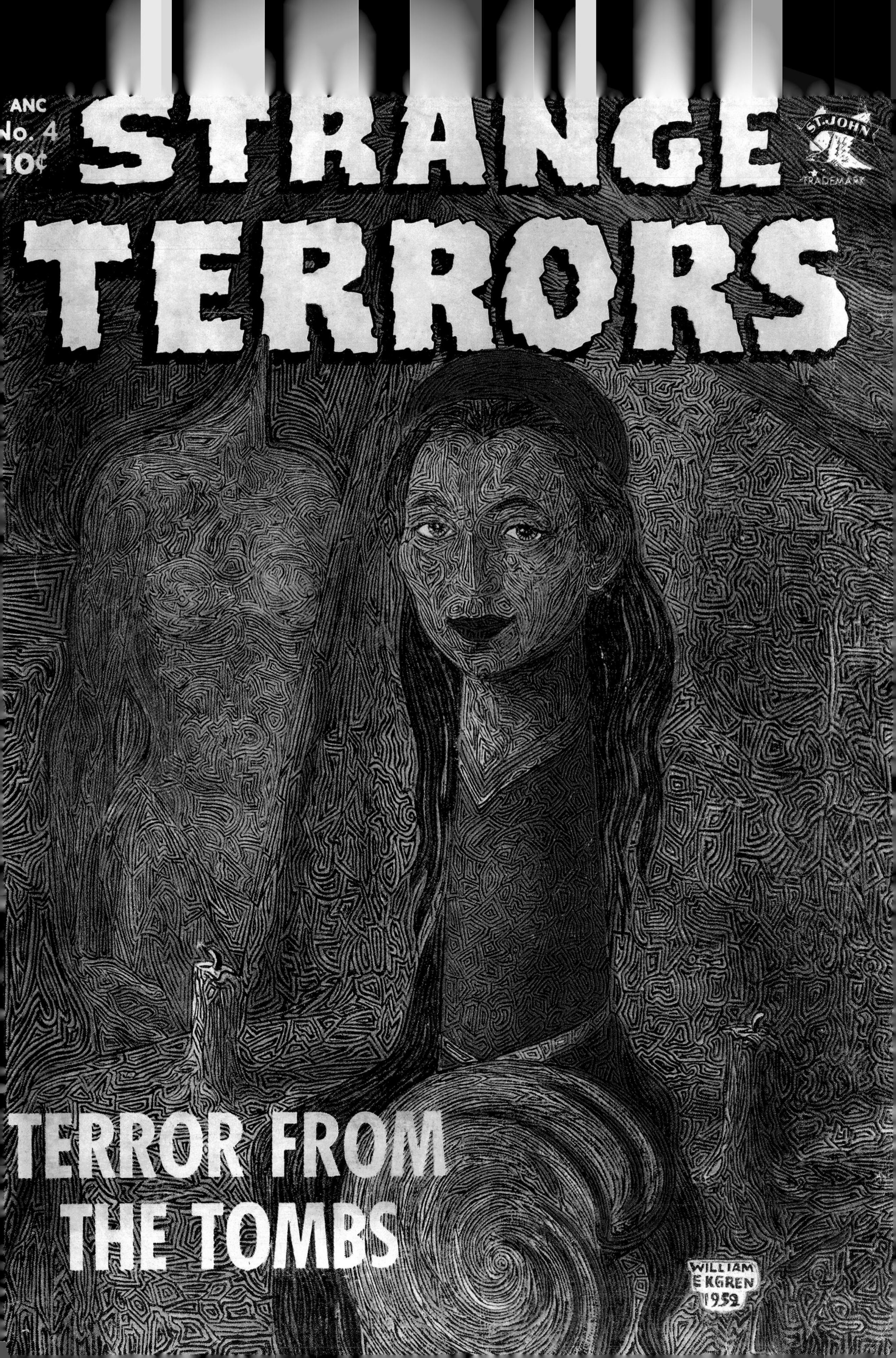
ANC
No. 4
10¢
STRANGE TERRORS
ST. JOHN
TRADEMARK
TERROR FROM THE TOMBS
WILLIAM EKGREN 1952

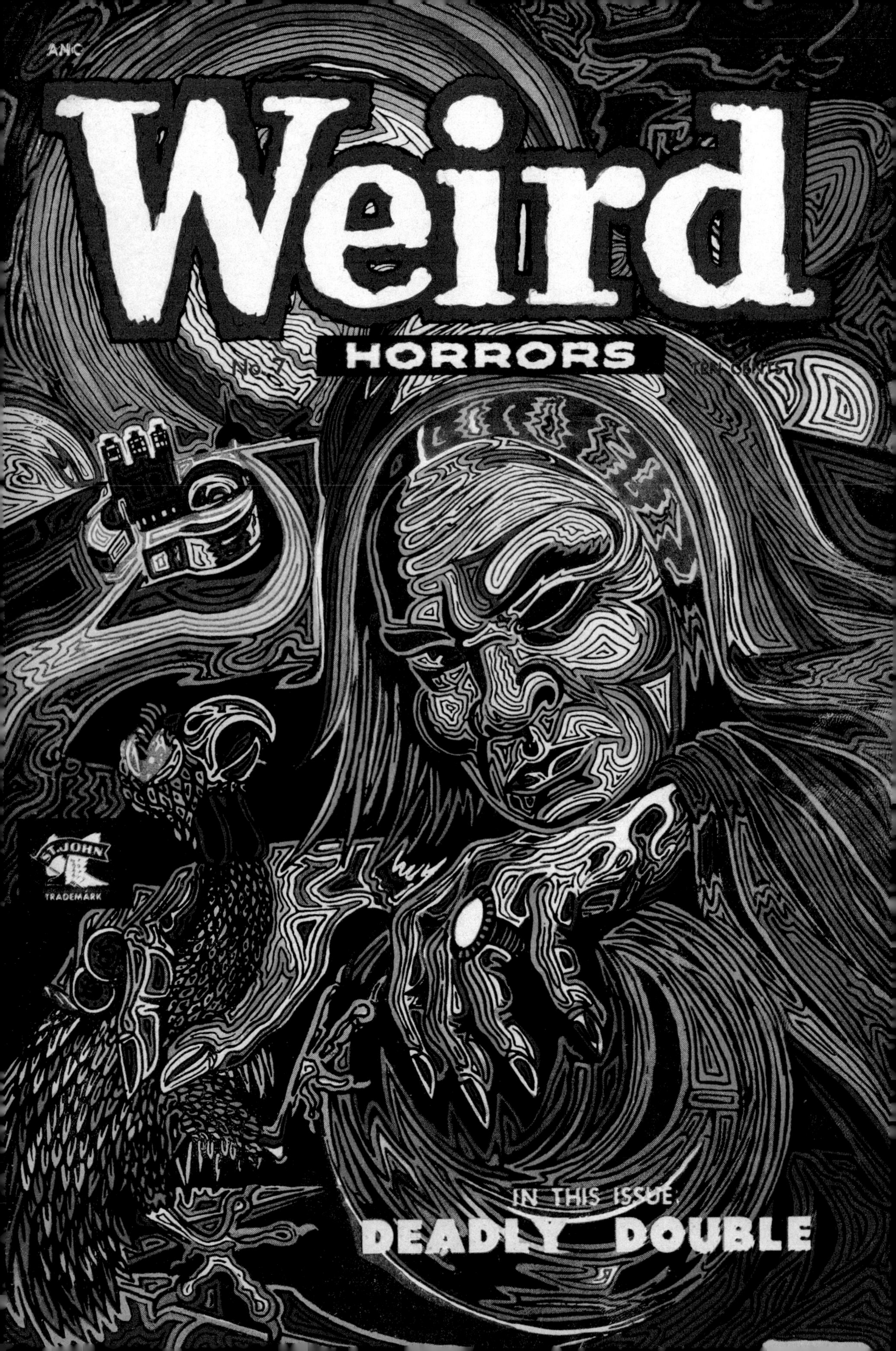
ANC
Weird
HORRORS
No. 7
TEN CENTS
ST. JOHN
TRADEMARK
IN THIS ISSUE:
DEADLY DOUBLE

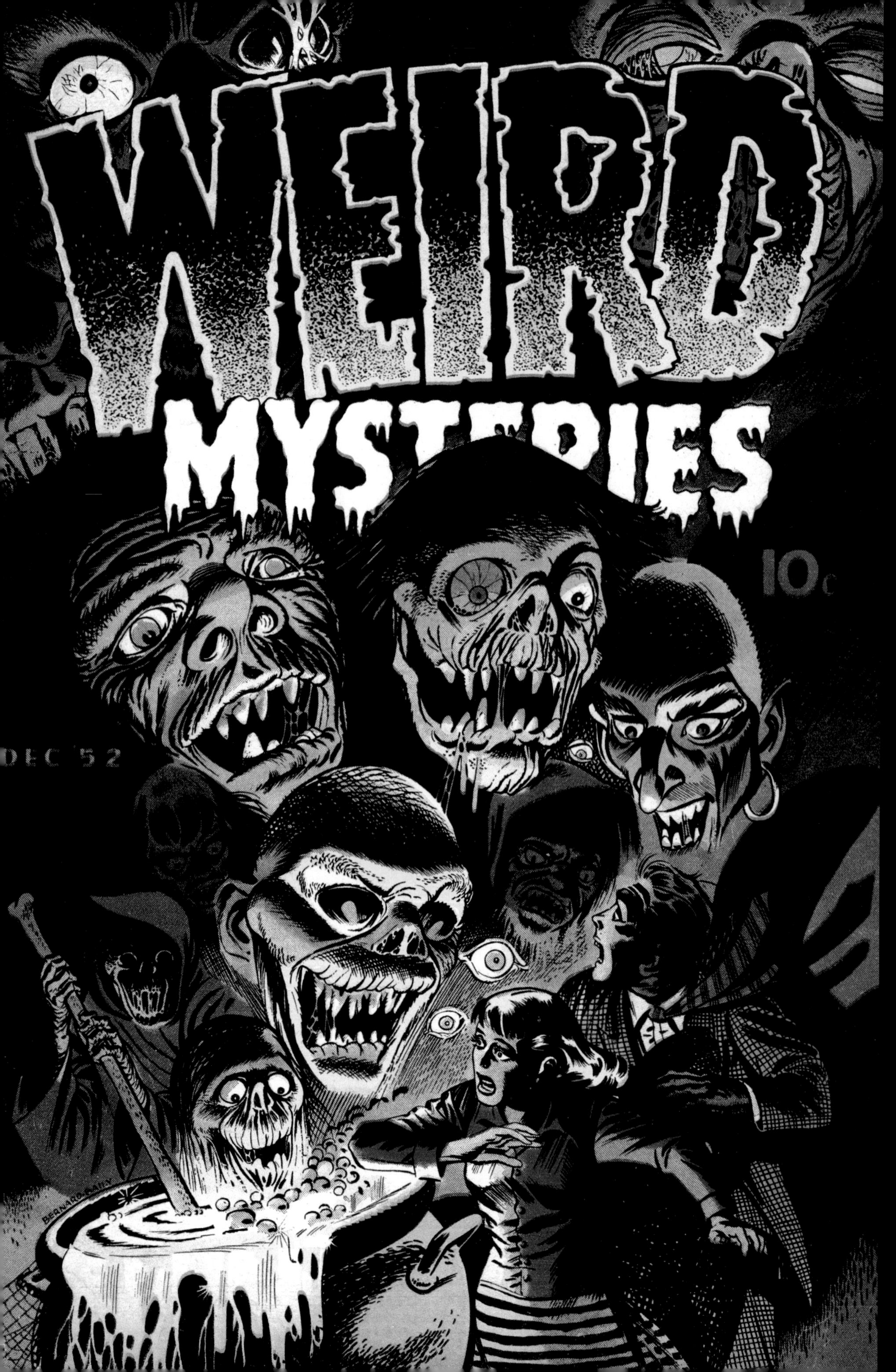
WEIRD
MYSTERIES
10c
DEC 52

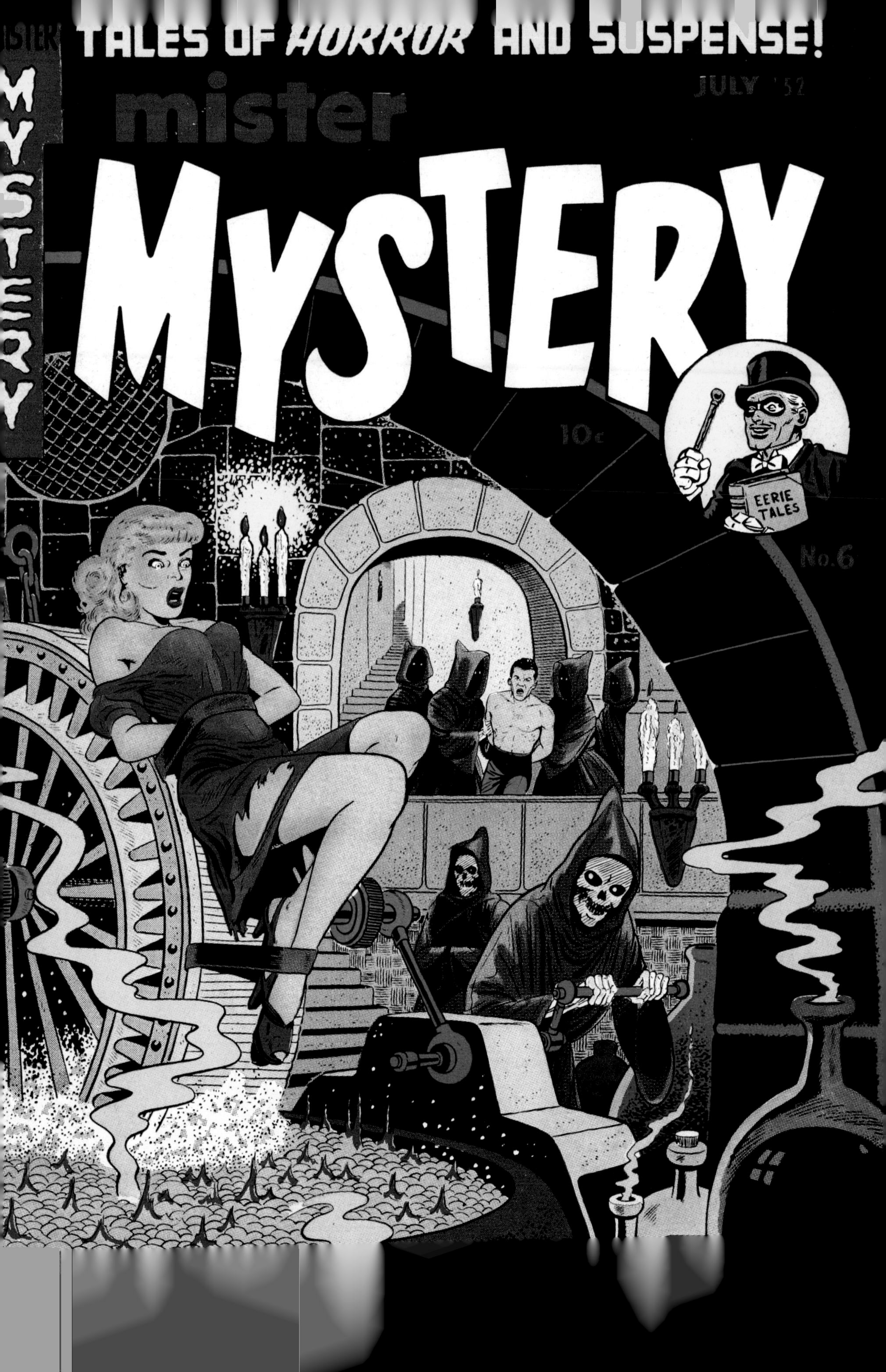

MISTER
TALES OF HORROR AND SUSPENSE!
JULY '52
mister
MYSTERY
10¢
EERIE TALES
No.6
MISTER MYSTERY

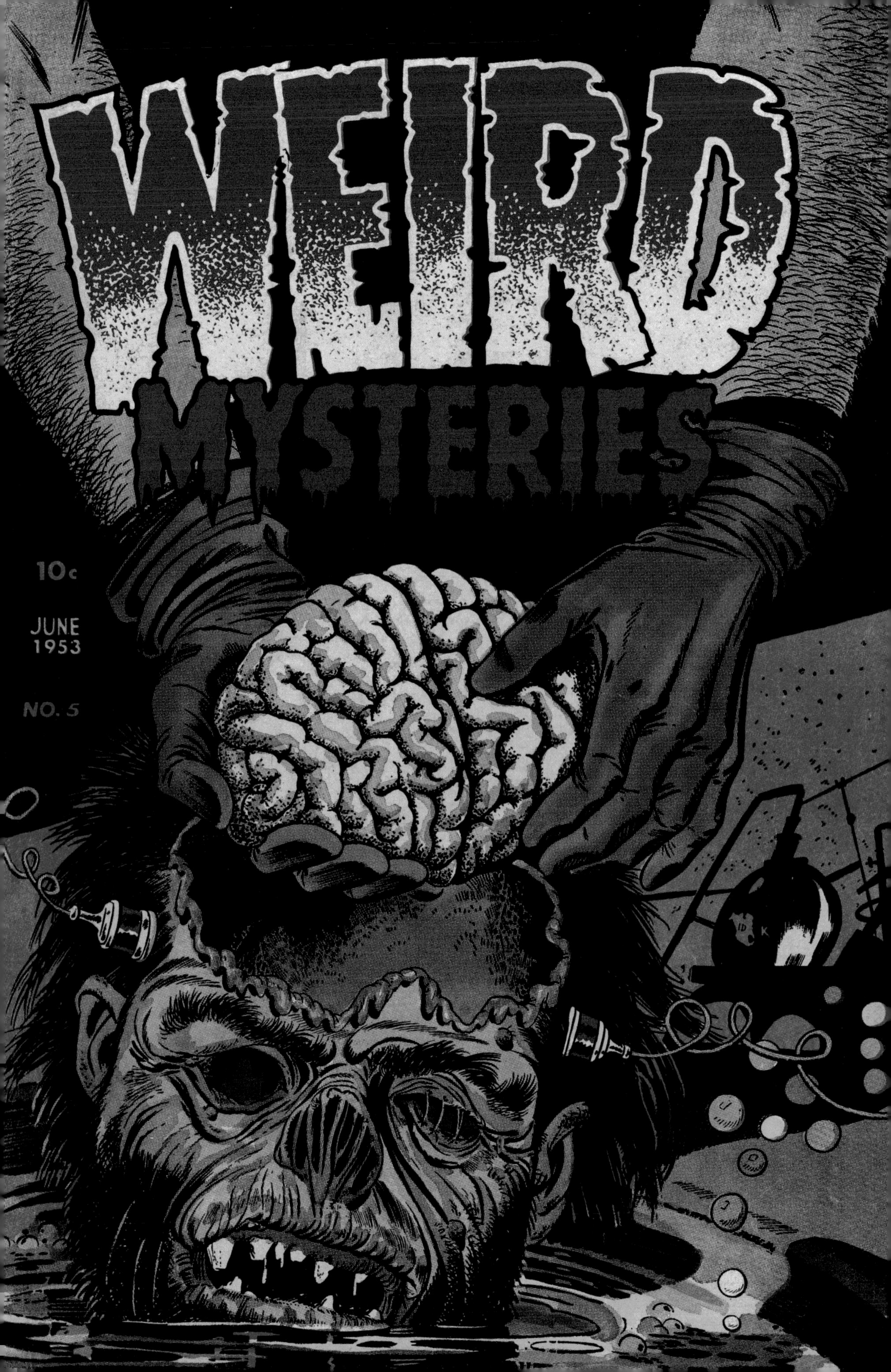
WEIRD
MYSTERIES
10c
JUNE
1953
NO. 5

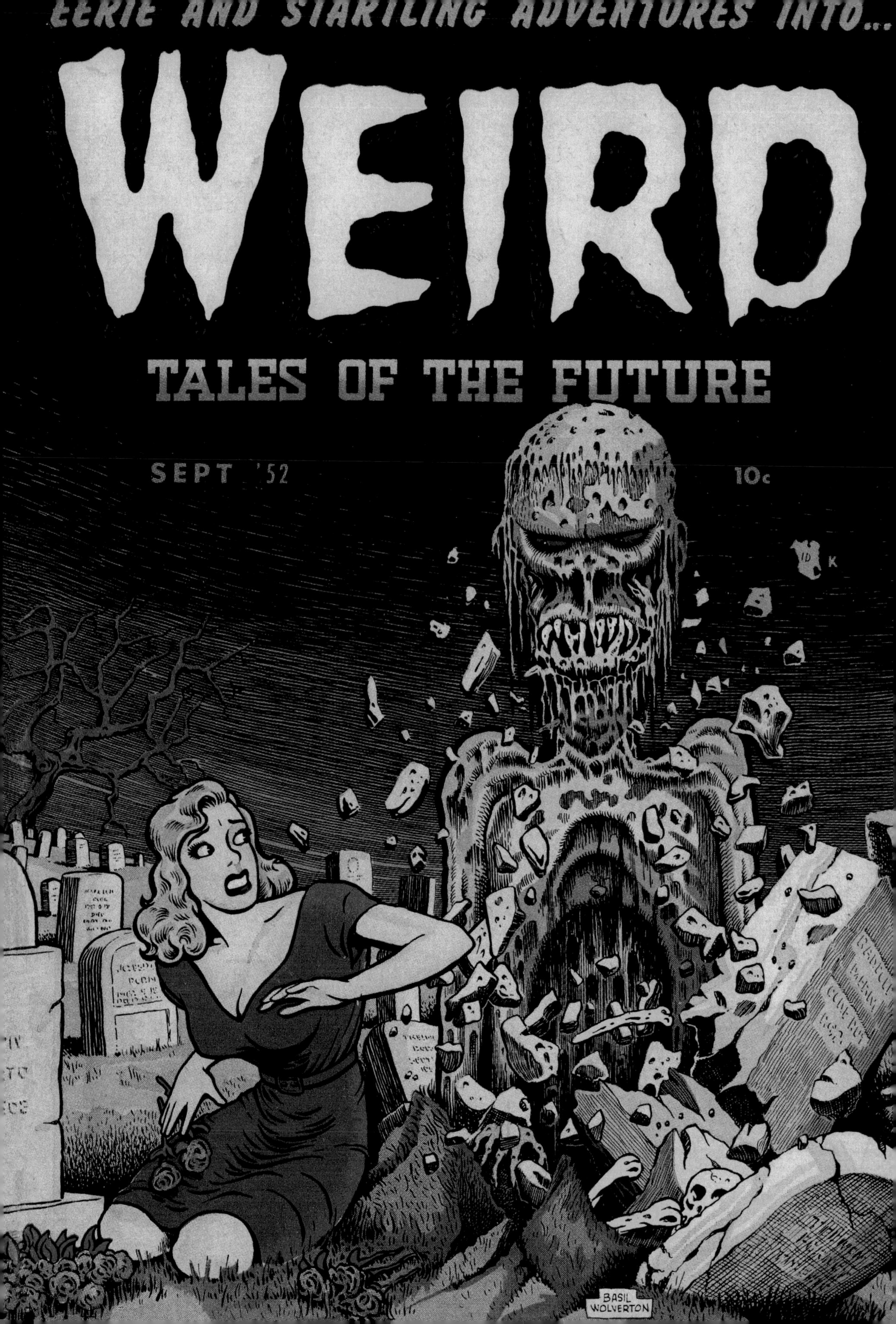
EERIE AND STARTLING ADVENTURES INTO...
WEIRD
TALES OF THE FUTURE
SEPT '52
10c
BASIL WOLVERTON

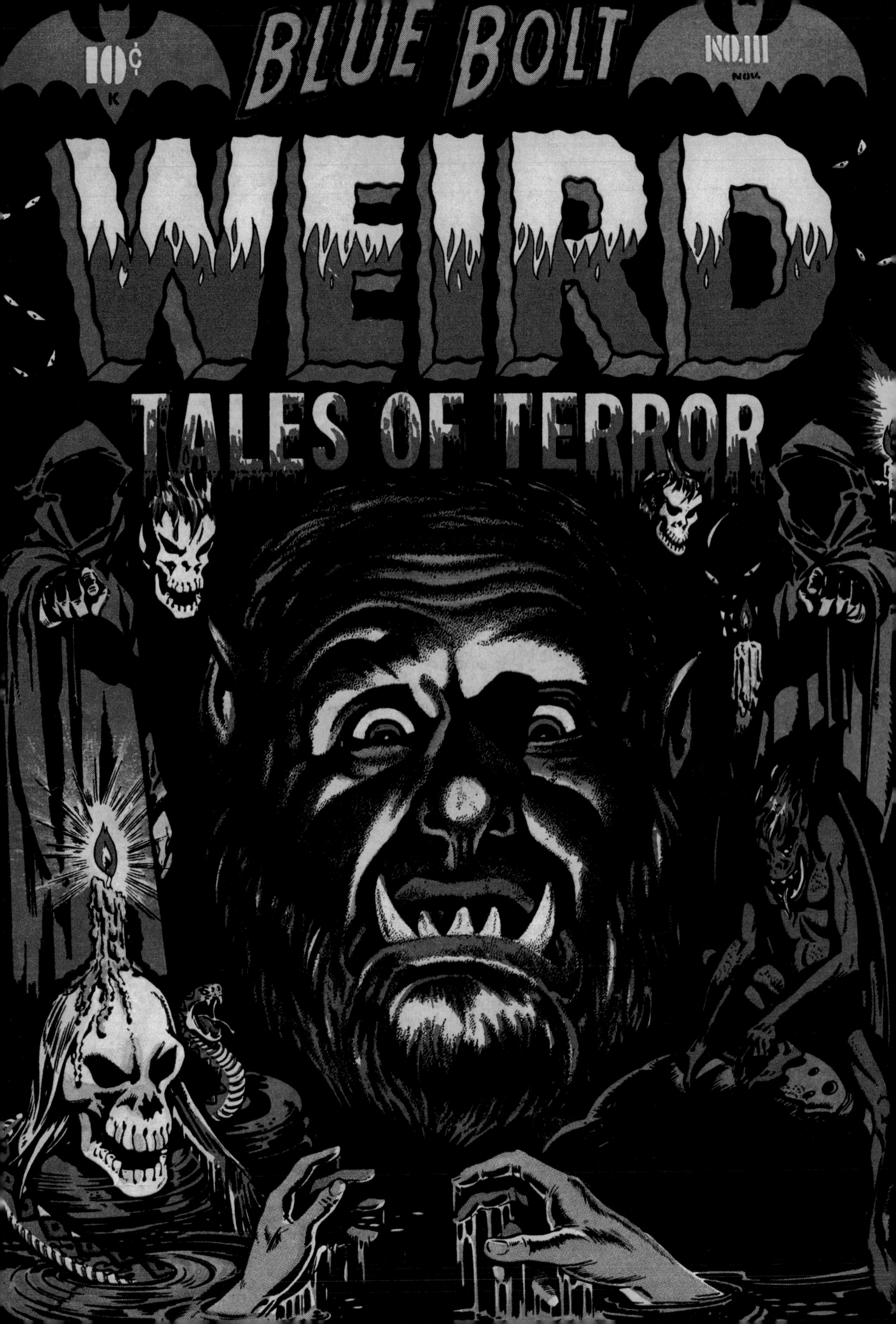
10¢
K
BLUE BOLT
NO.111
NOV.
WEIRD
TALES OF TERROR

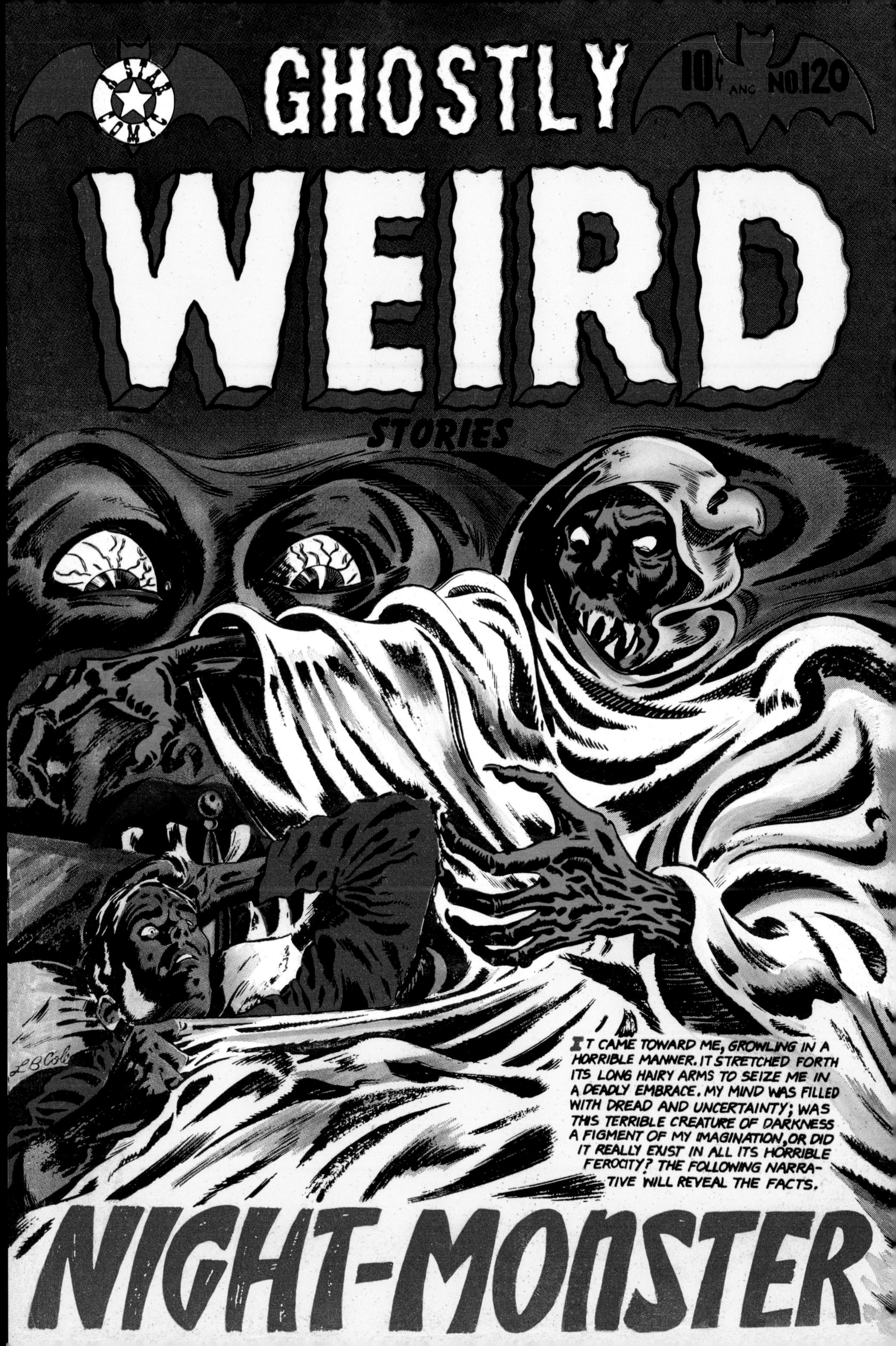

A STAR COMIC
GHOSTLY
10¢
ANC
NO. 120
WEIRD
STORIES
IT CAME TOWARD ME, GROWLING IN A HORRIBLE MANNER. IT STRETCHED FORTH ITS LONG HAIRY ARMS TO SEIZE ME IN A DEADLY EMBRACE. MY MIND WAS FILLED WITH DREAD AND UNCERTAINTY; WAS THIS TERRIBLE CREATURE OF DARKNESS A FIGMENT OF MY IMAGINATION, OR DID IT REALLY EXIST IN ALL ITS HORRIBLE FEROCITY? THE FOLLOWING NARRATIVE WILL REVEAL THE FACTS.
NIGHT-MONSTER

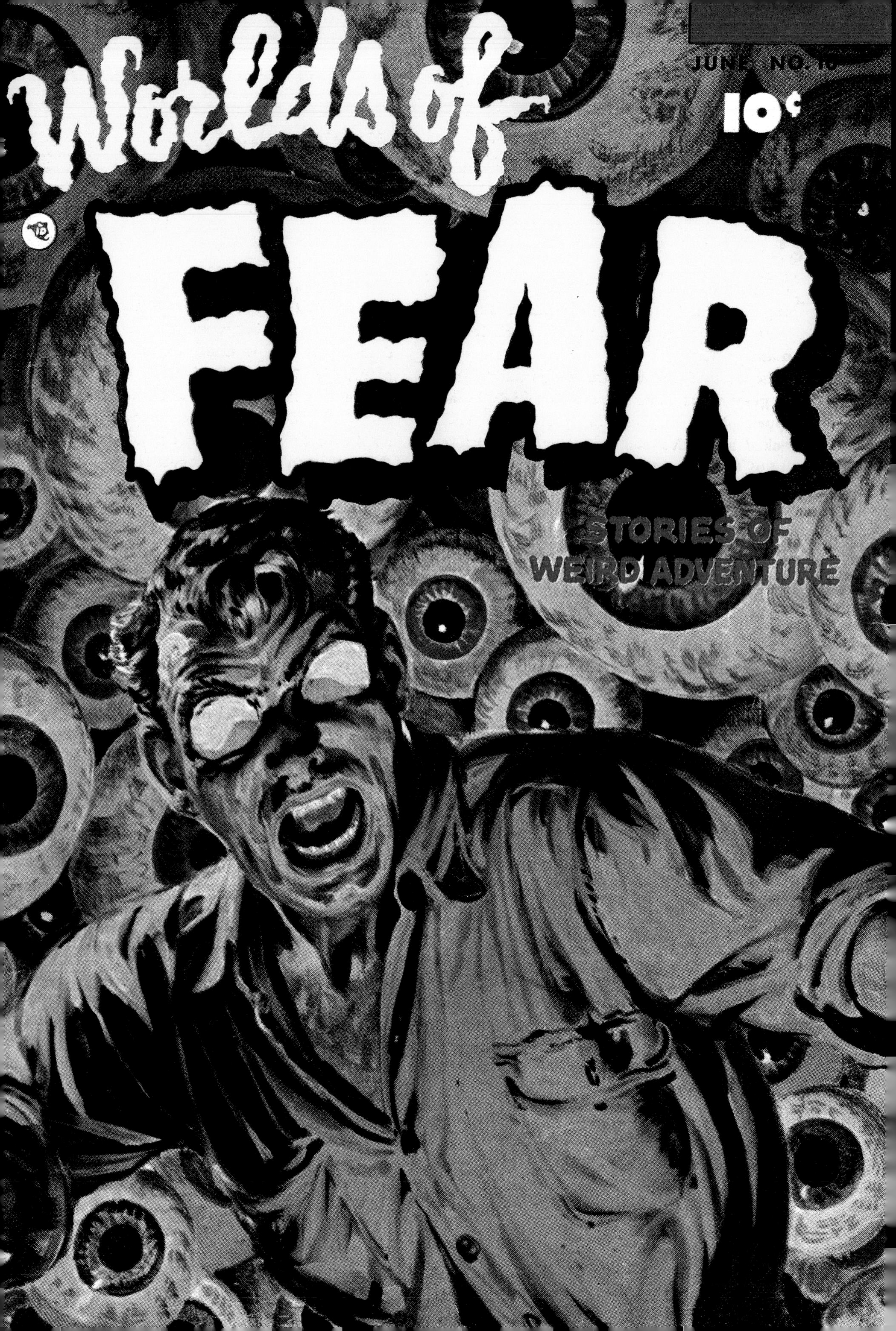
JUNE NO. 10
10¢
Worlds of
FEAR
STORIES OF
WEIRD ADVENTURE

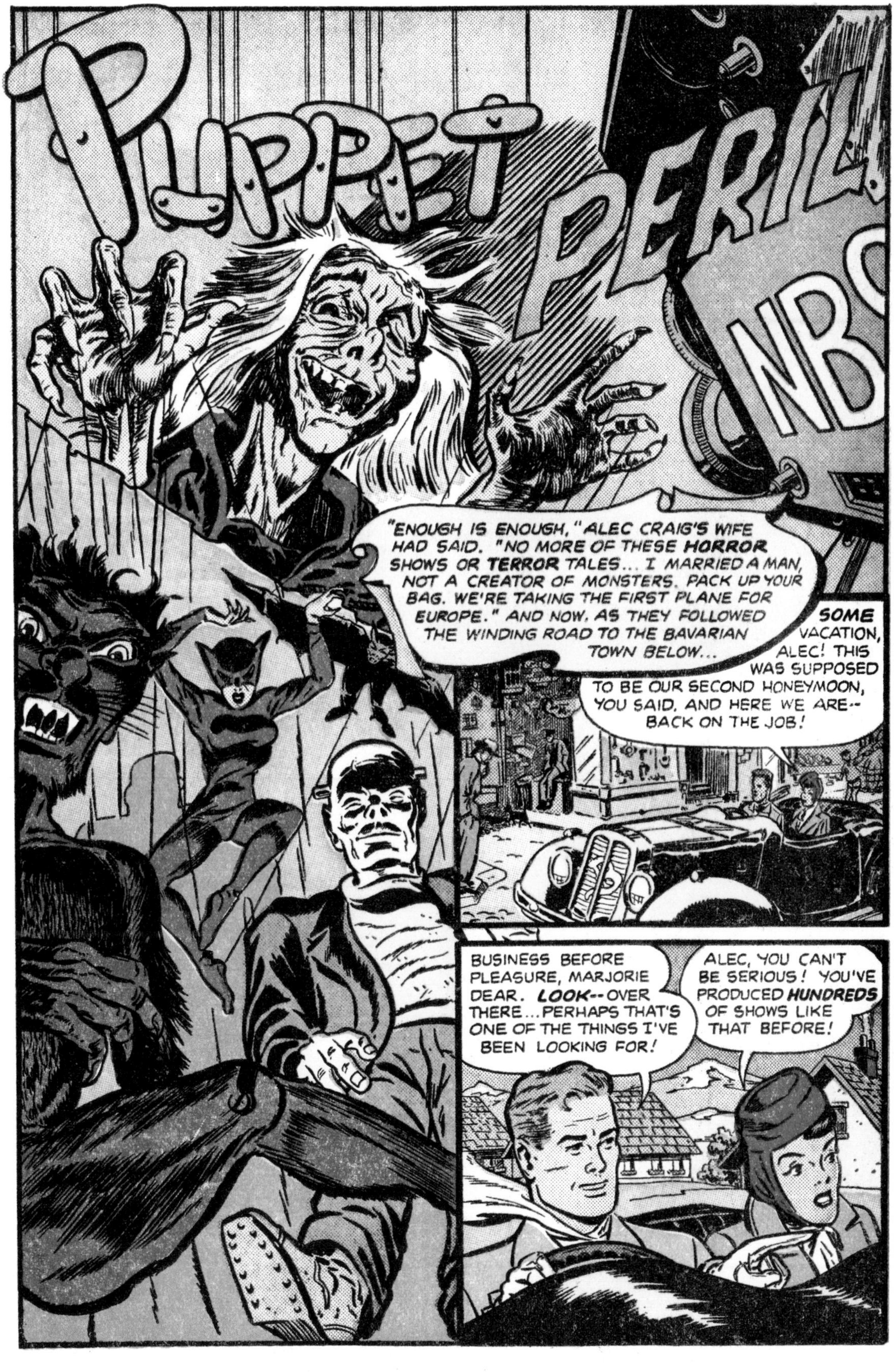
PUPPET PERIL!
"ENOUGH IS ENOUGH," ALEC CRAIG'S WIFE HAD SAID. "NO MORE OF THESE HORROR SHOWS OR TERROR TALES... I MARRIED A MAN, NOT A CREATOR OF MONSTERS. PACK UP YOUR BAG. WE'RE TAKING THE FIRST PLANE FOR EUROPE." AND NOW, AS THEY FOLLOWED THE WINDING ROAD TO THE BAVARIAN TOWN BELOW...
SOME VACATION, ALEC! THIS WAS SUPPOSED TO BE OUR SECOND HONEYMOON, YOU SAID, AND HERE WE ARE-- BACK ON THE JOB!
BUSINESS BEFORE PLEASURE, MARJORIE DEAR. LOOK-- OVER THERE... PERHAPS THAT'S ONE OF THE THINGS I'VE BEEN LOOKING FOR!
ALEC, YOU CAN'T BE SERIOUS! YOU'VE PRODUCED HUNDREDS OF SHOWS LIKE THAT BEFORE!

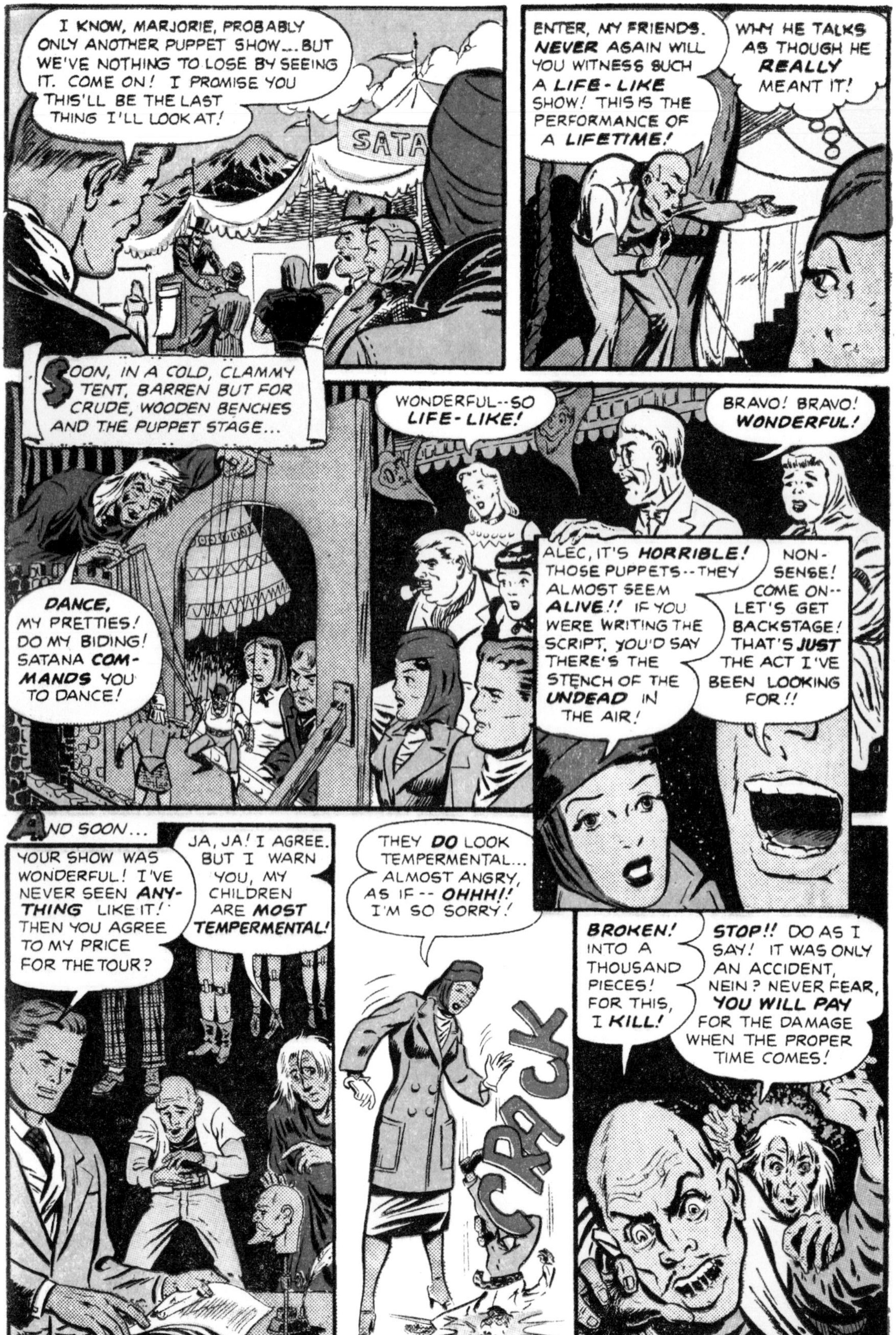
I KNOW, MARJORIE, PROBABLY ONLY ANOTHER PUPPET SHOW... BUT WE'VE NOTHING TO LOSE BY SEEING IT. COME ON! I PROMISE YOU THIS'LL BE THE LAST THING I'LL LOOK AT!
SATA
ENTER, MY FRIENDS. NEVER AGAIN WILL YOU WITNESS SUCH A LIFE-LIKE SHOW! THIS IS THE PERFORMANCE OF A LIFETIME!
WHY HE TALKS AS THOUGH HE REALLY MEANT IT!
SOON, IN A COLD, CLAMMY TENT, BARREN BUT FOR CRUDE, WOODEN BENCHES AND THE PUPPET STAGE...
DANCE, MY PRETTIES! DO MY BIDING! SATANA COMMANDS YOU TO DANCE!
WONDERFUL--SO LIFE-LIKE!
BRAVO! BRAVO! WONDERFUL!
ALEC, IT'S HORRIBLE! THOSE PUPPETS--THEY ALMOST SEEM ALIVE!! IF YOU WERE WRITING THE SCRIPT, YOU'D SAY THERE'S THE STENCH OF THE UNDEAD IN THE AIR!
NON-SENSE! COME ON-- LET'S GET BACKSTAGE! THAT'S JUST THE ACT I'VE BEEN LOOKING FOR!!
AND SOON...
YOUR SHOW WAS WONDERFUL! I'VE NEVER SEEN ANYTHING LIKE IT! THEN YOU AGREE TO MY PRICE FOR THE TOUR?
JA, JA! I AGREE. BUT I WARN YOU, MY CHILDREN ARE MOST TEMPERMENTAL!
THEY DO LOOK TEMPERMENTAL... ALMOST ANGRY, AS IF -- OHHH!! I'M SO SORRY!
CRACK
BROKEN! INTO A THOUSAND PIECES! FOR THIS, I KILL!
STOP!! DO AS I SAY! IT WAS ONLY AN ACCIDENT, NEIN? NEVER FEAR, YOU WILL PAY FOR THE DAMAGE WHEN THE PROPER TIME COMES!

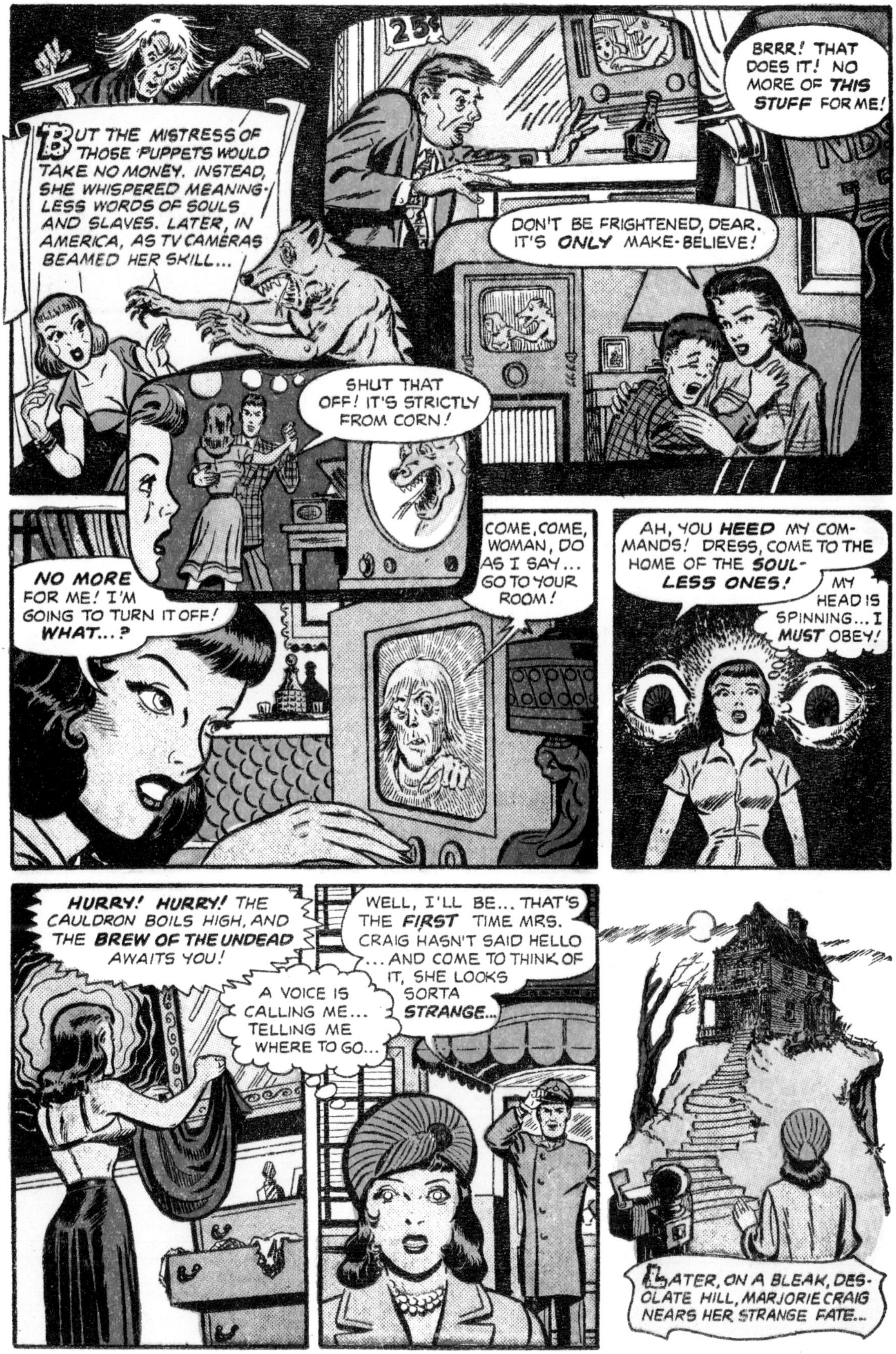
BUT THE MISTRESS OF THOSE PUPPETS WOULD TAKE NO MONEY. INSTEAD, SHE WHISPERED MEANINGLESS WORDS OF SOULS AND SLAVES. LATER, IN AMERICA, AS TV CAMERAS BEAMED HER SKILL...
25¢
BRRR! THAT DOES IT! NO MORE OF THIS STUFF FOR ME!
DON'T BE FRIGHTENED, DEAR. IT'S ONLY MAKE-BELIEVE!
SHUT THAT OFF! IT'S STRICTLY FROM CORN!
NO MORE FOR ME! I'M GOING TO TURN IT OFF! WHAT...?
COME, COME, WOMAN, DO AS I SAY... GO TO YOUR ROOM!
AH, YOU HEED MY COMMANDS! DRESS, COME TO THE HOME OF THE SOULLESS ONES!
MY HEAD IS SPINNING... I MUST OBEY!
HURRY! HURRY! THE CAULDRON BOILS HIGH, AND THE BREW OF THE UNDEAD AWAITS YOU!
A VOICE IS CALLING ME... TELLING ME WHERE TO GO...
WELL, I'LL BE... THAT'S THE FIRST TIME MRS. CRAIG HASN'T SAID HELLO ... AND COME TO THINK OF IT, SHE LOOKS SORTA STRANGE...
LATER, ON A BLEAK, DESOLATE HILL, MARJORIE CRAIG NEARS HER STRANGE FATE...

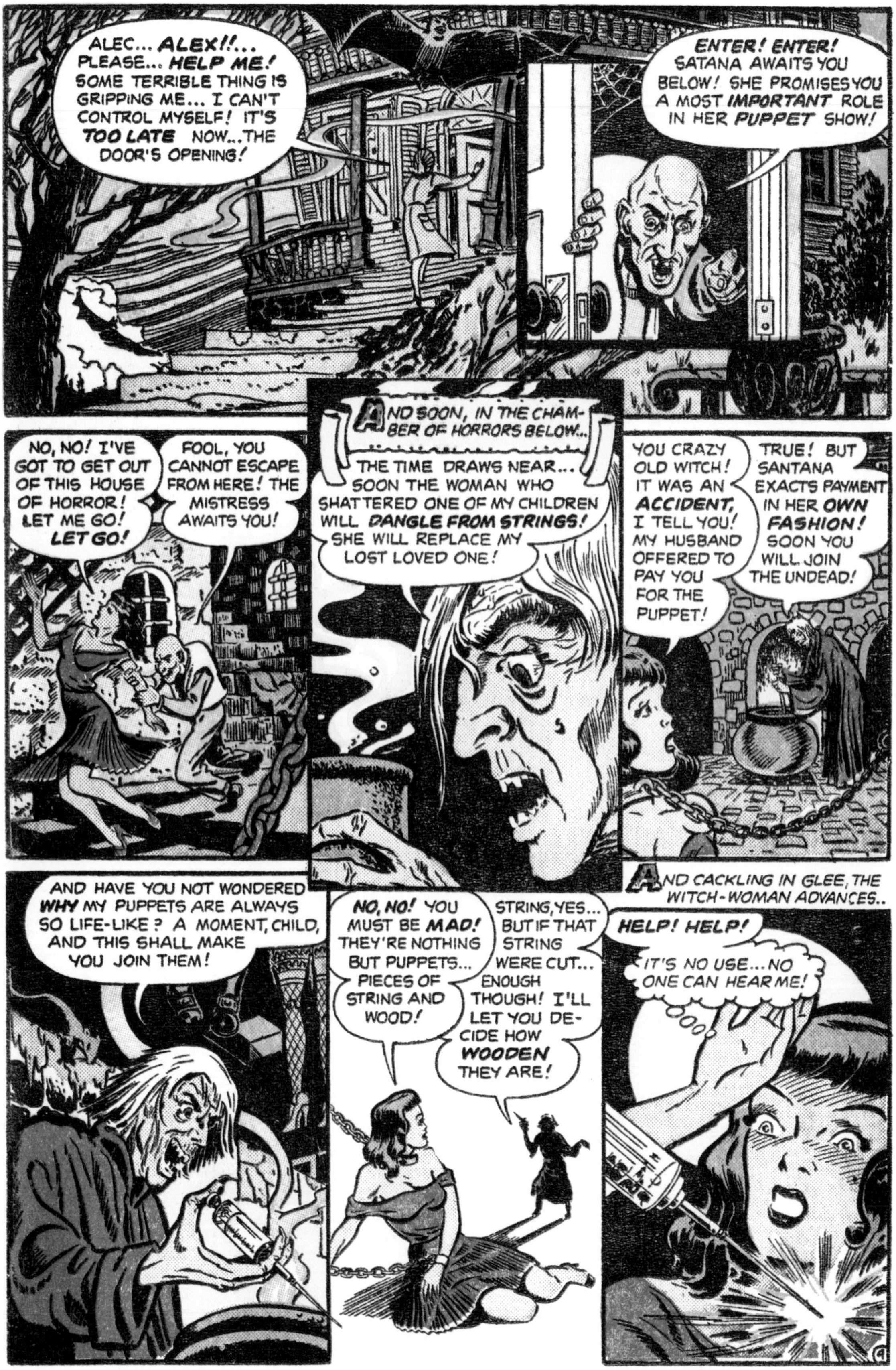
ALEC... ALEX!!... PLEASE... HELP ME! SOME TERRIBLE THING IS GRIPPING ME... I CAN'T CONTROL MYSELF! IT'S TOO LATE NOW... THE DOOR'S OPENING!
ENTER! ENTER! SATANA AWAITS YOU BELOW! SHE PROMISES YOU A MOST IMPORTANT ROLE IN HER PUPPET SHOW!
NO, NO! I'VE GOT TO GET OUT OF THIS HOUSE OF HORROR! LET ME GO! LET GO!
FOOL, YOU CANNOT ESCAPE FROM HERE! THE MISTRESS AWAITS YOU!
AND SOON, IN THE CHAMBER OF HORRORS BELOW...
THE TIME DRAWS NEAR... SOON THE WOMAN WHO SHATTERED ONE OF MY CHILDREN WILL DANGLE FROM STRINGS! SHE WILL REPLACE MY LOST LOVED ONE!
YOU CRAZY OLD WITCH! IT WAS AN ACCIDENT, I TELL YOU! MY HUSBAND OFFERED TO PAY YOU FOR THE PUPPET!
TRUE! BUT SANTANA EXACTS PAYMENT IN HER OWN FASHION! SOON YOU WILL JOIN THE UNDEAD!
AND CACKLING IN GLEE, THE WITCH-WOMAN ADVANCES..
AND HAVE YOU NOT WONDERED WHY MY PUPPETS ARE ALWAYS SO LIFE-LIKE? A MOMENT, CHILD, AND THIS SHALL MAKE YOU JOIN THEM!
NO, NO! YOU MUST BE MAD! THEY'RE NOTHING BUT PUPPETS... PIECES OF STRING AND WOOD!
STRING, YES... BUT IF THAT STRING WERE CUT... ENOUGH THOUGH! I'LL LET YOU DECIDE HOW WOODEN THEY ARE!
HELP! HELP!
IT'S NO USE... NO ONE CAN HEAR ME!
4

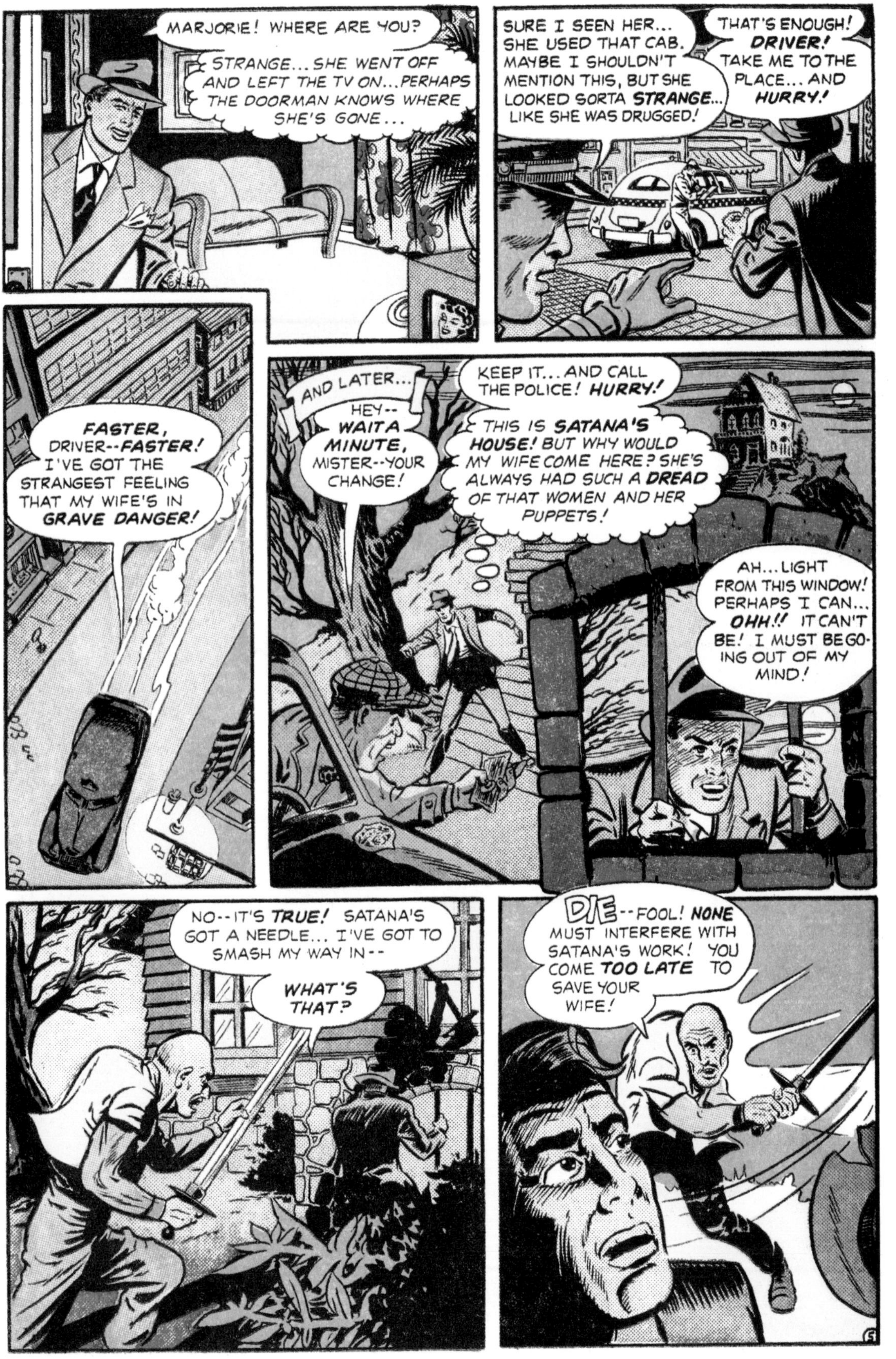
MARJORIE! WHERE ARE YOU?
STRANGE... SHE WENT OFF AND LEFT THE TV ON... PERHAPS THE DOORMAN KNOWS WHERE SHE'S GONE...
SURE I SEEN HER... SHE USED THAT CAB. MAYBE I SHOULDN'T MENTION THIS, BUT SHE LOOKED SORTA STRANGE... LIKE SHE WAS DRUGGED!
THAT'S ENOUGH! DRIVER! TAKE ME TO THE PLACE... AND HURRY!
FASTER, DRIVER--FASTER! I'VE GOT THE STRANGEST FEELING THAT MY WIFE'S IN GRAVE DANGER!
AND LATER...
HEY-- WAIT A MINUTE, MISTER--YOUR CHANGE!
KEEP IT... AND CALL THE POLICE! HURRY!
THIS IS SATANA'S HOUSE! BUT WHY WOULD MY WIFE COME HERE? SHE'S ALWAYS HAD SUCH A DREAD OF THAT WOMEN AND HER PUPPETS!
AH... LIGHT FROM THIS WINDOW! PERHAPS I CAN... OHH!! IT CAN'T BE! I MUST BE GOING OUT OF MY MIND!
NO--IT'S TRUE! SATANA'S GOT A NEEDLE... I'VE GOT TO SMASH MY WAY IN--
WHAT'S THAT?
DIE--FOOL! NONE MUST INTERFERE WITH SATANA'S WORK! YOU COME TOO LATE TO SAVE YOUR WIFE!
5

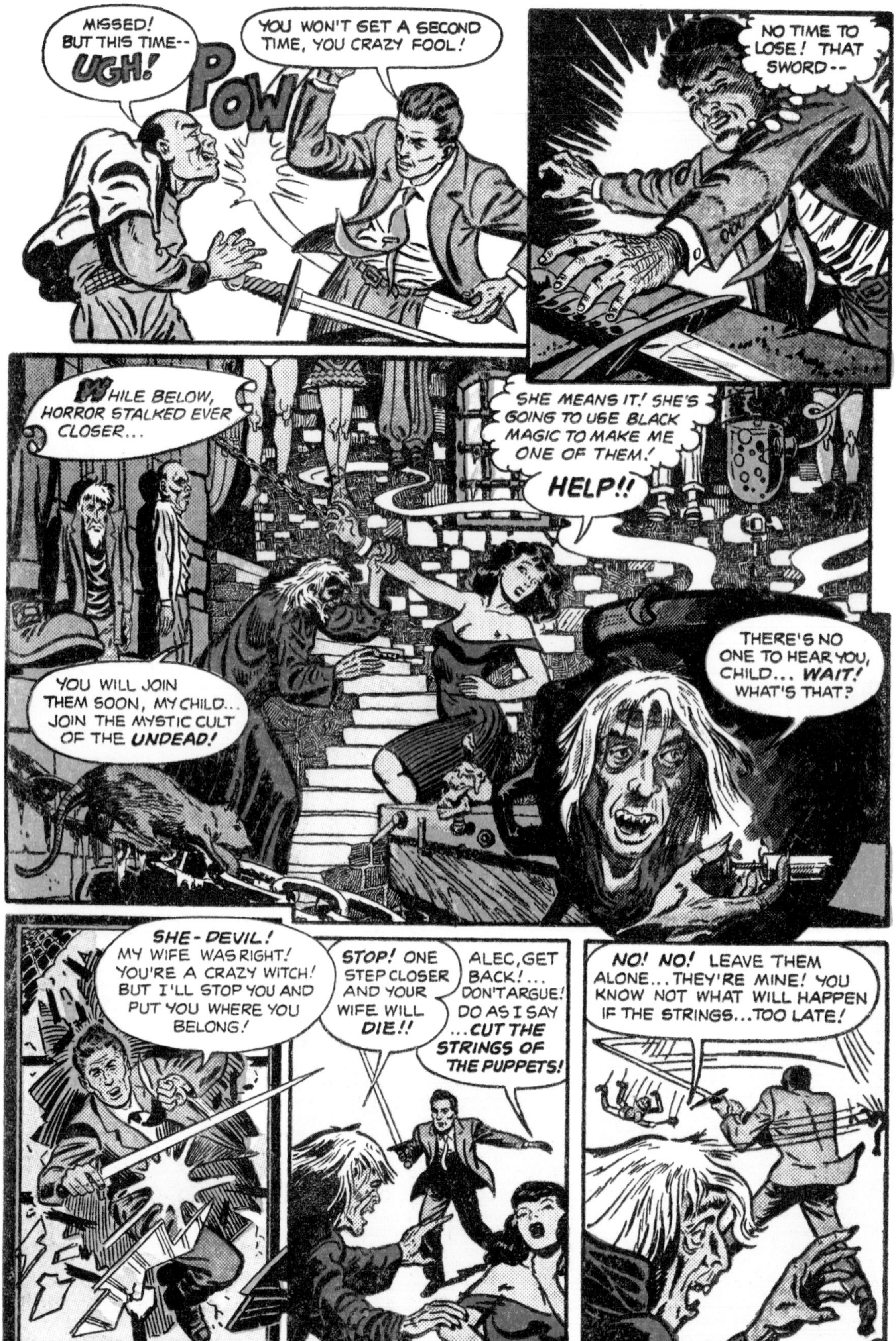
MISSED! BUT THIS TIME-- UGH!
POW
YOU WON'T GET A SECOND TIME, YOU CRAZY FOOL!
NO TIME TO LOSE! THAT SWORD--
WHILE BELOW, HORROR STALKED EVER CLOSER...
SHE MEANS IT! SHE'S GOING TO USE BLACK MAGIC TO MAKE ME ONE OF THEM!
HELP!!
YOU WILL JOIN THEM SOON, MY CHILD... JOIN THE MYSTIC CULT OF THE UNDEAD!
THERE'S NO ONE TO HEAR YOU, CHILD... WAIT! WHAT'S THAT?
SHE-DEVIL! MY WIFE WAS RIGHT! YOU'RE A CRAZY WITCH! BUT I'LL STOP YOU AND PUT YOU WHERE YOU BELONG!
STOP! ONE STEP CLOSER AND YOUR WIFE WILL DIE!!
ALEC, GET BACK!... DON'T ARGUE! DO AS I SAY ...CUT THE STRINGS OF THE PUPPETS!
NO! NO! LEAVE THEM ALONE... THEY'RE MINE! YOU KNOW NOT WHAT WILL HAPPEN IF THE STRINGS... TOO LATE!

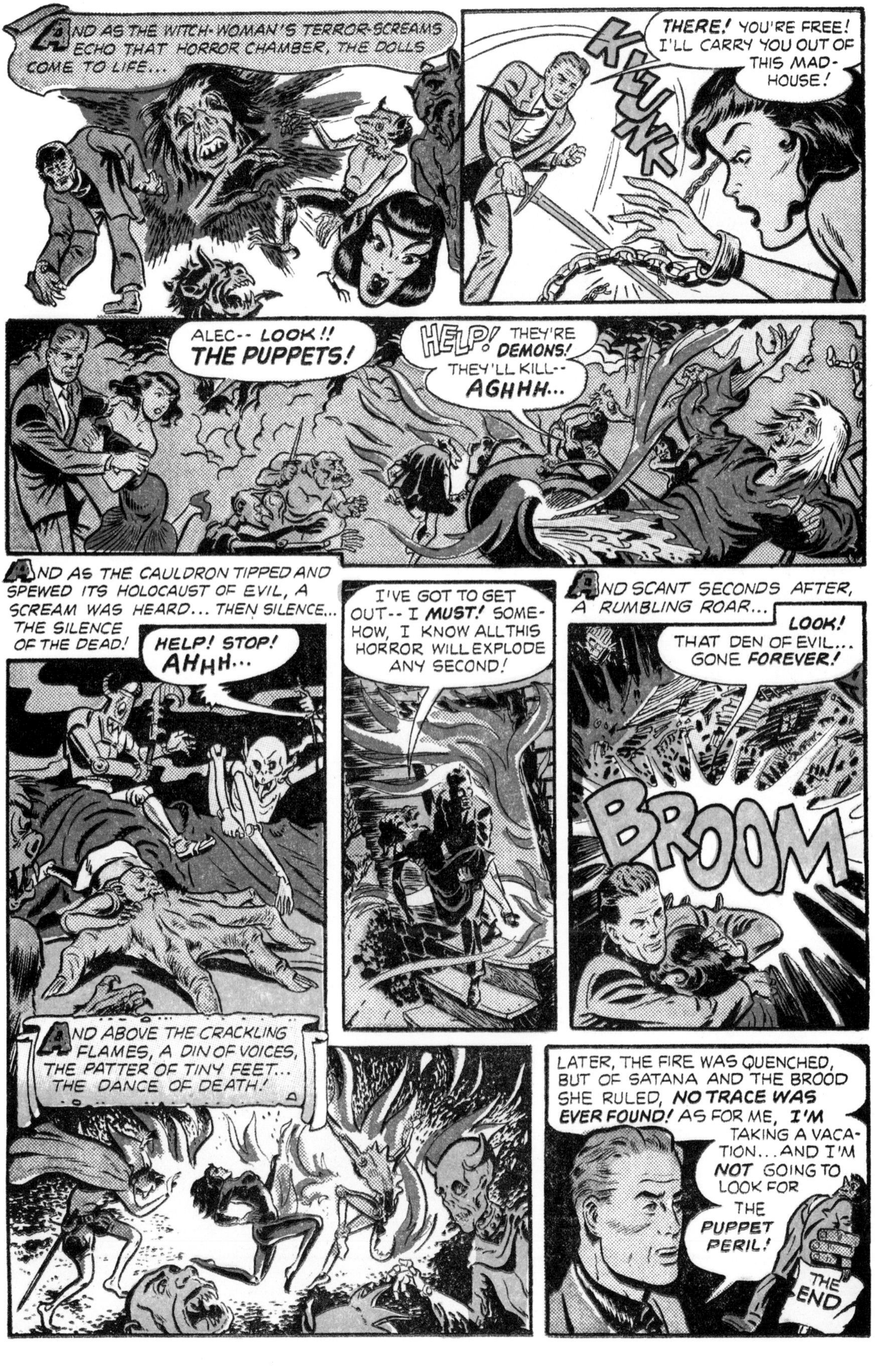
AND AS THE WITCH-WOMAN'S TERROR-SCREAMS ECHO THAT HORROR CHAMBER, THE DOLLS COME TO LIFE...
KLUNK
THERE! YOU'RE FREE! I'LL CARRY YOU OUT OF THIS MAD-HOUSE!
ALEC-- LOOK!! THE PUPPETS!
HELP! THEY'RE DEMONS! THEY'LL KILL-- AGHHH...
AND AS THE CAULDRON TIPPED AND SPEWED ITS HOLOCAUST OF EVIL, A SCREAM WAS HEARD... THEN SILENCE... THE SILENCE OF THE DEAD!
HELP! STOP! AHHH...
I'VE GOT TO GET OUT-- I MUST! SOMEHOW, I KNOW ALL THIS HORROR WILL EXPLODE ANY SECOND!
AND SCANT SECONDS AFTER, A RUMBLING ROAR...
LOOK! THAT DEN OF EVIL... GONE FOREVER!
BROOM
AND ABOVE THE CRACKLING FLAMES, A DIN OF VOICES, THE PATTER OF TINY FEET.. THE DANCE OF DEATH!
LATER, THE FIRE WAS QUENCHED, BUT OF SATANA AND THE BROOD SHE RULED, NO TRACE WAS EVER FOUND! AS FOR ME, I'M TAKING A VACATION... AND I'M NOT GOING TO LOOK FOR THE PUPPET PERIL!
THE END

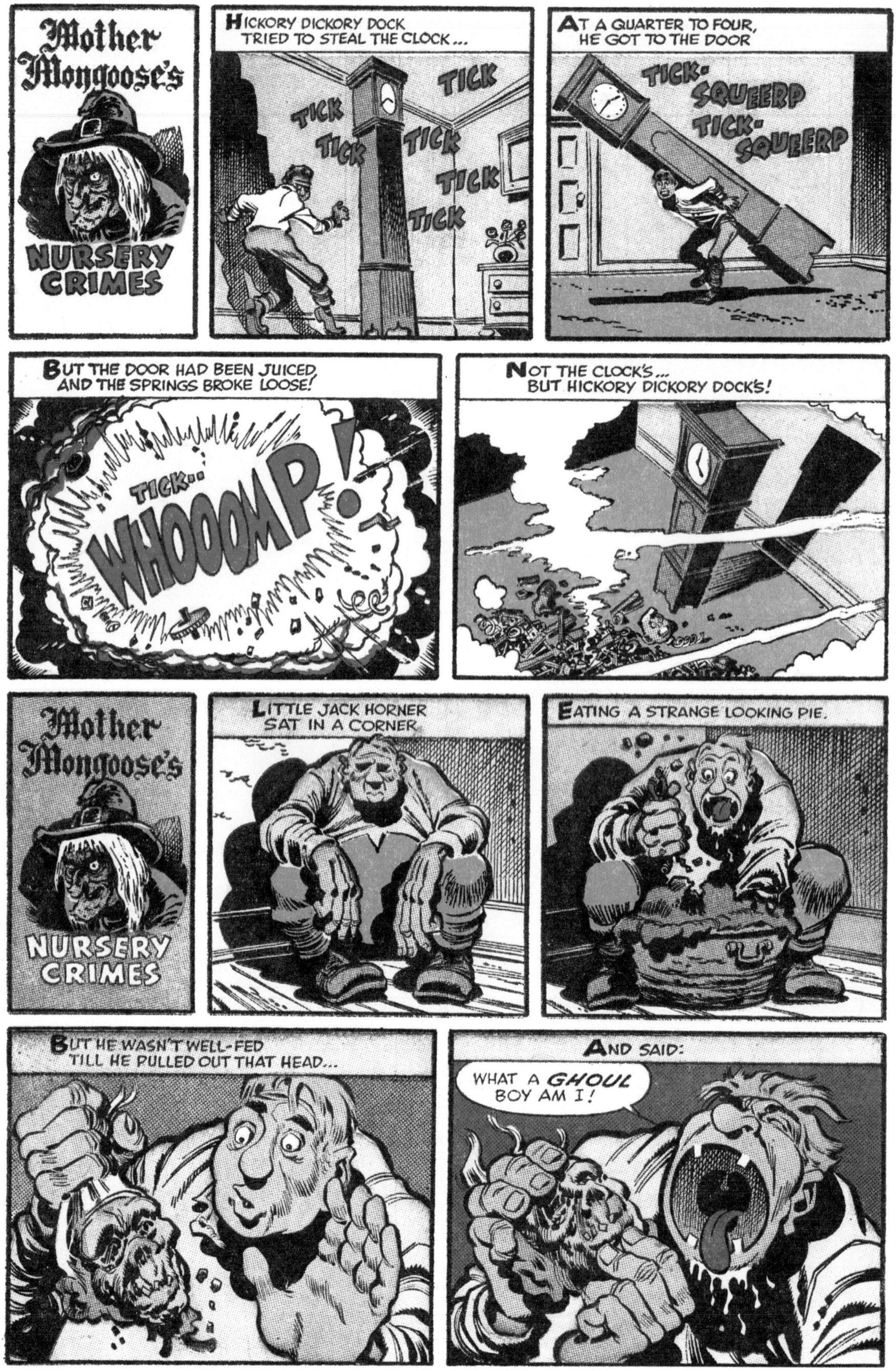
Mother Mongoose's
NURSERY CRIMES
HICKORY DICKORY DOCK
TRIED TO STEAL THE CLOCK...
TICK
TICK
TICK
TICK
TICK
TICK
AT A QUARTER TO FOUR,
HE GOT TO THE DOOR
TICK-SQUEERP
TICK-SQUEERP
BUT THE DOOR HAD BEEN JUICED,
AND THE SPRINGS BROKE LOOSE!
TICK...
WHOOOMP!
NOT THE CLOCK'S...
BUT HICKORY DICKORY DOCK'S!
Mother Mongoose's
NURSERY CRIMES
LITTLE JACK HORNER
SAT IN A CORNER
EATING A STRANGE LOOKING PIE.
BUT HE WASN'T WELL-FED
TILL HE PULLED OUT THAT HEAD...
AND SAID:
WHAT A GHOUL
BOY AM I!

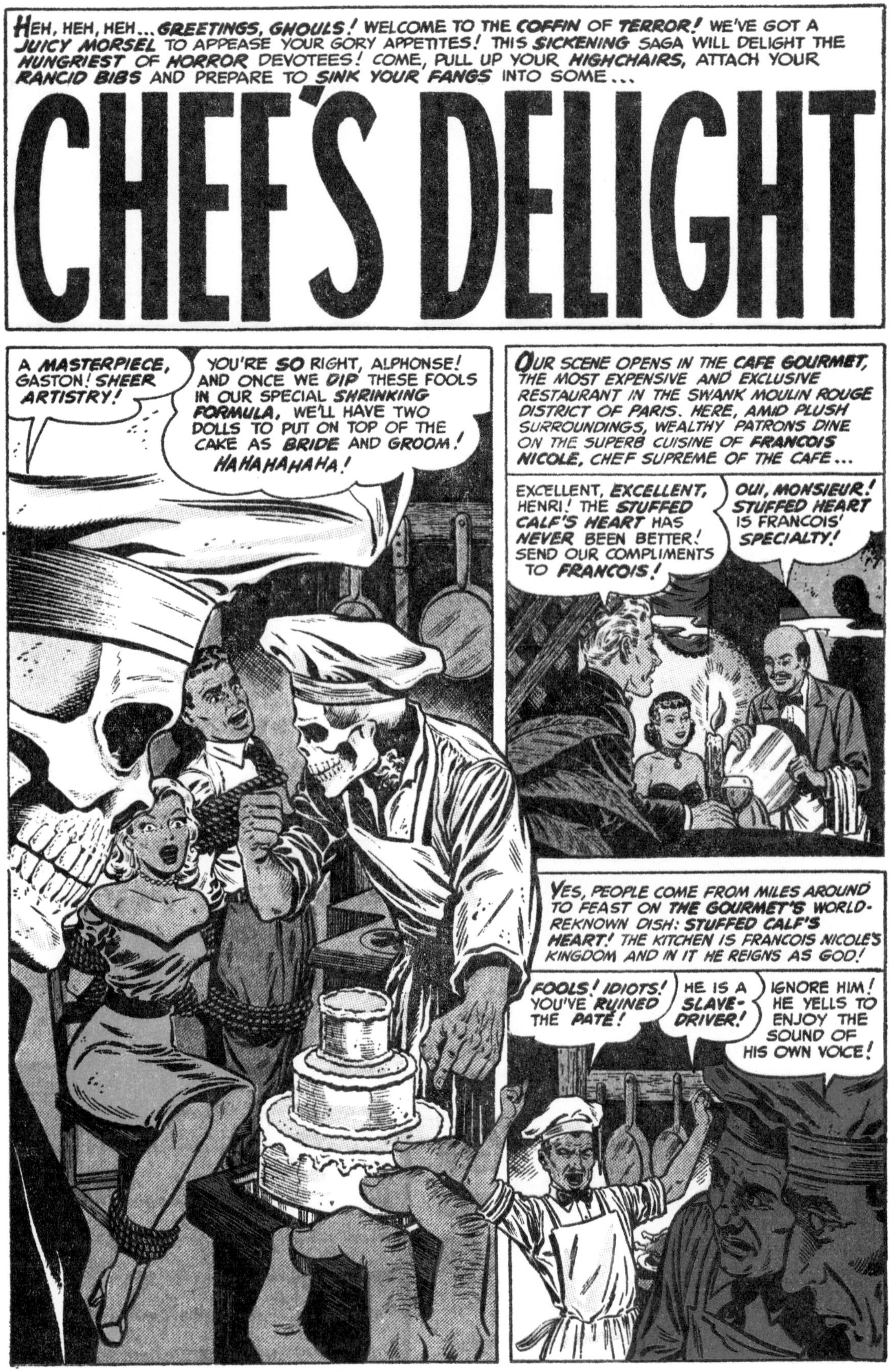
HEH, HEH, HEH... GREETINGS, GHOULS! WELCOME TO THE COFFIN OF TERROR! WE'VE GOT A JUICY MORSEL TO APPEASE YOUR GORY APPETITES! THIS SICKENING SAGA WILL DELIGHT THE HUNGRIEST OF HORROR DEVOTEES! COME, PULL UP YOUR HIGHCHAIRS, ATTACH YOUR RANCID BIBS AND PREPARE TO SINK YOUR FANGS INTO SOME...
CHEF'S DELIGHT
A MASTERPIECE, GASTON! SHEER ARTISTRY!
YOU'RE SO RIGHT, ALPHONSE! AND ONCE WE DIP THESE FOOLS IN OUR SPECIAL SHRINKING FORMULA, WE'LL HAVE TWO DOLLS TO PUT ON TOP OF THE CAKE AS BRIDE AND GROOM! HAHAHAHAHA!
OUR SCENE OPENS IN THE CAFE GOURMET, THE MOST EXPENSIVE AND EXCLUSIVE RESTAURANT IN THE SWANK MOULIN ROUGE DISTRICT OF PARIS. HERE, AMID PLUSH SURROUNDINGS, WEALTHY PATRONS DINE ON THE SUPERB CUISINE OF FRANCOIS NICOLE, CHEF SUPREME OF THE CAFE...
EXCELLENT, EXCELLENT, HENRI! THE STUFFED CALF'S HEART HAS NEVER BEEN BETTER! SEND OUR COMPLIMENTS TO FRANCOIS!
OUI, MONSIEUR! STUFFED HEART IS FRANCOIS' SPECIALTY!
YES, PEOPLE COME FROM MILES AROUND TO FEAST ON THE GOURMET'S WORLD-REKNOWN DISH: STUFFED CALF'S HEART! THE KITCHEN IS FRANCOIS NICOLE'S KINGDOM AND IN IT HE REIGNS AS GOD!
FOOLS! IDIOTS! YOU'VE RUINED THE PATÉ!
HE IS A SLAVE-DRIVER!
IGNORE HIM! HE YELLS TO ENJOY THE SOUND OF HIS OWN VOICE!

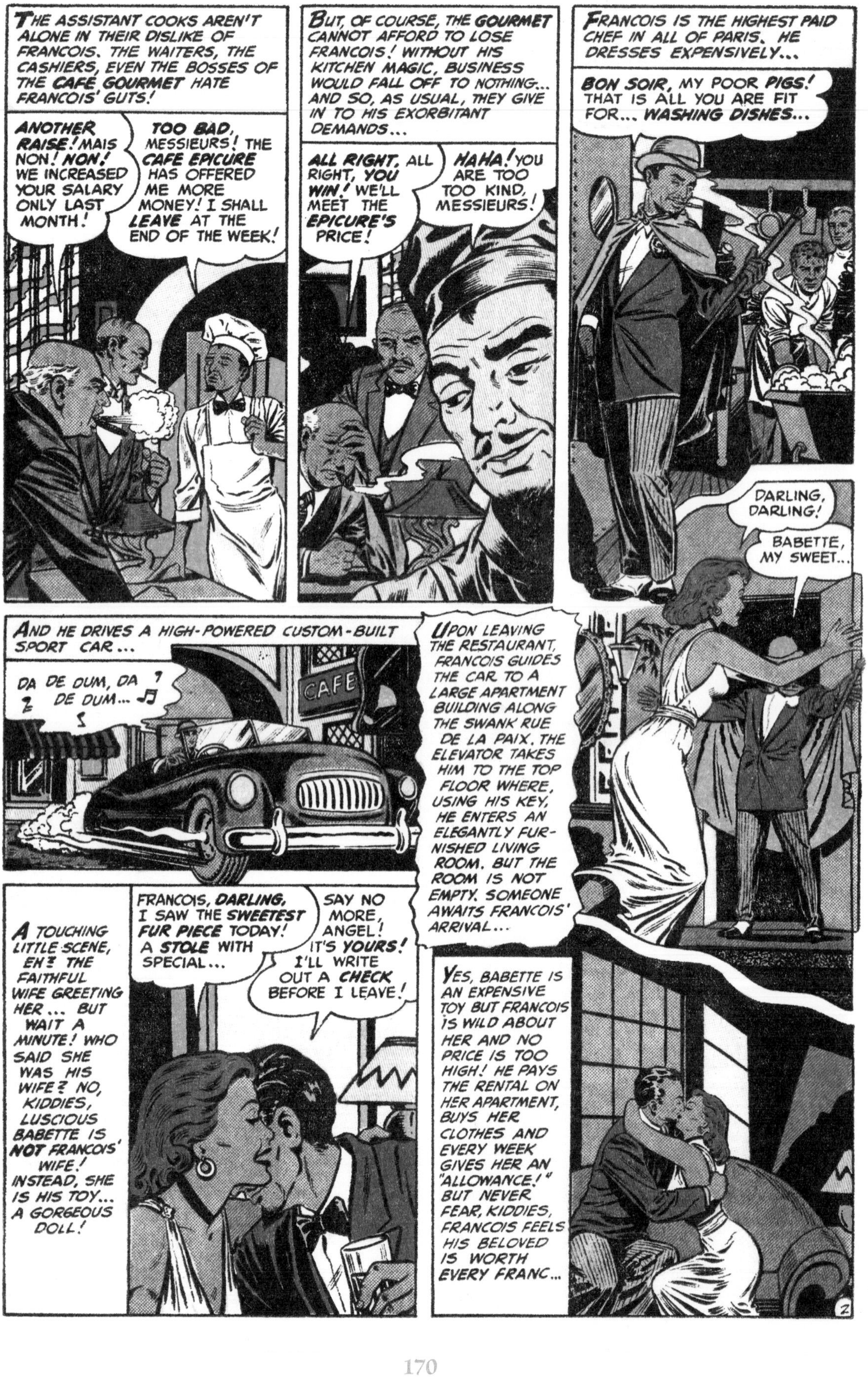
THE ASSISTANT COOKS AREN'T ALONE IN THEIR DISLIKE OF FRANCOIS. THE WAITERS, THE CASHIERS, EVEN THE BOSSES OF THE CAFÉ GOURMET HATE FRANCOIS' GUTS!
ANOTHER RAISE! MAIS NON! NON! WE INCREASED YOUR SALARY ONLY LAST MONTH!
TOO BAD, MESSIEURS! THE CAFE EPICURE HAS OFFERED ME MORE MONEY! I SHALL LEAVE AT THE END OF THE WEEK!
BUT, OF COURSE, THE GOURMET CANNOT AFFORD TO LOSE FRANCOIS! WITHOUT HIS KITCHEN MAGIC, BUSINESS WOULD FALL OFF TO NOTHING... AND SO, AS USUAL, THEY GIVE IN TO HIS EXORBITANT DEMANDS...
ALL RIGHT, ALL RIGHT, YOU WIN! WE'LL MEET THE EPICURE'S PRICE!
HAHA! YOU ARE TOO TOO KIND, MESSIEURS!
FRANCOIS IS THE HIGHEST PAID CHEF IN ALL OF PARIS. HE DRESSES EXPENSIVELY...
BON SOIR, MY POOR PIGS! THAT IS ALL YOU ARE FIT FOR... WASHING DISHES...
AND HE DRIVES A HIGH-POWERED CUSTOM-BUILT SPORT CAR...
DA DE DUM, DA DE DUM...
CAFE
UPON LEAVING THE RESTAURANT, FRANCOIS GUIDES THE CAR TO A LARGE APARTMENT BUILDING ALONG THE SWANK RUE DE LA PAIX. THE ELEVATOR TAKES HIM TO THE TOP FLOOR WHERE, USING HIS KEY, HE ENTERS AN ELEGANTLY FURNISHED LIVING ROOM. BUT THE ROOM IS NOT EMPTY. SOMEONE AWAITS FRANCOIS' ARRIVAL...
DARLING, DARLING!
BABETTE, MY SWEET...
A TOUCHING LITTLE SCENE, EH? THE FAITHFUL WIFE GREETING HER... BUT WAIT A MINUTE! WHO SAID SHE WAS HIS WIFE? NO, KIDDIES, LUSCIOUS BABETTE IS NOT FRANCOIS' WIFE! INSTEAD, SHE IS HIS TOY... A GORGEOUS DOLL!
FRANCOIS, DARLING, I SAW THE SWEETEST FUR PIECE TODAY! A STOLE WITH SPECIAL...
SAY NO MORE, ANGEL! IT'S YOURS! I'LL WRITE OUT A CHECK BEFORE I LEAVE!
YES, BABETTE IS AN EXPENSIVE TOY BUT FRANCOIS IS WILD ABOUT HER AND NO PRICE IS TOO HIGH! HE PAYS THE RENTAL ON HER APARTMENT, BUYS HER CLOTHES AND EVERY WEEK GIVES HER AN "ALLOWANCE!" BUT NEVER FEAR, KIDDIES, FRANCOIS FEELS HIS BELOVED IS WORTH EVERY FRANC...
2

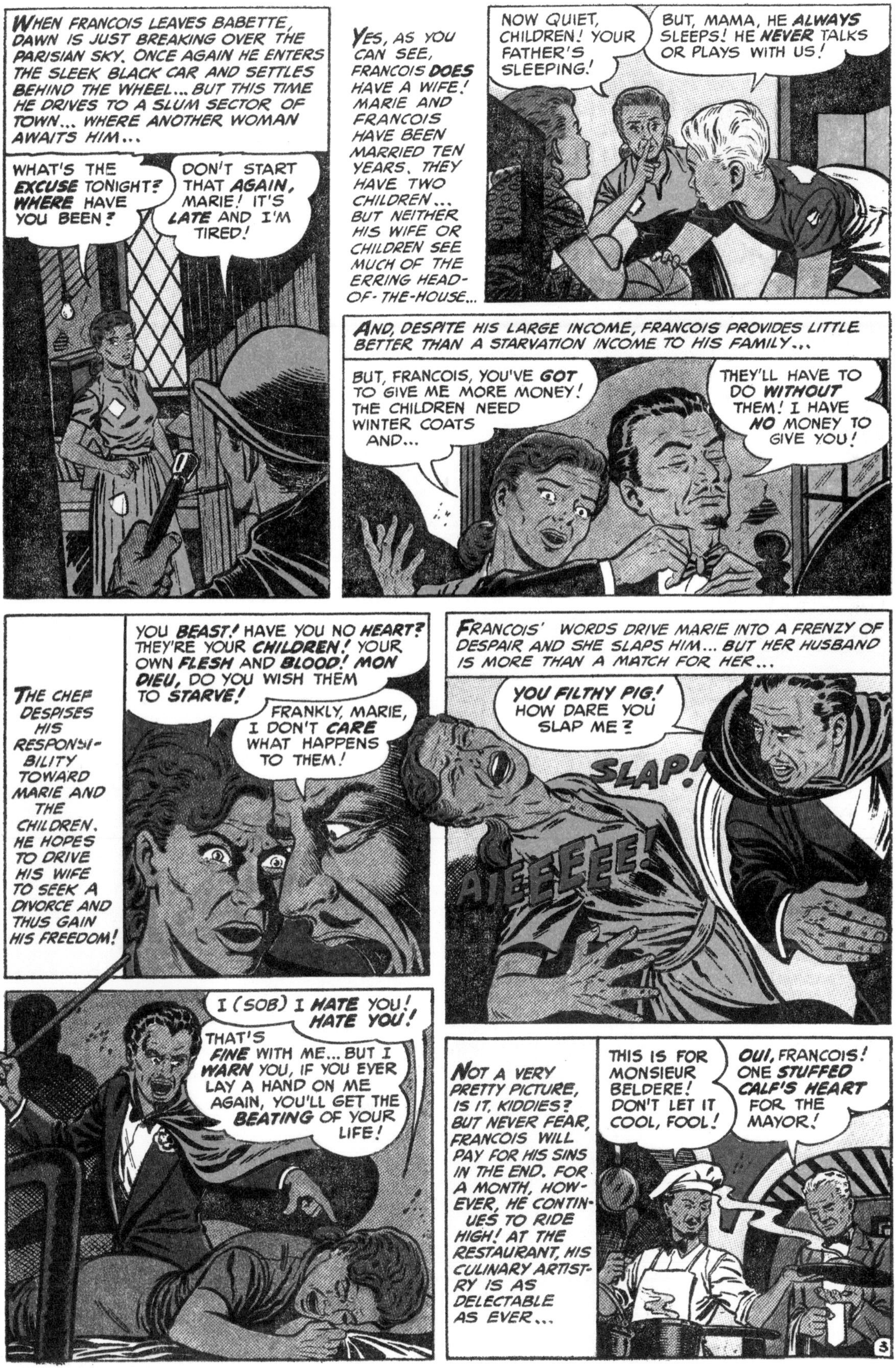

WHEN FRANCOIS LEAVES BABETTE, DAWN IS JUST BREAKING OVER THE PARISIAN SKY. ONCE AGAIN HE ENTERS THE SLEEK BLACK CAR AND SETTLES BEHIND THE WHEEL... BUT THIS TIME HE DRIVES TO A SLUM SECTOR OF TOWN... WHERE ANOTHER WOMAN AWAITS HIM...
WHAT'S THE EXCUSE TONIGHT? WHERE HAVE YOU BEEN?
DON'T START THAT AGAIN, MARIE! IT'S LATE AND I'M TIRED!
YES, AS YOU CAN SEE, FRANCOIS DOES HAVE A WIFE! MARIE AND FRANCOIS HAVE BEEN MARRIED TEN YEARS. THEY HAVE TWO CHILDREN... BUT NEITHER HIS WIFE OR CHILDREN SEE MUCH OF THE ERRING HEAD-OF-THE-HOUSE...
NOW QUIET, CHILDREN! YOUR FATHER'S SLEEPING!
BUT, MAMA, HE ALWAYS SLEEPS! HE NEVER TALKS OR PLAYS WITH US!
AND, DESPITE HIS LARGE INCOME, FRANCOIS PROVIDES LITTLE BETTER THAN A STARVATION INCOME TO HIS FAMILY...
BUT, FRANCOIS, YOU'VE GOT TO GIVE ME MORE MONEY! THE CHILDREN NEED WINTER COATS AND...
THEY'LL HAVE TO DO WITHOUT THEM! I HAVE NO MONEY TO GIVE YOU!
THE CHEF DESPISES HIS RESPONSIBILITY TOWARD MARIE AND THE CHILDREN. HE HOPES TO DRIVE HIS WIFE TO SEEK A DIVORCE AND THUS GAIN HIS FREEDOM!
YOU BEAST! HAVE YOU NO HEART? THEY'RE YOUR CHILDREN! YOUR OWN FLESH AND BLOOD! MON DIEU, DO YOU WISH THEM TO STARVE!
FRANKLY, MARIE, I DON'T CARE WHAT HAPPENS TO THEM!
FRANCOIS' WORDS DRIVE MARIE INTO A FRENZY OF DESPAIR AND SHE SLAPS HIM... BUT HER HUSBAND IS MORE THAN A MATCH FOR HER...
YOU FILTHY PIG! HOW DARE YOU SLAP ME?
SLAP!
AIEEEEEE!
I (SOB) I HATE YOU! HATE YOU!
THAT'S FINE WITH ME... BUT I WARN YOU, IF YOU EVER LAY A HAND ON ME AGAIN, YOU'LL GET THE BEATING OF YOUR LIFE!
NOT A VERY PRETTY PICTURE, IS IT, KIDDIES? BUT NEVER FEAR, FRANCOIS WILL PAY FOR HIS SINS IN THE END. FOR A MONTH, HOWEVER, HE CONTINUES TO RIDE HIGH! AT THE RESTAURANT, HIS CULINARY ARTISTRY IS AS DELECTABLE AS EVER...
THIS IS FOR MONSIEUR BELDERE! DON'T LET IT COOL, FOOL!
OUI, FRANCOIS! ONE STUFFED CALF'S HEART FOR THE MAYOR!
3

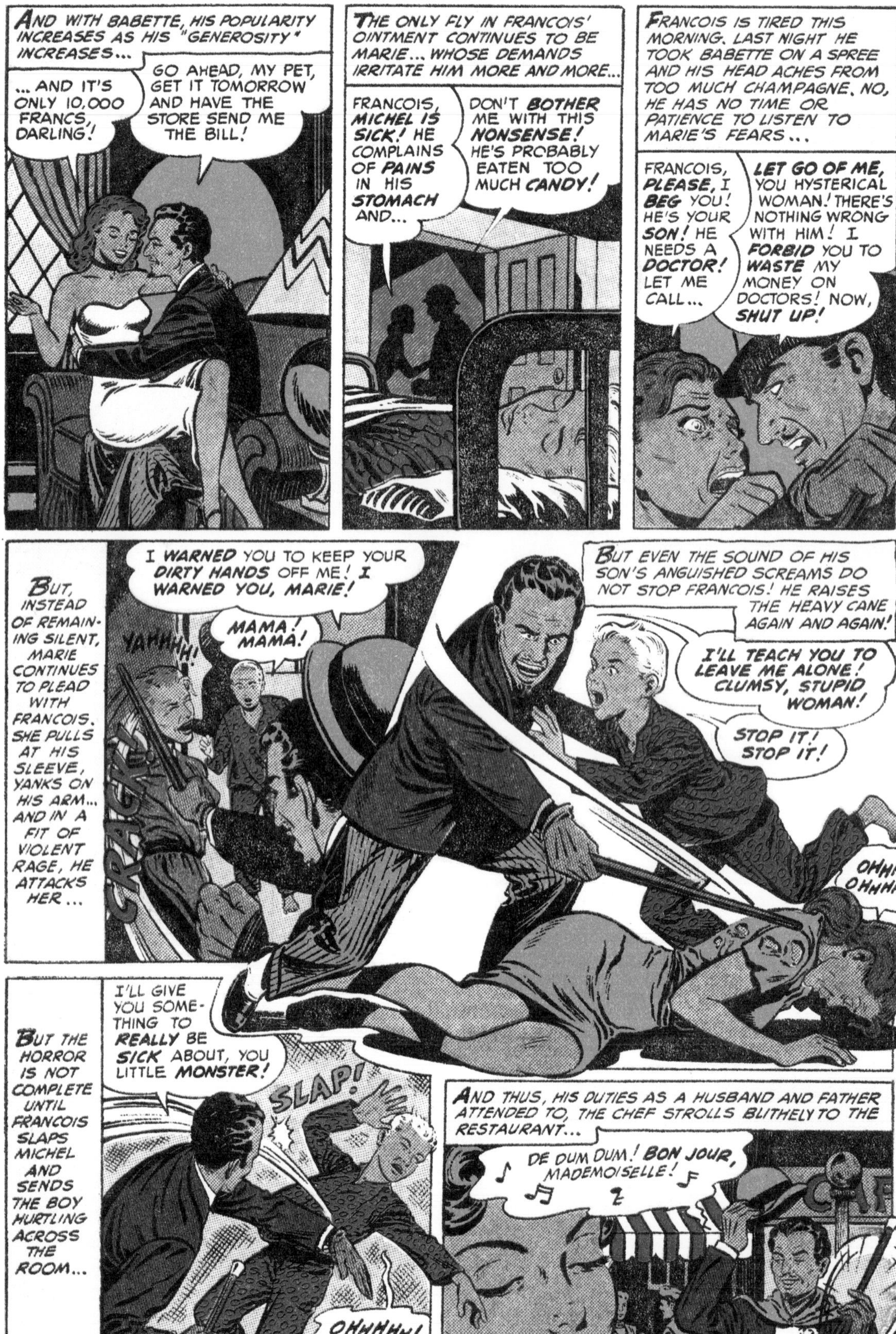
AND WITH BABETTE, HIS POPULARITY INCREASES AS HIS "GENEROSITY" INCREASES...
... AND IT'S ONLY 10,000 FRANCS, DARLING!
GO AHEAD, MY PET, GET IT TOMORROW AND HAVE THE STORE SEND ME THE BILL!
THE ONLY FLY IN FRANCOIS' OINTMENT CONTINUES TO BE MARIE... WHOSE DEMANDS IRRITATE HIM MORE AND MORE...
FRANCOIS, MICHEL IS SICK! HE COMPLAINS OF PAINS IN HIS STOMACH AND...
DON'T BOTHER ME WITH THIS NONSENSE! HE'S PROBABLY EATEN TOO MUCH CANDY!
FRANCOIS IS TIRED THIS MORNING. LAST NIGHT HE TOOK BABETTE ON A SPREE AND HIS HEAD ACHES FROM TOO MUCH CHAMPAGNE. NO, HE HAS NO TIME OR PATIENCE TO LISTEN TO MARIE'S FEARS...
FRANCOIS, PLEASE, I BEG YOU! HE'S YOUR SON! HE NEEDS A DOCTOR! LET ME CALL...
LET GO OF ME, YOU HYSTERICAL WOMAN! THERE'S NOTHING WRONG WITH HIM! I FORBID YOU TO WASTE MY MONEY ON DOCTORS! NOW, SHUT UP!
BUT, INSTEAD OF REMAINING SILENT, MARIE CONTINUES TO PLEAD WITH FRANCOIS. SHE PULLS AT HIS SLEEVE, YANKS ON HIS ARM... AND IN A FIT OF VIOLENT RAGE, HE ATTACKS HER...
I WARNED YOU TO KEEP YOUR DIRTY HANDS OFF ME! I WARNED YOU, MARIE!
YAHHHH!
MAMA! MAMA!
CRACK!
BUT EVEN THE SOUND OF HIS SON'S ANGUISHED SCREAMS DO NOT STOP FRANCOIS! HE RAISES THE HEAVY CANE AGAIN AND AGAIN!
I'LL TEACH YOU TO LEAVE ME ALONE! CLUMSY, STUPID WOMAN!
STOP IT! STOP IT!
OHHH.. OHHHH..
BUT THE HORROR IS NOT COMPLETE UNTIL FRANCOIS SLAPS MICHEL AND SENDS THE BOY HURTLING ACROSS THE ROOM...
I'LL GIVE YOU SOMETHING TO REALLY BE SICK ABOUT, YOU LITTLE MONSTER!
SLAP!
OHHHHH!
AND THUS, HIS DUTIES AS A HUSBAND AND FATHER ATTENDED TO, THE CHEF STROLLS BLITHELY TO THE RESTAURANT...
DE DUM DUM! BON JOUR, MADEMOISELLE!
4

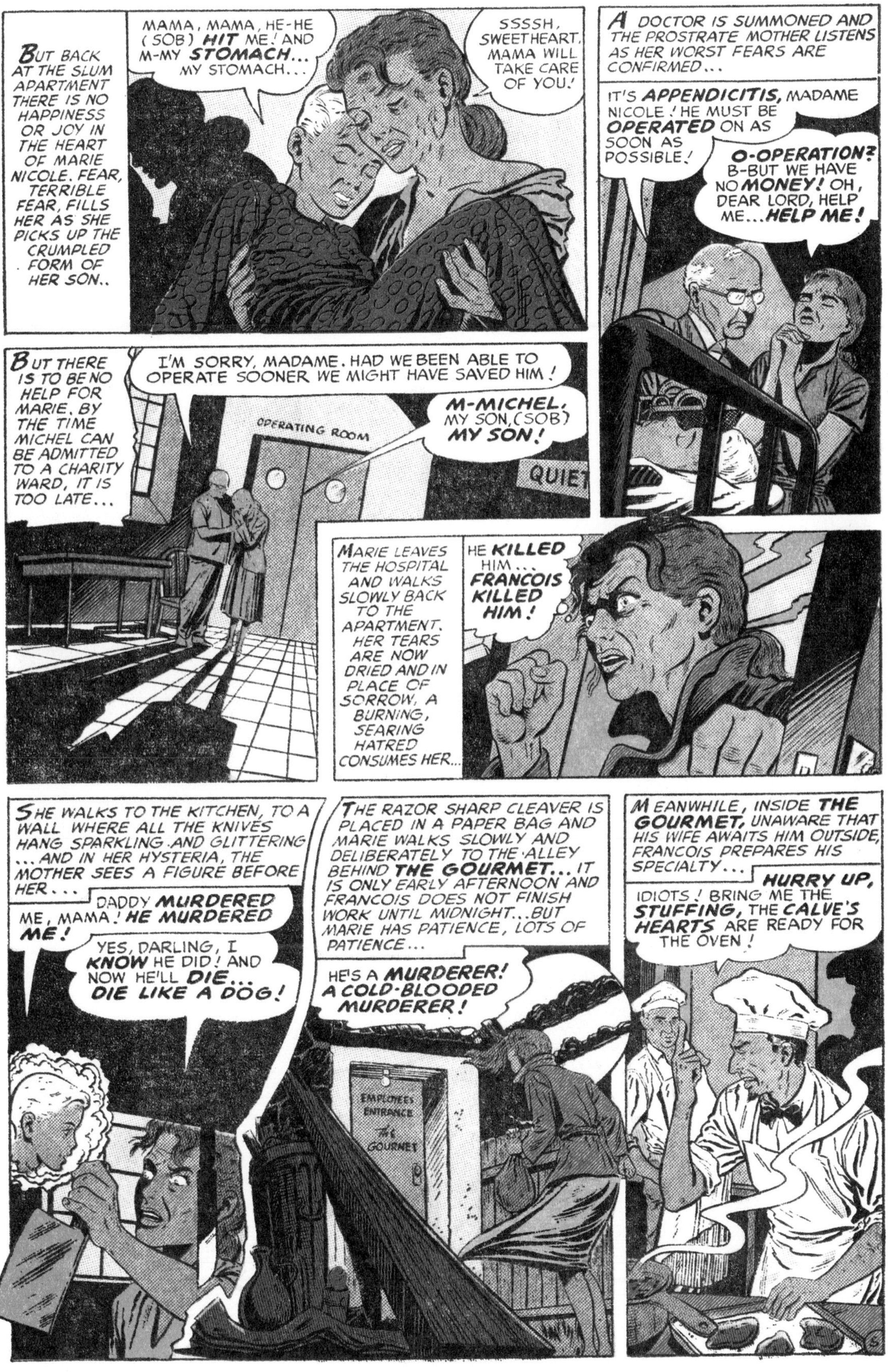
BUT BACK AT THE SLUM APARTMENT THERE IS NO HAPPINESS OR JOY IN THE HEART OF MARIE NICOLE. FEAR, TERRIBLE FEAR, FILLS HER AS SHE PICKS UP THE CRUMPLED FORM OF HER SON..
MAMA, MAMA, HE-HE (SOB) HIT ME! AND M-MY STOMACH... MY STOMACH...
SSSSH, SWEETHEART, MAMA WILL TAKE CARE OF YOU!
A DOCTOR IS SUMMONED AND THE PROSTRATE MOTHER LISTENS AS HER WORST FEARS ARE CONFIRMED...
IT'S APPENDICITIS, MADAME NICOLE! HE MUST BE OPERATED ON AS SOON AS POSSIBLE!
O-OPERATION? B-BUT WE HAVE NO MONEY! OH, DEAR LORD, HELP ME...HELP ME!
BUT THERE IS TO BE NO HELP FOR MARIE. BY THE TIME MICHEL CAN BE ADMITTED TO A CHARITY WARD, IT IS TOO LATE...
I'M SORRY, MADAME. HAD WE BEEN ABLE TO OPERATE SOONER WE MIGHT HAVE SAVED HIM!
M-MICHEL, MY SON, (SOB) MY SON!
OPERATING ROOM
QUIET
MARIE LEAVES THE HOSPITAL AND WALKS SLOWLY BACK TO THE APARTMENT. HER TEARS ARE NOW DRIED AND IN PLACE OF SORROW, A BURNING, SEARING HATRED CONSUMES HER...
HE KILLED HIM... FRANCOIS KILLED HIM!
SHE WALKS TO THE KITCHEN, TO A WALL WHERE ALL THE KNIVES HANG SPARKLING AND GLITTERING ...AND IN HER HYSTERIA, THE MOTHER SEES A FIGURE BEFORE HER...
DADDY MURDERED ME, MAMA! HE MURDERED ME!
YES, DARLING, I KNOW HE DID! AND NOW HE'LL DIE... DIE LIKE A DOG!
THE RAZOR SHARP CLEAVER IS PLACED IN A PAPER BAG AND MARIE WALKS SLOWLY AND DELIBERATELY TO THE ALLEY BEHIND THE GOURMET... IT IS ONLY EARLY AFTERNOON AND FRANCOIS DOES NOT FINISH WORK UNTIL MIDNIGHT...BUT MARIE HAS PATIENCE, LOTS OF PATIENCE...
HE'S A MURDERER! A COLD-BLOODED MURDERER!
EMPLOYEES ENTRANCE
THE GOURMET
MEANWHILE, INSIDE THE GOURMET, UNAWARE THAT HIS WIFE AWAITS HIM OUTSIDE, FRANCOIS PREPARES HIS SPECIALTY...
HURRY UP, IDIOTS! BRING ME THE STUFFING, THE CALVE'S HEARTS ARE READY FOR THE OVEN!

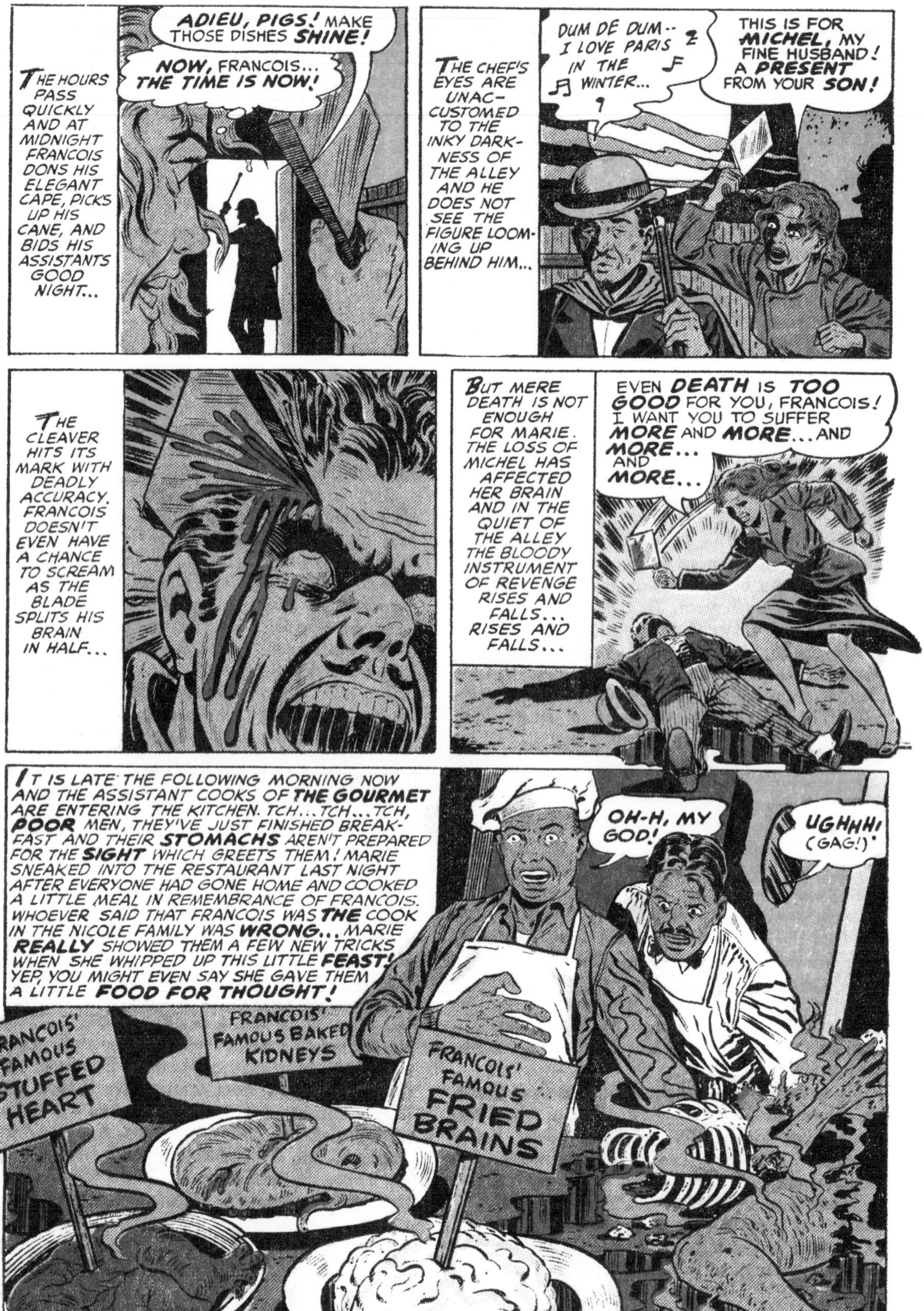
THE HOURS PASS QUICKLY AND AT MIDNIGHT FRANCOIS DONS HIS ELEGANT CAPE, PICKS UP HIS CANE, AND BIDS HIS ASSISTANTS GOOD NIGHT...
ADIEU, PIGS! MAKE THOSE DISHES SHINE!
NOW, FRANCOIS... THE TIME IS NOW!
THE CHEF'S EYES ARE UNACCUSTOMED TO THE INKY DARKNESS OF THE ALLEY AND HE DOES NOT SEE THE FIGURE LOOMING UP BEHIND HIM...
DUM DE DUM.. I LOVE PARIS IN THE WINTER...
THIS IS FOR MICHEL, MY FINE HUSBAND! A PRESENT FROM YOUR SON!
THE CLEAVER HITS ITS MARK WITH DEADLY ACCURACY. FRANCOIS DOESN'T EVEN HAVE A CHANCE TO SCREAM AS THE BLADE SPLITS HIS BRAIN IN HALF...
BUT MERE DEATH IS NOT ENOUGH FOR MARIE. THE LOSS OF MICHEL HAS AFFECTED HER BRAIN AND IN THE QUIET OF THE ALLEY THE BLOODY INSTRUMENT OF REVENGE RISES AND FALLS... RISES AND FALLS...
EVEN DEATH IS TOO GOOD FOR YOU, FRANCOIS! I WANT YOU TO SUFFER MORE AND MORE... AND MORE... AND MORE...
IT IS LATE THE FOLLOWING MORNING NOW AND THE ASSISTANT COOKS OF THE GOURMET ARE ENTERING THE KITCHEN. TCH... TCH, POOR MEN, THEY'VE JUST FINISHED BREAKFAST AND THEIR STOMACHS AREN'T PREPARED FOR THE SIGHT WHICH GREETS THEM! MARIE SNEAKED INTO THE RESTAURANT LAST NIGHT AFTER EVERYONE HAD GONE HOME AND COOKED A LITTLE MEAL IN REMEMBRANCE OF FRANCOIS. WHOEVER SAID THAT FRANCOIS WAS THE COOK IN THE NICOLE FAMILY WAS WRONG... MARIE REALLY SHOWED THEM A FEW NEW TRICKS WHEN SHE WHIPPED UP THIS LITTLE FEAST! YEP, YOU MIGHT EVEN SAY SHE GAVE THEM A LITTLE FOOD FOR THOUGHT!
OH-H, MY GOD!
UGHHH! (GAG!)
FRANCOIS' FAMOUS STUFFED HEART
FRANCOIS' FAMOUS BAKED KIDNEYS
FRANCOIS' FAMOUS FRIED BRAINS
THE END

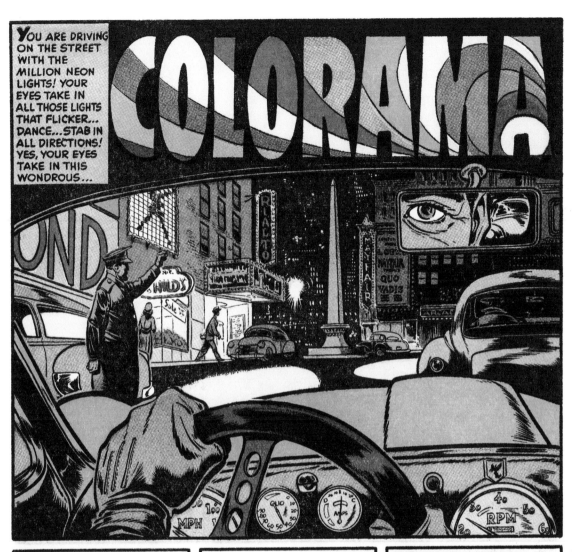

YOU ARE DRIVING ON THE STREET WITH THE MILLION NEON LIGHTS! YOUR EYES TAKE IN ALL THOSE LIGHTS THAT FLICKER... DANCE... STAB IN ALL DIRECTIONS! YES, YOUR EYES TAKE IN THIS WONDROUS...
COLORAMA
RIALTO
MAYFAIR
QUO VADIS
MPH
RPM
SUDDENLY... YOU SEE A NEW LIGHT... A DEEP, BLARING RED... THAT JABS LIKE AN ASTERISK!
RIALTO
YOU DRAW CLOSER... AND THE POINTS OF THE GROWING BALL BEGIN TO MELT... THEN DRIP...
IT SPLITS... INTO TINY PARTICLES. BUT... THE RED NUCLEUS IS STILL THERE! WHAT IS IT? WHERE DOES IT COME FROM?
1

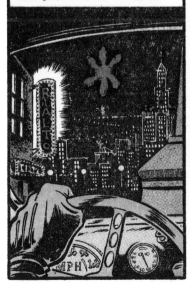

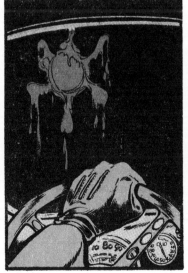

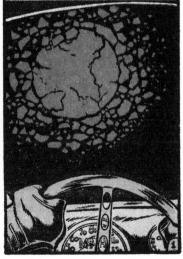

YOU APPLY THE BRAKES! BUT...THE RED BALL HAS DISAPPEARED...AND ALL YOU SEE IS A *TRAFFIC LIGHT*...A *RED* TRAFFIC LIGHT! YOU WONDER....?

WAS IT THE TRAFFIC LIGHT...ALL ALONG? YOU CAN'T THINK STRAIGHT! YOU STOP TO BLINK YOUR EYES...AND WHEN YOU OPEN THEM...YOU CATCH A GLIMPSE OF SOMETHING...

YOU TURN YOUR HEAD...AND SEE ...A SNAKE-LIKE GLOB OF *BLUE*...

AND...IT'S APPROACHING YOU. IT'S GROWING LARGER NOW... AND WIDENING...

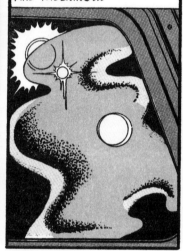

AND THEN...IT'S RIGHT ON TOP OF YOU...SMOTHERING YOU LIKE A WAD OF BLUE DOUGH...

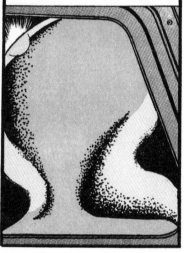

BUT...A VOICE MAKES IT VANISH...JUST AS THE HURT IN YOUR EYES RECEDE! AND...YOU SEE A *POLICEMAN*...IN A *BLUE* UNIFORM!

HEY, BUDDY! DON'T YOU KNOW YOU PASSED A *RED LIGHT?* LET'S SEE YOUR LICENSE!

YOU SHOW THE COP YOUR LICENSE, AND...YOU REMEMBER THAT IT READS...*20/20 VISION!* THEN...YOU KNOW IT! IT'S YOUR EYES...SOMETHING HAS GONE *WRONG* WITH *YOUR EYES!*

I'M GIVING YOU A TICKET, BUDDY! YOU *DESERVE* IT! MISSING THAT *LIGHT!* YOU *OUGHT TO HAVE YOUR EYES EXAMINED!*

2

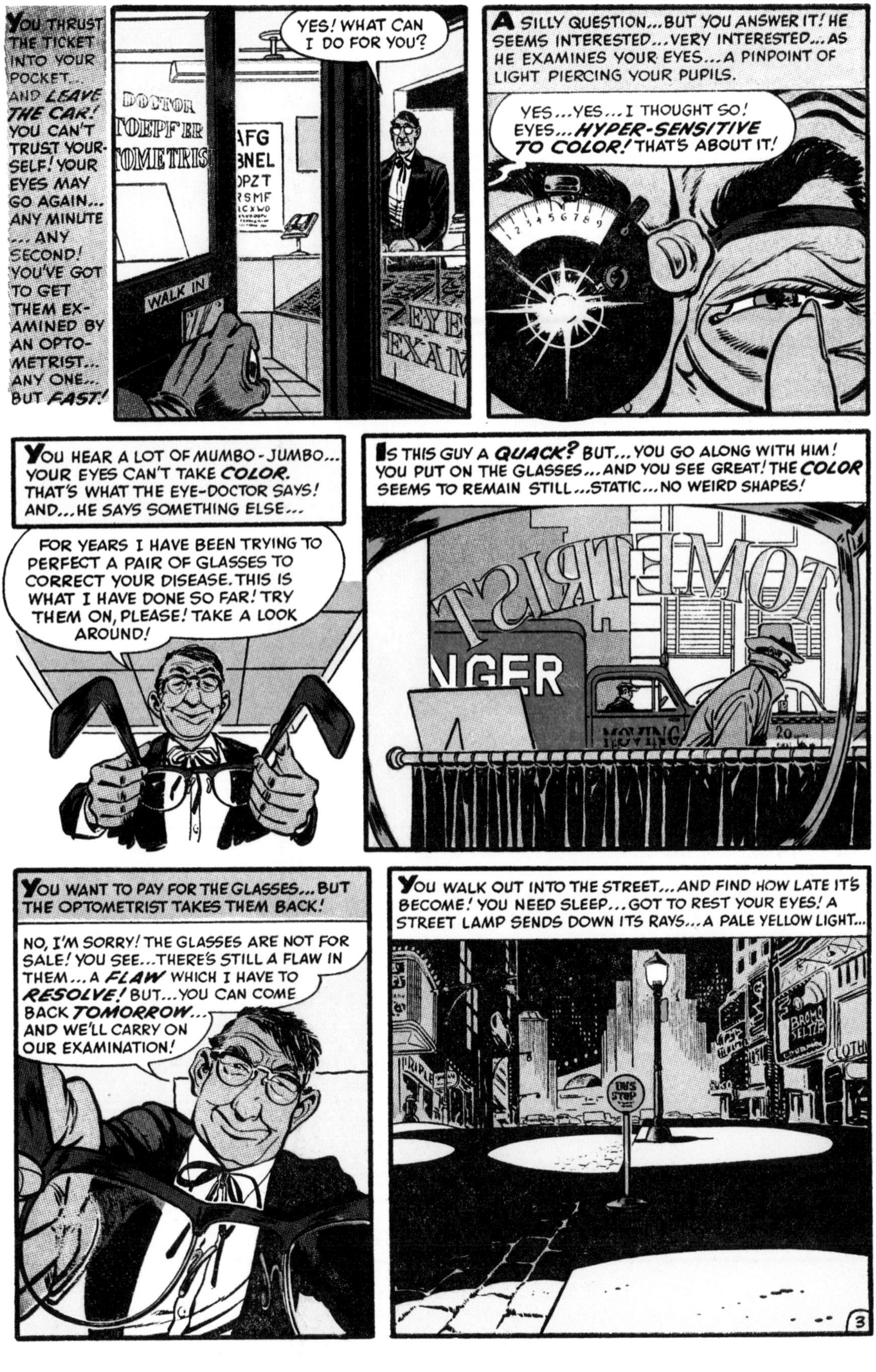
YOU THRUST THE TICKET INTO YOUR POCKET... AND LEAVE THE CAR! YOU CAN'T TRUST YOURSELF! YOUR EYES MAY GO AGAIN... ANY MINUTE ... ANY SECOND! YOU'VE GOT TO GET THEM EXAMINED BY AN OPTOMETRIST... ANY ONE... BUT FAST!
YES! WHAT CAN I DO FOR YOU?
DOCTOR
TOEPFER
TOMETRIST
WALK IN
EYE
EXAM
A SILLY QUESTION... BUT YOU ANSWER IT! HE SEEMS INTERESTED... VERY INTERESTED... AS HE EXAMINES YOUR EYES... A PINPOINT OF LIGHT PIERCING YOUR PUPILS.
YES... YES... I THOUGHT SO! EYES... HYPER-SENSITIVE TO COLOR! THAT'S ABOUT IT!
YOU HEAR A LOT OF MUMBO-JUMBO... YOUR EYES CAN'T TAKE COLOR. THAT'S WHAT THE EYE-DOCTOR SAYS! AND... HE SAYS SOMETHING ELSE...
FOR YEARS I HAVE BEEN TRYING TO PERFECT A PAIR OF GLASSES TO CORRECT YOUR DISEASE. THIS IS WHAT I HAVE DONE SO FAR! TRY THEM ON, PLEASE! TAKE A LOOK AROUND!
IS THIS GUY A QUACK? BUT... YOU GO ALONG WITH HIM! YOU PUT ON THE GLASSES... AND YOU SEE GREAT! THE COLOR SEEMS TO REMAIN STILL... STATIC... NO WEIRD SHAPES!
NGER
MOVING
YOU WANT TO PAY FOR THE GLASSES... BUT THE OPTOMETRIST TAKES THEM BACK!
NO, I'M SORRY! THE GLASSES ARE NOT FOR SALE! YOU SEE... THERE'S STILL A FLAW IN THEM... A FLAW WHICH I HAVE TO RESOLVE! BUT... YOU CAN COME BACK TOMORROW... AND WE'LL CARRY ON OUR EXAMINATION!
YOU WALK OUT INTO THE STREET... AND FIND HOW LATE IT'S BECOME! YOU NEED SLEEP... GOT TO REST YOUR EYES! A STREET LAMP SENDS DOWN ITS RAYS... A PALE YELLOW LIGHT...
BROMO SELTZER
BUS STOP
3

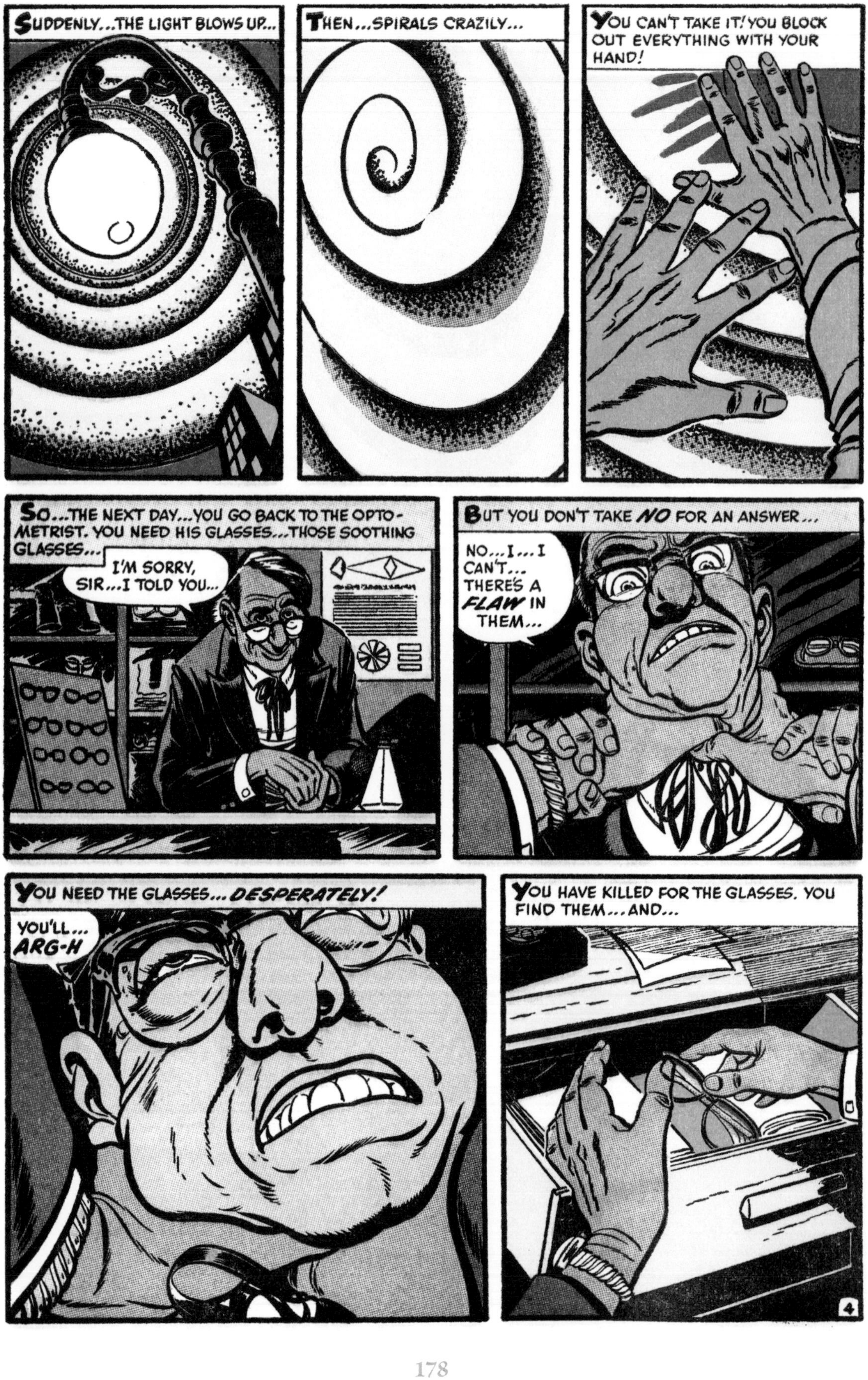
SUDDENLY...THE LIGHT BLOWS UP...
THEN...SPIRALS CRAZILY...
YOU CAN'T TAKE IT! YOU BLOCK OUT EVERYTHING WITH YOUR HAND!
SO...THE NEXT DAY...YOU GO BACK TO THE OPTOMETRIST. YOU NEED HIS GLASSES...THOSE SOOTHING GLASSES...
I'M SORRY, SIR...I TOLD YOU...
BUT YOU DON'T TAKE NO FOR AN ANSWER...
NO...I...I CAN'T... THERE'S A FLAW IN THEM...
YOU NEED THE GLASSES...DESPERATELY!
YOU'LL... ARG-H
YOU HAVE KILLED FOR THE GLASSES. YOU FIND THEM...AND...
4

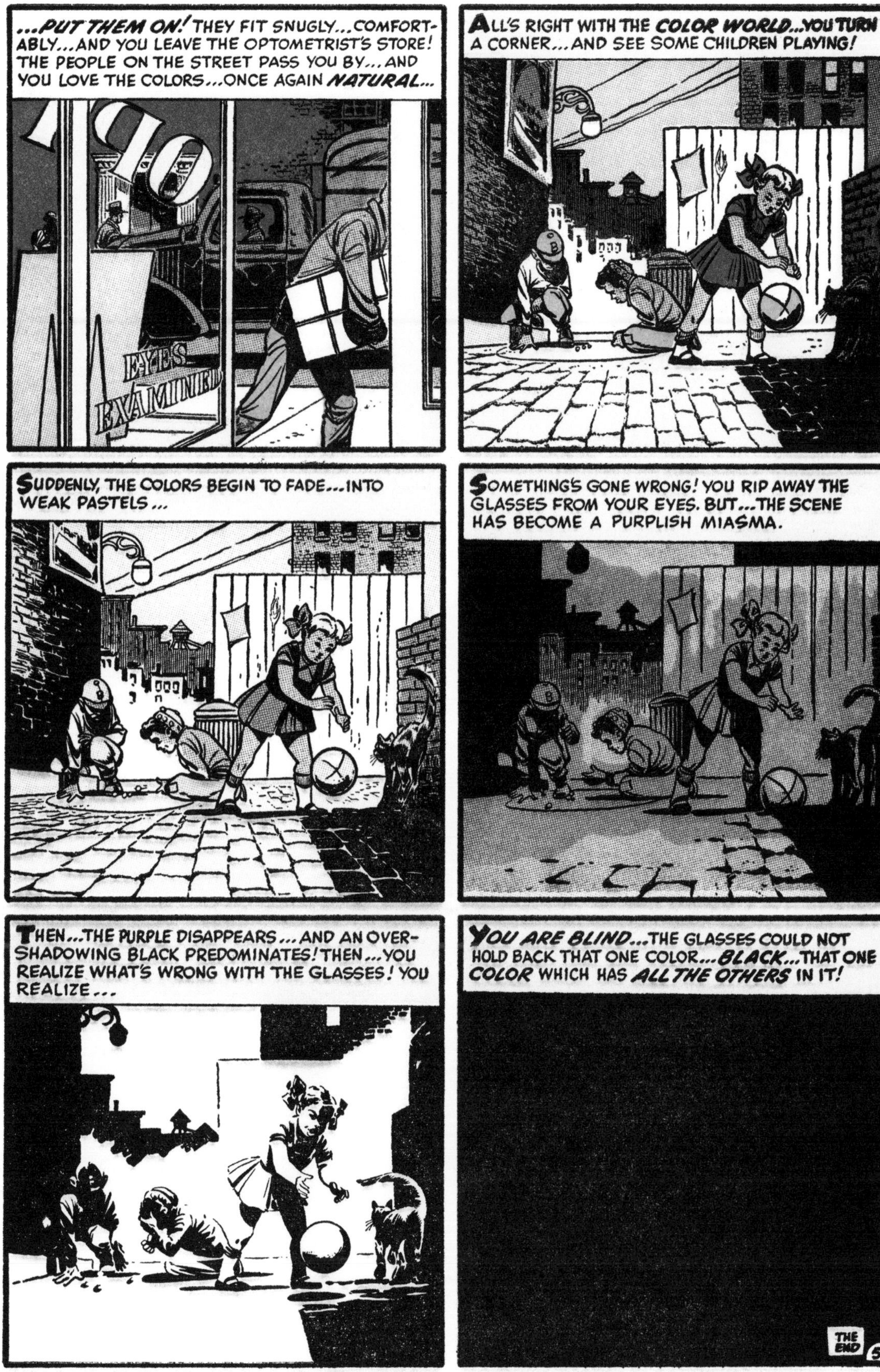
...PUT THEM ON! THEY FIT SNUGLY...COMFORTABLY...AND YOU LEAVE THE OPTOMETRIST'S STORE! THE PEOPLE ON THE STREET PASS YOU BY...AND YOU LOVE THE COLORS...ONCE AGAIN NATURAL...
EYES EXAMINED
ALL'S RIGHT WITH THE COLOR WORLD...YOU TURN A CORNER...AND SEE SOME CHILDREN PLAYING!
SUDDENLY, THE COLORS BEGIN TO FADE...INTO WEAK PASTELS...
SOMETHING'S GONE WRONG! YOU RIP AWAY THE GLASSES FROM YOUR EYES. BUT...THE SCENE HAS BECOME A PURPLISH MIASMA.
THEN...THE PURPLE DISAPPEARS...AND AN OVERSHADOWING BLACK PREDOMINATES! THEN...YOU REALIZE WHAT'S WRONG WITH THE GLASSES! YOU REALIZE...
YOU ARE BLIND...THE GLASSES COULD NOT HOLD BACK THAT ONE COLOR...BLACK...THAT ONE COLOR WHICH HAS ALL THE OTHERS IN IT!
THE END
5

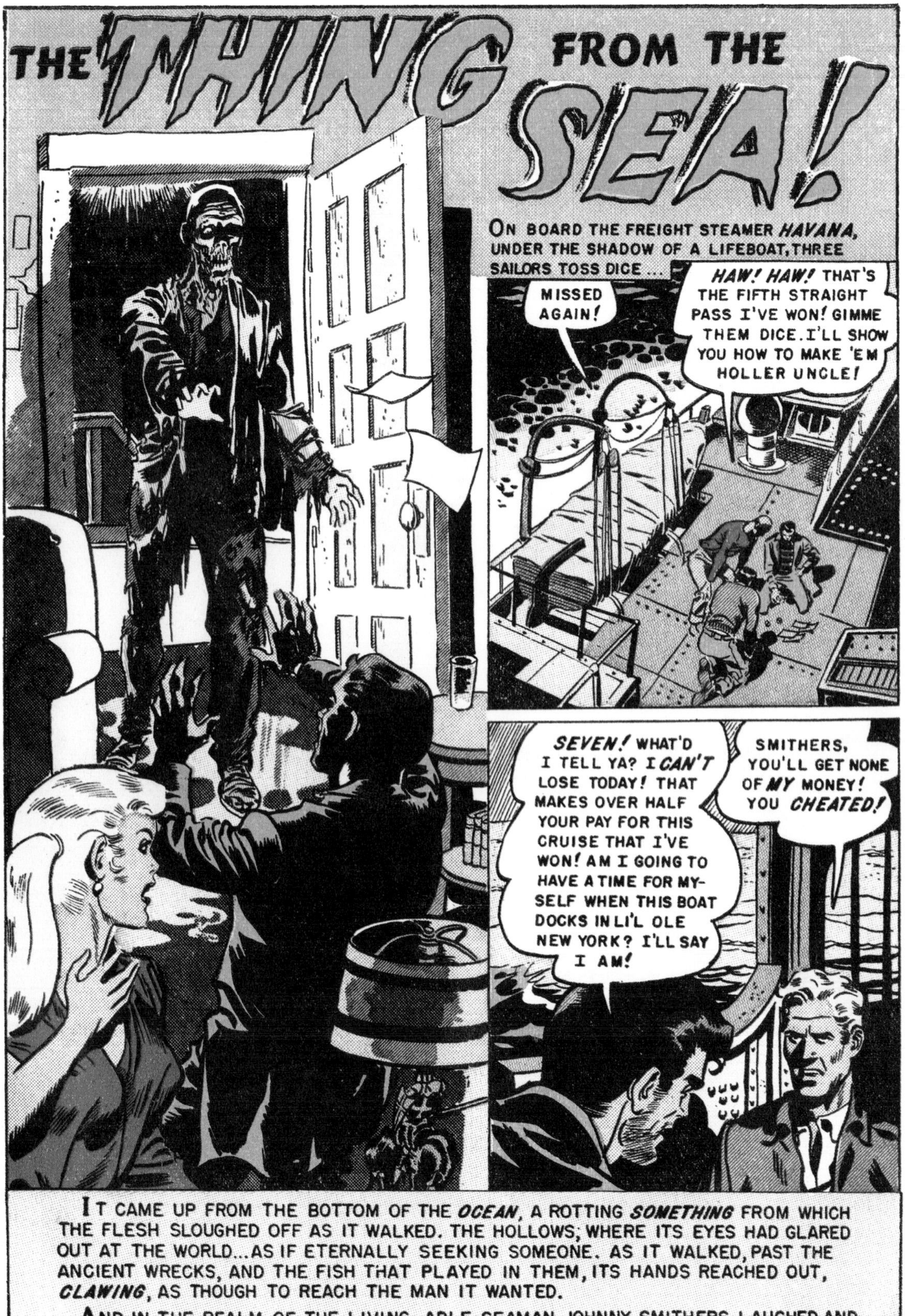
THE THING FROM THE SEA!
ON BOARD THE FREIGHT STEAMER HAVANA, UNDER THE SHADOW OF A LIFEBOAT, THREE SAILORS TOSS DICE ...
MISSED AGAIN!
HAW! HAW! THAT'S THE FIFTH STRAIGHT PASS I'VE WON! GIMME THEM DICE. I'LL SHOW YOU HOW TO MAKE 'EM HOLLER UNCLE!
SEVEN! WHAT'D I TELL YA? I CAN'T LOSE TODAY! THAT MAKES OVER HALF YOUR PAY FOR THIS CRUISE THAT I'VE WON! AM I GOING TO HAVE A TIME FOR MYSELF WHEN THIS BOAT DOCKS IN LI'L OLE NEW YORK? I'LL SAY I AM!
SMITHERS, YOU'LL GET NONE OF MY MONEY! YOU CHEATED!
IT CAME UP FROM THE BOTTOM OF THE OCEAN, A ROTTING SOMETHING FROM WHICH THE FLESH SLOUGHED OFF AS IT WALKED. THE HOLLOWS, WHERE ITS EYES HAD GLARED OUT AT THE WORLD...AS IF ETERNALLY SEEKING SOMEONE. AS IT WALKED, PAST THE ANCIENT WRECKS, AND THE FISH THAT PLAYED IN THEM, ITS HANDS REACHED OUT, CLAWING, AS THOUGH TO REACH THE MAN IT WANTED.
AND IN THE REALM OF THE LIVING, ABLE SEAMAN JOHNNY SMITHERS LAUGHED AND LOVED, NEVER DREAMING THAT DESTINY WAS COMING HIS WAY ON DEAD FEET. NO NEED FOR HIM TO WORRY...OR WAS THERE?
1

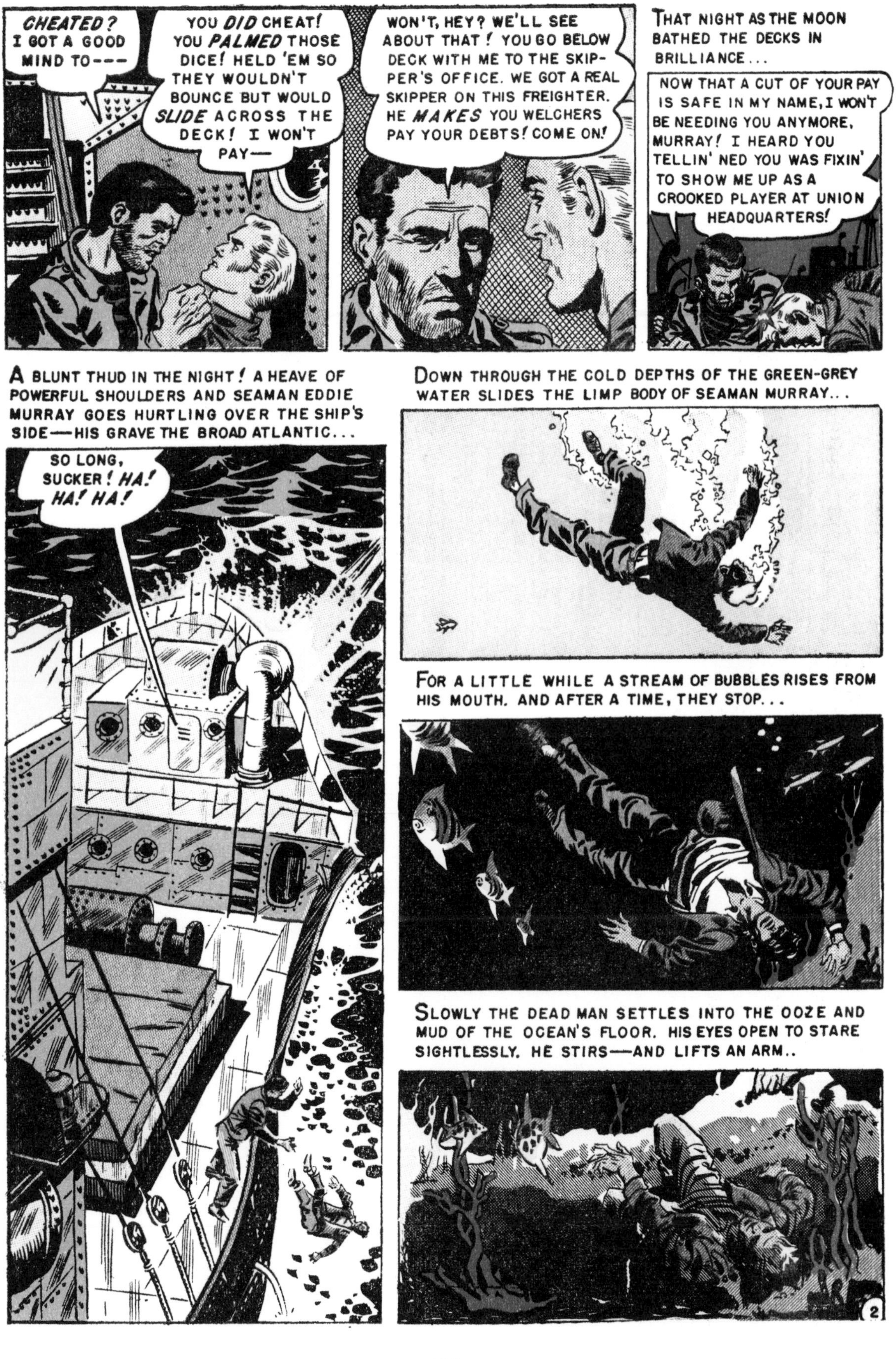
CHEATED? I GOT A GOOD MIND TO---
YOU DID CHEAT! YOU PALMED THOSE DICE! HELD 'EM SO THEY WOULDN'T BOUNCE BUT WOULD SLIDE ACROSS THE DECK! I WON'T PAY—
WON'T, HEY? WE'LL SEE ABOUT THAT! YOU GO BELOW DECK WITH ME TO THE SKIPPER'S OFFICE. WE GOT A REAL SKIPPER ON THIS FREIGHTER. HE MAKES YOU WELCHERS PAY YOUR DEBTS! COME ON!
THAT NIGHT AS THE MOON BATHED THE DECKS IN BRILLIANCE...
NOW THAT A CUT OF YOUR PAY IS SAFE IN MY NAME, I WON'T BE NEEDING YOU ANYMORE, MURRAY! I HEARD YOU TELLIN' NED YOU WAS FIXIN' TO SHOW ME UP AS A CROOKED PLAYER AT UNION HEADQUARTERS!
A BLUNT THUD IN THE NIGHT! A HEAVE OF POWERFUL SHOULDERS AND SEAMAN EDDIE MURRAY GOES HURTLING OVER THE SHIP'S SIDE—HIS GRAVE THE BROAD ATLANTIC...
SO LONG, SUCKER! HA! HA! HA!
DOWN THROUGH THE COLD DEPTHS OF THE GREEN-GREY WATER SLIDES THE LIMP BODY OF SEAMAN MURRAY...
FOR A LITTLE WHILE A STREAM OF BUBBLES RISES FROM HIS MOUTH. AND AFTER A TIME, THEY STOP...
SLOWLY THE DEAD MAN SETTLES INTO THE OOZE AND MUD OF THE OCEAN'S FLOOR. HIS EYES OPEN TO STARE SIGHTLESSLY. HE STIRS—AND LIFTS AN ARM..
2

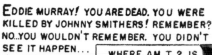

EDDIE MURRAY! YOU ARE DEAD. YOU WERE KILLED BY JOHNNY SMITHERS! REMEMBER? NO..YOU WOULDN'T REMEMBER. YOU DIDN'T SEE IT HAPPEN...

WHERE AM I? IS THIS *WATER* ALL AROUND ME? I'M NOT BREATHING... BUT I FEEL STRONG. AND THERE'S SOMETHING I WANT TO DO!

FISH NIBBLING AT MY FLESH... BUT I DON'T *FEEL* ANYTHING. JUST WANT TO WALK...UNTIL I FIND...WHAT I'M LOOKING FOR...

WHILE THE WALKING HORROR STALKS THE OCEAN BOTTOM, THE *HAVANA* DOCKS IN NEW YORK...

HE'S ON BOARD. I GOT HIS TELEGRAM WHEN THEY LEFT RIO. OH, EDDIE, IT'S BEEN SO LONG!

DO YOU KNOW A SEAMAN MURRAY? I'M HIS GIRL FRIEND. WE'RE GOING TO GET MARRIED...

SURE, I KNOW HIM. HE GOT DRUNK ONE NIGHT AND FELL OVERBOARD! HMMM.... DIDN'T KNOW HE HAD SUCH GOOD TASTE!

O-OVERBOARD...? ⸮SOB⸮ POOR EDDIE... OH, MY POOR DARLING!

NO SENSE CRYIN' OVER WHAT'S HAPPENED! COME ALONG WITH ME AND I'LL—TELL YOU ALL ABOUT IT!

EDDIE WAS A SWELL GUY. ONLY ONE TROUBLE—HE COULDN'T SHOOT DICE. MATTER OF FACT, IT WAS BECAUSE HE LOST SO MUCH MONEY THAT HE —FELL OVERBOARD!

HE WAS TRYING TO WIN MONEY SO WE COULD GET *MARRIED!*

MOVING SLOWLY PAST THE WRECK OF A LONG SUNKEN SHIP, FEET SLOGGING IN THE MUD, A THING THAT ONCE WAS HUMAN STALKS FORWARD..

HE'S OUT THERE SOMEWHERE...THE MAN WHO SENT ME DOWN HERE! I WONDER HOW HE'D LIKE TO WALK FOREVER ALONG THE BOTTOM OF THE OCEAN....WITH *ME?*

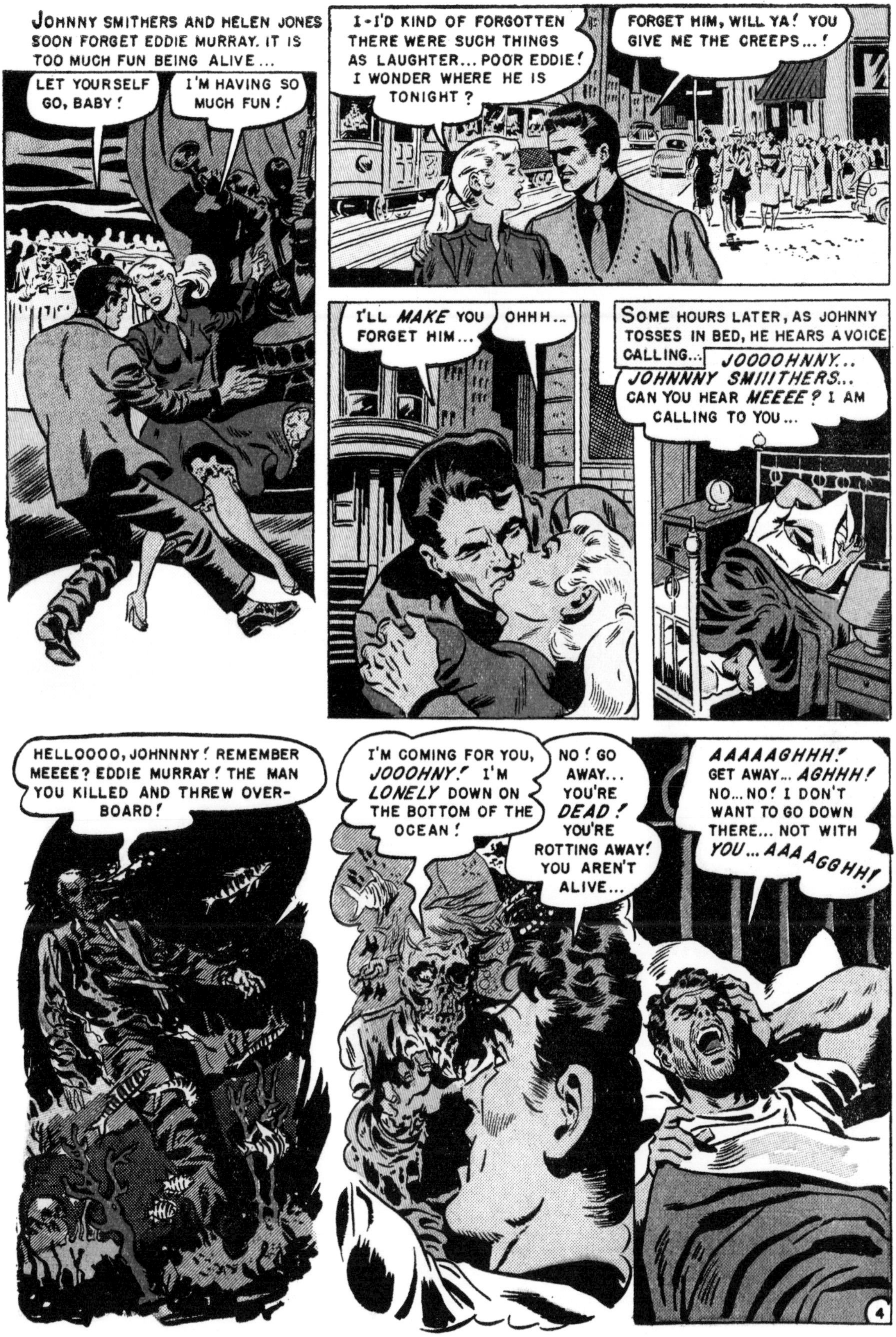

JOHNNY SMITHERS AND HELEN JONES SOON FORGET EDDIE MURRAY. IT IS TOO MUCH FUN BEING ALIVE...
LET YOURSELF GO, BABY!
I'M HAVING SO MUCH FUN!
I-I'D KIND OF FORGOTTEN THERE WERE SUCH THINGS AS LAUGHTER... POOR EDDIE! I WONDER WHERE HE IS TONIGHT?
FORGET HIM, WILL YA! YOU GIVE ME THE CREEPS...!
I'LL MAKE YOU FORGET HIM...
OHHH...
SOME HOURS LATER, AS JOHNNY TOSSES IN BED, HE HEARS A VOICE CALLING...
JOOOOHNNY... JOHNNNY SMIIITHERS... CAN YOU HEAR MEEEE? I AM CALLING TO YOU...
HELLOOOO, JOHNNNY! REMEMBER MEEEE? EDDIE MURRAY! THE MAN YOU KILLED AND THREW OVER-BOARD!
I'M COMING FOR YOU, JOOOHNY! I'M LONELY DOWN ON THE BOTTOM OF THE OCEAN!
NO! GO AWAY... YOU'RE DEAD! YOU'RE ROTTING AWAY! YOU AREN'T ALIVE...
AAAAAGHHH! GET AWAY... AGHHH! NO... NO! I DON'T WANT TO GO DOWN THERE... NOT WITH YOU... AAAAGGHH!
4

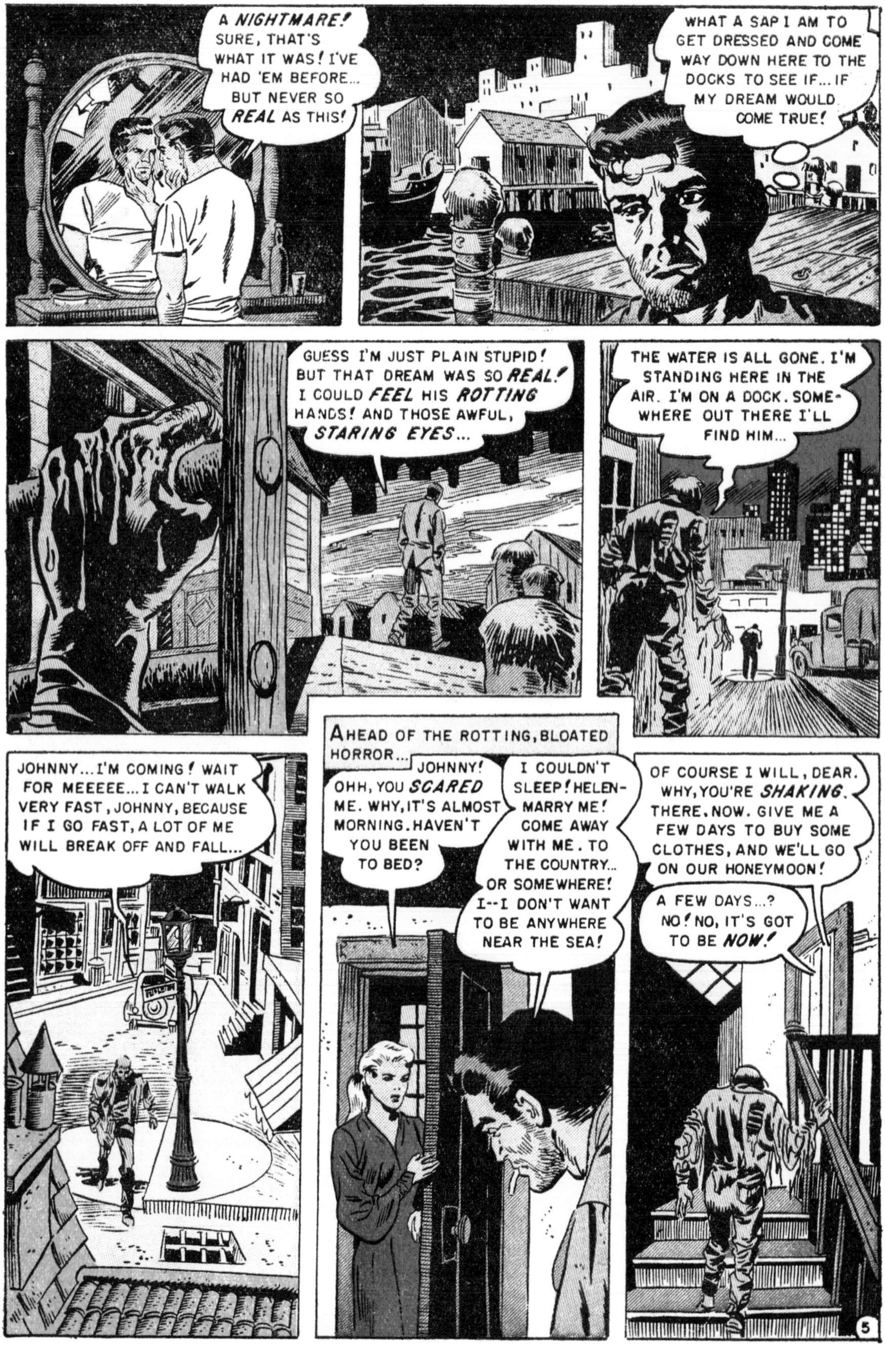

A NIGHTMARE! SURE, THAT'S WHAT IT WAS! I'VE HAD 'EM BEFORE... BUT NEVER SO REAL AS THIS!
WHAT A SAP I AM TO GET DRESSED AND COME WAY DOWN HERE TO THE DOCKS TO SEE IF... IF MY DREAM WOULD COME TRUE!
GUESS I'M JUST PLAIN STUPID! BUT THAT DREAM WAS SO REAL! I COULD FEEL HIS ROTTING HANDS! AND THOSE AWFUL, STARING EYES...
THE WATER IS ALL GONE. I'M STANDING HERE IN THE AIR. I'M ON A DOCK. SOMEWHERE OUT THERE I'LL FIND HIM...
JOHNNY...I'M COMING! WAIT FOR MEEEEE... I CAN'T WALK VERY FAST, JOHNNY, BECAUSE IF I GO FAST, A LOT OF ME WILL BREAK OFF AND FALL...
AHEAD OF THE ROTTING, BLOATED HORROR...
JOHNNY! OHH, YOU SCARED ME. WHY, IT'S ALMOST MORNING. HAVEN'T YOU BEEN TO BED?
I COULDN'T SLEEP! HELEN-MARRY ME! COME AWAY WITH ME. TO THE COUNTRY... OR SOMEWHERE! I--I DON'T WANT TO BE ANYWHERE NEAR THE SEA!
OF COURSE I WILL, DEAR. WHY, YOU'RE SHAKING. THERE. NOW. GIVE ME A FEW DAYS TO BUY SOME CLOTHES, AND WE'LL GO ON OUR HONEYMOON!
A FEW DAYS...? NO! NO, IT'S GOT TO BE NOW!
5

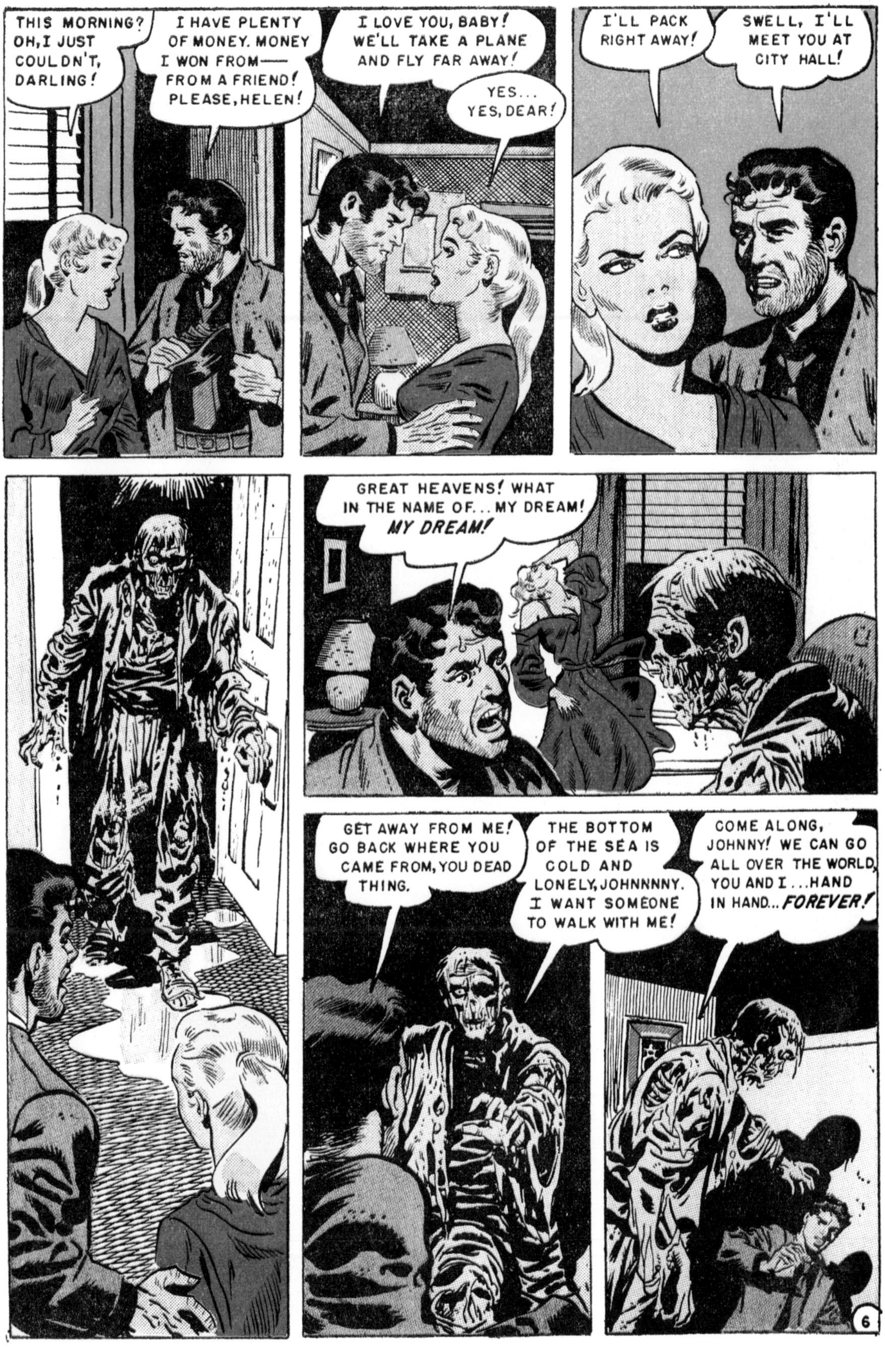
THIS MORNING? OH, I JUST COULDN'T, DARLING!
I HAVE PLENTY OF MONEY. MONEY I WON FROM—FROM A FRIEND! PLEASE, HELEN!
I LOVE YOU, BABY! WE'LL TAKE A PLANE AND FLY FAR AWAY!
YES... YES, DEAR!
I'LL PACK RIGHT AWAY!
SWELL, I'LL MEET YOU AT CITY HALL!
GREAT HEAVENS! WHAT IN THE NAME OF... MY DREAM! MY DREAM!
GET AWAY FROM ME! GO BACK WHERE YOU CAME FROM, YOU DEAD THING.
THE BOTTOM OF THE SEA IS COLD AND LONELY, JOHNNNNY. I WANT SOMEONE TO WALK WITH ME!
COME ALONG, JOHNNY! WE CAN GO ALL OVER THE WORLD, YOU AND I...HAND IN HAND...FOREVER!
6

HELEN! WAKE UP! CALL THE POLICE! HELP! PULL ME LOOSE FROM THIS HORROR! HIS FLESH IS ROTTEN! *HELP!*

JOHNNY SMITHERS GOES MAD! THE FEEL OF THAT COLD AND SLIMY HAND, SENDS COLD SHUDDERS DOWN HIS SPINE...

HELEN! IF YOU'LL ONLY GRAB MY HAND...I CAN BREAK FREE OF HIM. HELEN! WAKE UP---*HELEN!!*

IN THE EARLY DAWN OF A NEW YORK MORNING... WHILE THE CITY SLEEPS...

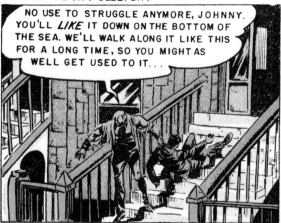

NO USE TO STRUGGLE ANYMORE, JOHNNY. YOU'LL *LIKE* IT DOWN ON THE BOTTOM OF THE SEA. WE'LL WALK ALONG IT LIKE THIS FOR A LONG TIME, SO YOU MIGHT AS WELL GET USED TO IT...

NO...*NO...NO!* I'LL GIVE YOU BACK YOUR MONEY...I WON'T SEE HELEN EVER AGAIN...JUST LET ME GO...*LET ME GO...*

I DON'T CARE ABOUT MONEY ANYMORE! I'VE FORGOTTEN HELEN, TOO! ALL I WANT IS *YOU*, JOHNNY...ON THE BOTTOM OF THE SEA!

JUST THINK, JOHNNY! YOU'RE GOING TO WALK THE OCEAN FLOOR WITH THE MAN YOU MURDERED!

NO...NO....

JOHNNY'S SCREAM GURGLES IN HIS THROAT. HE CLUTCHES EMPTY AIR...

AND THEN THERE IS JUST EMPTY WATER, ROLLING ENDLESSLY OVER THE OCEAN FLOOR WHERE TWO MEN WALK, FOREVER...

7

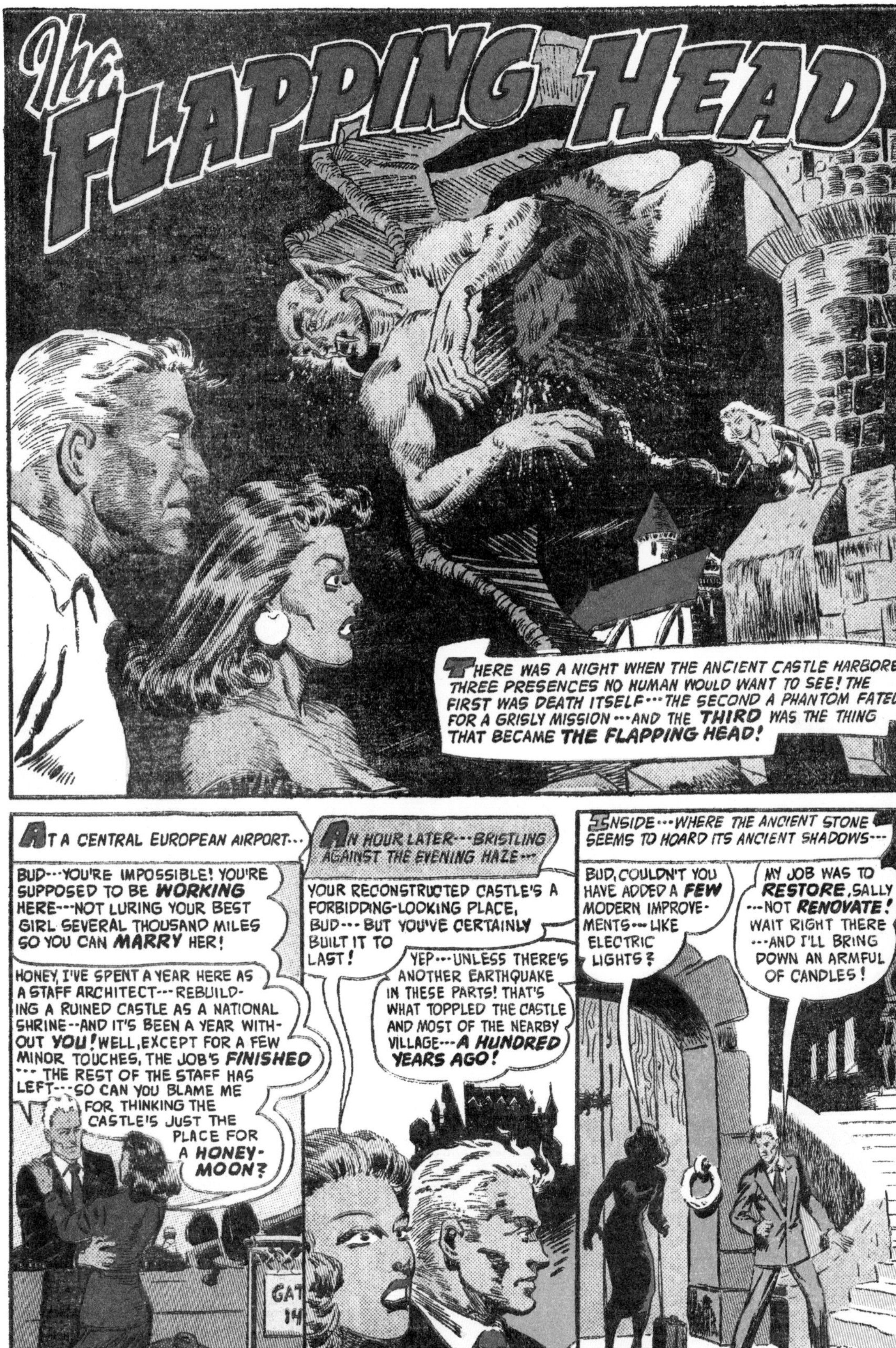
The FLAPPING HEAD
THERE WAS A NIGHT WHEN THE ANCIENT CASTLE HARBORED THREE PRESENCES NO HUMAN WOULD WANT TO SEE! THE FIRST WAS DEATH ITSELF--- THE SECOND A PHANTOM FATED FOR A GRISLY MISSION --- AND THE THIRD WAS THE THING THAT BECAME THE FLAPPING HEAD!
AT A CENTRAL EUROPEAN AIRPORT---
BUD---YOU'RE IMPOSSIBLE! YOU'RE SUPPOSED TO BE WORKING HERE---NOT LURING YOUR BEST GIRL SEVERAL THOUSAND MILES SO YOU CAN MARRY HER!
HONEY, I'VE SPENT A YEAR HERE AS A STAFF ARCHITECT--- REBUILDING A RUINED CASTLE AS A NATIONAL SHRINE--AND IT'S BEEN A YEAR WITHOUT YOU! WELL, EXCEPT FOR A FEW MINOR TOUCHES, THE JOB'S FINISHED --- THE REST OF THE STAFF HAS LEFT---SO CAN YOU BLAME ME FOR THINKING THE CASTLE'S JUST THE PLACE FOR A HONEYMOON?
AN HOUR LATER--- BRISTLING AGAINST THE EVENING HAZE---
YOUR RECONSTRUCTED CASTLE'S A FORBIDDING-LOOKING PLACE, BUD--- BUT YOU'VE CERTAINLY BUILT IT TO LAST!
YEP---UNLESS THERE'S ANOTHER EARTHQUAKE IN THESE PARTS! THAT'S WHAT TOPPLED THE CASTLE AND MOST OF THE NEARBY VILLAGE---A HUNDRED YEARS AGO!
INSIDE---WHERE THE ANCIENT STONE SEEMS TO HOARD ITS ANCIENT SHADOWS---
BUD, COULDN'T YOU HAVE ADDED A FEW MODERN IMPROVEMENTS--- LIKE ELECTRIC LIGHTS?
MY JOB WAS TO RESTORE, SALLY ---NOT RENOVATE! WAIT RIGHT THERE ---AND I'LL BRING DOWN AN ARMFUL OF CANDLES!
GAT 14

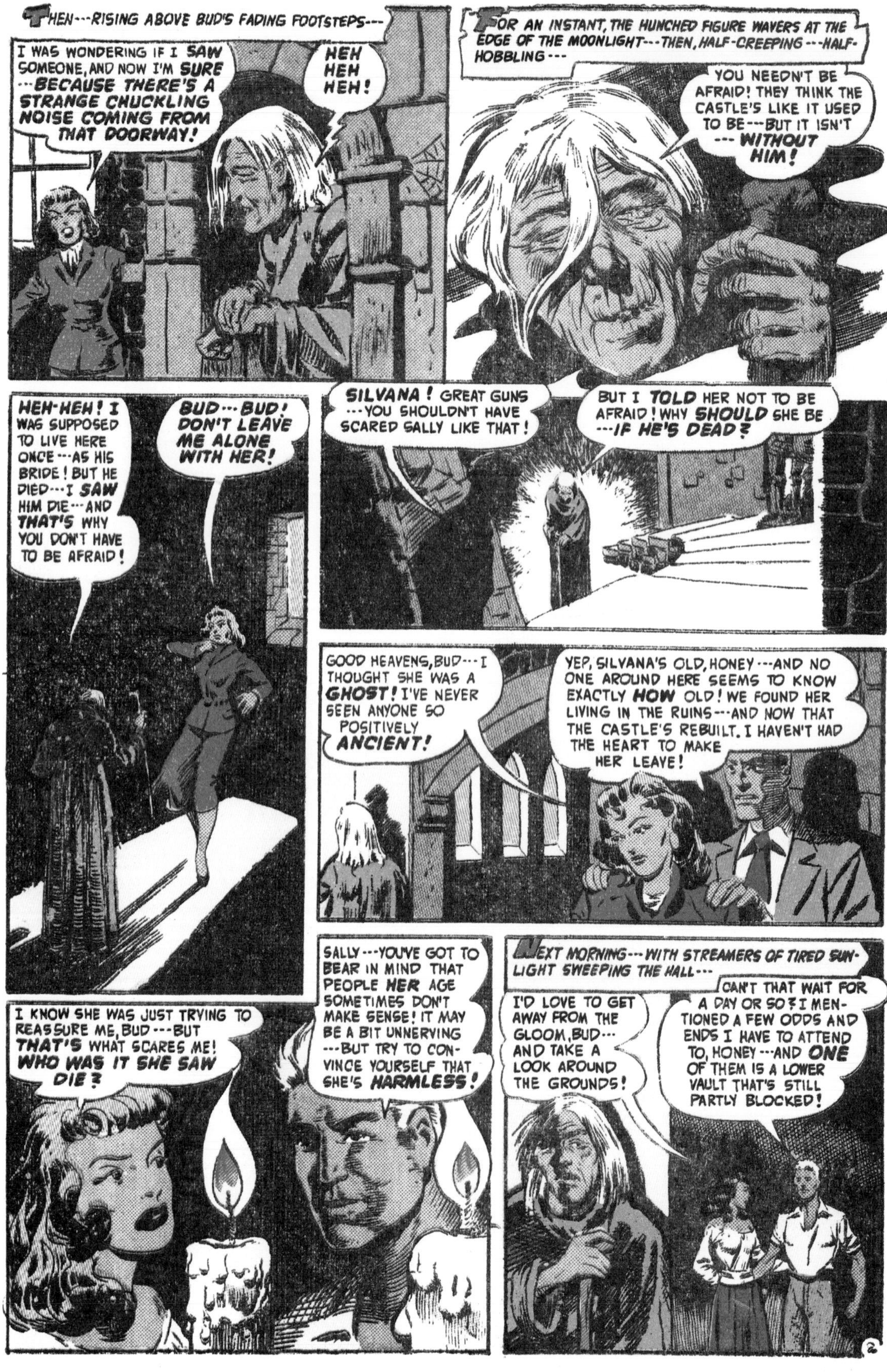
THEN---RISING ABOVE BUD'S FADING FOOTSTEPS---
I WAS WONDERING IF I SAW SOMEONE, AND NOW I'M SURE ---BECAUSE THERE'S A STRANGE CHUCKLING NOISE COMING FROM THAT DOORWAY!
HEH HEH HEH!
FOR AN INSTANT, THE HUNCHED FIGURE WAVERS AT THE EDGE OF THE MOONLIGHT---THEN, HALF-CREEPING---HALF-HOBBLING---
YOU NEEDN'T BE AFRAID! THEY THINK THE CASTLE'S LIKE IT USED TO BE---BUT IT ISN'T ---WITHOUT HIM!
HEH-HEH! I WAS SUPPOSED TO LIVE HERE ONCE---AS HIS BRIDE! BUT HE DIED---I SAW HIM DIE---AND THAT'S WHY YOU DON'T HAVE TO BE AFRAID!
BUD---BUD! DON'T LEAVE ME ALONE WITH HER!
SILVANA! GREAT GUNS ---YOU SHOULDN'T HAVE SCARED SALLY LIKE THAT!
BUT I TOLD HER NOT TO BE AFRAID! WHY SHOULD SHE BE ---IF HE'S DEAD?
GOOD HEAVENS, BUD---I THOUGHT SHE WAS A GHOST! I'VE NEVER SEEN ANYONE SO POSITIVELY ANCIENT!
YEP, SILVANA'S OLD, HONEY---AND NO ONE AROUND HERE SEEMS TO KNOW EXACTLY HOW OLD! WE FOUND HER LIVING IN THE RUINS---AND NOW THAT THE CASTLE'S REBUILT, I HAVEN'T HAD THE HEART TO MAKE HER LEAVE!
I KNOW SHE WAS JUST TRYING TO REASSURE ME, BUD---BUT THAT'S WHAT SCARES ME! WHO WAS IT SHE SAW DIE?
SALLY---YOU'VE GOT TO BEAR IN MIND THAT PEOPLE HER AGE SOMETIMES DON'T MAKE SENSE! IT MAY BE A BIT UNNERVING ---BUT TRY TO CONVINCE YOURSELF THAT SHE'S HARMLESS!
NEXT MORNING---WITH STREAMERS OF TIRED SUNLIGHT SWEEPING THE HALL---
I'D LOVE TO GET AWAY FROM THE GLOOM, BUD---AND TAKE A LOOK AROUND THE GROUNDS!
CAN'T THAT WAIT FOR A DAY OR SO? I MENTIONED A FEW ODDS AND ENDS I HAVE TO ATTEND TO, HONEY---AND ONE OF THEM IS A LOWER VAULT THAT'S STILL PARTLY BLOCKED!
2

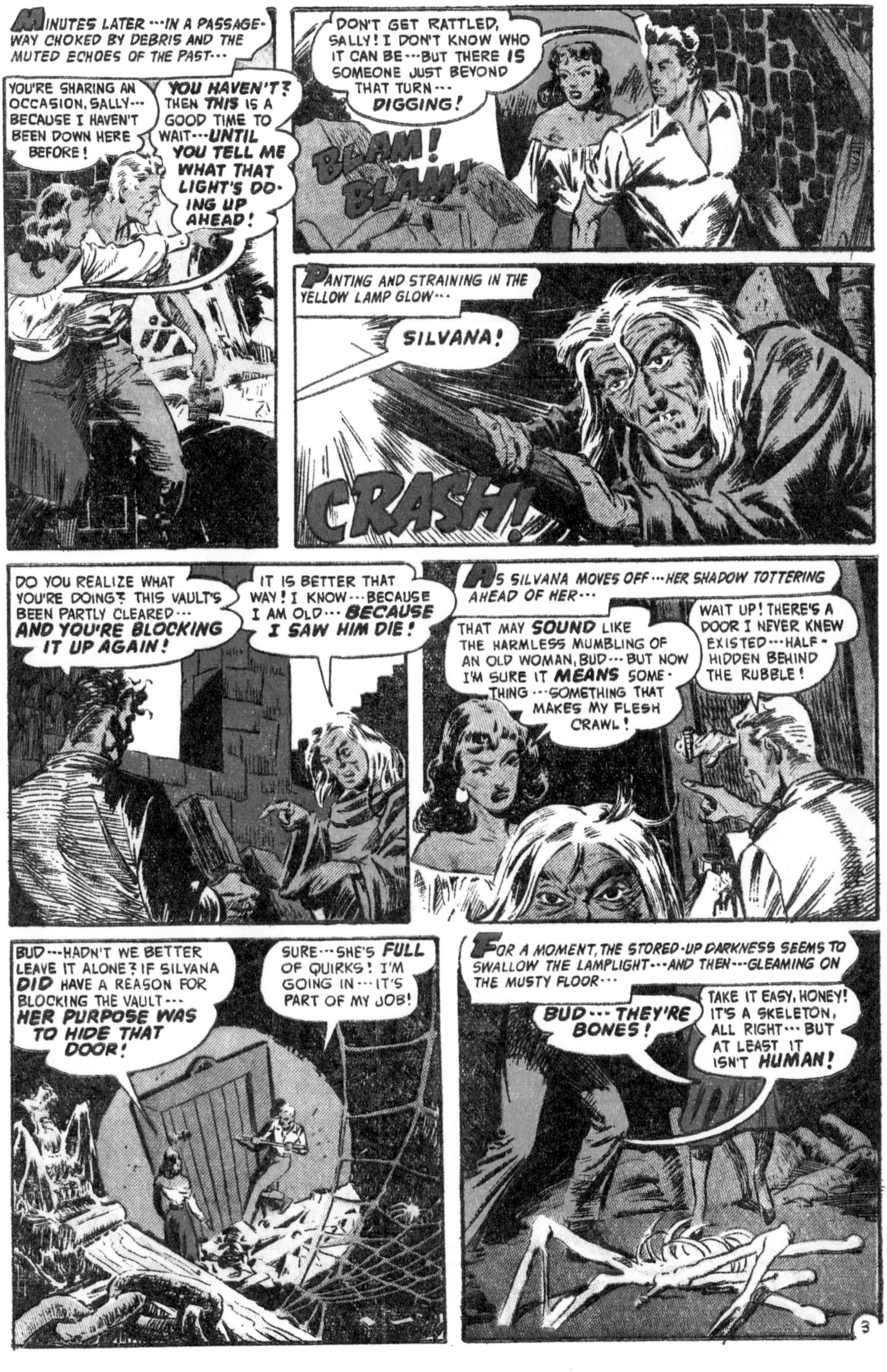
MINUTES LATER ··· IN A PASSAGE-WAY CHOKED BY DEBRIS AND THE MUTED ECHOES OF THE PAST ···
YOU'RE SHARING AN OCCASION, SALLY ··· BECAUSE I HAVEN'T BEEN DOWN HERE BEFORE!
YOU HAVEN'T? THEN THIS IS A GOOD TIME TO WAIT ··· UNTIL YOU TELL ME WHAT THAT LIGHT'S DOING UP AHEAD!
DON'T GET RATTLED, SALLY! I DON'T KNOW WHO IT CAN BE ··· BUT THERE IS SOMEONE JUST BEYOND THAT TURN ··· DIGGING!
BLAM! BLAM!
PANTING AND STRAINING IN THE YELLOW LAMP GLOW ···
SILVANA!
CRASH!
DO YOU REALIZE WHAT YOU'RE DOING? THIS VAULT'S BEEN PARTLY CLEARED ··· AND YOU'RE BLOCKING IT UP AGAIN!
IT IS BETTER THAT WAY! I KNOW ··· BECAUSE I AM OLD ··· BECAUSE I SAW HIM DIE!
AS SILVANA MOVES OFF ··· HER SHADOW TOTTERING AHEAD OF HER ···
THAT MAY SOUND LIKE THE HARMLESS MUMBLING OF AN OLD WOMAN, BUD ··· BUT NOW I'M SURE IT MEANS SOMETHING ··· SOMETHING THAT MAKES MY FLESH CRAWL!
WAIT UP! THERE'S A DOOR I NEVER KNEW EXISTED ··· HALF-HIDDEN BEHIND THE RUBBLE!
BUD ··· HADN'T WE BETTER LEAVE IT ALONE? IF SILVANA DID HAVE A REASON FOR BLOCKING THE VAULT ··· HER PURPOSE WAS TO HIDE THAT DOOR!
SURE ··· SHE'S FULL OF QUIRKS! I'M GOING IN ··· IT'S PART OF MY JOB!
FOR A MOMENT, THE STORED-UP DARKNESS SEEMS TO SWALLOW THE LAMPLIGHT ··· AND THEN ··· GLEAMING ON THE MUSTY FLOOR ···
BUD ··· THEY'RE BONES!
TAKE IT EASY, HONEY! IT'S A SKELETON, ALL RIGHT ··· BUT AT LEAST IT ISN'T HUMAN!
3

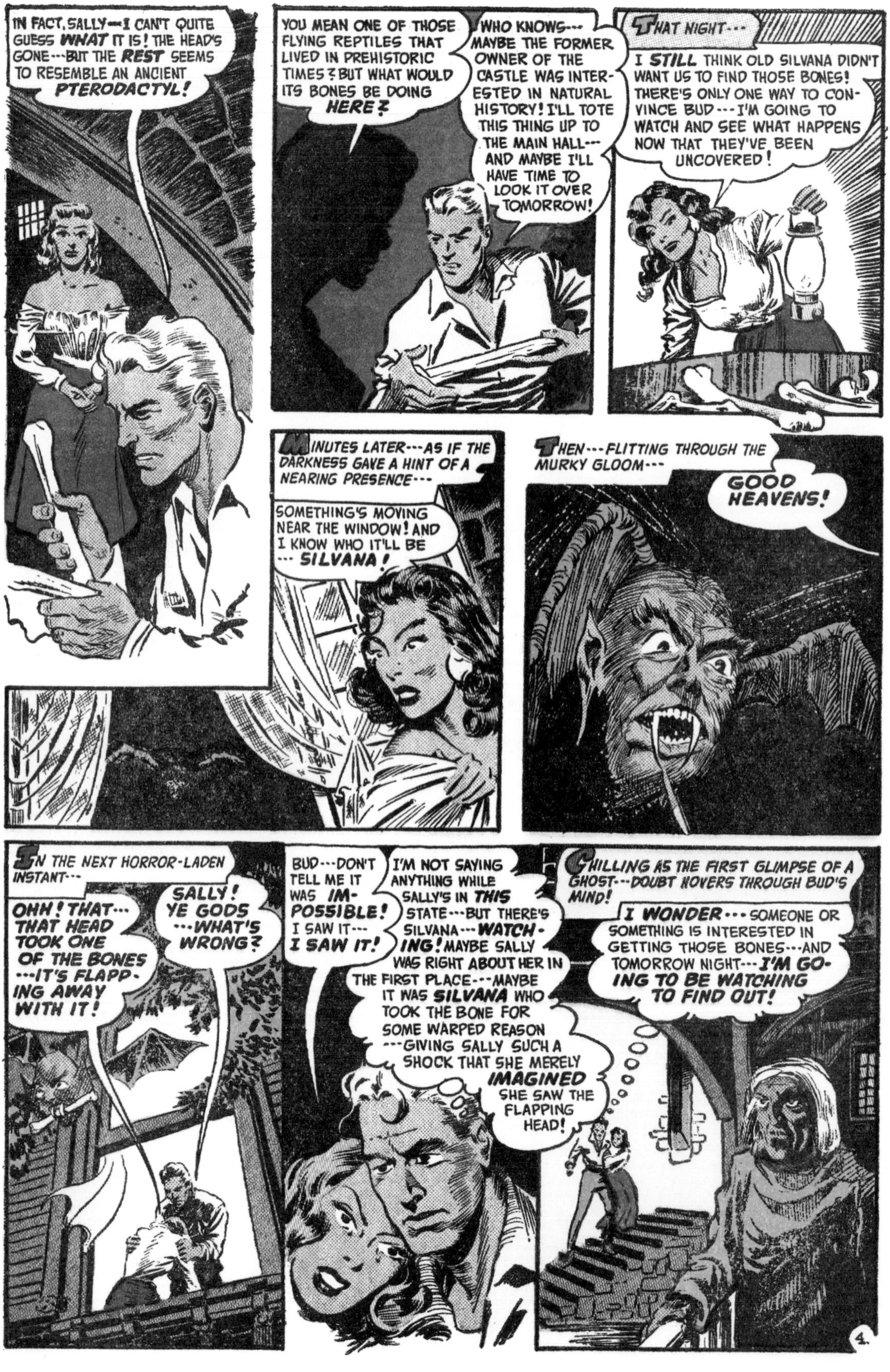
IN FACT, SALLY---I CAN'T QUITE GUESS WHAT IT IS! THE HEAD'S GONE---BUT THE REST SEEMS TO RESEMBLE AN ANCIENT PTERODACTYL!
YOU MEAN ONE OF THOSE FLYING REPTILES THAT LIVED IN PREHISTORIC TIMES? BUT WHAT WOULD ITS BONES BE DOING HERE?
WHO KNOWS--- MAYBE THE FORMER OWNER OF THE CASTLE WAS INTERESTED IN NATURAL HISTORY! I'LL TOTE THIS THING UP TO THE MAIN HALL--- AND MAYBE I'LL HAVE TIME TO LOOK IT OVER TOMORROW!
THAT NIGHT---
I STILL THINK OLD SILVANA DIDN'T WANT US TO FIND THOSE BONES! THERE'S ONLY ONE WAY TO CONVINCE BUD---I'M GOING TO WATCH AND SEE WHAT HAPPENS NOW THAT THEY'VE BEEN UNCOVERED!
MINUTES LATER---AS IF THE DARKNESS GAVE A HINT OF A NEARING PRESENCE---
SOMETHING'S MOVING NEAR THE WINDOW! AND I KNOW WHO IT'LL BE --- SILVANA!
THEN---FLITTING THROUGH THE MURKY GLOOM---
GOOD HEAVENS!
IN THE NEXT HORROR-LADEN INSTANT---
OHN! THAT--- THAT HEAD TOOK ONE OF THE BONES ---IT'S FLAPPING AWAY WITH IT!
SALLY! YE GODS ---WHAT'S WRONG?
BUD---DON'T TELL ME IT WAS IMPOSSIBLE! I SAW IT--- I SAW IT!
I'M NOT SAYING ANYTHING WHILE SALLY'S IN THIS STATE---BUT THERE'S SILVANA---WATCHING! MAYBE SALLY WAS RIGHT ABOUT HER IN THE FIRST PLACE---MAYBE IT WAS SILVANA WHO TOOK THE BONE FOR SOME WARPED REASON ---GIVING SALLY SUCH A SHOCK THAT SHE MERELY IMAGINED SHE SAW THE FLAPPING HEAD!
CHILLING AS THE FIRST GLIMPSE OF A GHOST---DOUBT HOVERS THROUGH BUD'S MIND!
I WONDER---SOMEONE OR SOMETHING IS INTERESTED IN GETTING THOSE BONES---AND TOMORROW NIGHT---I'M GOING TO BE WATCHING TO FIND OUT!
4.

THE FOLLOWING NIGHT---

I'M SURE WE WON'T SEE ANYTHING *YET*, BUD! WE'RE EARLY---IT WAS EXACTLY MIDNIGHT WHEN I SAW THE FLAPPING HEAD!

WAIT---HEAR *THAT*? SOUNDS LIKE SLOW FOOT-STEPS--- *COMING CLOSER!*

HUNCHED AND MUTTERING IN FEEBLE MOONLIGHT---

I WILL NOT SEE HIM DIE *AGAIN*---BUT HE *WILL* DIE--- *TONIGHT!*

Then, THROUGH THE BRISTLING GATEWAY---PAST THE RUSTLING HEDGES---

YOU CAN'T CALL *THIS* A QUIRK, BUD! SHE TOOK THE BONES--- *ALL OF THEM!*

SHE'S STOPPING AT A MOUND---IT'S A *GRAVE* IF I EVER SAW ONE---AND *THERE'S* THE BONE THAT DISAPPEARED LAST NIGHT ---*THRUST INTO THE TURF!*

LOOK---LOOK! SHE'S PUSHING THE OTHER BONES INTO THE MOUND---ONE BY ONE! BUD, WE NEEDN'T WONDER ANY MORE ABOUT SILVANA---THIS IS WITCHCRAFT--- *OR SOMETHING WORSE!*

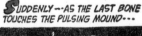

Suddenly---AS THE LAST BONE TOUCHES THE PULSING MOUND---

AAAGH!

CRRRAK!

FOR AN INSTANT, THE BONES CLATTER TOGETHER LIKE GRISLY DRUMBEATS IN THE MOONLIGHT---THEN---AS THEY MERGE---

HAA HA HA!

BUD, *THAT'S* THE FLAPPING HEAD I SAW--- BUT *NOW* IT HAS A BODY--- *IT'S A VAMPIRE!*

THAT EXPLAINS WHY THOSE BONES WE FOUND LACKED A *HEAD!* YOU WERE RIGHT ABOUT WHAT YOU SAW LAST NIGHT, SALLY! THE ONLY WAY THE FLAPPING HEAD COULD COLLECT ITS BONES WAS TO CARRY THEM OFF, ONE BY ONE---UNTIL SILVANA *BROUGHT* THEM HERE!

5

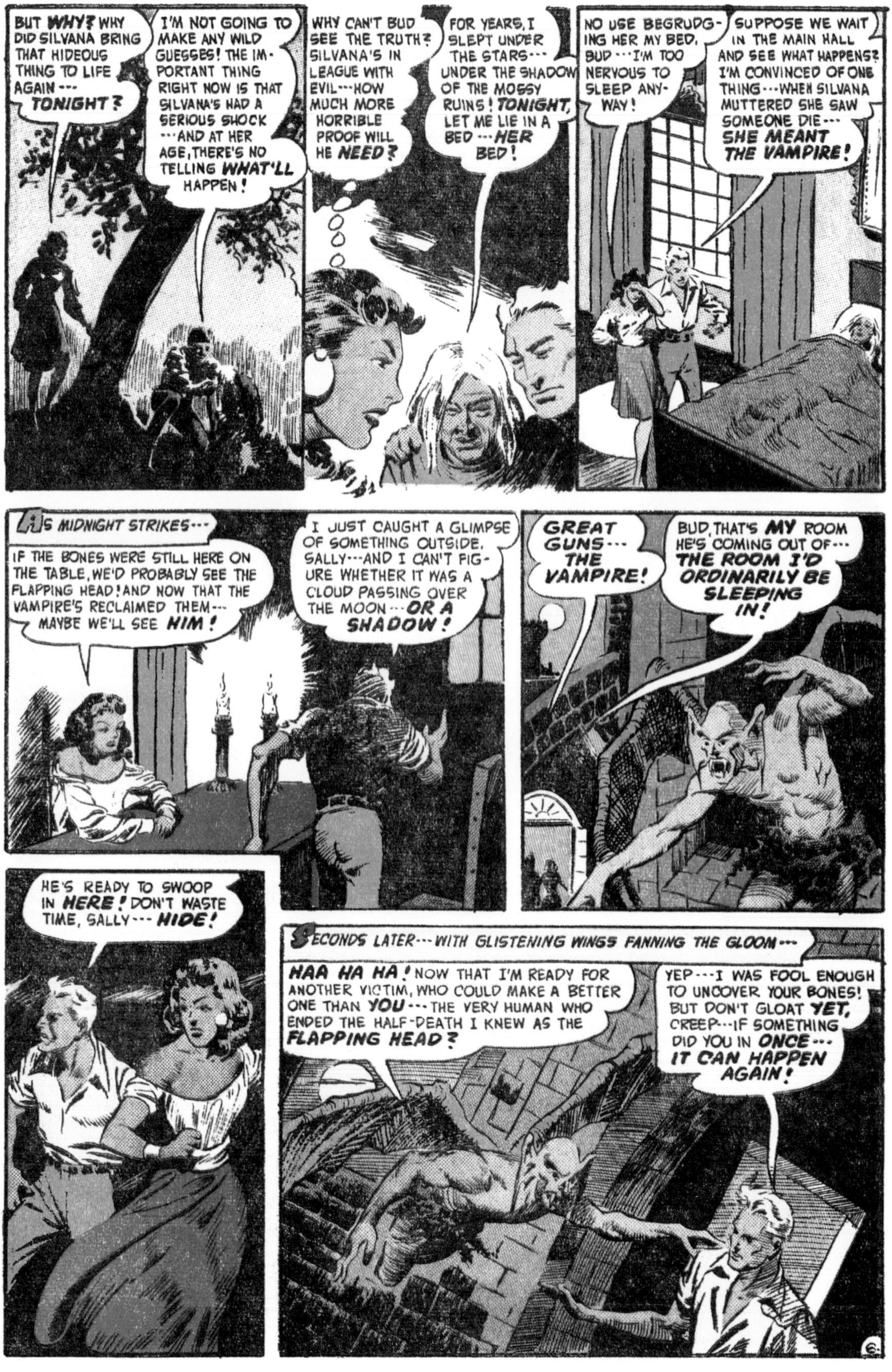
BUT WHY? WHY DID SILVANA BRING THAT HIDEOUS THING TO LIFE AGAIN --- TONIGHT?
I'M NOT GOING TO MAKE ANY WILD GUESSES! THE IMPORTANT THING RIGHT NOW IS THAT SILVANA'S HAD A SERIOUS SHOCK ---AND AT HER AGE, THERE'S NO TELLING WHAT'LL HAPPEN!
WHY CAN'T BUD SEE THE TRUTH? SILVANA'S IN LEAGUE WITH EVIL---HOW MUCH MORE HORRIBLE PROOF WILL HE NEED?
FOR YEARS, I SLEPT UNDER THE STARS--- UNDER THE SHADOW OF THE MOSSY RUINS! TONIGHT, LET ME LIE IN A BED ---HER BED!
NO USE BEGRUDGING HER MY BED, BUD ---I'M TOO NERVOUS TO SLEEP ANYWAY!
SUPPOSE WE WAIT IN THE MAIN HALL AND SEE WHAT HAPPENS? I'M CONVINCED OF ONE THING---WHEN SILVANA MUTTERED SHE SAW SOMEONE DIE--- SHE MEANT THE VAMPIRE!
AS MIDNIGHT STRIKES---
IF THE BONES WERE STILL HERE ON THE TABLE, WE'D PROBABLY SEE THE FLAPPING HEAD! AND NOW THAT THE VAMPIRE'S RECLAIMED THEM--- MAYBE WE'LL SEE HIM!
I JUST CAUGHT A GLIMPSE OF SOMETHING OUTSIDE, SALLY---AND I CAN'T FIGURE WHETHER IT WAS A CLOUD PASSING OVER THE MOON ---OR A SHADOW!
GREAT GUNS--- THE VAMPIRE!
BUD, THAT'S MY ROOM HE'S COMING OUT OF--- THE ROOM I'D ORDINARILY BE SLEEPING IN!
HE'S READY TO SWOOP IN HERE! DON'T WASTE TIME, SALLY--- HIDE!
SECONDS LATER---WITH GLISTENING WINGS FANNING THE GLOOM---
HAA HA HA! NOW THAT I'M READY FOR ANOTHER VICTIM, WHO COULD MAKE A BETTER ONE THAN YOU---THE VERY HUMAN WHO ENDED THE HALF-DEATH I KNEW AS THE FLAPPING HEAD?
YEP---I WAS FOOL ENOUGH TO UNCOVER YOUR BONES! BUT DON'T GLOAT YET, CREEP---IF SOMETHING DID YOU IN ONCE--- IT CAN HAPPEN AGAIN!
6

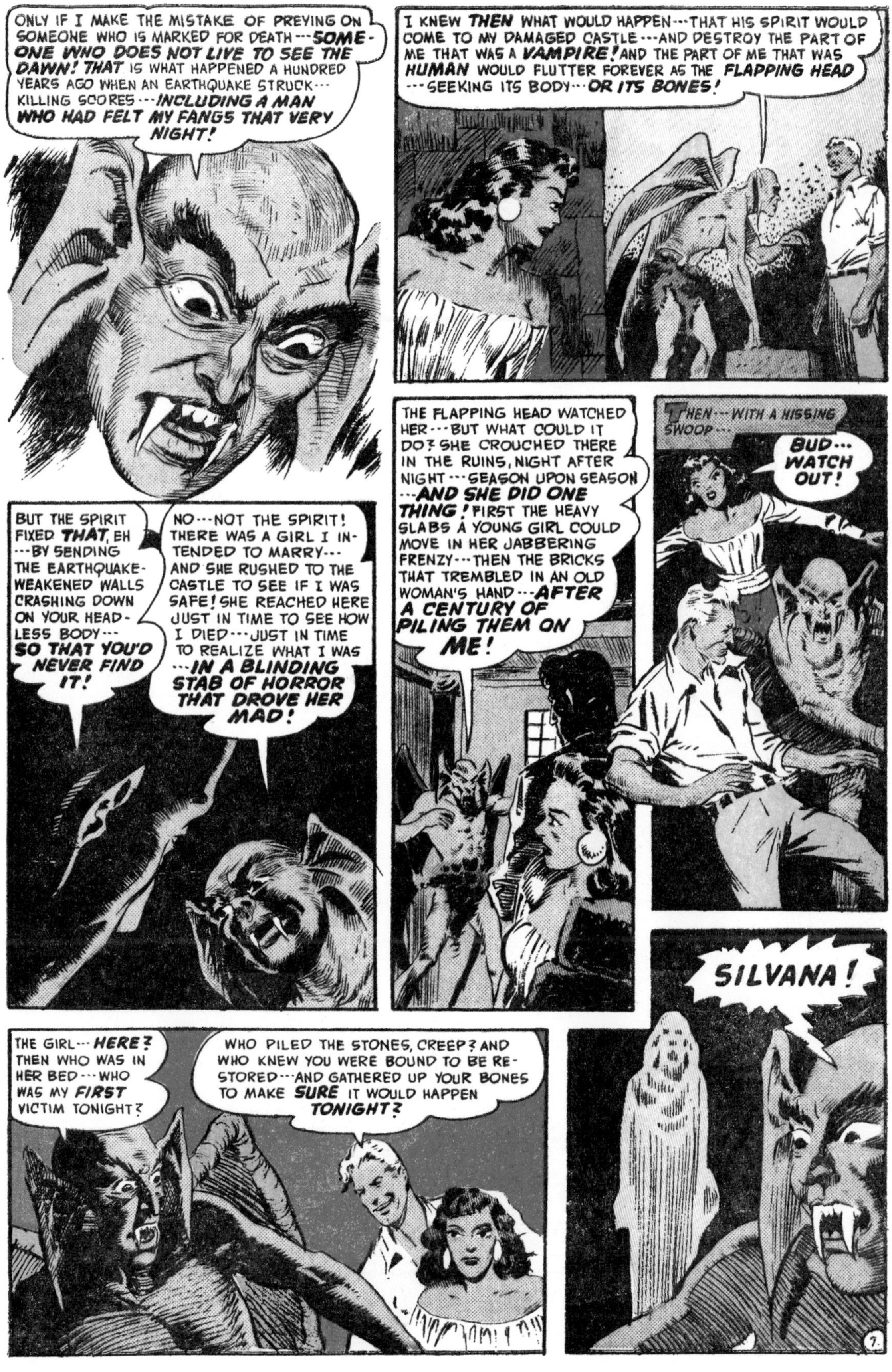

ONLY IF I MAKE THE MISTAKE OF PREYING ON SOMEONE WHO IS MARKED FOR DEATH --- SOMEONE WHO DOES NOT LIVE TO SEE THE DAWN! THAT IS WHAT HAPPENED A HUNDRED YEARS AGO WHEN AN EARTHQUAKE STRUCK --- KILLING SCORES --- INCLUDING A MAN WHO HAD FELT MY FANGS THAT VERY NIGHT!
I KNEW THEN WHAT WOULD HAPPEN --- THAT HIS SPIRIT WOULD COME TO MY DAMAGED CASTLE --- AND DESTROY THE PART OF ME THAT WAS A VAMPIRE! AND THE PART OF ME THAT WAS HUMAN WOULD FLUTTER FOREVER AS THE FLAPPING HEAD --- SEEKING ITS BODY --- OR ITS BONES!
BUT THE SPIRIT FIXED THAT, EH --- BY SENDING THE EARTHQUAKE-WEAKENED WALLS CRASHING DOWN ON YOUR HEADLESS BODY --- SO THAT YOU'D NEVER FIND IT!
NO --- NOT THE SPIRIT! THERE WAS A GIRL I INTENDED TO MARRY --- AND SHE RUSHED TO THE CASTLE TO SEE IF I WAS SAFE! SHE REACHED HERE JUST IN TIME TO SEE HOW I DIED --- JUST IN TIME TO REALIZE WHAT I WAS --- IN A BLINDING STAB OF HORROR THAT DROVE HER MAD!
THE FLAPPING HEAD WATCHED HER --- BUT WHAT COULD IT DO? SHE CROUCHED THERE IN THE RUINS, NIGHT AFTER NIGHT --- SEASON UPON SEASON --- AND SHE DID ONE THING! FIRST THE HEAVY SLABS A YOUNG GIRL COULD MOVE IN HER JABBERING FRENZY --- THEN THE BRICKS THAT TREMBLED IN AN OLD WOMAN'S HAND --- AFTER A CENTURY OF PILING THEM ON ME!
THEN --- WITH A HISSING SWOOP ---
BUD --- WATCH OUT!
THE GIRL --- HERE? THEN WHO WAS IN HER BED --- WHO WAS MY FIRST VICTIM TONIGHT?
WHO PILED THE STONES, CREEP? AND WHO KNEW YOU WERE BOUND TO BE RESTORED --- AND GATHERED UP YOUR BONES TO MAKE SURE IT WOULD HAPPEN TONIGHT?
SILVANA!
7.

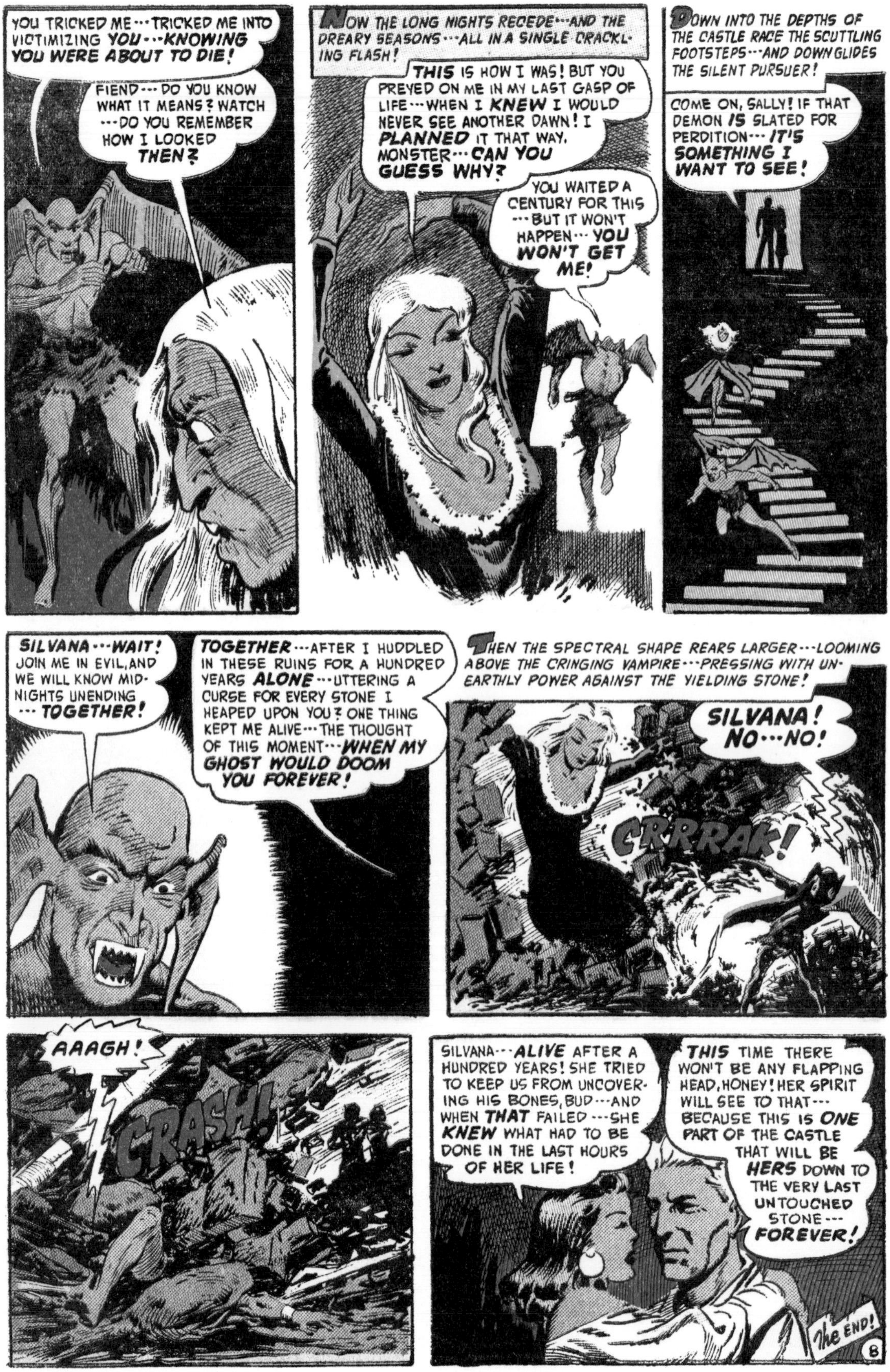

YOU TRICKED ME ··· TRICKED ME INTO VICTIMIZING YOU ··· KNOWING YOU WERE ABOUT TO DIE!
FIEND ··· DO YOU KNOW WHAT IT MEANS? WATCH ··· DO YOU REMEMBER HOW I LOOKED THEN?
NOW THE LONG NIGHTS RECEDE ··· AND THE DREARY SEASONS ··· ALL IN A SINGLE CRACKLING FLASH!
THIS IS HOW I WAS! BUT YOU PREYED ON ME IN MY LAST GASP OF LIFE ··· WHEN I KNEW I WOULD NEVER SEE ANOTHER DAWN! I PLANNED IT THAT WAY, MONSTER ··· CAN YOU GUESS WHY?
YOU WAITED A CENTURY FOR THIS ··· BUT IT WON'T HAPPEN ··· YOU WON'T GET ME!
DOWN INTO THE DEPTHS OF THE CASTLE RACE THE SCUTTLING FOOTSTEPS ··· AND DOWN GLIDES THE SILENT PURSUER!
COME ON, SALLY! IF THAT DEMON IS SLATED FOR PERDITION ··· IT'S SOMETHING I WANT TO SEE!
SILVANA ··· WAIT! JOIN ME IN EVIL, AND WE WILL KNOW MIDNIGHTS UNENDING ··· TOGETHER!
TOGETHER ··· AFTER I HUDDLED IN THESE RUINS FOR A HUNDRED YEARS ALONE ··· UTTERING A CURSE FOR EVERY STONE I HEAPED UPON YOU? ONE THING KEPT ME ALIVE ··· THE THOUGHT OF THIS MOMENT ··· WHEN MY GHOST WOULD DOOM YOU FOREVER!
THEN THE SPECTRAL SHAPE REARS LARGER ··· LOOMING ABOVE THE CRINGING VAMPIRE ··· PRESSING WITH UNEARTHLY POWER AGAINST THE YIELDING STONE!
SILVANA! NO ··· NO!
CRRRAK!
AAAGH!
CRASH!
SILVANA ··· ALIVE AFTER A HUNDRED YEARS! SHE TRIED TO KEEP US FROM UNCOVERING HIS BONES, BUD ··· AND WHEN THAT FAILED ··· SHE KNEW WHAT HAD TO BE DONE IN THE LAST HOURS OF HER LIFE!
THIS TIME THERE WON'T BE ANY FLAPPING HEAD, HONEY! HER SPIRIT WILL SEE TO THAT ··· BECAUSE THIS IS ONE PART OF THE CASTLE THAT WILL BE HERS DOWN TO THE VERY LAST UNTOUCHED STONE ··· FOREVER!
THE END!
8

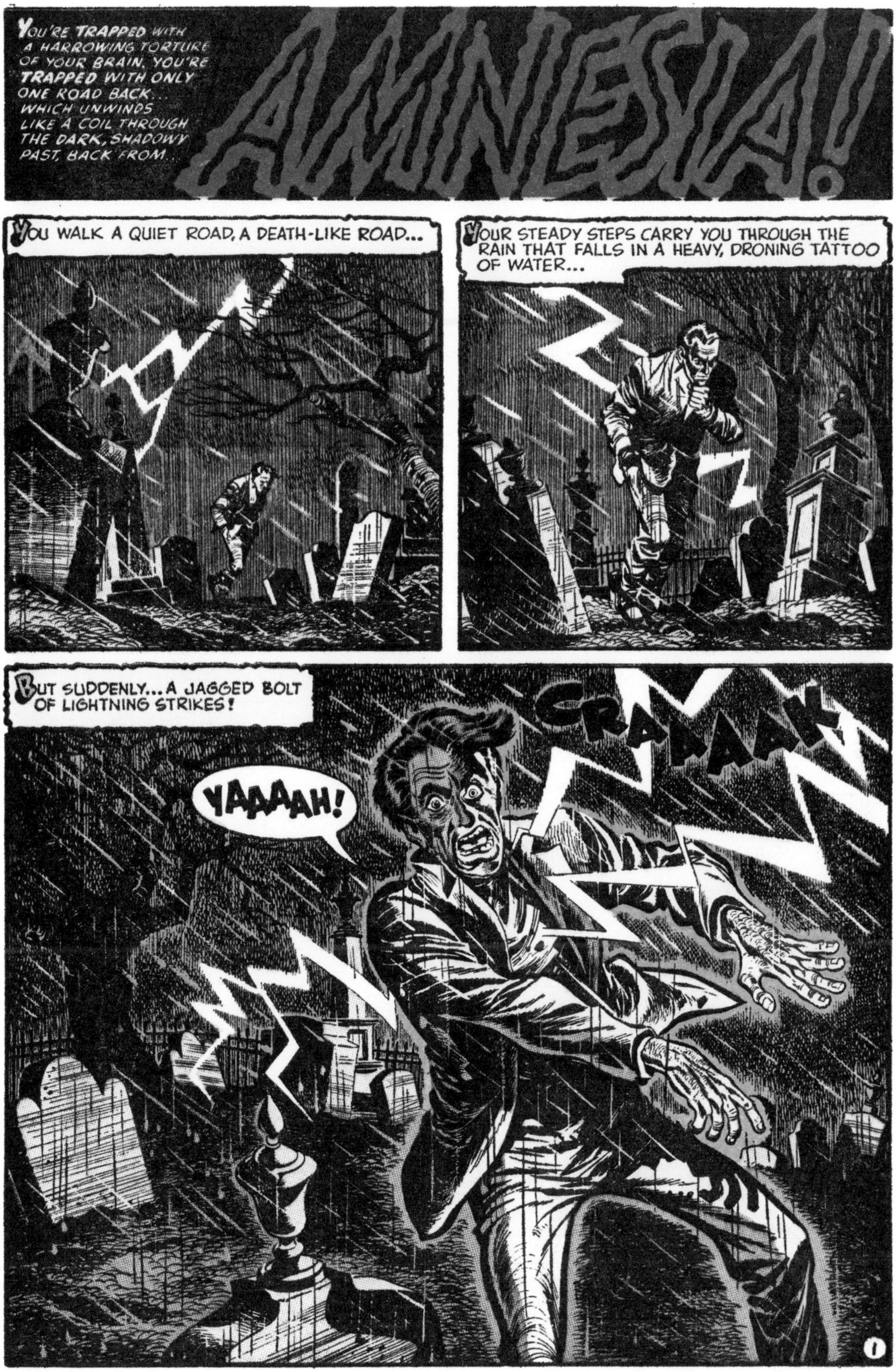

YOU'RE TRAPPED WITH A HARROWING TORTURE OF YOUR BRAIN. YOU'RE TRAPPED WITH ONLY ONE ROAD BACK... WHICH UNWINDS LIKE A COIL THROUGH THE DARK, SHADOWY PAST, BACK FROM...
AMNESIA!
YOU WALK A QUIET ROAD, A DEATH-LIKE ROAD...
YOUR STEADY STEPS CARRY YOU THROUGH THE RAIN THAT FALLS IN A HEAVY, DRONING TATTOO OF WATER...
BUT SUDDENLY... A JAGGED BOLT OF LIGHTNING STRIKES!
CRAAAAK!
YAAAAH!
1

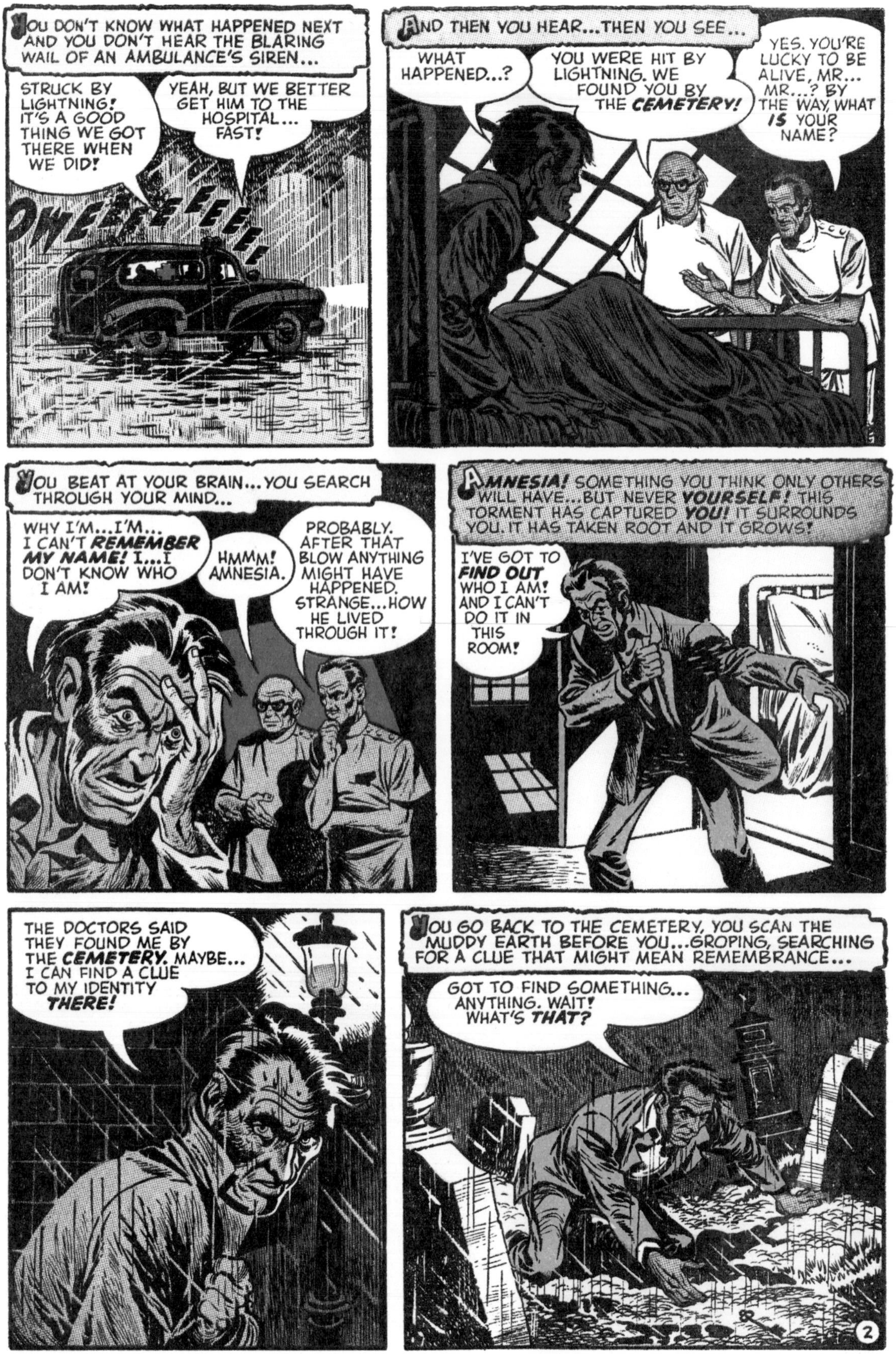
YOU DON'T KNOW WHAT HAPPENED NEXT AND YOU DON'T HEAR THE BLARING WAIL OF AN AMBULANCE'S SIREN...
STRUCK BY LIGHTNING! IT'S A GOOD THING WE GOT THERE WHEN WE DID!
YEAH, BUT WE BETTER GET HIM TO THE HOSPITAL... FAST!
OWEEEEEEE!
AND THEN YOU HEAR...THEN YOU SEE...
WHAT HAPPENED...?
YOU WERE HIT BY LIGHTNING. WE FOUND YOU BY THE CEMETERY!
YES. YOU'RE LUCKY TO BE ALIVE, MR... MR...? BY THE WAY, WHAT IS YOUR NAME?
YOU BEAT AT YOUR BRAIN...YOU SEARCH THROUGH YOUR MIND...
WHY I'M...I'M... I CAN'T REMEMBER MY NAME! I...I DON'T KNOW WHO I AM!
HMMM! AMNESIA.
PROBABLY. AFTER THAT BLOW ANYTHING MIGHT HAVE HAPPENED. STRANGE...HOW HE LIVED THROUGH IT!
AMNESIA! SOMETHING YOU THINK ONLY OTHERS WILL HAVE...BUT NEVER YOURSELF! THIS TORMENT HAS CAPTURED YOU! IT SURROUNDS YOU. IT HAS TAKEN ROOT AND IT GROWS!
I'VE GOT TO FIND OUT WHO I AM! AND I CAN'T DO IT IN THIS ROOM!
THE DOCTORS SAID THEY FOUND ME BY THE CEMETERY. MAYBE... I CAN FIND A CLUE TO MY IDENTITY THERE!
YOU GO BACK TO THE CEMETERY, YOU SCAN THE MUDDY EARTH BEFORE YOU...GROPING, SEARCHING FOR A CLUE THAT MIGHT MEAN REMEMBRANCE...
GOT TO FIND SOMETHING... ANYTHING. WAIT! WHAT'S THAT?
2

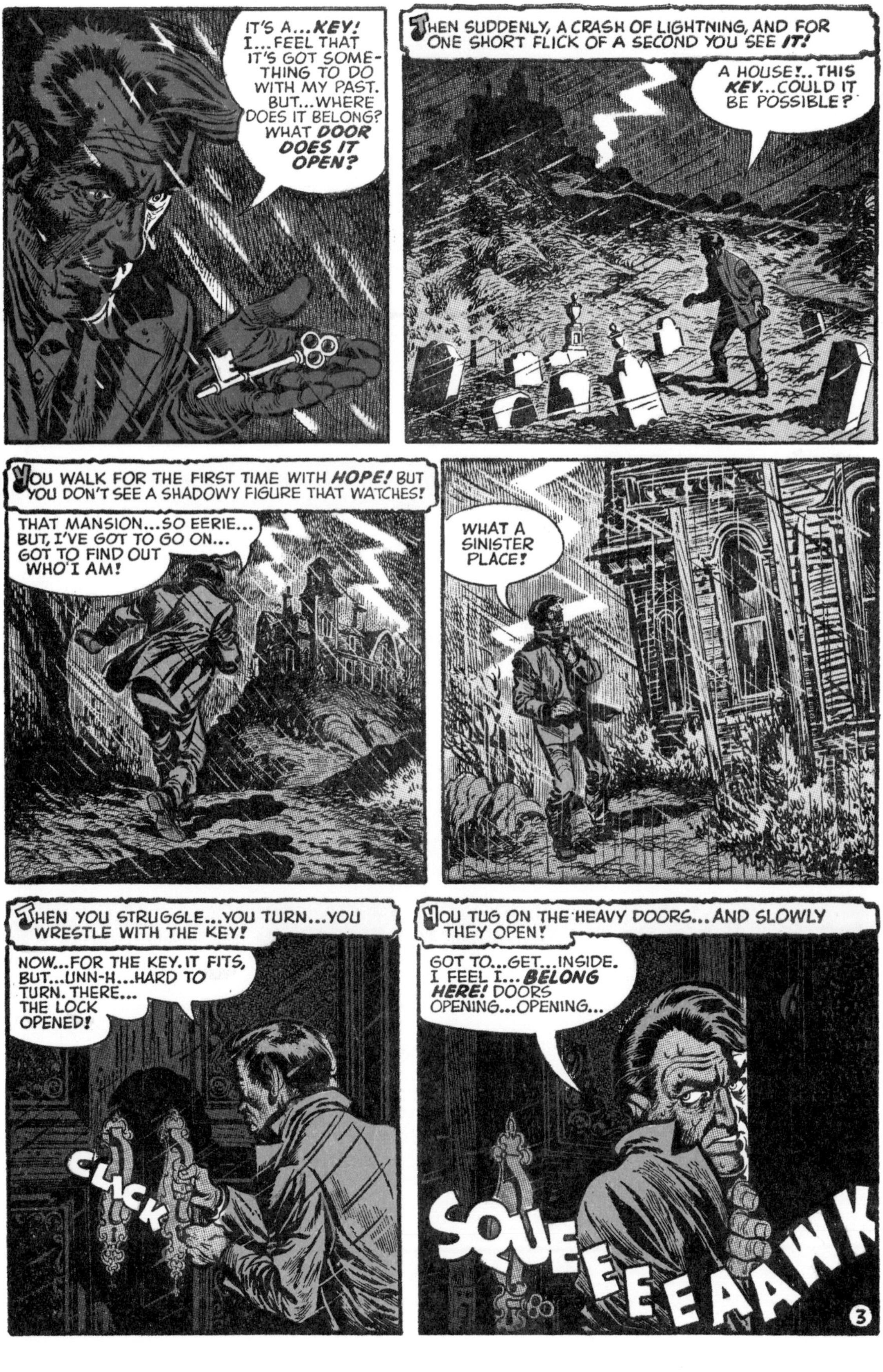
IT'S A...KEY! I...FEEL THAT IT'S GOT SOMETHING TO DO WITH MY PAST. BUT...WHERE DOES IT BELONG? WHAT DOOR DOES IT OPEN?
THEN SUDDENLY, A CRASH OF LIGHTNING, AND FOR ONE SHORT FLICK OF A SECOND YOU SEE IT!
A HOUSE!.. THIS KEY...COULD IT BE POSSIBLE?
YOU WALK FOR THE FIRST TIME WITH HOPE! BUT YOU DON'T SEE A SHADOWY FIGURE THAT WATCHES!
THAT MANSION...SO EERIE... BUT, I'VE GOT TO GO ON... GOT TO FIND OUT WHO I AM!
WHAT A SINISTER PLACE!
THEN YOU STRUGGLE...YOU TURN...YOU WRESTLE WITH THE KEY!
NOW...FOR THE KEY. IT FITS, BUT...UNN-H...HARD TO TURN. THERE... THE LOCK OPENED!
CLICK
YOU TUG ON THE HEAVY DOORS...AND SLOWLY THEY OPEN!
GOT TO...GET...INSIDE. I FEEL I...BELONG HERE! DOORS OPENING...OPENING...
SQUEEEEAAWK
3

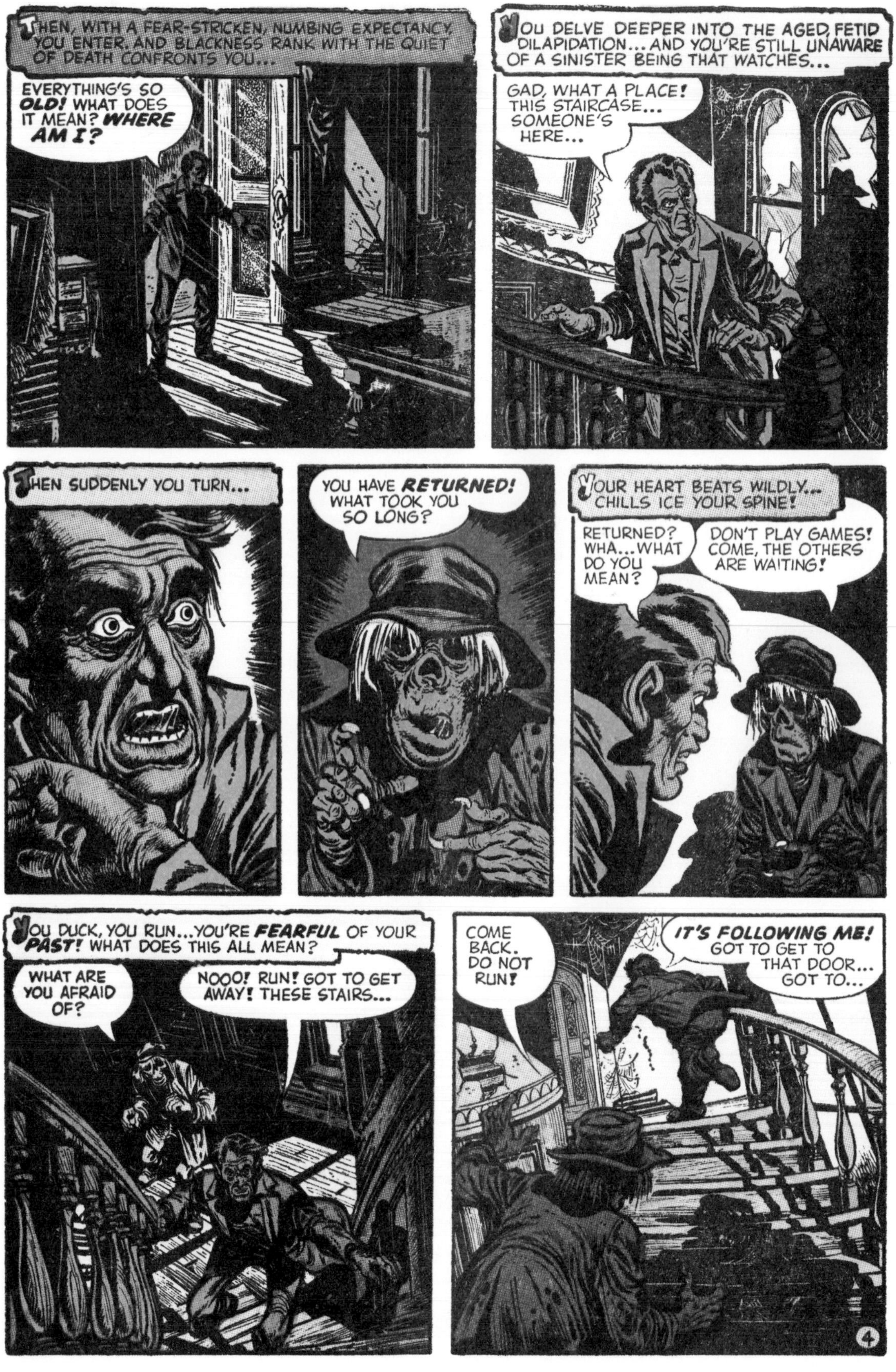
THEN, WITH A FEAR-STRICKEN, NUMBING EXPECTANCY YOU ENTER. AND BLACKNESS RANK WITH THE QUIET OF DEATH CONFRONTS YOU...
EVERYTHING'S SO OLD! WHAT DOES IT MEAN? WHERE AM I?
YOU DELVE DEEPER INTO THE AGED, FETID DILAPIDATION... AND YOU'RE STILL UNAWARE OF A SINISTER BEING THAT WATCHES...
GAD, WHAT A PLACE! THIS STAIRCASE... SOMEONE'S HERE...
THEN SUDDENLY YOU TURN...
YOU HAVE RETURNED! WHAT TOOK YOU SO LONG?
YOUR HEART BEATS WILDLY... CHILLS ICE YOUR SPINE!
RETURNED? WHA...WHAT DO YOU MEAN?
DON'T PLAY GAMES! COME, THE OTHERS ARE WAITING!
YOU DUCK, YOU RUN...YOU'RE FEARFUL OF YOUR PAST! WHAT DOES THIS ALL MEAN?
WHAT ARE YOU AFRAID OF?
NOOO! RUN! GOT TO GET AWAY! THESE STAIRS...
COME BACK. DO NOT RUN!
IT'S FOLLOWING ME! GOT TO GET TO THAT DOOR... GOT TO...
4

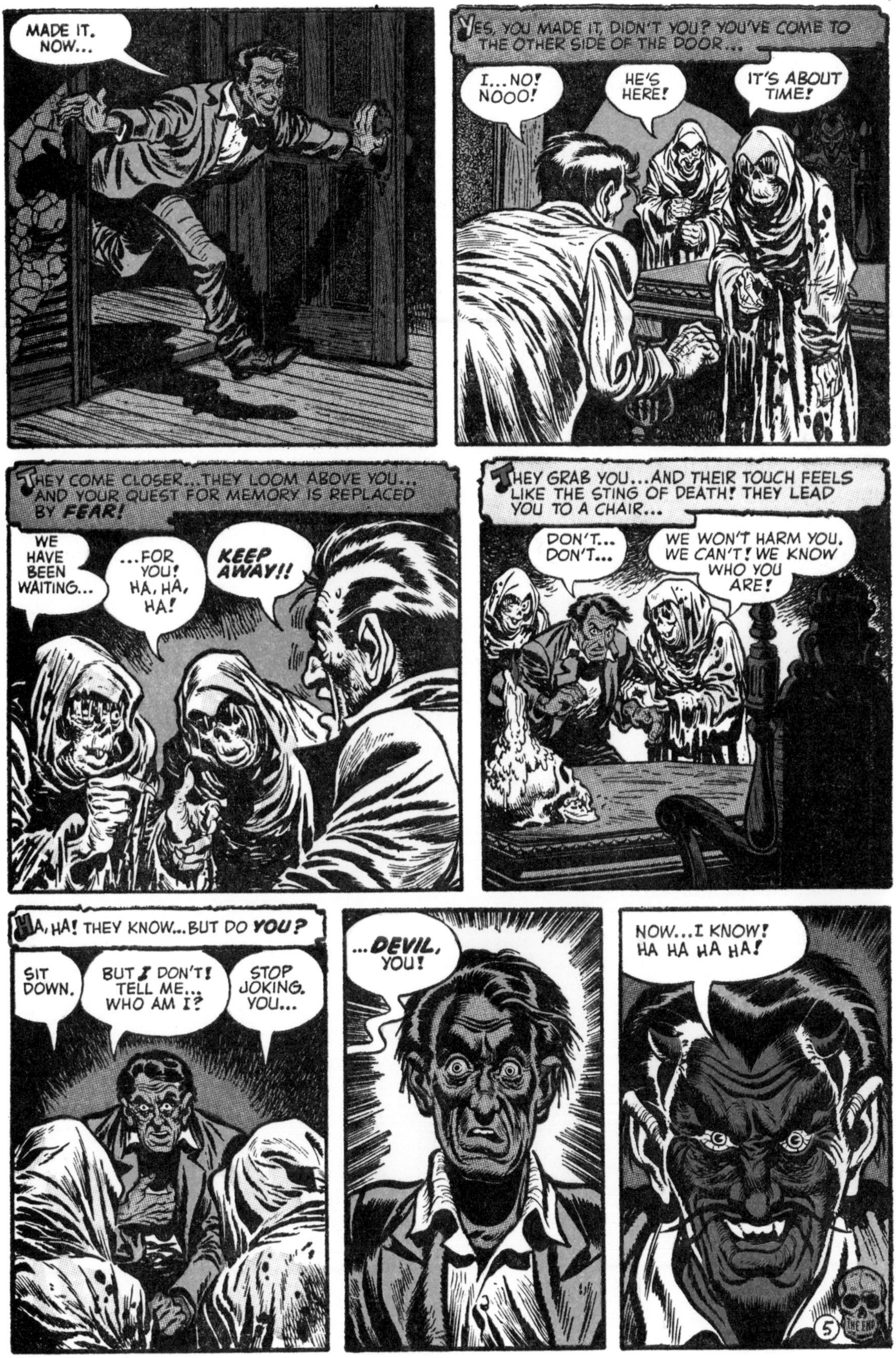
MADE IT. NOW...
YES, YOU MADE IT, DIDN'T YOU? YOU'VE COME TO THE OTHER SIDE OF THE DOOR...
I...NO! NOOO!
HE'S HERE!
IT'S ABOUT TIME!
THEY COME CLOSER...THEY LOOM ABOVE YOU... AND YOUR QUEST FOR MEMORY IS REPLACED BY FEAR!
WE HAVE BEEN WAITING...
...FOR YOU! HA, HA, HA!
KEEP AWAY!!
THEY GRAB YOU...AND THEIR TOUCH FEELS LIKE THE STING OF DEATH! THEY LEAD YOU TO A CHAIR...
DON'T... DON'T...
WE WON'T HARM YOU. WE CAN'T! WE KNOW WHO YOU ARE!
HA, HA! THEY KNOW...BUT DO YOU?
SIT DOWN.
BUT I DON'T! TELL ME... WHO AM I?
STOP JOKING. YOU...
...DEVIL, YOU!
NOW...I KNOW! HA HA HA HA!
5
THE END

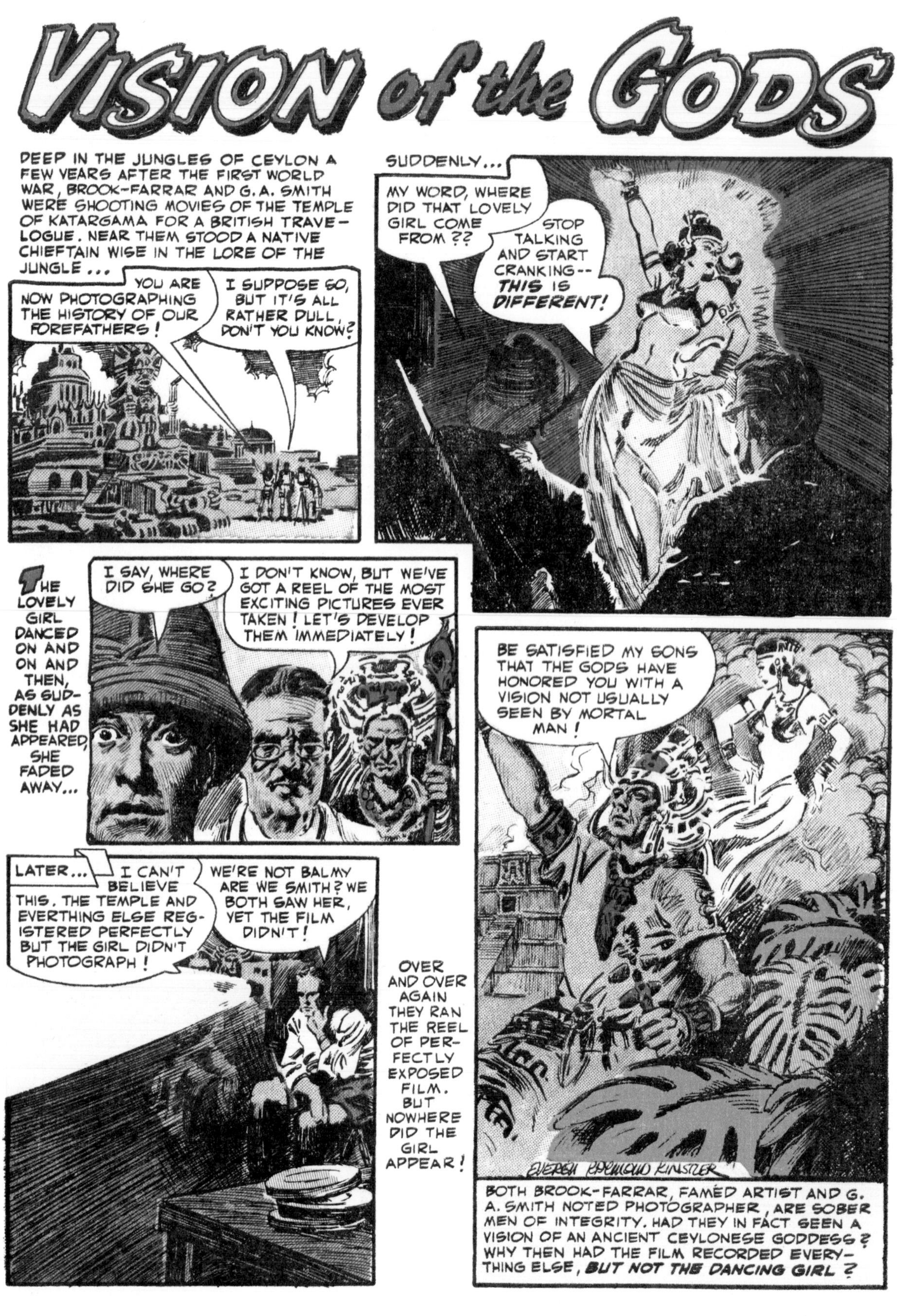
VISION of the GODS
DEEP IN THE JUNGLES OF CEYLON A FEW YEARS AFTER THE FIRST WORLD WAR, BROOK-FARRAR AND G. A. SMITH WERE SHOOTING MOVIES OF THE TEMPLE OF KATARGAMA FOR A BRITISH TRAVE-LOGUE. NEAR THEM STOOD A NATIVE CHIEFTAIN WISE IN THE LORE OF THE JUNGLE...
YOU ARE NOW PHOTOGRAPHING THE HISTORY OF OUR FOREFATHERS!
I SUPPOSE SO, BUT IT'S ALL RATHER DULL, DON'T YOU KNOW?
SUDDENLY...
MY WORD, WHERE DID THAT LOVELY GIRL COME FROM??
STOP TALKING AND START CRANKING-- THIS IS DIFFERENT!
THE LOVELY GIRL DANCED ON AND ON AND THEN, AS SUD-DENLY AS SHE HAD APPEARED, SHE FADED AWAY...
I SAY, WHERE DID SHE GO?
I DON'T KNOW, BUT WE'VE GOT A REEL OF THE MOST EXCITING PICTURES EVER TAKEN! LET'S DEVELOP THEM IMMEDIATELY!
BE SATISFIED MY SONS THAT THE GODS HAVE HONORED YOU WITH A VISION NOT USUALLY SEEN BY MORTAL MAN!
LATER...
I CAN'T BELIEVE THIS. THE TEMPLE AND EVERTHING ELSE REG-ISTERED PERFECTLY BUT THE GIRL DIDN'T PHOTOGRAPH!
WE'RE NOT BALMY ARE WE SMITH? WE BOTH SAW HER, YET THE FILM DIDN'T!
OVER AND OVER AGAIN THEY RAN THE REEL OF PER-FECTLY EXPOSED FILM. BUT NOWHERE DID THE GIRL APPEAR!
EVERETT RAYMOND KINSTLER
BOTH BROOK-FARRAR, FAMED ARTIST AND G. A. SMITH NOTED PHOTOGRAPHER, ARE SOBER MEN OF INTEGRITY. HAD THEY IN FACT SEEN A VISION OF AN ANCIENT CEYLONESE GODDESS? WHY THEN HAD THE FILM RECORDED EVERY-THING ELSE, BUT NOT THE DANCING GIRL?

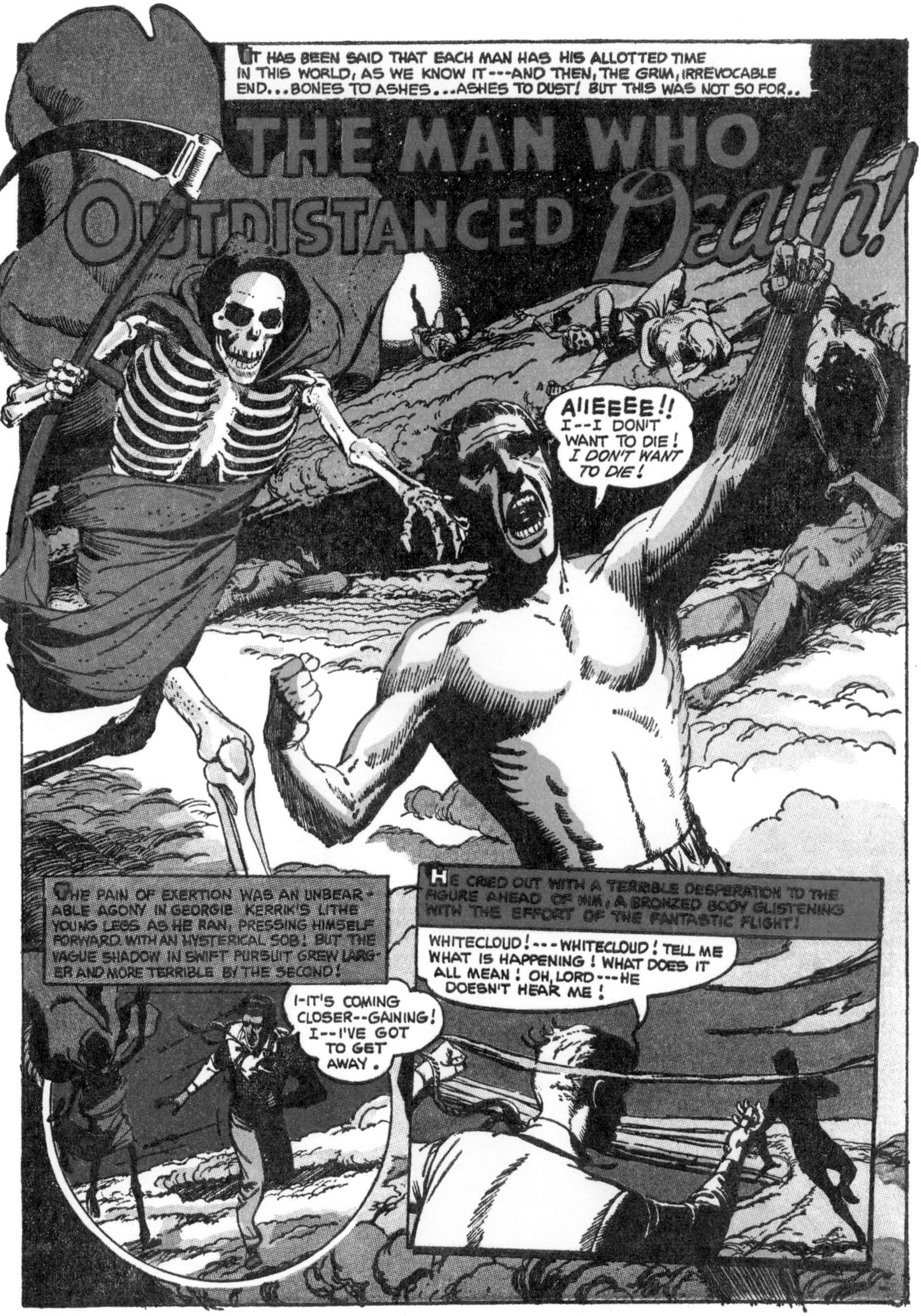
IT HAS BEEN SAID THAT EACH MAN HAS HIS ALLOTTED TIME IN THIS WORLD, AS WE KNOW IT---AND THEN, THE GRIM, IRREVOCABLE END...BONES TO ASHES...ASHES TO DUST! BUT THIS WAS NOT SO FOR..
THE MAN WHO OUTDISTANCED Death!
AIIEEEE!! I--I DON'T WANT TO DIE! I DON'T WANT TO DIE!
THE PAIN OF EXERTION WAS AN UNBEARABLE AGONY IN GEORGIE KERRIK'S LITHE YOUNG LEGS AS HE RAN, PRESSING HIMSELF FORWARD WITH AN HYSTERICAL SOB! BUT THE VAGUE SHADOW IN SWIFT PURSUIT GREW LARGER AND MORE TERRIBLE BY THE SECOND!
I-IT'S COMING CLOSER--GAINING! I--I'VE GOT TO GET AWAY.
HE CRIED OUT WITH A TERRIBLE DESPERATION TO THE FIGURE AHEAD OF HIM, A BRONZED BODY GLISTENING WITH THE EFFORT OF THE FANTASTIC FLIGHT!
WHITECLOUD!---WHITECLOUD! TELL ME WHAT IS HAPPENING! WHAT DOES IT ALL MEAN! OH, LORD---HE DOESN'T HEAR ME!

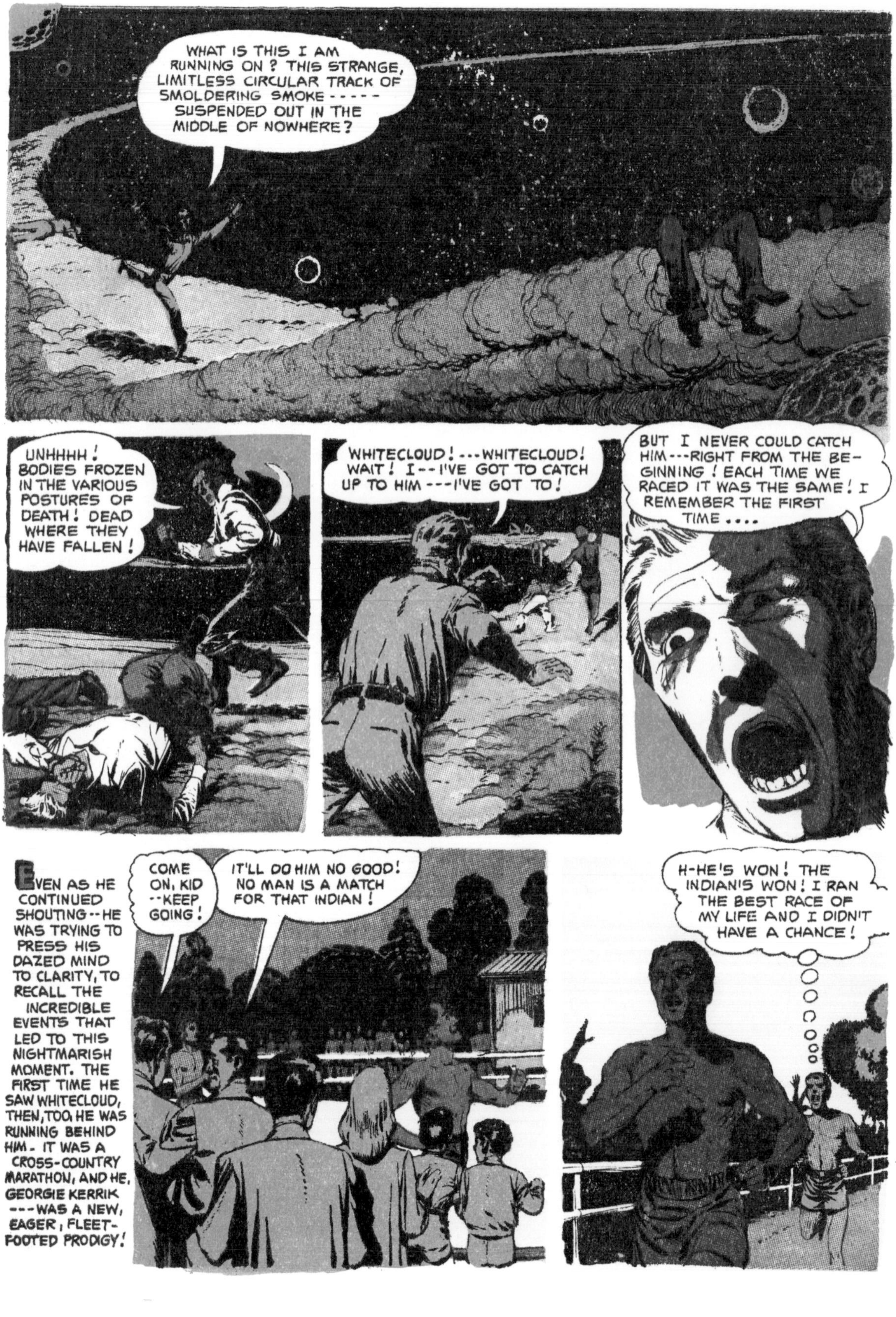
WHAT IS THIS I AM RUNNING ON? THIS STRANGE, LIMITLESS CIRCULAR TRACK OF SMOLDERING SMOKE----- SUSPENDED OUT IN THE MIDDLE OF NOWHERE?
UNHHHH! BODIES FROZEN IN THE VARIOUS POSTURES OF DEATH! DEAD WHERE THEY HAVE FALLEN!
WHITECLOUD! ---WHITECLOUD! WAIT! I--I'VE GOT TO CATCH UP TO HIM ---I'VE GOT TO!
BUT I NEVER COULD CATCH HIM---RIGHT FROM THE BE-GINNING! EACH TIME WE RACED IT WAS THE SAME! I REMEMBER THE FIRST TIME....
EVEN AS HE CONTINUED SHOUTING--HE WAS TRYING TO PRESS HIS DAZED MIND TO CLARITY, TO RECALL THE INCREDIBLE EVENTS THAT LED TO THIS NIGHTMARISH MOMENT. THE FIRST TIME HE SAW WHITECLOUD, THEN, TOO, HE WAS RUNNING BEHIND HIM. IT WAS A CROSS-COUNTRY MARATHON, AND HE, GEORGIE KERRIK ---WAS A NEW, EAGER, FLEET-FOOTED PRODIGY!
COME ON, KID --KEEP GOING!
IT'LL DO HIM NO GOOD! NO MAN IS A MATCH FOR THAT INDIAN!
H-HE'S WON! THE INDIAN'S WON! I RAN THE BEST RACE OF MY LIFE AND I DIDN'T HAVE A CHANCE!

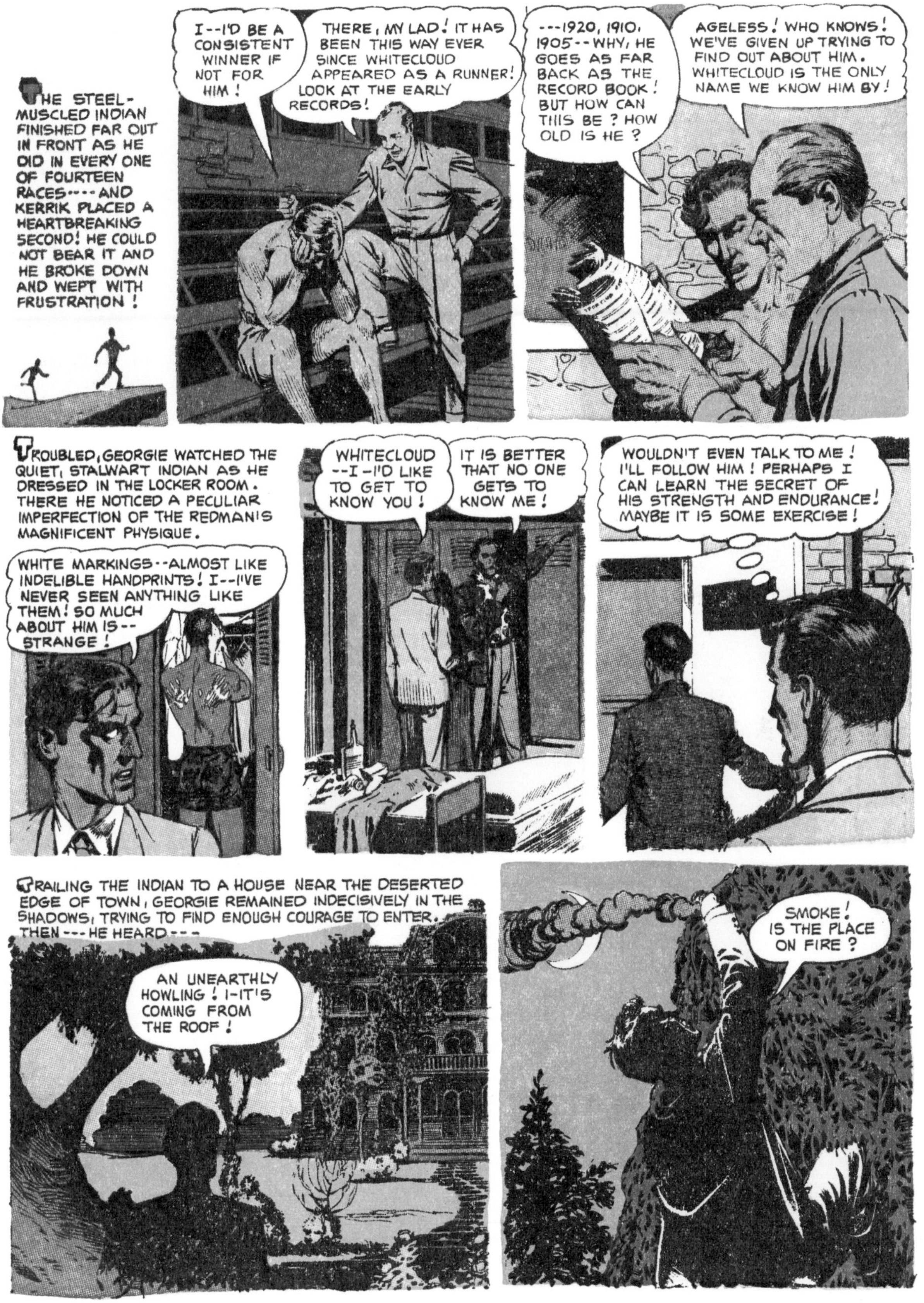
THE STEEL-MUSCLED INDIAN FINISHED FAR OUT IN FRONT AS HE DID IN EVERY ONE OF FOURTEEN RACES---- AND KERRIK PLACED A HEARTBREAKING SECOND! HE COULD NOT BEAR IT AND HE BROKE DOWN AND WEPT WITH FRUSTRATION!
I--I'D BE A CONSISTENT WINNER IF NOT FOR HIM!
THERE, MY LAD! IT HAS BEEN THIS WAY EVER SINCE WHITECLOUD APPEARED AS A RUNNER! LOOK AT THE EARLY RECORDS!
---1920, 1910, 1905--WHY, HE GOES AS FAR BACK AS THE RECORD BOOK! BUT HOW CAN THIS BE? HOW OLD IS HE?
AGELESS! WHO KNOWS! WE'VE GIVEN UP TRYING TO FIND OUT ABOUT HIM. WHITECLOUD IS THE ONLY NAME WE KNOW HIM BY!
TROUBLED, GEORGIE WATCHED THE QUIET, STALWART INDIAN AS HE DRESSED IN THE LOCKER ROOM. THERE HE NOTICED A PECULIAR IMPERFECTION OF THE REDMAN'S MAGNIFICENT PHYSIQUE.
WHITE MARKINGS--ALMOST LIKE INDELIBLE HANDPRINTS! I--I'VE NEVER SEEN ANYTHING LIKE THEM! SO MUCH ABOUT HIM IS--STRANGE!
WHITECLOUD--I--I'D LIKE TO GET TO KNOW YOU!
IT IS BETTER THAT NO ONE GETS TO KNOW ME!
WOULDN'T EVEN TALK TO ME! I'LL FOLLOW HIM! PERHAPS I CAN LEARN THE SECRET OF HIS STRENGTH AND ENDURANCE! MAYBE IT IS SOME EXERCISE!
TRAILING THE INDIAN TO A HOUSE NEAR THE DESERTED EDGE OF TOWN, GEORGIE REMAINED INDECISIVELY IN THE SHADOWS, TRYING TO FIND ENOUGH COURAGE TO ENTER. THEN---HE HEARD---
AN UNEARTHLY HOWLING! I-IT'S COMING FROM THE ROOF!
SMOKE! IS THE PLACE ON FIRE?

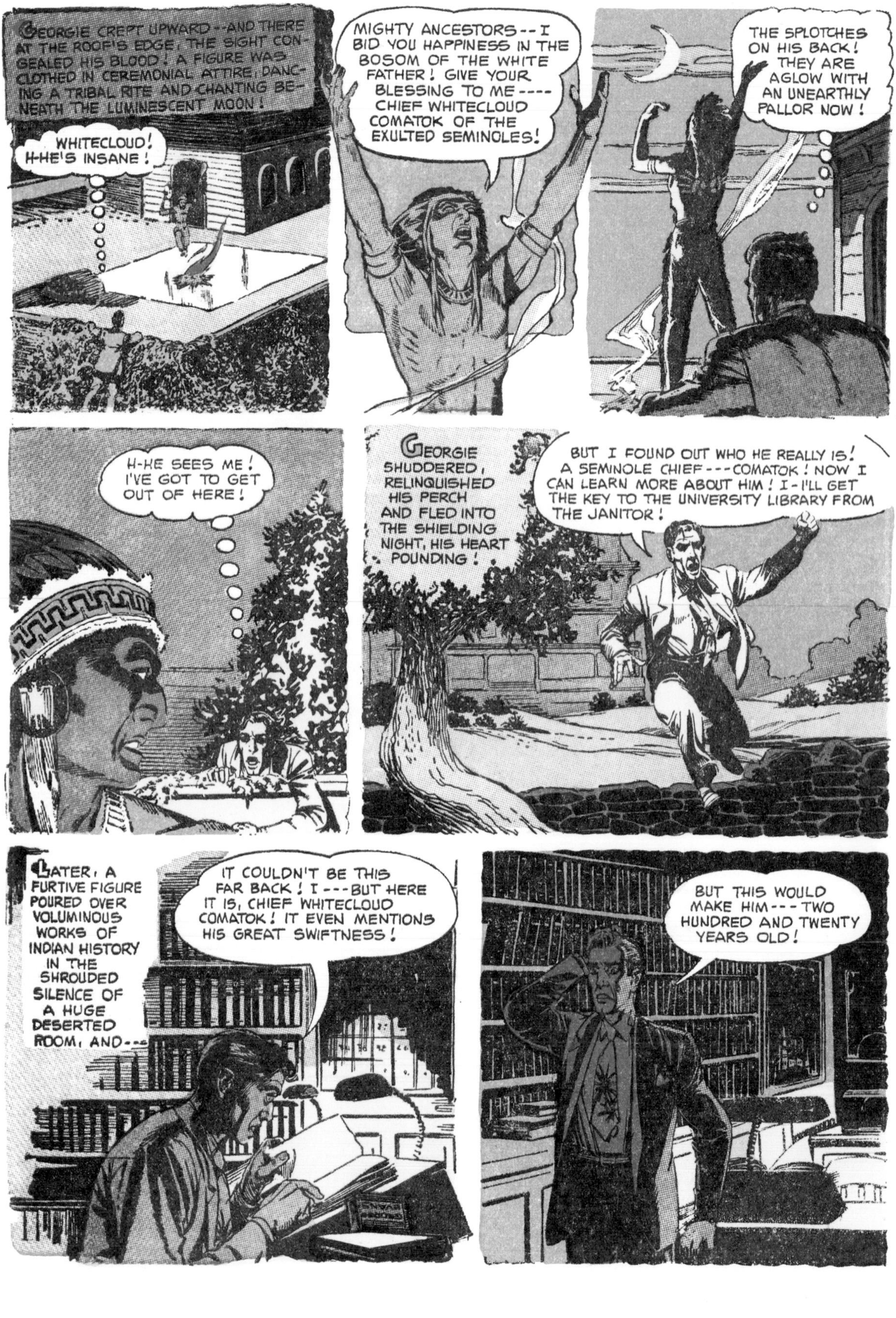
GEORGIE CREPT UPWARD--AND THERE AT THE ROOF'S EDGE, THE SIGHT CONGEALED HIS BLOOD! A FIGURE WAS CLOTHED IN CEREMONIAL ATTIRE, DANCING A TRIBAL RITE AND CHANTING BENEATH THE LUMINESCENT MOON!
WHITECLOUD! H-HE'S INSANE!
MIGHTY ANCESTORS--I BID YOU HAPPINESS IN THE BOSOM OF THE WHITE FATHER! GIVE YOUR BLESSING TO ME----CHIEF WHITECLOUD COMATOK OF THE EXULTED SEMINOLES!
THE SPLOTCHES ON HIS BACK! THEY ARE AGLOW WITH AN UNEARTHLY PALLOR NOW!
H-HE SEES ME! I'VE GOT TO GET OUT OF HERE!
GEORGIE SHUDDERED, RELINQUISHED HIS PERCH AND FLED INTO THE SHIELDING NIGHT, HIS HEART POUNDING!
BUT I FOUND OUT WHO HE REALLY IS! A SEMINOLE CHIEF---COMATOK! NOW I CAN LEARN MORE ABOUT HIM! I-I'LL GET THE KEY TO THE UNIVERSITY LIBRARY FROM THE JANITOR!
LATER, A FURTIVE FIGURE POURED OVER VOLUMINOUS WORKS OF INDIAN HISTORY IN THE SHROUDED SILENCE OF A HUGE DESERTED ROOM, AND--
IT COULDN'T BE THIS FAR BACK! I---BUT HERE IT IS, CHIEF WHITECLOUD COMATOK! IT EVEN MENTIONS HIS GREAT SWIFTNESS!
BUT THIS WOULD MAKE HIM---TWO HUNDRED AND TWENTY YEARS OLD!

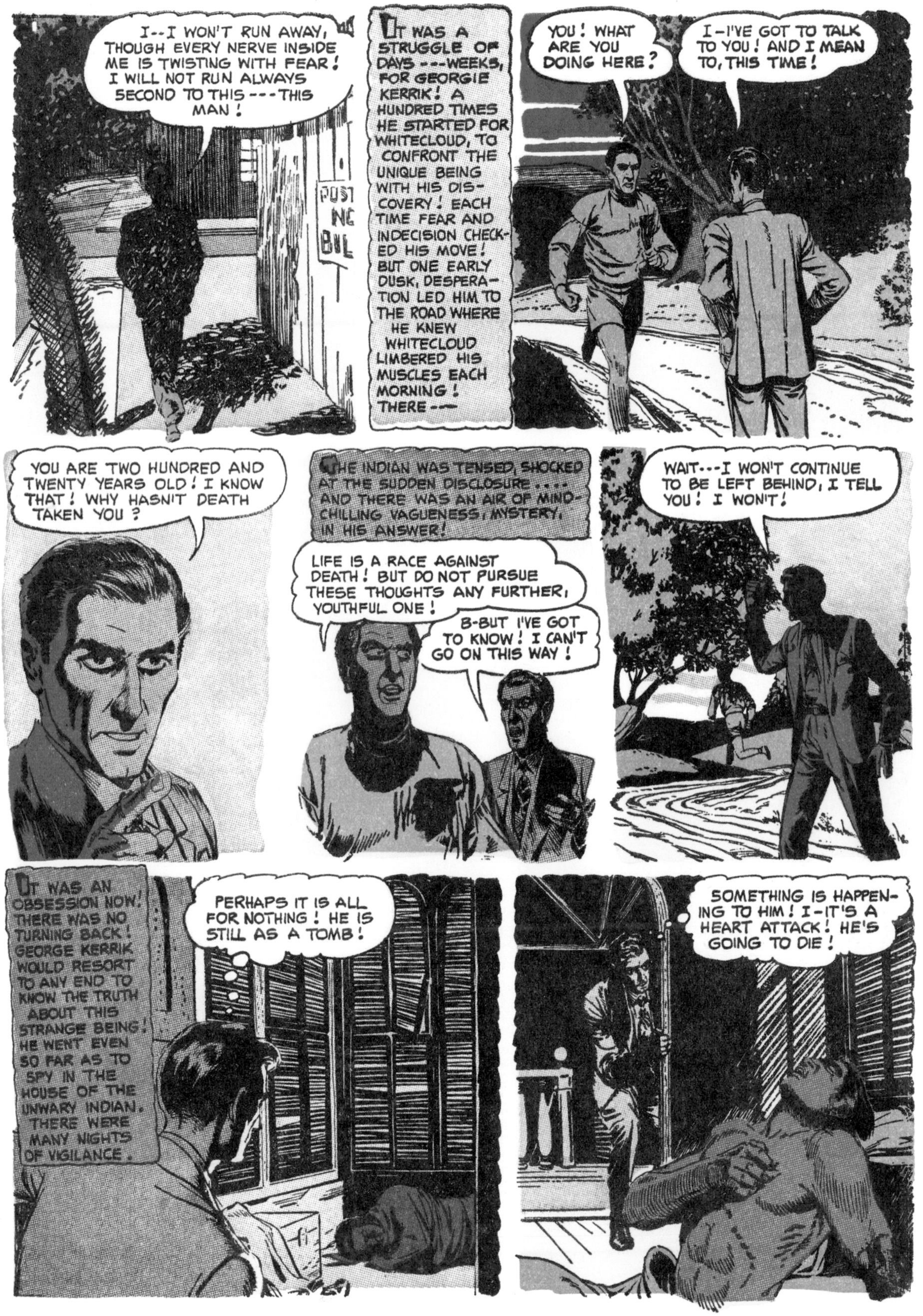
I--I WON'T RUN AWAY, THOUGH EVERY NERVE INSIDE ME IS TWISTING WITH FEAR! I WILL NOT RUN ALWAYS SECOND TO THIS---THIS MAN!
IT WAS A STRUGGLE OF DAYS---WEEKS, FOR GEORGIE KERRIK! A HUNDRED TIMES HE STARTED FOR WHITECLOUD, TO CONFRONT THE UNIQUE BEING WITH HIS DISCOVERY! EACH TIME FEAR AND INDECISION CHECKED HIS MOVE! BUT ONE EARLY DUSK, DESPERATION LED HIM TO THE ROAD WHERE HE KNEW WHITECLOUD LIMBERED HIS MUSCLES EACH MORNING! THERE--
YOU! WHAT ARE YOU DOING HERE?
I-I'VE GOT TO TALK TO YOU! AND I MEAN TO, THIS TIME!
YOU ARE TWO HUNDRED AND TWENTY YEARS OLD! I KNOW THAT! WHY HASN'T DEATH TAKEN YOU?
THE INDIAN WAS TENSED, SHOCKED AT THE SUDDEN DISCLOSURE.... AND THERE WAS AN AIR OF MIND-CHILLING VAGUENESS, MYSTERY, IN HIS ANSWER!
LIFE IS A RACE AGAINST DEATH! BUT DO NOT PURSUE THESE THOUGHTS ANY FURTHER, YOUTHFUL ONE!
B-BUT I'VE GOT TO KNOW! I CAN'T GO ON THIS WAY!
WAIT---I WON'T CONTINUE TO BE LEFT BEHIND, I TELL YOU! I WON'T!
IT WAS AN OBSESSION NOW! THERE WAS NO TURNING BACK! GEORGE KERRIK WOULD RESORT TO ANY END TO KNOW THE TRUTH ABOUT THIS STRANGE BEING! HE WENT EVEN SO FAR AS TO SPY IN THE HOUSE OF THE UNWARY INDIAN. THERE WERE MANY NIGHTS OF VIGILANCE.
PERHAPS IT IS ALL FOR NOTHING! HE IS STILL AS A TOMB!
SOMETHING IS HAPPENING TO HIM! I-IT'S A HEART ATTACK! HE'S GOING TO DIE!

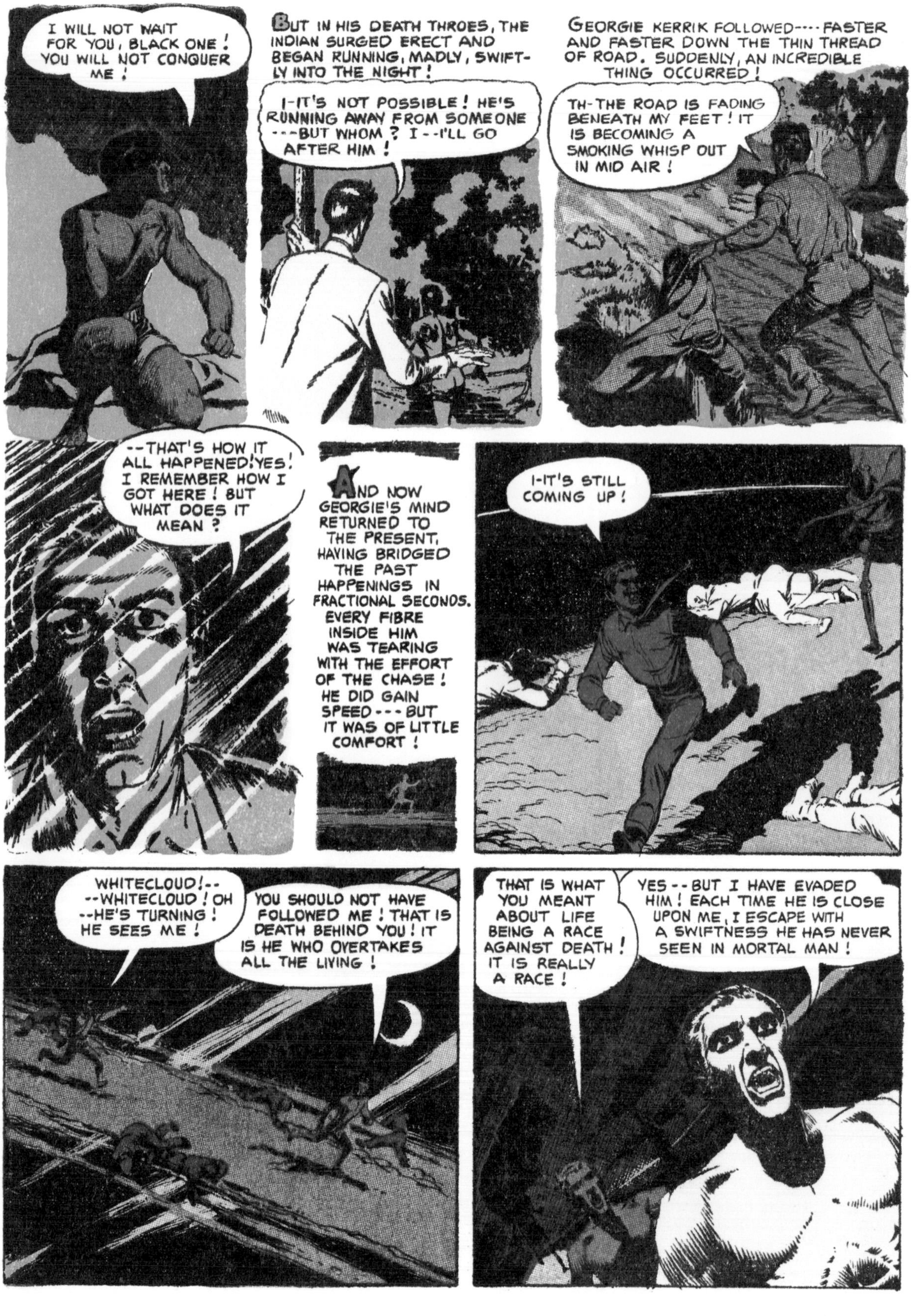
I WILL NOT WAIT FOR YOU, BLACK ONE! YOU WILL NOT CONQUER ME!
BUT IN HIS DEATH THROES, THE INDIAN SURGED ERECT AND BEGAN RUNNING, MADLY, SWIFTLY INTO THE NIGHT!
I-IT'S NOT POSSIBLE! HE'S RUNNING AWAY FROM SOMEONE ---BUT WHOM? I--I'LL GO AFTER HIM!
GEORGIE KERRIK FOLLOWED---- FASTER AND FASTER DOWN THE THIN THREAD OF ROAD. SUDDENLY, AN INCREDIBLE THING OCCURRED!
TH-THE ROAD IS FADING BENEATH MY FEET! IT IS BECOMING A SMOKING WHISP OUT IN MID AIR!
--THAT'S HOW IT ALL HAPPENED! YES! I REMEMBER HOW I GOT HERE! BUT WHAT DOES IT MEAN?
AND NOW GEORGIE'S MIND RETURNED TO THE PRESENT, HAVING BRIDGED THE PAST HAPPENINGS IN FRACTIONAL SECONDS. EVERY FIBRE INSIDE HIM WAS TEARING WITH THE EFFORT OF THE CHASE! HE DID GAIN SPEED---BUT IT WAS OF LITTLE COMFORT!
I-IT'S STILL COMING UP!
WHITECLOUD!-- --WHITECLOUD! OH --HE'S TURNING! HE SEES ME!
YOU SHOULD NOT HAVE FOLLOWED ME! THAT IS DEATH BEHIND YOU! IT IS HE WHO OVERTAKES ALL THE LIVING!
THAT IS WHAT YOU MEANT ABOUT LIFE BEING A RACE AGAINST DEATH! IT IS REALLY A RACE!
YES--BUT I HAVE EVADED HIM! EACH TIME HE IS CLOSE UPON ME, I ESCAPE WITH A SWIFTNESS HE HAS NEVER SEEN IN MORTAL MAN!

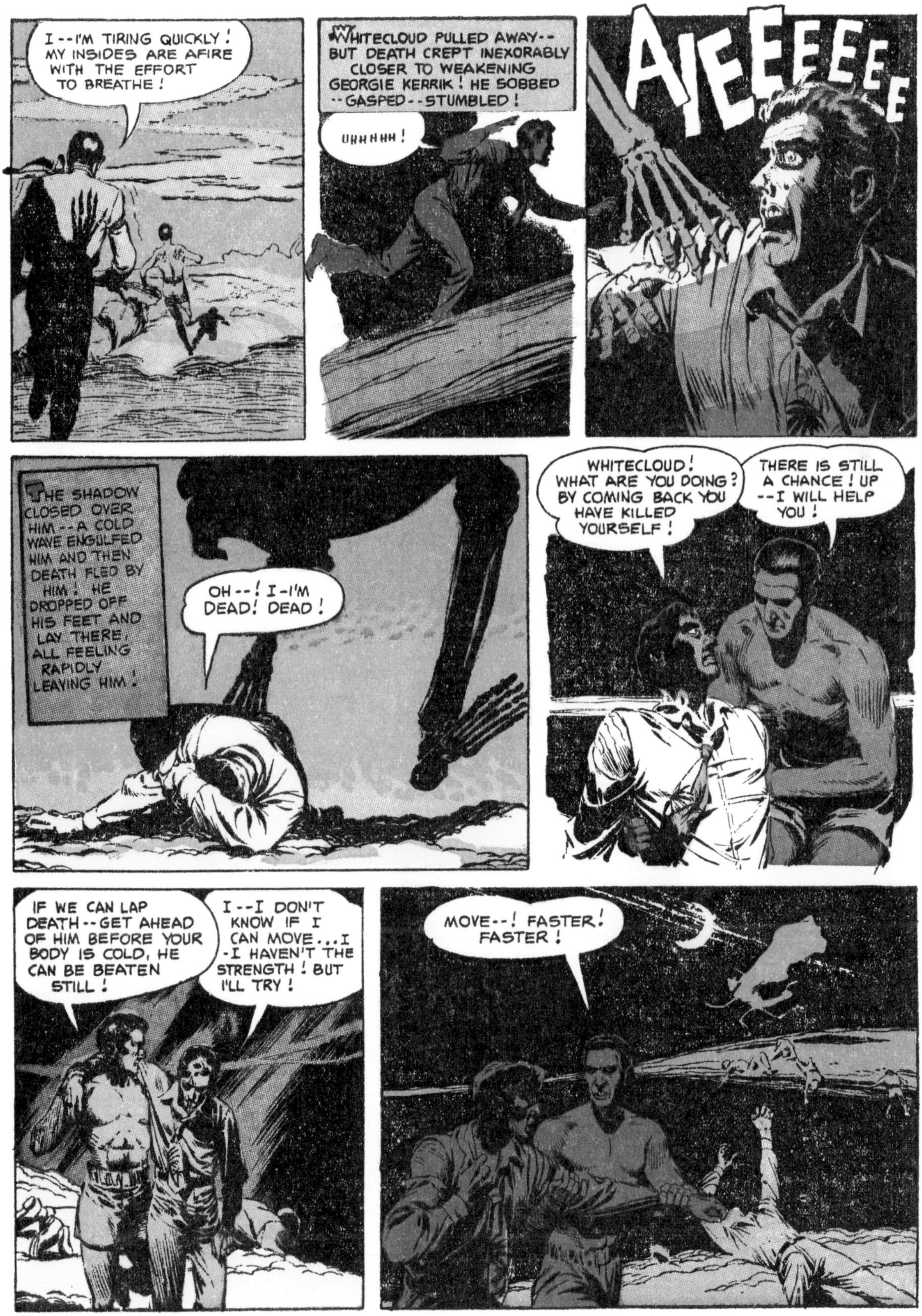
I--I'M TIRING QUICKLY! MY INSIDES ARE AFIRE WITH THE EFFORT TO BREATHE!
WHITECLOUD PULLED AWAY--BUT DEATH CREPT INEXORABLY CLOSER TO WEAKENING GEORGIE KERRIK! HE SOBBED--GASPED--STUMBLED!
UHHHHH!
AIEEEEEEE
THE SHADOW CLOSED OVER HIM--A COLD WAVE ENGULFED HIM AND THEN DEATH FLED BY HIM! HE DROPPED OFF HIS FEET AND LAY THERE, ALL FEELING RAPIDLY LEAVING HIM!
OH--! I-I'M DEAD! DEAD!
WHITECLOUD! WHAT ARE YOU DOING? BY COMING BACK YOU HAVE KILLED YOURSELF!
THERE IS STILL A CHANCE! UP--I WILL HELP YOU!
IF WE CAN LAP DEATH--GET AHEAD OF HIM BEFORE YOUR BODY IS COLD, HE CAN BE BEATEN STILL!
I--I DON'T KNOW IF I CAN MOVE...I-I HAVEN'T THE STRENGTH! BUT I'LL TRY!
MOVE--! FASTER! FASTER!

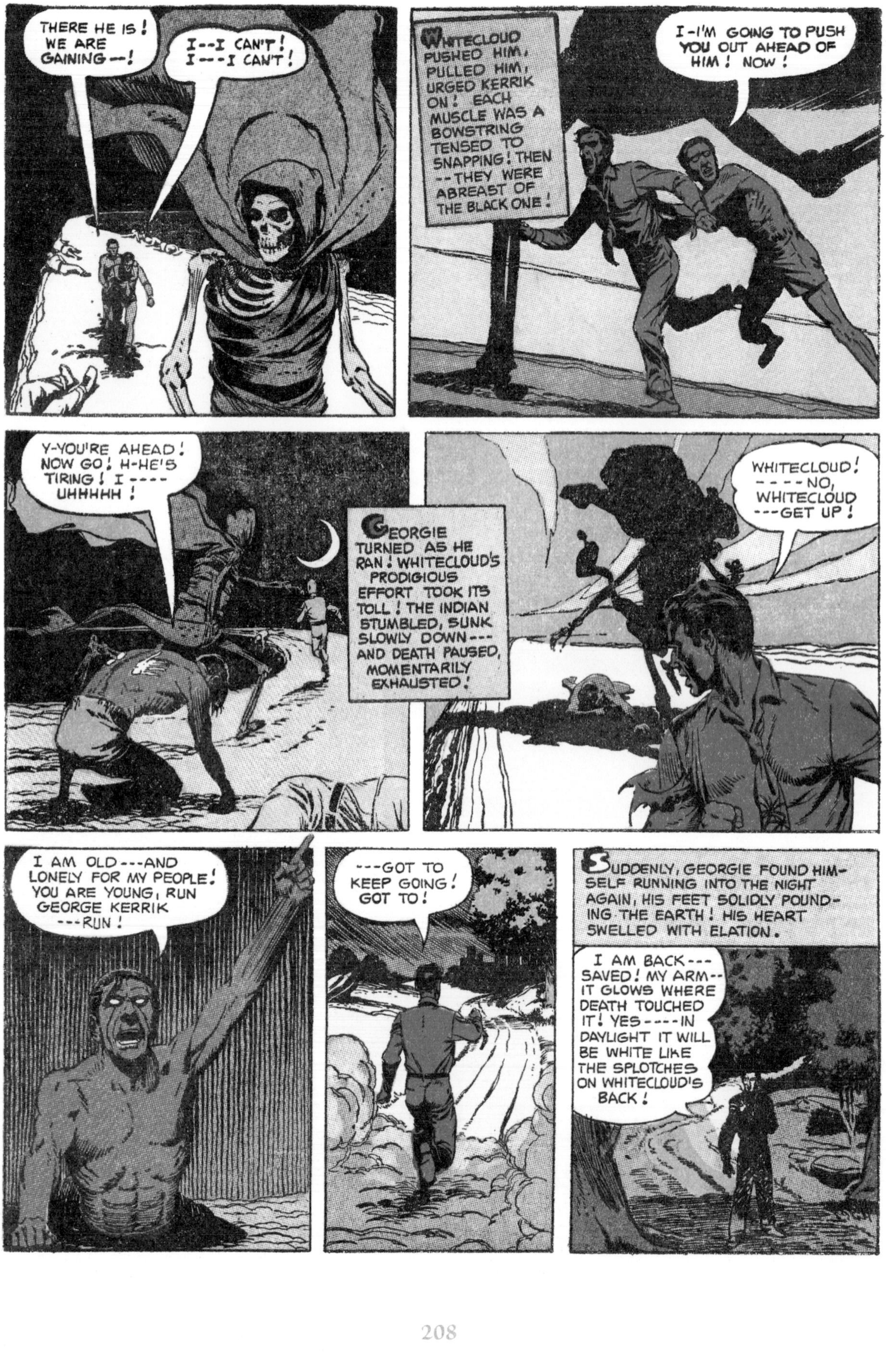
THERE HE IS! WE ARE GAINING--!
I--I CAN'T! I---I CAN'T!
WHITECLOUD PUSHED HIM, PULLED HIM, URGED KERRIK ON! EACH MUSCLE WAS A BOWSTRING TENSED TO SNAPPING! THEN --THEY WERE ABREAST OF THE BLACK ONE!
I-I'M GOING TO PUSH YOU OUT AHEAD OF HIM! NOW!
Y-YOU'RE AHEAD! NOW GO! H-HE'S TIRING! I ---- UHHHHH!
GEORGIE TURNED AS HE RAN! WHITECLOUD'S PRODIGIOUS EFFORT TOOK ITS TOLL! THE INDIAN STUMBLED, SUNK SLOWLY DOWN--- AND DEATH PAUSED, MOMENTARILY EXHAUSTED!
WHITECLOUD! ----NO, WHITECLOUD ---GET UP!
I AM OLD---AND LONELY FOR MY PEOPLE! YOU ARE YOUNG, RUN GEORGE KERRIK ---RUN!
---GOT TO KEEP GOING! GOT TO!
SUDDENLY, GEORGIE FOUND HIMSELF RUNNING INTO THE NIGHT AGAIN, HIS FEET SOLIDLY POUNDING THE EARTH! HIS HEART SWELLED WITH ELATION.
I AM BACK--- SAVED! MY ARM-- IT GLOWS WHERE DEATH TOUCHED IT! YES----IN DAYLIGHT IT WILL BE WHITE LIKE THE SPLOTCHES ON WHITECLOUD'S BACK!

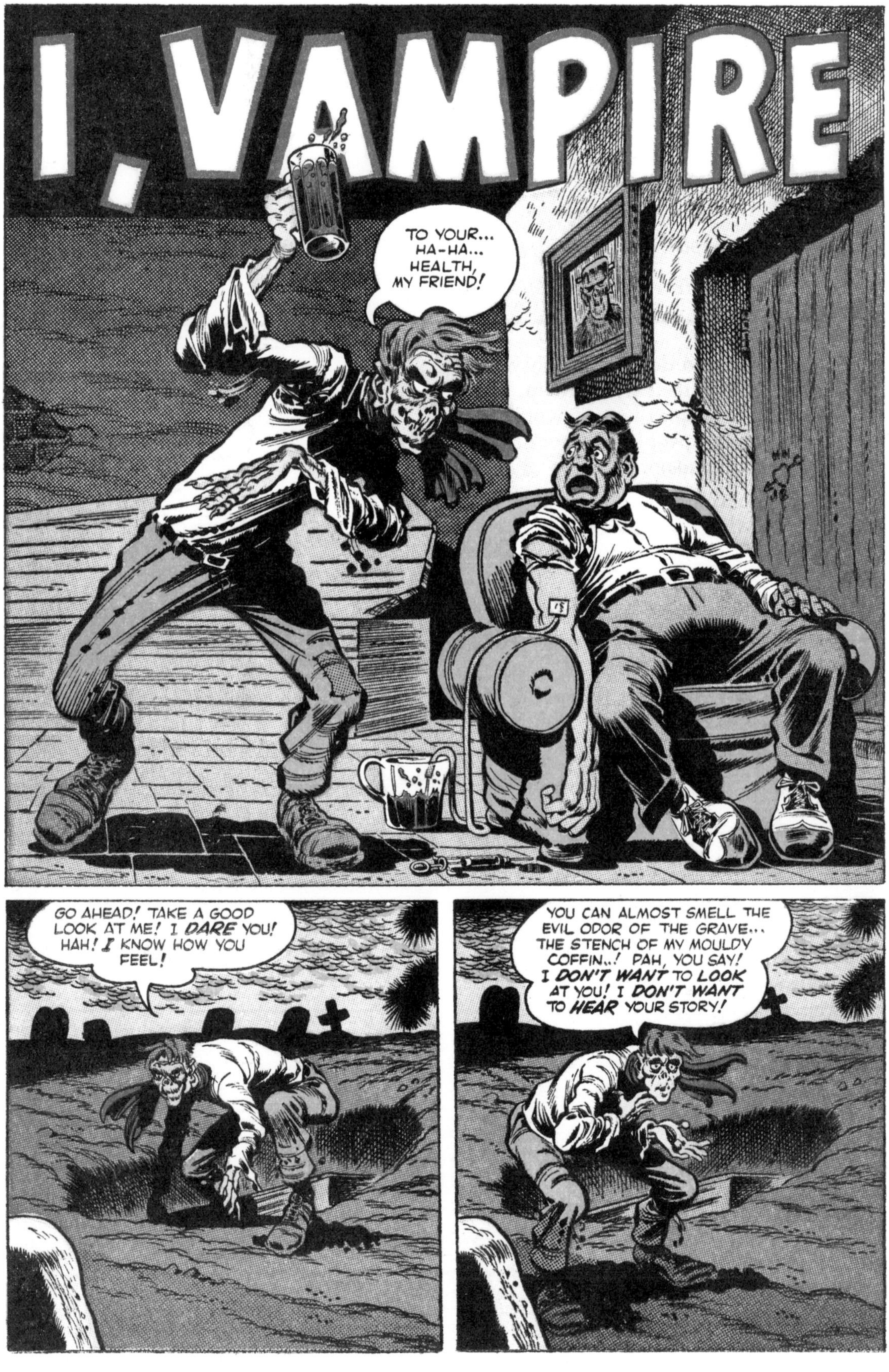
I, VAMPIRE
TO YOUR... HA-HA... HEALTH, MY FRIEND!
GO AHEAD! TAKE A GOOD LOOK AT ME! I DARE YOU! HAH! I KNOW HOW YOU FEEL!
YOU CAN ALMOST SMELL THE EVIL ODOR OF THE GRAVE... THE STENCH OF MY MOULDY COFFIN..! PAH, YOU SAY! I DON'T WANT TO LOOK AT YOU! I DON'T WANT TO HEAR YOUR STORY!

WELL, *LISTEN*, ANYHOW! MAYBE... THEN... YOU'LL INVITE ME TO YOUR HOME! AT LEAST... THAT'S WHAT I HOPE..!

"I KNOW WHY YOU HUMANS *SHUDDER AND SHAKE* WHEN YOU THINK OF US VAMPIRES! YOU PICTURE MY BONY HANDS CLUTCHING AT YOUR HAIR, PULLING YOUR HEAD BACK... BACK... BACK... "

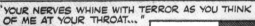

"YOUR NERVES WHINE WITH TERROR AS YOU THINK OF ME AT YOUR THROAT... "

"I CAN UNDERSTAND YOUR POINT OF VIEW. IT'S CERTAINLY NOT A *PLEASANT* EXPERIENCE. I CAN EVEN SYMPATHIZE WITH YOU FOR HATING US AND FOR HUNTING US DOWN!"

BUT DID YOU EVER THINK OF *OUR* SIDE OF THE STORY? DID YOU EVER TRY TO UNDERSTAND *US*... AS *I'M* TRYING TO UNDERSTAND *YOU*?

"JUST *TRY* TO SEE *OUR* PROBLEM! FIRST OF ALL, THE ONLY TIME WE CAN GO OUT IS AT *NIGHT*! OFTEN IT'S *BITTER COLD*! AND OUR SHROUDS ARE WORN *THIN*! THE WIND CUTS THROUGH OUR SCANT CLOTHING LIKE A KNIFE!"

BRRR! WHAT A NIGHT!

IF ONLY WE DIDN'T HAVE TO GO OUT! AHH... HOW PLEASANT IT WOULD BE TO SPEND THE EVENING IN OUR *NICE, WARM COFFINS*!

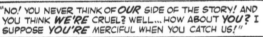

Panel 1:
"THEN, *WE* HAVE FEELINGS, TOO! IT HURTS US TO SEE THE EXPRESSIONS ON YOU HUMANS WHEN YOU CATCH A GLIMPSE OF US!"

AAAAAAHHH! VAMPIRES!

Panel 2:
"AND DID YOU EVER THINK WHAT IT'S LIKE TO BE CRAMPED ALL DAY IN SUCH A SMALL ROOM... NO WINDOWS... NO VENTILATION... NEVER TO SEE THE SUN..."

Panel 3:
"NO! YOU NEVER THINK OF *OUR* SIDE OF THE STORY! AND YOU THINK *WE'RE* CRUEL? WELL... HOW ABOUT *YOU?* I SUPPOSE *YOU'RE* MERCIFUL WHEN YOU CATCH US!"

A STAKE THROUGH THE HEART! *THAT'S* THE WAY...

THUDD

GRUUNNCH!

Panel 4:
DID YOU EVER TRY TO IMPROVE RELATIONS BETWEEN US? *DID* YOU? *NO!* BUT WE *ARE GOING TO!* WE'LL MAKE THE FIRST STEP TOWARD COOPERATION! JUST WAIT TILL YOU HEAR ABOUT OUR NEW IDEA!

Panel 5:
"THAT'S WHAT I WANT TO TELL YOU ABOUT... THAT *NEW IDEA!* YOU SEE, IN THE PAST WHEN WE LEFT A...ER...A DINING COMPANION... WE NEVER TOOK ANY MONEY!"

WHAT'S THE GOOD OF MONEY TO *US!*

NO... HEH...HEH...HEH... PLACE TO SPEND IT IN *OUR* NEIGHBORHOOD!

Panel 6:
"THEN ONE NIGHT *I* GOT THE *IDEA!* IT WAS DURING THE LAST WAR... AND WE FELT THE STRAIN, TOO! WITH SO MANY WOUNDED AND DEAD, EVEN *OUR* BLOOD SUPPLY WAS CUT DOWN! WE WERE LOTS MORE ACTIVE, AND HAD TO GO PLACES WE'D NEVER SEEN BEFORE!"

DO *YOU* SEE IT? IT--- IT'S A WONDERFUL IDEA!

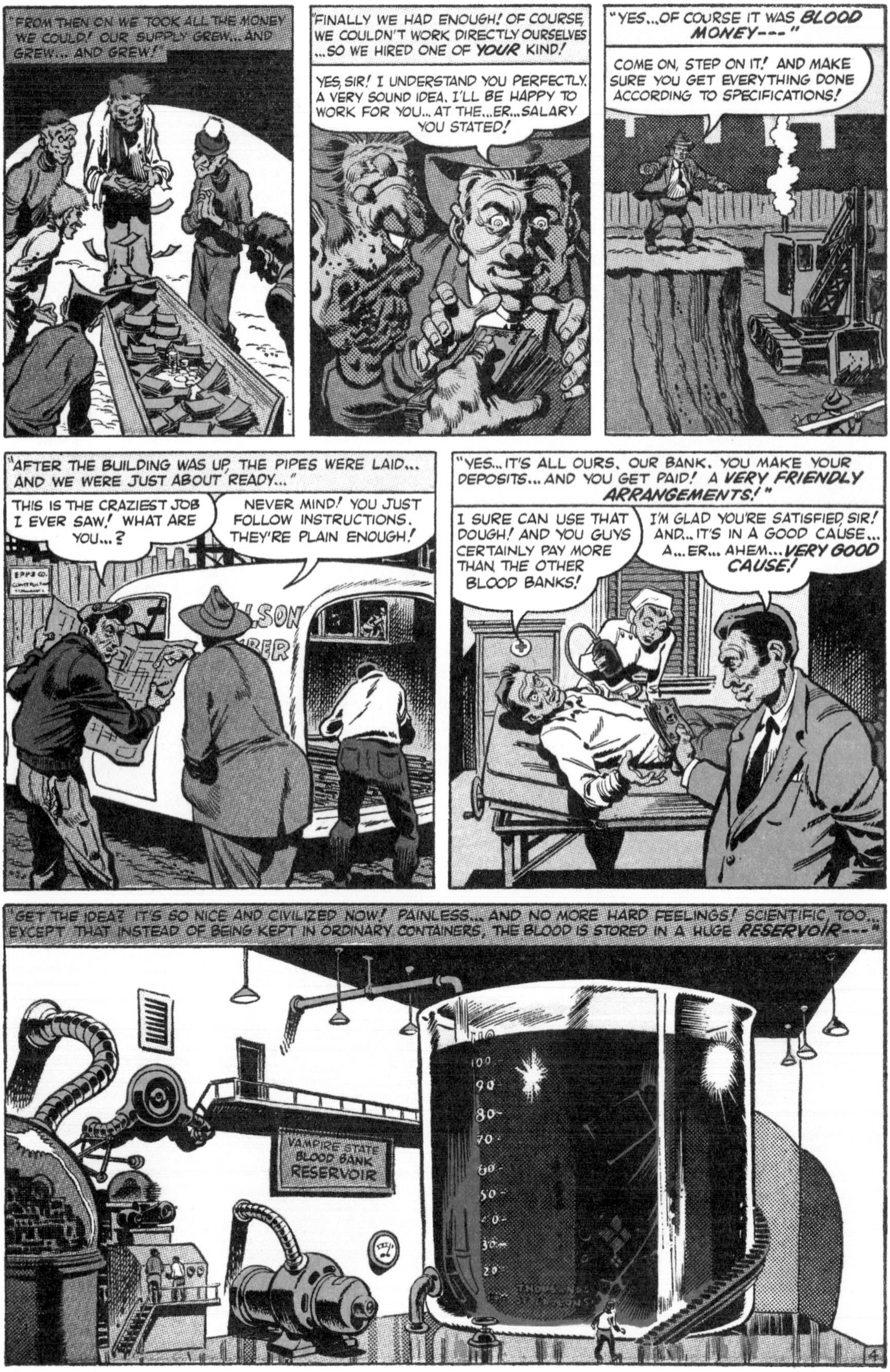

"FROM THEN ON WE TOOK ALL THE MONEY WE COULD! OUR SUPPLY GREW... AND GREW... AND GREW!"
"FINALLY WE HAD ENOUGH! OF COURSE, WE COULDN'T WORK DIRECTLY OURSELVES ...SO WE HIRED ONE OF YOUR KIND!
YES, SIR! I UNDERSTAND YOU PERFECTLY. A VERY SOUND IDEA. I'LL BE HAPPY TO WORK FOR YOU... AT THE...ER...SALARY YOU STATED!
"YES...OF COURSE IT WAS BLOOD MONEY---"
COME ON, STEP ON IT! AND MAKE SURE YOU GET EVERYTHING DONE ACCORDING TO SPECIFICATIONS!
"AFTER THE BUILDING WAS UP, THE PIPES WERE LAID... AND WE WERE JUST ABOUT READY..."
THIS IS THE CRAZIEST JOB I EVER SAW! WHAT ARE YOU...?
NEVER MIND! YOU JUST FOLLOW INSTRUCTIONS. THEY'RE PLAIN ENOUGH!
"YES... IT'S ALL OURS. OUR BANK. YOU MAKE YOUR DEPOSITS... AND YOU GET PAID! A VERY FRIENDLY ARRANGEMENTS!"
I SURE CAN USE THAT DOUGH! AND YOU GUYS CERTAINLY PAY MORE THAN THE OTHER BLOOD BANKS!
I'M GLAD YOU'RE SATISFIED, SIR! AND... IT'S IN A GOOD CAUSE... A...ER... AHEM...VERY GOOD CAUSE!
"GET THE IDEA? IT'S SO NICE AND CIVILIZED NOW! PAINLESS... AND NO MORE HARD FEELINGS! SCIENTIFIC, TOO... EXCEPT THAT INSTEAD OF BEING KEPT IN ORDINARY CONTAINERS, THE BLOOD IS STORED IN A HUGE RESERVOIR---"
VAMPIRE STATE BLOOD BANK RESERVOIR

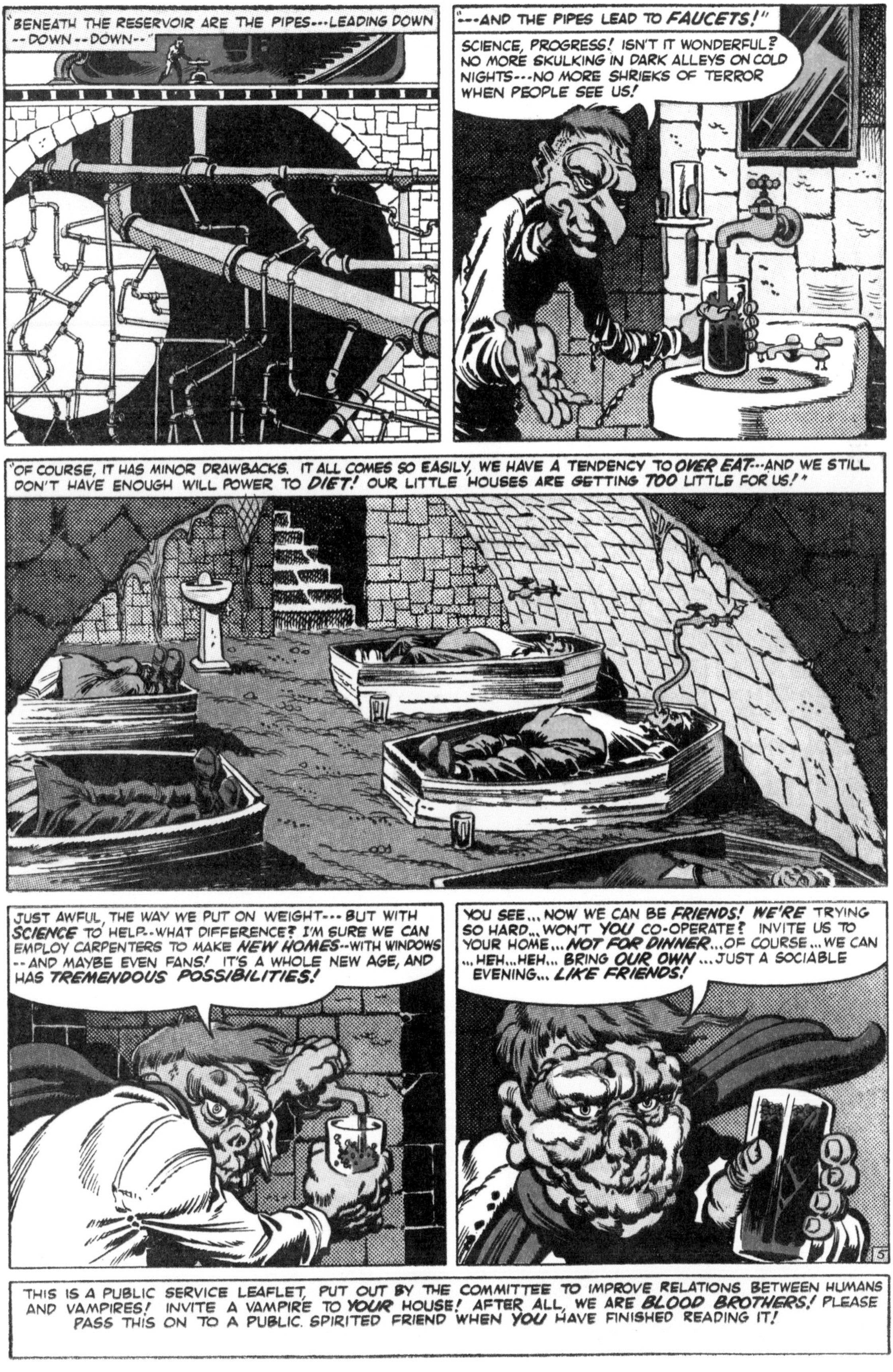
"BENEATH THE RESERVOIR ARE THE PIPES---LEADING DOWN --DOWN--DOWN--"
"---AND THE PIPES LEAD TO FAUCETS!"
SCIENCE, PROGRESS! ISN'T IT WONDERFUL? NO MORE SKULKING IN DARK ALLEYS ON COLD NIGHTS---NO MORE SHRIEKS OF TERROR WHEN PEOPLE SEE US!
"OF COURSE, IT HAS MINOR DRAWBACKS. IT ALL COMES SO EASILY, WE HAVE A TENDENCY TO OVER EAT---AND WE STILL DON'T HAVE ENOUGH WILL POWER TO DIET! OUR LITTLE HOUSES ARE GETTING TOO LITTLE FOR US!"
JUST AWFUL, THE WAY WE PUT ON WEIGHT--- BUT WITH SCIENCE TO HELP--WHAT DIFFERENCE? I'M SURE WE CAN EMPLOY CARPENTERS TO MAKE NEW HOMES--WITH WINDOWS --AND MAYBE EVEN FANS! IT'S A WHOLE NEW AGE, AND HAS TREMENDOUS POSSIBILITIES!
YOU SEE... NOW WE CAN BE FRIENDS! WE'RE TRYING SO HARD... WON'T YOU CO-OPERATE? INVITE US TO YOUR HOME... NOT FOR DINNER... OF COURSE... WE CAN ...HEH...HEH... BRING OUR OWN ... JUST A SOCIABLE EVENING... LIKE FRIENDS!
5
THIS IS A PUBLIC SERVICE LEAFLET, PUT OUT BY THE COMMITTEE TO IMPROVE RELATIONS BETWEEN HUMANS AND VAMPIRES! INVITE A VAMPIRE TO YOUR HOUSE! AFTER ALL, WE ARE BLOOD BROTHERS! PLEASE PASS THIS ON TO A PUBLIC. SPIRITED FRIEND WHEN YOU HAVE FINISHED READING IT!

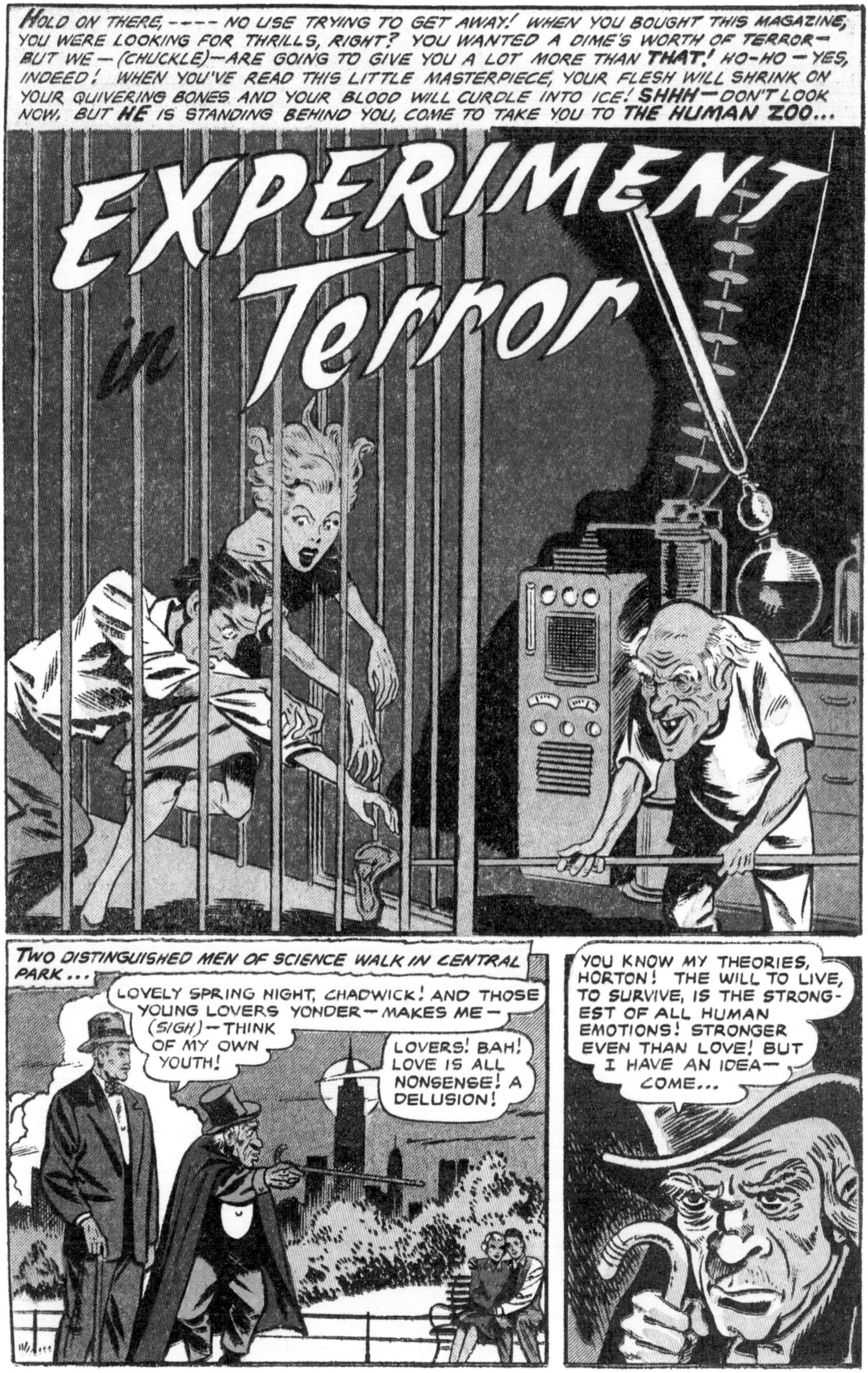
HOLD ON THERE, ---- NO USE TRYING TO GET AWAY! WHEN YOU BOUGHT THIS MAGAZINE, YOU WERE LOOKING FOR THRILLS, RIGHT? YOU WANTED A DIME'S WORTH OF TERROR—BUT WE—(CHUCKLE)—ARE GOING TO GIVE YOU A LOT MORE THAN THAT! HO-HO—YES, INDEED! WHEN YOU'VE READ THIS LITTLE MASTERPIECE, YOUR FLESH WILL SHRINK ON YOUR QUIVERING BONES AND YOUR BLOOD WILL CURDLE INTO ICE! SHHH—DON'T LOOK NOW, BUT HE IS STANDING BEHIND YOU, COME TO TAKE YOU TO THE HUMAN ZOO...
EXPERIMENT in Terror
TWO DISTINGUISHED MEN OF SCIENCE WALK IN CENTRAL PARK...
LOVELY SPRING NIGHT, CHADWICK! AND THOSE YOUNG LOVERS YONDER—MAKES ME—(SIGH)—THINK OF MY OWN YOUTH!
LOVERS! BAH! LOVE IS ALL NONSENSE! A DELUSION!
YOU KNOW MY THEORIES, HORTON! THE WILL TO LIVE, TO SURVIVE, IS THE STRONGEST OF ALL HUMAN EMOTIONS! STRONGER EVEN THAN LOVE! BUT I HAVE AN IDEA—COME...

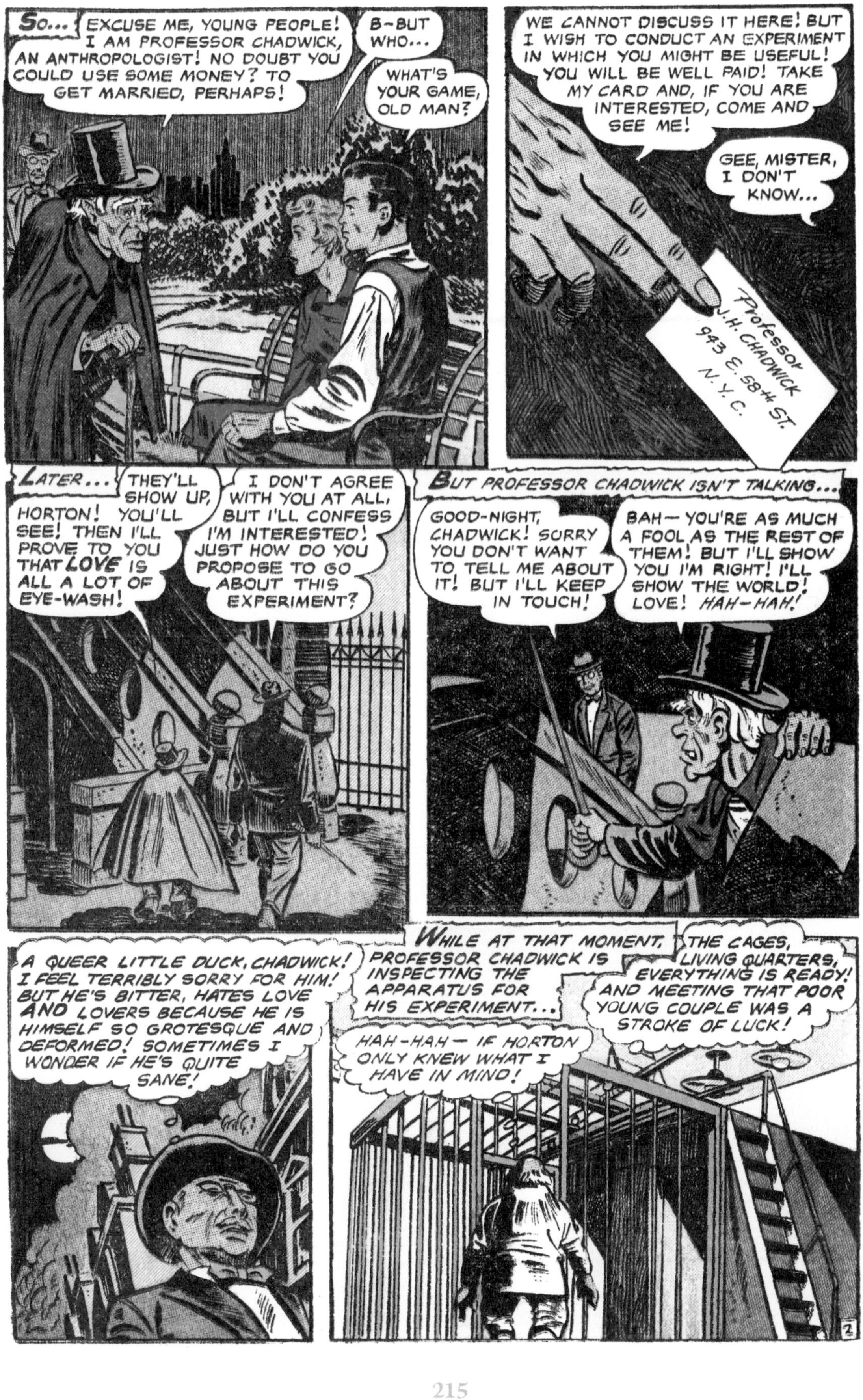

SO...
EXCUSE ME, YOUNG PEOPLE! I AM PROFESSOR CHADWICK, AN ANTHROPOLOGIST! NO DOUBT YOU COULD USE SOME MONEY? TO GET MARRIED, PERHAPS!
B-BUT WHO...
WHAT'S YOUR GAME, OLD MAN?
WE CANNOT DISCUSS IT HERE! BUT I WISH TO CONDUCT AN EXPERIMENT IN WHICH YOU MIGHT BE USEFUL! YOU WILL BE WELL PAID! TAKE MY CARD AND, IF YOU ARE INTERESTED, COME AND SEE ME!
GEE, MISTER, I DON'T KNOW...
Professor J.H. CHADWICK 943 E. 58th ST. N.Y.C.
LATER...
THEY'LL SHOW UP, HORTON! YOU'LL SEE! THEN I'LL PROVE TO YOU THAT LOVE IS ALL A LOT OF EYE-WASH!
I DON'T AGREE WITH YOU AT ALL, BUT I'LL CONFESS I'M INTERESTED! JUST HOW DO YOU PROPOSE TO GO ABOUT THIS EXPERIMENT?
BUT PROFESSOR CHADWICK ISN'T TALKING...
GOOD-NIGHT, CHADWICK! SORRY YOU DON'T WANT TO TELL ME ABOUT IT! BUT I'LL KEEP IN TOUCH!
BAH— YOU'RE AS MUCH A FOOL AS THE REST OF THEM! BUT I'LL SHOW YOU I'M RIGHT! I'LL SHOW THE WORLD! LOVE! HAH-HAH!
A QUEER LITTLE DUCK, CHADWICK! I FEEL TERRIBLY SORRY FOR HIM! BUT HE'S BITTER, HATES LOVE AND LOVERS BECAUSE HE IS HIMSELF SO GROTESQUE AND DEFORMED! SOMETIMES I WONDER IF HE'S QUITE SANE!
WHILE AT THAT MOMENT, PROFESSOR CHADWICK IS INSPECTING THE APPARATUS FOR HIS EXPERIMENT...
HAH-HAH— IF HORTON ONLY KNEW WHAT I HAVE IN MIND!
THE CAGES, LIVING QUARTERS, EVERYTHING IS READY! AND MEETING THAT POOR YOUNG COUPLE WAS A STROKE OF LUCK!
2

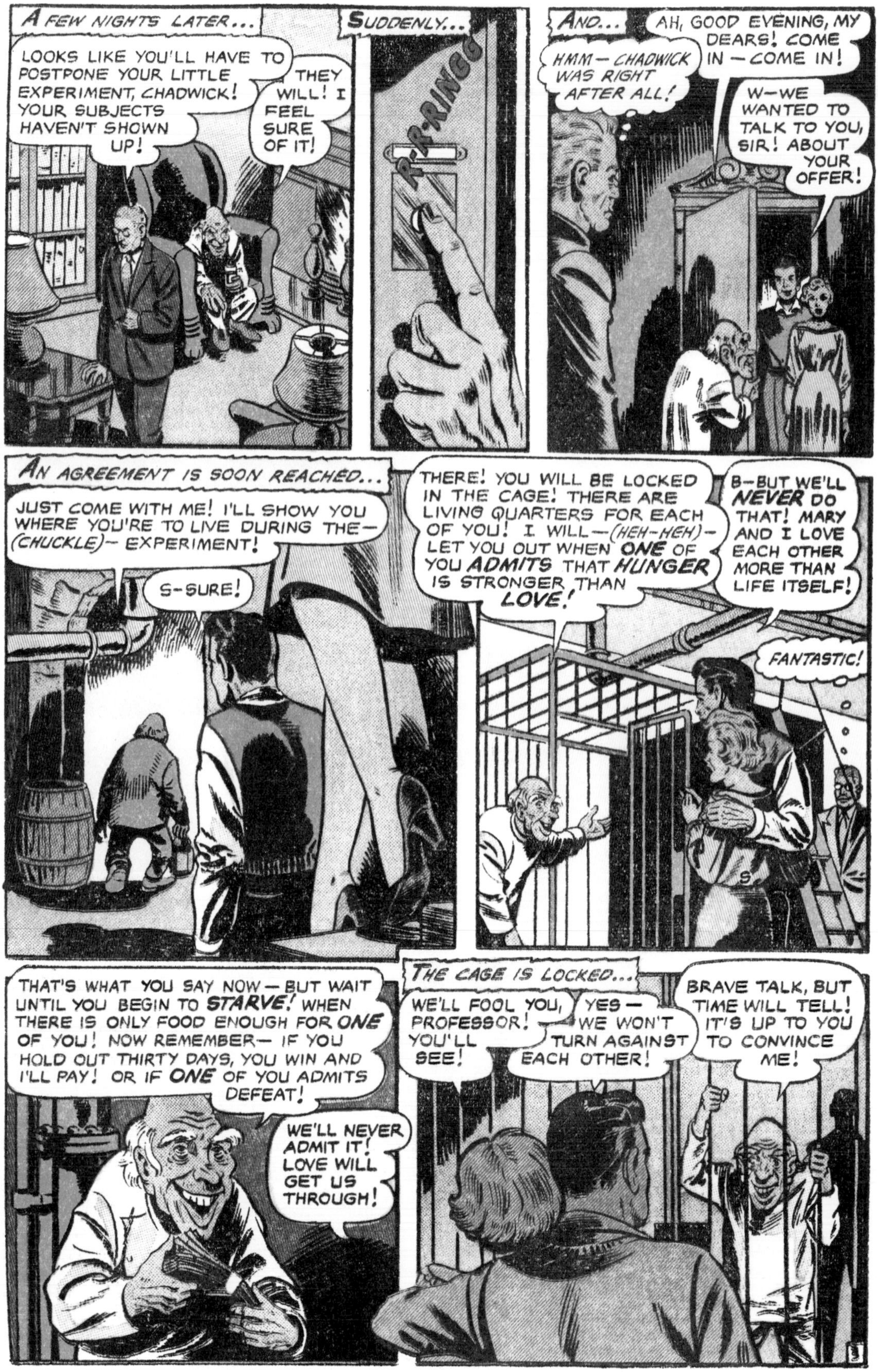
A FEW NIGHTS LATER...
LOOKS LIKE YOU'LL HAVE TO POSTPONE YOUR LITTLE EXPERIMENT, CHADWICK! YOUR SUBJECTS HAVEN'T SHOWN UP!
THEY WILL! I FEEL SURE OF IT!
SUDDENLY...
R-R-RINGG
AND...
HMM—CHADWICK WAS RIGHT AFTER ALL!
AH, GOOD EVENING, MY DEARS! COME IN—COME IN!
W-WE WANTED TO TALK TO YOU, SIR! ABOUT YOUR OFFER!
AN AGREEMENT IS SOON REACHED...
JUST COME WITH ME! I'LL SHOW YOU WHERE YOU'RE TO LIVE DURING THE—(CHUCKLE)—EXPERIMENT!
S-SURE!
THERE! YOU WILL BE LOCKED IN THE CAGE! THERE ARE LIVING QUARTERS FOR EACH OF YOU! I WILL—(HEH-HEH)—LET YOU OUT WHEN ONE OF YOU ADMITS THAT HUNGER IS STRONGER THAN LOVE!
B—BUT WE'LL NEVER DO THAT! MARY AND I LOVE EACH OTHER MORE THAN LIFE ITSELF!
FANTASTIC!
THAT'S WHAT YOU SAY NOW—BUT WAIT UNTIL YOU BEGIN TO STARVE! WHEN THERE IS ONLY FOOD ENOUGH FOR ONE OF YOU! NOW REMEMBER—IF YOU HOLD OUT THIRTY DAYS, YOU WIN AND I'LL PAY! OR IF ONE OF YOU ADMITS DEFEAT!
WE'LL NEVER ADMIT IT! LOVE WILL GET US THROUGH!
THE CAGE IS LOCKED...
WE'LL FOOL YOU, PROFESSOR! YOU'LL SEE!
YES—WE WON'T TURN AGAINST EACH OTHER!
BRAVE TALK, BUT TIME WILL TELL! IT'S UP TO YOU TO CONVINCE ME!
3

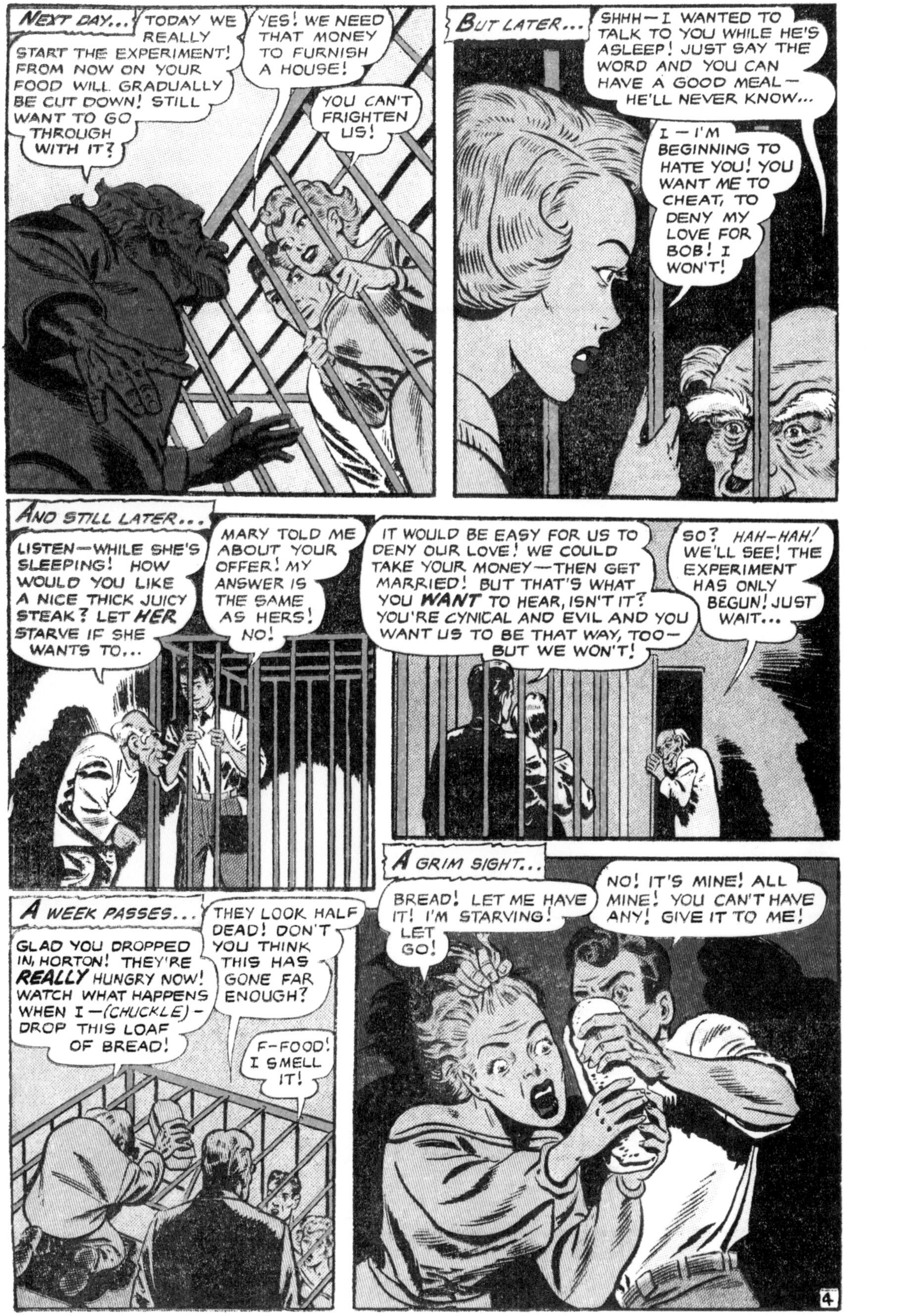
NEXT DAY...
TODAY WE REALLY START THE EXPERIMENT! FROM NOW ON YOUR FOOD WILL GRADUALLY BE CUT DOWN! STILL WANT TO GO THROUGH WITH IT?
YES! WE NEED THAT MONEY TO FURNISH A HOUSE!
YOU CAN'T FRIGHTEN US!
BUT LATER...
SHHH—I WANTED TO TALK TO YOU WHILE HE'S ASLEEP! JUST SAY THE WORD AND YOU CAN HAVE A GOOD MEAL—HE'LL NEVER KNOW...
I—I'M BEGINNING TO HATE YOU! YOU WANT ME TO CHEAT, TO DENY MY LOVE FOR BOB! I WON'T!
AND STILL LATER...
LISTEN—WHILE SHE'S SLEEPING! HOW WOULD YOU LIKE A NICE THICK JUICY STEAK? LET HER STARVE IF SHE WANTS TO...
MARY TOLD ME ABOUT YOUR OFFER! MY ANSWER IS THE SAME AS HERS! NO!
IT WOULD BE EASY FOR US TO DENY OUR LOVE! WE COULD TAKE YOUR MONEY—THEN GET MARRIED! BUT THAT'S WHAT YOU WANT TO HEAR, ISN'T IT? YOU'RE CYNICAL AND EVIL AND YOU WANT US TO BE THAT WAY, TOO—BUT WE WON'T!
SO? HAH-HAH! WE'LL SEE! THE EXPERIMENT HAS ONLY BEGUN! JUST WAIT...
A WEEK PASSES...
GLAD YOU DROPPED IN, HORTON! THEY'RE REALLY HUNGRY NOW! WATCH WHAT HAPPENS WHEN I—(CHUCKLE)—DROP THIS LOAF OF BREAD!
THEY LOOK HALF DEAD! DON'T YOU THINK THIS HAS GONE FAR ENOUGH?
F-FOOD! I SMELL IT!
A GRIM SIGHT...
BREAD! LET ME HAVE IT! I'M STARVING! LET GO!
NO! IT'S MINE! ALL MINE! YOU CAN'T HAVE ANY! GIVE IT TO ME!
4

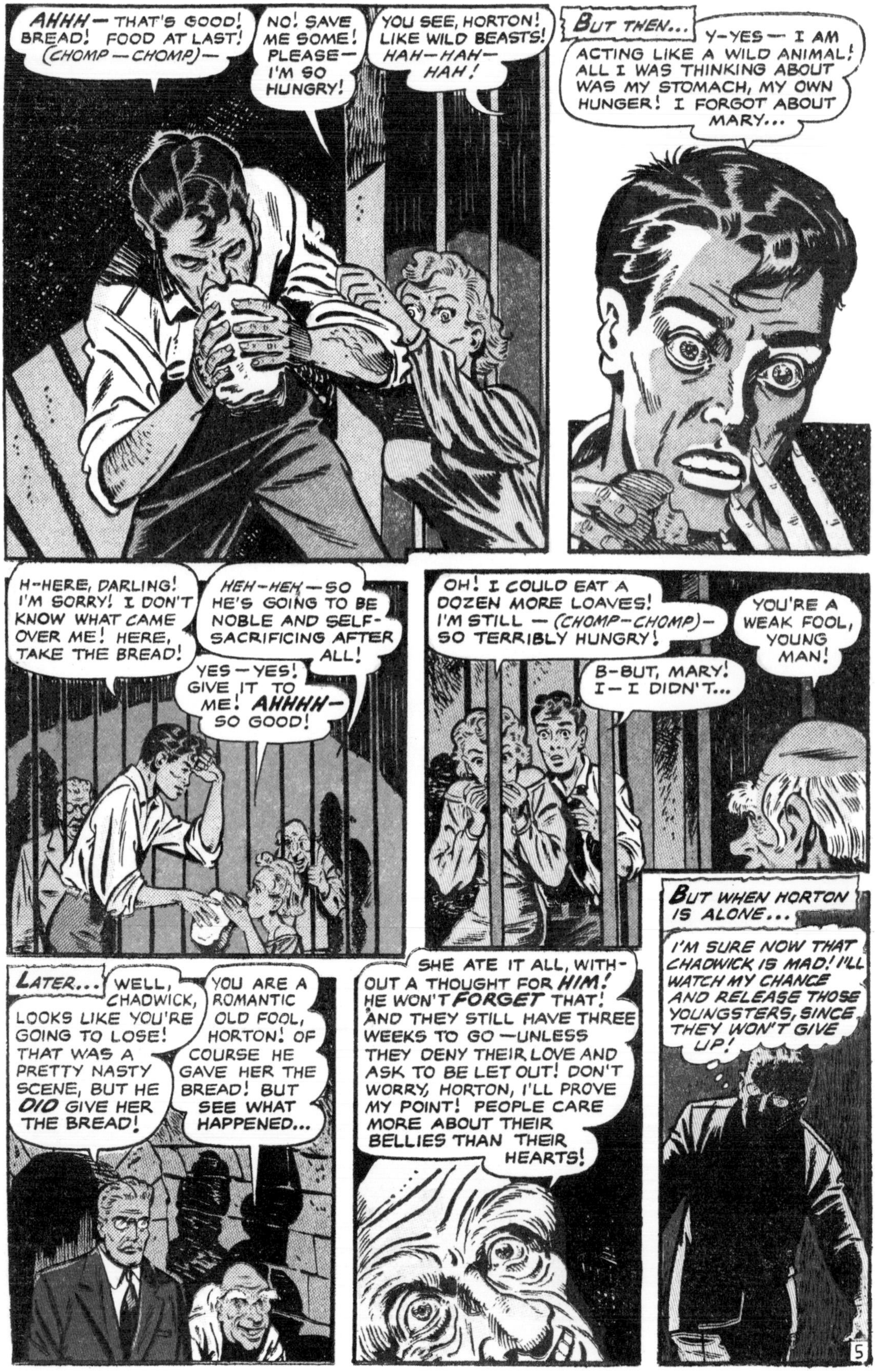
AHHH—THAT'S GOOD! BREAD! FOOD AT LAST! (CHOMP—CHOMP)—
NO! SAVE ME SOME! PLEASE—I'M SO HUNGRY!
YOU SEE, HORTON! LIKE WILD BEASTS! HAH-HAH-HAH!
BUT THEN...
Y-YES—I AM ACTING LIKE A WILD ANIMAL! ALL I WAS THINKING ABOUT WAS MY STOMACH, MY OWN HUNGER! I FORGOT ABOUT MARY...
H-HERE, DARLING! I'M SORRY! I DON'T KNOW WHAT CAME OVER ME! HERE, TAKE THE BREAD!
HEH-HEH—SO HE'S GOING TO BE NOBLE AND SELF-SACRIFICING AFTER ALL!
YES—YES! GIVE IT TO ME! AHHHH—SO GOOD!
OH! I COULD EAT A DOZEN MORE LOAVES! I'M STILL—(CHOMP-CHOMP)—SO TERRIBLY HUNGRY!
B-BUT, MARY! I—I DIDN'T...
YOU'RE A WEAK FOOL, YOUNG MAN!
BUT WHEN HORTON IS ALONE...
I'M SURE NOW THAT CHADWICK IS MAD! I'LL WATCH MY CHANCE AND RELEASE THOSE YOUNGSTERS, SINCE THEY WON'T GIVE UP!
LATER...
WELL, CHADWICK, LOOKS LIKE YOU'RE GOING TO LOSE! THAT WAS A PRETTY NASTY SCENE, BUT HE DID GIVE HER THE BREAD!
YOU ARE A ROMANTIC OLD FOOL, HORTON! OF COURSE HE GAVE HER THE BREAD! BUT SEE WHAT HAPPENED...
SHE ATE IT ALL, WITHOUT A THOUGHT FOR HIM! HE WON'T FORGET THAT! AND THEY STILL HAVE THREE WEEKS TO GO—UNLESS THEY DENY THEIR LOVE AND ASK TO BE LET OUT! DON'T WORRY, HORTON, I'LL PROVE MY POINT! PEOPLE CARE MORE ABOUT THEIR BELLIES THAN THEIR HEARTS!
5

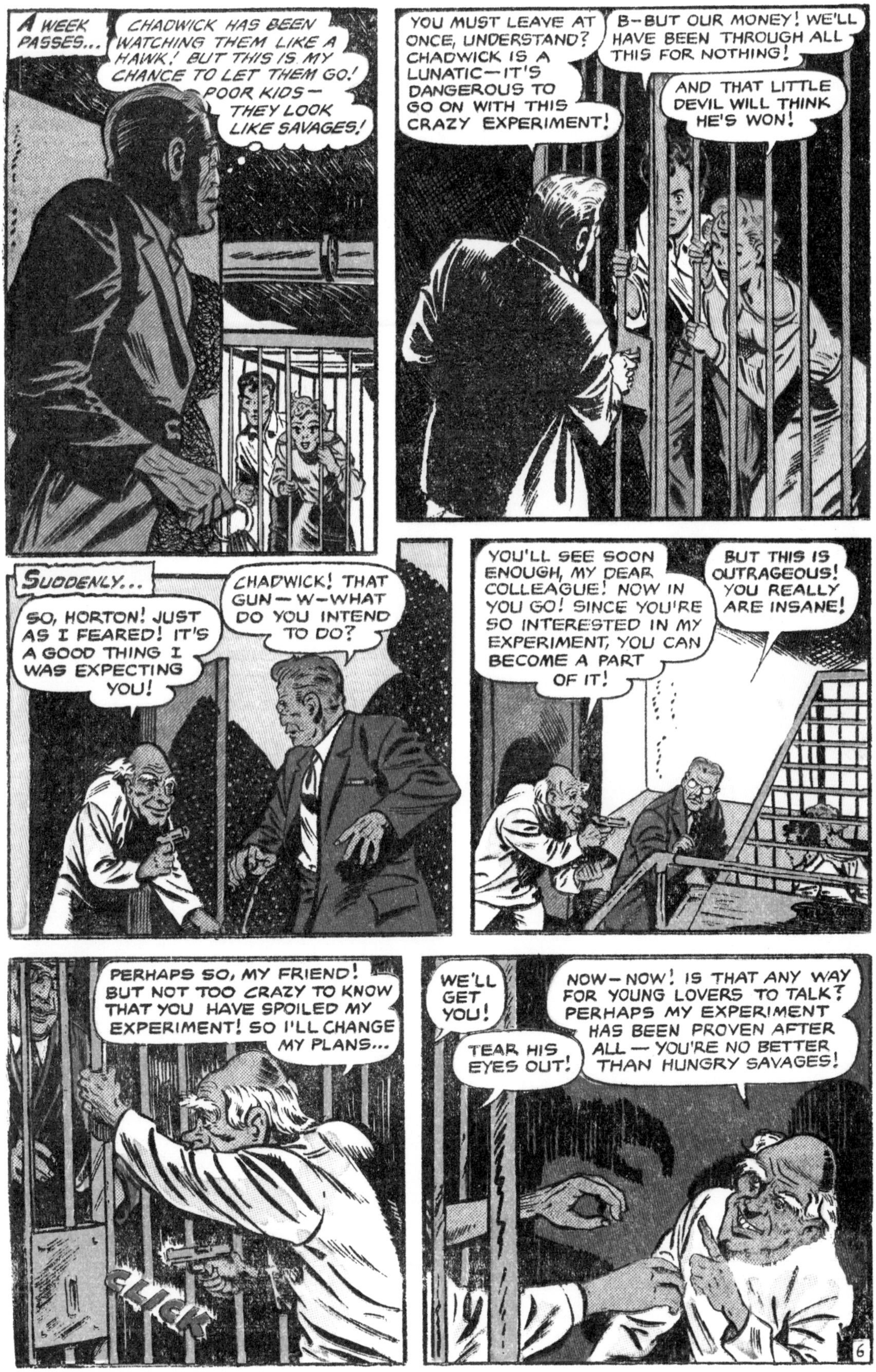
A WEEK PASSES...
CHADWICK HAS BEEN WATCHING THEM LIKE A HAWK! BUT THIS IS MY CHANCE TO LET THEM GO! POOR KIDS— THEY LOOK LIKE SAVAGES!
YOU MUST LEAVE AT ONCE, UNDERSTAND? CHADWICK IS A LUNATIC—IT'S DANGEROUS TO GO ON WITH THIS CRAZY EXPERIMENT!
B—BUT OUR MONEY! WE'LL HAVE BEEN THROUGH ALL THIS FOR NOTHING!
AND THAT LITTLE DEVIL WILL THINK HE'S WON!
SUDDENLY...
SO, HORTON! JUST AS I FEARED! IT'S A GOOD THING I WAS EXPECTING YOU!
CHADWICK! THAT GUN—W—WHAT DO YOU INTEND TO DO?
YOU'LL SEE SOON ENOUGH, MY DEAR COLLEAGUE! NOW IN YOU GO! SINCE YOU'RE SO INTERESTED IN MY EXPERIMENT, YOU CAN BECOME A PART OF IT!
BUT THIS IS OUTRAGEOUS! YOU REALLY ARE INSANE!
PERHAPS SO, MY FRIEND! BUT NOT TOO CRAZY TO KNOW THAT YOU HAVE SPOILED MY EXPERIMENT! SO I'LL CHANGE MY PLANS...
CLICK
WE'LL GET YOU!
TEAR HIS EYES OUT!
NOW—NOW! IS THAT ANY WAY FOR YOUNG LOVERS TO TALK? PERHAPS MY EXPERIMENT HAS BEEN PROVEN AFTER ALL — YOU'RE NO BETTER THAN HUNGRY SAVAGES!
6

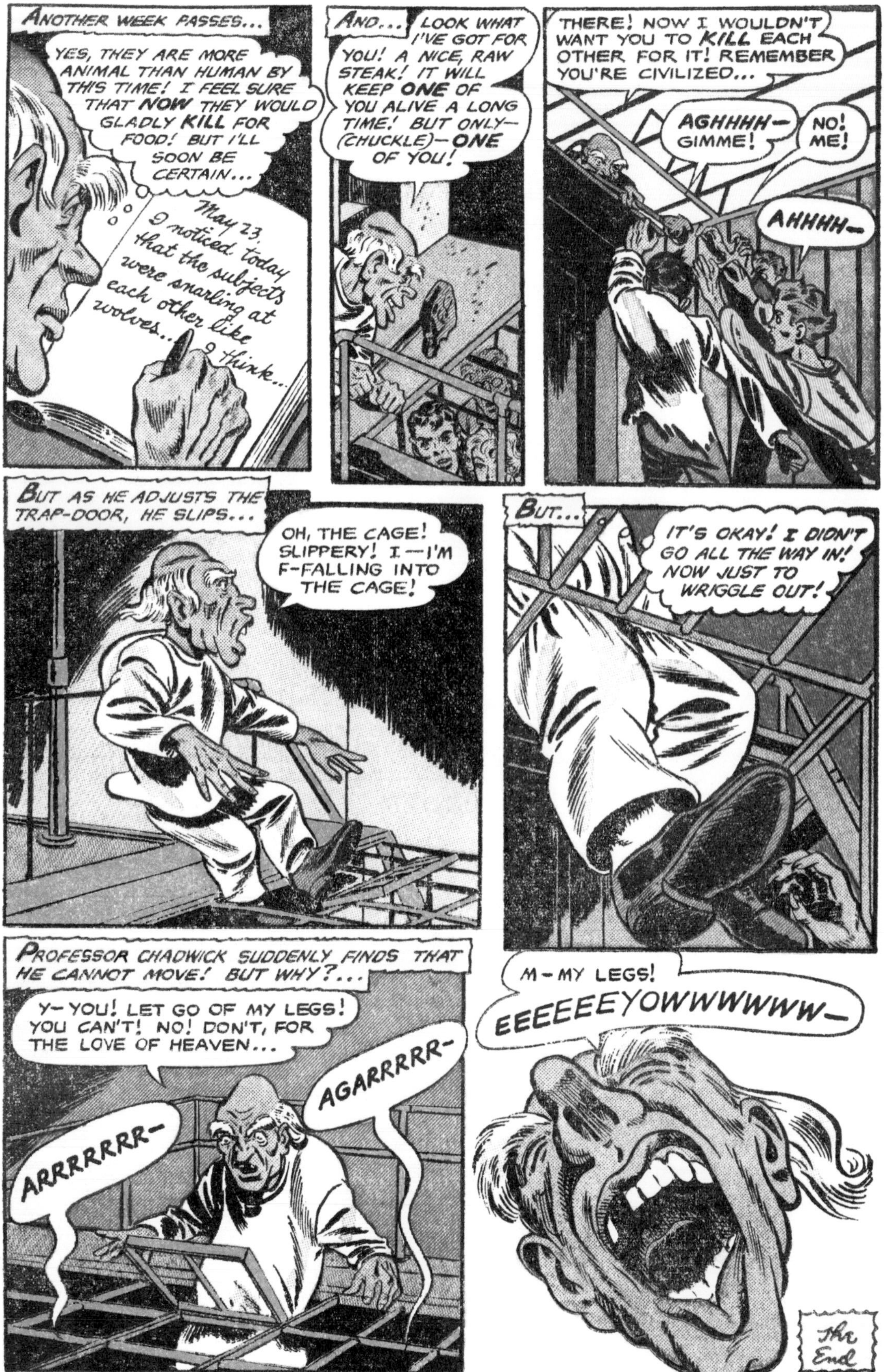
ANOTHER WEEK PASSES...
YES, THEY ARE MORE ANIMAL THAN HUMAN BY THIS TIME! I FEEL SURE THAT NOW THEY WOULD GLADLY KILL FOR FOOD! BUT I'LL SOON BE CERTAIN...
May 23. I noticed today that the subjects were snarling at each other like wolves... I think...
AND...
LOOK WHAT I'VE GOT FOR YOU! A NICE, RAW STEAK! IT WILL KEEP ONE OF YOU ALIVE A LONG TIME! BUT ONLY-(CHUCKLE)-ONE OF YOU!
THERE! NOW I WOULDN'T WANT YOU TO KILL EACH OTHER FOR IT! REMEMBER YOU'RE CIVILIZED...
AGHHHH- GIMME!
NO! ME!
AHHHH-
BUT AS HE ADJUSTS THE TRAP-DOOR, HE SLIPS...
OH, THE CAGE! SLIPPERY! I--I'M F-FALLING INTO THE CAGE!
BUT...
IT'S OKAY! I DIDN'T GO ALL THE WAY IN! NOW JUST TO WRIGGLE OUT!
PROFESSOR CHADWICK SUDDENLY FINDS THAT HE CANNOT MOVE! BUT WHY?...
Y-YOU! LET GO OF MY LEGS! YOU CAN'T! NO! DON'T, FOR THE LOVE OF HEAVEN...
AGARRRRR-
ARRRRRRR-
M-MY LEGS!
EEEEEEYOWWWWWW-
The End

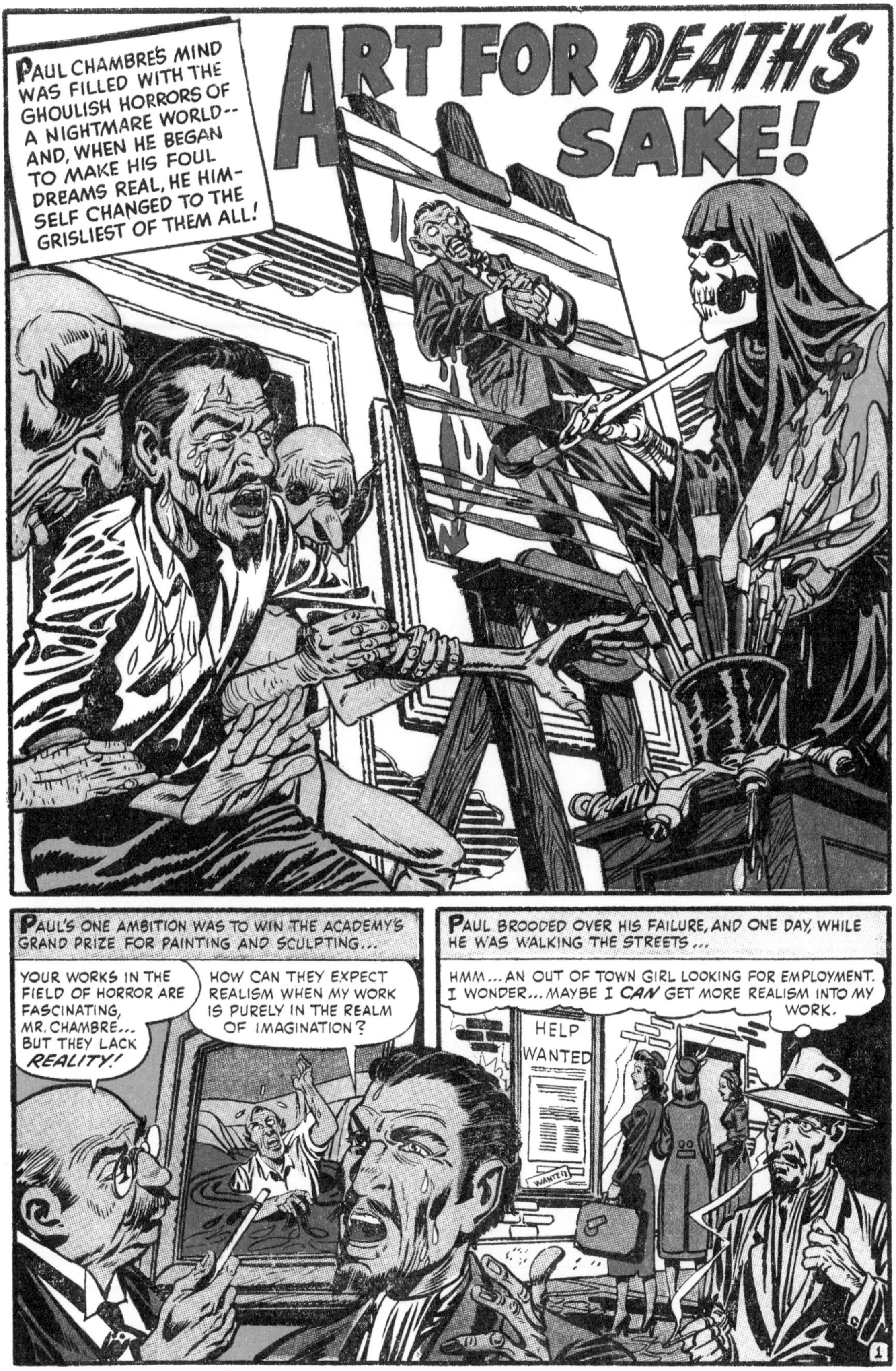

PAUL CHAMBRE'S MIND WAS FILLED WITH THE GHOULISH HORRORS OF A NIGHTMARE WORLD-- A NIGHTMARE WORLD-- AND, WHEN HE BEGAN TO MAKE HIS FOUL DREAMS REAL, HE HIMSELF CHANGED TO THE GRISLIEST OF THEM ALL!
ART FOR DEATH'S SAKE!
PAUL'S ONE AMBITION WAS TO WIN THE ACADEMY'S GRAND PRIZE FOR PAINTING AND SCULPTING...
YOUR WORKS IN THE FIELD OF HORROR ARE FASCINATING, MR. CHAMBRE... BUT THEY LACK REALITY!
HOW CAN THEY EXPECT REALISM WHEN MY WORK IS PURELY IN THE REALM OF IMAGINATION?
PAUL BROODED OVER HIS FAILURE, AND ONE DAY, WHILE HE WAS WALKING THE STREETS...
HMM... AN OUT OF TOWN GIRL LOOKING FOR EMPLOYMENT. I WONDER... MAYBE I CAN GET MORE REALISM INTO MY WORK.
HELP WANTED
WANTED
1

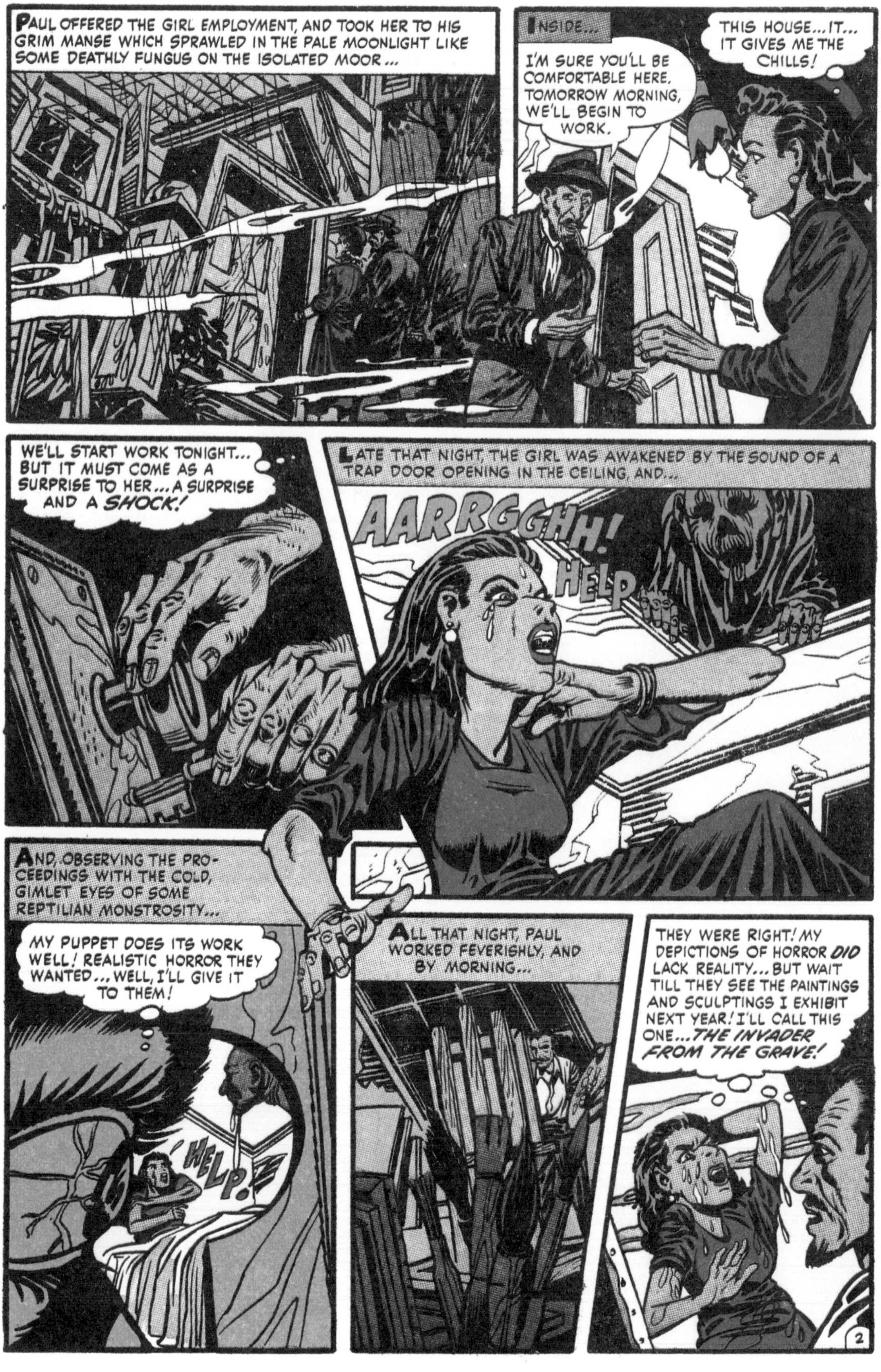
PAUL OFFERED THE GIRL EMPLOYMENT, AND TOOK HER TO HIS GRIM MANSE WHICH SPRAWLED IN THE PALE MOONLIGHT LIKE SOME DEATHLY FUNGUS ON THE ISOLATED MOOR...
INSIDE...
I'M SURE YOU'LL BE COMFORTABLE HERE. TOMORROW MORNING, WE'LL BEGIN TO WORK.
THIS HOUSE... IT... IT GIVES ME THE CHILLS!
WE'LL START WORK TONIGHT... BUT IT MUST COME AS A SURPRISE TO HER... A SURPRISE AND A SHOCK!
LATE THAT NIGHT, THE GIRL WAS AWAKENED BY THE SOUND OF A TRAP DOOR OPENING IN THE CEILING, AND...
AARRGGHH!
HELP
AND, OBSERVING THE PROCEEDINGS WITH THE COLD, GIMLET EYES OF SOME REPTILIAN MONSTROSITY...
MY PUPPET DOES ITS WORK WELL! REALISTIC HORROR THEY WANTED... WELL, I'LL GIVE IT TO THEM!
HELP!
ALL THAT NIGHT, PAUL WORKED FEVERISHLY, AND BY MORNING...
THEY WERE RIGHT! MY DEPICTIONS OF HORROR DID LACK REALITY... BUT WAIT TILL THEY SEE THE PAINTINGS AND SCULPTINGS I EXHIBIT NEXT YEAR! I'LL CALL THIS ONE... THE INVADER FROM THE GRAVE!
2

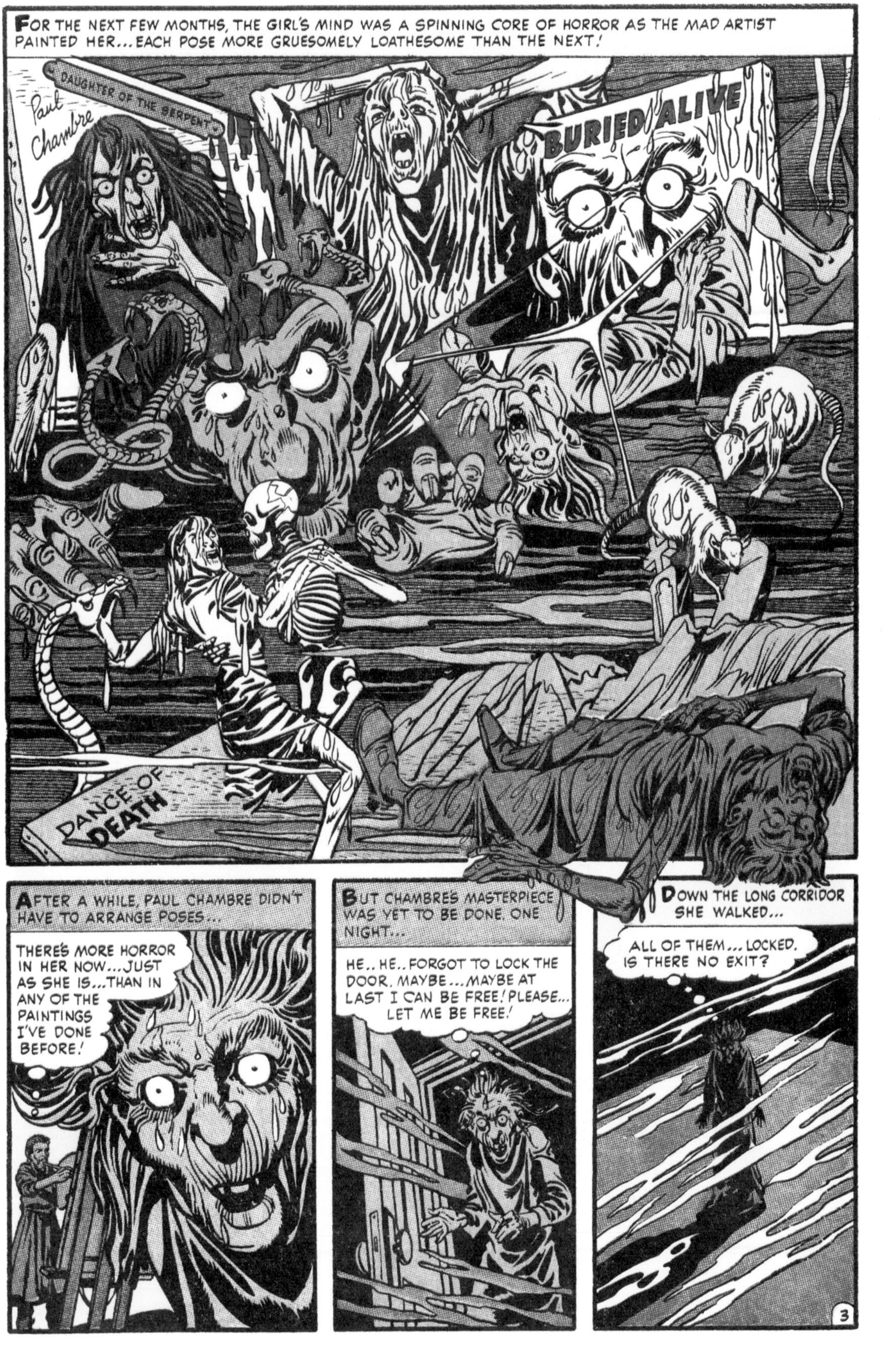

FOR THE NEXT FEW MONTHS, THE GIRL'S MIND WAS A SPINNING CORE OF HORROR AS THE MAD ARTIST PAINTED HER... EACH POSE MORE GRUESOMELY LOATHESOME THAN THE NEXT!
Paul Chambre
DAUGHTER OF THE SERPENT
BURIED ALIVE
DANCE OF DEATH
AFTER A WHILE, PAUL CHAMBRE DIDN'T HAVE TO ARRANGE POSES...
THERE'S MORE HORROR IN HER NOW... JUST AS SHE IS... THAN IN ANY OF THE PAINTINGS I'VE DONE BEFORE!
BUT CHAMBRE'S MASTERPIECE WAS YET TO BE DONE. ONE NIGHT...
HE.. HE.. FORGOT TO LOCK THE DOOR. MAYBE... MAYBE AT LAST I CAN BE FREE! PLEASE... LET ME BE FREE!
DOWN THE LONG CORRIDOR SHE WALKED...
ALL OF THEM... LOCKED. IS THERE NO EXIT?
3

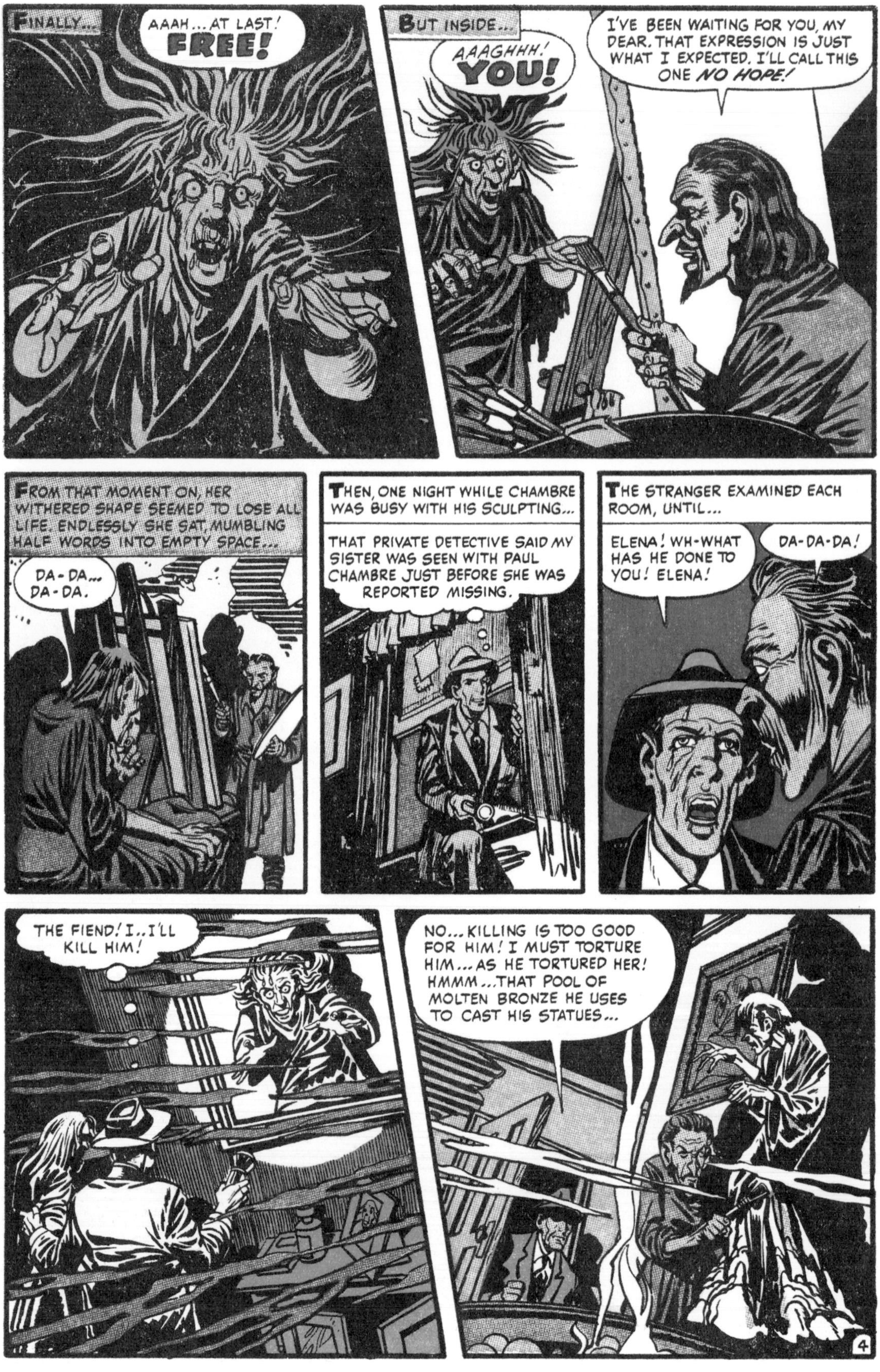
FINALLY...
AAAH... AT LAST! FREE!
BUT INSIDE...
AAAGHHH! YOU!
I'VE BEEN WAITING FOR YOU, MY DEAR. THAT EXPRESSION IS JUST WHAT I EXPECTED. I'LL CALL THIS ONE NO HOPE!
FROM THAT MOMENT ON, HER WITHERED SHAPE SEEMED TO LOSE ALL LIFE. ENDLESSLY SHE SAT, MUMBLING HALF WORDS INTO EMPTY SPACE...
DA-DA... DA-DA.
THEN, ONE NIGHT WHILE CHAMBRE WAS BUSY WITH HIS SCULPTING...
THAT PRIVATE DETECTIVE SAID MY SISTER WAS SEEN WITH PAUL CHAMBRE JUST BEFORE SHE WAS REPORTED MISSING.
THE STRANGER EXAMINED EACH ROOM, UNTIL...
ELENA! WH-WHAT HAS HE DONE TO YOU! ELENA!
DA-DA-DA!
THE FIEND! I..I'LL KILL HIM!
NO... KILLING IS TOO GOOD FOR HIM! I MUST TORTURE HIM... AS HE TORTURED HER! HMMM... THAT POOL OF MOLTEN BRONZE HE USES TO CAST HIS STATUES...
4

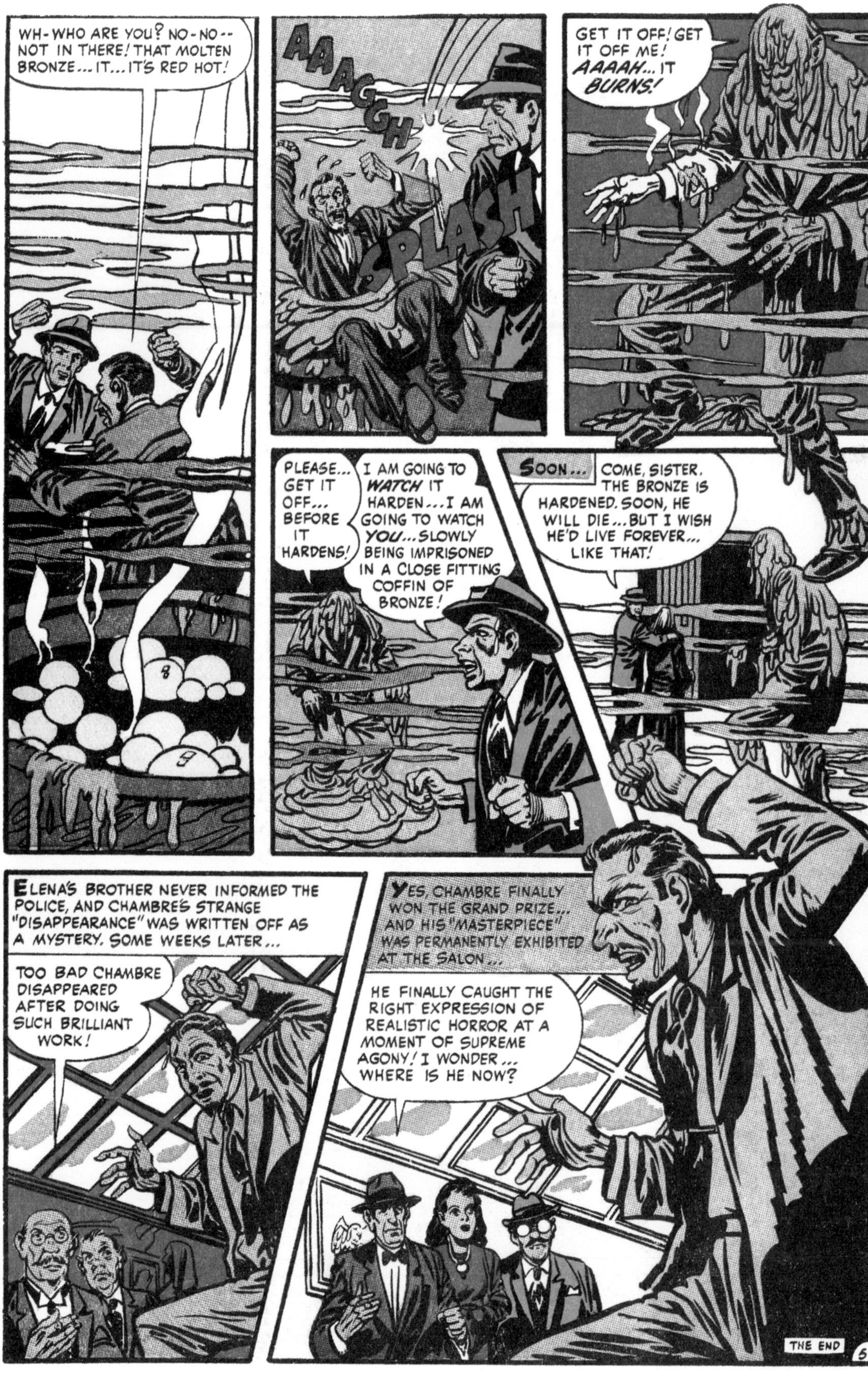

WH-WHO ARE YOU? NO-NO--NOT IN THERE! THAT MOLTEN BRONZE... IT... IT'S RED HOT!
AAAAGGH
SPLASH
GET IT OFF! GET IT OFF ME! AAAAH... IT BURNS!
PLEASE... GET IT OFF... BEFORE IT HARDENS!
I AM GOING TO WATCH IT HARDEN... I AM GOING TO WATCH YOU... SLOWLY BEING IMPRISONED IN A CLOSE FITTING COFFIN OF BRONZE!
SOON...
COME, SISTER. THE BRONZE IS HARDENED. SOON, HE WILL DIE... BUT I WISH HE'D LIVE FOREVER... LIKE THAT!
ELENA'S BROTHER NEVER INFORMED THE POLICE, AND CHAMBRE'S STRANGE "DISAPPEARANCE" WAS WRITTEN OFF AS A MYSTERY. SOME WEEKS LATER...
TOO BAD CHAMBRE DISAPPEARED AFTER DOING SUCH BRILLIANT WORK!
YES, CHAMBRE FINALLY WON THE GRAND PRIZE... AND HIS "MASTERPIECE" WAS PERMANENTLY EXHIBITED AT THE SALON...
HE FINALLY CAUGHT THE RIGHT EXPRESSION OF REALISTIC HORROR AT A MOMENT OF SUPREME AGONY! I WONDER... WHERE IS HE NOW?
THE END
5

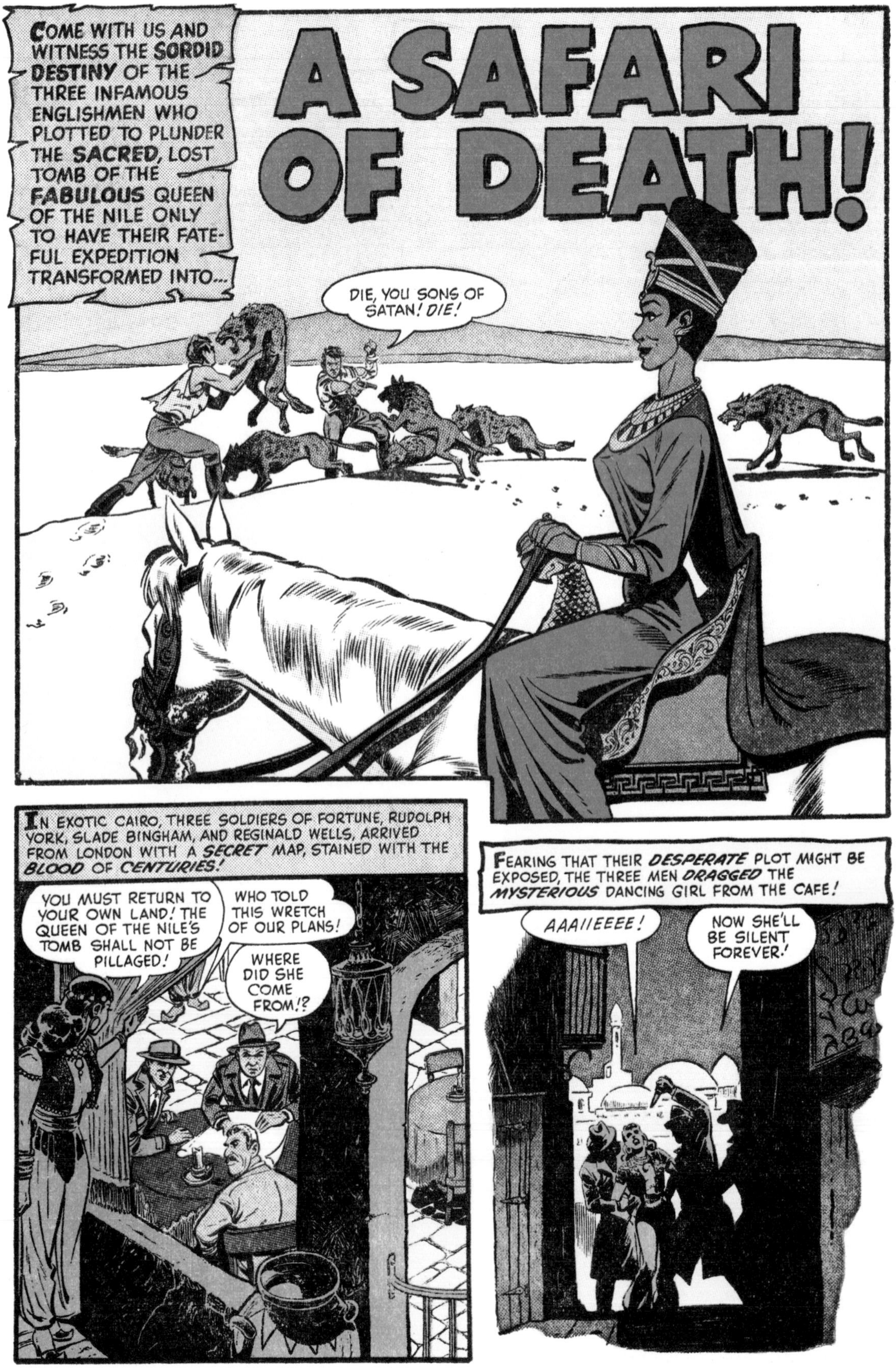
COME WITH US AND WITNESS THE SORDID DESTINY OF THE THREE INFAMOUS ENGLISHMEN WHO PLOTTED TO PLUNDER THE SACRED, LOST TOMB OF THE FABULOUS QUEEN OF THE NILE ONLY TO HAVE THEIR FATEFUL EXPEDITION TRANSFORMED INTO...
A SAFARI OF DEATH!
DIE, YOU SONS OF SATAN! DIE!
IN EXOTIC CAIRO, THREE SOLDIERS OF FORTUNE, RUDOLPH YORK, SLADE BINGHAM, AND REGINALD WELLS, ARRIVED FROM LONDON WITH A SECRET MAP, STAINED WITH THE BLOOD OF CENTURIES!
YOU MUST RETURN TO YOUR OWN LAND! THE QUEEN OF THE NILE'S TOMB SHALL NOT BE PILLAGED!
WHO TOLD THIS WRETCH OF OUR PLANS!
WHERE DID SHE COME FROM!?
FEARING THAT THEIR DESPERATE PLOT MIGHT BE EXPOSED, THE THREE MEN DRAGGED THE MYSTERIOUS DANCING GIRL FROM THE CAFE!
AAAIIEEEE!
NOW SHE'LL BE SILENT FOREVER!

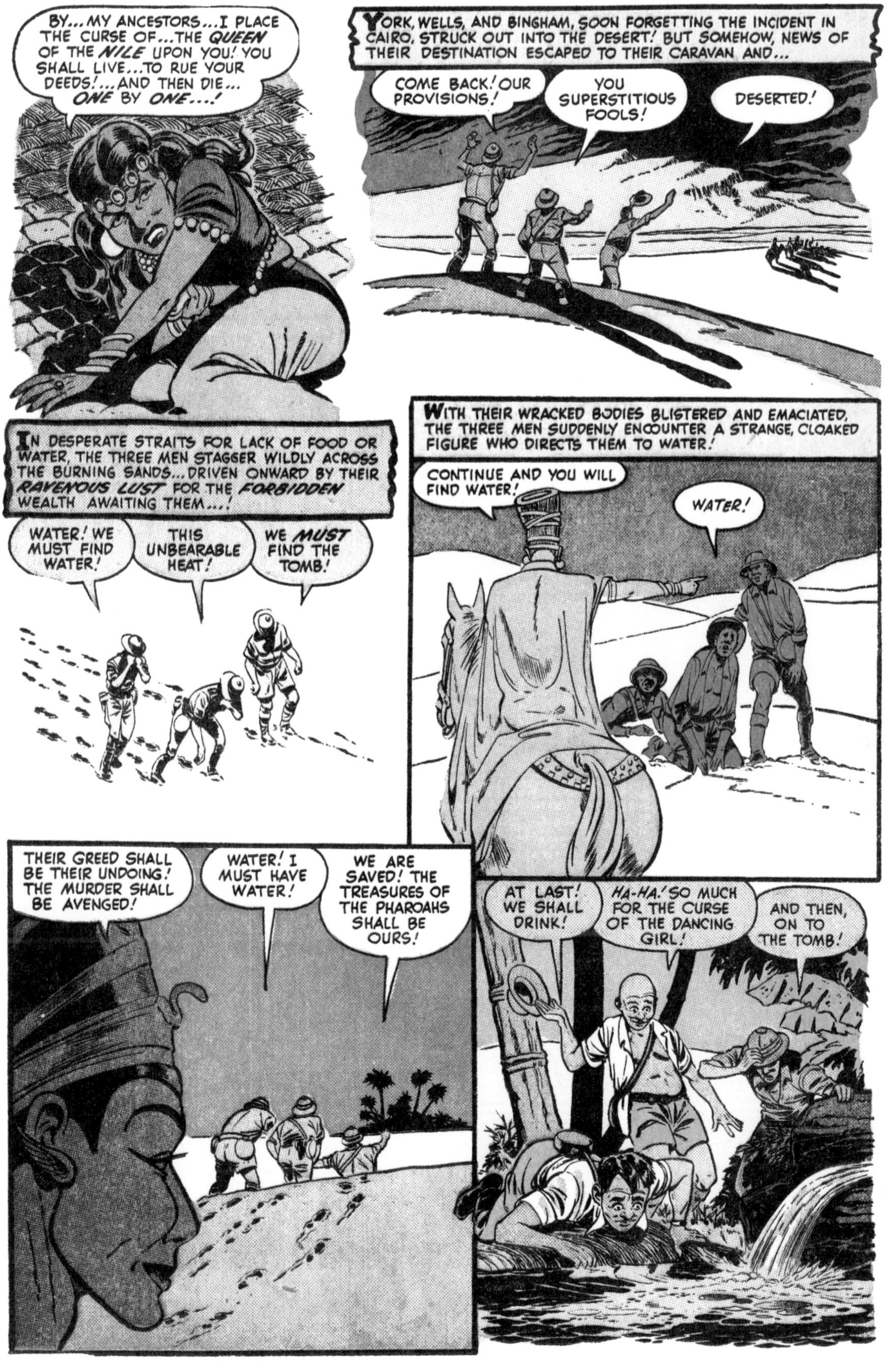

BY... MY ANCESTORS... I PLACE THE CURSE OF... THE QUEEN OF THE NILE UPON YOU! YOU SHALL LIVE... TO RUE YOUR DEEDS!... AND THEN DIE... ONE BY ONE...!
YORK, WELLS, AND BINGHAM, SOON FORGETTING THE INCIDENT IN CAIRO, STRUCK OUT INTO THE DESERT! BUT SOMEHOW, NEWS OF THEIR DESTINATION ESCAPED TO THEIR CARAVAN AND...
COME BACK! OUR PROVISIONS!
YOU SUPERSTITIOUS FOOLS!
DESERTED!
IN DESPERATE STRAITS FOR LACK OF FOOD OR WATER, THE THREE MEN STAGGER WILDLY ACROSS THE BURNING SANDS... DRIVEN ONWARD BY THEIR RAVENOUS LUST FOR THE FORBIDDEN WEALTH AWAITING THEM...!
WATER! WE MUST FIND WATER!
THIS UNBEARABLE HEAT!
WE MUST FIND THE TOMB!
WITH THEIR WRACKED BODIES BLISTERED AND EMACIATED, THE THREE MEN SUDDENLY ENCOUNTER A STRANGE, CLOAKED FIGURE WHO DIRECTS THEM TO WATER!
CONTINUE AND YOU WILL FIND WATER!
WATER!
THEIR GREED SHALL BE THEIR UNDOING! THE MURDER SHALL BE AVENGED!
WATER! I MUST HAVE WATER!
WE ARE SAVED! THE TREASURES OF THE PHARAOHS SHALL BE OURS!
AT LAST! WE SHALL DRINK!
HA-HA! SO MUCH FOR THE CURSE OF THE DANCING GIRL!
AND THEN, ON TO THE TOMB!

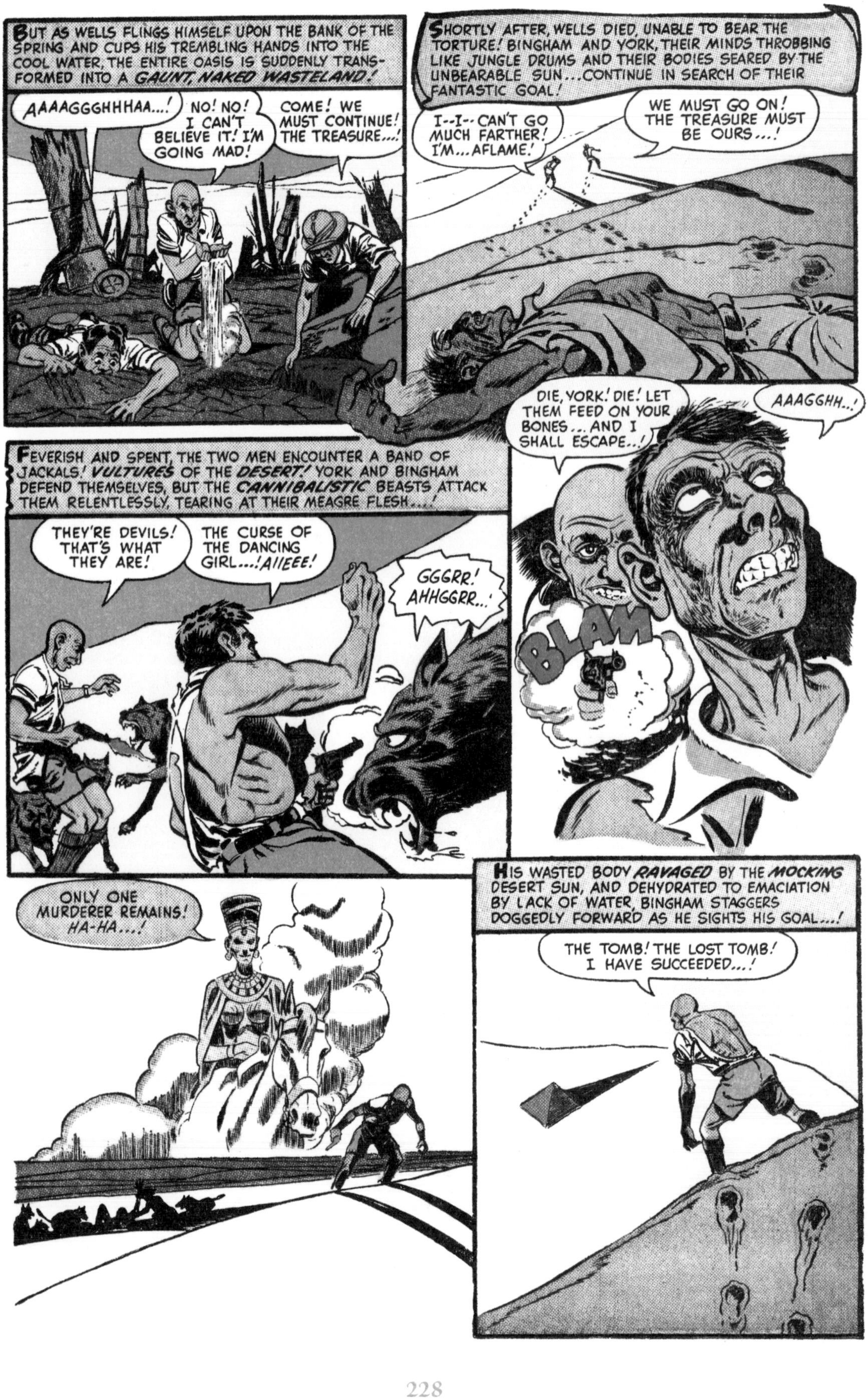
BUT AS WELLS FLINGS HIMSELF UPON THE BANK OF THE SPRING AND CUPS HIS TREMBLING HANDS INTO THE COOL WATER, THE ENTIRE OASIS IS SUDDENLY TRANSFORMED INTO A GAUNT, NAKED WASTELAND!
AAAAGGGHHHAA...!
NO! NO! I CAN'T BELIEVE IT! I'M GOING MAD!
COME! WE MUST CONTINUE! THE TREASURE...!
SHORTLY AFTER, WELLS DIED, UNABLE TO BEAR THE TORTURE! BINGHAM AND YORK, THEIR MINDS THROBBING LIKE JUNGLE DRUMS AND THEIR BODIES SEARED BY THE UNBEARABLE SUN... CONTINUE IN SEARCH OF THEIR FANTASTIC GOAL!
I--I-- CAN'T GO MUCH FARTHER! I'M... AFLAME!
WE MUST GO ON! THE TREASURE MUST BE OURS...!
FEVERISH AND SPENT, THE TWO MEN ENCOUNTER A BAND OF JACKALS! VULTURES OF THE DESERT! YORK AND BINGHAM DEFEND THEMSELVES, BUT THE CANNIBALISTIC BEASTS ATTACK THEM RELENTLESSLY, TEARING AT THEIR MEAGRE FLESH...!
THEY'RE DEVILS! THAT'S WHAT THEY ARE!
THE CURSE OF THE DANCING GIRL...! AIIEEE!
GGGRR! AHHGGRR...!
DIE, YORK! DIE! LET THEM FEED ON YOUR BONES... AND I SHALL ESCAPE...!
AAAGGHH...!
BLAM
ONLY ONE MURDERER REMAINS! HA-HA...!
HIS WASTED BODY RAVAGED BY THE MOCKING DESERT SUN, AND DEHYDRATED TO EMACIATION BY LACK OF WATER, BINGHAM STAGGERS DOGGEDLY FORWARD AS HE SIGHTS HIS GOAL...!
THE TOMB! THE LOST TOMB! I HAVE SUCCEEDED...!

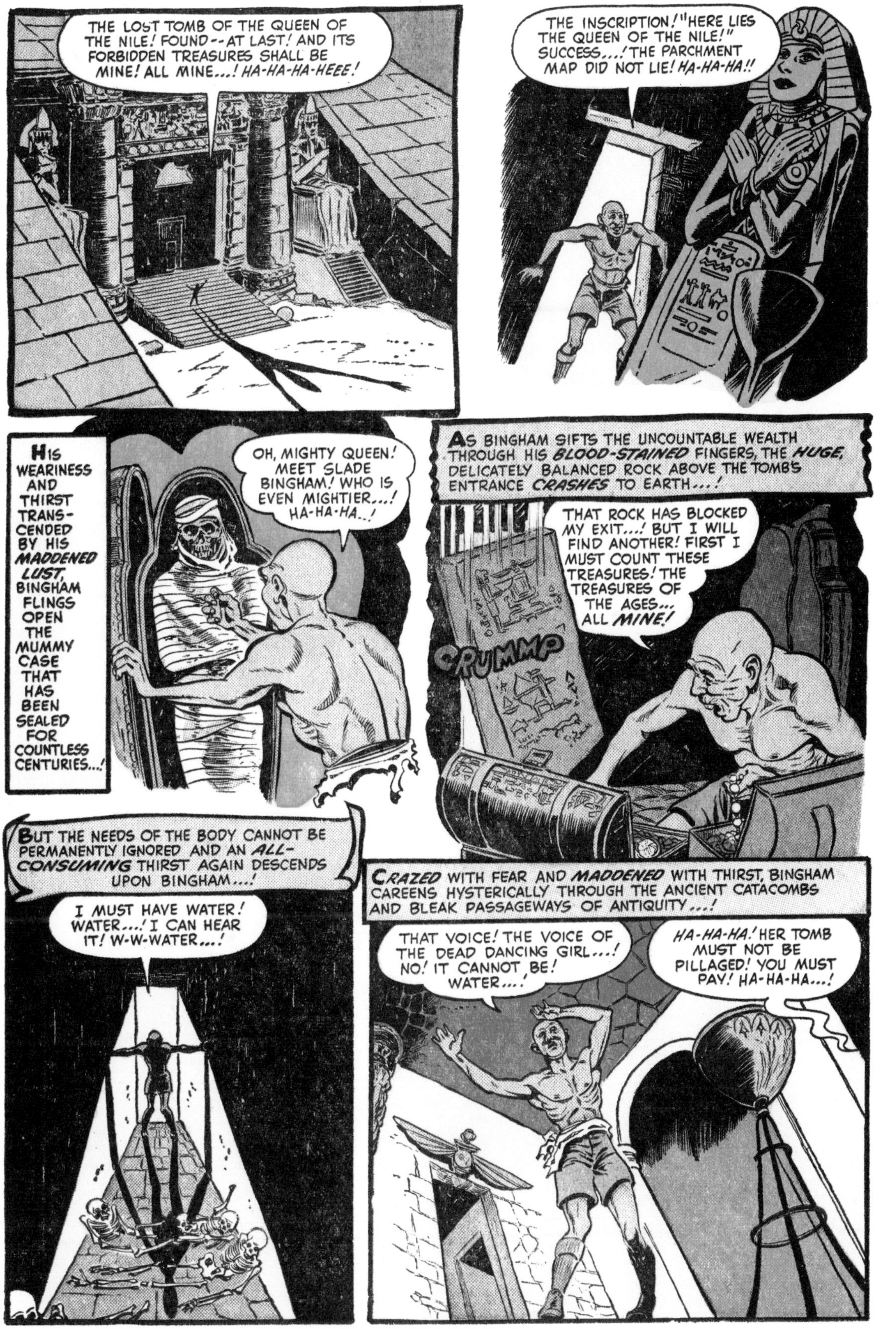

THE LOST TOMB OF THE QUEEN OF THE NILE! FOUND--AT LAST! AND ITS FORBIDDEN TREASURES SHALL BE MINE! ALL MINE...! HA-HA-HA-HEEE!
THE INSCRIPTION! "HERE LIES THE QUEEN OF THE NILE!" SUCCESS...! THE PARCHMENT MAP DID NOT LIE! HA-HA-HA!!
HIS WEARINESS AND THIRST TRANSCENDED BY HIS MADDENED LUST, BINGHAM FLINGS OPEN THE MUMMY CASE THAT HAS BEEN SEALED FOR COUNTLESS CENTURIES...!
OH, MIGHTY QUEEN! MEET SLADE BINGHAM! WHO IS EVEN MIGHTIER...! HA-HA-HA..!
AS BINGHAM SIFTS THE UNCOUNTABLE WEALTH THROUGH HIS BLOOD-STAINED FINGERS, THE HUGE, DELICATELY BALANCED ROCK ABOVE THE TOMB'S ENTRANCE CRASHES TO EARTH...!
CRUMMP
THAT ROCK HAS BLOCKED MY EXIT...! BUT I WILL FIND ANOTHER! FIRST I MUST COUNT THESE TREASURES! THE TREASURES OF THE AGES... ALL MINE!
BUT THE NEEDS OF THE BODY CANNOT BE PERMANENTLY IGNORED AND AN ALL-CONSUMING THIRST AGAIN DESCENDS UPON BINGHAM...!
I MUST HAVE WATER! WATER...! I CAN HEAR IT! W-W-WATER...!
CRAZED WITH FEAR AND MADDENED WITH THIRST, BINGHAM CAREENS HYSTERICALLY THROUGH THE ANCIENT CATACOMBS AND BLEAK PASSAGEWAYS OF ANTIQUITY...!
THAT VOICE! THE VOICE OF THE DEAD DANCING GIRL...! NO! IT CANNOT BE! WATER...!
HA-HA-HA! HER TOMB MUST NOT BE PILLAGED! YOU MUST PAY! HA-HA-HA...!

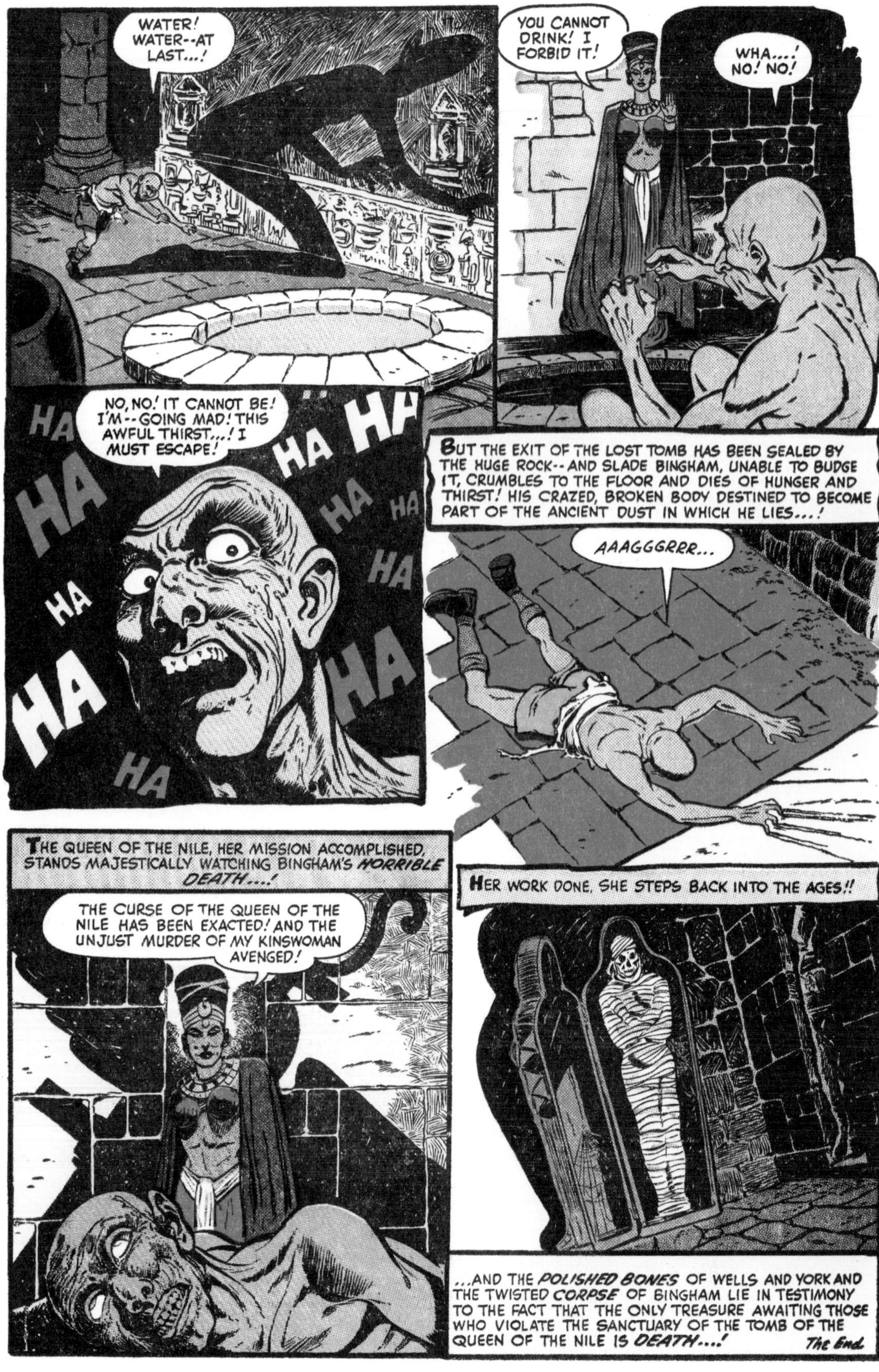
WATER! WATER--AT LAST...!
YOU CANNOT DRINK! I FORBID IT!
WHA...! NO! NO!
NO, NO! IT CANNOT BE! I'M--GOING MAD! THIS AWFUL THIRST...! I MUST ESCAPE!
HA HA HA HA HA HA HA HA HA HA HA HA
BUT THE EXIT OF THE LOST TOMB HAS BEEN SEALED BY THE HUGE ROCK--AND SLADE BINGHAM, UNABLE TO BUDGE IT, CRUMBLES TO THE FLOOR AND DIES OF HUNGER AND THIRST! HIS CRAZED, BROKEN BODY DESTINED TO BECOME PART OF THE ANCIENT DUST IN WHICH HE LIES...!
AAAGGGRRR...
THE QUEEN OF THE NILE, HER MISSION ACCOMPLISHED, STANDS MAJESTICALLY WATCHING BINGHAM'S HORRIBLE DEATH...!
THE CURSE OF THE QUEEN OF THE NILE HAS BEEN EXACTED! AND THE UNJUST MURDER OF MY KINSWOMAN AVENGED!
HER WORK DONE, SHE STEPS BACK INTO THE AGES!!
...AND THE POLISHED BONES OF WELLS AND YORK AND THE TWISTED CORPSE OF BINGHAM LIE IN TESTIMONY TO THE FACT THAT THE ONLY TREASURE AWAITING THOSE WHO VIOLATE THE SANCTUARY OF THE TOMB OF THE QUEEN OF THE NILE IS DEATH...!
The End

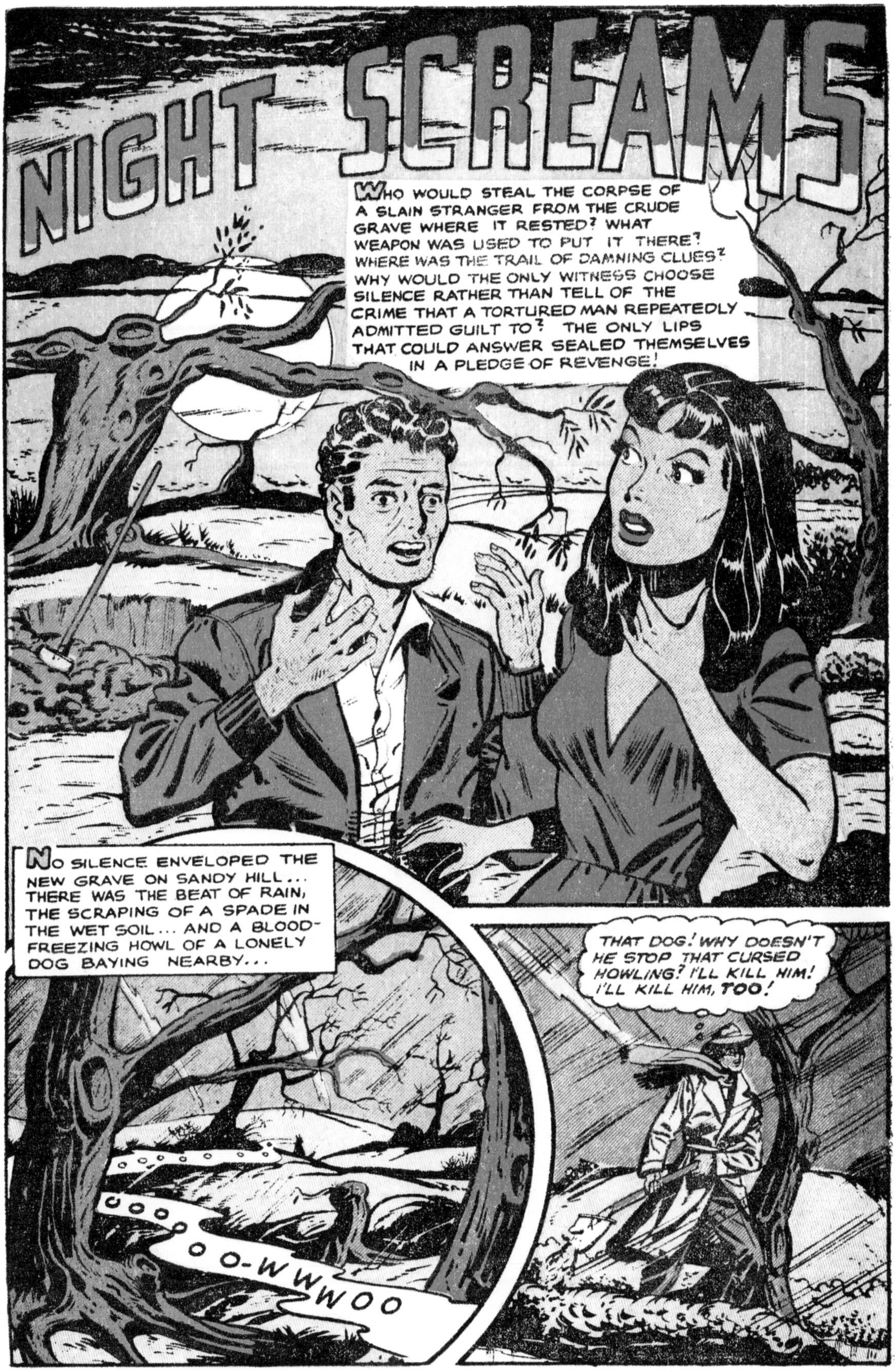
NIGHT SCREAMS
WHO WOULD STEAL THE CORPSE OF A SLAIN STRANGER FROM THE CRUDE GRAVE WHERE IT RESTED? WHAT WEAPON WAS USED TO PUT IT THERE? WHERE WAS THE TRAIL OF DAMNING CLUES? WHY WOULD THE ONLY WITNESS CHOOSE SILENCE RATHER THAN TELL OF THE CRIME THAT A TORTURED MAN REPEATEDLY ADMITTED GUILT TO? THE ONLY LIPS THAT COULD ANSWER SEALED THEMSELVES IN A PLEDGE OF REVENGE!
NO SILENCE ENVELOPED THE NEW GRAVE ON SANDY HILL... THERE WAS THE BEAT OF RAIN, THE SCRAPING OF A SPADE IN THE WET SOIL... AND A BLOOD-FREEZING HOWL OF A LONELY DOG BAYING NEARBY...
OOOOOOOOO-WWWOO
THAT DOG! WHY DOESN'T HE STOP THAT CURSED HOWLING? I'LL KILL HIM! I'LL KILL HIM, TOO!

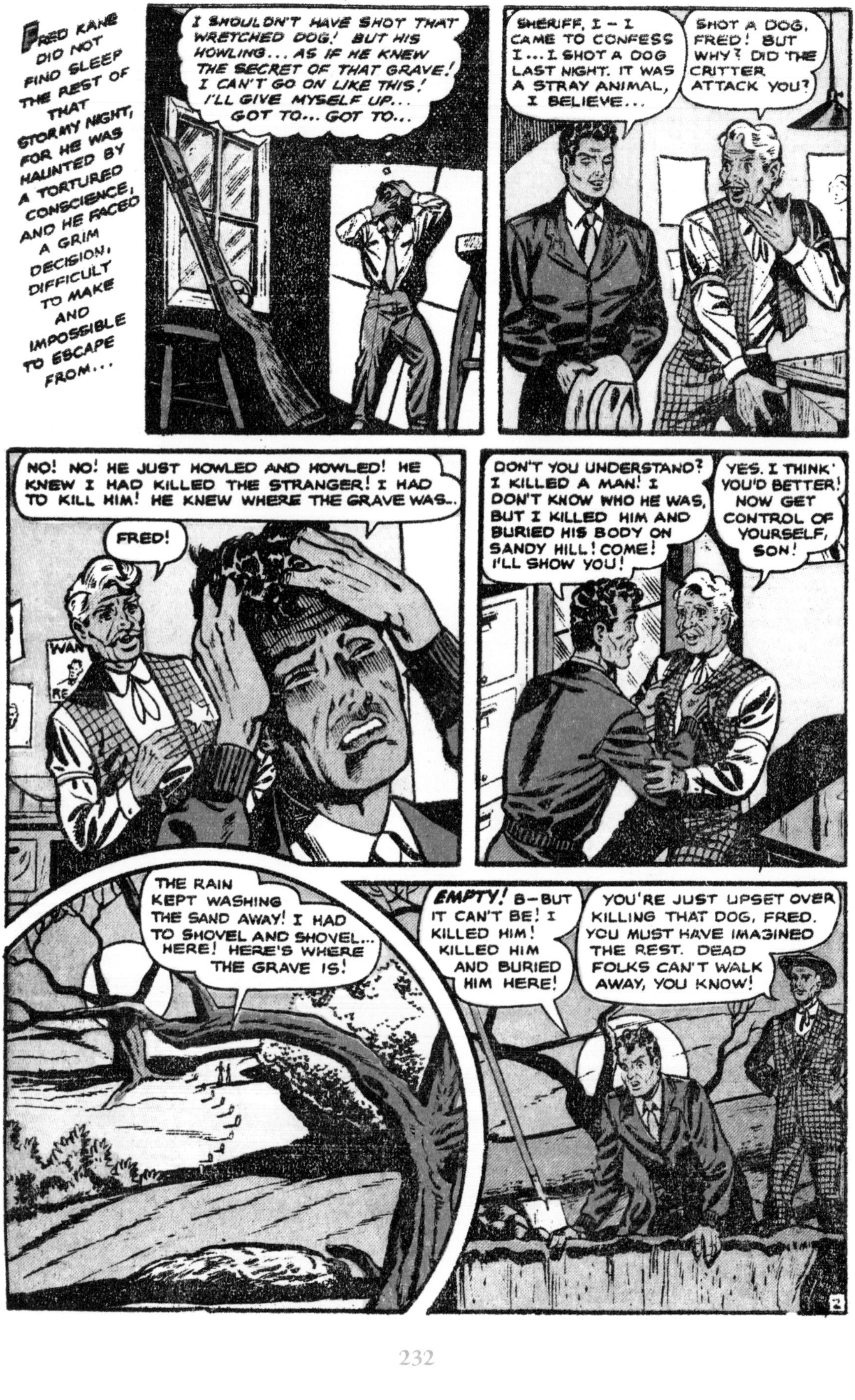
FRED KANE DID NOT FIND SLEEP THE REST OF THAT STORMY NIGHT, FOR HE WAS HAUNTED BY A TORTURED CONSCIENCE, AND HE FACED A GRIM DECISION, DIFFICULT TO MAKE AND IMPOSSIBLE TO ESCAPE FROM...
I SHOULDN'T HAVE SHOT THAT WRETCHED DOG! BUT HIS HOWLING... AS IF HE KNEW THE SECRET OF THAT GRAVE! I CAN'T GO ON LIKE THIS! I'LL GIVE MYSELF UP... GOT TO... GOT TO...
SHERIFF, I -- I CAME TO CONFESS I... I SHOT A DOG LAST NIGHT. IT WAS A STRAY ANIMAL, I BELIEVE...
SHOT A DOG, FRED! BUT WHY? DID THE CRITTER ATTACK YOU?
NO! NO! HE JUST HOWLED AND HOWLED! HE KNEW I HAD KILLED THE STRANGER! I HAD TO KILL HIM! HE KNEW WHERE THE GRAVE WAS..
FRED!
DON'T YOU UNDERSTAND? I KILLED A MAN! I DON'T KNOW WHO HE WAS, BUT I KILLED HIM AND BURIED HIS BODY ON SANDY HILL! COME! I'LL SHOW YOU!
YES. I THINK YOU'D BETTER! NOW GET CONTROL OF YOURSELF, SON!
THE RAIN KEPT WASHING THE SAND AWAY! I HAD TO SHOVEL AND SHOVEL... HERE! HERE'S WHERE THE GRAVE IS!
EMPTY! B-BUT IT CAN'T BE! I KILLED HIM! KILLED HIM AND BURIED HIM HERE!
YOU'RE JUST UPSET OVER KILLING THAT DOG, FRED. YOU MUST HAVE IMAGINED THE REST. DEAD FOLKS CAN'T WALK AWAY, YOU KNOW!
2

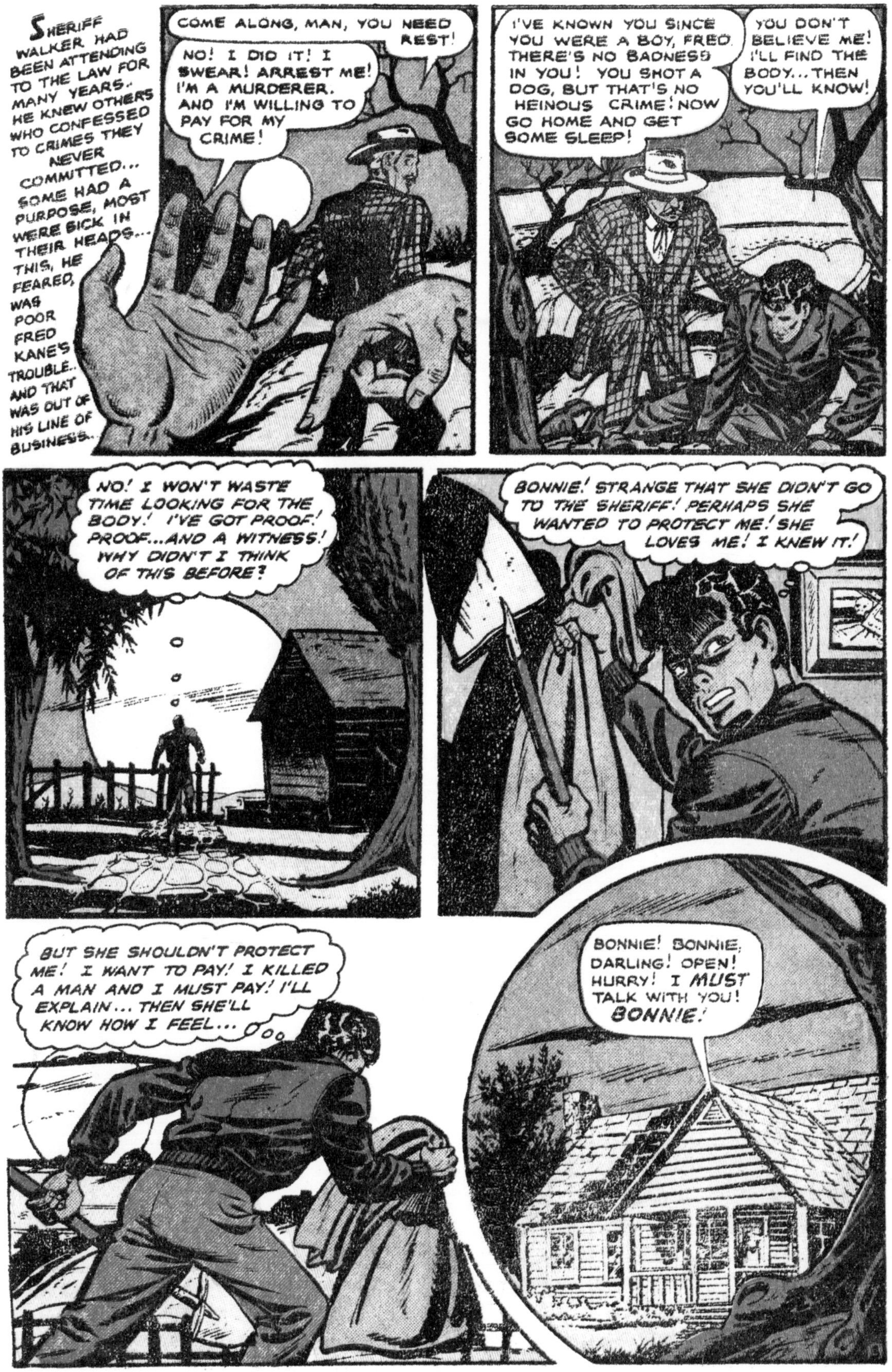
SHERIFF WALKER HAD BEEN ATTENDING TO THE LAW FOR MANY YEARS.. HE KNEW OTHERS WHO CONFESSED TO CRIMES THEY NEVER COMMITTED... SOME HAD A PURPOSE, MOST WERE SICK IN THEIR HEADS... THIS, HE FEARED, WAS POOR FRED KANE'S TROUBLE.. AND THAT WAS OUT OF HIS LINE OF BUSINESS..
COME ALONG, MAN, YOU NEED REST!
NO! I DID IT! I SWEAR! ARREST ME! I'M A MURDERER. AND I'M WILLING TO PAY FOR MY CRIME!
I'VE KNOWN YOU SINCE YOU WERE A BOY, FRED. THERE'S NO BADNESS IN YOU! YOU SHOT A DOG, BUT THAT'S NO HEINOUS CRIME! NOW GO HOME AND GET SOME SLEEP!
YOU DON'T BELIEVE ME! I'LL FIND THE BODY... THEN YOU'LL KNOW!
NO! I WON'T WASTE TIME LOOKING FOR THE BODY! I'VE GOT PROOF! PROOF... AND A WITNESS! WHY DIDN'T I THINK OF THIS BEFORE?
BONNIE! STRANGE THAT SHE DIDN'T GO TO THE SHERIFF! PERHAPS SHE WANTED TO PROTECT ME! SHE LOVES ME! I KNEW IT!
BUT SHE SHOULDN'T PROTECT ME! I WANT TO PAY! I KILLED A MAN AND I MUST PAY! I'LL EXPLAIN... THEN SHE'LL KNOW HOW I FEEL...
BONNIE! BONNIE, DARLING! OPEN! HURRY! I MUST TALK WITH YOU! BONNIE!

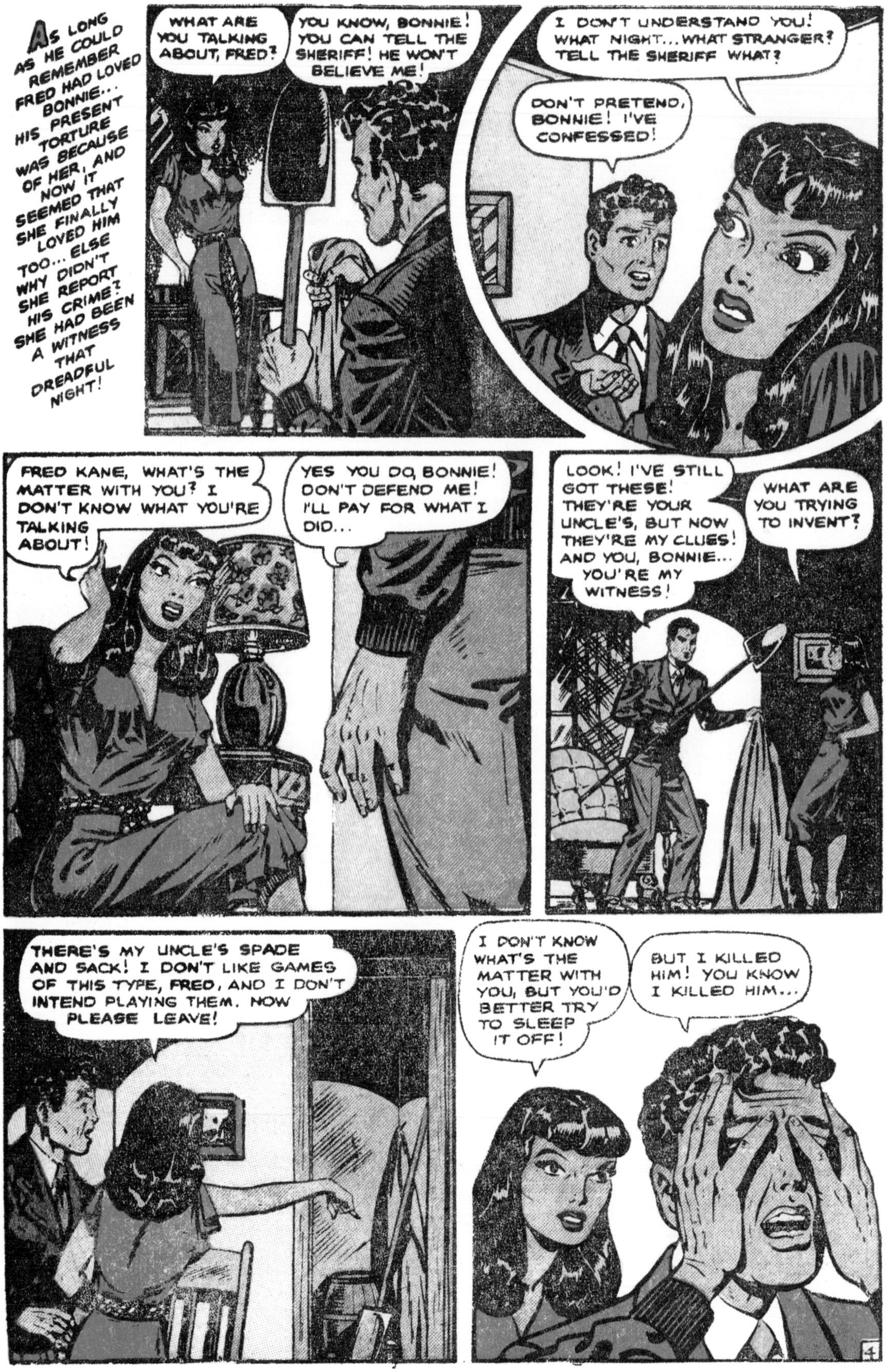
As long as he could remember Fred had loved Bonnie... his present torture was because of her, and now it seemed that she finally loved him too... else why didn't she report his crime? She had been a witness that dreadful night!
WHAT ARE YOU TALKING ABOUT, FRED?
YOU KNOW, BONNIE! YOU CAN TELL THE SHERIFF! HE WON'T BELIEVE ME!
I DON'T UNDERSTAND YOU! WHAT NIGHT... WHAT STRANGER? TELL THE SHERIFF WHAT?
DON'T PRETEND, BONNIE! I'VE CONFESSED!
FRED KANE, WHAT'S THE MATTER WITH YOU? I DON'T KNOW WHAT YOU'RE TALKING ABOUT!
YES YOU DO, BONNIE! DON'T DEFEND ME! I'LL PAY FOR WHAT I DID...
LOOK! I'VE STILL GOT THESE! THEY'RE YOUR UNCLE'S, BUT NOW THEY'RE MY CLUES! AND YOU, BONNIE... YOU'RE MY WITNESS!
WHAT ARE YOU TRYING TO INVENT?
THERE'S MY UNCLE'S SPADE AND SACK! I DON'T LIKE GAMES OF THIS TYPE, FRED, AND I DON'T INTEND PLAYING THEM. NOW PLEASE LEAVE!
I DON'T KNOW WHAT'S THE MATTER WITH YOU, BUT YOU'D BETTER TRY TO SLEEP IT OFF!
BUT I KILLED HIM! YOU KNOW I KILLED HIM...
4

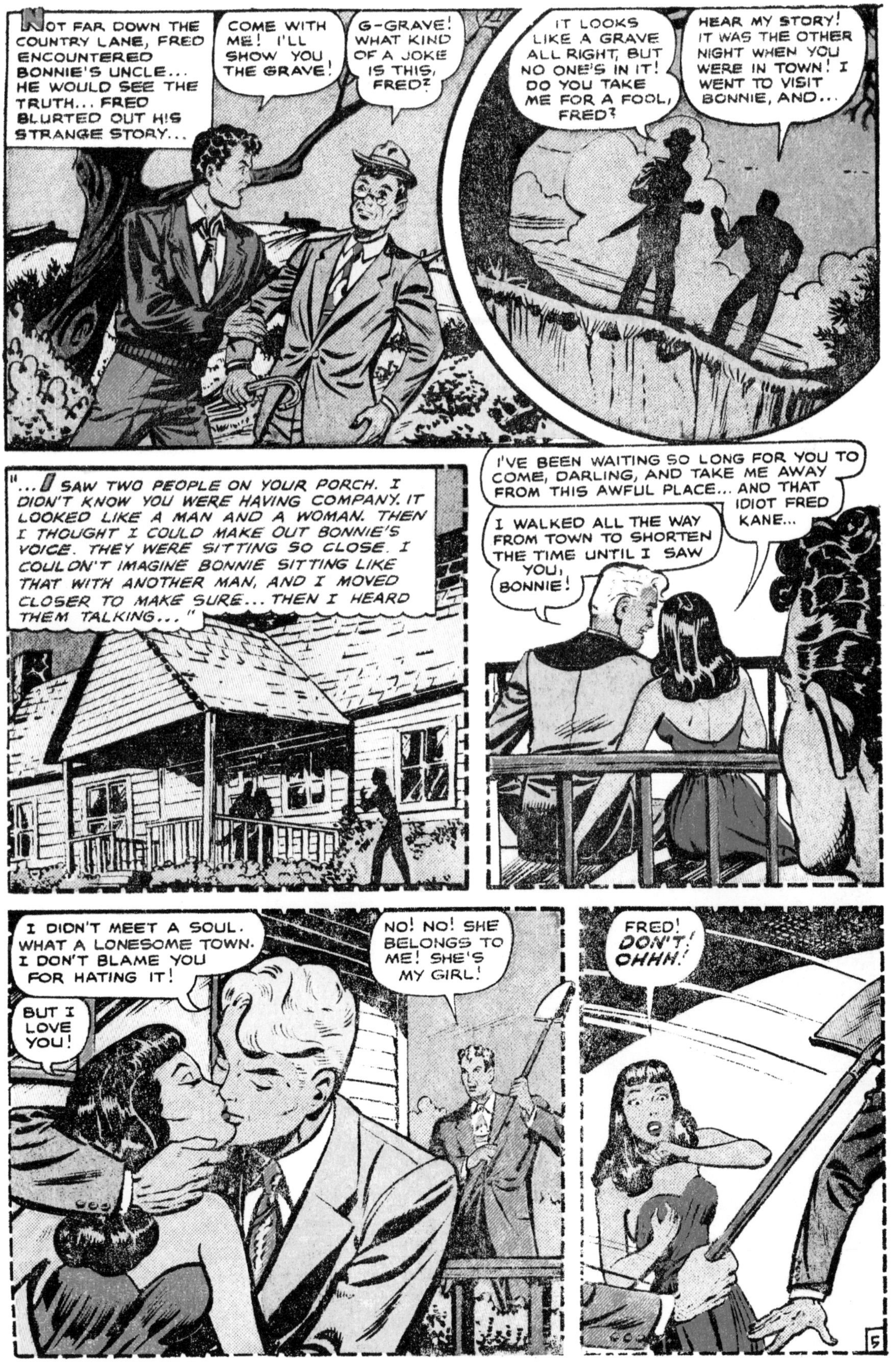
NOT FAR DOWN THE COUNTRY LANE, FRED ENCOUNTERED BONNIE'S UNCLE... HE WOULD SEE THE TRUTH... FRED BLURTED OUT HIS STRANGE STORY...
COME WITH ME! I'LL SHOW YOU THE GRAVE!
G-GRAVE! WHAT KIND OF A JOKE IS THIS, FRED?
IT LOOKS LIKE A GRAVE ALL RIGHT, BUT NO ONE'S IN IT! DO YOU TAKE ME FOR A FOOL, FRED?
HEAR MY STORY! IT WAS THE OTHER NIGHT WHEN YOU WERE IN TOWN! I WENT TO VISIT BONNIE, AND...
"...I SAW TWO PEOPLE ON YOUR PORCH. I DIDN'T KNOW YOU WERE HAVING COMPANY. IT LOOKED LIKE A MAN AND A WOMAN. THEN I THOUGHT I COULD MAKE OUT BONNIE'S VOICE. THEY WERE SITTING SO CLOSE. I COULDN'T IMAGINE BONNIE SITTING LIKE THAT WITH ANOTHER MAN, AND I MOVED CLOSER TO MAKE SURE... THEN I HEARD THEM TALKING..."
I WALKED ALL THE WAY FROM TOWN TO SHORTEN THE TIME UNTIL I SAW YOU, BONNIE!
I'VE BEEN WAITING SO LONG FOR YOU TO COME, DARLING, AND TAKE ME AWAY FROM THIS AWFUL PLACE... AND THAT IDIOT FRED KANE...
I DIDN'T MEET A SOUL. WHAT A LONESOME TOWN. I DON'T BLAME YOU FOR HATING IT!
BUT I LOVE YOU!
NO! NO! SHE BELONGS TO ME! SHE'S MY GIRL!
FRED! DON'T! OHHH!
5

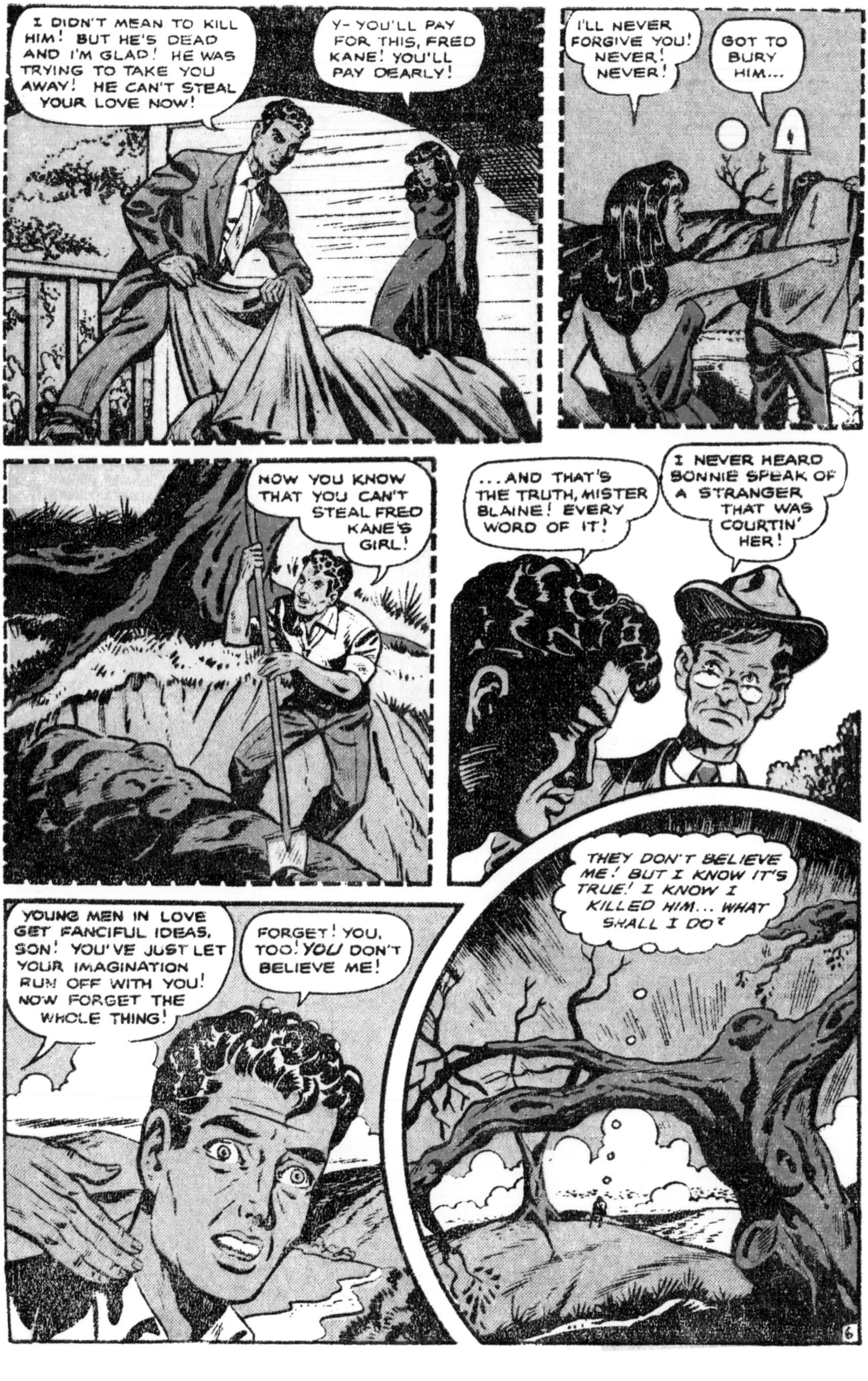
I DIDN'T MEAN TO KILL HIM! BUT HE'S DEAD AND I'M GLAD! HE WAS TRYING TO TAKE YOU AWAY! HE CAN'T STEAL YOUR LOVE NOW!
Y- YOU'LL PAY FOR THIS, FRED KANE! YOU'LL PAY DEARLY!
I'LL NEVER FORGIVE YOU! NEVER! NEVER!
GOT TO BURY HIM...
NOW YOU KNOW THAT YOU CAN'T STEAL FRED KANE'S GIRL!
...AND THAT'S THE TRUTH, MISTER BLAINE! EVERY WORD OF IT!
I NEVER HEARD BONNIE SPEAK OF A STRANGER THAT WAS COURTIN' HER!
YOUNG MEN IN LOVE GET FANCIFUL IDEAS, SON! YOU'VE JUST LET YOUR IMAGINATION RUN OFF WITH YOU! NOW FORGET THE WHOLE THING!
FORGET! YOU, TOO! YOU DON'T BELIEVE ME!
THEY DON'T BELIEVE ME! BUT I KNOW IT'S TRUE! I KNOW I KILLED HIM... WHAT SHALL I DO?
6

LIFE HAD TURNED INTO A NIGHTMARE FOR FRED KANE, THE REPENTANT KILLER WHO SOUGHT PUNISHMENT, BUT WAS ONLY LASHED BY HIS OWN CONSCIENCE AND DISBELIEVED BY HIS FELLOW MEN...

BONNIE SAW ME! SHE WAS THERE!

I DON'T KNOW WHO HE WAS! BUT I KILLED HIM! I'VE GOT TO BE PUNISHED!

MURDERER! I'VE **GOT** TO MAKE BONNIE REMEMBER!

I KILLED HIM.

HERE SHE COMES! I'LL MAKE HER GO WITH ME TO THE SHERIFF IF I HAVE TO...

DON'T HIDE, FRED. I KNOW YOU'RE THERE!

YOU'RE COMING WITH ME, BONNIE! TO THE SHERIFF!

LET GO OF ME, YOU FOOL! YOU'RE CRAZY!

I WILL BE CRAZY IF YOU DON'T HELP ME! YOU SAW ME! YOU KNOW I KILLED A MAN!

TAKE YOUR HANDS OFF ME! I HATE YOU!

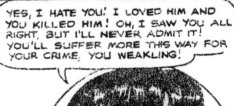

YES, I HATE YOU! I LOVED HIM AND YOU KILLED HIM! OH, I SAW YOU ALL RIGHT, BUT I'LL NEVER ADMIT IT! YOU'LL SUFFER MORE THIS WAY FOR YOUR CRIME, YOU WEAKLING!

7

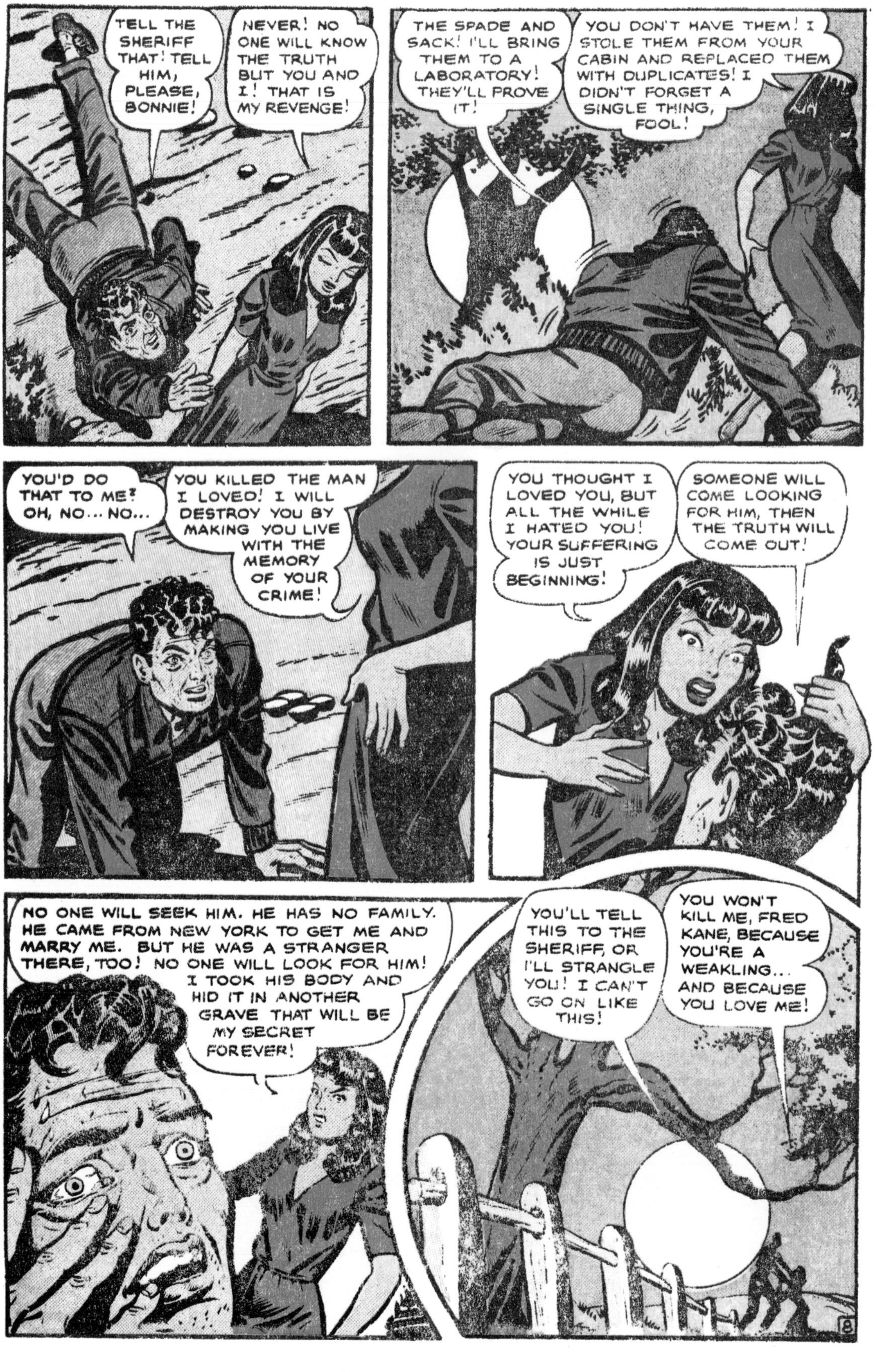
TELL THE SHERIFF THAT! TELL HIM, PLEASE, BONNIE!
NEVER! NO ONE WILL KNOW THE TRUTH BUT YOU AND I! THAT IS MY REVENGE!
THE SPADE AND SACK! I'LL BRING THEM TO A LABORATORY! THEY'LL PROVE IT!
YOU DON'T HAVE THEM! I STOLE THEM FROM YOUR CABIN AND REPLACED THEM WITH DUPLICATES! I DIDN'T FORGET A SINGLE THING, FOOL!
YOU'D DO THAT TO ME? OH, NO... NO...
YOU KILLED THE MAN I LOVED! I WILL DESTROY YOU BY MAKING YOU LIVE WITH THE MEMORY OF YOUR CRIME!
YOU THOUGHT I LOVED YOU, BUT ALL THE WHILE I HATED YOU! YOUR SUFFERING IS JUST BEGINNING!
SOMEONE WILL COME LOOKING FOR HIM, THEN THE TRUTH WILL COME OUT!
NO ONE WILL SEEK HIM. HE HAS NO FAMILY. HE CAME FROM NEW YORK TO GET ME AND MARRY ME. BUT HE WAS A STRANGER THERE, TOO! NO ONE WILL LOOK FOR HIM! I TOOK HIS BODY AND HID IT IN ANOTHER GRAVE THAT WILL BE MY SECRET FOREVER!
YOU'LL TELL THIS TO THE SHERIFF, OR I'LL STRANGLE YOU! I CAN'T GO ON LIKE THIS!
YOU WON'T KILL ME, FRED KANE, BECAUSE YOU'RE A WEAKLING... AND BECAUSE YOU LOVE ME!
8

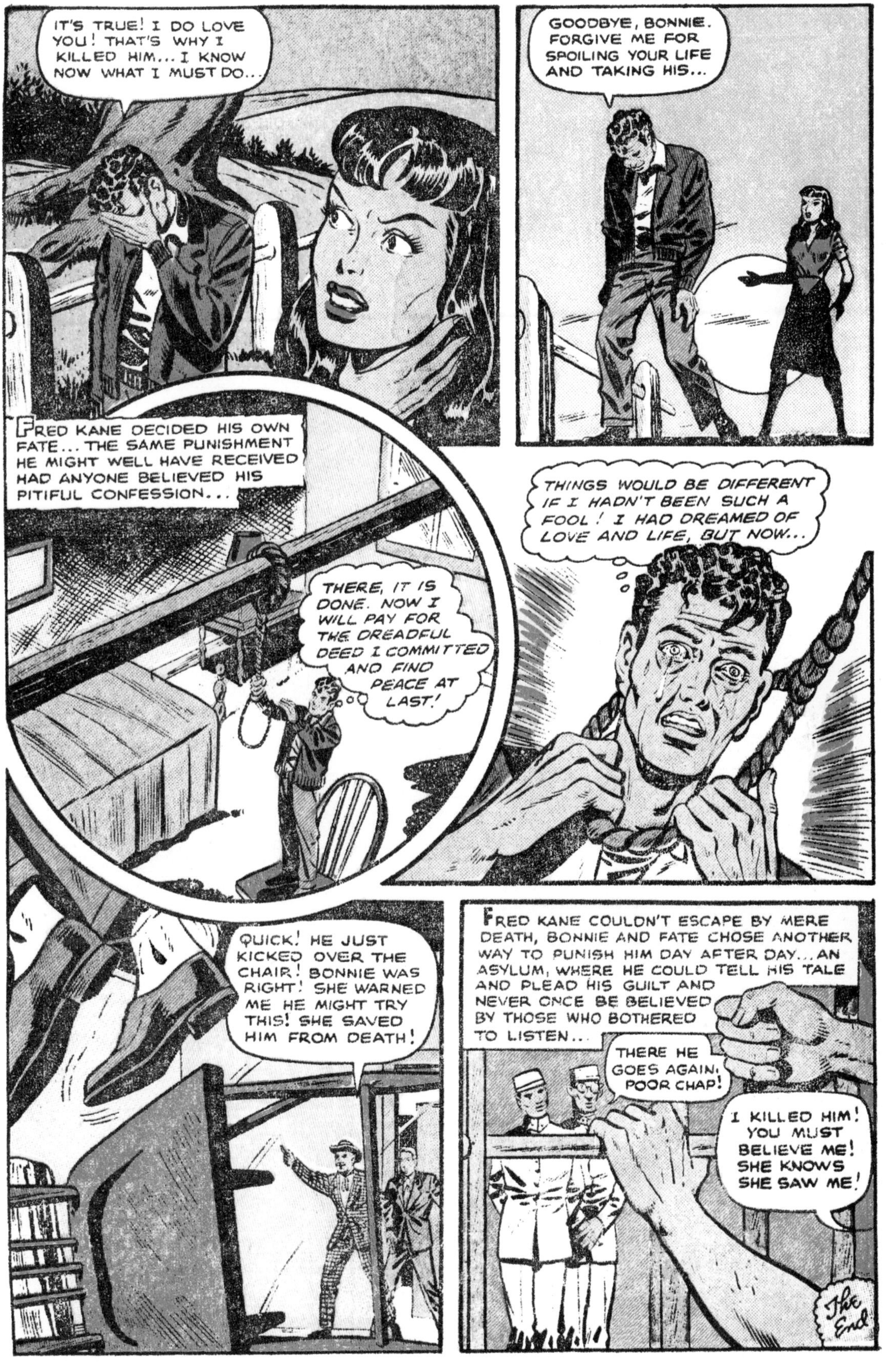
IT'S TRUE! I DO LOVE YOU! THAT'S WHY I KILLED HIM... I KNOW NOW WHAT I MUST DO...
GOODBYE, BONNIE. FORGIVE ME FOR SPOILING YOUR LIFE AND TAKING HIS...
FRED KANE DECIDED HIS OWN FATE... THE SAME PUNISHMENT HE MIGHT WELL HAVE RECEIVED HAD ANYONE BELIEVED HIS PITIFUL CONFESSION...
THERE, IT IS DONE. NOW I WILL PAY FOR THE DREADFUL DEED I COMMITTED AND FIND PEACE AT LAST!
THINGS WOULD BE DIFFERENT IF I HADN'T BEEN SUCH A FOOL! I HAD DREAMED OF LOVE AND LIFE, BUT NOW...
QUICK! HE JUST KICKED OVER THE CHAIR! BONNIE WAS RIGHT! SHE WARNED ME HE MIGHT TRY THIS! SHE SAVED HIM FROM DEATH!
FRED KANE COULDN'T ESCAPE BY MERE DEATH, BONNIE AND FATE CHOSE ANOTHER WAY TO PUNISH HIM DAY AFTER DAY... AN ASYLUM, WHERE HE COULD TELL HIS TALE AND PLEAD HIS GUILT AND NEVER ONCE BE BELIEVED BY THOSE WHO BOTHERED TO LISTEN...
THERE HE GOES AGAIN, POOR CHAP!
I KILLED HIM! YOU MUST BELIEVE ME! SHE KNOWS SHE SAW ME!
The End

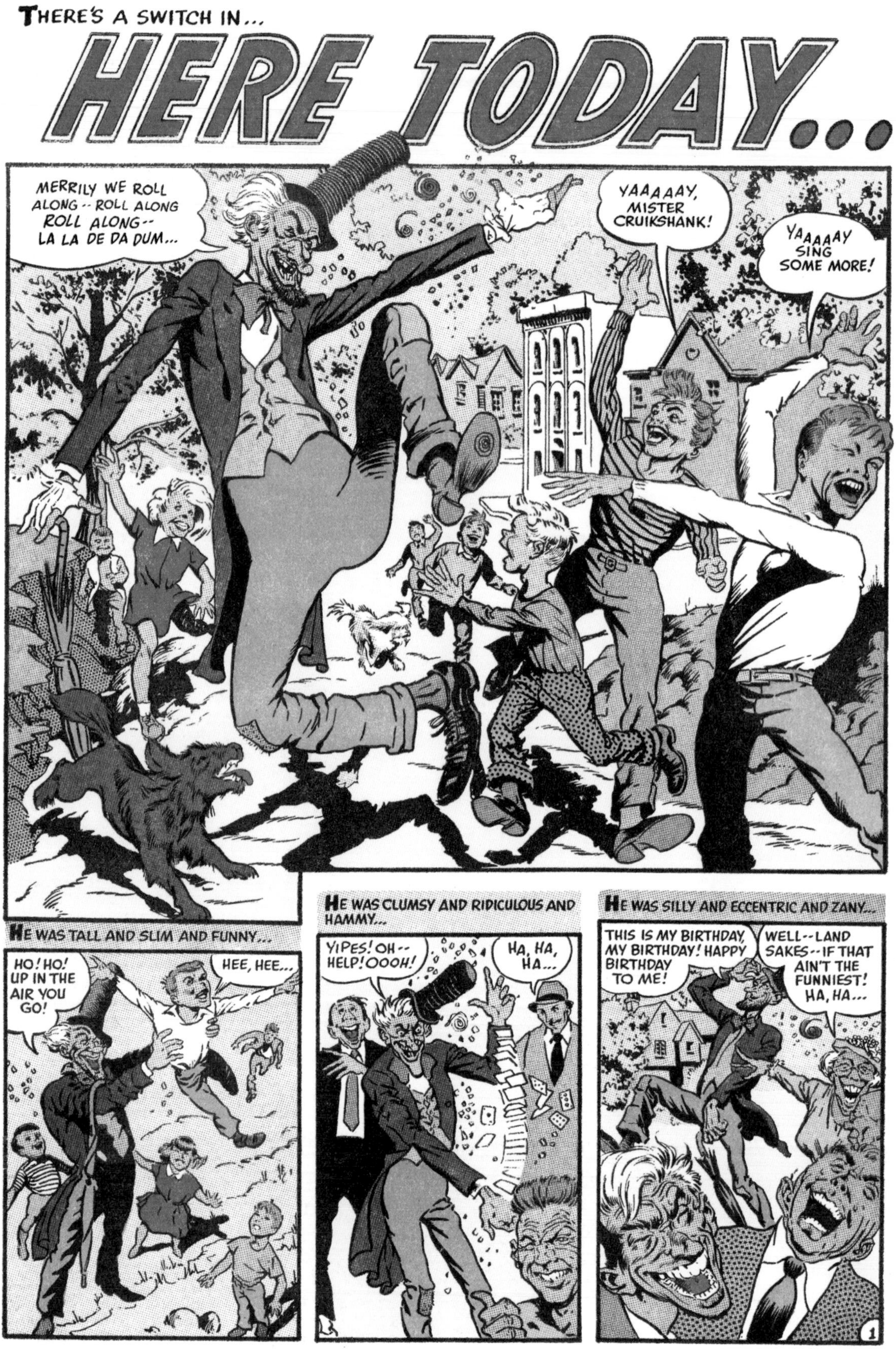

THERE'S A SWITCH IN...
HERE TODAY...
MERRILY WE ROLL ALONG -- ROLL ALONG ROLL ALONG -- LA LA DE DA DUM...
YAAAAAY, MISTER CRUIKSHANK!
YAAAAAY SING SOME MORE!
HE WAS TALL AND SLIM AND FUNNY...
HO! HO! UP IN THE AIR YOU GO!
HEE, HEE...
HE WAS CLUMSY AND RIDICULOUS AND HAMMY...
YIPES! OH -- HELP! OOOH!
HA, HA, HA...
HE WAS SILLY AND ECCENTRIC AND ZANY...
THIS IS MY BIRTHDAY, MY BIRTHDAY! HAPPY BIRTHDAY TO ME!
WELL -- LAND SAKES -- IF THAT AIN'T THE FUNNIEST! HA, HA...
1

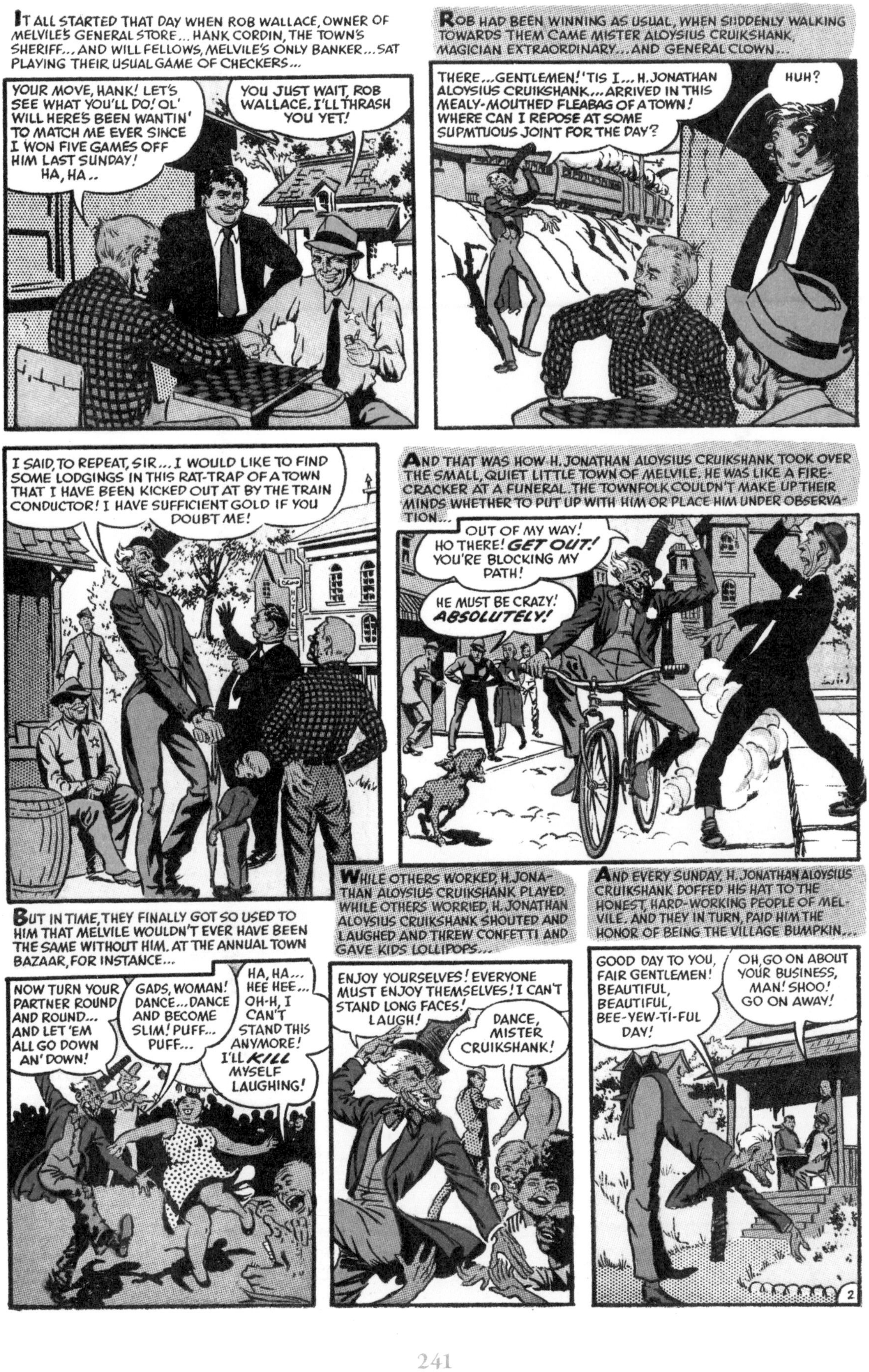
IT ALL STARTED THAT DAY WHEN ROB WALLACE, OWNER OF MELVILE'S GENERAL STORE... HANK CORDIN, THE TOWN'S SHERIFF... AND WILL FELLOWS, MELVILE'S ONLY BANKER... SAT PLAYING THEIR USUAL GAME OF CHECKERS...
YOUR MOVE, HANK! LET'S SEE WHAT YOU'LL DO! OL' WILL HERE'S BEEN WANTIN' TO MATCH ME EVER SINCE I WON FIVE GAMES OFF HIM LAST SUNDAY! HA, HA..
YOU JUST WAIT, ROB WALLACE. I'LL THRASH YOU YET!
ROB HAD BEEN WINNING AS USUAL, WHEN SUDDENLY WALKING TOWARDS THEM CAME MISTER ALOYSIUS CRUIKSHANK, MAGICIAN EXTRAORDINARY... AND GENERAL CLOWN...
THERE... GENTLEMEN! 'TIS I... H. JONATHAN ALOYSIUS CRUIKSHANK... ARRIVED IN THIS MEALY-MOUTHED FLEABAG OF A TOWN! WHERE CAN I REPOSE AT SOME SUPMTUOUS JOINT FOR THE DAY?
HUH?
I SAID, TO REPEAT, SIR... I WOULD LIKE TO FIND SOME LODGINGS IN THIS RAT-TRAP OF A TOWN THAT I HAVE BEEN KICKED OUT AT BY THE TRAIN CONDUCTOR! I HAVE SUFFICIENT GOLD IF YOU DOUBT ME!
AND THAT WAS HOW H. JONATHAN ALOYSIUS CRUIKSHANK TOOK OVER THE SMALL, QUIET LITTLE TOWN OF MELVILE. HE WAS LIKE A FIRE-CRACKER AT A FUNERAL. THE TOWNFOLK COULDN'T MAKE UP THEIR MINDS WHETHER TO PUT UP WITH HIM OR PLACE HIM UNDER OBSERVATION...
OUT OF MY WAY! HO THERE! GET OUT! YOU'RE BLOCKING MY PATH!
HE MUST BE CRAZY! ABSOLUTELY!
BUT IN TIME, THEY FINALLY GOT SO USED TO HIM THAT MELVILE WOULDN'T EVER HAVE BEEN THE SAME WITHOUT HIM. AT THE ANNUAL TOWN BAZAAR, FOR INSTANCE...
NOW TURN YOUR PARTNER ROUND AND ROUND... AND LET 'EM ALL GO DOWN AN' DOWN!
GADS, WOMAN! DANCE... DANCE AND BECOME SLIM! PUFF... PUFF...
HA, HA... HEE HEE... OH-H, I CAN'T STAND THIS ANYMORE! I'LL KILL MYSELF LAUGHING!
WHILE OTHERS WORKED H. JONATHAN ALOYSIUS CRUIKSHANK PLAYED. WHILE OTHERS WORRIED, H. JONATHAN ALOYSIUS CRUIKSHANK SHOUTED AND LAUGHED AND THREW CONFETTI AND GAVE KIDS LOLLIPOPS...
ENJOY YOURSELVES! EVERYONE MUST ENJOY THEMSELVES! I CAN'T STAND LONG FACES! LAUGH!
DANCE, MISTER CRUIKSHANK!
AND EVERY SUNDAY, H. JONATHAN ALOYSIUS CRUIKSHANK DOFFED HIS HAT TO THE HONEST, HARD-WORKING PEOPLE OF MELVILE. AND THEY IN TURN, PAID HIM THE HONOR OF BEING THE VILLAGE BUMPKIN...
GOOD DAY TO YOU, FAIR GENTLEMEN! BEAUTIFUL, BEAUTIFUL, BEE-YEW-TI-FUL DAY!
OH, GO ON ABOUT YOUR BUSINESS, MAN! SHOO! GO ON AWAY!
2

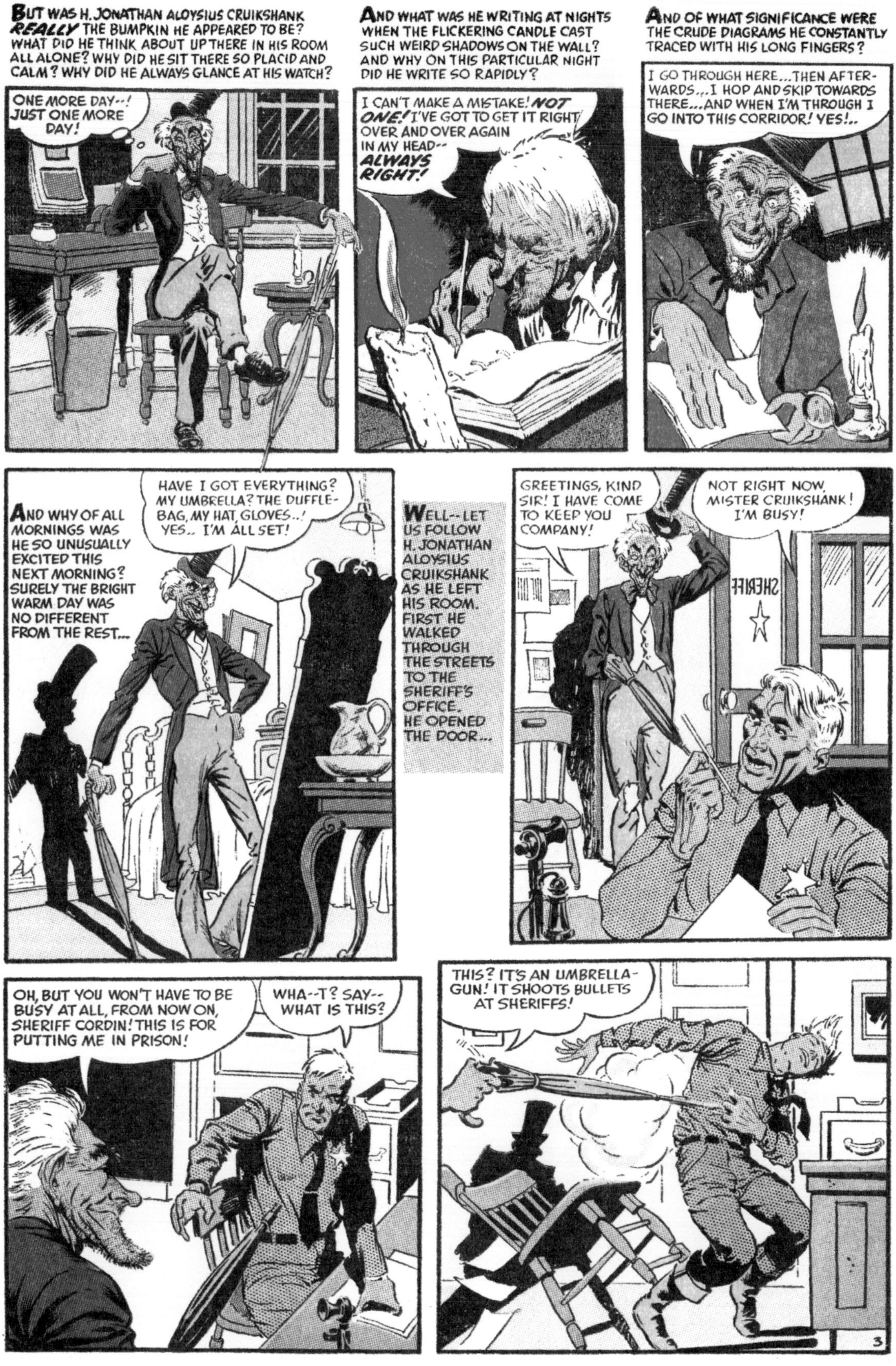
BUT WAS H. JONATHAN ALOYSIUS CRUIKSHANK REALLY THE BUMPKIN HE APPEARED TO BE? WHAT DID HE THINK ABOUT UP THERE IN HIS ROOM ALL ALONE? WHY DID HE SIT THERE SO PLACID AND CALM? WHY DID HE ALWAYS GLANCE AT HIS WATCH?
ONE MORE DAY--! JUST ONE MORE DAY!
AND WHAT WAS HE WRITING AT NIGHTS WHEN THE FLICKERING CANDLE CAST SUCH WEIRD SHADOWS ON THE WALL? AND WHY ON THIS PARTICULAR NIGHT DID HE WRITE SO RAPIDLY?
I CAN'T MAKE A MISTAKE! NOT ONE! I'VE GOT TO GET IT RIGHT OVER AND OVER AGAIN IN MY HEAD-- ALWAYS RIGHT!
AND OF WHAT SIGNIFICANCE WERE THE CRUDE DIAGRAMS HE CONSTANTLY TRACED WITH HIS LONG FINGERS?
I GO THROUGH HERE... THEN AFTER-WARDS... I HOP AND SKIP TOWARDS THERE... AND WHEN I'M THROUGH I GO INTO THIS CORRIDOR! YES!..
AND WHY OF ALL MORNINGS WAS HE SO UNUSUALLY EXCITED THIS NEXT MORNING? SURELY THE BRIGHT WARM DAY WAS NO DIFFERENT FROM THE REST...
HAVE I GOT EVERYTHING? MY UMBRELLA? THE DUFFLE-BAG, MY HAT, GLOVES..! YES.. I'M ALL SET!
WELL--LET US FOLLOW H. JONATHAN ALOYSIUS CRUIKSHANK AS HE LEFT HIS ROOM. FIRST HE WALKED THROUGH THE STREETS TO THE SHERIFF'S OFFICE. HE OPENED THE DOOR...
GREETINGS, KIND SIR! I HAVE COME TO KEEP YOU COMPANY!
NOT RIGHT NOW, MISTER CRUIKSHANK! I'M BUSY!
SHERIFF
OH, BUT YOU WON'T HAVE TO BE BUSY AT ALL, FROM NOW ON, SHERIFF CORDIN! THIS IS FOR PUTTING ME IN PRISON!
WHA--T? SAY-- WHAT IS THIS?
THIS? IT'S AN UMBRELLA-GUN! IT SHOOTS BULLETS AT SHERIFFS!
3

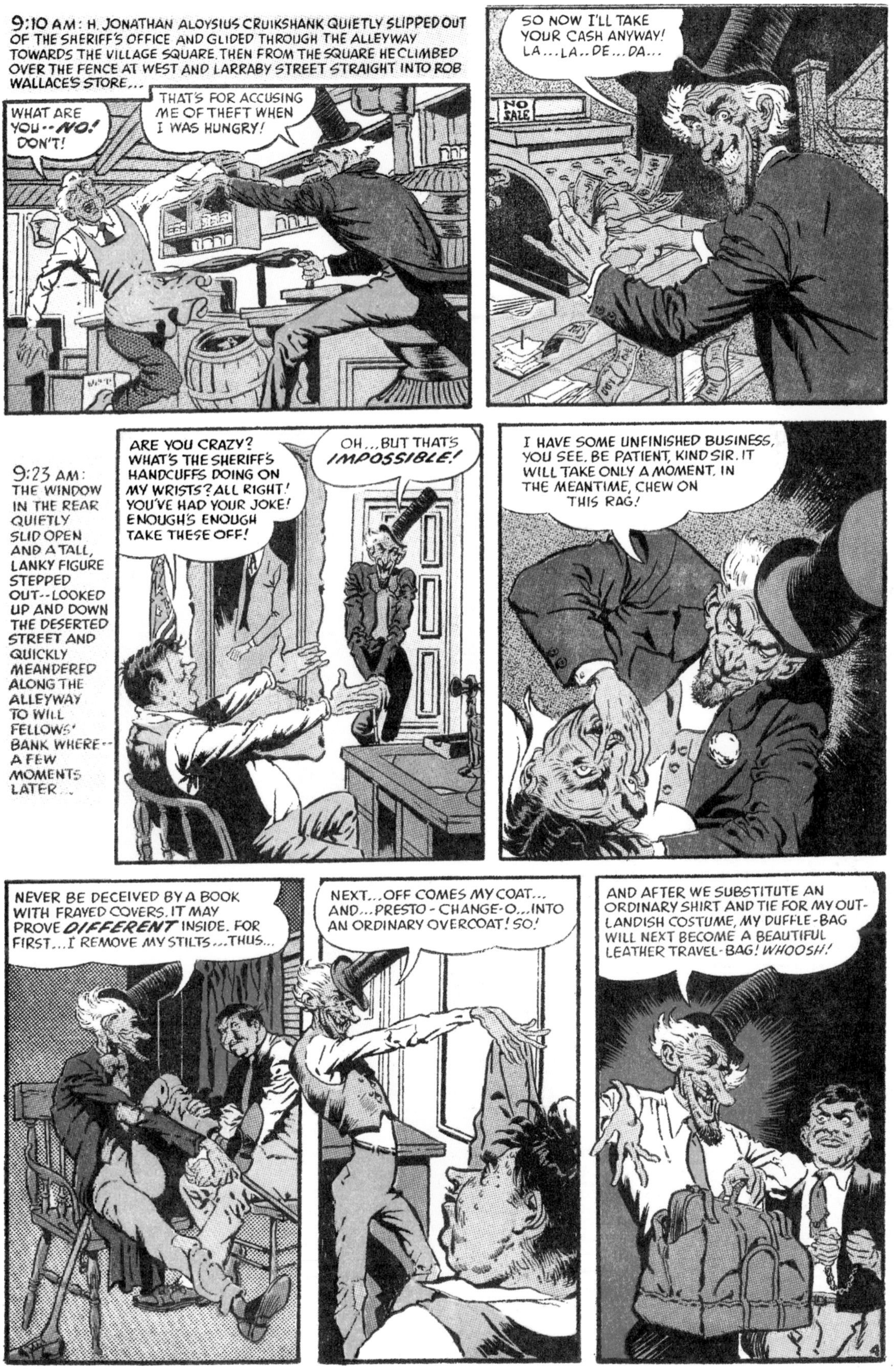
9:10 AM: H. JONATHAN ALOYSIUS CRUIKSHANK QUIETLY SLIPPED OUT OF THE SHERIFF'S OFFICE AND GLIDED THROUGH THE ALLEYWAY TOWARDS THE VILLAGE SQUARE. THEN FROM THE SQUARE HE CLIMBED OVER THE FENCE AT WEST AND LARRABY STREET STRAIGHT INTO ROB WALLACE'S STORE...
WHAT ARE YOU--NO! DON'T!
THAT'S FOR ACCUSING ME OF THEFT WHEN I WAS HUNGRY!
SO NOW I'LL TAKE YOUR CASH ANYWAY! LA...LA..DE...DA...
NO SALE
9:23 AM: THE WINDOW IN THE REAR QUIETLY SLID OPEN AND A TALL, LANKY FIGURE STEPPED OUT--LOOKED UP AND DOWN THE DESERTED STREET AND QUICKLY MEANDERED ALONG THE ALLEYWAY TO WILL FELLOWS' BANK WHERE--A FEW MOMENTS LATER...
ARE YOU CRAZY? WHAT'S THE SHERIFF'S HANDCUFFS DOING ON MY WRISTS? ALL RIGHT! YOU'VE HAD YOUR JOKE! ENOUGH'S ENOUGH TAKE THESE OFF!
OH...BUT THAT'S IMPOSSIBLE!
I HAVE SOME UNFINISHED BUSINESS, YOU SEE. BE PATIENT, KIND SIR. IT WILL TAKE ONLY A MOMENT. IN THE MEANTIME, CHEW ON THIS RAG!
NEVER BE DECEIVED BY A BOOK WITH FRAYED COVERS. IT MAY PROVE DIFFERENT INSIDE. FOR FIRST...I REMOVE MY STILTS...THUS...
NEXT...OFF COMES MY COAT...AND...PRESTO-CHANGE-O...INTO AN ORDINARY OVERCOAT! SO!
AND AFTER WE SUBSTITUTE AN ORDINARY SHIRT AND TIE FOR MY OUTLANDISH COSTUME, MY DUFFLE-BAG WILL NEXT BECOME A BEAUTIFUL LEATHER TRAVEL-BAG! WHOOSH!

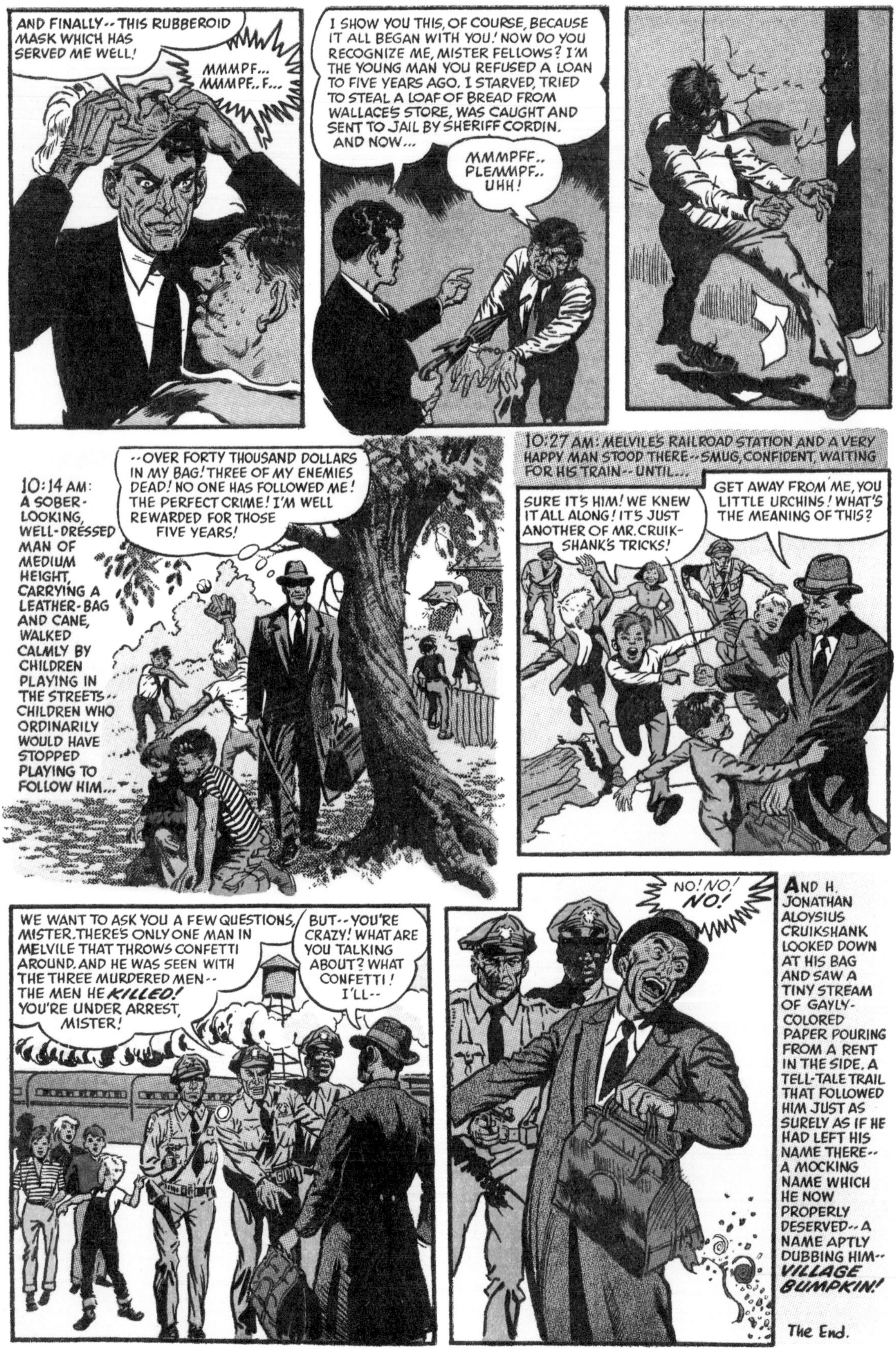

AND FINALLY-- THIS RUBBEROID MASK WHICH HAS SERVED ME WELL!
MMMPF... MMMPF.. F...
I SHOW YOU THIS, OF COURSE, BECAUSE IT ALL BEGAN WITH YOU! NOW DO YOU RECOGNIZE ME, MISTER FELLOWS? I'M THE YOUNG MAN YOU REFUSED A LOAN TO FIVE YEARS AGO. I STARVED, TRIED TO STEAL A LOAF OF BREAD FROM WALLACE'S STORE, WAS CAUGHT AND SENT TO JAIL BY SHERIFF CORDIN. AND NOW...
MMMPFF.. PLEMMPF.. UHH!
10:14 AM: A SOBER-LOOKING, WELL-DRESSED MAN OF MEDIUM HEIGHT, CARRYING A LEATHER-BAG AND CANE, WALKED CALMLY BY CHILDREN PLAYING IN THE STREETS-- CHILDREN WHO ORDINARILY WOULD HAVE STOPPED PLAYING TO FOLLOW HIM...
--OVER FORTY THOUSAND DOLLARS IN MY BAG! THREE OF MY ENEMIES DEAD! NO ONE HAS FOLLOWED ME! THE PERFECT CRIME! I'M WELL REWARDED FOR THOSE FIVE YEARS!
10:27 AM: MELVILE'S RAILROAD STATION AND A VERY HAPPY MAN STOOD THERE-- SMUG, CONFIDENT, WAITING FOR HIS TRAIN-- UNTIL...
SURE IT'S HIM! WE KNEW IT ALL ALONG! IT'S JUST ANOTHER OF MR. CRUIKSHANK'S TRICKS!
GET AWAY FROM ME, YOU LITTLE URCHINS! WHAT'S THE MEANING OF THIS?
WE WANT TO ASK YOU A FEW QUESTIONS, MISTER. THERE'S ONLY ONE MAN IN MELVILE THAT THROWS CONFETTI AROUND. AND HE WAS SEEN WITH THE THREE MURDERED MEN-- THE MEN HE KILLED! YOU'RE UNDER ARREST, MISTER!
BUT-- YOU'RE CRAZY! WHAT ARE YOU TALKING ABOUT? WHAT CONFETTI! I'LL--
NO! NO! NO!
AND H. JONATHAN ALOYSIUS CRUIKSHANK LOOKED DOWN AT HIS BAG AND SAW A TINY STREAM OF GAYLY-COLORED PAPER POURING FROM A RENT IN THE SIDE. A TELL-TALE TRAIL THAT FOLLOWED HIM JUST AS SURELY AS IF HE HAD LEFT HIS NAME THERE-- A MOCKING NAME WHICH HE NOW PROPERLY DESERVED-- A NAME APTLY DUBBING HIM-- VILLAGE BUMPKIN!
The End.

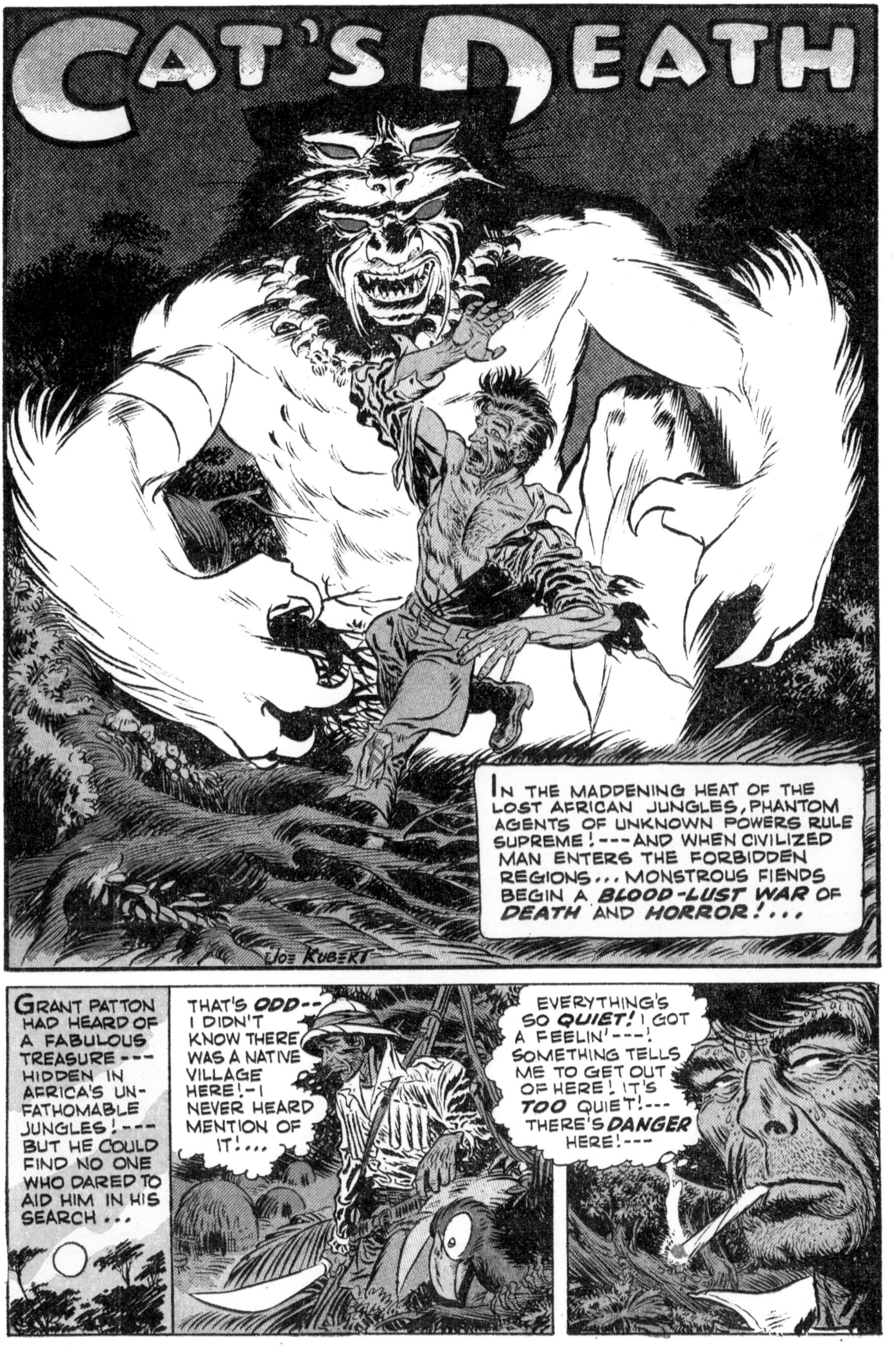
CAT'S DEATH
IN THE MADDENING HEAT OF THE LOST AFRICAN JUNGLES, PHANTOM AGENTS OF UNKNOWN POWERS RULE SUPREME! ---AND WHEN CIVILIZED MAN ENTERS THE FORBIDDEN REGIONS... MONSTROUS FIENDS BEGIN A BLOOD-LUST WAR OF DEATH AND HORROR!...
JOE KUBERT
GRANT PATTON HAD HEARD OF A FABULOUS TREASURE --- HIDDEN IN AFRICA'S UN-FATHOMABLE JUNGLES! --- BUT HE COULD FIND NO ONE WHO DARED TO AID HIM IN HIS SEARCH...
THAT'S ODD-- I DIDN'T KNOW THERE WAS A NATIVE VILLAGE HERE!-I NEVER HEARD MENTION OF IT!...
EVERYTHING'S SO QUIET! I GOT A FEELIN'---! SOMETHING TELLS ME TO GET OUT OF HERE! IT'S TOO QUIET!--- THERE'S DANGER HERE!---

SUDDENLY--OUT OF THE MATTED JUNGLE UNDERGROWTH, STRONG BLACK ARMS REACH OUT AND...

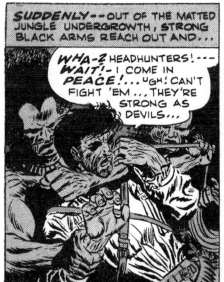

WHA--? HEADHUNTERS!--- WAIT!--I COME IN PEACE!...UGH! CAN'T FIGHT 'EM...THEY'RE STRONG AS DEVILS...

THEY'RE...THEY'RE LEADING ME TO THE VILLAGE!--HERE IT COMES, PATTON--- HERE IT COMES!

SILENTLY, THE GIANT BLACKS LEAD HIM THROUGH THE VILLAGE...PAST HOSTILE, STARING EYES...

WHERE WILL THEY TAKE ME NOW? I NEVER FIGURED TO DIE LIKE THIS---!

UMBA! ULLAKA WALU!--TUMM!

HOLY--! THIS MUST BE WHERE THEIR MEDICINE-MAN LIVES! THEY SEEM AFRAID TO ENTER-!

THEY'RE CALLING WHOEVER'S INSIDE BY HITTING THAT DRUM!...SOMETHING IS MOVING INSIDE! SOMEONE'S COMING!

WHO CALLS ME? WHO CALLS PAN-THA?

BOOMBOOMBOOMB

AWALLA CHUMBA! TAHARU CHUMBA!

INTRUDERS ARE NOT WELCOME HERE, MY FRIEND! YOUR -ER- PRESUMPTIVENESS WILL PROVE FATAL TO YOU!---

AM I HEARING THINGS? YOU SPEAK ENGLISH!-

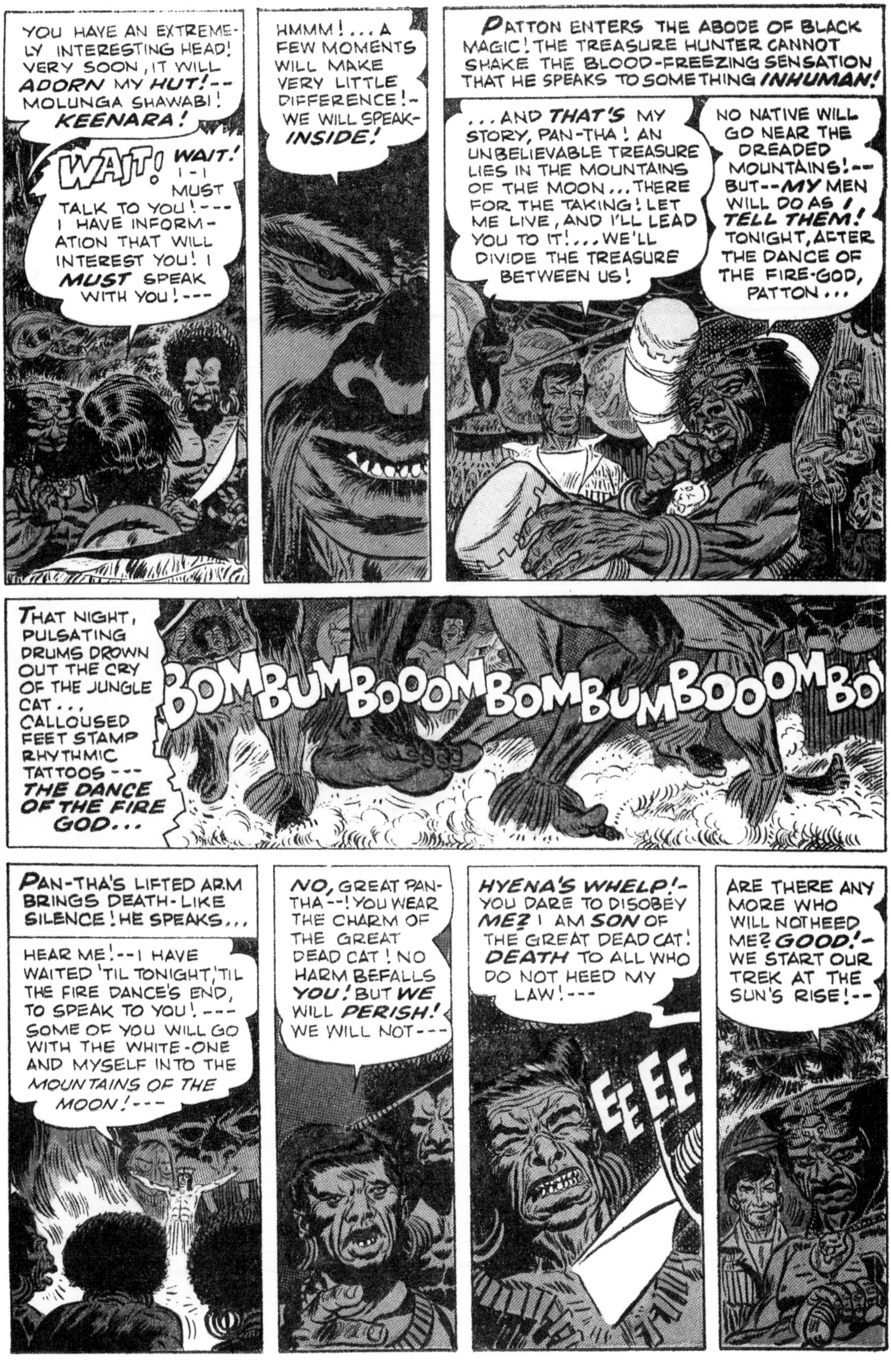
YOU HAVE AN EXTREMELY INTERESTING HEAD! VERY SOON, IT WILL ADORN MY HUT!-- MOLUNGA SHAWABI! KEENARA!
WAIT! WAIT! I-I MUST TALK TO YOU!--- I HAVE INFORMATION THAT WILL INTEREST YOU! I MUST SPEAK WITH YOU!---
HMMM!... A FEW MOMENTS WILL MAKE VERY LITTLE DIFFERENCE!- WE WILL SPEAK-INSIDE!
PATTON ENTERS THE ABODE OF BLACK MAGIC! THE TREASURE HUNTER CANNOT SHAKE THE BLOOD-FREEZING SENSATION THAT HE SPEAKS TO SOMETHING INHUMAN!
...AND THAT'S MY STORY, PAN-THA! AN UNBELIEVABLE TREASURE LIES IN THE MOUNTAINS OF THE MOON...THERE FOR THE TAKING! LET ME LIVE, AND I'LL LEAD YOU TO IT!...WE'LL DIVIDE THE TREASURE BETWEEN US!
NO NATIVE WILL GO NEAR THE DREADED MOUNTAINS!-- BUT--MY MEN WILL DO AS I TELL THEM! TONIGHT, AFTER THE DANCE OF THE FIRE-GOD, PATTON...
THAT NIGHT, PULSATING DRUMS DROWN OUT THE CRY OF THE JUNGLE CAT... CALLOUSED FEET STAMP RHYTHMIC TATTOOS --- THE DANCE OF THE FIRE GOD...
BOMBUMBOOOMBOMBUMBOOOMBO
PAN-THA'S LIFTED ARM BRINGS DEATH-LIKE SILENCE! HE SPEAKS...
HEAR ME!--I HAVE WAITED 'TIL TONIGHT,'TIL THE FIRE DANCE'S END, TO SPEAK TO YOU!--- SOME OF YOU WILL GO WITH THE WHITE-ONE AND MYSELF INTO THE MOUNTAINS OF THE MOON!---
NO, GREAT PAN-THA--! YOU WEAR THE CHARM OF THE GREAT DEAD CAT! NO HARM BEFALLS YOU! BUT WE WILL PERISH! WE WILL NOT---
HYENA'S WHELP!- YOU DARE TO DISOBEY ME? I AM SON OF THE GREAT DEAD CAT! DEATH TO ALL WHO DO NOT HEED MY LAW!---
EEEE
ARE THERE ANY MORE WHO WILL NOT HEED ME? GOOD!- WE START OUR TREK AT THE SUN'S RISE!--

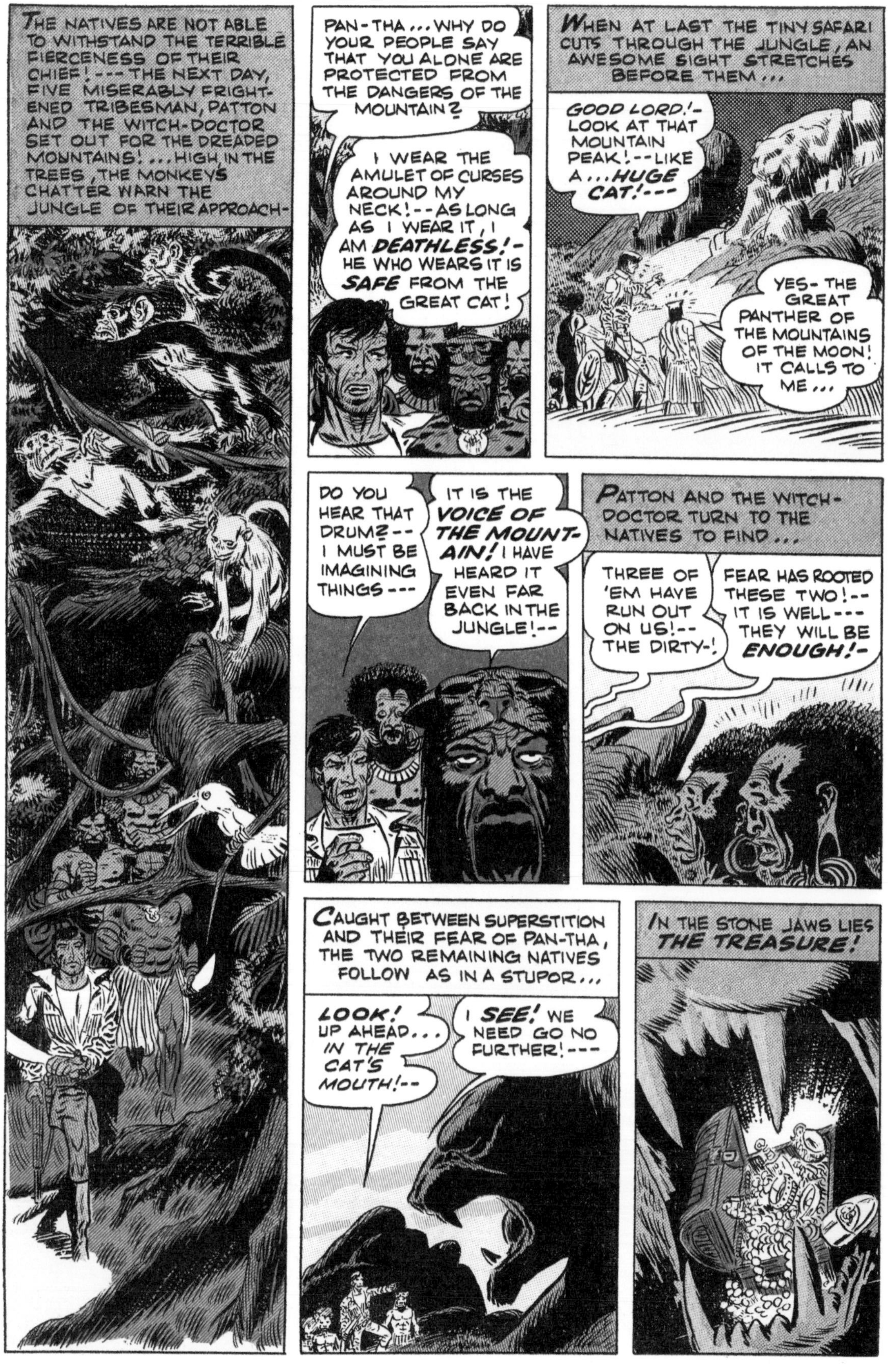

THE NATIVES ARE NOT ABLE TO WITHSTAND THE TERRIBLE FIERCENESS OF THEIR CHIEF! --- THE NEXT DAY, FIVE MISERABLY FRIGHTENED TRIBESMAN, PATTON AND THE WITCH-DOCTOR SET OUT FOR THE DREADED MOUNTAINS! ... HIGH IN THE TREES, THE MONKEYS CHATTER WARN THE JUNGLE OF THEIR APPROACH-
PAN-THA ... WHY DO YOUR PEOPLE SAY THAT YOU ALONE ARE PROTECTED FROM THE DANGERS OF THE MOUNTAIN?
I WEAR THE AMULET OF CURSES AROUND MY NECK! -- AS LONG AS I WEAR IT, I AM DEATHLESS! - HE WHO WEARS IT IS SAFE FROM THE GREAT CAT!
WHEN AT LAST THE TINY SAFARI CUTS THROUGH THE JUNGLE, AN AWESOME SIGHT STRETCHES BEFORE THEM ...
GOOD LORD! - LOOK AT THAT MOUNTAIN PEAK! -- LIKE A ... HUGE CAT! ---
YES- THE GREAT PANTHER OF THE MOUNTAINS OF THE MOON! IT CALLS TO ME ...
DO YOU HEAR THAT DRUM? -- I MUST BE IMAGINING THINGS ---
IT IS THE VOICE OF THE MOUNTAIN! I HAVE HEARD IT EVEN FAR BACK IN THE JUNGLE! --
PATTON AND THE WITCH-DOCTOR TURN TO THE NATIVES TO FIND ...
THREE OF 'EM HAVE RUN OUT ON US! -- THE DIRTY-!
FEAR HAS ROOTED THESE TWO! -- IT IS WELL --- THEY WILL BE ENOUGH! -
CAUGHT BETWEEN SUPERSTITION AND THEIR FEAR OF PAN-THA, THE TWO REMAINING NATIVES FOLLOW AS IN A STUPOR ...
LOOK! UP AHEAD ... IN THE CAT'S MOUTH! --
I SEE! WE NEED GO NO FURTHER! ---
IN THE STONE JAWS LIES THE TREASURE!

UNGALLA! BWAMBA!-- INTO THE JAWS AND BRING OUT THE TREASURE! QUICKLY!

THEY'RE ALMOST PETRIFIED WITH FEAR! BUT--- THEY'LL DO AS HE SAYS! ---

THE J-JAWS ARE MOVING! TH-THEY'RE CLOSING!

NO ONE CAN TELL OF THE TREASURE NOW! NO ONE BUT US!-

BUMBOMBOOMBUMBOMBO

THEY'RE GONE! GONE! WAIT!- ARE YOU MAD? D-DON'T GO IN THERE!

HAVE NO FEAR ... NOTICE THAT THE DEATH-DRUM HAS STOPPED? AS LONG AS I WEAR THE AMULET, I CANNOT BE HARMED!---

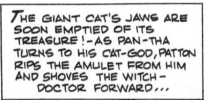

THE GIANT CAT'S JAWS ARE SOON EMPTIED OF ITS TREASURE!-AS PAN-THA TURNS TO HIS CAT-GOD, PATTON RIPS THE AMULET FROM HIM AND SHOVES THE WITCH-DOCTOR FORWARD...

NOW I HAVE THE AMULET! ...THE TREASURE WILL BE ALL MINE!

WHAT IS --? NO! NO!

EEEAAAR!

BOOM BOM BUM BOOOM

HAHAHA YOU FOOL! NOW I CONTROL THE GODS OF THE MOUNTAINS OF THE MOON!-

MY MIND MUST BE PLAYING TRICKS ON ME! ---I FEEL THAT WITCH DOCTOR'S PRESENCE! I'VE GOT TO GET AWAY FROM HERE! ---

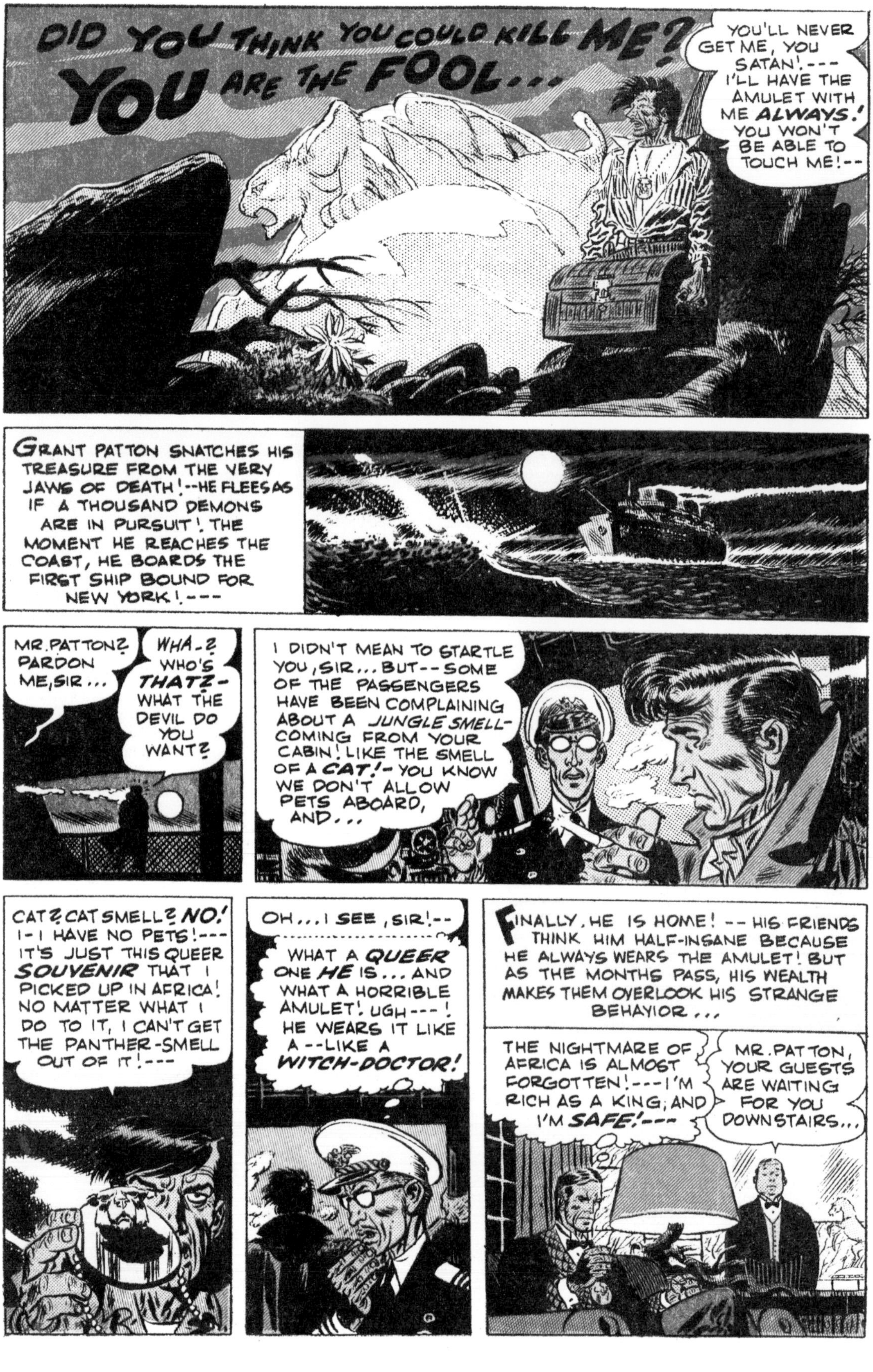
DID YOU THINK YOU COULD KILL ME? YOU ARE THE FOOL...
YOU'LL NEVER GET ME, YOU SATAN!--- I'LL HAVE THE AMULET WITH ME ALWAYS! YOU WON'T BE ABLE TO TOUCH ME!--
GRANT PATTON SNATCHES HIS TREASURE FROM THE VERY JAWS OF DEATH!--HE FLEES AS IF A THOUSAND DEMONS ARE IN PURSUIT! THE MOMENT HE REACHES THE COAST, HE BOARDS THE FIRST SHIP BOUND FOR NEW YORK!---
MR. PATTON? PARDON ME, SIR...
WHA-? WHO'S THAT?- WHAT THE DEVIL DO YOU WANT?
I DIDN'T MEAN TO STARTLE YOU, SIR... BUT--SOME OF THE PASSENGERS HAVE BEEN COMPLAINING ABOUT A JUNGLE SMELL- COMING FROM YOUR CABIN! LIKE THE SMELL OF A CAT!- YOU KNOW WE DON'T ALLOW PETS ABOARD, AND...
CAT? CAT SMELL? NO! I-I HAVE NO PETS!--- IT'S JUST THIS QUEER SOUVENIR THAT I PICKED UP IN AFRICA! NO MATTER WHAT I DO TO IT, I CAN'T GET THE PANTHER-SMELL OUT OF IT!---
OH... I SEE, SIR!--
WHAT A QUEER ONE HE IS... AND WHAT A HORRIBLE AMULET! UGH---! HE WEARS IT LIKE A--LIKE A WITCH-DOCTOR!
FINALLY, HE IS HOME! --HIS FRIENDS THINK HIM HALF-INSANE BECAUSE HE ALWAYS WEARS THE AMULET! BUT AS THE MONTHS PASS, HIS WEALTH MAKES THEM OVERLOOK HIS STRANGE BEHAVIOR...
THE NIGHTMARE OF AFRICA IS ALMOST FORGOTTEN!---I'M RICH AS A KING, AND I'M SAFE!---
MR. PATTON, YOUR GUESTS ARE WAITING FOR YOU DOWNSTAIRS...

Panel 1: HUH?---OH, YES...THANKS, BRIGGS! PERHAPS A LITTLE FUN WILL CLEAR MY MIND!-- TELL 'EM I'LL BE RIGHT DOWN!...

Panel 2: SOME TIME LATER, GRANT PATTON AND HIS GUESTS ARRIVE AT THE ZOO THAT GRANT HAD RENTED FOR HIS PARTY...

Panel 3: GRANT, WHAT A WONDERFUL IDEA THIS IS!

I FEEL LIKE A KID AGAIN!--HAVEN'T DONE ANYTHING LIKE THIS IN YEARS!

OOOH--THE LION HOUSE! LET'S GO IN AND SAY 'HELLO' TO THE KITTIES!

Panel 4: THE CAGES STIR WITH JUNGLE LIFE, AS GRANT AND HIS PARTY ENTER THE LION HOUSE...

Panel 5: GRANT!--THAT ANIMAL'S GONE NUTS! HE'S--HE'S TRYING TO GET AT YOU!--

Panel 6: LISTEN! D-DOES ANYONE H-HEAR--- D-DRUMS?

DRUMS? I DON'T HEAR ANY---! GRANT! ARE YOU ILL?

Panel 7: TODAY IS THE ANNIVERSARY OF PAN-THA'S CURSE! THOSE BIG CATS KNOW....AND THEY SMELL--- DEATH!!

BOMBUMBOOOOMBOMBUMBOM

Panel 8: MR. PATTON-- IS SOME-THING WRONG, SIR?...

DRUMS...CURSE.. WHA-? N-NO, I'M FINE...! LISTEN--DON'T LET ANYONE IN HERE, BRIGGS! I'M GOING INTO MY STUDY, AND I DON'T WANT TO BE DISTURBED!

Panel 9: ONCE IN HIS STUDY, GRANT COVERS HIS EARS TO STOP THE BEATING OF...

THOSE DRUMS! DRIVING ME CRAZY!--SO LOUD! THE AMULET...IT'S-IT'S GETTING SO HOT,...AND HEAVY...HEAVY...

BOOM! BUMBOOMBO

Panel 10: IN THE APARTMENT....

DR. JOHNSON? COULD YOU COME TO MR. GRANT PATTON'S HOME AT ONCE? HE'S ...OH, THANK YOU!-- I'LL SEE THAT NO ONE DISTURBS HIM UNTIL YOU ARRIVE, DOCTOR!---

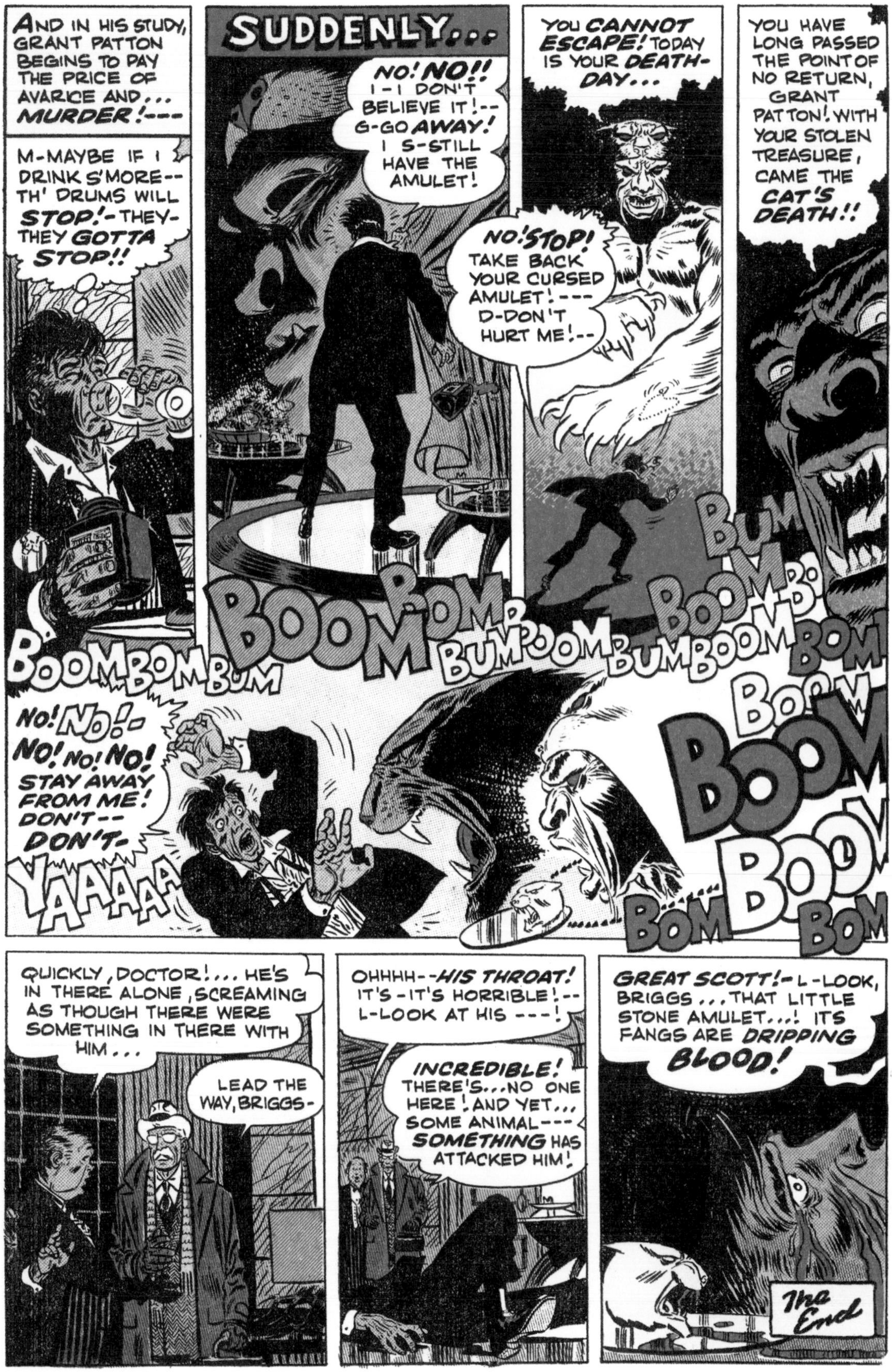

AND IN HIS STUDY, GRANT PATTON BEGINS TO PAY THE PRICE OF AVARICE AND... MURDER!---
M-MAYBE IF I DRINK S'MORE-- TH' DRUMS WILL STOP!- THEY- THEY GOTTA STOP!!
SUDDENLY...
NO! NO!! I-I DON'T BELIEVE IT!-- G-GO AWAY! I S-STILL HAVE THE AMULET!
YOU CANNOT ESCAPE! TODAY IS YOUR DEATH-DAY...
NO! STOP! TAKE BACK YOUR CURSED AMULET!--- D-DON'T HURT ME!--
YOU HAVE LONG PASSED THE POINT OF NO RETURN, GRANT PATTON! WITH YOUR STOLEN TREASURE, CAME THE CAT'S DEATH!!
BOOMBOMBUM
BOOM BOMB
BUMBOOM
BUM
BOOMBO
BUMBOOM
BOM
BOOM
NO! NO!- NO! NO! NO! STAY AWAY FROM ME! DON'T-- DON'T-
YAAAAA
BOOM
BOOM
BOM
BOM
QUICKLY, DOCTOR!... HE'S IN THERE ALONE, SCREAMING AS THOUGH THERE WERE SOMETHING IN THERE WITH HIM...
LEAD THE WAY, BRIGGS-
OHHHH--HIS THROAT! IT'S-IT'S HORRIBLE!-- L-LOOK AT HIS---!
INCREDIBLE! THERE'S... NO ONE HERE! AND YET... SOME ANIMAL--- SOMETHING HAS ATTACKED HIM!
GREAT SCOTT!- L-LOOK, BRIGGS... THAT LITTLE STONE AMULET...! ITS FANGS ARE DRIPPING BLOOD!
The End

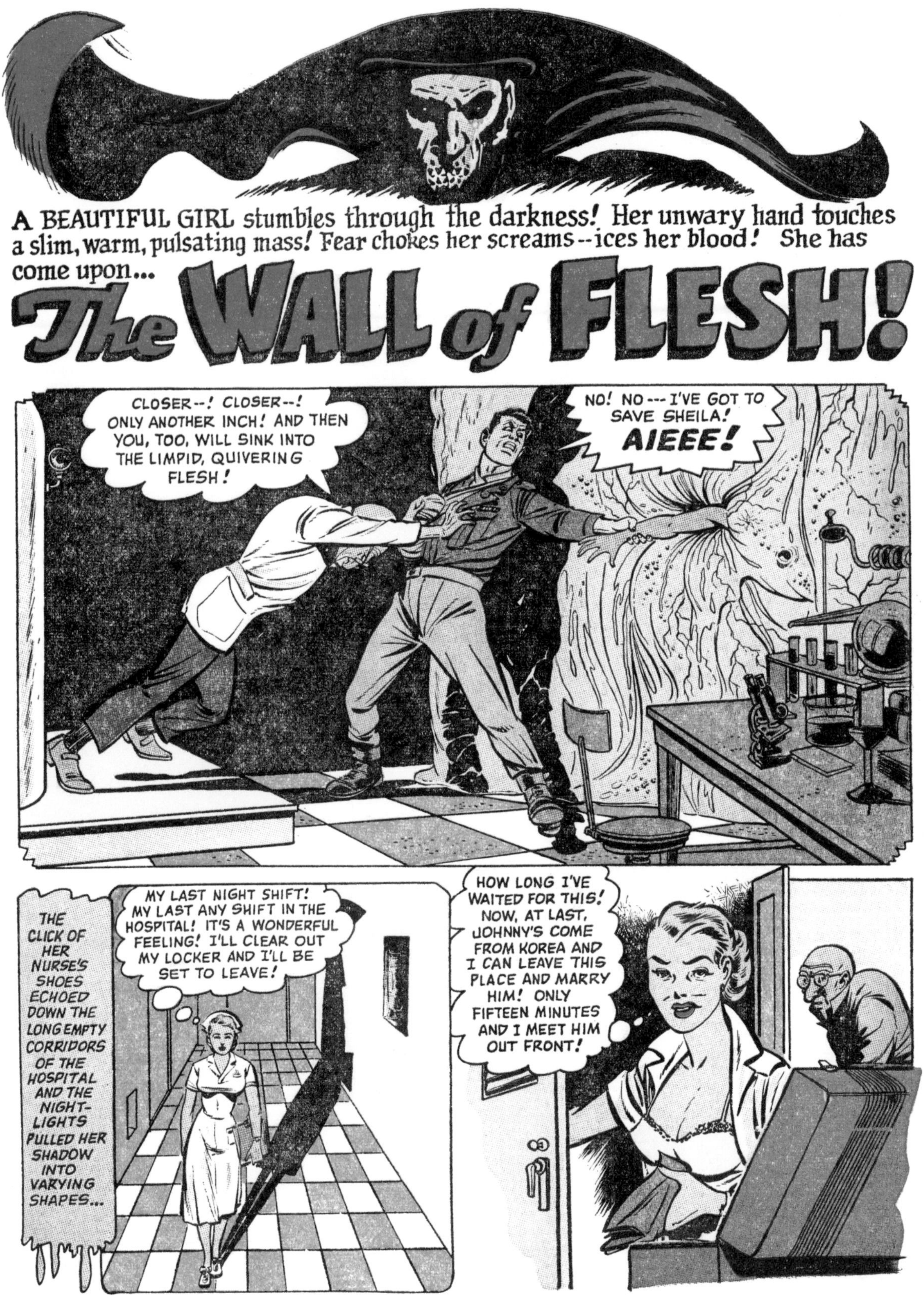
A BEAUTIFUL GIRL stumbles through the darkness! Her unwary hand touches a slim, warm, pulsating mass! Fear chokes her screams--ices her blood! She has come upon...
The WALL of FLESH!
CLOSER--! CLOSER--! ONLY ANOTHER INCH! AND THEN YOU, TOO, WILL SINK INTO THE LIMPID, QUIVERING FLESH!
NO! NO--- I'VE GOT TO SAVE SHEILA! AIEEE!
THE CLICK OF HER NURSE'S SHOES ECHOED DOWN THE LONG EMPTY CORRIDORS OF THE HOSPITAL AND THE NIGHT-LIGHTS PULLED HER SHADOW INTO VARYING SHAPES...
MY LAST NIGHT SHIFT! MY LAST ANY SHIFT IN THE HOSPITAL! IT'S A WONDERFUL FEELING! I'LL CLEAR OUT MY LOCKER AND I'LL BE SET TO LEAVE!
HOW LONG I'VE WAITED FOR THIS! NOW, AT LAST, JOHNNY'S COME FROM KOREA AND I CAN LEAVE THIS PLACE AND MARRY HIM! ONLY FIFTEEN MINUTES AND I MEET HIM OUT FRONT!

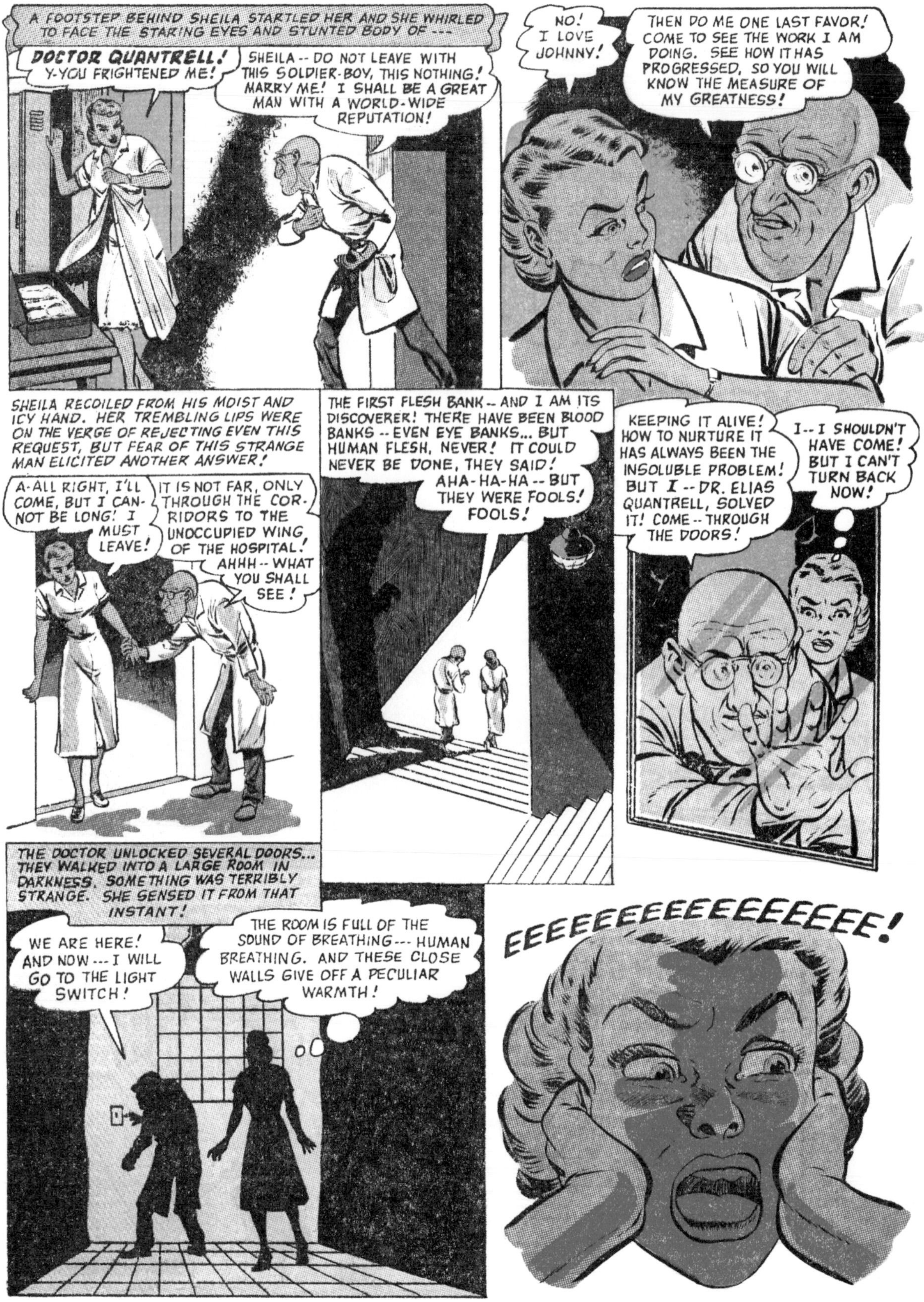

A FOOTSTEP BEHIND SHEILA STARTLED HER AND SHE WHIRLED TO FACE THE STARING EYES AND STUNTED BODY OF ---
DOCTOR QUANTRELL! Y-YOU FRIGHTENED ME!
SHEILA -- DO NOT LEAVE WITH THIS SOLDIER-BOY, THIS NOTHING! MARRY ME! I SHALL BE A GREAT MAN WITH A WORLD-WIDE REPUTATION!
NO! I LOVE JOHNNY!
THEN DO ME ONE LAST FAVOR! COME TO SEE THE WORK I AM DOING. SEE HOW IT HAS PROGRESSED, SO YOU WILL KNOW THE MEASURE OF MY GREATNESS!
SHEILA RECOILED FROM HIS MOIST AND ICY HAND. HER TREMBLING LIPS WERE ON THE VERGE OF REJECTING EVEN THIS REQUEST, BUT FEAR OF THIS STRANGE MAN ELICITED ANOTHER ANSWER!
A-ALL RIGHT, I'LL COME, BUT I CANNOT BE LONG! I MUST LEAVE!
IT IS NOT FAR, ONLY THROUGH THE CORRIDORS TO THE UNOCCUPIED WING, OF THE HOSPITAL! AHHH -- WHAT YOU SHALL SEE!
THE FIRST FLESH BANK -- AND I AM ITS DISCOVERER! THERE HAVE BEEN BLOOD BANKS -- EVEN EYE BANKS... BUT HUMAN FLESH, NEVER! IT COULD NEVER BE DONE, THEY SAID!
AHA-HA-HA -- BUT THEY WERE FOOLS! FOOLS!
KEEPING IT ALIVE! HOW TO NURTURE IT HAS ALWAYS BEEN THE INSOLUBLE PROBLEM! BUT I -- DR. ELIAS QUANTRELL, SOLVED IT! COME -- THROUGH THE DOORS!
I -- I SHOULDN'T HAVE COME! BUT I CAN'T TURN BACK NOW!
THE DOCTOR UNLOCKED SEVERAL DOORS... THEY WALKED INTO A LARGE ROOM IN DARKNESS. SOMETHING WAS TERRIBLY STRANGE. SHE SENSED IT FROM THAT INSTANT!
WE ARE HERE! AND NOW --- I WILL GO TO THE LIGHT SWITCH!
THE ROOM IS FULL OF THE SOUND OF BREATHING --- HUMAN BREATHING. AND THESE CLOSE WALLS GIVE OFF A PECULIAR WARMTH!
EEEEEEEEEEEEEEEEE!

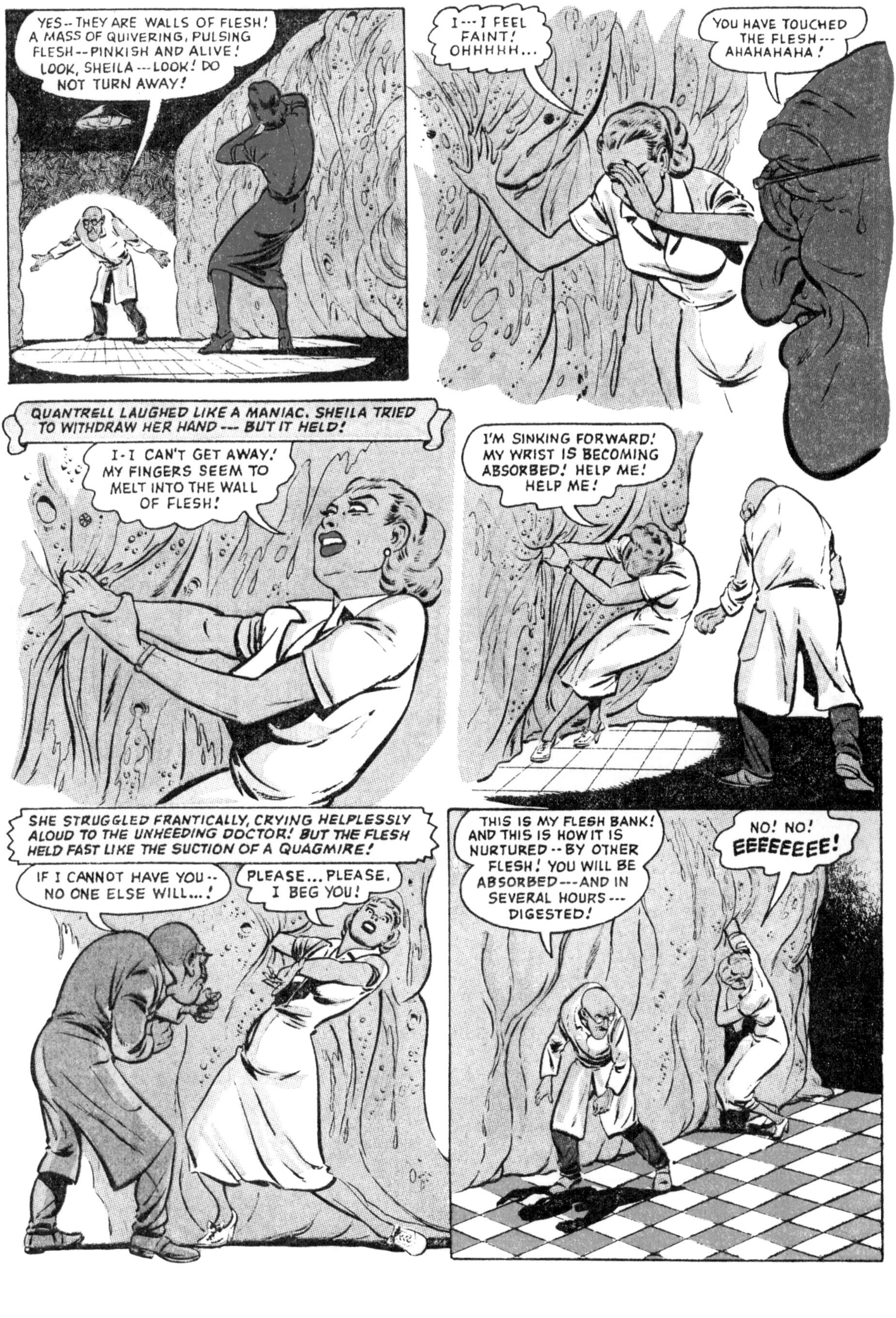

YES-- THEY ARE WALLS OF FLESH! A MASS OF QUIVERING, PULSING FLESH--PINKISH AND ALIVE! LOOK, SHEILA---LOOK! DO NOT TURN AWAY!
I---I FEEL FAINT! OHHHHH...
YOU HAVE TOUCHED THE FLESH--- AHAHAHAHA!
QUANTRELL LAUGHED LIKE A MANIAC. SHEILA TRIED TO WITHDRAW HER HAND --- BUT IT HELD!
I-I CAN'T GET AWAY! MY FINGERS SEEM TO MELT INTO THE WALL OF FLESH!
I'M SINKING FORWARD! MY WRIST IS BECOMING ABSORBED! HELP ME! HELP ME!
SHE STRUGGLED FRANTICALLY, CRYING HELPLESSLY ALOUD TO THE UNHEEDING DOCTOR! BUT THE FLESH HELD FAST LIKE THE SUCTION OF A QUAGMIRE!
IF I CANNOT HAVE YOU-- NO ONE ELSE WILL...!
PLEASE... PLEASE, I BEG YOU!
THIS IS MY FLESH BANK! AND THIS IS HOW IT IS NURTURED--BY OTHER FLESH! YOU WILL BE ABSORBED---AND IN SEVERAL HOURS--- DIGESTED!
NO! NO! EEEEEEEE!

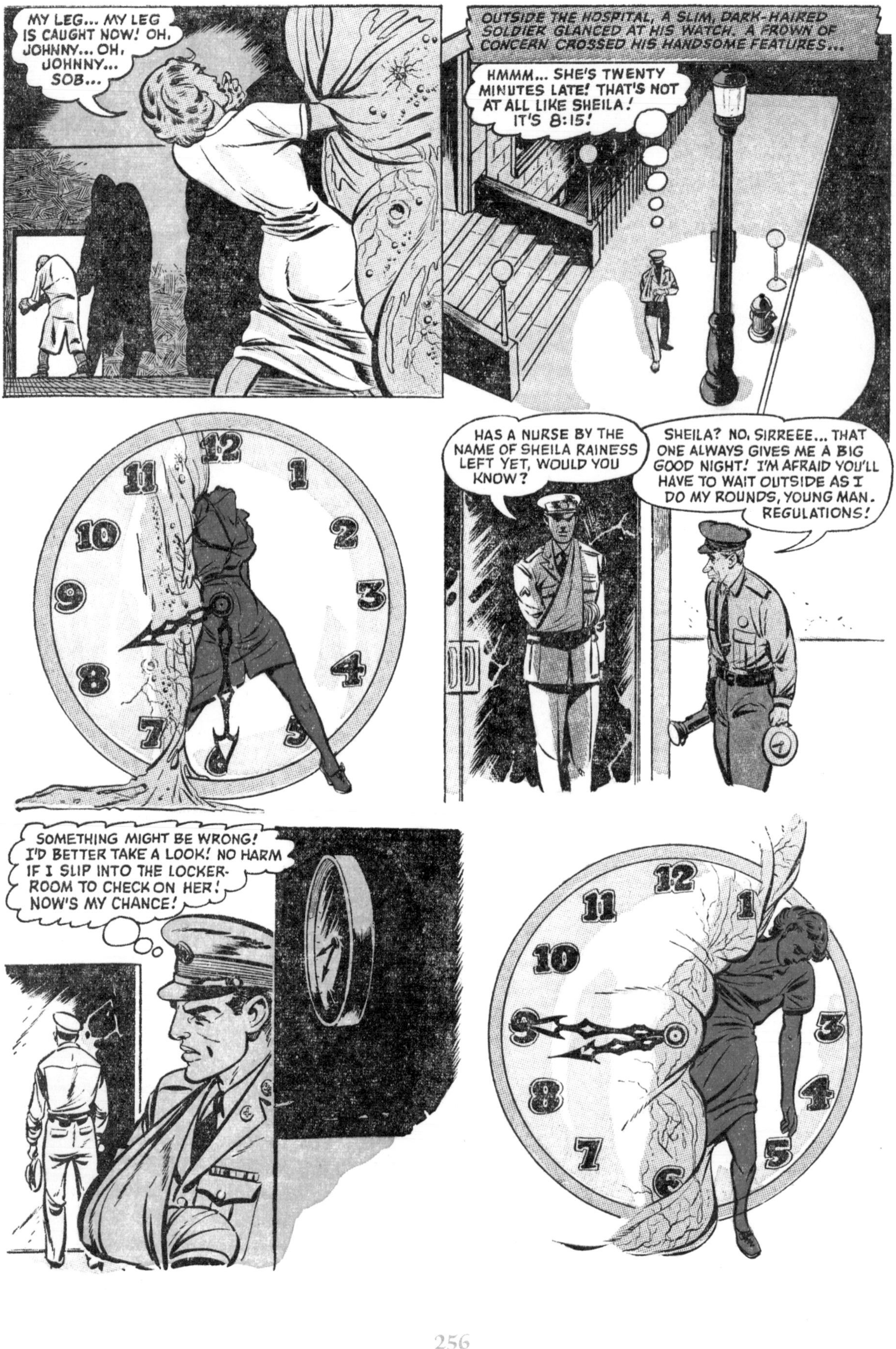
MY LEG... MY LEG IS CAUGHT NOW! OH, JOHNNY... OH, JOHNNY... SOB...
OUTSIDE THE HOSPITAL, A SLIM, DARK-HAIRED SOLDIER GLANCED AT HIS WATCH. A FROWN OF CONCERN CROSSED HIS HANDSOME FEATURES...
HMMM... SHE'S TWENTY MINUTES LATE! THAT'S NOT AT ALL LIKE SHEILA! IT'S 8:15!
12
1
2
3
4
5
6
7
8
9
10
11
HAS A NURSE BY THE NAME OF SHEILA RAINESS LEFT YET, WOULD YOU KNOW?
SHEILA? NO, SIRREEE... THAT ONE ALWAYS GIVES ME A BIG GOOD NIGHT! I'M AFRAID YOU'LL HAVE TO WAIT OUTSIDE AS I DO MY ROUNDS, YOUNG MAN. REGULATIONS!
SOMETHING MIGHT BE WRONG! I'D BETTER TAKE A LOOK! NO HARM IF I SLIP INTO THE LOCKER-ROOM TO CHECK ON HER! NOW'S MY CHANCE!
12
1
3
4
5
6
7
8
9
10
11

THESE ARE HER THINGS--- PARTIALLY PACKED! BUT SHE'S NOT AROUND! WHAT'S THAT---? A FOOTSTEP! MAYBE IT'S THE NIGHT-MAN! I'D BETTER DUCK!
I'LL DISPOSE OF HER THINGS... AND SHE WILL HAVE VANISHED! VANISHED! AHHAHA!
VANISHED? SOMETHING IS COCKEYED! I'D BETTER FOLLOW THIS CHARACTER!
I--I COULD JUMP HIM... BUT I'VE GOT TO BE SURE OF WHAT'S GOING ON! AND THIS ARM OF MINE! WHAT A TIME TO HAVE A WAR WOUND!

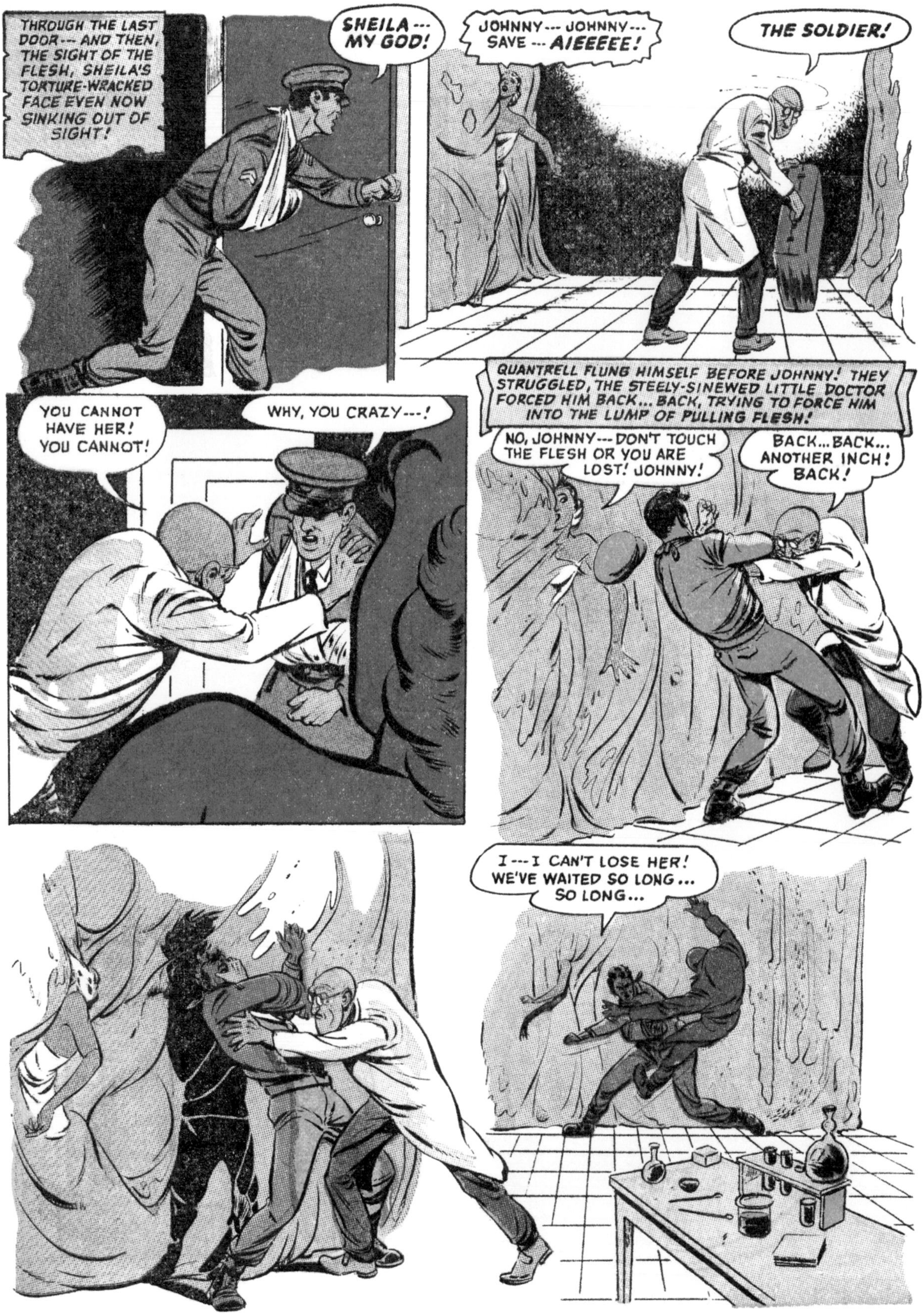
THROUGH THE LAST DOOR --- AND THEN, THE SIGHT OF THE FLESH, SHEILA'S TORTURE-WRACKED FACE EVEN NOW SINKING OUT OF SIGHT!
SHEILA --- MY GOD!
JOHNNY --- JOHNNY --- SAVE --- AIEEEEE!
THE SOLDIER!
YOU CANNOT HAVE HER! YOU CANNOT!
WHY, YOU CRAZY ---!
QUANTRELL FLUNG HIMSELF BEFORE JOHNNY! THEY STRUGGLED, THE STEELY-SINEWED LITTLE DOCTOR FORCED HIM BACK... BACK, TRYING TO FORCE HIM INTO THE LUMP OF PULLING FLESH!
NO, JOHNNY --- DON'T TOUCH THE FLESH OR YOU ARE LOST! JOHNNY!
BACK... BACK... ANOTHER INCH! BACK!
I --- I CAN'T LOSE HER! WE'VE WAITED SO LONG... SO LONG...

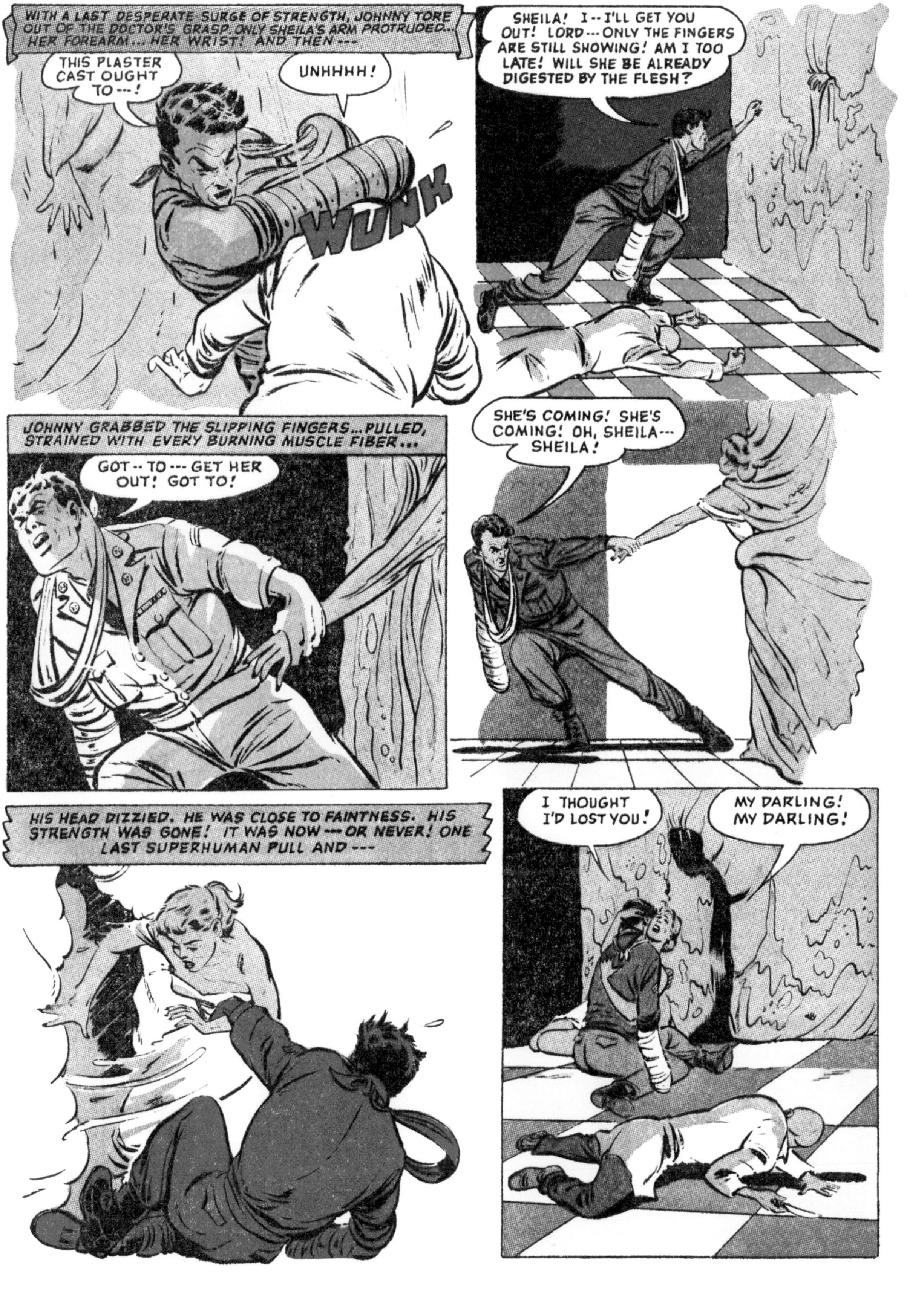
WITH A LAST DESPERATE SURGE OF STRENGTH, JOHNNY TORE OUT OF THE DOCTOR'S GRASP. ONLY SHEILA'S ARM PROTRUDED... HER FOREARM... HER WRIST! AND THEN---
THIS PLASTER CAST OUGHT TO---!
UNHHHH!
WUNK
SHEILA! I--I'LL GET YOU OUT! LORD---ONLY THE FINGERS ARE STILL SHOWING! AM I TOO LATE! WILL SHE BE ALREADY DIGESTED BY THE FLESH?
JOHNNY GRABBED THE SLIPPING FINGERS...PULLED, STRAINED WITH EVERY BURNING MUSCLE FIBER...
GOT--TO---GET HER OUT! GOT TO!
SHE'S COMING! SHE'S COMING! OH, SHEILA--- SHEILA!
HIS HEAD DIZZIED. HE WAS CLOSE TO FAINTNESS. HIS STRENGTH WAS GONE! IT WAS NOW---OR NEVER! ONE LAST SUPERHUMAN PULL AND---
I THOUGHT I'D LOST YOU!
MY DARLING! MY DARLING!

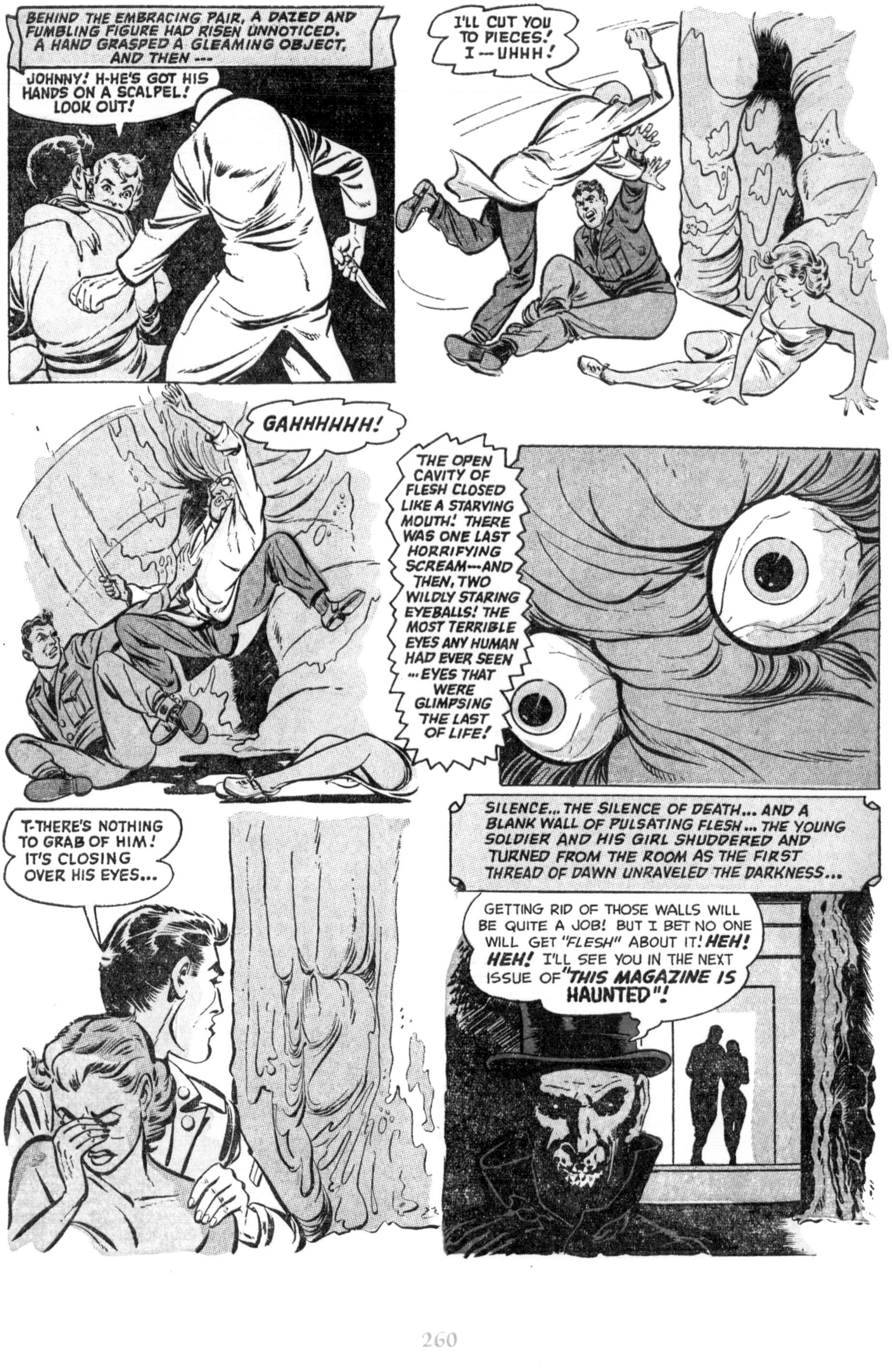
BEHIND THE EMBRACING PAIR, A DAZED AND FUMBLING FIGURE HAD RISEN UNNOTICED. A HAND GRASPED A GLEAMING OBJECT, AND THEN ---
JOHNNY! H-HE'S GOT HIS HANDS ON A SCALPEL! LOOK OUT!
I'LL CUT YOU TO PIECES! I --- UHHH!
GAHHHHHH!
THE OPEN CAVITY OF FLESH CLOSED LIKE A STARVING MOUTH! THERE WAS ONE LAST HORRIFYING SCREAM---AND THEN, TWO WILDLY STARING EYEBALLS! THE MOST TERRIBLE EYES ANY HUMAN HAD EVER SEEN ... EYES THAT WERE GLIMPSING THE LAST OF LIFE!
T-THERE'S NOTHING TO GRAB OF HIM! IT'S CLOSING OVER HIS EYES...
SILENCE... THE SILENCE OF DEATH... AND A BLANK WALL OF PULSATING FLESH... THE YOUNG SOLDIER AND HIS GIRL SHUDDERED AND TURNED FROM THE ROOM AS THE FIRST THREAD OF DAWN UNRAVELED THE DARKNESS...
GETTING RID OF THOSE WALLS WILL BE QUITE A JOB! BUT I BET NO ONE WILL GET "FLESH" ABOUT IT! HEH! HEH! I'LL SEE YOU IN THE NEXT ISSUE OF "THIS MAGAZINE IS HAUNTED"!

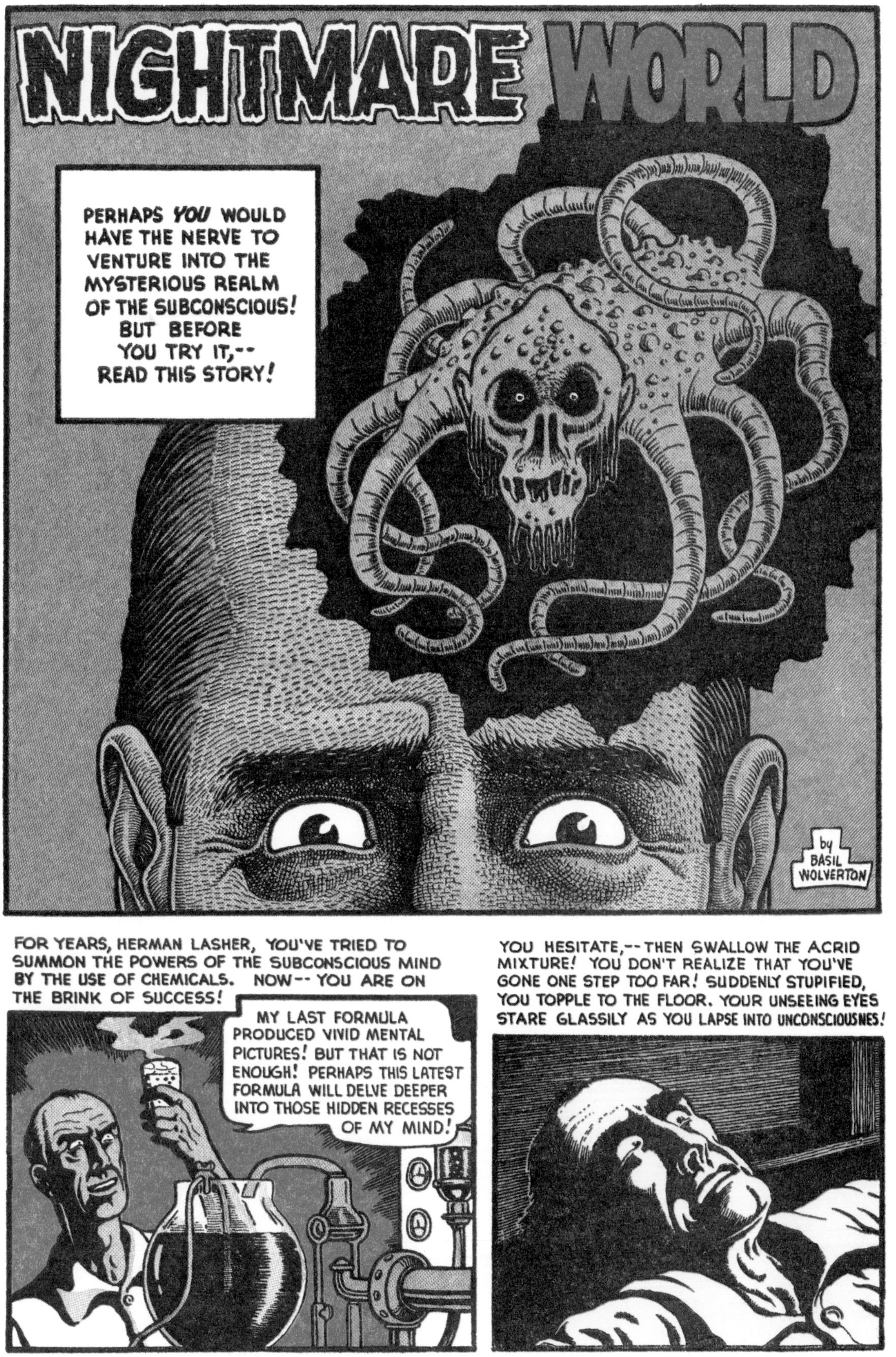
NIGHTMARE WORLD
PERHAPS YOU WOULD HAVE THE NERVE TO VENTURE INTO THE MYSTERIOUS REALM OF THE SUBCONSCIOUS! BUT BEFORE YOU TRY IT,-- READ THIS STORY!
by BASIL WOLVERTON
FOR YEARS, HERMAN LASHER, YOU'VE TRIED TO SUMMON THE POWERS OF THE SUBCONSCIOUS MIND BY THE USE OF CHEMICALS. NOW-- YOU ARE ON THE BRINK OF SUCCESS!
MY LAST FORMULA PRODUCED VIVID MENTAL PICTURES! BUT THAT IS NOT ENOUGH! PERHAPS THIS LATEST FORMULA WILL DELVE DEEPER INTO THOSE HIDDEN RECESSES OF MY MIND!
YOU HESITATE,-- THEN SWALLOW THE ACRID MIXTURE! YOU DON'T REALIZE THAT YOU'VE GONE ONE STEP TOO FAR! SUDDENLY STUPIFIED, YOU TOPPLE TO THE FLOOR. YOUR UNSEEING EYES STARE GLASSILY AS YOU LAPSE INTO UNCONSCIOUSNES!

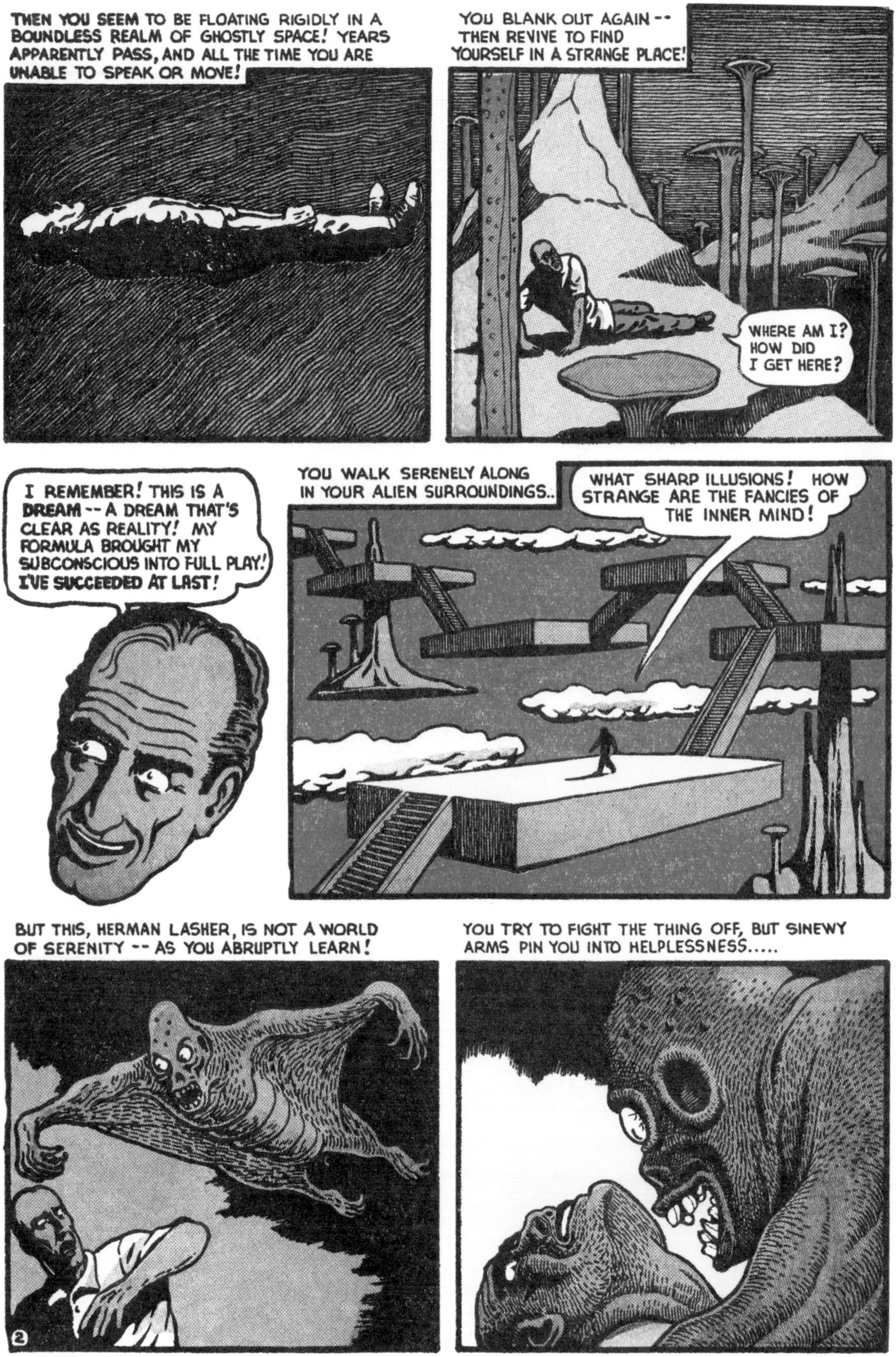
THEN YOU SEEM TO BE FLOATING RIGIDLY IN A BOUNDLESS REALM OF GHOSTLY SPACE! YEARS APPARENTLY PASS, AND ALL THE TIME YOU ARE UNABLE TO SPEAK OR MOVE!
YOU BLANK OUT AGAIN -- THEN REVIVE TO FIND YOURSELF IN A STRANGE PLACE!
WHERE AM I? HOW DID I GET HERE?
I REMEMBER! THIS IS A DREAM -- A DREAM THAT'S CLEAR AS REALITY! MY FORMULA BROUGHT MY SUBCONSCIOUS INTO FULL PLAY! I'VE SUCCEEDED AT LAST!
YOU WALK SERENELY ALONG IN YOUR ALIEN SURROUNDINGS..
WHAT SHARP ILLUSIONS! HOW STRANGE ARE THE FANCIES OF THE INNER MIND!
BUT THIS, HERMAN LASHER, IS NOT A WORLD OF SERENITY -- AS YOU ABRUPTLY LEARN!
2
YOU TRY TO FIGHT THE THING OFF, BUT SINEWY ARMS PIN YOU INTO HELPLESSNESS.....

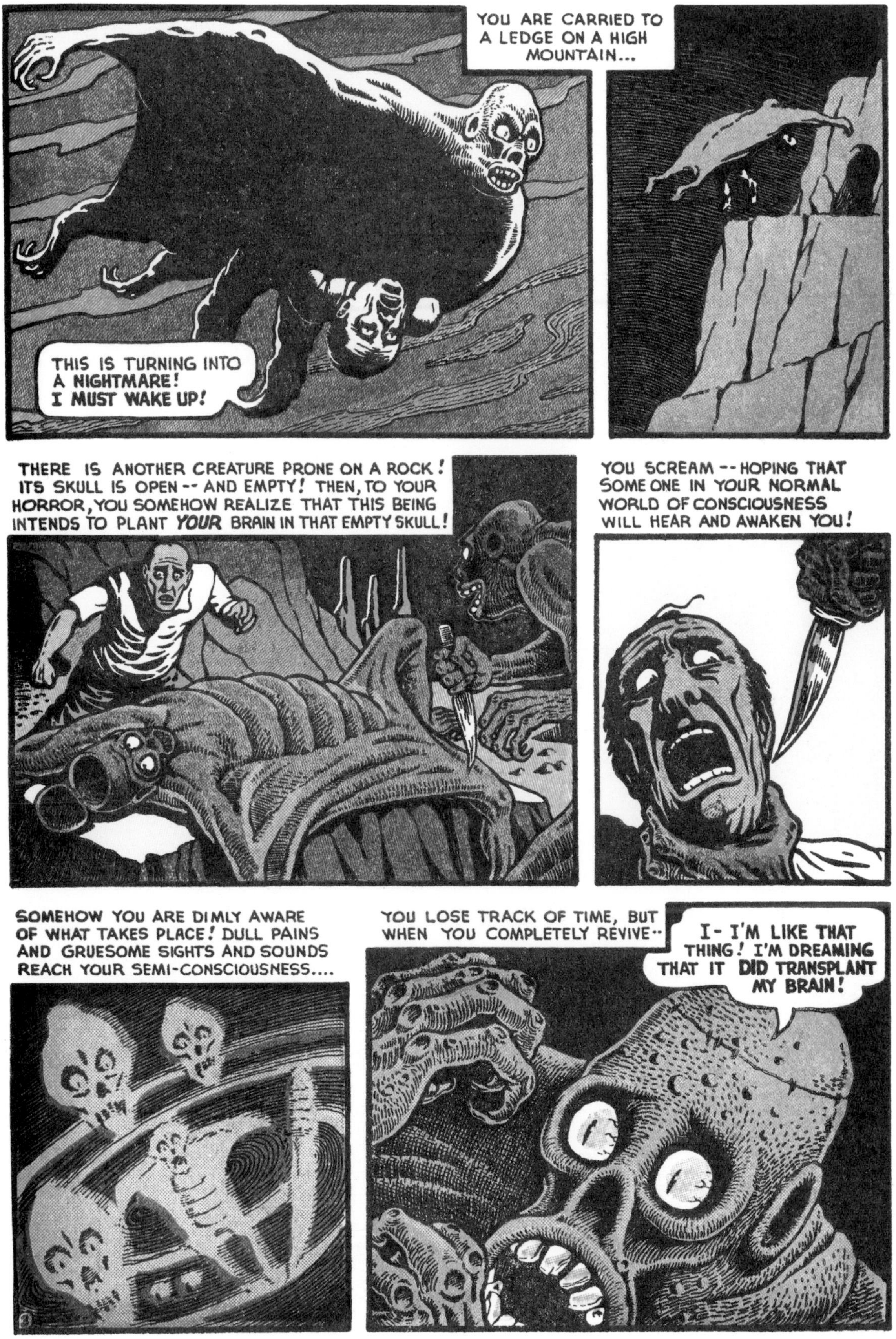
YOU ARE CARRIED TO A LEDGE ON A HIGH MOUNTAIN...
THIS IS TURNING INTO A NIGHTMARE! I MUST WAKE UP!
THERE IS ANOTHER CREATURE PRONE ON A ROCK! ITS SKULL IS OPEN -- AND EMPTY! THEN, TO YOUR HORROR, YOU SOMEHOW REALIZE THAT THIS BEING INTENDS TO PLANT YOUR BRAIN IN THAT EMPTY SKULL!
YOU SCREAM -- HOPING THAT SOME ONE IN YOUR NORMAL WORLD OF CONSCIOUSNESS WILL HEAR AND AWAKEN YOU!
SOMEHOW YOU ARE DIMLY AWARE OF WHAT TAKES PLACE! DULL PAINS AND GRUESOME SIGHTS AND SOUNDS REACH YOUR SEMI-CONSCIOUSNESS....
YOU LOSE TRACK OF TIME, BUT WHEN YOU COMPLETELY REVIVE--
I- I'M LIKE THAT THING! I'M DREAMING THAT IT DID TRANSPLANT MY BRAIN!

YOU TURN TO SEE THE OTHER CREATURE REGARDING YOU! BEHIND IT LIES A CRUMPLED BODY--*YOUR* BODY!

STRENGTHENED WITH RAGE, YOU LEAP AT THE OTHER, AND CLAW ITS THROAT OPEN WITH ONE SWIFT SLASH OF YOUR SHARP TALONS!

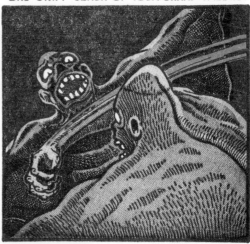

THEN, DETERMINED TO END THE NIGHTMARE, YOU PLUNGE OFF THE LEDGE!

YOU FALL AND FALL INTO WHAT SEEMS TO BE A BOTTOMLESS PIT! AGAIN YOU FEEL AS THOUGH YOU ARE TRAPPED IN TIME.....

YOU OPEN YOUR EYES. YOU ARE LYING ON A HARD FLOOR. A SENSE OF TREMENDOUS RELIEF SWEEPS OVER YOU AS YOU RECOGNIZE FAMILIAR OBJECTS IN YOUR LAB! YOU ARE BACK IN YOUR WORLD OF NORMAL CONSCIOUSNESS! YOUR NIGHTMARE IS OVER!

BUT--AS YOU GET TO YOUR FEET, YOU CAN'T HELP BUT NOTICE YOURSELF--AND YOU RECEIVE THE SUPREME SHOCK! THEN YOU REALIZE, HERMAN LASHER, THAT YOUR LONG-SOUGHT FORMULA HAS RESULTED IN MUCH MORE THAN JUST A NIGHTMARE!

THE END

264

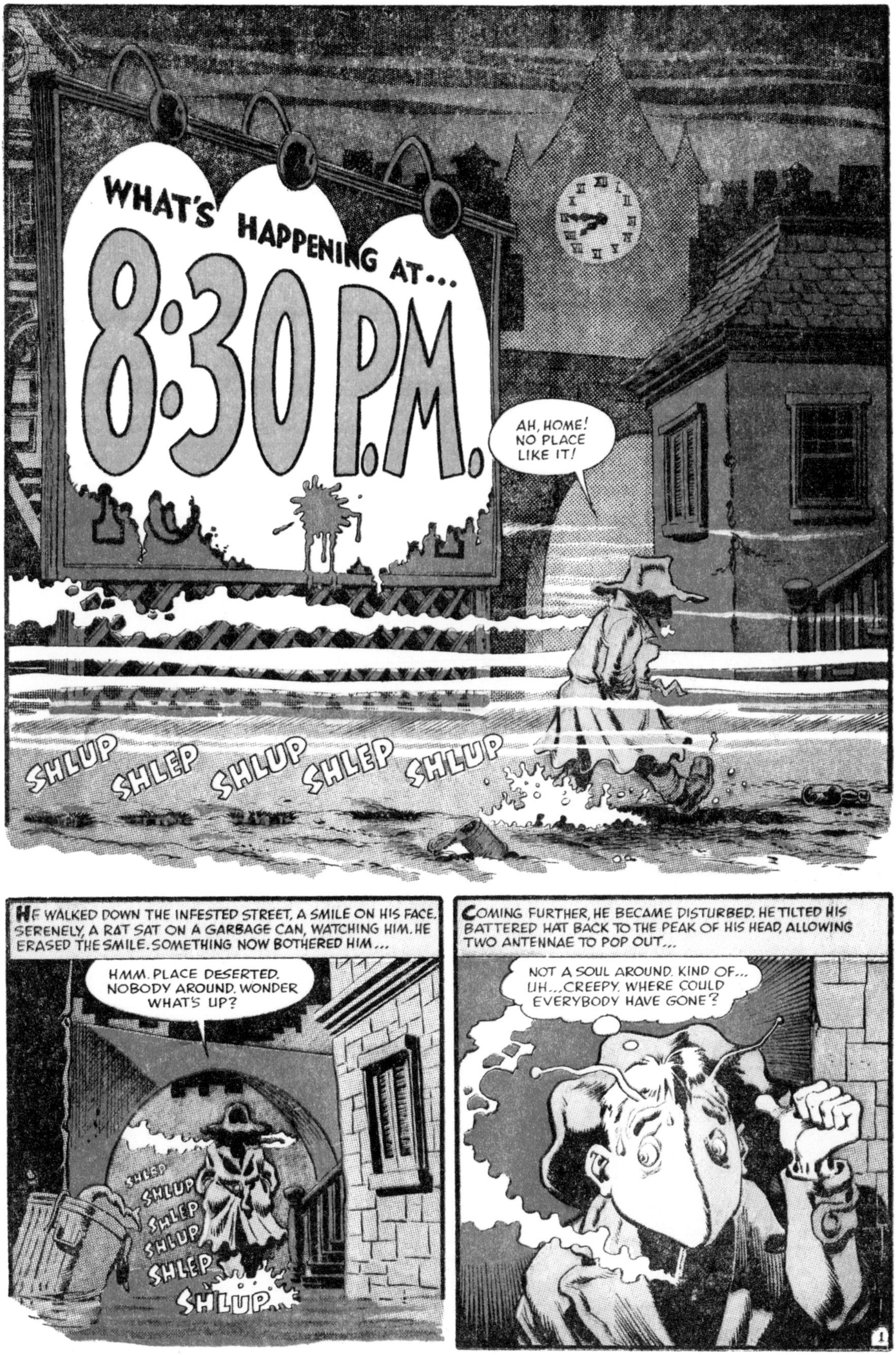
WHAT'S HAPPENING AT... 8:30 P.M.
AH, HOME! NO PLACE LIKE IT!
SHLUP SHLEP SHLUP SHLEP SHLUP
HE WALKED DOWN THE INFESTED STREET, A SMILE ON HIS FACE. SERENELY, A RAT SAT ON A GARBAGE CAN, WATCHING HIM. HE ERASED THE SMILE. SOMETHING NOW BOTHERED HIM...
HMM. PLACE DESERTED. NOBODY AROUND. WONDER WHAT'S UP?
SHLEP SHLUP SHLEP SHLUP SHLEP SHLUP
COMING FURTHER, HE BECAME DISTURBED. HE TILTED HIS BATTERED HAT BACK TO THE PEAK OF HIS HEAD, ALLOWING TWO ANTENNAE TO POP OUT...
NOT A SOUL AROUND. KIND OF... UH...CREEPY. WHERE COULD EVERYBODY HAVE GONE?
1

EVEN AS HE ROUNDED A CORNER, FACING A DILAPIDATED STREET, THERE WAS A STILLNESS AND AN EMPTINESS THAT DISTURBED HIM. SUDDENLY, A SHAFT OF LIGHT PEEKED DOWN. A YOUNG BOY WAS LOOKING OUT, TOWARDS HIM...

HEY!

QUICKLY, AS IF TERROR WERE GOADING HER, THE BOY'S MOTHER PULLED HIM AWAY...

TOMMY! WHAT'S THE MATTER WITH YOU? DON'T STAY THERE!

TWO SHUTTERS SLAMMED, KNIFING THE SHAFT OF LIGHT INTO DARKNESS...

WHAT GIVES HERE?

SLAM!

PERPLEXED, AGITATED BY THE EMPTINESS THAT HUNG LIKE A SHROUD OVER EVERY STREET HE WALKED UPON, THE MAN SEEMED TO WANDER AIMLESSLY. A BELFRY CLOCK SOMEWHERE TOLLED EIGHT TIMES...

BONG BONG BONG BONG BONG BONG BONG BONG

SHLEP SHLUP
SHLEP SHLUP
SHLEP SHLUP

THEN HE STOPPED, A CREASE OF A SMILE EASING INTO HIS FACE. A SHORT DISTANCE AWAY WAS A MAN, WARMING HIMSELF BY A BRIGHT, ORANGE FIRE...

WELL, HALLELUJAH! A PERSON!

HE DIDN'T KNOW WHY HE SHUFFLED SILENTLY TO THE FIRE. IT JUST SEEMED TO FIT THE VILLAGE'S FOREBODING TONE. SLOWLY, HE TAPPED THE MAN ON THE SHOULDER. THE MAN TURNED AROUND, THE LOOK OF FEAR ON HIS FACE...

UM, EXCUSE ME.

TAP TAP

YOOOUU!!

HE EXPLAINED, WANTING TO KNOW WHERE EVERYBODY WAS. THE STRANGER EASED UP A LITTLE, STILL SLIGHTLY CAUTIOUS HE WAS INVITED TO SIT DOWN. THE FIRE'S GLOW WAS WARM...

SURE, IT'S LONELY, BUSTER! YOU BETTER SIT DOWN. DON'T YOU KNOW WHAT'S HAPPENING AT 8:30 PM?!

THANKS, WHAT DO YOU MEAN... 8:30?!! WHAT'S GOING ON? WHAT'S HAPPENING?!!

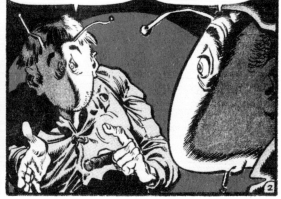

266

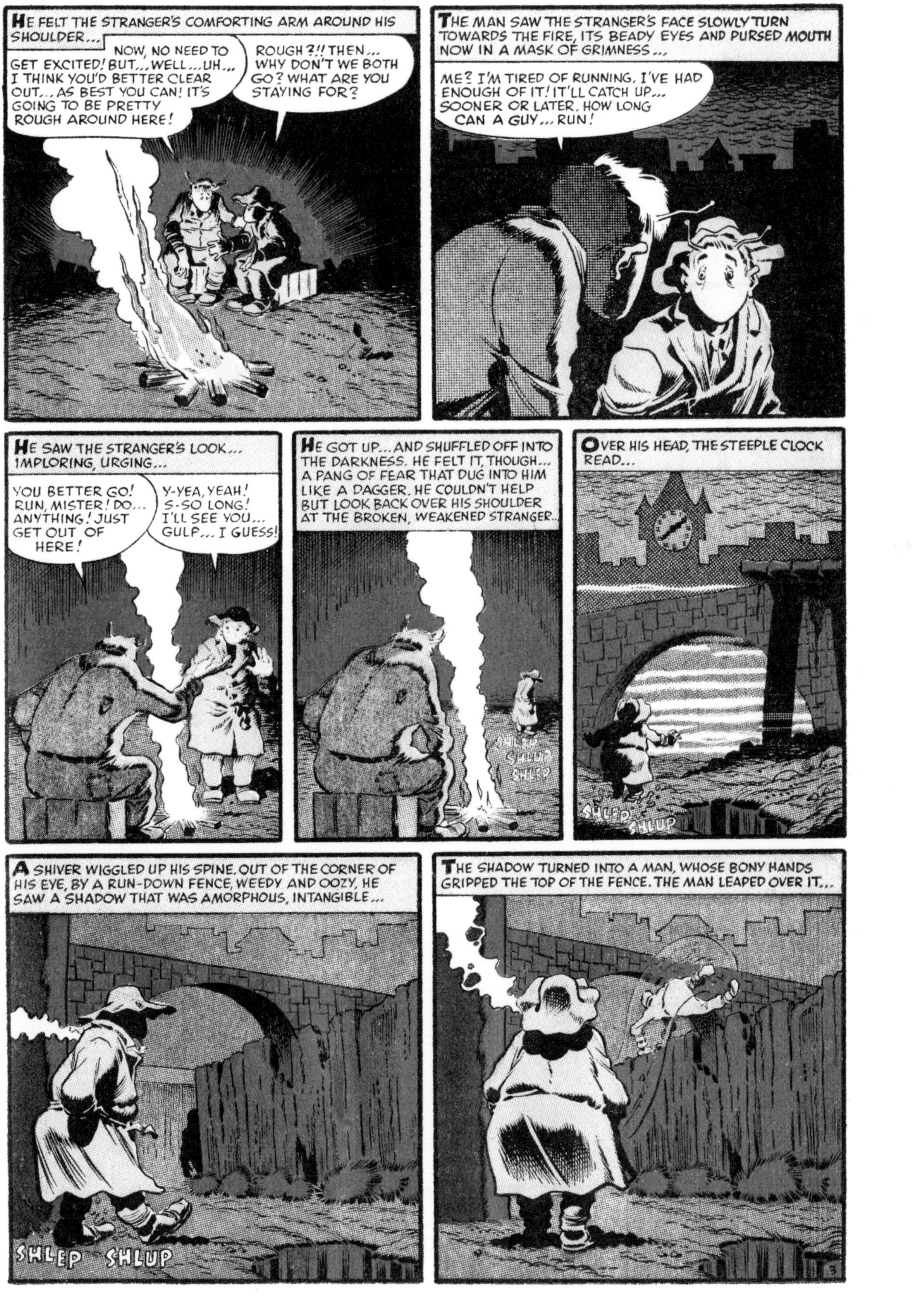
HE FELT THE STRANGER'S COMFORTING ARM AROUND HIS SHOULDER...
NOW, NO NEED TO GET EXCITED! BUT... WELL... UH... I THINK YOU'D BETTER CLEAR OUT... AS BEST YOU CAN! IT'S GOING TO BE PRETTY ROUGH AROUND HERE!
ROUGH?!! THEN... WHY DON'T WE BOTH GO? WHAT ARE YOU STAYING FOR?
THE MAN SAW THE STRANGER'S FACE SLOWLY TURN TOWARDS THE FIRE, ITS BEADY EYES AND PURSED MOUTH NOW IN A MASK OF GRIMNESS...
ME? I'M TIRED OF RUNNING. I'VE HAD ENOUGH OF IT! IT'LL CATCH UP... SOONER OR LATER. HOW LONG CAN A GUY... RUN!
HE SAW THE STRANGER'S LOOK... IMPLORING, URGING...
YOU BETTER GO! RUN, MISTER! DO... ANYTHING! JUST GET OUT OF HERE!
Y-YEA, YEAH! S-SO LONG! I'LL SEE YOU... GULP... I GUESS!
HE GOT UP... AND SHUFFLED OFF INTO THE DARKNESS. HE FELT IT, THOUGH... A PANG OF FEAR THAT DUG INTO HIM LIKE A DAGGER. HE COULDN'T HELP BUT LOOK BACK OVER HIS SHOULDER AT THE BROKEN, WEAKENED STRANGER...
SHLUP
SHLEP
OVER HIS HEAD, THE STEEPLE CLOCK READ...
SHLEP SHLUP
A SHIVER WIGGLED UP HIS SPINE. OUT OF THE CORNER OF HIS EYE, BY A RUN-DOWN FENCE, WEEDY AND OOZY, HE SAW A SHADOW THAT WAS AMORPHOUS, INTANGIBLE...
SHLEP SHLUP
THE SHADOW TURNED INTO A MAN, WHOSE BONY HANDS GRIPPED THE TOP OF THE FENCE. THE MAN LEAPED OVER IT...

THE GUY WAS RUNNING. HE WAS SURE OF IT. SUDDENLY, HE FELT A SCURRYING BEHIND HIM AND THE TRAMPLE OF FEET MOVING RAPIDLY... HE WHIRLED...

SHLOP
SHLOP SHLUP
SHLOP SHLUP SHLOP

SOMETHING WAS HAPPENING. IT WAS LIKE A SNOWBALL ON A HILL, ROLLING DOWNWARD AND GETTING BIGGER. SOMEBODY ELSE BRUSHED BY HIM...AND RAN OFF...

HE PUT HIS GRIMY FINGERNAILS TO HIS MOUTH. SWEAT BEADS FORMED ON HIS INKY BROW. FEAR:...COLD AND ABSOLUTE ...CHOKED HIM, KNOTTING HIS THROAT IN AN UNCONSUMING BALL...

LORD...LORD...!

AND... HE BEGAN TO RUN...

SHLEP SHLEP
SHLUP SHLUP
SHLEP
SHLUP
SHLEP SHLEP
SHLUP
SHLEP SHLUP
SHLEP SHLEP
SHLUP.

BUT,... HE DIDN'T KNOW WHERE TO GO. EVERY AVENUE SEEMED BLOCKED, EVERY DIRECTION SEEMED TO END IN A MAZE. HE HEADED FOR AN ALLEY, TRIPPING OVER AN ASH-CAN. THE METALLIC DIN RESOUNDED IN CLAMOR...

CRASSHH!

SHLEP
SHLUP SHLEP
SHLUP SHLEP
SHLUP SHLEP
SHLUP SHLEP

HE VEERED, SLUSHING AWAY FROM A RED GLASS EYE, AND RAN WITH INCREASED FERVOR. HE CHURNED THE GROUND BENEATH HIM IN HUGE GLOBS OF WETNESS, HEADING INTO DARKNESS AND BLIND DIRECTION...

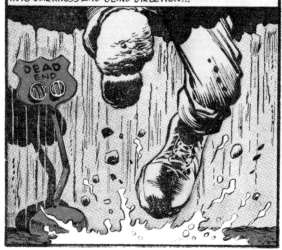

DEAD END

UNTIL HE FACED AN EMPTY FETID STREET. HE STOOD ALONE... HORRIBLY ALONE... IN THE MUCK THAT HAD THE SWEET SCENT OF HOME...

WH-WHERE CAN I GO? WHY AM I RUNNING? WHAT THE BLAZES IS GOING ON, ANY HOW?

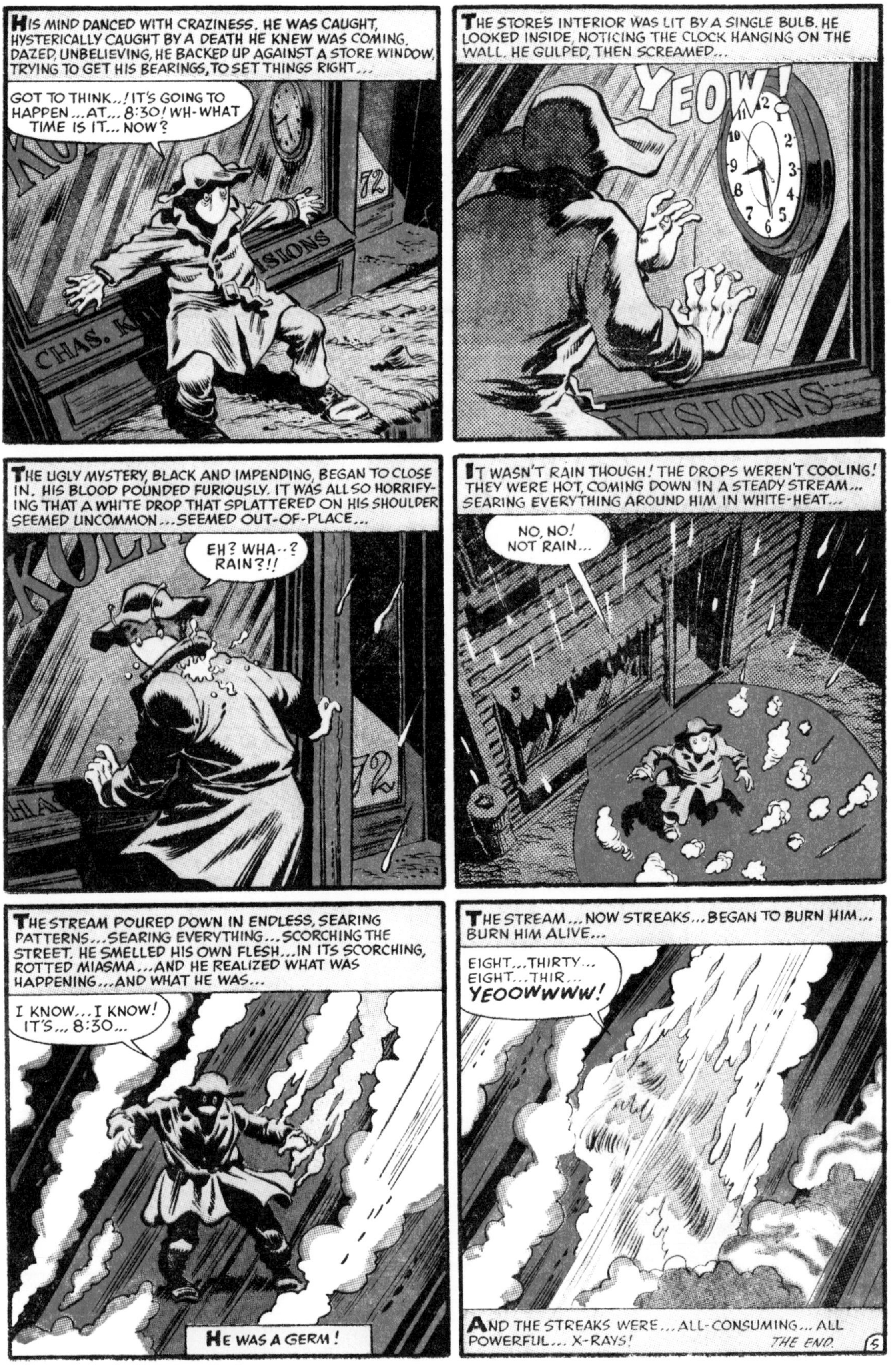
HIS MIND DANCED WITH CRAZINESS. HE WAS CAUGHT, HYSTERICALLY CAUGHT BY A DEATH HE KNEW WAS COMING. DAZED, UNBELIEVING, HE BACKED UP AGAINST A STORE WINDOW, TRYING TO GET HIS BEARINGS, TO SET THINGS RIGHT...
GOT TO THINK..! IT'S GOING TO HAPPEN...AT...8:30! WH-WHAT TIME IS IT...NOW?
72
CHAS. K
VISIONS
THE STORE'S INTERIOR WAS LIT BY A SINGLE BULB. HE LOOKED INSIDE, NOTICING THE CLOCK HANGING ON THE WALL. HE GULPED, THEN SCREAMED...
YEOW!
VISIONS
THE UGLY MYSTERY, BLACK AND IMPENDING, BEGAN TO CLOSE IN. HIS BLOOD POUNDED FURIOUSLY. IT WAS ALL SO HORRIFYING THAT A WHITE DROP THAT SPLATTERED ON HIS SHOULDER SEEMED UNCOMMON...SEEMED OUT-OF-PLACE...
EH? WHA--? RAIN?!!
72
IT WASN'T RAIN THOUGH! THE DROPS WEREN'T COOLING! THEY WERE HOT, COMING DOWN IN A STEADY STREAM... SEARING EVERYTHING AROUND HIM IN WHITE-HEAT...
NO, NO! NOT RAIN...
THE STREAM POURED DOWN IN ENDLESS, SEARING PATTERNS...SEARING EVERYTHING...SCORCHING THE STREET. HE SMELLED HIS OWN FLESH...IN ITS SCORCHING, ROTTED MIASMA...AND HE REALIZED WHAT WAS HAPPENING...AND WHAT HE WAS...
I KNOW...I KNOW! IT'S...8:30...
HE WAS A GERM!
THE STREAM...NOW STREAKS...BEGAN TO BURN HIM... BURN HIM ALIVE...
EIGHT...THIRTY... EIGHT...THIR... YEOOWWWW!
AND THE STREAKS WERE...ALL-CONSUMING...ALL POWERFUL...X-RAYS!
THE END.
5

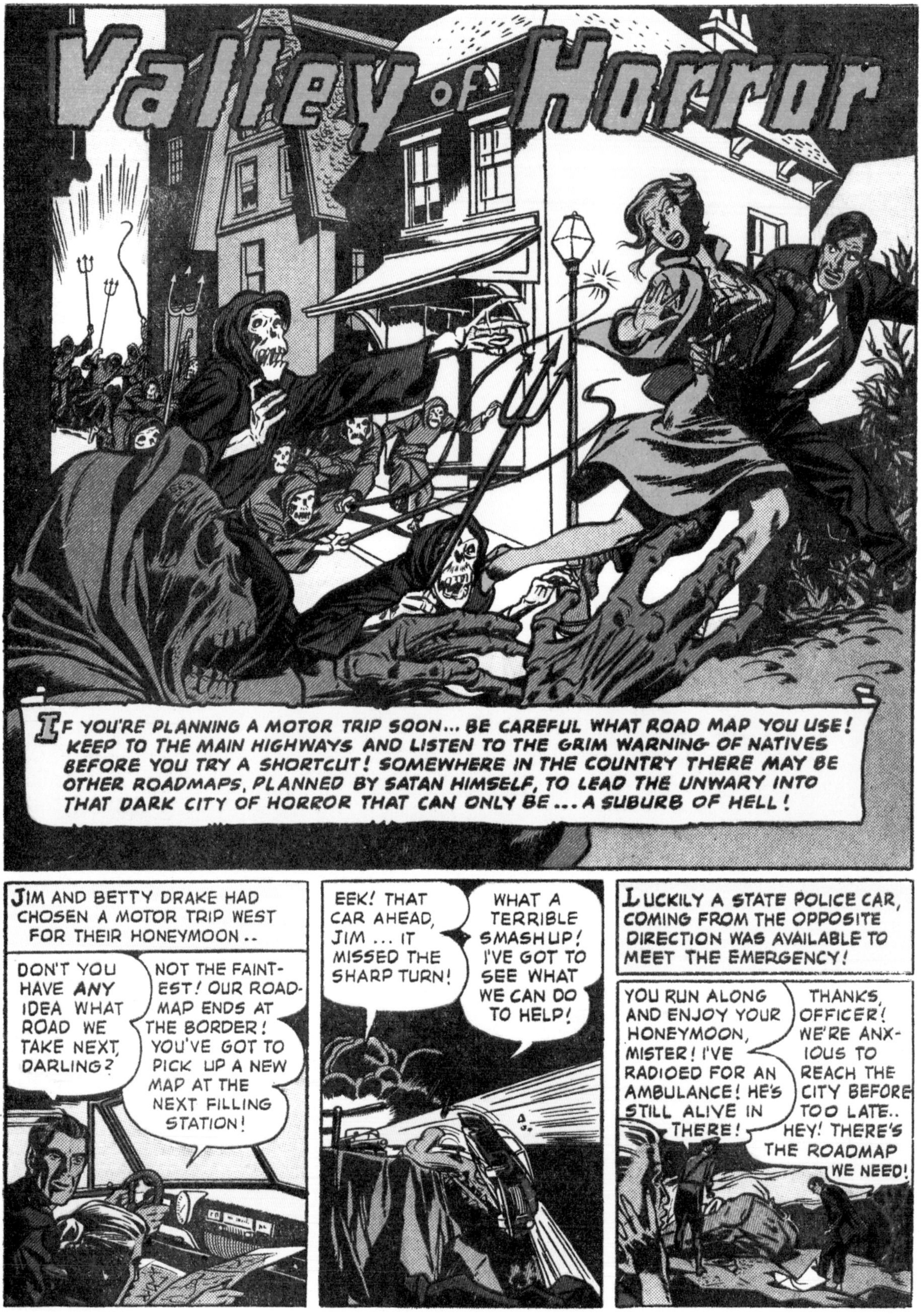
Valley of Horror
If you're planning a motor trip soon... be careful what road map you use! Keep to the main highways and listen to the grim warning of natives before you try a shortcut! Somewhere in the country there may be other roadmaps, planned by Satan himself, to lead the unwary into that dark city of horror that can only be ... a suburb of hell!
Jim and Betty Drake had chosen a motor trip west for their honeymoon..
Don't you have any idea what road we take next, darling?
Not the faintest! Our roadmap ends at the border! You've got to pick up a new map at the next filling station!
Eek! That car ahead, Jim ... it missed the sharp turn!
What a terrible smashup! I've got to see what we can do to help!
Luckily a state police car, coming from the opposite direction was available to meet the emergency!
You run along and enjoy your honeymoon, mister! I've radioed for an ambulance! He's still alive in there!
Thanks, officer! We're anxious to reach the city before too late.. Hey! There's the roadmap we need!

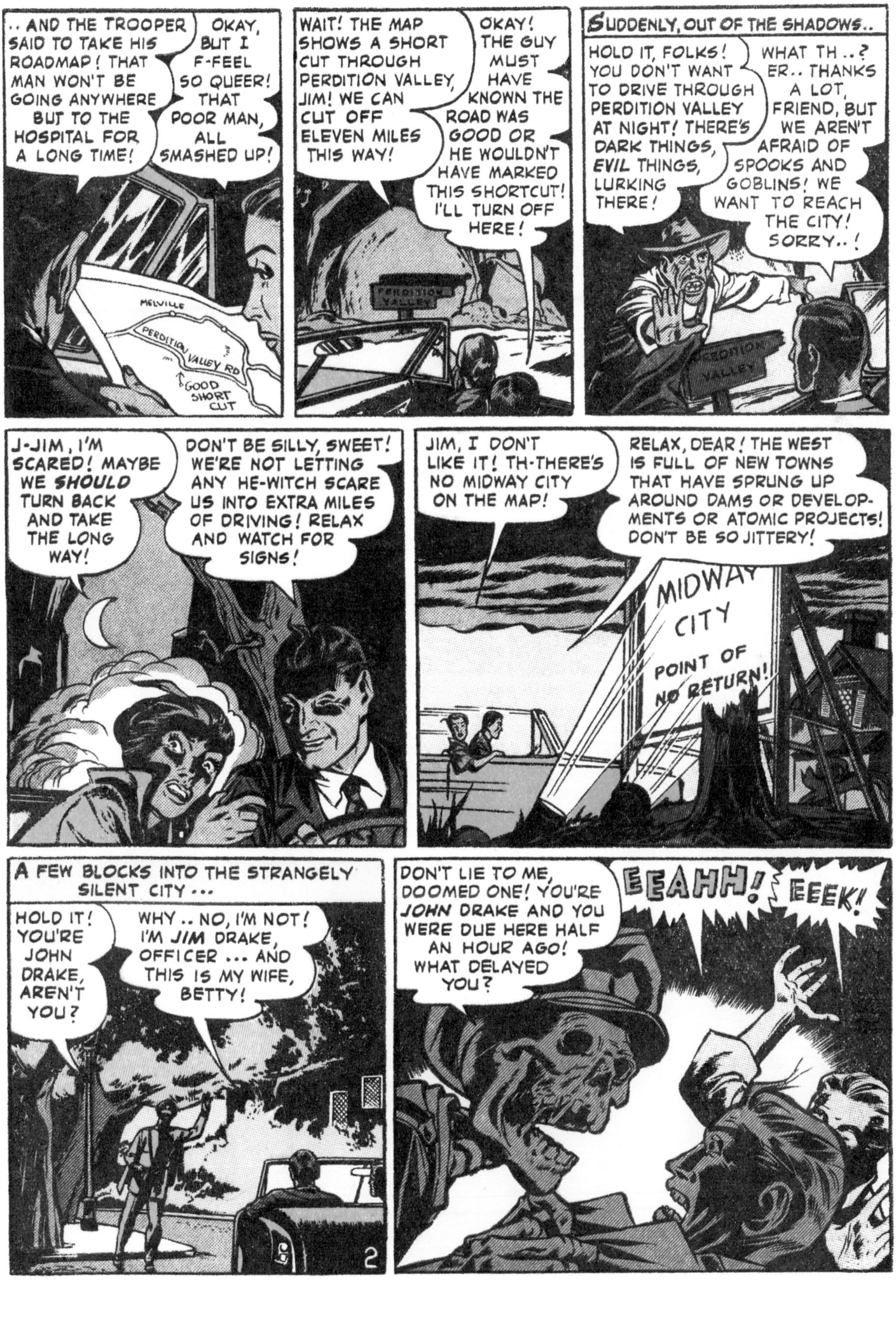
.. AND THE TROOPER SAID TO TAKE HIS ROADMAP! THAT MAN WON'T BE GOING ANYWHERE BUT TO THE HOSPITAL FOR A LONG TIME!
OKAY, BUT I F-FEEL SO QUEER! THAT POOR MAN, ALL SMASHED UP!
MELVILLE
PERDITION VALLEY RD
GOOD SHORT CUT
WAIT! THE MAP SHOWS A SHORT CUT THROUGH PERDITION VALLEY, JIM! WE CAN CUT OFF ELEVEN MILES THIS WAY!
OKAY! THE GUY MUST HAVE KNOWN THE ROAD WAS GOOD OR HE WOULDN'T HAVE MARKED THIS SHORTCUT! I'LL TURN OFF HERE!
SUDDENLY, OUT OF THE SHADOWS..
HOLD IT, FOLKS! YOU DON'T WANT TO DRIVE THROUGH PERDITION VALLEY AT NIGHT! THERE'S DARK THINGS, EVIL THINGS, LURKING THERE!
WHAT TH ..? ER.. THANKS A LOT, FRIEND, BUT WE AREN'T AFRAID OF SPOOKS AND GOBLINS! WE WANT TO REACH THE CITY! SORRY..!
J-JIM, I'M SCARED! MAYBE WE SHOULD TURN BACK AND TAKE THE LONG WAY!
DON'T BE SILLY, SWEET! WE'RE NOT LETTING ANY HE-WITCH SCARE US INTO EXTRA MILES OF DRIVING! RELAX AND WATCH FOR SIGNS!
JIM, I DON'T LIKE IT! TH-THERE'S NO MIDWAY CITY ON THE MAP!
RELAX, DEAR! THE WEST IS FULL OF NEW TOWNS THAT HAVE SPRUNG UP AROUND DAMS OR DEVELOPMENTS OR ATOMIC PROJECTS! DON'T BE SO JITTERY!
MIDWAY CITY
POINT OF NO RETURN!
A FEW BLOCKS INTO THE STRANGELY SILENT CITY ...
HOLD IT! YOU'RE JOHN DRAKE, AREN'T YOU?
WHY .. NO, I'M NOT! I'M JIM DRAKE, OFFICER ... AND THIS IS MY WIFE, BETTY!
2
DON'T LIE TO ME, DOOMED ONE! YOU'RE JOHN DRAKE AND YOU WERE DUE HERE HALF AN HOUR AGO! WHAT DELAYED YOU?
EEAHH!
EEEK!

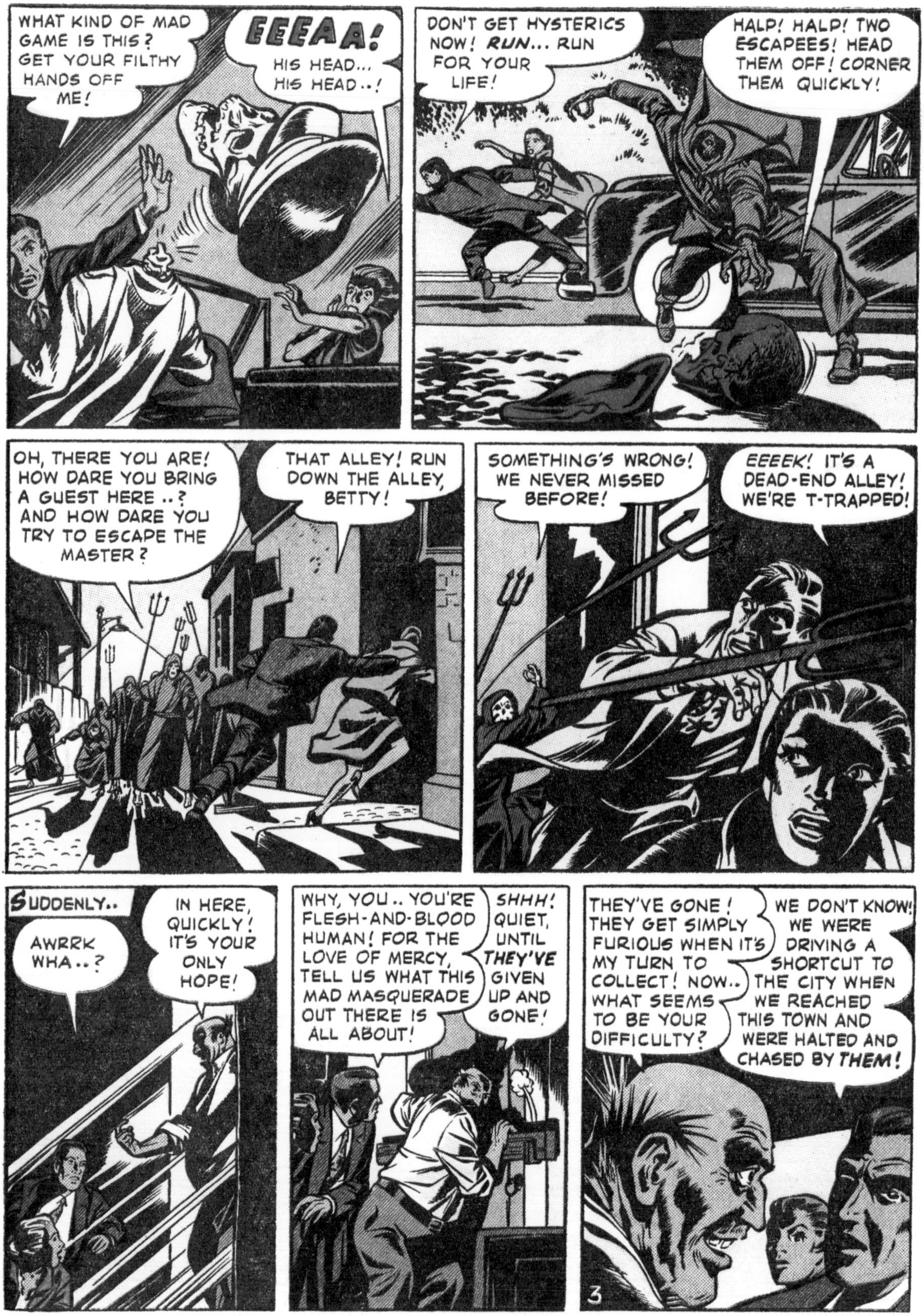

WHAT KIND OF MAD GAME IS THIS? GET YOUR FILTHY HANDS OFF ME!
EEEAA!
HIS HEAD... HIS HEAD..!
DON'T GET HYSTERICS NOW! RUN... RUN FOR YOUR LIFE!
HALP! HALP! TWO ESCAPEES! HEAD THEM OFF! CORNER THEM QUICKLY!
OH, THERE YOU ARE! HOW DARE YOU BRING A GUEST HERE..? AND HOW DARE YOU TRY TO ESCAPE THE MASTER?
THAT ALLEY! RUN DOWN THE ALLEY, BETTY!
SOMETHING'S WRONG! WE NEVER MISSED BEFORE!
EEEEK! IT'S A DEAD-END ALLEY! WE'RE T-TRAPPED!
SUDDENLY..
AWRRK WHA..?
IN HERE, QUICKLY! IT'S YOUR ONLY HOPE!
WHY, YOU.. YOU'RE FLESH-AND-BLOOD HUMAN! FOR THE LOVE OF MERCY, TELL US WHAT THIS MAD MASQUERADE OUT THERE IS ALL ABOUT!
SHHH! QUIET, UNTIL THEY'VE GIVEN UP AND GONE!
THEY'VE GONE! THEY GET SIMPLY FURIOUS WHEN IT'S MY TURN TO COLLECT! NOW.. WHAT SEEMS TO BE YOUR DIFFICULTY?
WE DON'T KNOW! WE WERE DRIVING A SHORTCUT TO THE CITY WHEN WE REACHED THIS TOWN AND WERE HALTED AND CHASED BY THEM!
3

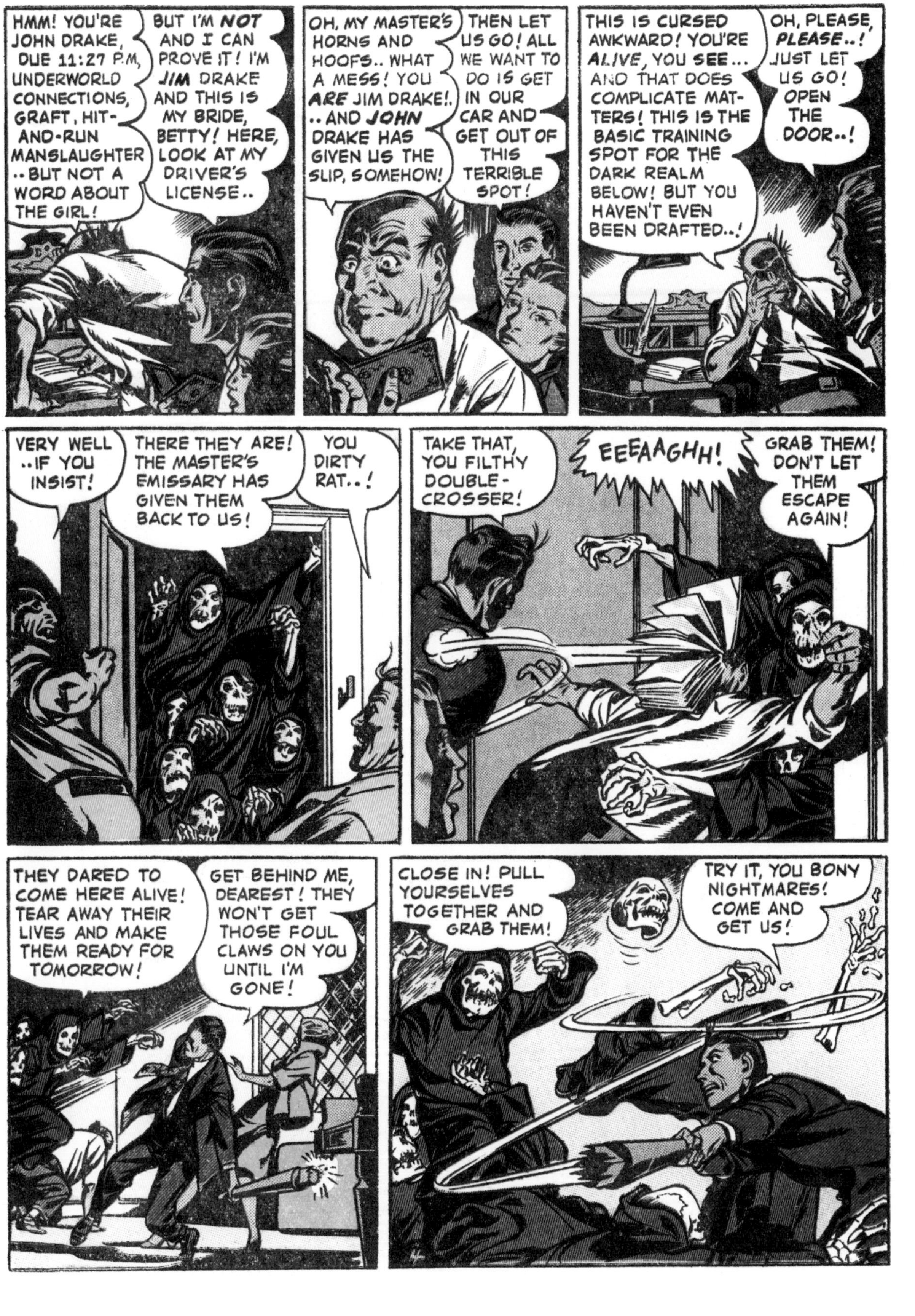
HMM! YOU'RE JOHN DRAKE, DUE 11:27 P.M, UNDERWORLD CONNECTIONS, GRAFT, HIT-AND-RUN MANSLAUGHTER ..BUT NOT A WORD ABOUT THE GIRL!
BUT I'M NOT AND I CAN PROVE IT! I'M JIM DRAKE AND THIS IS MY BRIDE, BETTY! HERE, LOOK AT MY DRIVER'S LICENSE..
OH, MY MASTER'S HORNS AND HOOFS.. WHAT A MESS! YOU ARE JIM DRAKE!. ..AND JOHN DRAKE HAS GIVEN US THE SLIP, SOMEHOW!
THEN LET US GO! ALL WE WANT TO DO IS GET IN OUR CAR AND GET OUT OF THIS TERRIBLE SPOT!
THIS IS CURSED AWKWARD! YOU'RE ALIVE, YOU SEE... AND THAT DOES COMPLICATE MATTERS! THIS IS THE BASIC TRAINING SPOT FOR THE DARK REALM BELOW! BUT YOU HAVEN'T EVEN BEEN DRAFTED..!
OH, PLEASE, PLEASE..! JUST LET US GO! OPEN THE DOOR..!
VERY WELL ..IF YOU INSIST!
THERE THEY ARE! THE MASTER'S EMISSARY HAS GIVEN THEM BACK TO US!
YOU DIRTY RAT..!
TAKE THAT, YOU FILTHY DOUBLE-CROSSER!
EEEAAGHH!
GRAB THEM! DON'T LET THEM ESCAPE AGAIN!
THEY DARED TO COME HERE ALIVE! TEAR AWAY THEIR LIVES AND MAKE THEM READY FOR TOMORROW!
GET BEHIND ME, DEAREST! THEY WON'T GET THOSE FOUL CLAWS ON YOU UNTIL I'M GONE!
CLOSE IN! PULL YOURSELVES TOGETHER AND GRAB THEM!
TRY IT, YOU BONY NIGHTMARES! COME AND GET US!

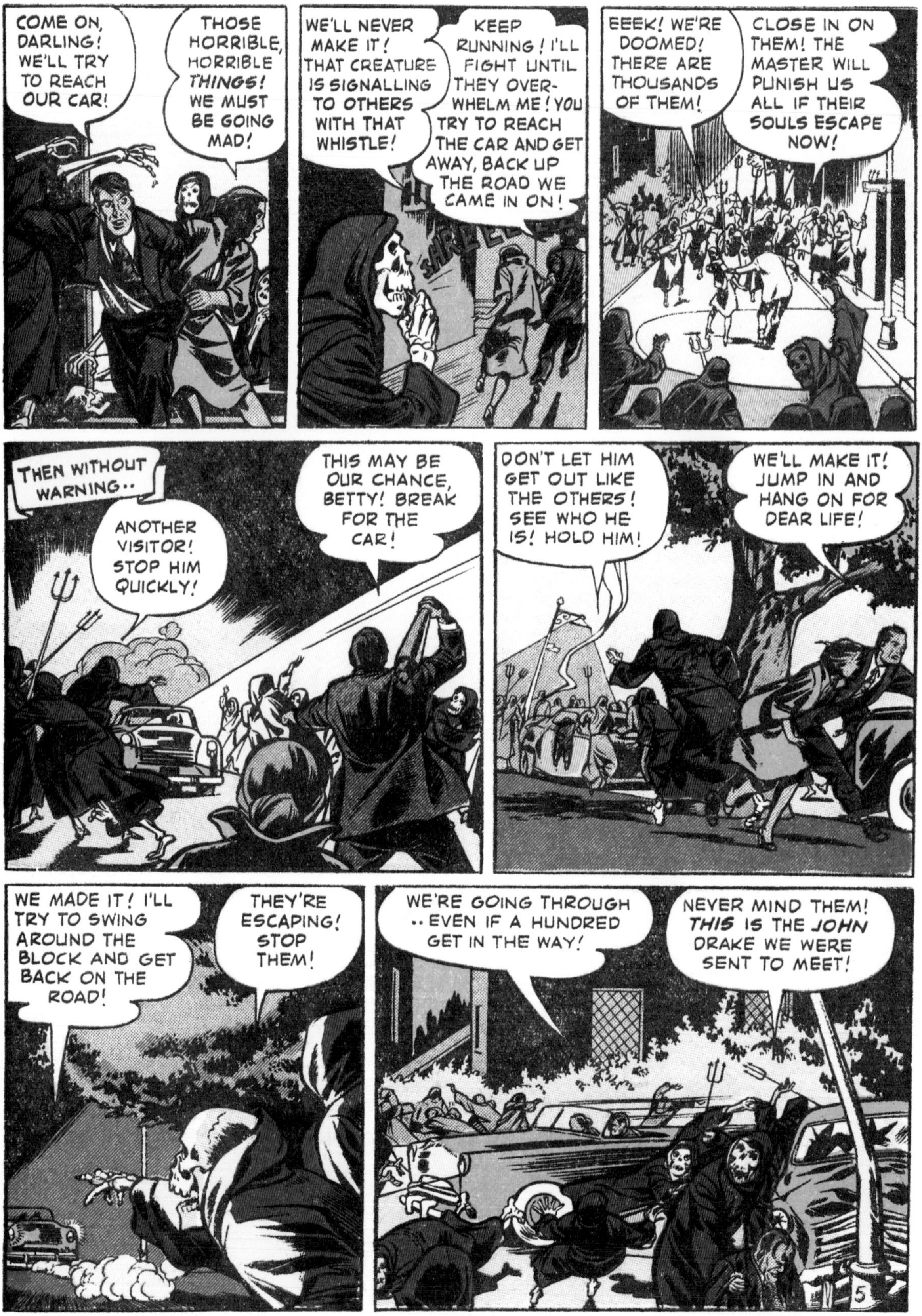
COME ON, DARLING! WE'LL TRY TO REACH OUR CAR!
THOSE HORRIBLE, HORRIBLE THINGS! WE MUST BE GOING MAD!
WE'LL NEVER MAKE IT! THAT CREATURE IS SIGNALLING TO OTHERS WITH THAT WHISTLE!
KEEP RUNNING! I'LL FIGHT UNTIL THEY OVER-WHELM ME! YOU TRY TO REACH THE CAR AND GET AWAY, BACK UP THE ROAD WE CAME IN ON!
SHREEEE
EEEK! WE'RE DOOMED! THERE ARE THOUSANDS OF THEM!
CLOSE IN ON THEM! THE MASTER WILL PUNISH US ALL IF THEIR SOULS ESCAPE NOW!
THEN WITHOUT WARNING..
ANOTHER VISITOR! STOP HIM QUICKLY!
THIS MAY BE OUR CHANCE, BETTY! BREAK FOR THE CAR!
DON'T LET HIM GET OUT LIKE THE OTHERS! SEE WHO HE IS! HOLD HIM!
WE'LL MAKE IT! JUMP IN AND HANG ON FOR DEAR LIFE!
WE MADE IT! I'LL TRY TO SWING AROUND THE BLOCK AND GET BACK ON THE ROAD!
THEY'RE ESCAPING! STOP THEM!
WE'RE GOING THROUGH ..EVEN IF A HUNDRED GET IN THE WAY!
NEVER MIND THEM! THIS IS THE JOHN DRAKE WE WERE SENT TO MEET!
5

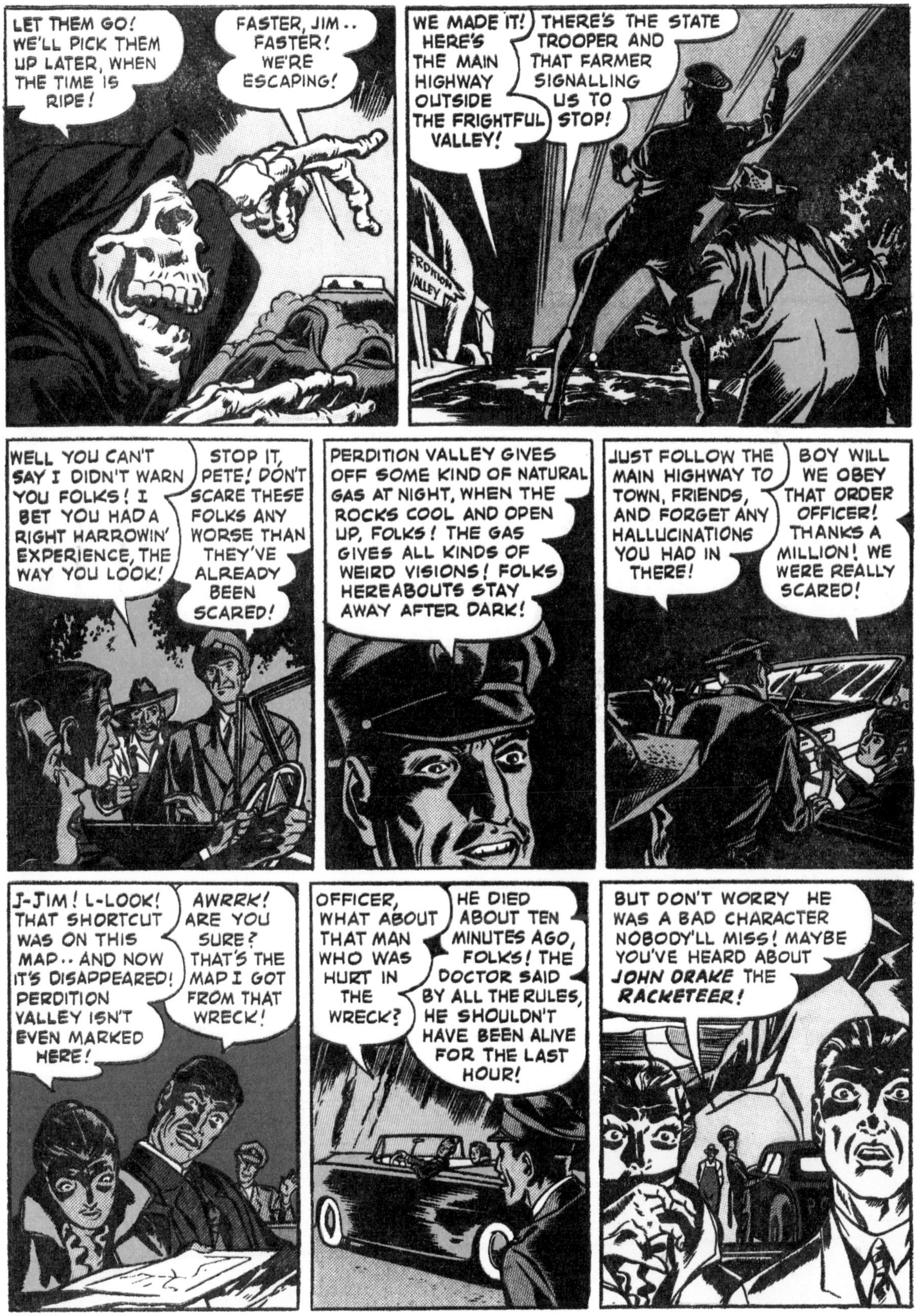
LET THEM GO! WE'LL PICK THEM UP LATER, WHEN THE TIME IS RIPE!
FASTER, JIM.. FASTER! WE'RE ESCAPING!
WE MADE IT! HERE'S THE MAIN HIGHWAY OUTSIDE THE FRIGHTFUL VALLEY!
THERE'S THE STATE TROOPER AND THAT FARMER SIGNALLING US TO STOP!
WELL YOU CAN'T SAY I DIDN'T WARN YOU FOLKS! I BET YOU HAD A RIGHT HARROWIN' EXPERIENCE, THE WAY YOU LOOK!
STOP IT, PETE! DON'T SCARE THESE FOLKS ANY WORSE THAN THEY'VE ALREADY BEEN SCARED!
PERDITION VALLEY GIVES OFF SOME KIND OF NATURAL GAS AT NIGHT, WHEN THE ROCKS COOL AND OPEN UP, FOLKS! THE GAS GIVES ALL KINDS OF WEIRD VISIONS! FOLKS HEREABOUTS STAY AWAY AFTER DARK!
JUST FOLLOW THE MAIN HIGHWAY TO TOWN, FRIENDS, AND FORGET ANY HALLUCINATIONS YOU HAD IN THERE!
BOY WILL WE OBEY THAT ORDER OFFICER! THANKS A MILLION! WE WERE REALLY SCARED!
J-JIM! L-LOOK! THAT SHORTCUT WAS ON THIS MAP.. AND NOW IT'S DISAPPEARED! PERDITION VALLEY ISN'T EVEN MARKED HERE!
AWRRK! ARE YOU SURE? THAT'S THE MAP I GOT FROM THAT WRECK!
OFFICER, WHAT ABOUT THAT MAN WHO WAS HURT IN THE WRECK?
HE DIED ABOUT TEN MINUTES AGO, FOLKS! THE DOCTOR SAID BY ALL THE RULES, HE SHOULDN'T HAVE BEEN ALIVE FOR THE LAST HOUR!
BUT DON'T WORRY HE WAS A BAD CHARACTER NOBODY'LL MISS! MAYBE YOU'VE HEARD ABOUT JOHN DRAKE THE RACKETEER!

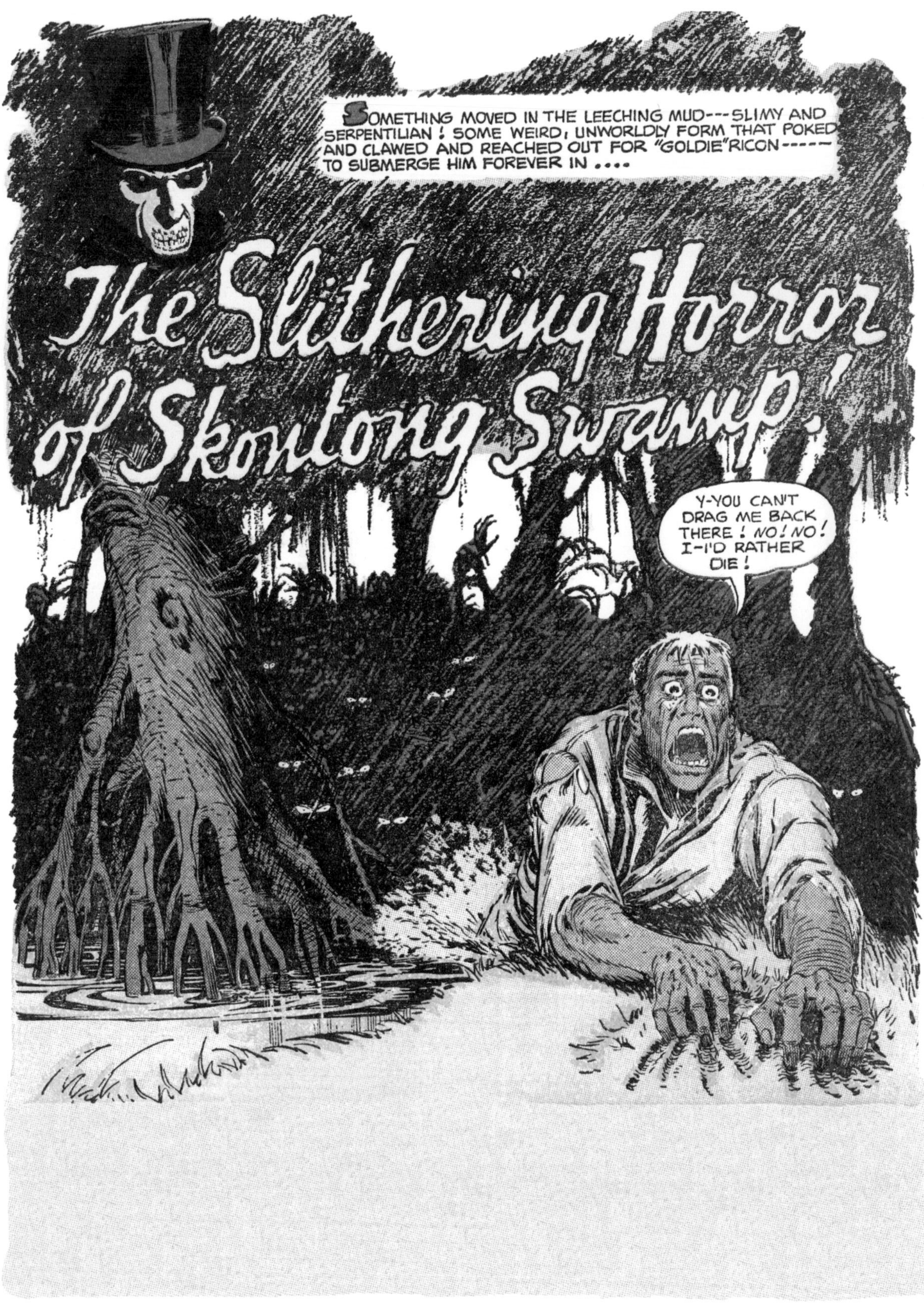
SOMETHING MOVED IN THE LEECHING MUD---SLIMY AND SERPENTILIAN! SOME WEIRD, UNWORLDLY FORM THAT POKED AND CLAWED AND REACHED OUT FOR "GOLDIE" RICON----- TO SUBMERGE HIM FOREVER IN ....
The Slithering Horror of Skontong Swamp!
Y-YOU CAN'T DRAG ME BACK THERE! NO! NO! I-I'D RATHER DIE!

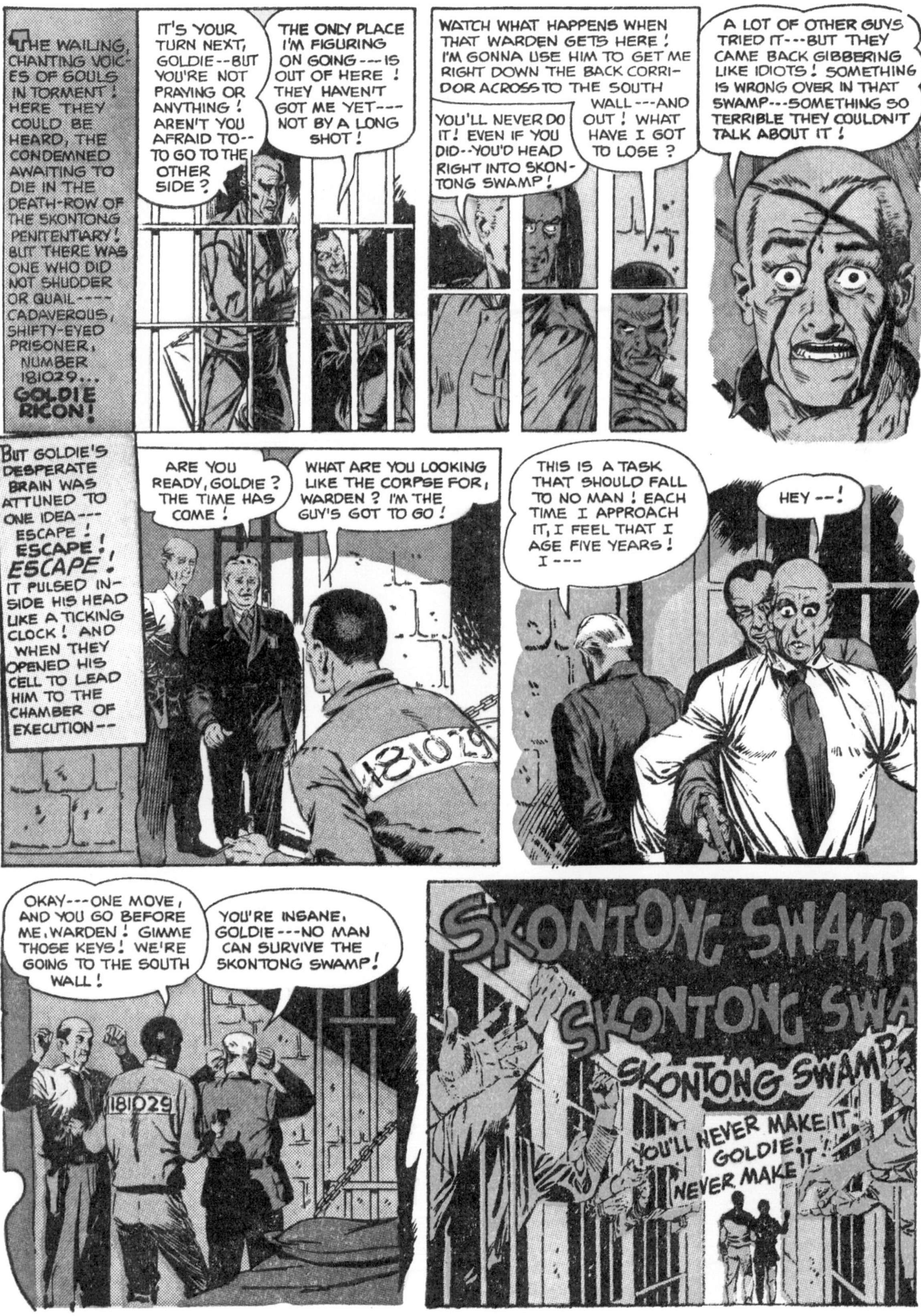
THE WAILING, CHANTING VOICES OF SOULS IN TORMENT! HERE THEY COULD BE HEARD, THE CONDEMNED AWAITING TO DIE IN THE DEATH-ROW OF THE SKONTONG PENITENTIARY! BUT THERE WAS ONE WHO DID NOT SHUDDER OR QUAIL---- CADAVEROUS, SHIFTY-EYED PRISONER, NUMBER 181029... GOLDIE RICON!
IT'S YOUR TURN NEXT, GOLDIE--BUT YOU'RE NOT PRAYING OR ANYTHING! AREN'T YOU AFRAID TO--TO GO TO THE OTHER SIDE?
THE ONLY PLACE I'M FIGURING ON GOING---IS OUT OF HERE! THEY HAVEN'T GOT ME YET---NOT BY A LONG SHOT!
WATCH WHAT HAPPENS WHEN THAT WARDEN GETS HERE! I'M GONNA USE HIM TO GET ME RIGHT DOWN THE BACK CORRIDOR ACROSS TO THE SOUTH WALL---AND OUT! WHAT HAVE I GOT TO LOSE?
YOU'LL NEVER DO IT! EVEN IF YOU DID--YOU'D HEAD RIGHT INTO SKONTONG SWAMP!
A LOT OF OTHER GUYS TRIED IT---BUT THEY CAME BACK GIBBERING LIKE IDIOTS! SOMETHING IS WRONG OVER IN THAT SWAMP---SOMETHING SO TERRIBLE THEY COULDN'T TALK ABOUT IT!
BUT GOLDIE'S DESPERATE BRAIN WAS ATTUNED TO ONE IDEA--- ESCAPE! ESCAPE! ESCAPE! IT PULSED INSIDE HIS HEAD LIKE A TICKING CLOCK! AND WHEN THEY OPENED HIS CELL TO LEAD HIM TO THE CHAMBER OF EXECUTION--
ARE YOU READY, GOLDIE? THE TIME HAS COME!
WHAT ARE YOU LOOKING LIKE THE CORPSE FOR, WARDEN? I'M THE GUY'S GOT TO GO!
181029
THIS IS A TASK THAT SHOULD FALL TO NO MAN! EACH TIME I APPROACH IT, I FEEL THAT I AGE FIVE YEARS! I---
HEY--!
OKAY---ONE MOVE, AND YOU GO BEFORE ME, WARDEN! GIMME THOSE KEYS! WE'RE GOING TO THE SOUTH WALL!
YOU'RE INSANE, GOLDIE---NO MAN CAN SURVIVE THE SKONTONG SWAMP!
181029
SKONTONG SWAMP
SKONTONG SWA
SKONTONG SWAMP
YOU'LL NEVER MAKE IT, GOLDIE! NEVER MAKE IT!

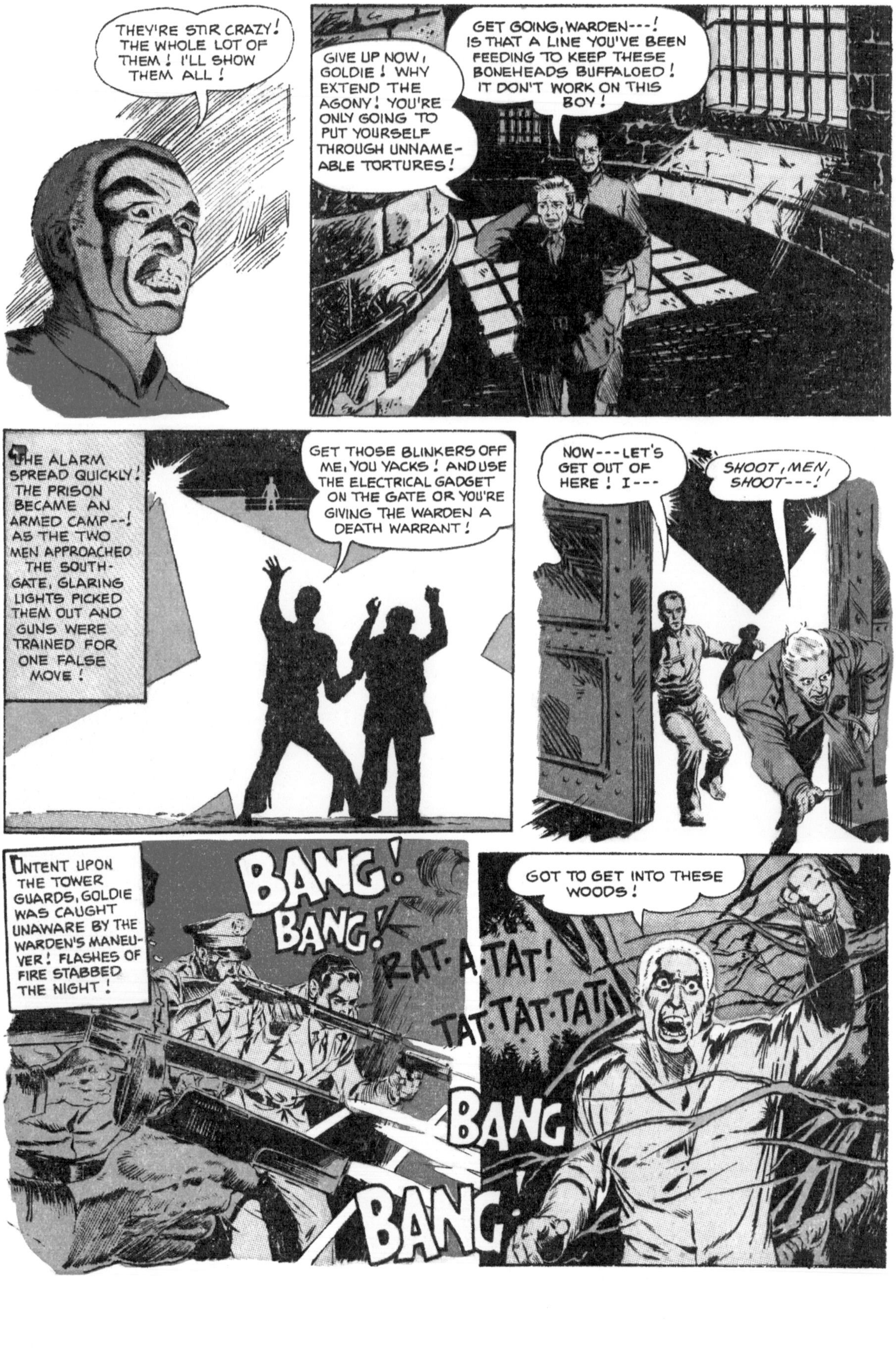
THEY'RE STIR CRAZY! THE WHOLE LOT OF THEM! I'LL SHOW THEM ALL!
GIVE UP NOW, GOLDIE! WHY EXTEND THE AGONY! YOU'RE ONLY GOING TO PUT YOURSELF THROUGH UNNAMEABLE TORTURES!
GET GOING, WARDEN---! IS THAT A LINE YOU'VE BEEN FEEDING TO KEEP THESE BONEHEADS BUFFALOED! IT DON'T WORK ON THIS BOY!
THE ALARM SPREAD QUICKLY! THE PRISON BECAME AN ARMED CAMP--! AS THE TWO MEN APPROACHED THE SOUTH-GATE, GLARING LIGHTS PICKED THEM OUT AND GUNS WERE TRAINED FOR ONE FALSE MOVE!
GET THOSE BLINKERS OFF ME, YOU YACKS! AND USE THE ELECTRICAL GADGET ON THE GATE OR YOU'RE GIVING THE WARDEN A DEATH WARRANT!
NOW---LET'S GET OUT OF HERE! I---
SHOOT, MEN, SHOOT---!
INTENT UPON THE TOWER GUARDS, GOLDIE WAS CAUGHT UNAWARE BY THE WARDEN'S MANEUVER! FLASHES OF FIRE STABBED THE NIGHT!
BANG!
BANG!
RAT-A-TAT!
TAT-TAT-TAT!
BANG
BANG!
GOT TO GET INTO THESE WOODS!

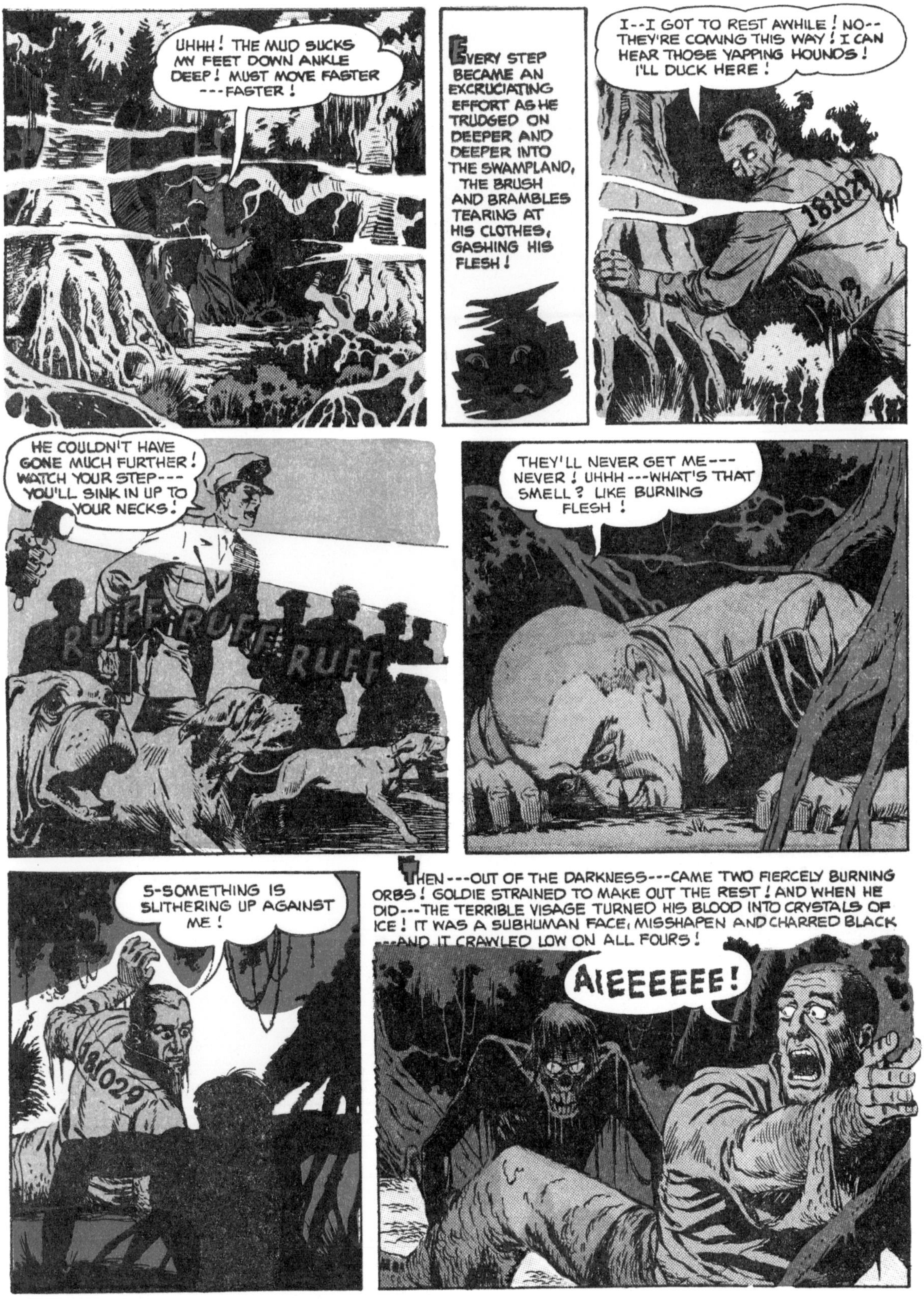
UHHH! THE MUD SUCKS MY FEET DOWN ANKLE DEEP! MUST MOVE FASTER ---FASTER!
EVERY STEP BECAME AN EXCRUCIATING EFFORT AS HE TRUDGED ON DEEPER AND DEEPER INTO THE SWAMPLAND, THE BRUSH AND BRAMBLES TEARING AT HIS CLOTHES, GASHING HIS FLESH!
I--I GOT TO REST AWHILE! NO--THEY'RE COMING THIS WAY! I CAN HEAR THOSE YAPPING HOUNDS! I'LL DUCK HERE!
18102
HE COULDN'T HAVE GONE MUCH FURTHER! WATCH YOUR STEP---YOU'LL SINK IN UP TO YOUR NECKS!
RUFF RUFF RUFF RUFF
THEY'LL NEVER GET ME---NEVER! UHHH---WHAT'S THAT SMELL? LIKE BURNING FLESH!
S-SOMETHING IS SLITHERING UP AGAINST ME!
181029
THEN---OUT OF THE DARKNESS---CAME TWO FIERCELY BURNING ORBS! GOLDIE STRAINED TO MAKE OUT THE REST! AND WHEN HE DID---THE TERRIBLE VISAGE TURNED HIS BLOOD INTO CRYSTALS OF ICE! IT WAS A SUBHUMAN FACE, MISSHAPEN AND CHARRED BLACK ---AND IT CRAWLED LOW ON ALL FOURS!
AIEEEEEE!

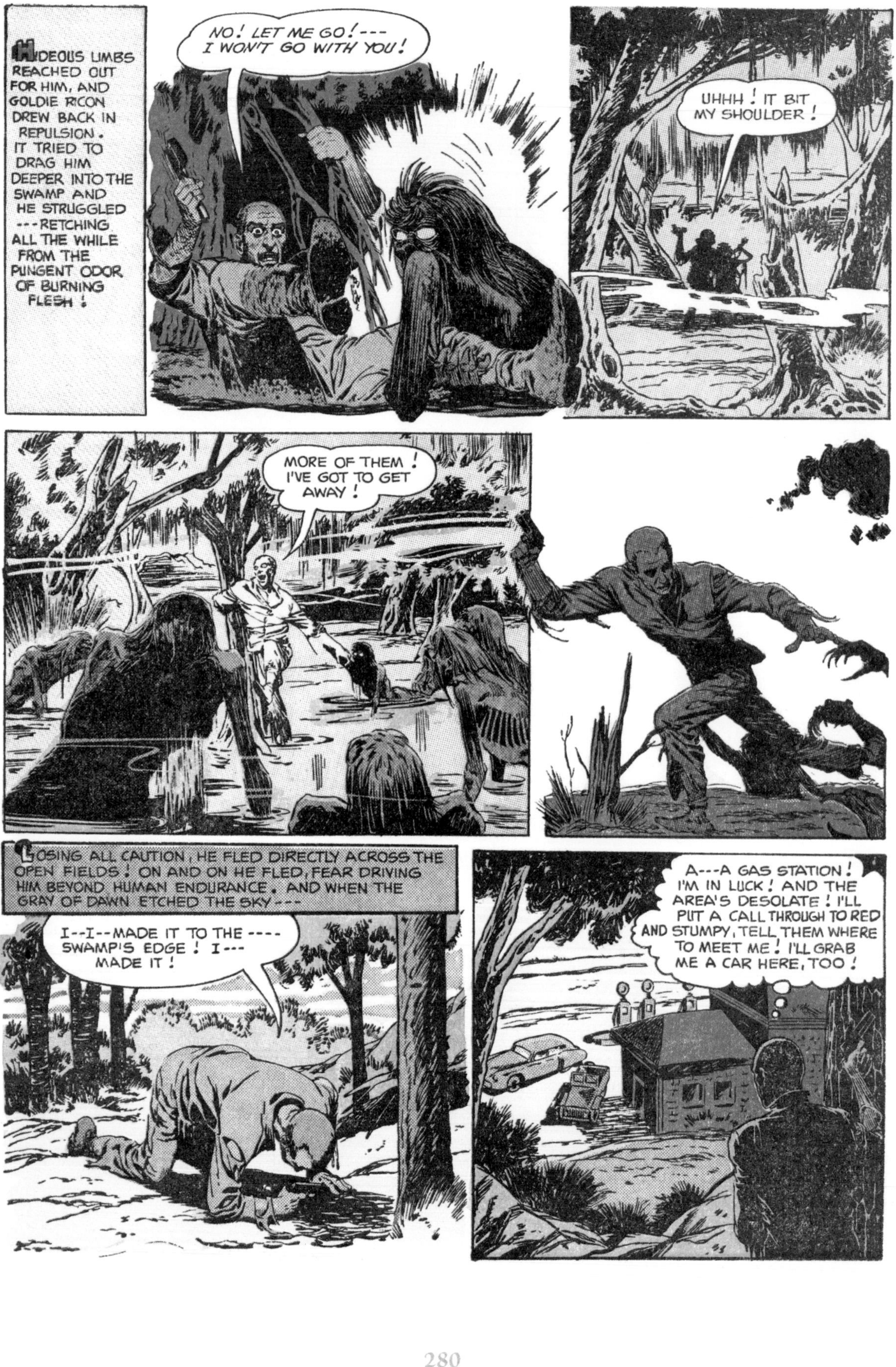
HIDEOUS LIMBS REACHED OUT FOR HIM, AND GOLDIE RICON DREW BACK IN REPULSION. IT TRIED TO DRAG HIM DEEPER INTO THE SWAMP AND HE STRUGGLED ---RETCHING ALL THE WHILE FROM THE PUNGENT ODOR OF BURNING FLESH!
NO! LET ME GO!--- I WON'T GO WITH YOU!
UHHH! IT BIT MY SHOULDER!
MORE OF THEM! I'VE GOT TO GET AWAY!
LOSING ALL CAUTION, HE FLED DIRECTLY ACROSS THE OPEN FIELDS! ON AND ON HE FLED, FEAR DRIVING HIM BEYOND HUMAN ENDURANCE. AND WHEN THE GRAY OF DAWN ETCHED THE SKY---
I--I--MADE IT TO THE---- SWAMP'S EDGE! I--- MADE IT!
A---A GAS STATION! I'M IN LUCK! AND THE AREA'S DESOLATE! I'LL PUT A CALL THROUGH TO RED AND STUMPY, TELL THEM WHERE TO MEET ME! I'LL GRAB ME A CAR HERE, TOO!

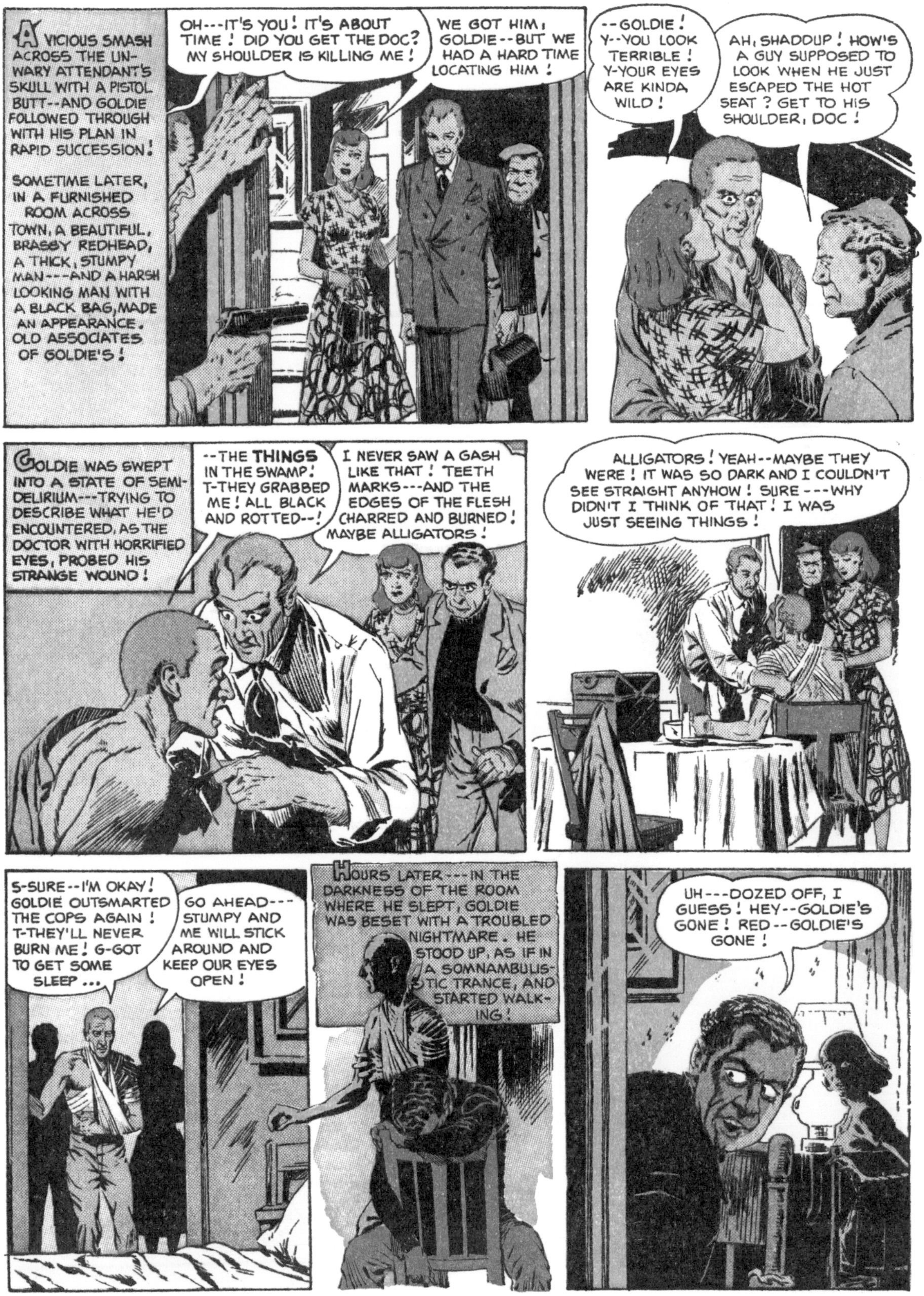
A VICIOUS SMASH ACROSS THE UNWARY ATTENDANT'S SKULL WITH A PISTOL BUTT--AND GOLDIE FOLLOWED THROUGH WITH HIS PLAN IN RAPID SUCCESSION!
SOMETIME LATER, IN A FURNISHED ROOM ACROSS TOWN, A BEAUTIFUL, BRASSY REDHEAD, A THICK, STUMPY MAN---AND A HARSH LOOKING MAN WITH A BLACK BAG, MADE AN APPEARANCE. OLD ASSOCIATES OF GOLDIE'S!
OH---IT'S YOU! IT'S ABOUT TIME! DID YOU GET THE DOC? MY SHOULDER IS KILLING ME!
WE GOT HIM, GOLDIE--BUT WE HAD A HARD TIME LOCATING HIM!
--GOLDIE! Y--YOU LOOK TERRIBLE! Y-YOUR EYES ARE KINDA WILD!
AH, SHADDUP! HOW'S A GUY SUPPOSED TO LOOK WHEN HE JUST ESCAPED THE HOT SEAT? GET TO HIS SHOULDER, DOC!
GOLDIE WAS SWEPT INTO A STATE OF SEMI-DELIRIUM---TRYING TO DESCRIBE WHAT HE'D ENCOUNTERED, AS THE DOCTOR WITH HORRIFIED EYES, PROBED HIS STRANGE WOUND!
--THE THINGS IN THE SWAMP! T-THEY GRABBED ME! ALL BLACK AND ROTTED--!
I NEVER SAW A GASH LIKE THAT! TEETH MARKS---AND THE EDGES OF THE FLESH CHARRED AND BURNED! MAYBE ALLIGATORS!
ALLIGATORS! YEAH--MAYBE THEY WERE! IT WAS SO DARK AND I COULDN'T SEE STRAIGHT ANYHOW! SURE---WHY DIDN'T I THINK OF THAT! I WAS JUST SEEING THINGS!
S-SURE--I'M OKAY! GOLDIE OUTSMARTED THE COPS AGAIN! T-THEY'LL NEVER BURN ME! G-GOT TO GET SOME SLEEP...
GO AHEAD--- STUMPY AND ME WILL STICK AROUND AND KEEP OUR EYES OPEN!
HOURS LATER---IN THE DARKNESS OF THE ROOM WHERE HE SLEPT, GOLDIE WAS BESET WITH A TROUBLED NIGHTMARE. HE STOOD UP, AS IF IN A SOMNAMBULISTIC TRANCE, AND STARTED WALKING!
UH---DOZED OFF, I GUESS! HEY--GOLDIE'S GONE! RED--GOLDIE'S GONE!

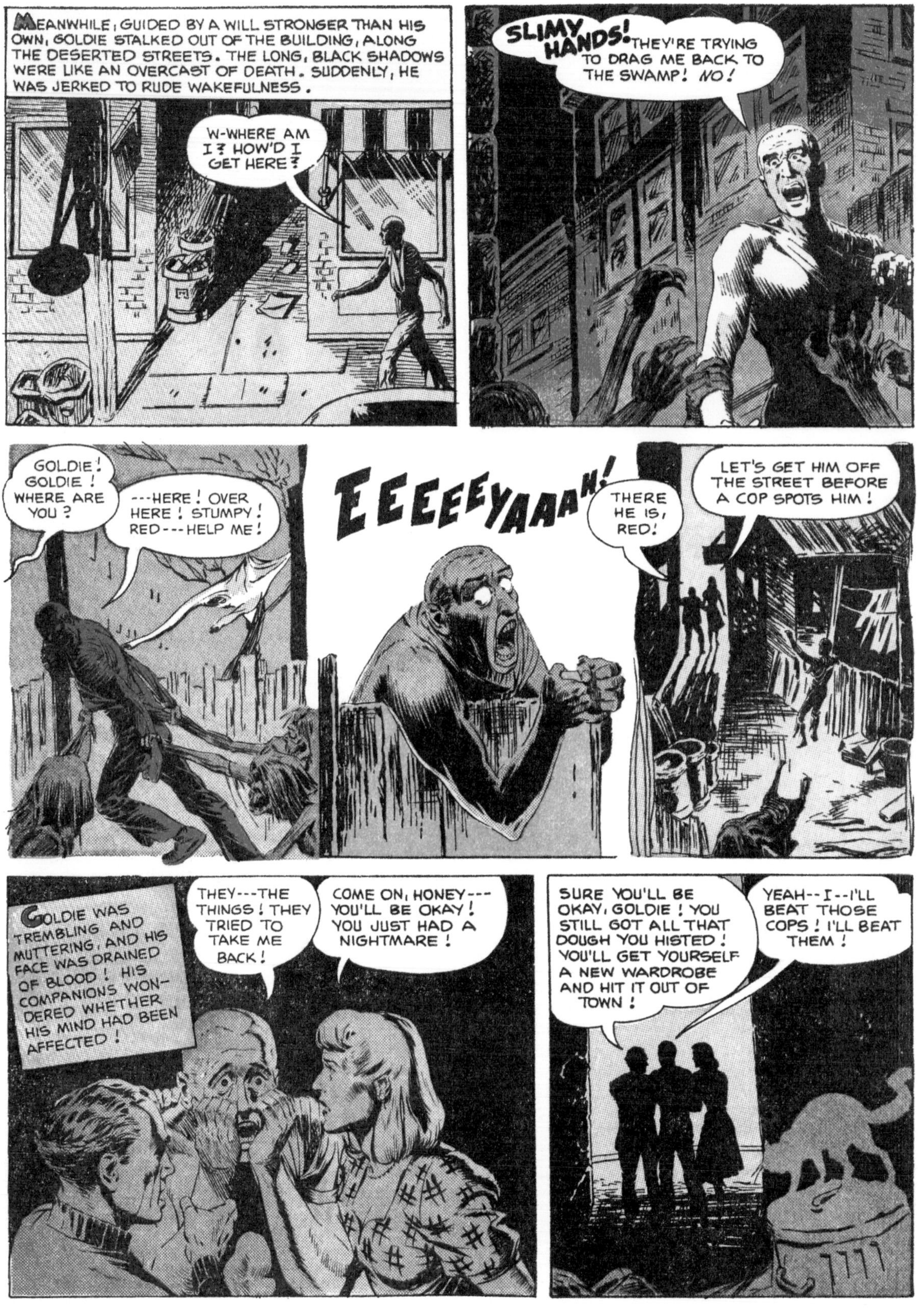
MEANWHILE, GUIDED BY A WILL STRONGER THAN HIS OWN, GOLDIE STALKED OUT OF THE BUILDING, ALONG THE DESERTED STREETS. THE LONG, BLACK SHADOWS WERE LIKE AN OVERCAST OF DEATH. SUDDENLY, HE WAS JERKED TO RUDE WAKEFULNESS.
W-WHERE AM I? HOW'D I GET HERE?
SLIMY HANDS! THEY'RE TRYING TO DRAG ME BACK TO THE SWAMP! NO!
GOLDIE! GOLDIE! WHERE ARE YOU?
---HERE! OVER HERE! STUMPY! RED---HELP ME!
EEEEEYAAAH!
THERE HE IS, RED!
LET'S GET HIM OFF THE STREET BEFORE A COP SPOTS HIM!
GOLDIE WAS TREMBLING AND MUTTERING, AND HIS FACE WAS DRAINED OF BLOOD! HIS COMPANIONS WONDERED WHETHER HIS MIND HAD BEEN AFFECTED!
THEY---THE THINGS! THEY TRIED TO TAKE ME BACK!
COME ON, HONEY--- YOU'LL BE OKAY! YOU JUST HAD A NIGHTMARE!
SURE YOU'LL BE OKAY, GOLDIE! YOU STILL GOT ALL THAT DOUGH YOU HISTED! YOU'LL GET YOURSELF A NEW WARDROBE AND HIT IT OUT OF TOWN!
YEAH-- I--I'LL BEAT THOSE COPS! I'LL BEAT THEM!

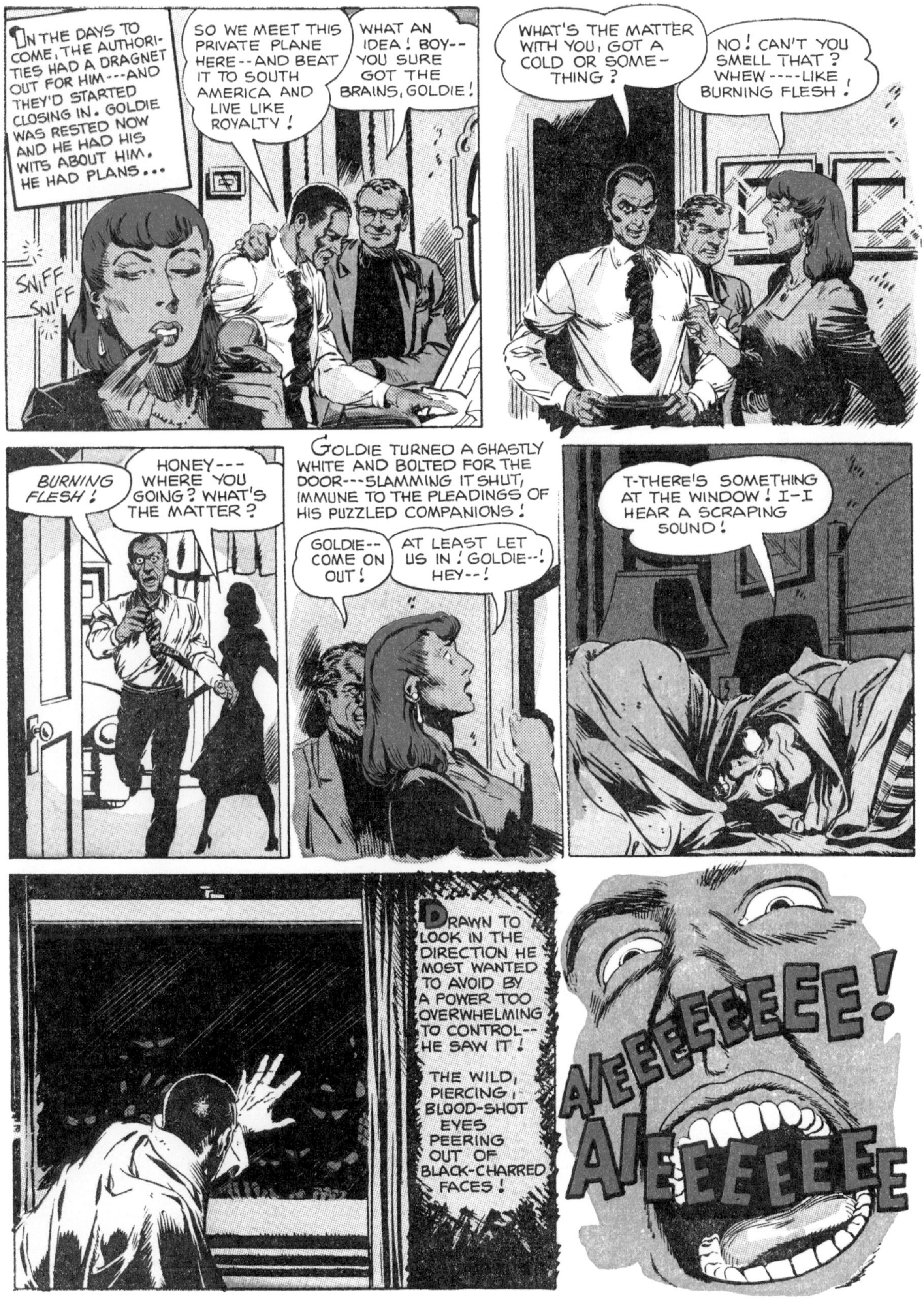
IN THE DAYS TO COME, THE AUTHORITIES HAD A DRAGNET OUT FOR HIM---AND THEY'D STARTED CLOSING IN. GOLDIE WAS RESTED NOW AND HE HAD HIS WITS ABOUT HIM. HE HAD PLANS...
SO WE MEET THIS PRIVATE PLANE HERE--AND BEAT IT TO SOUTH AMERICA AND LIVE LIKE ROYALTY!
WHAT AN IDEA! BOY--YOU SURE GOT THE BRAINS, GOLDIE!
SNIFF SNIFF
WHAT'S THE MATTER WITH YOU, GOT A COLD OR SOMETHING?
NO! CAN'T YOU SMELL THAT? WHEW----LIKE BURNING FLESH!
BURNING FLESH!
HONEY---WHERE YOU GOING? WHAT'S THE MATTER?
GOLDIE TURNED A GHASTLY WHITE AND BOLTED FOR THE DOOR---SLAMMING IT SHUT, IMMUNE TO THE PLEADINGS OF HIS PUZZLED COMPANIONS!
GOLDIE--COME ON OUT!
AT LEAST LET US IN! GOLDIE--! HEY--!
T-THERE'S SOMETHING AT THE WINDOW! I-I HEAR A SCRAPING SOUND!
DRAWN TO LOOK IN THE DIRECTION HE MOST WANTED TO AVOID BY A POWER TOO OVERWHELMING TO CONTROL--HE SAW IT!
THE WILD, PIERCING, BLOOD-SHOT EYES PEERING OUT OF BLACK-CHARRED FACES!
AIEEEEEEEE! AIEEEEEEE

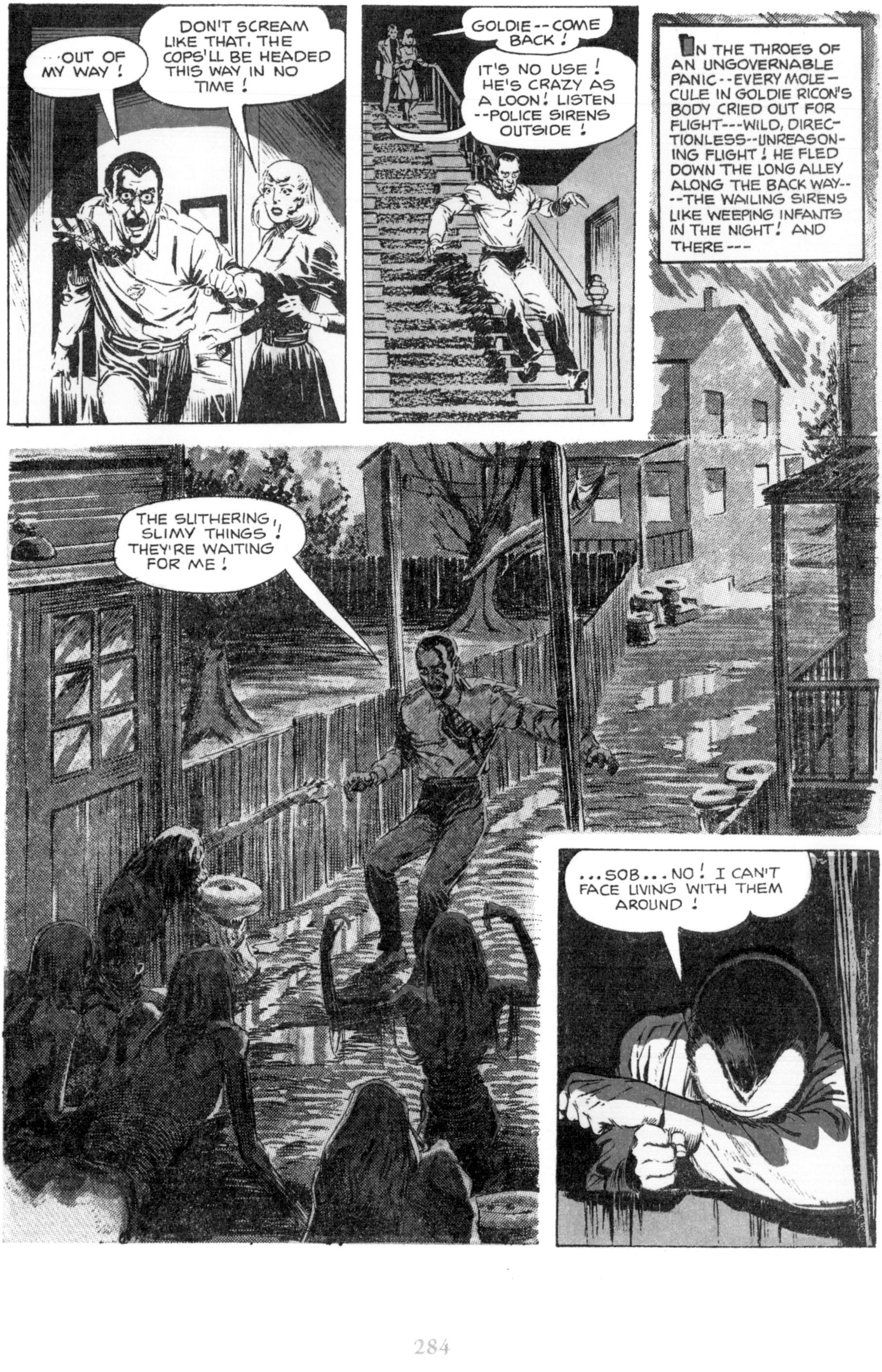
...OUT OF MY WAY!
DON'T SCREAM LIKE THAT, THE COPS'LL BE HEADED THIS WAY IN NO TIME!
GOLDIE--COME BACK!
IT'S NO USE! HE'S CRAZY AS A LOON! LISTEN --POLICE SIRENS OUTSIDE!
IN THE THROES OF AN UNGOVERNABLE PANIC--EVERY MOLE-CULE IN GOLDIE RICON'S BODY CRIED OUT FOR FLIGHT---WILD, DIREC-TIONLESS--UNREASON-ING FLIGHT! HE FLED DOWN THE LONG ALLEY ALONG THE BACK WAY-- --THE WAILING SIRENS LIKE WEEPING INFANTS IN THE NIGHT! AND THERE---
THE SLITHERING, SLIMY THINGS! THEY'RE WAITING FOR ME!
...SOB...NO! I CAN'T FACE LIVING WITH THEM AROUND!

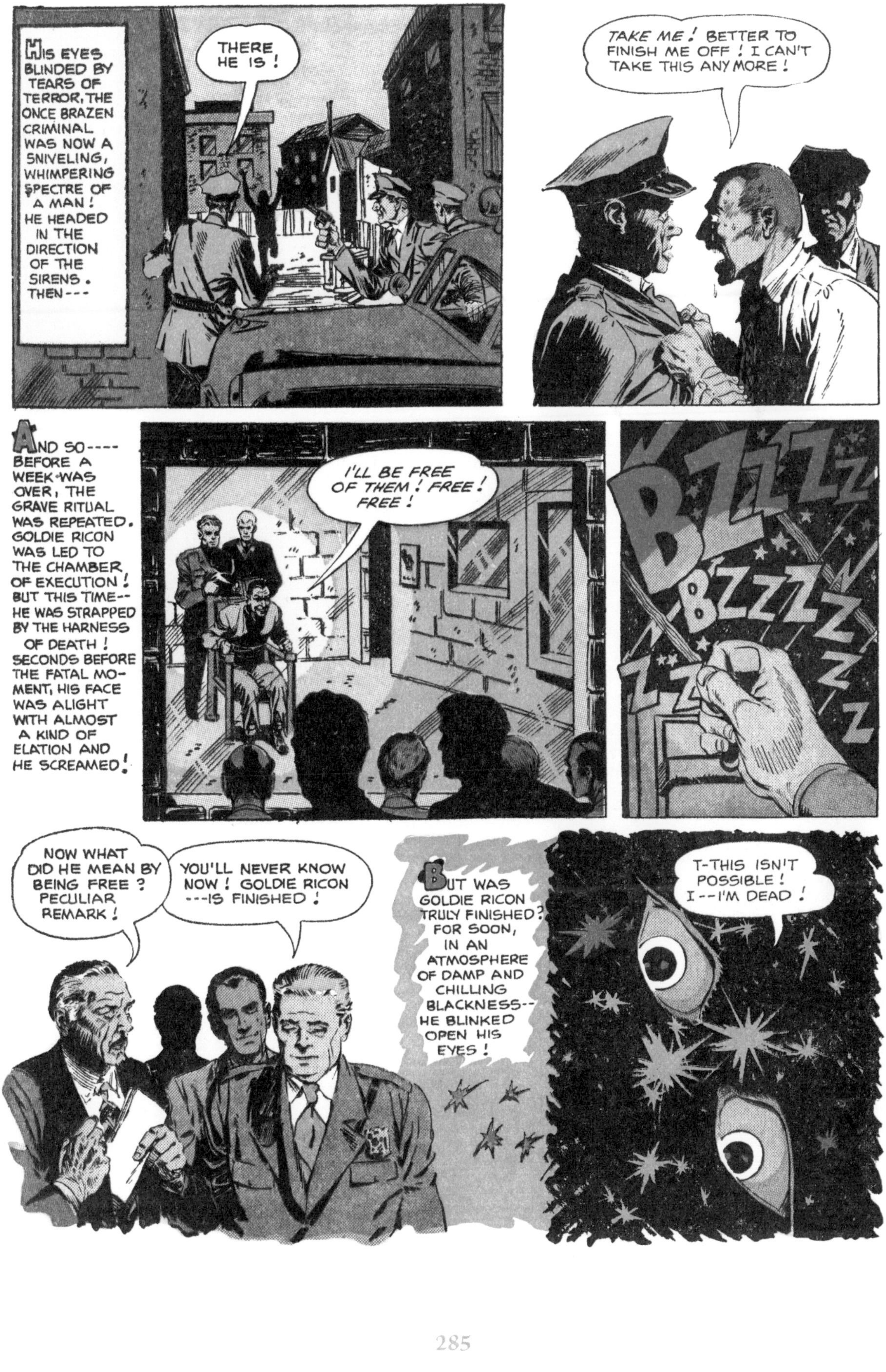
HIS EYES BLINDED BY TEARS OF TERROR, THE ONCE BRAZEN CRIMINAL WAS NOW A SNIVELING, WHIMPERING SPECTRE OF A MAN! HE HEADED IN THE DIRECTION OF THE SIRENS. THEN---
THERE HE IS!
TAKE ME! BETTER TO FINISH ME OFF! I CAN'T TAKE THIS ANYMORE!
AND SO---- BEFORE A WEEK WAS OVER, THE GRAVE RITUAL WAS REPEATED. GOLDIE RICON WAS LED TO THE CHAMBER OF EXECUTION! BUT THIS TIME-- HE WAS STRAPPED BY THE HARNESS OF DEATH! SECONDS BEFORE THE FATAL MOMENT, HIS FACE WAS ALIGHT WITH ALMOST A KIND OF ELATION AND HE SCREAMED!
I'LL BE FREE OF THEM! FREE! FREE!
BZZZZ
BZZZZ
ZZZZZ
NOW WHAT DID HE MEAN BY BEING FREE? PECULIAR REMARK!
YOU'LL NEVER KNOW NOW! GOLDIE RICON ---IS FINISHED!
BUT WAS GOLDIE RICON TRULY FINISHED? FOR SOON, IN AN ATMOSPHERE OF DAMP AND CHILLING BLACKNESS-- HE BLINKED OPEN HIS EYES!
T-THIS ISN'T POSSIBLE! I--I'M DEAD!

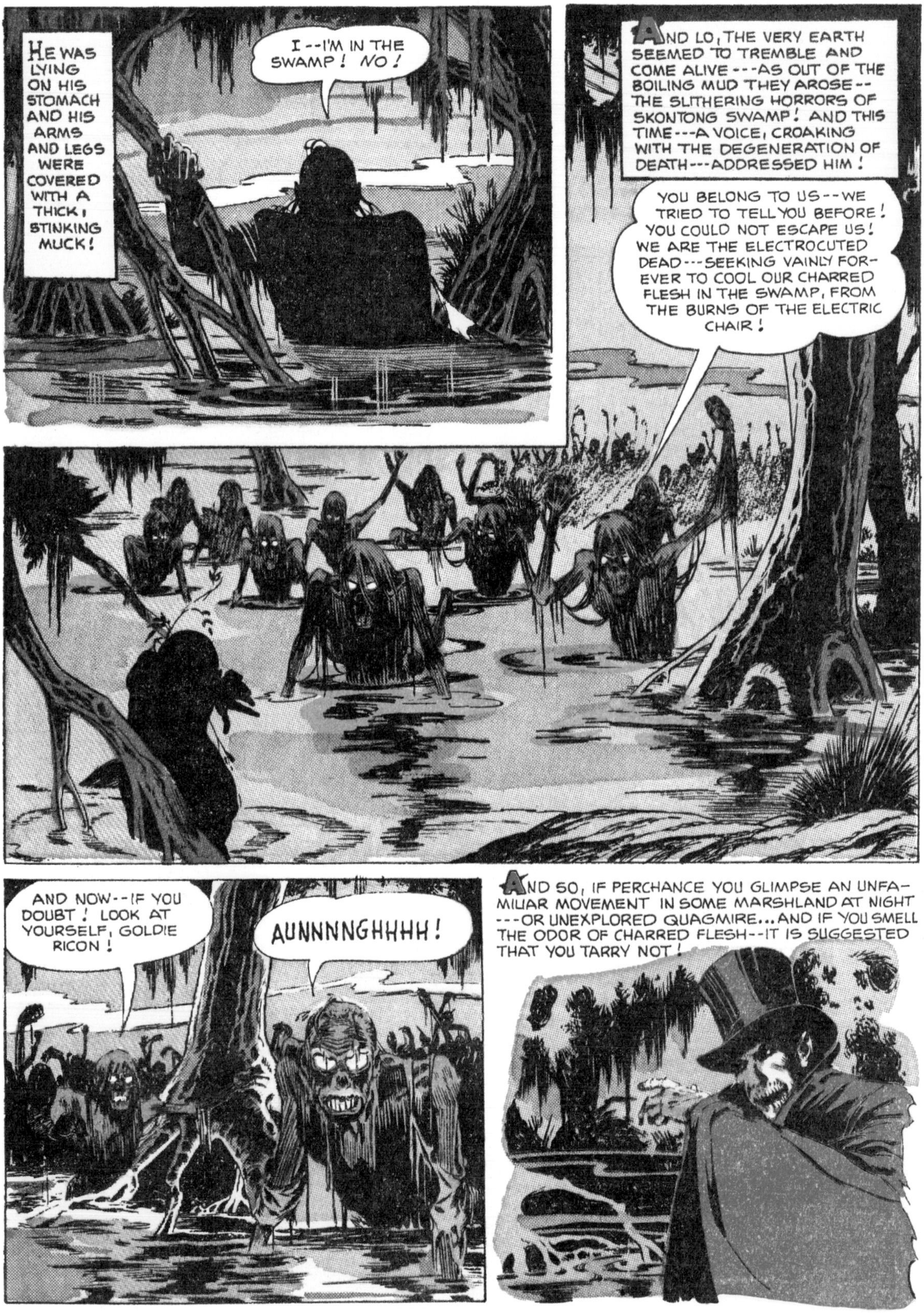
HE WAS LYING ON HIS STOMACH AND HIS ARMS AND LEGS WERE COVERED WITH A THICK, STINKING MUCK!
I--I'M IN THE SWAMP! NO!
AND LO, THE VERY EARTH SEEMED TO TREMBLE AND COME ALIVE---AS OUT OF THE BOILING MUD THEY AROSE--THE SLITHERING HORRORS OF SKONTONG SWAMP! AND THIS TIME---A VOICE, CROAKING WITH THE DEGENERATION OF DEATH---ADDRESSED HIM!
YOU BELONG TO US--WE TRIED TO TELL YOU BEFORE! YOU COULD NOT ESCAPE US! WE ARE THE ELECTROCUTED DEAD---SEEKING VAINLY FOREVER TO COOL OUR CHARRED FLESH IN THE SWAMP, FROM THE BURNS OF THE ELECTRIC CHAIR!
AND NOW--IF YOU DOUBT! LOOK AT YOURSELF, GOLDIE RICON!
AUNNNNGHHHH!
AND SO, IF PERCHANCE YOU GLIMPSE AN UNFAMILIAR MOVEMENT IN SOME MARSHLAND AT NIGHT---OR UNEXPLORED QUAGMIRE...AND IF YOU SMELL THE ODOR OF CHARRED FLESH--IT IS SUGGESTED THAT YOU TARRY NOT!

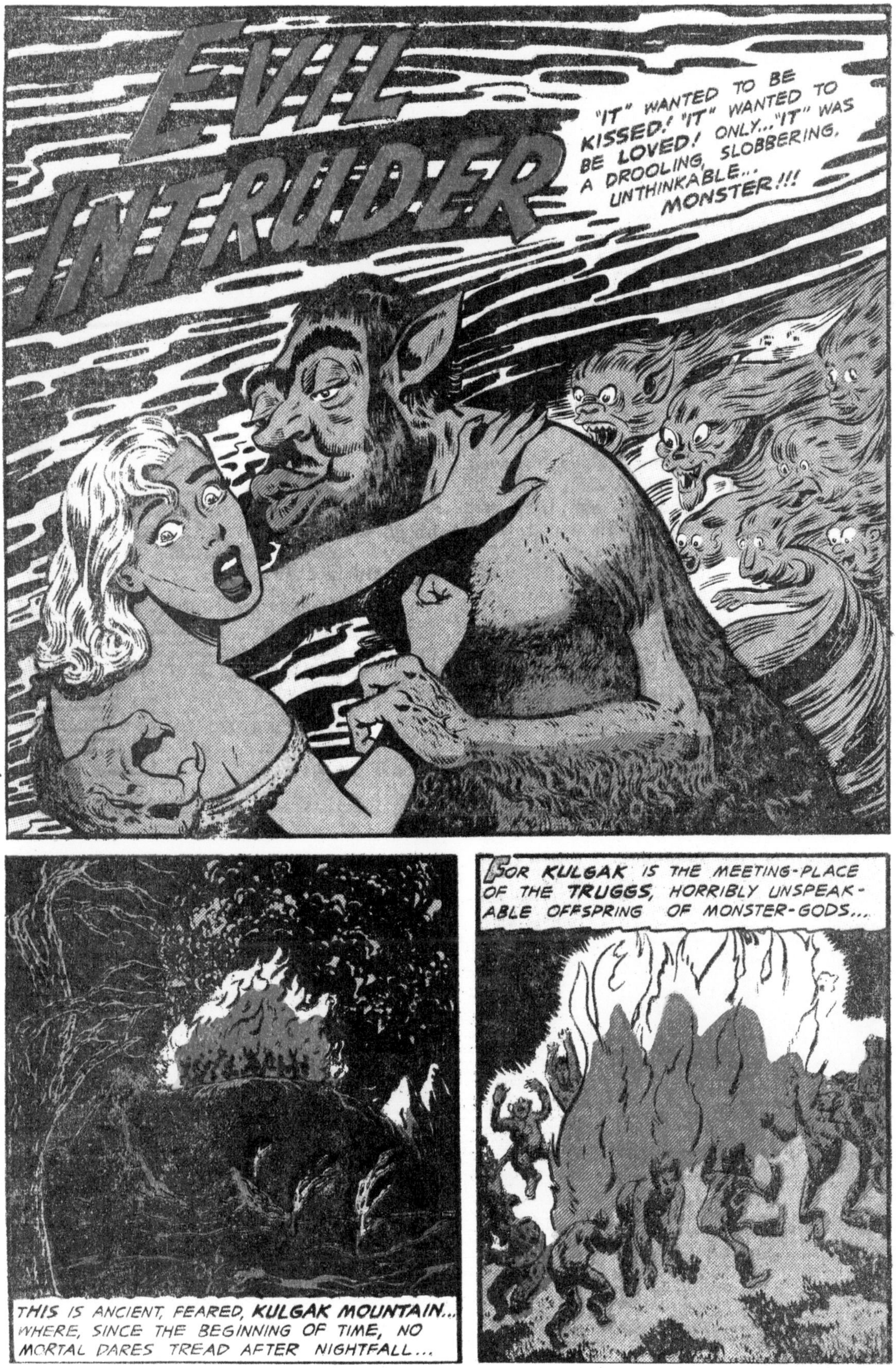
EVIL INTRUDER
"IT" WANTED TO BE KISSED! "IT" WANTED TO BE LOVED! ONLY..."IT" WAS A DROOLING, SLOBBERING, UNTHINKABLE... MONSTER!!!
THIS IS ANCIENT, FEARED, KULGAK MOUNTAIN... WHERE, SINCE THE BEGINNING OF TIME, NO MORTAL DARES TREAD AFTER NIGHTFALL...
FOR KULGAK IS THE MEETING-PLACE OF THE TRUGGS, HORRIBLY UNSPEAK-ABLE OFFSPRING OF MONSTER-GODS...

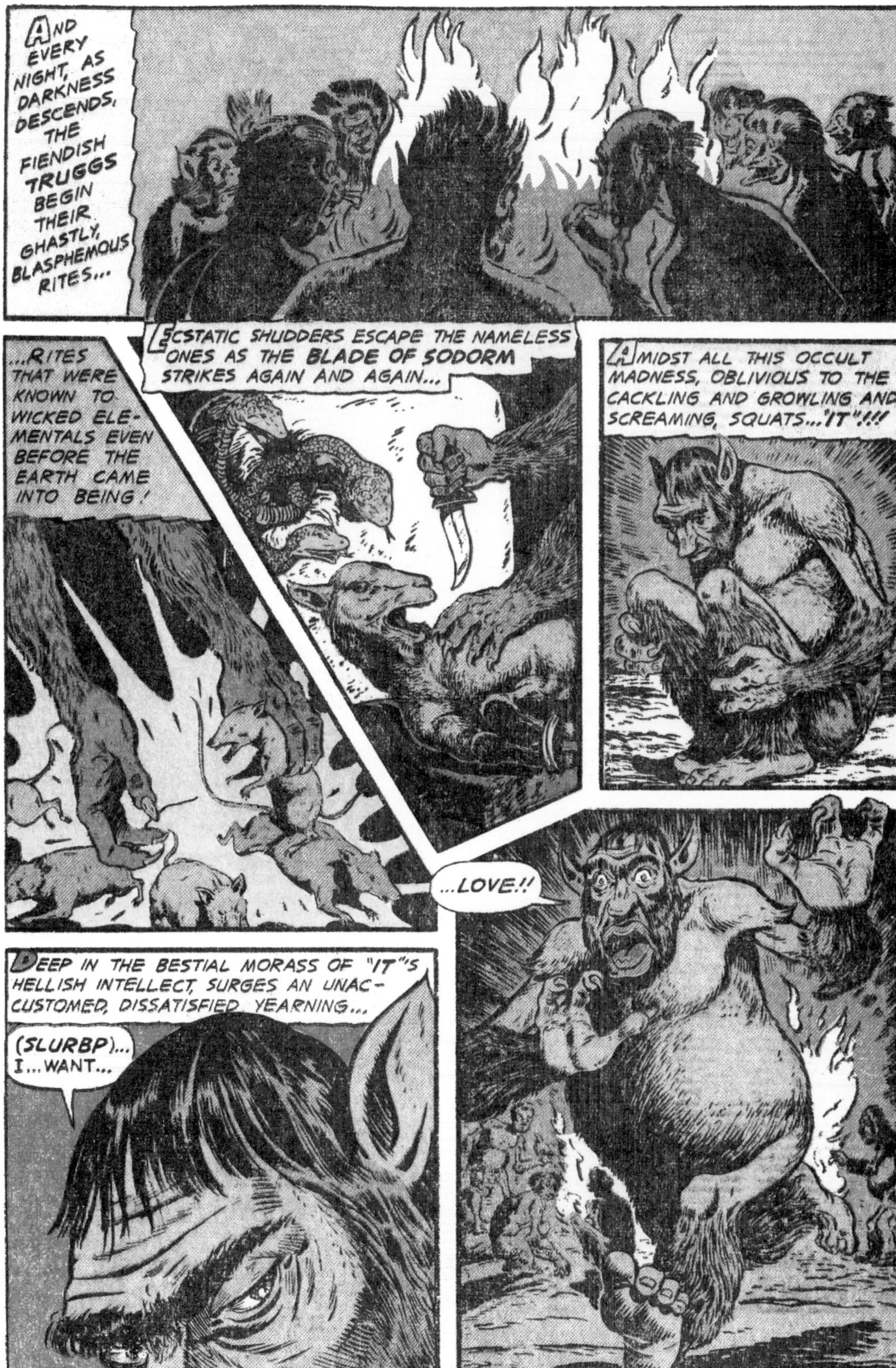
AND EVERY NIGHT, AS DARKNESS DESCENDS, THE FIENDISH TRUGGS BEGIN THEIR GHASTLY, BLASPHEMOUS RITES...
...RITES THAT WERE KNOWN TO WICKED ELEMENTALS EVEN BEFORE THE EARTH CAME INTO BEING!
ECSTATIC SHUDDERS ESCAPE THE NAMELESS ONES AS THE BLADE OF SODORM STRIKES AGAIN AND AGAIN...
AMIDST ALL THIS OCCULT MADNESS, OBLIVIOUS TO THE CACKLING AND GROWLING AND SCREAMING, SQUATS..."IT"!!!
DEEP IN THE BESTIAL MORASS OF "IT"'S HELLISH INTELLECT, SURGES AN UNACCUSTOMED, DISSATISFIED YEARNING...
(SLURBP)... I...WANT...
...LOVE!!
2

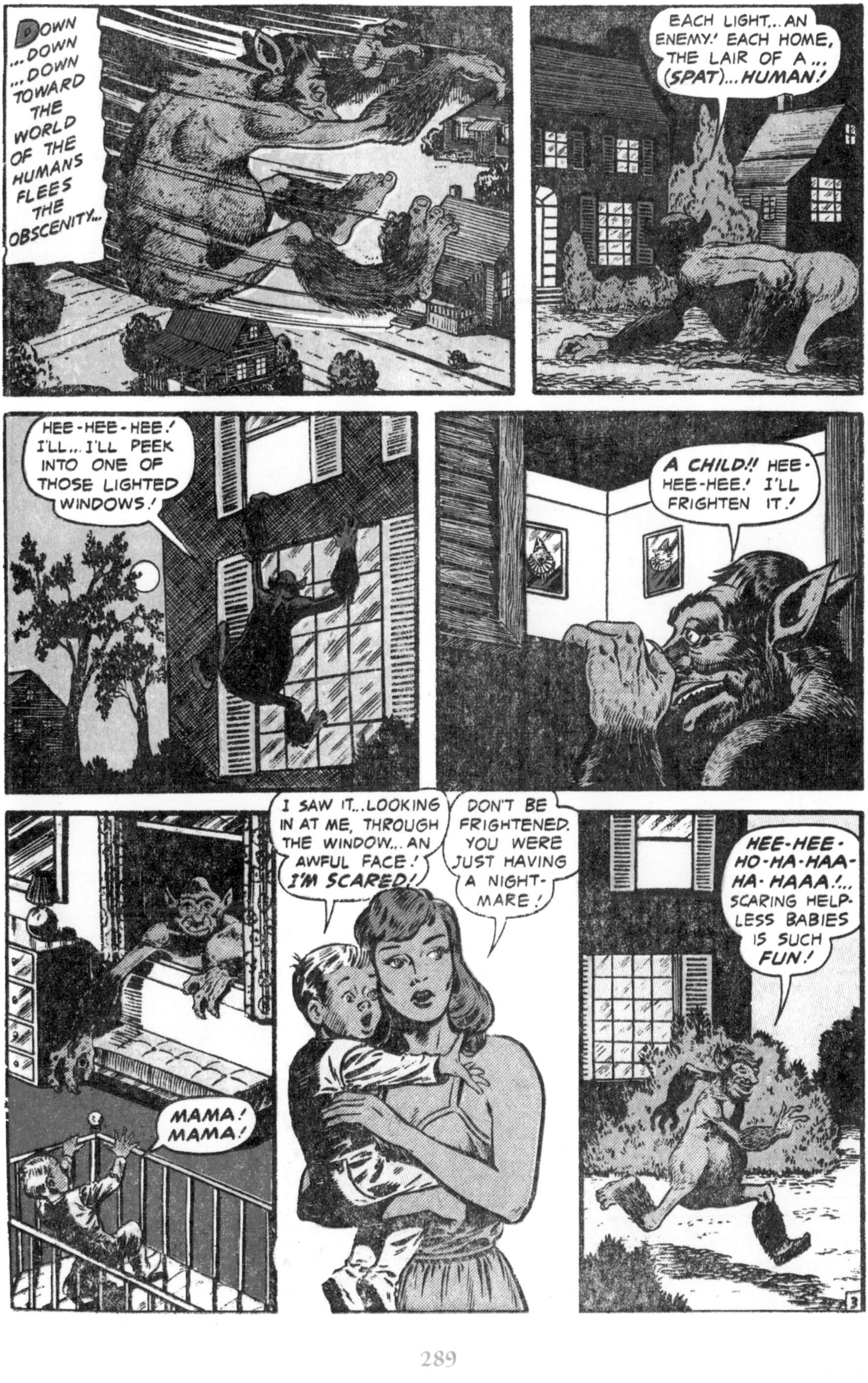
DOWN ...DOWN ...DOWN TOWARD THE WORLD OF THE HUMANS FLEES THE OBSCENITY...
EACH LIGHT... AN ENEMY! EACH HOME, THE LAIR OF A... (SPAT)... HUMAN!
HEE-HEE-HEE! I'LL... I'LL PEEK INTO ONE OF THOSE LIGHTED WINDOWS!
A CHILD!! HEE-HEE-HEE! I'LL FRIGHTEN IT!
MAMA! MAMA!
I SAW IT... LOOKING IN AT ME, THROUGH THE WINDOW... AN AWFUL FACE! I'M SCARED!
DON'T BE FRIGHTENED. YOU WERE JUST HAVING A NIGHT-MARE!
HEE-HEE-HO-HA-HAA-HA-HAAA!... SCARING HELP-LESS BABIES IS SUCH FUN!
3

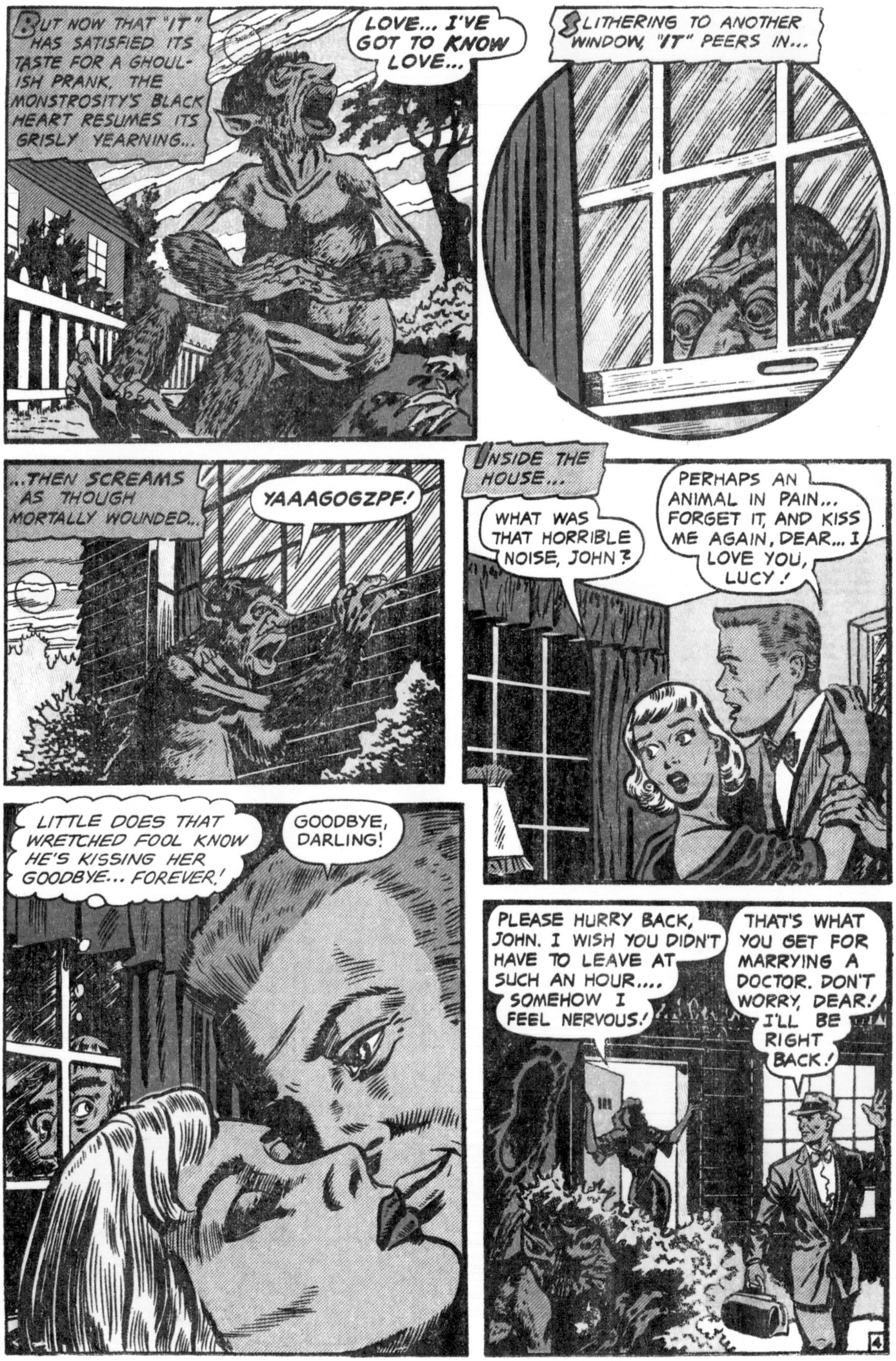
BUT NOW THAT "IT" HAS SATISFIED ITS TASTE FOR A GHOULISH PRANK, THE MONSTROSITY'S BLACK HEART RESUMES ITS GRISLY YEARNING...
LOVE... I'VE GOT TO KNOW LOVE...
SLITHERING TO ANOTHER WINDOW, "IT" PEERS IN...
...THEN SCREAMS AS THOUGH MORTALLY WOUNDED...
YAAAGOGZPF!
INSIDE THE HOUSE...
WHAT WAS THAT HORRIBLE NOISE, JOHN?
PERHAPS AN ANIMAL IN PAIN... FORGET IT, AND KISS ME AGAIN, DEAR... I LOVE YOU, LUCY!
LITTLE DOES THAT WRETCHED FOOL KNOW HE'S KISSING HER GOODBYE... FOREVER!
GOODBYE, DARLING!
PLEASE HURRY BACK, JOHN. I WISH YOU DIDN'T HAVE TO LEAVE AT SUCH AN HOUR.... SOMEHOW I FEEL NERVOUS!
THAT'S WHAT YOU GET FOR MARRYING A DOCTOR. DON'T WORRY, DEAR! I'LL BE RIGHT BACK!
4

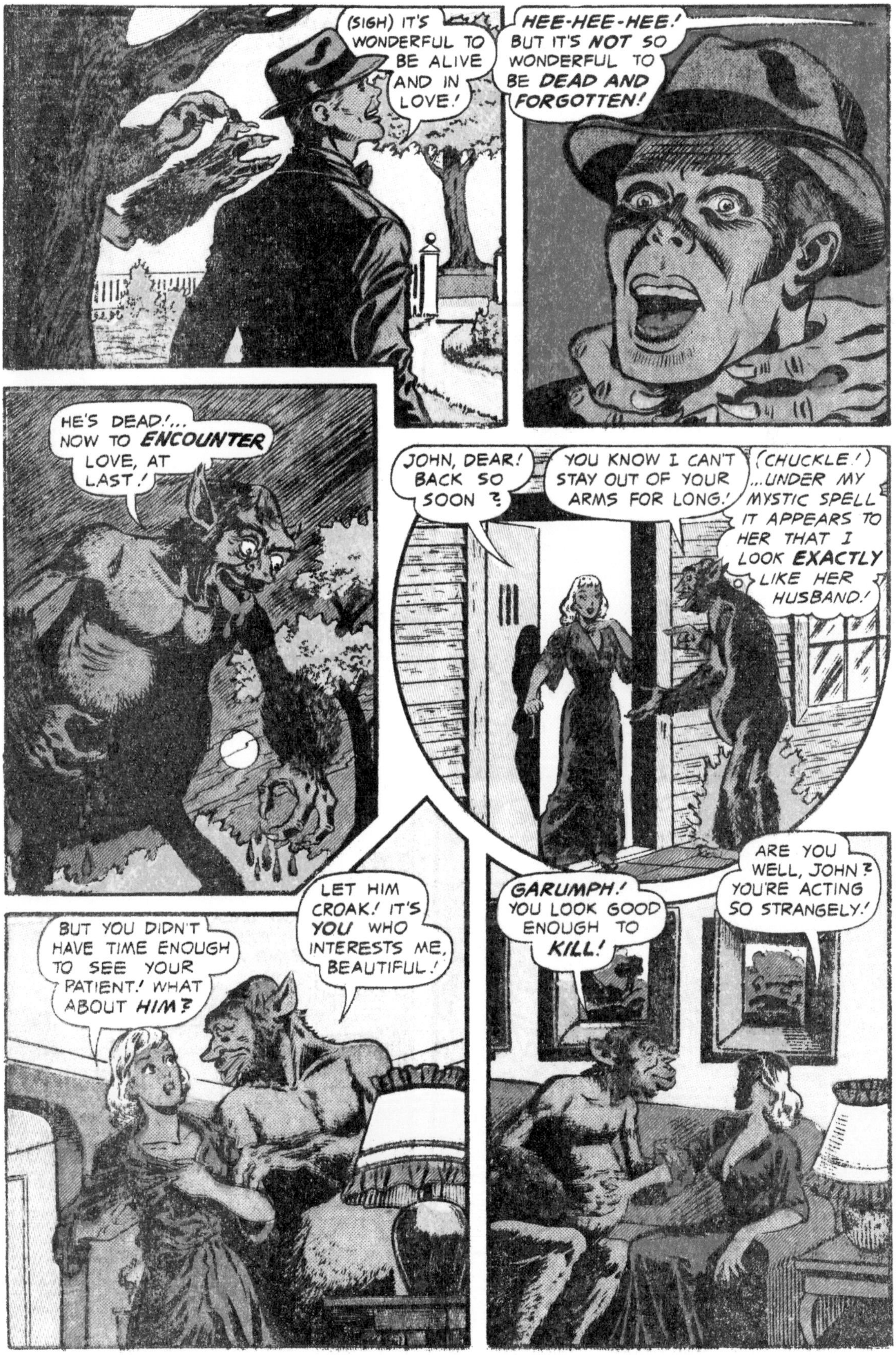
(SIGH) IT'S WONDERFUL TO BE ALIVE AND IN LOVE!
HEE-HEE-HEE! BUT IT'S NOT SO WONDERFUL TO BE DEAD AND FORGOTTEN!
HE'S DEAD!... NOW TO ENCOUNTER LOVE, AT LAST!
JOHN, DEAR! BACK SO SOON?
YOU KNOW I CAN'T STAY OUT OF YOUR ARMS FOR LONG!
(CHUCKLE!) ...UNDER MY MYSTIC SPELL IT APPEARS TO HER THAT I LOOK EXACTLY LIKE HER HUSBAND!
BUT YOU DIDN'T HAVE TIME ENOUGH TO SEE YOUR PATIENT! WHAT ABOUT HIM?
LET HIM CROAK! IT'S YOU WHO INTERESTS ME, BEAUTIFUL!
ARE YOU WELL, JOHN? YOU'RE ACTING SO STRANGELY!
GARUMPH! YOU LOOK GOOD ENOUGH TO KILL!

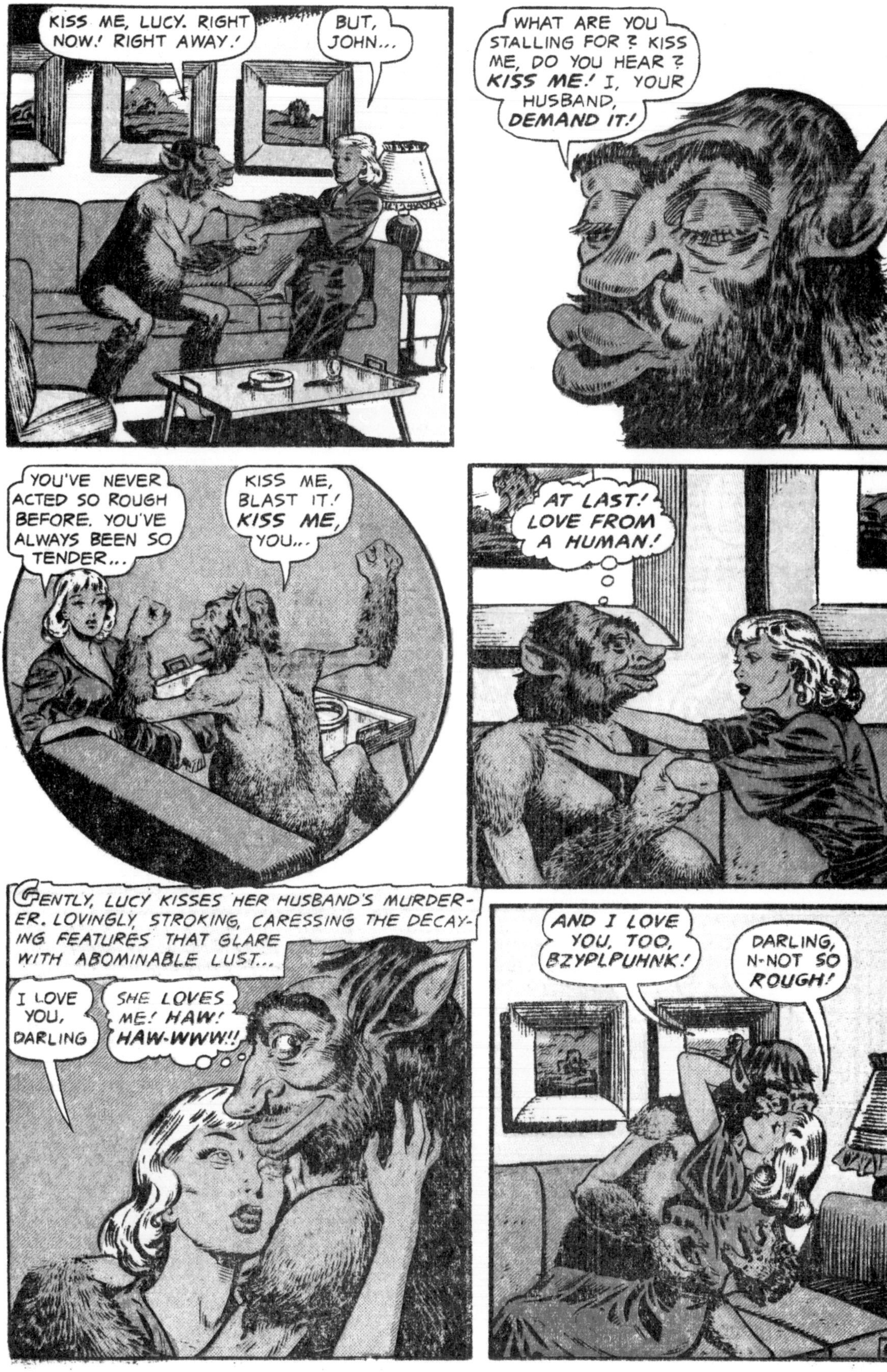
KISS ME, LUCY. RIGHT NOW! RIGHT AWAY!
BUT, JOHN...
WHAT ARE YOU STALLING FOR? KISS ME, DO YOU HEAR? KISS ME! I, YOUR HUSBAND, DEMAND IT!
YOU'VE NEVER ACTED SO ROUGH BEFORE. YOU'VE ALWAYS BEEN SO TENDER...
KISS ME, BLAST IT! KISS ME, YOU...
AT LAST! LOVE FROM A HUMAN!
GENTLY, LUCY KISSES HER HUSBAND'S MURDERER. LOVINGLY, STROKING, CARESSING THE DECAYING FEATURES THAT GLARE WITH ABOMINABLE LUST...
I LOVE YOU, DARLING
SHE LOVES ME! HAW! HAW-WWW!!
AND I LOVE YOU, TOO, BZYPLPUHNK!
DARLING, N-NOT SO ROUGH!

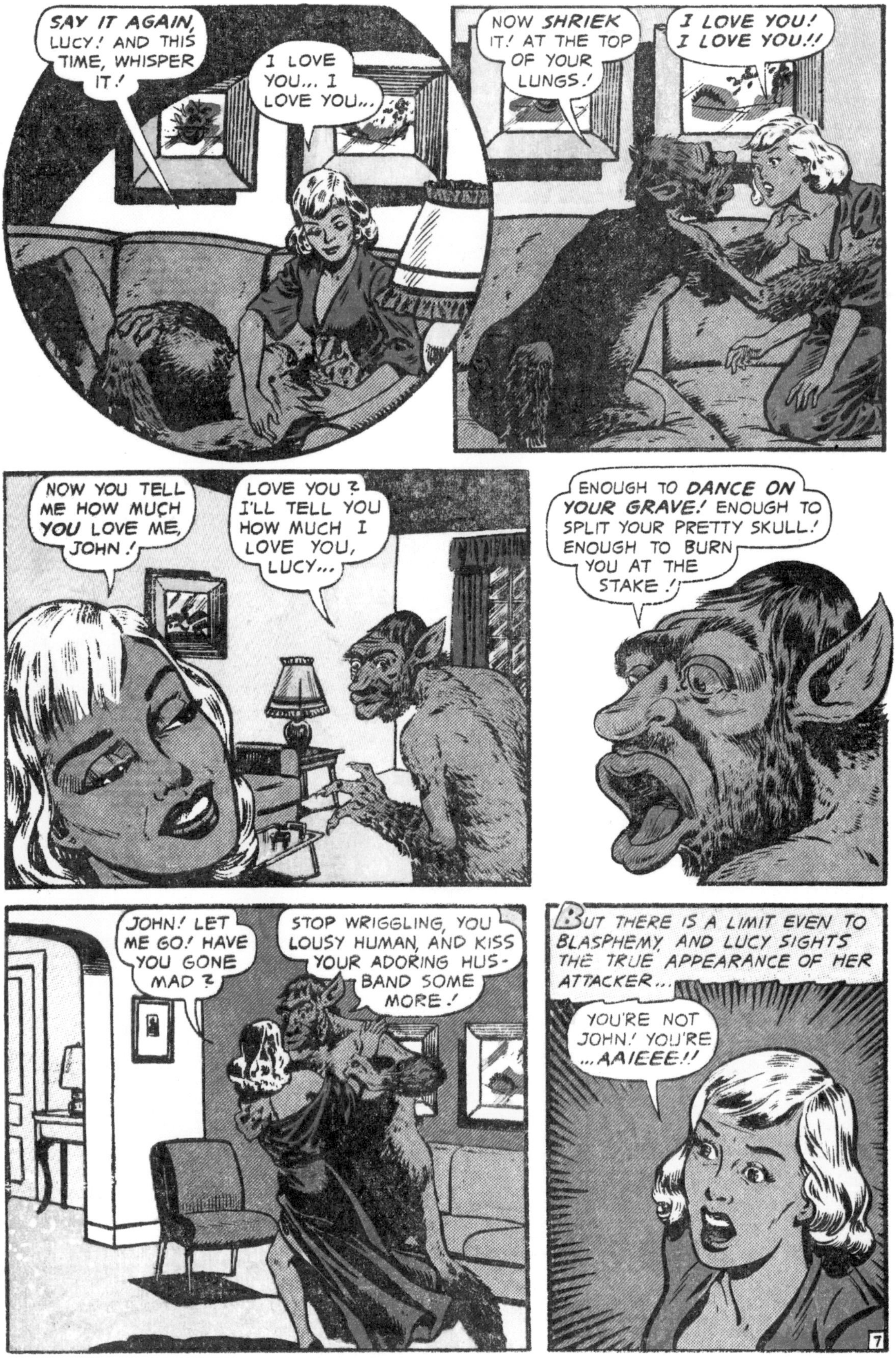

SAY IT AGAIN, LUCY! AND THIS TIME, WHISPER IT!
I LOVE YOU... I LOVE YOU...
NOW SHRIEK IT! AT THE TOP OF YOUR LUNGS!
I LOVE YOU! I LOVE YOU!!
NOW YOU TELL ME HOW MUCH YOU LOVE ME, JOHN!
LOVE YOU? I'LL TELL YOU HOW MUCH I LOVE YOU, LUCY...
ENOUGH TO DANCE ON YOUR GRAVE! ENOUGH TO SPLIT YOUR PRETTY SKULL! ENOUGH TO BURN YOU AT THE STAKE!
JOHN! LET ME GO! HAVE YOU GONE MAD?
STOP WRIGGLING, YOU LOUSY HUMAN, AND KISS YOUR ADORING HUS-BAND SOME MORE!
BUT THERE IS A LIMIT EVEN TO BLASPHEMY, AND LUCY SIGHTS THE TRUE APPEARANCE OF HER ATTACKER...
YOU'RE NOT JOHN! YOU'RE ...AAIEEE!!
7

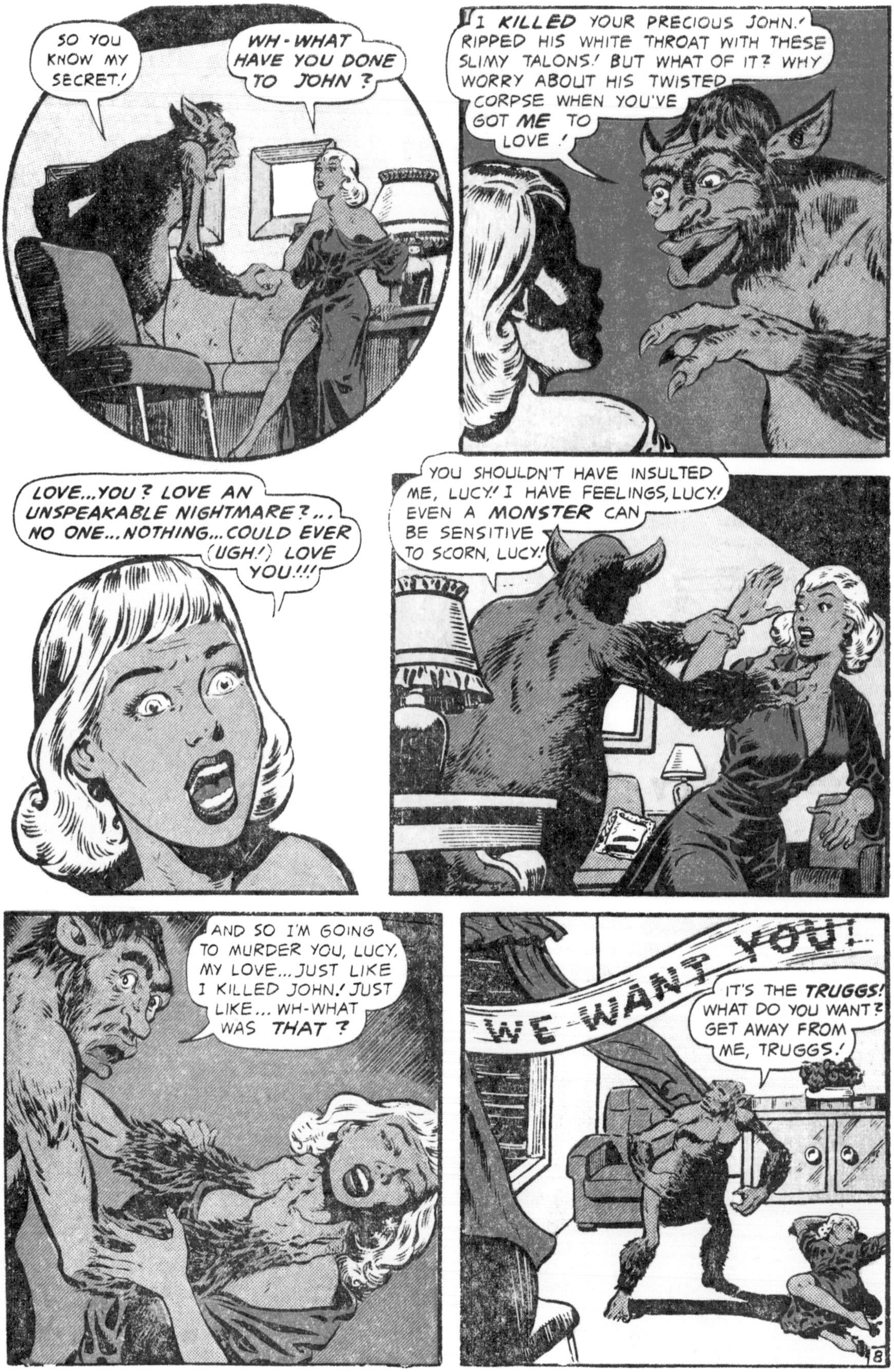
SO YOU KNOW MY SECRET!
WH-WHAT HAVE YOU DONE TO JOHN?
I KILLED YOUR PRECIOUS JOHN! RIPPED HIS WHITE THROAT WITH THESE SLIMY TALONS! BUT WHAT OF IT? WHY WORRY ABOUT HIS TWISTED CORPSE WHEN YOU'VE GOT ME TO LOVE!
LOVE...YOU? LOVE AN UNSPEAKABLE NIGHTMARE?... NO ONE...NOTHING...COULD EVER (UGH!) LOVE YOU!!!
YOU SHOULDN'T HAVE INSULTED ME, LUCY! I HAVE FEELINGS, LUCY! EVEN A MONSTER CAN BE SENSITIVE TO SCORN, LUCY!
AND SO I'M GOING TO MURDER YOU, LUCY, MY LOVE...JUST LIKE I KILLED JOHN! JUST LIKE... WH-WHAT WAS THAT?
WE WANT YOU!...
IT'S THE TRUGGS! WHAT DO YOU WANT? GET AWAY FROM ME, TRUGGS!
8

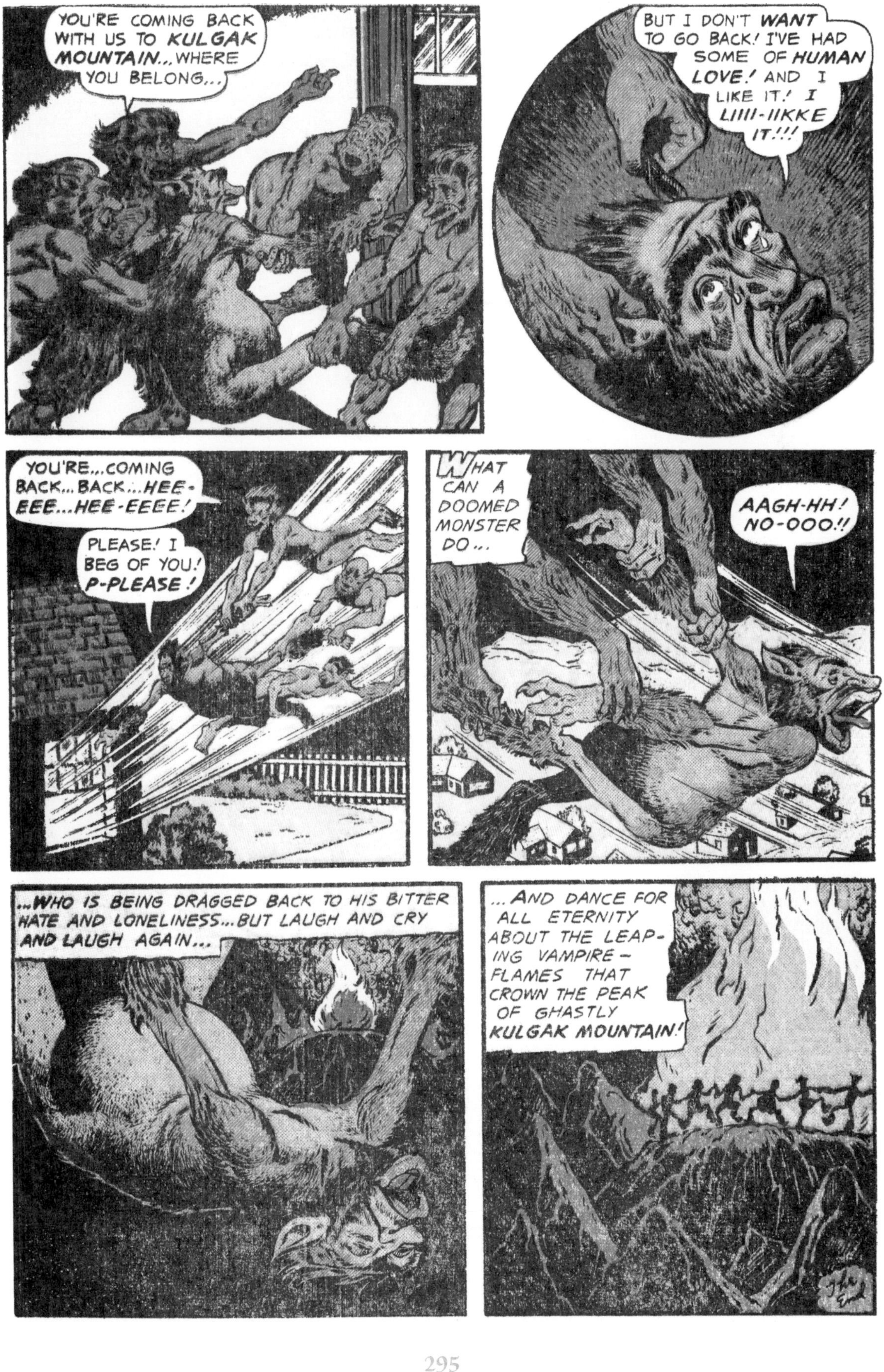
YOU'RE COMING BACK WITH US TO KULGAK MOUNTAIN... WHERE YOU BELONG...
BUT I DON'T WANT TO GO BACK! I'VE HAD SOME OF HUMAN LOVE! AND I LIKE IT! I LIIII-IIKKE IT!!!
YOU'RE...COMING BACK...BACK...HEE-EEE...HEE-EEEE!
PLEASE! I BEG OF YOU! P-PLEASE!
WHAT CAN A DOOMED MONSTER DO...
AAGH-HH! NO-OOO!!
...WHO IS BEING DRAGGED BACK TO HIS BITTER HATE AND LONELINESS...BUT LAUGH AND CRY AND LAUGH AGAIN...
...AND DANCE FOR ALL ETERNITY ABOUT THE LEAP-ING VAMPIRE-FLAMES THAT CROWN THE PEAK OF GHASTLY KULGAK MOUNTAIN!
The End

Notes

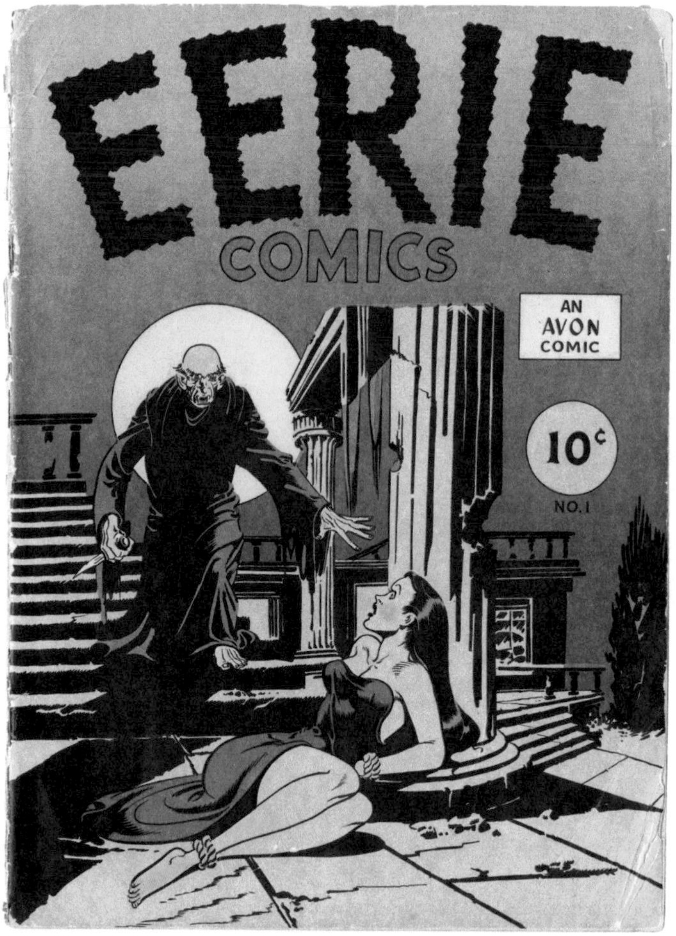
EERIE
COMICS
AN
AVON
COMIC
10¢
NO.1
Eerie Comics no.1, January 1947. Cover by Bob Fujitani

THERE WAS ONCE A TIME WHEN THE birth of horror comics in the fifties seemed an easy tale to tell. It went like this: Bill Gaines, at the age of 25, had inherited the Entertaining Comics company (EC) after his father Max was killed in a boating accident. When young Bill began to reshape the company, he hired a young artist-writer named Al Feldstein, and as the two talked over what they'd like to do, they each remembered *The Old Witch's Tale* and other mystery and horror radio shows. In the December 1949-January 1950 issues of EC's crime comics they introduced horror tales in a new back-up feature, "The Vault of Horror," followed by "The Crypt of Terror" a month later. Reader response was so strong that two issues later, with the April-May 1950 issues, the titles of these features became the titles of the comics themselves. The substantial sales of these and a third EC title added a month later, *The Haunt of Fear*, made the industry take note, and soon everyone started publishing horror comics.

This straightforward scenario, true as far as it goes, took a big hit when artist Shelly Moldoff came forward in the early nineties to describe how he had come to Gaines with an idea for comics titled *Tales of the Supernatural* and *This Magazine Is Haunted* over a year and a half before the first "Vault" and "Crypt" features appeared, and even signed a contract with Gaines to produce those titles, casting doubt on the oft-told source of Gaines' inspiration.

An examination of the record reveals further problems with this simple scenario. However much EC may deserve its reputation for causing the horror onslaught, it cannot take credit for being first. We're not referring to such antecedents as the horror stories in various Harry "A" Chesler comics or the horror series in Charlton's *Yellowjacket Comics*, both in the mid-1940s. We're not even including Avon's one-shot *Eerie Comics* 1 (January 1947), which is now generally considered the first horror comic book (although Avon did publish a multiple-issue series with that title starting in 1951). We're talking about genuine 1950s-type horror comics.

The first continuing horror comic was ACG's *Adventures into the Unknown*, which began in Fall 1948 and had published nine issues by the time EC started their horror comics. Significantly, the third issue, dated February-March 1949, contained a horror story illustrated by Al Feldstein, the very same who later became the editor and chief writer of EC's horror line. And Martin Goodman's Atlas Comics started up three continuing horror titles in mid-1949 which combined had brought out eight issues before EC began theirs. (Atlas' early entry in the genre gives lie to the popular image of Goodman merely copying popular trends started by others.) Atlas went on to be the most prolific horror publisher, producing over 25 per cent of all pre-Code horror comics, more than the next three most prolific companies combined.

There is, of course, no problem in defining the *end* of the horror comics era. Things came to an abrupt halt when the Comics Code was instituted. Horror comics were gone from the newsstands by the end of 1954, though some carry early-1955 dates due to advance dating. John Benson

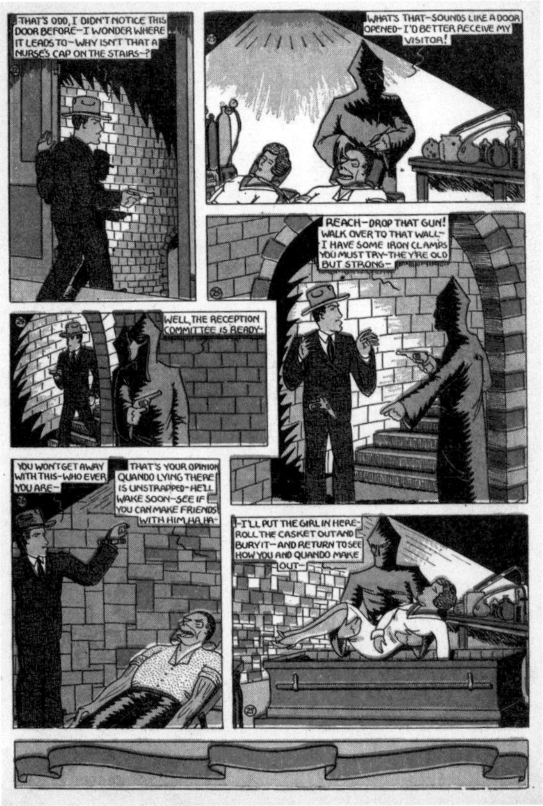
THAT'S ODD, I DIDN'T NOTICE THIS DOOR BEFORE—I WONDER WHERE IT LEADS TO—WHY ISN'T THAT A NURSE'S CAP ON THE STAIRS—?
WHAT'S THAT—SOUNDS LIKE A DOOR OPENED—I'D BETTER RECEIVE MY VISITOR!
REACH—DROP THAT GUN! WALK OVER TO THAT WALL—I HAVE SOME IRON CLAMPS YOU MUST TRY—THEY'RE OLD BUT STRONG—
WELL, THE RECEPTION COMMITTEE IS READY—
YOU WON'T GET AWAY WITH THIS—WHO EVER YOU ARE—
THAT'S YOUR OPINION QUANDO LYING THERE IS UNSTRAPPED—HE'LL WAKE SOON—SEE IF YOU CAN MAKE FRIENDS WITH HIM HA HA—
—I'LL PUT THE GIRL IN HERE—ROLL THE CASKET OUT AND BURY IT—AND RETURN TO SEE HOW YOU AND QUANDO MAKE OUT—

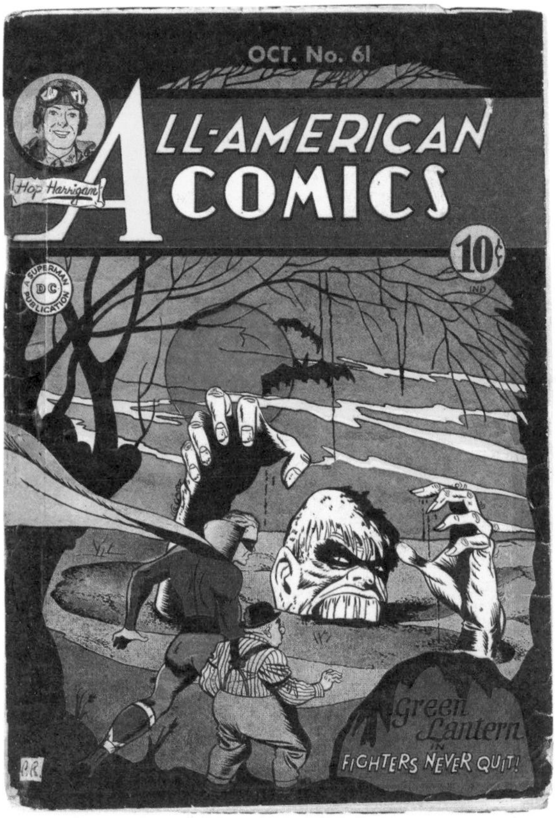
OCT. No. 61
ALL-AMERICAN COMICS
Hop Harrigan
10¢
SUPERMAN DC PUBLICATION
Green Lantern
FIGHTERS NEVER QUIT!

© DC Comics

Horror has been a theme in comic book anthology titles stretching back to its earliest days. Left: page four of "The Madhouse Murder Mystery," by E.F. Webster, for Centaur Publications' *Amazing Mystery Funnies* vol.2 no.3 (March 1939); right: Paul Reinman's cover to DC's *All-American Comics* no.61 (October 1944), featuring Green Lantern's Frankensteinian nemesis, Solomon Grundy. Harry "A" Chesler, one of the earliest comic book packagers, also featured horror themes in his titles from late 1936 into the early postwar years.

Page 8. Ajax/Farrell house ad, featured in comic books dated early 1954

ACG, Atlas, EC, Fawcett, and Harvey regularly promoted their horror lines with house ads, but few examples exist from smaller companies, who never knew when the bottom would fall out from the horror craze and preferred to use their non-story pages for paid advertising. Ajax/Farrell did just this one to herald its complete horror line.

Page 9. "The Strange Case of Henpecked Harry" (*Eerie Comics* 1, January 1947) Art by Fred Kida (1920-2014)

This story first appeared in what is now considered the very first true horror comic, and is the only story in this volume that did not appear during the 1950s. Though it features murder, a bloody apparition, and a phantom train, the title doesn't quite fit the horror mold. Avon rectified this error when they reprinted the story a few years later, retitling it "Subway Terror."

We can't help comparing this story to the oft-reprinted Al Feldstein-written, Bernard Krigstein-illustrated "Master Race" (*Impact* 1, March–April 1955), which also utilized most of a page to depict someone falling into the path of a subway train. Surely, *this* is the proper way to do it: varied angles and hiked skirts!

Page 17. "Pit of the Damned" (*Chamber of Chills* 7, April 1952) Art by Bob Powell (1916-1967)

The Harvey horror comics can easily be divided into two eras, before and after the arrival of Sid Jacobson, who took over as editor with issues dated in the Spring of 1953. Recurring pictorial motifs before Jacobson included elaborate arched stone dungeons (see "Servants of the Tomb" and "The Body Maker") and all-encompassing fire, as seen here in "Pit of the Damned." Powell wrote as well as drew the classic *Mr. Mystic* strip for the Sunday newspaper *Spirit* section and also wrote other features, so it's just possible that he wrote this and his other two pre-Jacobson stories chosen for this book, "Servants of the Tomb" and "A Safari of Death." Powell was at the peak of his powers in the early 1950s, and these stories represent some of his most imaginative work.

Bob Powell got his 1937 start in comics at the Will Eisner-Jerry Iger shop, and when Eisner left in 1939 to start a smaller studio, he took Powell with him. Powell established his own shop in 1945, which by the 1950s included talented assistants George Siefringer, Marvin Epp, and Howard Nostrand. In an interview for the 1981 Pleasure Dome Convention program, Nostrand described how the Powell team worked on a page: "Bob would pencil the thing. I would ink the figures, George inked the backgrounds and

Marty would work along with George and me on the backgrounds and Powell put the faces in."

In this story Powell works in the standard six-panels-per-page layout, but like Eisner's *Spirit,* he keeps it fresh with thoughtful page designs and by eradicating most panel borders. The penultimate page is often where comic book stories reach their climax, and Powell's page six is breathtaking, with a sense of drama and the skewed perspectives worthy of his mentor. Powell was also able to get in some rather racy figure drawings throughout, both male and female.

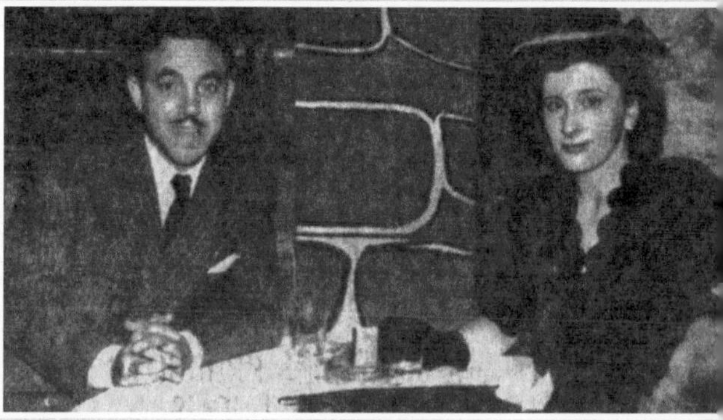

Jerry Iger and Ruth Roche at a Manhattan restaurant, 1942 (photo courtesy of Jay Disbrow)

Page 24. "Corpses... Coast to Coast" (*Voodoo* 14, March-April 1954) Art by Iger studio

This first of six entries by the Jerry Iger studio is also the most ambitious, as it pictorializes an undertaker's Nazi-inspired dream of zombie world domination. *Voodoo* typically featured zombie stories, but here the ancient science of zombifying reaches a streamlined industrial level, with millions of the living dead voting in elections and infiltrating all government agencies.

Typical of the Iger studio, this story's art is primarily influenced by the earlier work of Iger alumni Matt Baker and Jack Kamen, both of whom had left the studio by the early 1950s. Even by 1954 standards, Iger horror art has a distinctly anachronistic quality, eternally stuck in the postwar period of the 1940s. But pairing this with an almost underground sensibility gives their horror graphics an unsettling creepiness unique to this company. For instance, the death-mask visage and black-hole eye slits of this story's "Big Z" could have come from no other outfit.

Page 31. "A Pact with the Devil" (*Web of Evil* 9, December 1953) Art by Jack Cole (1914-1958)

Among the many superhero characters Jack Cole created and worked on during the "Golden Age" of comics, he is best remembered for the quirky, amusing, super-stretch Plastic Man. His brief foray into crime comics is also fairly well known, especially his innovative and outrageous story "Murder, Morphine and Me," for *True Crime Comics,* which became a prime exhibit of comic-book excess during the 1950s crackdown. His horror comics for Quality are unjustly overlooked, and three of his best are in this volume. Throughout his career Cole often wrote his own scripts, including quite possibly these horror stories.

When the comics market drastically shrank in 1954, Cole found a new career as one of *Playboy's* premier cartoonists, and in 1958 he realized his dream of selling a syndicated strip with *Betsy and Me.* That August, Cole committed suicide. His reasons for this precipitous act are unknown; his suicide note to his wife has never been released. This has led some to look to his work for clues, and a number of *Plastic Man* stories featuring suicide have been chronicled. "A Pact with the Devil" is another example, if indeed it was written by him.

Like Bob Powell, Cole had been in comic books almost from the industry's beginning, joining Harry "A" Chesler's seminal shop in 1937. Apart from his considerable technical gifts, the sheer enthusiasm with which he approached his craft inspired an entire generation of artists, including a young Alex Toth, who at 15 managed to sneak into Cole's cubicle at Quality for some advice and counsel, which the busy artist cheerfully provided. Toth never forgot the gesture and often championed Cole as a major influence.

Following a luxuriant full-page splash panel, "A Pact with the Devil" opens with a portentous two-panel intro, then proceeds at breakneck speed until the two-panel windup. The characters in this story never walk – they're either running or immobilized with fear. Furthering this kinetic pace is Cole's use of the blue gremlins, hanging on to the devil's coattails for the full eight-page ride, mugging, observing, and spurring on the inevitable suicide.

Wearing his ubiquitous eyeshades, Bob Powell confers with his assistants (left to right) Marty Epp, George Siefringer, and Howard Nostrand, c.1951 (photo courtesy of Seth Powell)

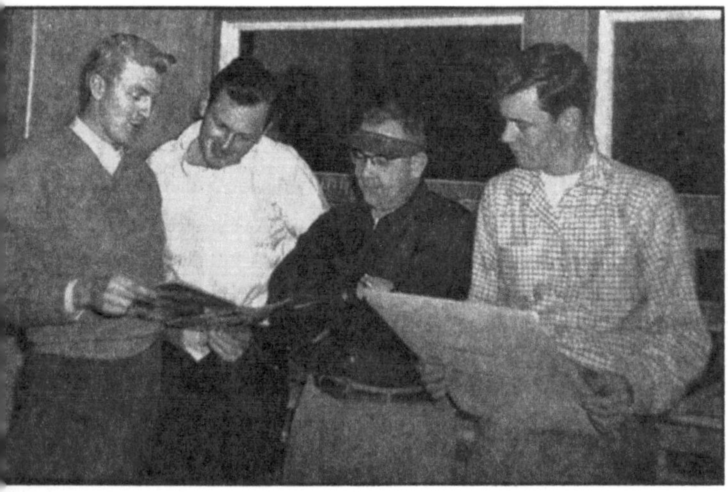

Page 40. "The Corpse That Came to Dinner" (*Out of the Shadows* 9, July 1953) Art by Reed Crandall (1917-1982), **inked by Mike Peppe**

Reed Crandall started in the late 1930s with the Eisner and Iger shop, supplying art for Fiction House's *Planet, Jumbo, Jungle,* and *Wings* before starting a solo career for Busy Arnold at Quality. Leaving Quality in 1953, he was quickly hired by EC, doing his first story, "Carrion Death," for the

Ruth Roche and the Iger Studio

SOME FIFTIES HORROR COMICS DID NOT LIST AN EDITOR in the indicia and even stated "Editor: None" in the required annual circulation statement. The Ajax/Farrell titles did list an editor: Ruth Roche. But Roche was not an employee of Farrell, she was part of the Iger Studio that supplied Ajax/Farrell and Superior with the content of their books in the 1950s, not only for the horror titles but for all genres.

Samuel Maxwell "Jerry" Iger (1903-1990) started one of the original comic book shops in partnership with Will Eisner in 1936. After Eisner left in late 1939 to start a smaller studio and create his newspaper feature *The Spirit*, Iger continued to package comic books and run a small newspaper syndicate. In a shop, one artist might pencil the figures, another the faces, still another the backgrounds, and the inking might be similarly apportioned out. Complete issues created this way were then sold to publishers as a package. Though shops were common in the early days of comics, the Iger Studio was the last shop standing when these stories were produced.

Ruth Roche (1921-1983) started with Iger at the age of 20 shortly after he split with Eisner, and by the 1950s she was a partner in the enterprise. The two were also reportedly romantically linked. Although Roche was a prolific writer, the sheer volume of the Iger output meant that she also served as script editor for other writers (such as Manning Lee Stokes). So while it's not possible to say with certainty that she wrote every Iger story in this volume, her imprint is on all of them.

One of the hardest tasks in editing this book was keeping the number of Iger-Roche stories down to a manageable level. Roche dealt in truly creepy, unsettling concepts, and often created narratives with an eerie, nightmare atmosphere. Many 1950s horror comics featured violence, gore and menace for their own sake, but in Roche's world, they were often only suggested, for they were merely manifestations of her real subject: the unbridled evil and chaos that was always lurking just beneath the surface, waiting to escape into the world. The innocent died with the guilty in her stories, and sometimes the particular personification of evil would still be at large at the story's end. A chilling variation on the theme of hidden chaos is the discovery that a loved-one or trusted figure is actually "the other" (a theme effectively used in the movie *Invasion of the Body Snatchers* a few years later). "Evil Intruder" (pg. 287) tellingly develops this theme and is one of the more horrifying stories in the whole genre.

What makes "Corpses...Coast to Coast" (pg. 24) so disturbing is the character of the narrator himself, who relishes his megalomaniacal, fascist, wish-fantasy daydream. This could have been a simple comic-book horror story without a narrator, but the story repeatedly emphasizes that the events depicted are merely his imaginings – the story is really about *the character*. For without him it would simply be a wild fantasy that couldn't really happen, but as it's written you know it certainly *could* happen, that a man could be daydreaming of violent world domination by "dehumanizing" the population. Grim as the imagery is, the story has many playful touches such as the U.W.Z. (the explanation of the initials coyly withheld until page 4) and such phrases as "making the world safe for zombiocracy." Those playful aspects of the Roche œuvre come to the fore in "Green Horror" (pg. 124), a story that deals with the eternal triangle: man, woman, and...cactus.

"Death Deals a Hand" (pg. 71) is loosely based on Robert Louis Stevenson's "Story of the Young Man with the Cream Tarts," one of three stories collectively known as "The Suicide Club." The setup of the club comes directly from Stevenson, including the ace of spades representing the victim and the ace of clubs representing the killer. There's evidence in other Iger-shop stories that Roche had read Stevenson and absorbed elements of his style, although it's possible that adaptations on radio (*Escape* in 1947) or television (*Suspense* in 1950) were the scriptwriter's immediate source. At 11,000 words Stevenson's story is a leisurely affair, at times even humorous. The Iger version goes directly to the essence of the story's implicit horrific nature, much as does the recent, acclaimed French film *13 Tzameti*, which powerfully employs the same theme.

With the opening lines of "Experiment in Terror" (pg. 214) – "When you bought this magazine...you wanted a dime's worth of terror: but we...are going to give you a lot more..." – Roche gives notice that the story will go well beyond simple entertainment to tackle some (dare one say) meaty issues. Reading it, one cannot help but think of Art Spiegelman's concentration camp-survivor father Vladek, in *Maus*, saying, "Friends? If you lock them together with no food for a week, then you could see what it is, friends." There is no caption in the final panel to say that the couple who were in love at the start of the story are now devouring the scientist's legs, but by this point no caption is needed. In this Roche think-piece the chaos just below the surface of the civilized world erupts in a particularly realistic, disturbing way.

Roche stories often were psychologically astute. "Night Screams" (pg. 231) deals with guilt and the compulsion to confess, and the narrative unfolds in a subtle progression from the howling of the dog, to the protagonist wanting to kill the dog, to him caught in the light of the window agonizing about the need to confess, to his confession to the killing of the dog, only admitting to his greater crime almost parenthetically in explaining why he killed the dog. The story continues to develop psychologically; the sheriff thinking of his confession in psychiatric terms, the young girl taunting the murderer, with her final deadly act of revenge a purely psychological one.

The art in these stories is not always elegant, but it's a full partner in their success, and only after reading the stories is this apparent. The art on "Corpses" (largely by Robert Webb and David Heames, per comic art historian Hames Ware) is an imaginative, detailed pictorializing of the dream, and the depiction of the sly, weary, corrupt sophistication of the narrator is key to the story's strength. Likewise, the devilish personality given to the card dealer (again Webb and Heames) is what makes "Death Deals a Hand" so potent. The truly disgusting, naked, hairy-limbed, nameless "It" in "Evil Intruder," with its protruding lips and lascivious expression (by Maurice Gutwirth et al., per Ware), carries that story's effrontery to a whole new level. In "Green Horror" the subtle facial expressions of the cactus and the impish insertion of a fine arts icon match the story's arch premise (art on this and "Experiment in Terror" largely by Ken Battefield, per Ware). And in "Night Screams" the unreal and exaggerated landscapes reinforce the dreamlike aspect of the narrative. In all these stories, the art is an essential component of their total effectiveness. J.B.

CARRION DEATH!

MY LIPS ARE PARCHED AND SWOLLEN AND CRACKED, MY TONGUE IS DRY AND SEARCHES MY MOUTH FOR MOISTURE, BUT FINDS NONE. I LIE ON THE BURNING HOT SAND, STARING UP AT THE CLOUDLESS SKY. THE GLARING SUN BAKES DOWN, AND MY EYES SMART BUT THEY DO NOT TEAR, FOR I HAVE HAD NO WATER FOR FOUR DAYS. I LIE ON THE STEAMING DESERT BADLANDS AND I WATCH THE BUZZARDS CIRCLING LAZILY, SCREAMING AND SOARING, SWOOPING HUNGRILY. AND I WAIT...

C'MON, YOU LOUSY VULTURES! C'MON DOWN HERE AND *FEAST!* C'MON DOWN HERE AND *SET ME FREE!*

I TRY TO REMEMBER HOW IT ALL BEGAN... HOW I CAME TO BE LYING HERE, IN THE MIDDLE OF NOWHERE, WAITING FOR THE CARRION BIRDS TO DROP DOWN AND SINK THEIR RAZOR SHARP TALONS INTO FLESH AND TEAR AND RIP AND FREE ME FROM THE JAWS OF DEATH. I SEE IT NOW... THE RIBBON OF CONCRETE STRETCHING ACROSS THE DESERT, SWEEPING BENEATH MY SPEEDING CARWHEELS...

HE'S *GAINING* ON ME! I'LL NEVER *MAKE* IT!

BESIDE ME, ON THE CAR SEAT, THIRTY THOUSAND DOLLARS RESTED IN A BLACK SATCHEL... THIRTY THOUSAND DOLLARS FOR WHICH I'D HELD UP A BANK AND MURDERED A GUARD. AHEAD, EASY LIVING AND WOMEN AND FANCY CLOTHES WAITED, SMILING, BECKONING. BUT RIGHT BEHIND ME, CLOSING THE GAP BETWEEN US, HIS SIREN WAILING, CAME THE STATE TROOPER...

YOU'LL *NEVER GET ME*, COPPER. I'LL...*KILL* YOU FIRST!

© William M. Gaines, Agent, Inc.

REED CRANDALL

"Carrion Death," *ShockSuspenstories* no.9 (June–July 1953), art by Reed Crandall; story by Bill Gaines and Al Feldstein

Page 48. "The Maze Master" (*Baffling Mysteries* 20, April 1954) Art by Lou Cameron (1924-2010)

Lou Cameron did his first comics story ("The Corpse's Embrace," *Dark Mysteries* 1, June–July 1951) for publisher Bill Friedman, whose company assumed several mastheads (Master, Merit, Premiere, Story). As Cameron told interviewer Jim Amash, "...a lot of people went through Billy's company on the way up. It was a place to break in. It was very difficult to do that in most places. You could not break in, say, at Ace unless you had some published work."

After a year at Friedman's, Cameron switched to Ace Periodicals. A.A. Wyn created that company out of Magazine Publishers, where he had been an editor, after owner Harold Hersey died in 1929. In 1940 Wyn branched out into comics, aided by his wife Rose (Cameron knew her as "Ma Wyn"). Ace was located on the 6th floor of a building on West 47th Street, now the heart of New York's Diamond District.

Though Cameron dealt directly with editor Mac Phillips, an episode with managing editor Fred Gardener stuck with him 50 years later:

"Jerry Siegel showed up at Ace one time, and demanded to speak to their comics editor. He had an idea for a comic book, and wanted to speak to Mac Phillips. I was waiting to see Phillips, but somebody was in there, talking to him. The receptionist said to Siegel, 'Well, sit down and I'll tell him you're here.' He said, 'I'm not accustomed to waiting. I am Jerry Siegel. I created Superman comics, and I do not wait in waiting rooms.' He was fussing at this poor little girl, and Gardener came in. He said, 'What the hell is going on? Who are you? What are you yelling about?' And he said, 'I am Jerry Siegel, the creator of Superman, and this impertinent receptionist won't send me in as soon as I – ' Fred says, 'I know who you are. Get out of my office and as I draw breath, you will never do anything for Ace Publications.' He threw him out, and he told the girl, 'You don't have to take crap off of these people. If they give you a hard time, call me. I'll throw them out.' ...Gardener would not suffer fools, and if people raised hell, he threw them down the stairs. He wouldn't put up with any nonsense."

Ace's star artist, Lou Cameron was always assigned the page-one story, his striking splash panels (often full-page) calculated to grab the potential buyer's attention. He was also a born storyteller, as this story shows. A writer at heart, Cameron left comics in the late 1950s to become a successful author of Westerns, creating the popular *Longarm* series under the

ninth issue of *Shock SuspenStories*. Shortly before securing the EC account, he turned in the remarkable "Corpse That Came to Dinner" to Standard Comics.

In comparing "Corpse" to "Carrion Death," one is struck by the differences in storytelling techniques. Unlike other companies, EC did not simply give its artists typewritten scripts for them to break down into panels. Its two editors, Al Feldstein and Harvey Kurtzman, also laid out each story page by page, with Kurtzman even going to the extent of supplying thumbnail drawings of every panel. Feldstein's pages were fully lettered, but he left the panels empty for the artists.

Feldstein had fallen under the intoxicating spell of writer Ray Bradbury, and while this accounted for many classic stories and a substantial part of EC's success, it also tended to make the art seem at times almost incidental. In "Carrion Death" every single panel has a paragraph of descriptive text over it, which can't help but intrude on the artist's approach. In "The Corpse" overhead text is kept to a minimum, leaving Crandall free to tell the story with dialogue and imagery.

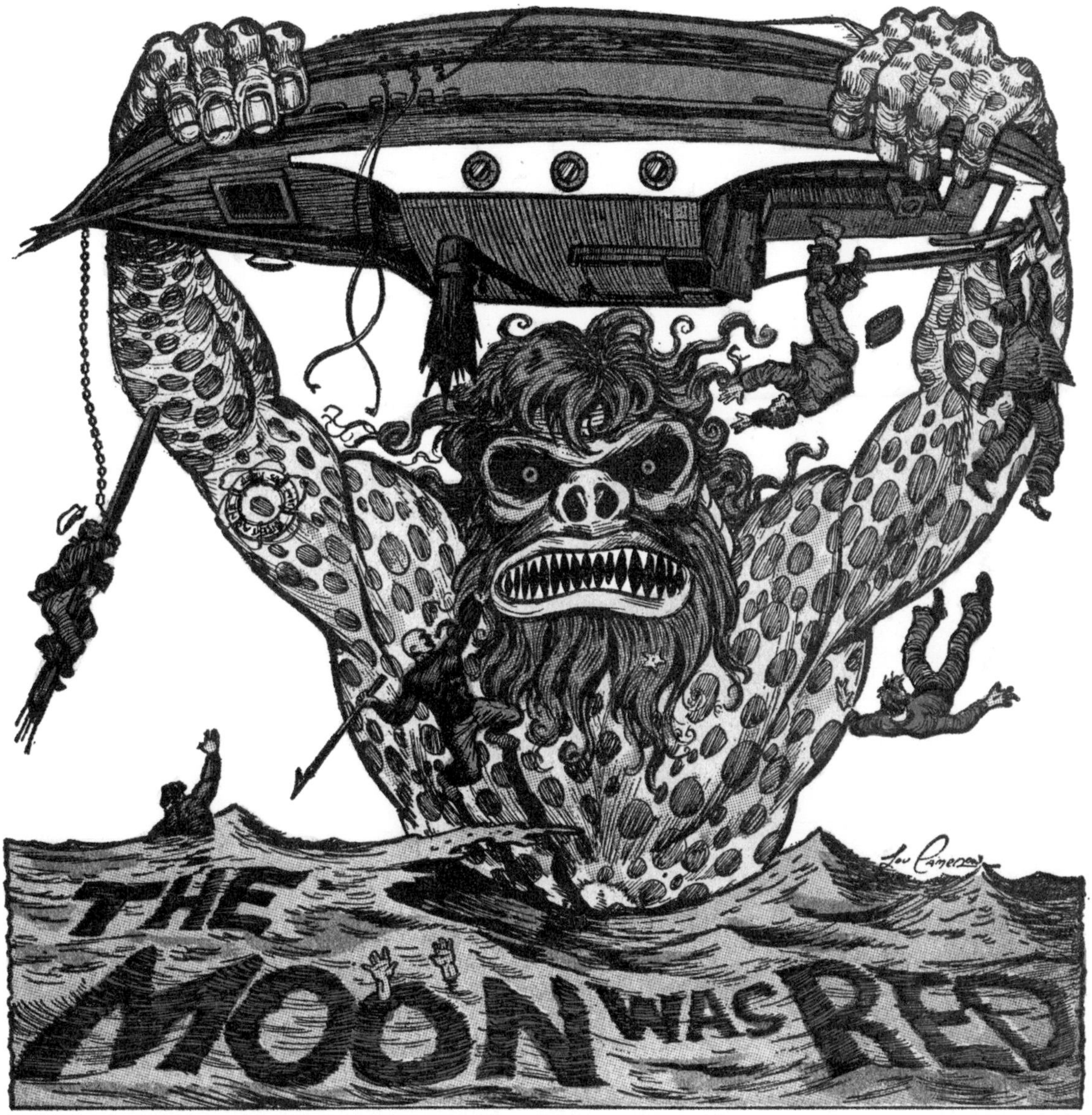
THE MOON WAS RED
Lou Cameron
"The Moon Was Red," *Web of Mystery* no. 18 (May 1953), Lou Cameron splash panel

pen name Tabor Evans. During his period in comics, he generally worked from others' scripts, but he may have written the surreal "Maze Master." [*All quotes in this entry were taken from an interview with Lou Cameron conducted by Jim Amash that appeared in* Alter-Ego *79 and 80 (July and August 2008).*]

Incidentally, that half-page "filler" house ad on the last page was taken from Harvey, not Ace.

Page 55. "Swamp Monster" (*Weird Mysteries* 5, June 1953) Art by Basil Wolverton (1909-1978)

Weird Mysteries was published by Stanley Morse under the banner of Gillmor (at times spelled Gilmor) Magazines, a combination of the names of Morse and managing editor Gilbert Singer. Other Morse comic book imprints included Aragon, Key, Media, S.P.M., and Stanmor. Accountants by trade, Morse and his brother (and future business manager) Michael were so impressed by the profitable ledgers for several comic book clients that they decided in mid-1952 to publish their own horror, romance, war, and Western titles.

This issue of *Weird Mysteries* featured a text feature, "The Blackboard," ostensibly as a continuing give-and-take forum with their readers. The letter printed (from Miss Lucy Hurley) read in part, "Why do you print trash like that? How can you justify lowering yourselves and your readers by offering them the horrible fare that *Weird Mysteries* provides?"

Morse (or Singer) patiently explained that it was simply a matter of supply and demand, and that what Gillmor printed continued a literary tradition:

"First, let me say that the principal aim in publishing our magazine is to give the readers what they want to read. If we didn't do this, we wouldn't (and couldn't) stay in business.

"The type of stories that we are publishing are not chosen by us arbitrarily, but rather after considerable research and investigation into what is marketable on the newsstands. If

HORROR
STORY
RROR
HIDEOUS CRIMES
GHOUL STORIES
Ghastly TALES
YOU, LEO GRANT, ARE THE EDITOR OF "GHASTLY TALES" MAGAZINE ··· YOU SIT IN YOUR OFFICE ON A DARK, DISMAL DAY, READING A SCRIPT ··· YOU'VE READ A LOT OF SCRIPTS IN YOUR TIME, BUT NEVER ONE LIKE THIS! THIS ONE GETS TO YOU ··· MAKES YOUR HAIR STAND ON END! AS YOU READ, YOU SEEM TO SMELL THE MUSTY ODOR OF YAWNING GRAVES WEAVING A HORRID MIST AROUND YOU···

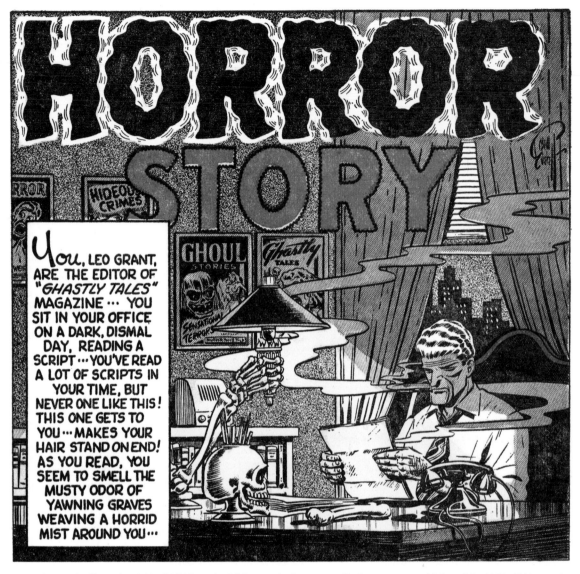

"Horror Story," *Spellbound* no.2 (April 1952), art by Bill Everett. As the most prolific horror comic publisher of the 1950s (389 issues), Atlas is conspicuous by its absence in this book. But the Atlas output is so vast that we felt it would be better served in a separate volume devoted entirely to the company.

MYSTERY and HORROR are what the readers want then we are obliged to comply. In short then, it is the reader who determines what the publisher prints.

"The implication in your letter, and on the part of many people and groups who have taken exception to the bulk of comic magazine material, is that it is 'worthless trash,' having harmful effects on the youth of our country... contributing even to delinquency. If you (and they) will take the trouble to analyze the so-called 'prescribed' reading for children, I am sure you would conclude that comic magazine stories are no more unacceptable than they are.

"For instance, let's study fairy tales:

"1. LITTLE RED RIDING HOOD... in which a vicious wolf devours an old invalid woman and then attempts to do the same to her grand-daughter.

"2. HANSEL AND GRETEL... in which a wicked witch attempts to roast alive two children in a red hot oven with the purpose of eating them afterwards.

"3. SNOW WHITE AND THE SEVEN DWARVES... in which a wicked queen assigns a woodsman to butcher Snow White. Failing in this, she then feeds the girl a poisoned apple.

"There are many, many more... too many to go into in this limited space.

"Surely, horror and violence in this form is no less harmful... IF HARMFUL IT IS... than what you find in comics. Let's remember that we, now adults, were raised on these fairy tales.

"The crux of the matter lies in a child's upbringing. A child who is inclined to delinquency or other types of neurotic behavior does not need comic books to express these tendencies. Comics are no more contributory than anything else in the child's environment.

"Limitations of space stop the discussion at this point. However, we hope we have stimulated enough interest and thought so that other readers, especially parents, will write us their opinions on the topic."

"The Blackboard" may have been a fabricated plant by Morse to answer horror critics. It was never heard from again.

Page 61. "Discovery" (*Black Cat Mystery* 46, October 1953) Art by Manny Stallman (1927-1997), **inked by John Giunta** (1920-1970)

Harvey editor Sid Jacobson fostered a friendly rivalry among his artists, and many of them noticeably improved during his tenure. A good example is Manny Stallman, a veteran comic book artist who had been with Harvey since the inception of the horror era. He did some of the best work of his career under Jacobson, as seen in this story's ambitious splash panel and detailed pencils.

HEARTLINE
THIS IS THE HEART...
THIS IS THE GIRL...
THESE ARE MY HANDS...

"Heartline," *Chamber of Chills* no. 23 (May 1954), art by Manny Stallman, inked by John Giunta. Stark graphics by the Stallman "factory" for Harvey Publications.

Manny Stallman started in comics in the early 1940s as a production assistant for MLJ, then began penciling at Lev Gleason for his superhero and crime titles. By the end of the decade he was working in a variety of styles at Prize under Simon and Kirby's direction (*Charlie Chan, Headline, Justice Traps the Guilty*). Stallman and artist John Giunta forged a small shop in the early 1950s, contributing to Atlas, Avon, and DC. Sid Jacobson felt that Stallman did "sensational things" for Harvey: "...[Manny] was inspired by what was going on, and [the artists] paid attention to each other. Stallman used to have like a little factory. He had several people working for him, John Giunta being one. And then John did some [stories] alone."

Stallman continued to work in comics for Tower and DC into the 1960s and 1970s, then rode out his career producing giveaway promotional eight-page comics for the ice-cream store Baskin-Robbins (*Basky and Robin*) and Bob's Big Boy restaurant (*The Adventures of Big Boy*). As Mark Evanier writes, "For more than a decade, Manny Stallman was the writer-artist-editor of the comic book with the widest circulation of any comic in America. Each month, somewhere between two and three million copies of *Big Boy* were disseminated in hamburger emporiums across the land."

Page 66. "Death Sentence" (*Tomb of Terror* 14, March 1954) Art by Sid Check

Sid Check began in comics c.1949, assisting Wallace Wood and Joe Orlando on jobs for Fox and Avon (including the 25-page Avon one-shot *The Mask of Fu Manchu*). Check was a capable illustrator, but he never seemed to shake the weight of his influences, particularly Wood, as evidenced in this story (depending on the story, he could also ape the styles of Orlando and Al Williamson).

Check's gangly style is well suited to the twisted images of galloping protoplasm in "Death Sentence." One would figure him as a natural fit for Harvey, since editor Jacobson openly encouraged his staff to mimic EC artists, but Check did only three stories for them.

Page 71. "Death Deals a Hand" (*Strange Mysteries* 18, July 1954) Art by Iger studio

When artist Jay Disbrow worked as an inker for Jerry Iger in the early 1950s, all penciling was done by freelancers, and Iger's seven-member staff consisted of five inkers, a letterer, and editor Ruth Roche. As Disbrow notes in his 1985 book, *The Iger Comics Kingdom*:

"Sometimes more than one inker worked on the same page. When hectic schedules prevailed, as many as three or four worked on a single page. All inkers strove to maintain the same technique (at least they were told to), with one artist inking only characters' faces, etc. When the stories were completed, somehow the style of the penciler showed through in the finished product, and every story had the distinctive 'Iger look' to it."

Among its inherent flaws, the shop system left itself open to faulty continuities. On pages six and seven of this story, the inker (or inkers) can't decide whether or not the victim is completely bald.

Page 80. "Custodian of the Dead" (*Web of Evil* 1, November 1952) Art by Jack Cole

The ending of "Custodian of the Dead" is based on Henry Kuttner's classic tale "The Graveyard Rats." In 1950 EC ran a story from the same source, scripted by Gardner Fox and illustrated by Graham Ingels ("Rats Have Sharp Teeth," *Vault of Horror* 14). Both comics versions add unneeded plot complications to Kuttner's straightforward horror tale, but on the whole we think Cole's version is better.

Reportedly, others had been inking Cole's pencils by this time, but since this appears to be his lettering, Cole probably inked it as well.

Page 87. "Servants of the Tomb" (*Witches Tales* 6, November 1951) Art by Bob Powell

Most of the really impressive stories in Harvey's pre-Jacobson period were produced by Bob Powell and his assistants. Powell wrote as well as drew his *Mr. Mystic* strip for the Sunday newspaper *Spirit* section and he also wrote some other features, so it's just possible that he wrote the three early Harvey stories presented in this volume, "Servants of the Tomb," "Pit of the Damned," and "A Safari of Death."

Page 94. "Nightmare" (*Adventures into the Unknown* 51, January 1954) Art by Harry Lazarus

By the time this story appeared, the 3-D comics craze had already come and gone. St. John had started it six months earlier, made a fortune, and lost it just as fast when the fad almost immediately died. Other companies went straight to the losing part. The 3-D comics cost a quarter rather than

the usual dime, and did create a gimmicky effect if produced properly (which they often weren't), but they were in monochrome and provided no long-term entertainment value. The Polaroid 3-D movies that inspired the comics were usually in color with better glasses, and lasted longer, the cycle running over a year before dying out.

Successful 3-D movies like *Hondo* and *Kiss Me Kate* were in the theatres when American Comics Group figured a new way to capitalize on the craze, coming up with the full-color gimmick "Truevision." This is the first story in the format, and Lazarus, who devised the process and did many of the Truevision stories, tried harder to use the technique imaginatively here than he did later. It was used in nine issues of *Adventures into the Unknown* and a few romance titles, more or less ending with the last 3-D movies. Although Harry Lazarus told Jim Amash in 2005 that he wrote some of the Truevision stories, this one seems to have editor Richard Hughes' touch. Hughes wrote many of the ACG stories, and had a way of taking familiar themes and going in a slightly unexpected direction, giving the reader food for thought. This story's twist ending might lead the reader to ponder just what constitutes greed.   J.B.

Page 102. "Me, Ghost" (*Adventures into Darkness* 10, June 1953) Art by Jack Katz (b. 1927)

In the late 1940s, artist Jack Katz apprenticed at King Features Syndicate, learning a thing or two from the great Hal Foster of *Prince Valiant* fame. He did stories for Fawcett, MLJ, Marvel, and, here, for Standard. Katz left the field to paint and teach, but was inspired by the 1960s underground comix movement to create twenty-four issues of *The First Kingdom*, now seen as the first independently published graphic novel.

Page 107. "Dust unto Dust" (*Chamber of Chills* 23, May 1954) Art by Howard Nostrand (1929-1984)

It was Sid Jacobson who gave Howard Nostrand the chance to leave Bob Powell's studio in March 1952 and work on his own, while encouraging him to emulate EC artists Jack

LI MOVES UP THE RIDGE! HIS HEART BEATS LOUDLY! HE IS EXHILERATED! HAPPY!

THE THOUGHT OF KILLING A MAN PLEASES HIM! HE FEELS A STRANGE PERVERTED JOY!

FIRING IS GOING ON ALL AROUND! LI'S BREATHING COMES QUICKLY! SOON... SOON...

THERE! NOW! AN AMERICAN! HIS WHOLE BODY TREMBLING! LI MOVES IN! HE MUSTN'T MISS!

"Kill!" *Two-Fisted Tales* no. 23 (Sept.–Oct. 1951), art by Harvey Kurtzman. Kurtzman's "stationary camera" technique is employed liberally by disciple Howard Nostrand in "Dust unto Dust" (page 107).

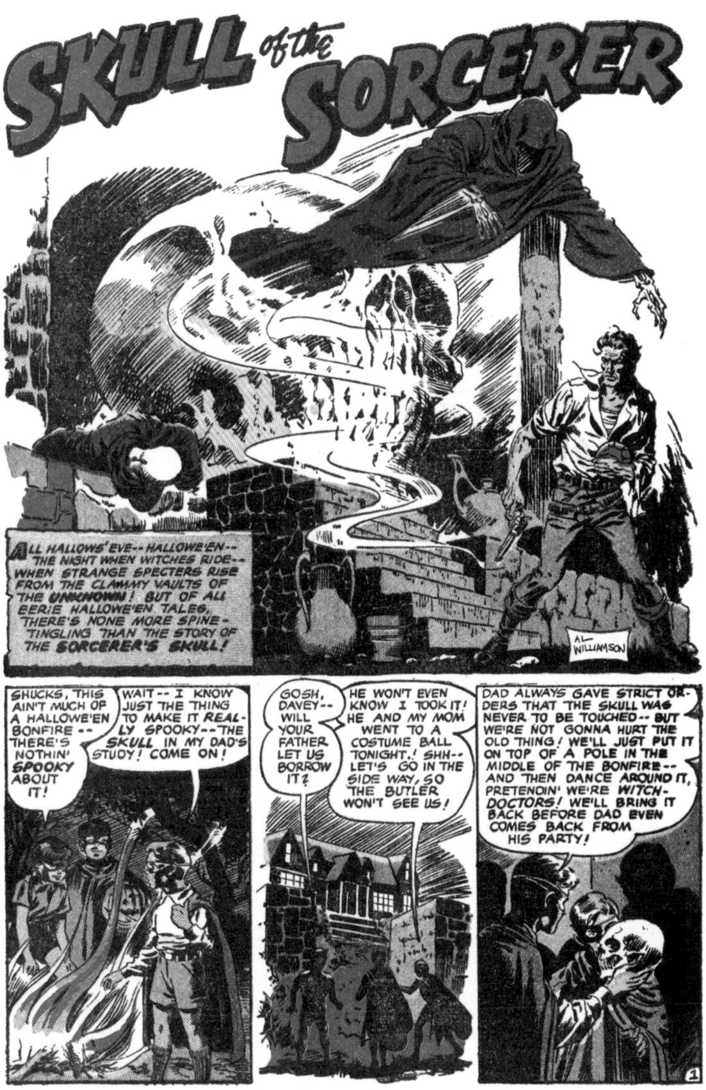
SKULL of the SORCERER
ALL HALLOWS' EVE-- HALLOWE'EN-- THE NIGHT WHEN WITCHES RIDE-- WHEN STRANGE SPECTERS RISE FROM THE CLAMMY VAULTS OF THE UNKNOWN! BUT OF ALL EERIE HALLOWE'EN TALES, THERE'S NONE MORE SPINE-TINGLING THAN THE STORY OF THE SORCERER'S SKULL!
AL WILLIAMSON
SHUCKS, THIS AIN'T MUCH OF A HALLOWE'EN BONFIRE -- THERE'S NOTHIN' SPOOKY ABOUT IT!
WAIT -- I KNOW JUST THE THING TO MAKE IT REALLY SPOOKY -- THE SKULL IN MY DAD'S STUDY! COME ON!
GOSH, DAVEY -- WILL YOUR FATHER LET US BORROW IT?
HE WON'T EVEN KNOW I TOOK IT! HE AND MY MOM WENT TO A COSTUME BALL TONIGHT.! SHH-- LET'S GO IN THE SIDE WAY, SO THE BUTLER WON'T SEE US!
DAD ALWAYS GAVE STRICT ORDERS THAT THE SKULL WAS NEVER TO BE TOUCHED -- BUT WE'RE NOT GONNA HURT THE OLD THING! WE'LL JUST PUT IT ON TOP OF A POLE IN THE MIDDLE OF THE BONFIRE -- AND THEN DANCE AROUND IT, PRETENDIN' WE'RE WITCH-DOCTORS! WE'LL BRING IT BACK BEFORE DAD EVEN COMES BACK FROM HIS PARTY!
1

"Skull of the Sorcerer," *Forbidden Worlds* no.3 (Nov.–Dec.1951) Signed by Williamson, this ACG story was a collaboration with Joe Orlando and Wallace Wood.

Davis and Wallace Wood. As Jacobson remembers, "I think we all looked at EC, and tried to say 'what are they doing that's so interesting?' I became totally enamored with Jack Davis. And Wally Wood. Those were the foremost, and I think Jack Davis was also part of the Will Eisner tradition. Different, but it was the visual strength; he had *style*. And so many artists looked so much alike. But here he had style and realism. And that's what I tried to say, 'Look at these people and see…'"

Nostrand was an avid EC fan, particularly of editor Harvey Kurtzman's war books and *Mad*. In "Dust unto Dust" he tells virtually the entire story with Kurtzman's technique of repeating a scene with slight changes across a tier of panels (a device Kurtzman used much more sparingly).

Page 112. "Drum of Doom" (*Out of the Night* 2, April-May 1952) Art by Al Williamson (1931-2010), **inked by King Ward** (*The attribution of Ward is based on analysis of the work itself, not on objective records.*)

Al Williamson's pre-EC work is notoriously inconsistent, but "Drum of Doom" is one of his better efforts. The artist often cited the 1933 RKO movie *King Kong* as one of his great influences, so it figures that he would be inspired by a tale whose plot closely follows the film, only with a big drum replacing the big ape.

ACG editor Richard Hughes made a profound impression on Williamson, who in 1995 told interviewer Michael Vance that he questioned his mid-1952 decision to work exclusively for EC. "In a way I have mixed emotions about having worked for EC. But, of course, you're young, you're 21, and working with all of these great people. You figure, this is it. [EC] paid better than ACG. And they were very nice people. But Mr. Hughes was exceptional.

"He was a very sweet man. I think he was a very honest man. I understand he wrote some of the stories. The editor that I think I like best – this is not putting down EC guys at all – the one that I feel I should have done more work for, should have been the better artist for, is Richard Hughes.

"But I was young and stupid. I wanted to work for EC, and they asked me to work for them, and not to do any work for anybody else. I remember taking a job in to Mr. Hughes. I said, 'Well, this will be my last job, 'cause I'll be working for EC now.' He said, 'Oh, I really am very, very sorry that you are.' He wished me success."

Page 117. "The Body Maker" (*Black Cat Mystery* 39, September 1952) Art by Warren Kremer (1921-2003)

Before the arrival of Jacobson, variations on traditional horror themes reigned at Harvey, as seen in the use of the Frankenstein theme in "The Body Maker," a typically brutal story from this period.

After graduating from New York's School of Industrial Arts, Kremer got a job at Ace Magazines doing layouts and lettering. He became a full-time artist when the company expanded into comic books in the early 1940s, doing stories and covers for *Hap Hazard, Four Favorites*, and *Super-Mystery*. Kremer moved to Harvey in 1948, was promoted to art editor in 1950, and remained at the company for over 35 years.

Page 124. "Green Horror" (*Fantastic Fears* 8, July-August 1954) Art by Iger studio

Another Iger story in which the innocent die with the guilty, although in this case the guilty is a cactus. In his *Iger Comics Kingdom*, Jay Disbrow described the Iger studio:

"… Ruth Roche wrote scripts, which were translated into finished comics stories. Supplemental scripts were supplied by the respective publishers, and from freelance writers.

"Each script was a complete story, containing narration (the captions) and dialogue ('word balloons' containing the characters' lines). Instructions for the pencilers (scene setting, background, characters, and panel layout) were also included in the script. Note: The artists frequently ignored these instructions, to render the story as they saw fit.

"Scripts were given to pencilers (layout artists), many of whom did the assignments on a freelance basis in their home studios. The stories were penciled 50% larger than a printed page, on bristol board. The finished pencils were then returned to the Iger Studios for lettering of the copy. The pages were then passed out to the inkers, who carefully inked the penciler's drawing. From there it was on to an apprentice for the clean-up process: erasing all pencil marks, opaquing extraneous blemishes, and – last but not least – restoring inked lines that were erased during the clean-up process. Finally, the pages were reviewed by Jerry Iger or Ruth Roche and returned to the publisher."

WEIRD ADVENTURES
SPINE-CHILLING TALES OF MYSTERY–
WEIRD ADVENTURES
AUG.
10¢
PL
WEB OF HORROR!
PUPPET PERIL!
Weird Adventures no.2 (Aug.1951), cover by Ernie Bache and Harry Harrison

Page 161. "Puppet Peril" (*Weird Adventures* 2, July-August 1951) Art by Ernie Bache (?–1968), **inked by Harry Harrison** (1925-2012)

In *Graphic Story Magazine* 15 (Summer 1973) artist/writer/editor Harry Harrison told interviewers Bill Spicer and Pete Serniuk how he broke into comics. "Around 1946 or '47… Burne Hogarth had a drawing class at a little school in New York City… It was an accredited art school, but with dumbhead instructors – only [Burne] had a good class there and everyone with any real interest or talent ended up in it. We were all just a lot of ex-G.I.s riding the G.I. Bill. He transferred us to this one little room first and then started his own school called the Cartoonists and Illustrators School. I think they've changed the name now to something a little more elegant [The School of Visual Arts]. But Burne got the money and a partner and the G.I. backing and moved into an old Bell Telephone building, opened his own school, and bit by bit everyone came to it. The first guy I met was Ernie Bache, and we wound up working together for a few years after that. Then Al Williamson appeared…then Wally Wood, Ross Andru, Mike Esposito, Roy Krenkel, John Severin…we were all just living on the G.I. Bill, 75 bucks a month for a single guy, 15 more for art supplies. We mostly bought art books and sold them for cash, keeping just one pencil and one brush. But very quickly the guys who were going to make it made it.

"I started working with Wally Wood at this time, a very facile guy who really had a natural talent. At that time comics were going great guns, and we started selling art to Victor Fox, our first professional comics work. Anybody could work at Fox, whether they could draw well or not. We worked together because neither of us could hack it alone. We were a complete team, we did everything together. In the beginning I think he penciled and I inked, and then he got very good with inking and did the heads and hands. He'd break down the pages very tight with the figures, and we'd pass the pages back and forth, each handling certain kinds of swipes."

The Wood/Harrison team (with Krenkel backgrounds) made its debut on 1949 Fox romance titles, doing their final stories about a year later for early EC sci-fi books. After the split, Harrison started a small shop, packaging and editing titles for Premiere, Story, and Youthful. He also edited the 1951 one-shot *Captain Rocket* for P.L. Publishing, who published the three-issue run of *Weird Adventures*. With covers by Bache/Harrison (the third issue's can be found in our covers section), this may have been another Harrison-edited package.

"Puppet Peril" takes a "kitchen sink" approach, cramming in just about everything a comic book horror story could contain: a mittel-European setting, an old dark house, a dungeon, a hunchback, a witch at a cauldron, hypnotism, a hypodermic needle, a lingerie panel, bondage, the undead, demons, and fire – not to mention sinister puppets.

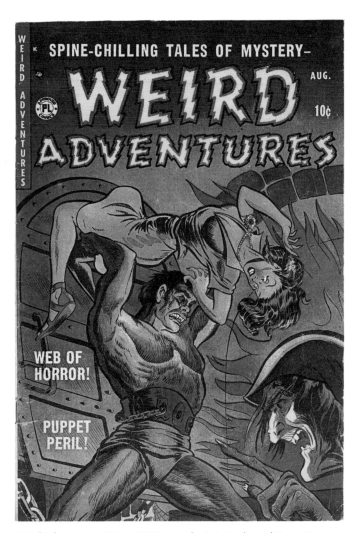

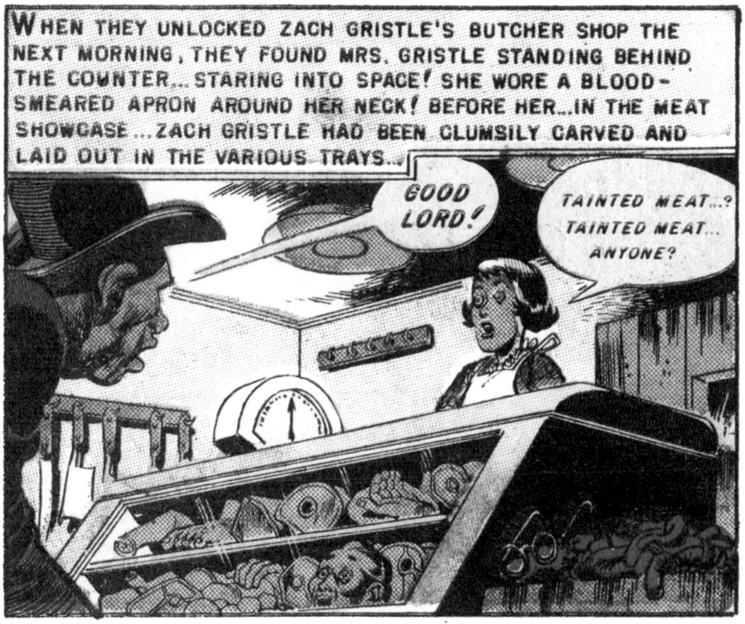
WHEN THEY UNLOCKED ZACH GRISTLE'S BUTCHER SHOP THE NEXT MORNING, THEY FOUND MRS. GRISTLE STANDING BEHIND THE COUNTER... STARING INTO SPACE! SHE WORE A BLOOD-SMEARED APRON AROUND HER NECK! BEFORE HER...IN THE MEAT SHOWCASE... ZACH GRISTLE HAD BEEN CLUMSILY CARVED AND LAID OUT IN THE VARIOUS TRAYS...
GOOD LORD!
TAINTED MEAT...? TAINTED MEAT... ANYONE?

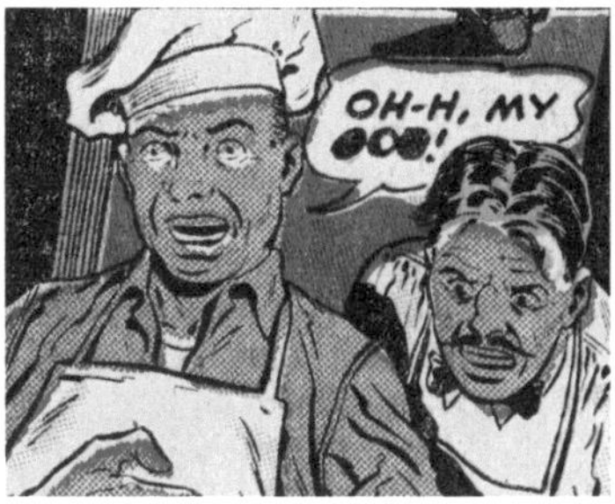
OH-H, MY GOD!

Above: "Tain't the Meat...It's the Humanity," *Tales from the Crypt* no.32 (Oct.–Nov.1952), art by Jack Davis, story by Bill Gaines and Al Feldstein; right: self-censored balloon from last panel of "Chef's Delight"

Page 168. "Mother Mongoose's Nursery Crimes" (*Witches Tales* 25, June 1954) Art by Howard Nostrand

When Sid Jacobson became Harvey editor, classic horror themes and rampant fantasy were moderated by a more contemporary attitude and a definite sense of humor. This latter, as seen in "Mother Mongoose's Nursery Crimes," was not only influenced by EC's phenomenally popular *Mad* (then a comic) but by the macabre humor in many of their horror stories, especially the "Grim Fairy Tales" series. The writers under Jacobson's editorship included Nat Barnett, Dick Kahn, Ted Senitsky [later Sennett], and Art Wallace. Jacobson recalls Barnett as writing "all the really super scripts... [and] those with a real sense of humor, because he had a terrific sense of humor." On this basis, it seems probable that Barnett wrote "I, Vampire," and "What's Happening at 8:30."

Page 169. "Chef's Delight" (*Mysterious Adventures* 20, June 1954) Art by Dick Beck, inked by Bill Savage (*The art attribution is based on analysis of the work itself, not on objective records.*)

As pointed out in the introduction, the other companies' conception of horror was generally quite different from that found in the EC comics. One company, Story Comics, was the exception, and this story is typical of their later output. EC specialized in stories in which someone is driven by the actions of a thoroughly nasty character to exact violent revenge, usually involving physical dismemberment with an obvious ironic twist. Miserable marriages and unfaithful spouses often figured in these stories. "Chef's Delight" mixes these in a plot that draws on EC's "Tain't the Meat... It's the Humanity" (*Tales from the Crypt* 32, Oct-Nov 1952) – the nasty butcher, the dead son, the wife driven mad, innocents opening the store next morning to find the neatly arranged carnage – and "An Ample Sample" (*Vault of Horror* 32, Nov-Dec 1953) – the spouse who spends freely while the other has to scrimp, again the spouse driven mad, and the signs labeling the various body parts.

But the plot similarities are only the beginning. A pastiche of another artist's style was not unknown in comics (see Nostrand's Wood-Davis-Kurtzman style in "Dust Unto Dust"), but the Story Comics writer did something unique in comics – he created an extraordinarily close pastiche of EC's editor-writer Al Feldstein's idiosyncratic *writing* style. Every panel has a text-heavy caption, and many words are almost randomly emphasized in larger, darker italics ("their *stomachs* aren't prepared for the *sight* which greets them"), both Feldstein hallmarks. (Some Story stories even used the LeRoy lettering employed by EC.) Though there is no pictorialized teller-of-tales, the above-title text is an exact copy of the patter used by EC's GhouLunatic hosts. And like EC, the teller sarcastically comments on the characters and the action all through the story, and even speaks directly to the reader: "Yes, as you can see, Francois *does* have a wife!" "Not a very pretty picture, is it, kiddies?" The style is pure EC, down to the "Yes" and "kiddies." Even the EC endings, which traditionally had the innocents saying, "Good Lord!" and "*choke*" is paralleled here with "My God!" and "(gag)."

Still, there *are* some differences. The splash panel sports a horror concept that is completely different and incompatible with the story. And Story went further in the outright gore and bad taste. EC would never have used the horrific image of the meat cleaver hacking into the chef's head, with blood spurting out. Feldstein and Gaines would have withheld the gore until their bad-taste "joke" conclusion in which they *intentionally* defied good taste. Story used gore without irony. It seems, incidentally, that the word God in the last panel was tampered with in the original printing, an apparent self-censorship of "blasphemy." J.B.

Page 175. "Colorama" (*Black Cat Mystery* 45, August 1953) Art by Bob Powell

"Colorama" is probably the most famous Harvey horror story, having been reprinted numerous times in black and white; Harvey reprinted it twice in color, though only a censored post-Comics Code version. *The Comics Journal* did finally reprint the original in 2008 (though most, if not all,

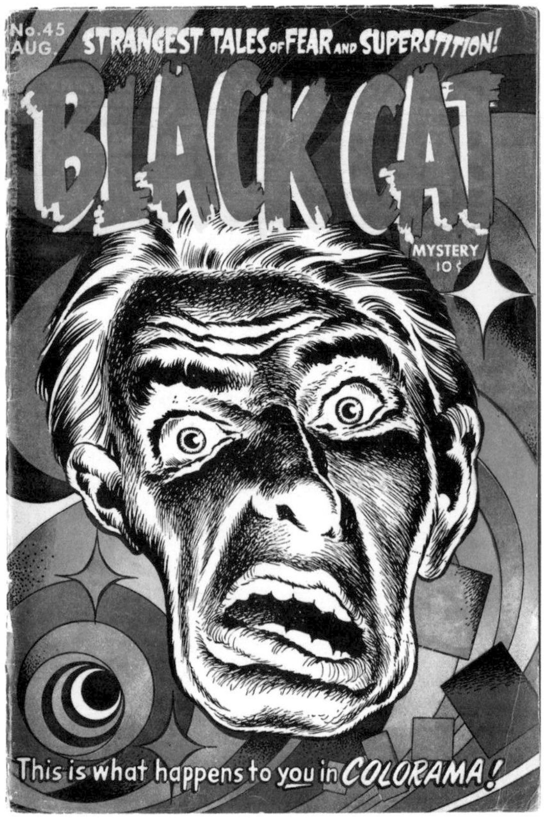
No. 45 AUG.
STRANGEST TALES OF FEAR AND SUPERSTITION!
BLACK CAT
MYSTERY 10¢
This is what happens to you in COLORAMA!

Black Cat Mystery no. 45 (Aug. 1953), cover by Warren Kremer. Harvey editor Sid Jacobson: "The 'Colorama' cover is a self-portait of of Warren Kremer, the twisted face. What he did was draw himself and then go like that (*crumples a piece of paper*) and throw it on the floor. And then he drew it."

of the other stories in this volume have not been reprinted in color since they first appeared).

Howard Nostrand pointed out Powell's resemblance to the story's murder victim. "He looked like the eyeglass-maker in 'Colorama.' He wore glasses and had kind of a round face. I wouldn't say he was fat; he was a little overweight for his size."

Editor Sid Jacobson himself claimed authorship of "Colorama," and the storytelling is an amalgam of devices used by EC editors Al Feldstein (text narration in the second person but told visually from a first person perspective) and Harvey Kurtzman ("fixed camera" panels on page one, each tier on page two, and most of page five; the absence of color in the final panel). It is even drawn by Powell in a style reminiscent of EC's Johnny Craig.

Jacobson readily admitted EC's influence. "I think that, before [my arrival], everyone knew they were doing hack things, and then I came in, new to the whole business, and I looked at EC and I said, 'Oh my God!' I mean, no one else knew anything, except they. And I said, 'Why don't we strive to do this?' ...That's what we were trying to emulate. At that time no one else was doing anything worthwhile... there was nothing at any of the other companies. And EC was superb. And that's what you try to do. And I think we came closest to it."

Page 180. "The Thing from the Sea" (*Eerie* 2, August-September 1951) Art by Wallace Wood (1927-1982)

Before moving exclusively to EC in early 1952, the prolific Wallace Wood created comics for Avon, Fox, Trojan, Youthful, and Ziff-Davis. Much of his early work is collaborative, and Joe Orlando and Sid Check may have helped out on this Avon assignment, especially as it's unsigned. Other than a few stories for early issues of the EC horror titles, Wood did very little in the genre, much preferring science fiction.

Page 187. "The Flapping Head" (*Forbidden Worlds* 6, May-June 1952) Art by Al Williamson, with Larry Woromay and King Ward

The idea of a "flapping head" is another example of taking a traditional theme in a slightly unexpected direction, a trademark of ACG editor Richard Hughes. Though the supernatural could be threatening at ACG, it was treated completely differently from Ruth Roche's world of evil and chaos hiding just beneath the veneer of civilization. Here, supernatural elements were clearly separate from our workaday world but still subject to orderly rules: the head must fly exactly at midnight, the events must occur exactly 100 years later than the initial events, and the vampire can be vanquished if he preys on someone who would not live out the night. After their initial surprise, the protagonists earnestly try to figure out the rules that they know will restore the natural order of the world, and natural order was indeed always restored at the end of ACG stories.

Al Williamson was certainly involved in this story, but the other art attribution is based on analysis of the work itself, not on objective records. Some have suggested that Harry Harrison also lent a hand. J.B.

Page 195. "Amnesia" (*Chamber of Chills* 17, May 1953) Art by Warren Kremer

A longtime Harvey staffer that editor Jacobson worked closely with was Warren Kremer, an all-around creative dynamo who served as art editor, created cover and story logos, illustrated covers and stories, and developed ideas for cover artist Lee Elias. Though later the mainstay of the Harvey young-kids line (*Casper, Little Audrey,* etc.), even taking credit for inventing Richie Rich, Kremer was also an able horror practitioner, as his atmospherically creepy "Amnesia" attests.

Page 200. "Vision of the Gods" (*Nightmare* 1, Summer 1952) Art by Everett Raymond Kinstler (b.1926)

This page, probably inspired by H. Rider Haggard's famous novel *She*, is typical of the detailed illustrational style that Kinstler brought to comics. Much of his best comics work was for the many black-and-white pictorial "table of contents" inside front covers that he did for Avon. In the 1960s Kinstler made a career change that led to his becoming one of the top portrait artists of his time, painting the official portraits of Gerald Ford and Ronald Reagan. Readers are referred to *Everett Raymond Kinstler; The Artist's Journey Through Popular Culture* by Kinstler and Jim Vadeboncoeur, Jr.

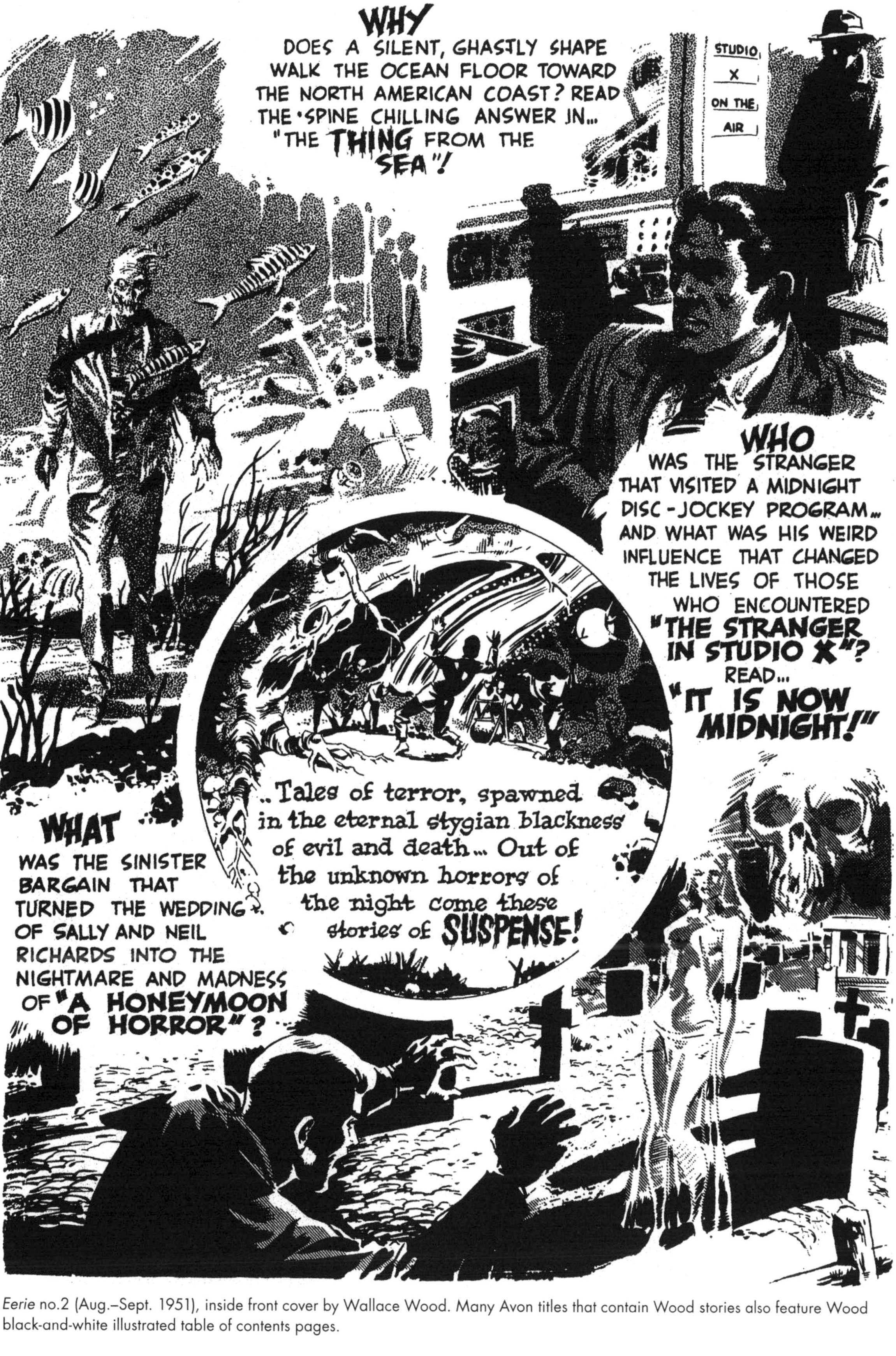
WHY DOES A SILENT, GHASTLY SHAPE WALK THE OCEAN FLOOR TOWARD THE NORTH AMERICAN COAST? READ THE SPINE CHILLING ANSWER IN... "THE THING FROM THE SEA"!
STUDIO X ON THE AIR
WHO WAS THE STRANGER THAT VISITED A MIDNIGHT DISC-JOCKEY PROGRAM... AND WHAT WAS HIS WEIRD INFLUENCE THAT CHANGED THE LIVES OF THOSE WHO ENCOUNTERED "THE STRANGER IN STUDIO X"? READ... "IT IS NOW MIDNIGHT!"
..Tales of terror, spawned in the eternal stygian blackness of evil and death... Out of the unknown horrors of the night come these stories of SUSPENSE!
WHAT WAS THE SINISTER BARGAIN THAT TURNED THE WEDDING OF SALLY AND NEIL RICHARDS INTO THE NIGHTMARE AND MADNESS OF "A HONEYMOON OF HORROR"?

Eerie no.2 (Aug.–Sept. 1951), inside front cover by Wallace Wood. Many Avon titles that contain Wood stories also feature Wood black-and-white illustrated table of contents pages.

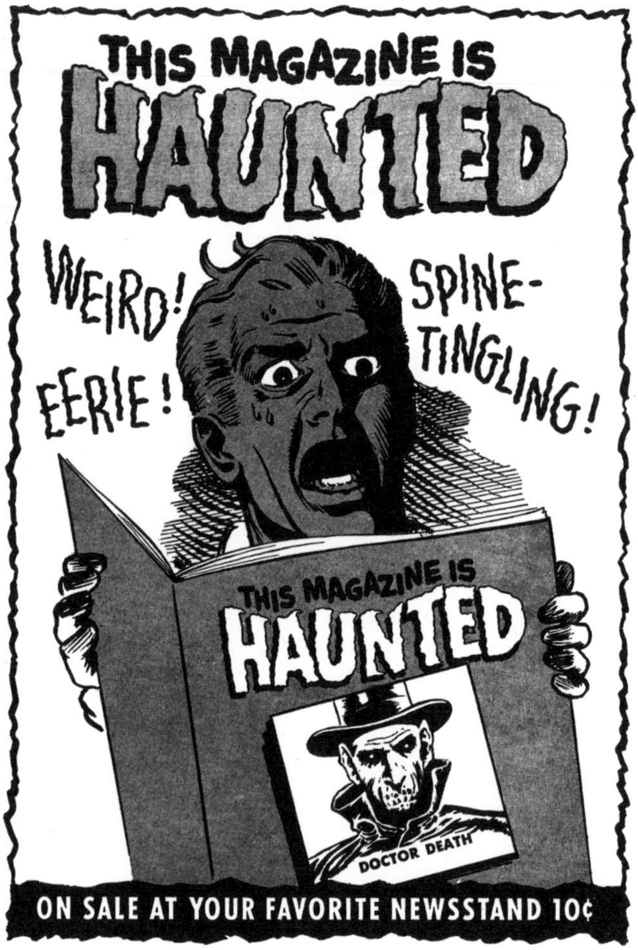
THIS MAGAZINE IS
HAUNTED
WEIRD!
SPINE-TINGLING!
EERIE!
THIS MAGAZINE IS
HAUNTED
DOCTOR DEATH
ON SALE AT YOUR FAVORITE NEWSSTAND 10¢

Fawcett inside-cover house ad with art by George Evans, 1952

Page 201. "The Man Who Outdistanced Death" (*Strange Suspense Stories* 4, December 1952) Art by George Evans (1920-2001)

George Evans started in comics during the postwar years, drawing stories for Fiction House. By late 1949 he had settled in comfortably at Fawcett, but in 1952 the company was on the verge of losing a 12-year-old copyright infringement lawsuit filed by DC, which claimed Fawcett's hero Captain Marvel was based on Superman. Forced to cancel its flagship title, Fawcett shut down its comics division in 1953.

As Evans told interviewer Paul Wardle, "I had no idea of [Fawcett's] financial state. In fact, I don't think it had been decided, but Al Williamson, who cruised everywhere, and wherever he went he was as much a salesman for me and my stuff as he was for his own, and he wanted me to go up to EC and he said: 'Fawcett appears to be going to lose this suit and it will probably put them out of business.' So, he took me up to EC and introduced me to Bill [Gaines] and Al [Feldstein] and we hit it off from the first. It was like walking into a friendly house, just people sitting around, and we talked and they said, 'Well, we got a script here, do you want to try it?' So I talked to the people at Fawcett and they said, yes, it was true that things were going to be bad and if I had the chance it would probably be wise to take it. They were good people up at Fawcett. I liked every one of them."

Page 209. "I, Vampire" (*Chamber of Chills* 24, July 1954) Art by Howard Nostrand

Another engaging Harvey story by Howard Nostrand in the Jack Davis mold. Warren Kremer remembers Sid Jacobson steering Nostrand in that artistic direction. "When [Nostrand] came to us, his inking was just like Powell's. And Sid said to him, 'Look, we're trying to do what EC does. Look at this guy Jack Davis, he's got a terrific technique. Why don't you style your stuff after him?' And Nostand went home and imitated Jack Davis. He did all the wrinkles and the lines, and then he kept drawing like Davis. He had all those little bubbles in the ground, all of that."

Page 214. "Experiment in Terror" (*Haunted Thrills* 13, January 1954) Art by Iger studio

Manhattanite Jerry Iger lavished a portion of his considerable bank account on dancing and dining, and fancied himself a man about town. Jay Disbrow recalls, "Jerry was fascinated with show business, and he knew many people who were actively involved in the Broadway scene. He had a fondness for bringing actors, actresses, singers, and dancers to his studios to show them off to us. I don't think he knew many of the top performers of that day, but he knew many who were on their way up, and a few who were on their way down."

Quality editor Al Grenet, who got his 1938 start at Eisner and Iger's studio, remembers Iger as a guy who never let his diminutive stature prevent him from throwing his weight around. As he told interviewer Jim Amash, "Jerry Iger was a little fellow... but was a very strict boss. This was in the days of the Depression when we worried about our jobs. He'd come in about 10:00, look around and see that some of the guys were talking and some were working. Iger spoke with a lisp. He'd say [*imitating Iger*] 'Jeethuth Crythte! This is Monday, tomorrow's Tuesday, and Wednesday's coming. Half the week's shot to hell and nothing's done!' That's the way he used to talk. People used to make fun of him. He was tyrannical in that sense.

"I remember one time when Iger invited all of us to his house – [artist] Aldo Rubano, me, and some others. Iger had a servant working for him named Rufus, who also worked in the office. We sat down for dinner and Rufus served us some soup. Iger asked Rufus, 'Where's the crackers?' Rufus

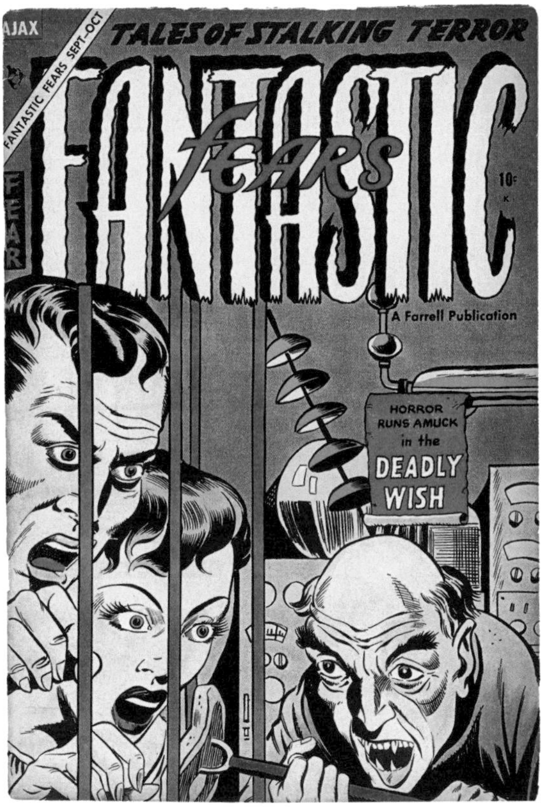
AJAX
TALES OF STALKING TERROR
FANTASTIC FEARS SEPT-OCT
FANTASTIC
FEARS
10¢
A Farrell Publication
HORROR RUNS AMUCK in the
DEADLY WISH

Fantastic Fears no.9 (Sept.–Oct. 1954), cover by Iger studio. This cover inexplicably illustrates the story "Experiment in Terror," which had appeared eight months earlier in a different Iger title.

said there weren't any more, and Iger said, 'What do you mean there aren't any more? You ate all the crackers?' We were embarrassed because Iger was yelling at poor Rufus, but Iger used to yell at everybody. He was lucky that he never got beaten up, because there were a few guys who wanted to...I remember one guy threatened to beat him up, and Iger was such a little guy, he was shaking in his pants." [*All quotes in this entry were taken from an interview with Al Grenet conducted by Jim Amash that appeared in* Alter-Ego 89 *(October 2009).*]

Page 221. "Art for Death's Sake" (*Witches Tales* 15, October 1952) Art by Rudy Palais (1921-2004)

Born in Hoboken, NJ, Rudy Palais learned his craft as a teenager working for an art studio that designed movie theatre and commercial business fronts. One of its clients was Warner Brothers, and Palais was soon creating movie posters for the studio, and meeting movie stars such as James Cagney, Bette Davis, and Edward G. Robinson. In 1992 he told interviewer Jim Amash, "That was great. Here I was in my twenties and I'm meeting these God-like people off the screen."

After a strike forced Palais to leave Warners, he worked part-time in the display department of Brooklyn's Medal Gold Ice Cream Company, designing its *Popsicle* logo, a variant of which is still in use today. The artist then spent five years at Columbia Pictures painting over 750 grade-B movie posters.

His brother Walter had been working as an artist at the Iger shop, and got Palais his start in comics in the early 1940s. "Walter told them about me, and they asked him to tell me to drop in sometime, which I did. I became so interested in the work these young men were doing that I decided to jump into the comics game. It opened up a new horizon of all kinds of things I could be drawing. It was different from doing movie posters, which was something you constantly did from photographs. That didn't do a whole lot for your imagination other than making new layouts."

Palais left Iger after about nine months, then worked on staff for Quality shortly before commencing a busy freelance career, doing work for editors L.B. Cole at Holyoke (*Captain Aero, Cat-Man, Terrific*), Charles Biro at Lev Gleason (*Crime Does Not Pay*), and Ed Cronin at Hillman (*Air Fighters, Clue*), as well as work for Ace, Harvey, and Fox, and several issues of *Classics Illustrated* under editor Alex Blum.

Palais enjoyed the challenges of horror. "I really had fun doing that work. Horror stories lend themselves to creativity. I like crime, drama, and horror stories...I always envisioned the characters in my head and that helped me tell the story. Sometimes I found the stories a little lacking, and I'd add things to punch up the drama. I would exaggerate things as I felt necessary to add mood to the story."

When asked why his characters sweated so much (as they do in this story), Palais replied matter-of-factly, "Well, I added that to emphasize the stress that the characters were going through." [*All quotes in this entry were taken from an interview with Rudy Palais conducted by Jim Amash that appeared in* Alter-Ego 62 *(October 2006).*]

Page 226. "A Safari of Death" (*Chamber of Chills* 8, May 1952) Art by Bob Powell

Another accomplished story by the Powell team during the pre-Jacobson era, "A Safari of Death" has particularly fine inks by Howard Nostrand, who a few months later would be embarking on a solo career.

You may have noticed that all Harvey stories are five pages long. According to Sid Jacobson, that was no accident. "That's an old Harvey trick. All Harvey stories were five pages. Because it was broken down to leave you filler material and advertising [on the same flat]. The advertising flats were on one or two, I think...it always remained that way." Flats are the large full sheets that are cut down and arranged into a book. This would explain why Harvey books so often began with text material, usually a table of contents and an ad.

Page 231. "Night Screams" (*Journey into Fear* 2, July 1951) Art by Iger studio

Of Iger's two horror accounts, Ajax/Farrell and Superior, the latter Canadian company was decidedly more of a fly-by-night operation, with inferior printing, covers that were often cobbled together from interior story panels, and the frequent reprinting of old stories. Superior's "Statement of Ownership" lists its editor as Harry L. Cohen, with a Brooklyn address. Cohen was probably the agent between Iger and the publisher, as the stories were unquestionably edited by Ruth Roche.

"Night Screams" is the earliest Iger story in this collection, appearing in the second issue of Superior's first horror title, *Journey into Fear.* The penultimate page eight has a distinct sexuality to it, with the protagonist prostrate in supplication before his scornful ex-girlfriend, and her pulling him up by his hair to her breast. Just enough, perhaps, to entice a pubescent youth to part with his dime.

Page 240. "Here Today..." (*Black Cat Mystery* 50, June 1954) Art by Sid Check, inked by Frank Frazetta (1928-2010)

Another artist Sid Check admired was Frank Frazetta, and they worked together on at least two stories plus the classic *Beware* cover presented in our cover section.

In a 2002 interview with Heritage Auctions, Frazetta recalled, "I don't remember that much about Sid Check. I only knew him for a few weeks...I do recall helping him on several stories and, I believe, a cover of some sort...You have to remember that I helped out a lot of guys during those days. Everybody did some inking on last-minute deadline jobs as favors to friends, or to make a little extra money. If you look carefully at the faces, or scenes with action, you can usually see where I was inking. My stuff is easy to notice if you know where to look. I never tried to change someone else's lines if I was inking them. Sometimes there would be areas that needed my approach, and these were left open for me to do what I wanted. I was often asked to ink the faces. I enjoyed giving the faces some unique character."

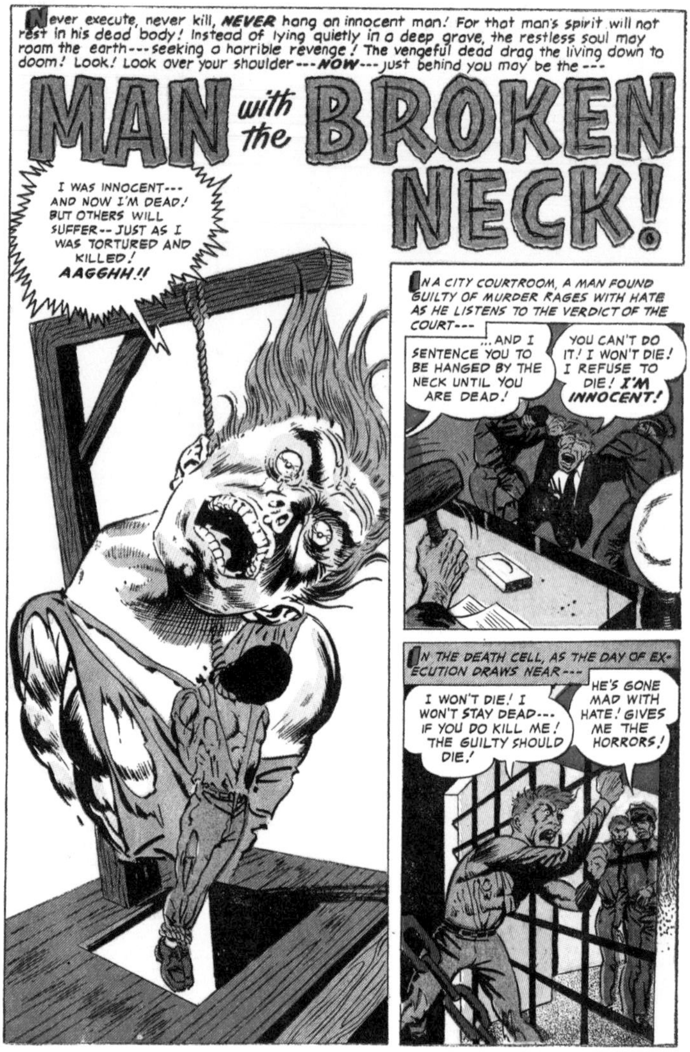

Never execute, never kill, NEVER hang an innocent man! For that man's spirit will not rest in his dead body! Instead of lying quietly in a deep grave, the restless soul may roam the earth---seeking a horrible revenge! The vengeful dead drag the living down to doom! Look! Look over your shoulder---NOW---just behind you may be the---
MAN with the BROKEN NECK!
I WAS INNOCENT--- AND NOW I'M DEAD! BUT OTHERS WILL SUFFER-- JUST AS I WAS TORTURED AND KILLED! AAGGHH!!
IN A CITY COURTROOM, A MAN FOUND GUILTY OF MURDER RAGES WITH HATE AS HE LISTENS TO THE VERDICT OF THE COURT---
...AND I SENTENCE YOU TO BE HANGED BY THE NECK UNTIL YOU ARE DEAD!
YOU CAN'T DO IT! I WON'T DIE! I REFUSE TO DIE! I'M INNOCENT!
IN THE DEATH CELL, AS THE DAY OF EXECUTION DRAWS NEAR---
I WON'T DIE! I WON'T STAY DEAD--- IF YOU DO KILL ME! THE GUILTY SHOULD DIE!
HE'S GONE MAD WITH HATE! GIVES ME THE HORRORS!

Beware no.10 (July 1954), "Man with the Broken Neck," art by Sid Check and Frank Frazetta. Another dynamic collaboration from the short-lived team.

Frazetta appears to have done some penciling here as well, the most obvious example being the gracefully falling figure in the last panel of page three. Even though Frazetta's input is substantial, the storytelling is Check's achievement, and may be his best work in comics.

"Here Today..." is based rather closely on the 1952 George K. Arthur short film *The Stranger Left No Card*, and equals if not exceeds the sinister whimsy of the film.

Page 245. "Cat's Death" (*Strange Terrors* 7, March 1953) Art by Joe Kubert (b.1926)

Publisher Archer St. John (who was educated at St. Albans, an Illinois Episcopal boarding school) had a strong sense of good taste, and undoubtedly found most horror comics distasteful. Of the roughly 700 issues of over 75 titles of pre-Code comics that he published, only 20 issues of two titles were horror comics. He even changed the title of the longer running one from *Weird Horrors* to the decidedly milder *Nightmare*, and, later, to *Amazing Ghost Stories*. St. John also considered himself an innovator, and the bizarre covers (seen in the cover section of this book) by two artists who otherwise never worked in comics are certainly different!

Joe Kubert and his partner Norman Maurer had a long association with St. John, starting in 1949, when Kubert sold the publisher several comics issues as complete packages. In the Summer of 1953, Kubert and Maurer approached St. John with a proposal to publish comics in 3-D, and entered into a profit-sharing agreement to produce both 3-D and regular comics, notably their own titles, *Tor, Whack,* and *The Three Stooges.* In between these two periods of special contractual arrangements, Kubert served a two-year stint in the Army, during which he was an occasional freelancer for the St. John horror books. Kubert liked working for St. John, and had complete freedom to lay out the scripts given to him as he chose. The result is some of his best work of the period, particularly this story with its intense narrative style, elaborate panel layouts and especially the creative use of lettering throughout. For more on Kubert, see *Man of Rock: a Biography of Joe Kubert* by Bill Schelly (Fantagraphics Books). J.B.

Page 253. "The Wall of Flesh" (*This Magazine Is Haunted* 12, August 1953) Art by Bob Powell

Bob Powell worked for a number of publishers during the 1950s. In addition to Harvey, his accounts included Atlas, Hillman, Magazine Enterprises, and Fawcett. For the latter he did some excellent horror stories with intriguing concepts, a fine example of which is "Wall of Flesh."

There was a lot more to Fawcett Publications than *Captain Marvel,* though they were heavily invested in the success of that title. Some of the most challenging and off-beat stories of the period came from this family-owned business, one that treated its workers decently and encouraged a convivial atmosphere. As production man Emilio Squeglio told interviewer Jim Amash, "Al Allard [Fawcett art director] was a wonderful man – very honest and fair. Ralph Daigh was the editorial director, and he really supervised the comics. He was committed to making sure he had the best writers, and that their work was up to Fawcett's standards. His heart was in his work. Mr. Daigh was a stern, quiet man – very fastidious, but a nice man. He never ventured out of his office unless there was a particular reason. He didn't walk up and down the halls. Now, Al used to fly around the place. He'd have one pant leg inside his boot and one outside, and had long hair. He was a good-looking man who always wore black or brown shirts – that kind of thing – the 'arty' type. But inwardly, he was a very fine man. Will Lieberson was the executive director. Will was a fun guy. He was kind of short, and dressed up for parties, because he liked to clown around. Fawcett was great for parties. They kept the entire 11th floor unrented just for parties. They'd have a party at the drop of a hat. It was a fun company."

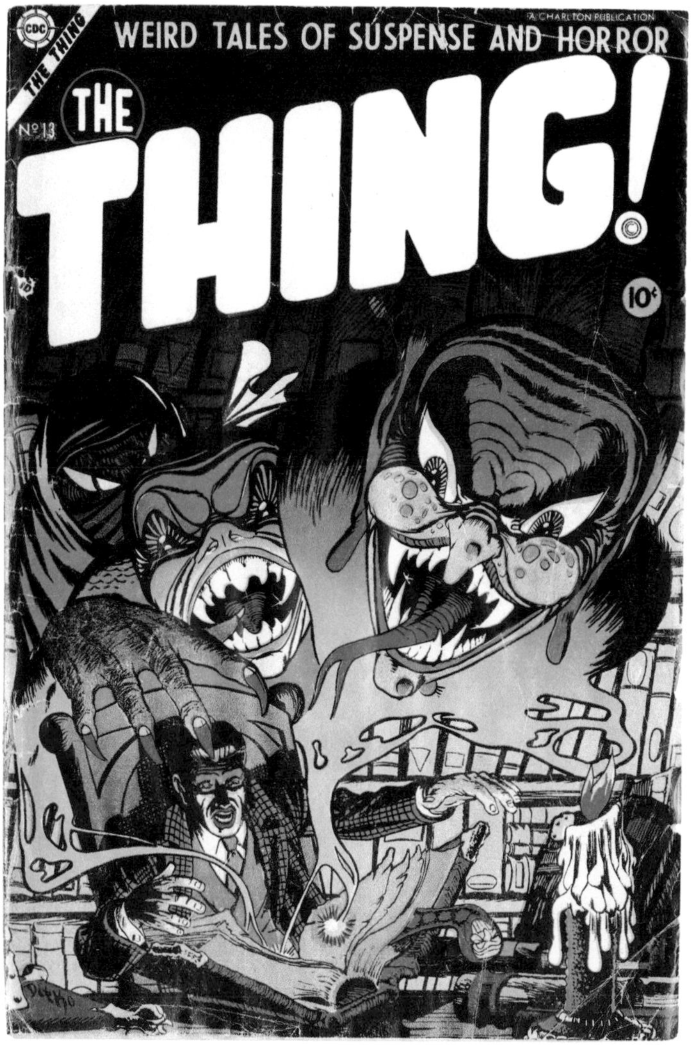
A CHARLTON PUBLICATION
CDC
THE THING
WEIRD TALES OF SUSPENSE AND HORROR
No 13
THE THING!
10¢
The Thing no.13 (April 1954), cover by Steve Ditko. Another glaring omission from this book is the work of comic book horror master Steve Ditko, readily available in the multi-volume *Steve Ditko Archives* (Fantagraphics Books).

When Squeglio arrived at Fawcett in 1947, DC's lawsuit had already been hanging over the company for six years, and wouldn't be resolved for another five. Squeglio said a damaging rumor had circulated that a Fawcett artist swiped a *Superman* layout into *Captain Marvel,* and that DC was using this as evidence to cement its case. "We never knew how true it was. They never told us who did it...We never found out who it was, or whether or not it was really true. I know [circulation director] Roscoe Fawcett believed it was so, and he didn't want to fight it anymore. He didn't want to lose any more money on this suit. If they'd kept fighting, [the entire company] might have been ruined. I think the story was put out to scare Fawcett into settling the case [which they did]. I don't think DC really had that much against Fawcett. The two characters were so different that I didn't see any similarities. [But] let's face it, Fawcett was a major competitor to DC. They were pushing DC hard in the sales. From what Roscoe told us, *Captain Marvel* was really the big money maker and was carrying the department. The rest of the comics couldn't. There wouldn't be enough money coming in to keep it profitable in terms of staff, materials, and so forth. That's why they stopped doing comics." [*All quotes in this entry were taken from an interview with Emilio Squeglio conducted by Jim Amash that appeared in* Alter Ego *41 (October 2004).*]

Page 261. "Nightmare World" (*Weird Tales of the Future* 3, September 1952) Art by Basil Wolverton

One of Wolverton's most infamous stories for its LSD-like theme, "Nightmare World" appeared in the third issue of Stanley Morse's *Weird Tales of the Future.* Wolverton figured heavily in its eight-issue run, doing three covers and as many as three stories per issue. He had been losing interest in comic books around this time, and was busy trying to come up with a syndicated strip, when the chance arose to work on titles in which artists would share in the profits. As he told interviewer Dick Voll, "Somebody in New York tried to talk me into joining a very small group of artists and writers who would be their own publishers. Among them was Mickey Spillane. I declined. I heard later that it didn't work out. Nevertheless, I unwisely joined another group for the same purpose. For a year I batted out comic book pages. Five new titles of ours went on the stands for several months, including *Weird Tales of the Future*. They simply added to the already glutted market. The comic book market was starting to topple for too many publishers."

Three of the other four Morse titles that featured Wolverton were *Mr. Mystery, Weird Mysteries,* and *Weird Chills*. Editor Ray Gill, a Wolverton fan since the early 1940s when the pair worked together at Lloyd Jacquet's studio, was the brains behind the failed cooperative and responsible for Wolverton's last non-humorous work in comics.

ME
In this issue
THE GHOST RIDER
10¢
BOBBY BENSON'S
B-Bar-B
RIDERS
No. 14

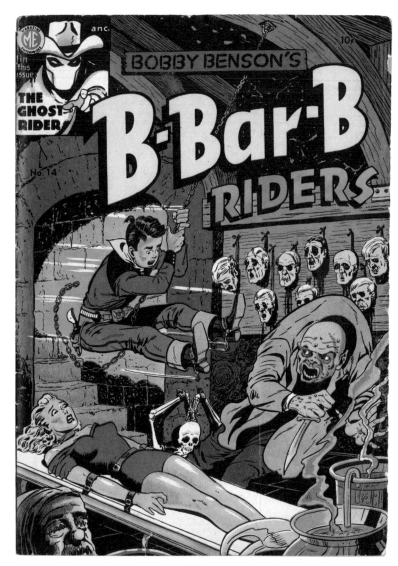

Bobby Benson's B-Bar-B Riders no. 14 (1952), cover attributed to Bob Powell. This Western title took a stab at horror perhaps a bit too earnestly, taking the prize for most severed heads on a cover. Publisher Vin Sullivan's Magazine Enterprises omitted the cover month to prolong its newsstand shelf life.

Page 265. "What's Happening at...8:30 P.M." (*Witches Tales* 25, June 1954) Art by Howard Nostrand

In his 1968 interview with Bhob Stewart, Howard Nostrand complained that, compared to EC, Harvey never went quite far enough in its horror books: "Harvey had a sort of chicken attitude about horror stuff. Like, it should be horrible but not *too* horrible. Granted, they get a little ghastly every once in a while, but I suppose they wanted to keep it in fairly good taste. When you look at ["8:30 P.M."] there's nothing particularly horrible about it. It's a little germ wandering around. And the fact that the germ gets killed, nobody's going to lie awake at night thinking about it."

Nostrand pointed out the influence of movie directors on the artists. "Powell was a great fan of Hitchcock's, same way that Eisner was. You look at an old Hitchcock movie...the first thing you do is set the scene. This is what I tried to do in a lot of these things. You set a mood for the whole thing. With about the first three shots, you set the mood, and then you go from there." He went on to say that the splash-panel title lettering was influenced by Eisner's *Spirit*. "Eisner used to get his titles in the opening panel there...the [overall] treatment is strictly Eisner. But then again, the background and all that is EC." As for the coloring's crimson palette, Nostrand explained, "It's supposed to be on the inside of a body, and so everything is kind of reddish...the only thing that isn't red is this foreign body."

Page 270. "Valley of Horror" (*Web of Evil* 8, November 1953) Art by Jack Cole

Artist Alex Kotzky, who helped Cole package two issues of the infamous 1947 *True Crime Comics*, told interviewer Jim Amash that he was in awe of Cole's speed and accuracy with a brush. "Jack worked very roughly. He did a lot of the drawing with the brush. The sketches were just there with all the essential action on the page. As far as the details that you would normally put in with the pencil, he just did it with the brush. He used a very small brush...a number one or two...that smaller brush gave him the opportunity to put in more detail over rough penciling. I was always amazed at the

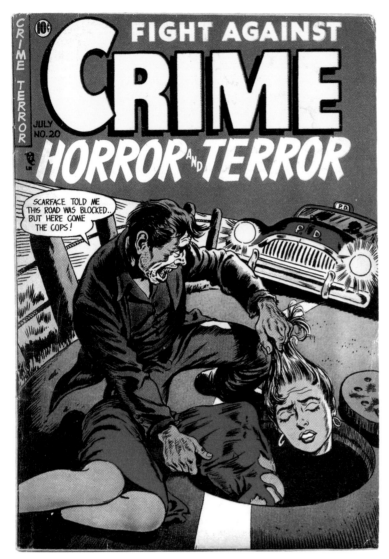

10¢
FIGHT AGAINST
CRIME
CRIME TERROR
JULY
NO.20
HORROR AND TERROR
SCARFACE TOLD ME THIS ROAD WAS BLOCKED.. BUT HERE COME THE COPS!
P.D.

Fight Against Crime no.20 (July 1954), cover attributed to Dick Beck. Most crime books incorporated horror at some point, including this notorious title from publisher Bill Friedman often cited for its classic extreme violence. Imagine your mom catching you with *this* one.

spontaneity Jack had with his brushwork. If he had done it any other way, he might have lost that quality. The last time I saw Jack was about 1954 or '55 at the Illustrators Club in New York. Just by chance he happened to show up to one of the meetings there. He had trimmed down, because he had quite a waistline. He looked great. The same old Jack. Cheerful, talkative. I couldn't imagine why he would kill himself a few years later."

Although possibly coincidental, this story is very reminiscent of Dashiell Hammett's novelette, *Nightmare Town*. There's nothing supernatural in Hammett's tale, but it has an equally nightmarish quality, with an innocent man and woman trapped in a purely evil town and a final scene of the two being chased by a crowd and barely making an escape by car. The thuggish, overweight, balding Devil's envoy here would be right at home in Hammett's tale, too, which is about a town in which the entire population is in on a series of crooked schemes.

For more on Jack Cole, see *Forms Stretched to their Limits: Jack Cole and Plastic Man* by Art Spiegelman and Chip Kidd (Chronicle Books).

Page 276. "The Slithering Horror of Skontong Swamp" (*This Magazine is Haunted* 5, June 1952) Art by George Evans

As with Crandall's "The Corpse That Came to Dinner," it's interesting to compare Evans' layouts with his later text-heavy horror work for EC. While this story also utilizes descriptive text boxes, Evans keeps them out of the picture area whenever possible, making them substantially less intrusive. And the expansive full-page spread on page nine would have been impossible at EC, where artists had to conform to Feldstein's and Kurtzman's layouts. Equally expansive is the story's eleven-page length, a fairly common occurrence at Fawcett but something unthinkable at EC, with its self-imposed eight-page limit.

Page 287. "Evil Intruder" (*Journey into Fear* 12, March 1953) Art by Iger studio

What better way to end a 1950s horror collection than with the slobbering impotent love-starved homicidal "It"? And this time in an Iger/Roche story, only the *innocent* get killed.

Most comic book companies had folded by 1956, due to the rise of television and the 1954 establishment of the Comics Code Authority, which in no uncertain terms abolished horror themes. The industry lost most of its relevancy until the superhero resurgence of the 1960s. Horror was left to fend for itself in other media – which of course it still does, with continued great success. G.S. (*and J.B. where noted*)

References: Alter Ego (www.twomorrows.com) vol. 3, nos. 34, 41, 61, 62, 79, 89; *The Comic Book in America: An Illustrated History* by Mike Benton (Taylor Publishing); *The Comics Journal* (www.tcj.com), various issues; *Confessions, Romances, Secrets, and Temptations: Archer St. John and the St. John Romance Comics* by John Benson; Heritage Auctions website (www.ha.com); *Graphic Story Magazine* nos.14 and 15; *The Iger Comics Kingdom* by Jay Disbrow; Lambiek Comiclopedia (www.lambiek.com); Mark Evanier's POVonline (www.povonline.com). Thanks to Jim Amash, John Benson, Bill Spicer, Pete Serniuk, Bhob Stewart, Michael Vance, Dick Voll, and Paul Wardle for the use of quotes from their interviews with comic book veterans.

Cover Section Key

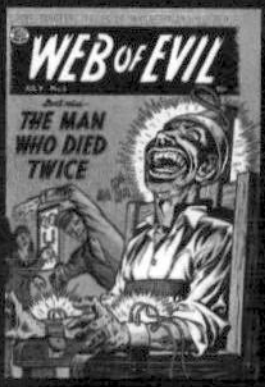
WEB OF EVIL
THE MAN WHO DIED TWICE

***Web of Evil* 5, Oct-Nov 1952**
Jack Cole
Cole finished his comic book career at Quality's single horror title, doing four covers and over two dozen stories, a fitting conclusion to the pioneering work of this manic, over-the-top master.

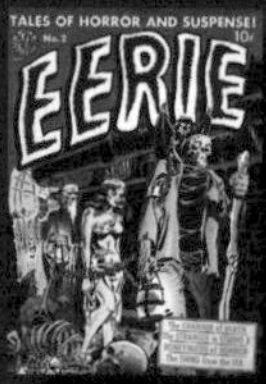
TALES OF HORROR AND SUSPENSE!
EERIE

***Eerie* 2, Aug-Sep 1951**
Wallace Wood
This is the first of Wood's three covers for Avon's *Eerie*, and the only one he signed. Unlike his better-known EC covers for editor Al Feldstein, in which block logos take up more than a third of the cover area, here Wood is allowed to work full canvas.

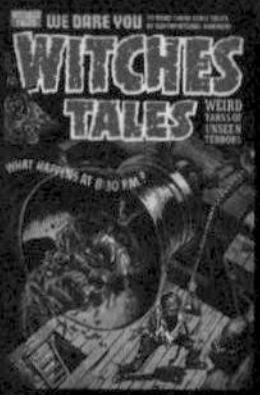
WE DARE YOU
WITCHES TALES

***Witches Tales* 25, June 1954**
Warren Kremer
Harvey art editor Howard Kremer gave cover artist Lee Elias a thumbnail sketch of this cover to work from, but the Harvey front office wasn't pleased with the result, and Kremer did the final version himself.

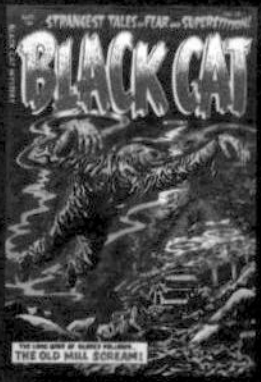
BLACK CAT

***Black Cat Mystery* 51, Aug 1954**
Lee Elias
Like many of Elias' Harvey covers, this one originated from a sketch by Warren Kremer. Editor Sid Jacobson noted, "Elias was not an idea man in terms of covers. He followed what we told him to do."

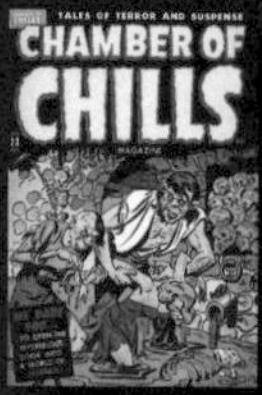
TALES OF TERROR AND SUSPENSE
CHAMBER OF CHILLS

***Chamber of Chills* 3, Oct 1951**
Al Avison
Along with Elias, Avison was one of Harvey's two primary cover artists during their horror period. Before joining the company in the late 1940s, Avison did a great deal of Timely superhero work. He left the field in mid-1954.

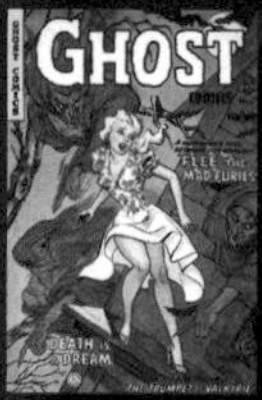
GHOST

***Ghost Comics* 4, Fall 1952**
Maurice Whitman
Pulp magazine publisher Fiction House entered comic books with its 1939 debut of *Jungle Comics*, an Eisner & Iger package. Their covers retained the more upscale printing process of pulp covers.

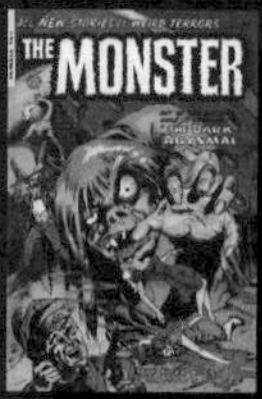
THE MONSTER

***The Monster* 2, 1953**
Maurice Whitman
The most striking Fiction House horror covers were by artist Maurice Whitman, who began at the Chesler and Iger shops in the early 1940s. He continued to work in comics for another four decades, including a stint at Wallace Wood's studio.

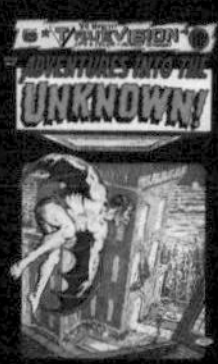
ADVENTURES INTO THE UNKNOWN!

***Adventures into the Unknown* 53, March 1953**
Harry Lazarus
This is the third issue of *Adventures into the Unknown* that featured *Truevision*, a simulated 3-D process. ACG regular Harry Lazarus became something of a specialist in the "deep dish" covers and stories.

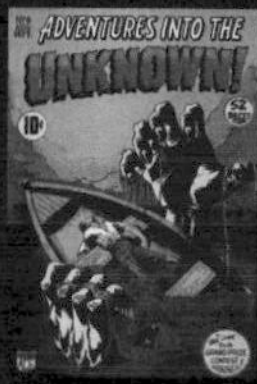
ADVENTURES INTO THE UNKNOWN!

***Adventures into the Unknown* 6, Aug-Sep 1948**
Edvard Moritz
Moritz started c. 1942 on superhero titles for Ned Pines' Better Publications. He did the first eleven covers of this seminal horror title before being replaced by Ogden Whitney, a competent artist who lacked Moritz's gift for drama and staging.

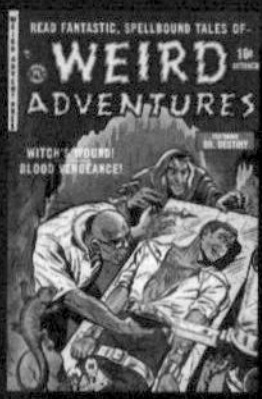
WEIRD ADVENTURES

***Weird Adventures* 3, Oct 1951**
Ernie Bache and Harry Harrison
Exciting graphics punched up by vivid saturated color schemes are hallmarks of this title's three covers. You'll find a tiny "HH" sneaked in at center-left bottom, to the left of the vacuum tubes.

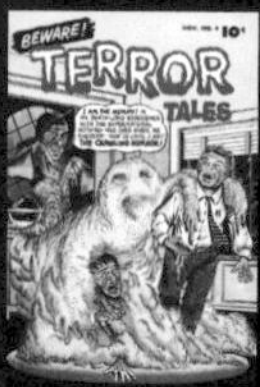
BEWARE!
TERROR
TALES

***Beware Terror Tales* 4, Nov 1952**
Bernard Baily
Baily had been in comic books from the very beginning, hired by the Eisner & Iger shop in 1936. He achieved some notoriety in 1940 as co-creator (with Jerry Siegel) of DC's creepy superhero The Spectre, then started his own shop in the early 1940s.

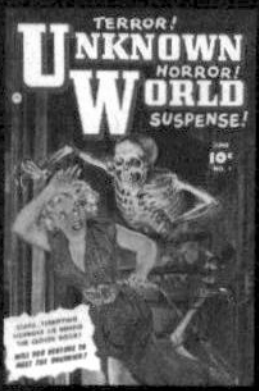
TERROR!
UNKNOWN
HORROR!
WORLD
SUSPENSE!

***Unknown World* 1, June 1952**
Norman Saunders
Saunders began illustrating for Minneapolis publisher William Fawcett c. 1927, then followed him to New York in 1934. After studying with Howard Pyle protégé Harvey Dunn, Saunders produced hundreds of cover paintings for pulps, magazines, paperbacks, and comics.

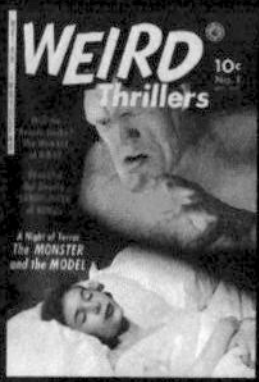
WEIRD
Thrillers

***Weird Thrillers* 1, Sep-Oct 1951**
Photo Cover
Photo covers were fairly common on Western, romance, and crime titles, but aside from this bizarre Ziff-Davis offering, non-existent on superhero and horror books.

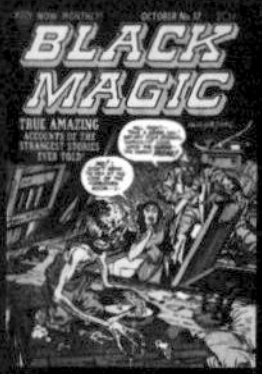
BLACK MAGIC

***Black Magic* 17, Oct 1952**
Jack Kirby and Joe Simon
Published by Crestwood, Prize Publications' Simon-and-Kirby offshoot, this popular title lasted well into the post-Code era, ending just on the eve of the superhero resurgence in 1961.

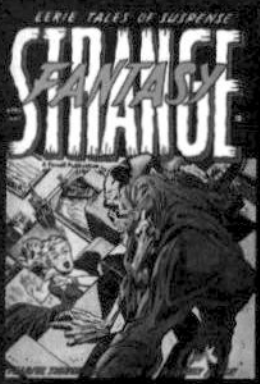
EERIE TALES OF SUSPENSE
STRANGE
FANTASY

***Strange Fantasy* 11, April-May 1953**
Iger Studio
One of the more unusual Iger covers due to its combined bird's-eye and rear-end views – though a blonde with her mouth agape is a typical Iger cover device.

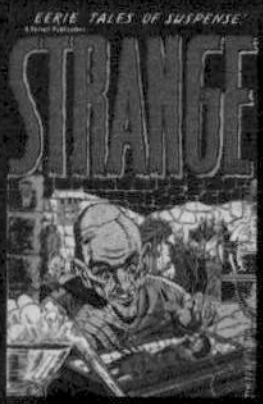
EERIE TALES OF SUSPENSE
STRANGE

***Strange Fantasy* 2 (1), Aug 1952**
Iger Studio
Despite its indication as no. 2 in the indicia, this is the premiere issue of Ajax/Farrell's *Strange Fantasy*. The shrunken-female motif was repeated on several Iger horror covers.

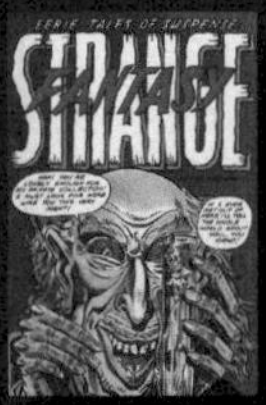
STRANGE

***Strange Fantasy* 9, Dec 1953**
IGER STUDIO
Another reduced-female Iger cover, this time given word balloons. "Big head" covers were prevalent at the time; publisher Comic Media cover artist Don Heck (*Horrific, Weird Terror*) churned them out almost exclusively.

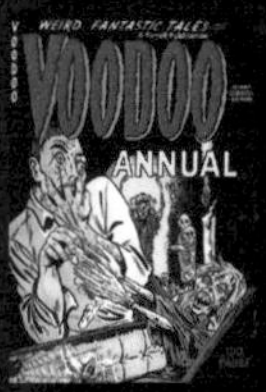
VOODOO
ANNUAL

***Voodoo Annual*, 1952**
IGER STUDIO
Annuals were created by combining four issues of newsstand-returned books into a 25-cent 100-page package. This was Ajax/Farrell's only horror annual.

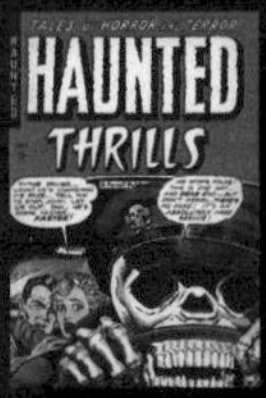
HAUNTED
THRILLS

***Haunted Thrills* 13, July 1954**
IGER STUDIO
If one could own just one Iger book, this might be it. Apart from this classic cover, you'll find "Experiment in Terror" (reprinted in this volume) and "Death Do Us Part," a tale of consensual human-baboon love that just missed the cut.

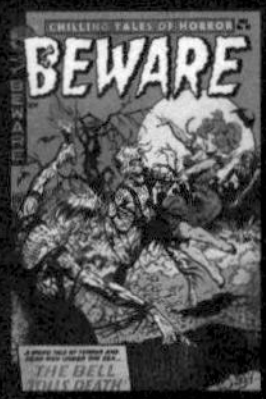
BEWARE

***Beware* 10, July 1954**
FRANK FRAZETTA AND SID CHECK
Check roughed out the drawing, then left Frazetta to his own devices, enough so for Frank to place his signature on top. That gravity-defying female could have come from no other artist.

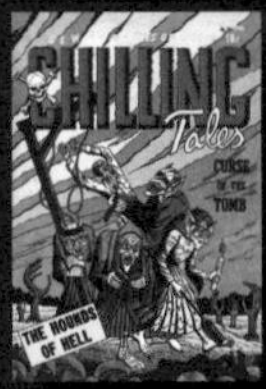
CHILLING
Tales

***Chilling Tales* 15, April 1953**
MATT FOX
This is the second of three *Chilling Tales* covers from the pulp (*Weird Tales*) cover specialist. Fox's body of comics work also includes 40 known stories (23 as inker), all but one for Atlas and Marvel, and a single Atlas cover.

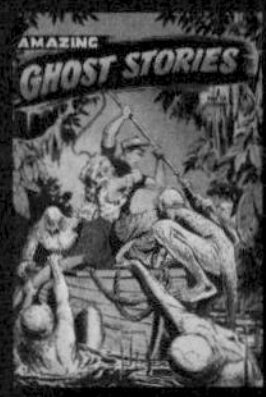
AMAZING
GHOST STORIES

***Amazing Ghost Stories* 14, Oct 1954**
MATT BAKER
Though he had worked in all genres, by the 1950s Matt Baker was a romance specialist, capitalizing on his considerable deftness in drawing the female anatomy. This is apparently his only horror cover.

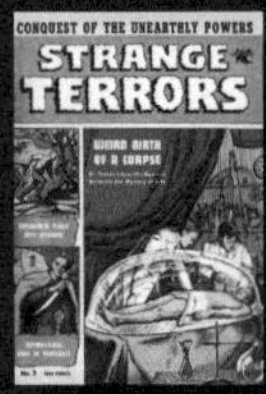
STRANGE
TERRORS

***Strange Terrors* 2, July 1952**
GEORGE MEYERRIECKS
Publisher Archer St. John wasn't afraid to take chances, and this is reflected by some of his company's highly unusual cover art. This is one of three St. John covers by the prolific book illustrator Meyerriecks.

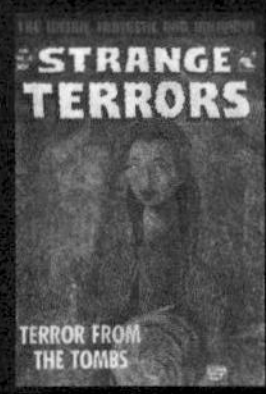
STRANGE
TERRORS
TERROR FROM
THE TOMBS

***Strange Terrors* 4, Sep 1952**
WILLIAM EKGREN
Historian Ken Quattro: "Ekgren was displaying in the Greenwich Village artists' market when four people (including Archer St. John) approached him and asked if he would sell them three of his paintings to use as covers for comic books." *(continued in next entry)*

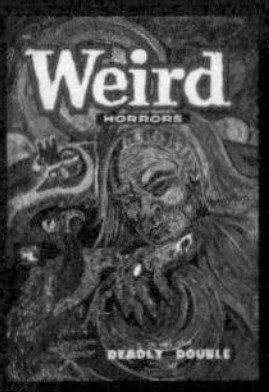
Weird

***Weird Horrors* 7, June 1953**
WILLIAM EKGREN
(*cont.*) "The next week they returned with his paintings, but they didn't want their money back. They gave the art back so it could be re-sold. So somewhere out there, the three paintings hang in art collections." As of this writing (August 2016), Ekgren, now 98, lives and paints in Stockholm.

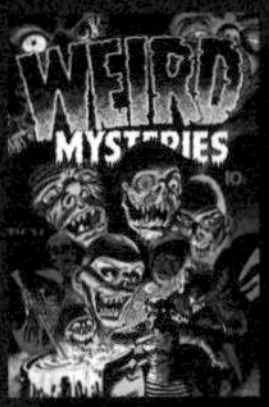
WEIRD
MYSTERIES

***Weird Mysteries* 2, Dec 1952**
BERNARD BAILY
One of Baily's most effective covers, for publisher Stanley Morse's imprint Gillmor. By this time Baily was exclusively a cover artist, but he also packaged and edited a few titles.

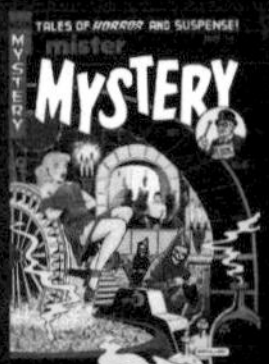
MYSTERY

***Mister Mystery* 6, July 1952**
TONY MORTELLARO
Mortellaro got started in the early 1950s at Trojan and some of the Stanley Morse titles, then joined Timely and remained there through its Atlas and Marvel incarnations, into the 1970s.

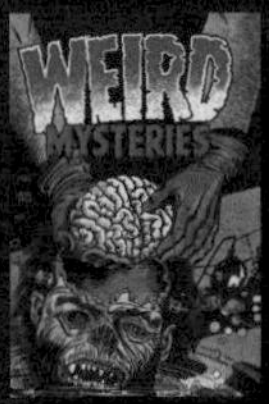
WEIRD
MYSTERIES

***Weird Mysteries* 5, June 1953**
BERNARD BAILY
When you're a kid cruising the comics stands, nothing quite says "buy me" like an exposed brain. Baily usually signed his covers, but he may have had qualms about being traced back to this one.

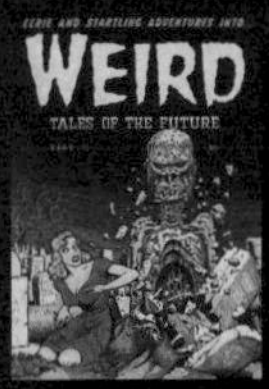
WEIRD

***Weird Tales of the Future* 3, Sep 1952**
BASIL WOLVERTON
Wolverton was assigned only a handful of covers during his comics career. Stanley Morse published Wolverton's final non-humorous comics, including this cover, his second to last.

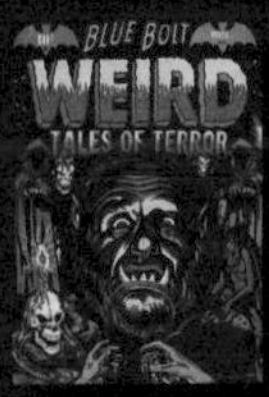
BLUE BOLT
WEIRD
TALES OF TERROR

***Blue Bolt Weird Tales of Terror* 111, Nov 1951**
L.B. COLE
In 1949, Cole established Star Publications with partner Jerry Kramer by buying the Novelty catalog from magazine powerhouse Curtis Publishing. Star produced a number of titles over the next six years, sporting new Cole covers but primarily containing Novelty unused inventory and reprints.

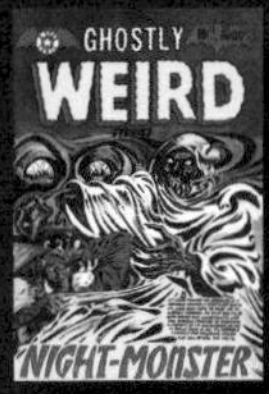
GHOSTLY
WEIRD
NIGHT-MONSTER

***Ghostly Weird Stories* 120, Sep 1953**
L.B. COLE
With Star Publications titles, the interior seemed almost irrelevant – and it often was. What sold these books were the poster-like covers of L.B. Cole, who claimed he did over 1500 throughout his career, then re-created many of them for collectors in the 1980s.

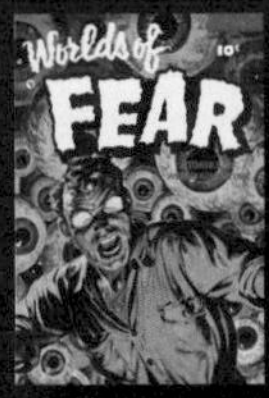
Worlds of
FEAR

***Worlds of Fear* 10, June 1953**
NORMAN SAUNDERS
We end with another Fawcett classic by the king of painted covers. 2009 saw the publication of *Norman Saunders*, an essential 368-page profusely illustrated *catalogue raisonné* written by his son David.

The Pre-Code Horror Comics

The term "horror comic" is somewhat elastic, but this list is generally exclusive rather than inclusive. It does not include the many science fiction, crime and jungle comics with horror overtones, or comics of other genres that had an occasional horror story or horror–themed cover. The continuing non–humor issues of Prize's *Frankenstein* are included, but *Classics Illustrated*'s adaptation of the Mary Shelley novel and of other horror literature are not (on the grounds that their primary appeal was in being able to write a book report without actually reading the original). A tough-to-call borderline title is Trojan's *Crime Mysteries* which had horror themes on most covers, but any supernatural elements in the stories were generally explained away. Several Atlas titles gradually drifted in and out of the horror genre, and it is a matter of judgement which issues are true horror comics. Lastly, even the number of companies publishing comics is open to question, since some individual publishers used different company names. Listed below are 1,371 pre-Code issues, representing 110 titles from 30 companies. Issues approved by the Comics Code Authority (CCA) are shown in brackets but not included in the totals or date-ranges.   J.B.

ACE 97 issues
Baffling Mysteries 5 to 24 (Nov. 1951 – Jan. 1955) [25, 26 approved by CCA]
The Beyond 1 to 30 (Nov. 1950 – Jan. 1955)
Challenge of the Unknown 6 (Sep. 1950)
Hand of Fate 8 to 25, 25 (Dec. 1951 – Mar. 1955)
Web of Mystery 1 to 27 (Feb. 1951 – Nov. 1954) [28, 29 approved by CCA]

AMERICAN COMICS GROUP 119 issues
Adventures into the Unknown 1 to 61 (Fall 1948 – Jan.–Feb. 1955) [62 to 174 approved by CCA]
The Clutching Hand 1 (July – Aug. 1954)
Forbidden Worlds 1 to 34 (July–Aug. 1951 – Oct.–Nov. 1954) [35 to 145 approved by CCA]
Out of the Night 1 to 17 (Feb.–Mar. 1952 – Oct.–Nov. 1954)
Skeleton Hand 1 to 6 (Sep.–Oct. 1952 – July–Aug. 1953)

AJAX–FARRELL 62 issues
Fantastic Fears 7, 8, 3 to 9 (May 1953 – Sep.–Oct. 1954)
Fantastic 10, 11 (Nov.–Dec. 1954 – Jan.–Feb. 1955)
Haunted Thrills 1 to 18 (June 1952 – Nov.–Dec. 1954)
Strange Fantasy 2 (1), 2 to 14 (Aug. 1952 – Oct.–Nov. 1954)
Voodoo 1 to 18 (May 1952–Nov. – Dec. 1954) [19 features *Seven Seas* reprints and other non–horror fare]
Voodoo Annual 1 (1952)

ATLAS 389 issues
Adventures into Terror 43, 44, 3 to 31 (Nov. 1950 – May 1954)
Adventures into Weird Worlds 1 to 30 (Jan. 1952 – June 1954)
Amazing Detective Cases 11 to 14 (Mar. 1952 – Sep. 1952) [1 to 10 feature crime stories]
Amazing Mysteries 32, 33 (May 1949 – July 1949) [34, 35 feature crime stories]
Astonishing 6 to 37 (Oct. 1951 – Feb. 1955) [3 to 5 feature Marvel Boy; 6, listed here, has a straight horror cover with

Marvel Boy still in the stories; 38 to 63 approved by CCA]
Captain America's Weird Tales 74, 75 (Oct. 1949 – Feb. 1950)
Journey into Mystery 1 to 22 (June 1952 – Feb. 1955) [23 to 125 approved by CCA]
Journey into Unknown Worlds 4 to 33 (Apr. 1951 – Feb. 1955) [1 to 3 feature s–f stories; 34 to 59 approved by CCA]
Marvel Tales 93 to 131 (Aug. 1949 – Feb. 1955) [132 to 159 approved by CCA]
Menace 1 to 11 (Mar. 1953 – May 1954)
Men's Adventures 21 to 26 (May 1953 – Mar. 1954) [1 to 20 feature war and adventure stories; 21 to 26 feature horror with adventure overtones; 27, 28 feature The Human Torch]
Mystery Tales 1 to 26 (Mar. 1952 – Feb. 1955) [27 to 54 approved by CCA]
Mystic 1 to 36 (Mar. 1951 – Mar. 1955) [37 to 61 approved by CCA]
Spellbound 1 to 23 (Mar. 1952 – June 1954) [24 to 34 approved by CCA]
Strange Tales 1 to 34 (June 1951 – Feb. 1955) [35 to 188 approved by CCA]
Suspense 3 to 29 (May 1950 – Apr. 1953) [1, 2 feature mystery–adventure stories; the title gradually morphed into a horror comic; the line "based on CBS radio television series" was carried on the cover through issue 11.]
Uncanny Tales 1 to 28 (June 1952 – Jan. 1955) [29 to 56 approved by CCA]
Venus 14 to 19 (June 1951 – Apr. 1952) [early issues feature romantic fantasy; with issue 10 the title becomes increasingly adventure with horror overtones; the last six (listed here) feature horror stories and the final three also have pure horror covers]

AVON 30 issues
City of the Living Dead (1952)
The Dead Who Walk (1952)
Diary of Horror 1 (Dec. 1952)
Eerie Comics 1 (Jan. 1947)
Eerie 1 to 17 (May 1951 – Aug.–Sep. 1954)
Night of Mystery (1953)
Phantom Witch Doctor 1 (1952)
Secret Diary of Eerie Adventures (1953)
Witchcraft 1 to 6 (Mar. 1952–Mar. 1953)

CHARLTON 32 issues
Strange Suspense Stories 16 to 22 (Jan.–Feb. 1954 – Nov. 1954 [23 to 26 do not exist; 27 to 77 approved by CCA]
The Thing 1 to 17 (Feb. 1952 – Nov. 1954)
This is Suspense 23 (Feb. 1955) [24 to 26 approved by CCA]
This Magazine Is Haunted 15 to 21 (Mar. 1954 – Nov. 1954)

COMIC MEDIA 27 issues
Horrific 1 to 13 (Sep. 1952 – Sep. 1954)
Terrific 14 (Dec. 1954)
Weird Terror 1 to 13 (Sep. 1952 – Sep. 1954)

DS/PL 3 issues
Weird Adventures 1 to 3 (May–June 1951 – Sep.–Oct. 1951)

EC 91 issues
Crypt of Terror 17 to 19 (Apr.–May 1950 – Aug.–Sep. 1950)
Haunt of Fear 15 to 17, 4 to 28 (May–June 1950 –
   Nov.–Dec. 1954)
Tales from the Crypt 20 to 46 (Oct.–Nov. 1950 –
   Feb.–Mar. 1955)
Tales of Terror Annual 1 to 3 (1951 – 1953)
Three–Dimensional Tales from the Crypt of Terror
   3–D no. 2 (Spring 1954)
Vault of Horror 12 to 40 (Apr.–May 1950 –
   Dec. 1954–Jan. 1955)

FAWCETT 42 issues
Beware Terror Tales 1 to 8 (May 1952 – July 1953)
Strange Stories from Another World 2 to 5 (Aug. 1952 – Feb. 1953)
Strange Suspense Stories 1 to 5 (June 1952 – Feb. 1953)
This Magazine Is Haunted 1 to 14 (Oct. 1951 – Dec. 1953)
Unknown World 1 (June 1952)
Worlds Beyond 1 (Nov. 1951)
Worlds of Fear 2 to 10 (Jan. 1952 – June 1953)

FICTION HOUSE 13 issues
Ghost Comics 1 to 11 (1951 – 1954)
The Monster 1, 2 (1953)

FOX 1 issue
A Star Presentation 3 (*Dr. Jekyll and Mr. Hyde*) (May 1950)

GILLMOR 12 issues
Weird Mysteries 1 to 12 (Oct. 1952 – Sep. 1954)

HARVEY 96 issues
Black Cat Mystery 30 to 53 (Aug. 1951 – Dec. 1954)
Chamber of Chills 21 to 24, 5 to 26 (June 1951 – Dec. 1954)
Thrills of Tomorrow 17, 18 (Oct. 1954 – Dec. 1954)
Tomb of Terror 1 to 16 (June 1952 – July 1954)
Witches Tales 1 to 28 (Jan. 1951 – Dec. 1954)

HILLMAN 1 issue
Monster Crime Comics 1 (Oct. 1952)

KEY 3 issues
Weird Chills 1 to 3 (July 1954 – Nov. 1954)

MASTER 22 issues
Dark Mysteries 1 to 22 (June 1951 – Mar. 1955) [23, 24
   approved by CCA]

PREMIER 2 issues
Horror from the Tomb 1 (Sep. 1954)
Mysterious Stories 2 (Dec. 1954) [3 to 7 approved by CCA]

PRIZE 53 issues
Black Magic 1 to 33 (Oct.–Nov. 1950 – Nov.–Dec. 1954)
   [34 to 50 approved by CCA]
Frankenstein 18 to 33 (Mar. 1952 – Oct.–Nov. 1954)
   [1 to 17 feature humorous stories about the monster]
Strange World of Your Dreams 1 to 4 (Aug. 1952 – Jan.–Feb. 1953)

QUALITY 22 issues
Intrigue 1 (Jan. 1955)
Web of Evil 1 to 21 (Nov. 1952 – Dec. 1954)

STANDARD 31 issues
Adventures into Darkness 5 to 14 (Aug. 1952 – June 1954)
Out of the Shadows 5 to 14 (July 1952 – Aug. 1954)
The Unseen 5 to 15 (1952 – July 1954)

STANLEY MORSE 27 issues
Mister Mystery 1 to 19 (Sep. 1951 – Oct. 1954)
Weird Tales of the Future 1 to 8 (Mar. 1952 – July 1953)

STAR 36 issues
Blue Bolt Weird Tales 111 to 119 (Nov. 1951 – May–June
   1953)
Ghostly Weird Stories 120 to 124 (Sep. 1953 – Sep. 1954)
Spook 22 to 30 (Jan. 1953 – Oct. 1954)
Startling Terror Tales 10 to 14, 4 to 11 (May 1952 – Nov. 1954)

STERLING 2 issues
The Tormented 1, 2 (July 1954 – Sep. 1954)

STORY 36 issues
Fight Against Crime 9 to 21 (Sep. 1952 – Sep. 1954) [1 to 8
   feature crime stories]
Mysterious Adventures 1 to 23 (Mar. 1951 – Dec. 1954)
   [24, 25 approved by CCA]

ST. JOHN 25 issues
Amazing Ghost Stories 14 to 16 (Oct. 1954 – Feb. 1955)
House of Terror 1 (Oct. 1953)
Nightmare 3, 10 to 13 (Oct. 1953 – Aug. 1954)
Strange Terrors 1 to 7 (June 1952 – Mar. 1953)
Weird Horrors 1 to 9 (June 1952 – Oct. 1953)

SUPERIOR 53 issues
Journey into Fear 1 to 21 (May 1951 – Sep. 1954)
Mysteries (Weird and Strange) 1 to 11 (May 1953 – Jan. 1955)
Strange Mysteries 1 to 21 (Sep. 1951 – Jan. 1955)

TOBY 14 issues
Tales of Horror 1 to 13 (June 1952 – Oct. 1954)
Tales of Terror 1 (1952)

YOUTHFUL/TROJAN 22 issues
Beware 10 to 16, 5 to 14 (June 1952 – Mar. 1955)
   [15 approved by CCA]
Chilling Tales 13 to 17 (Dec. 1952 – Oct. 1953)

ZIFF–DAVIS 8 issues
Eerie Adventures 1 (Winter 1951)
Nightmare 1, 2 (Summer 1952 – Fall 1952)
Weird Thrillers 1 to 5 (Sep. 1951 – Oct.–Nov. 1952)

[Checklist compiled by John Benson]

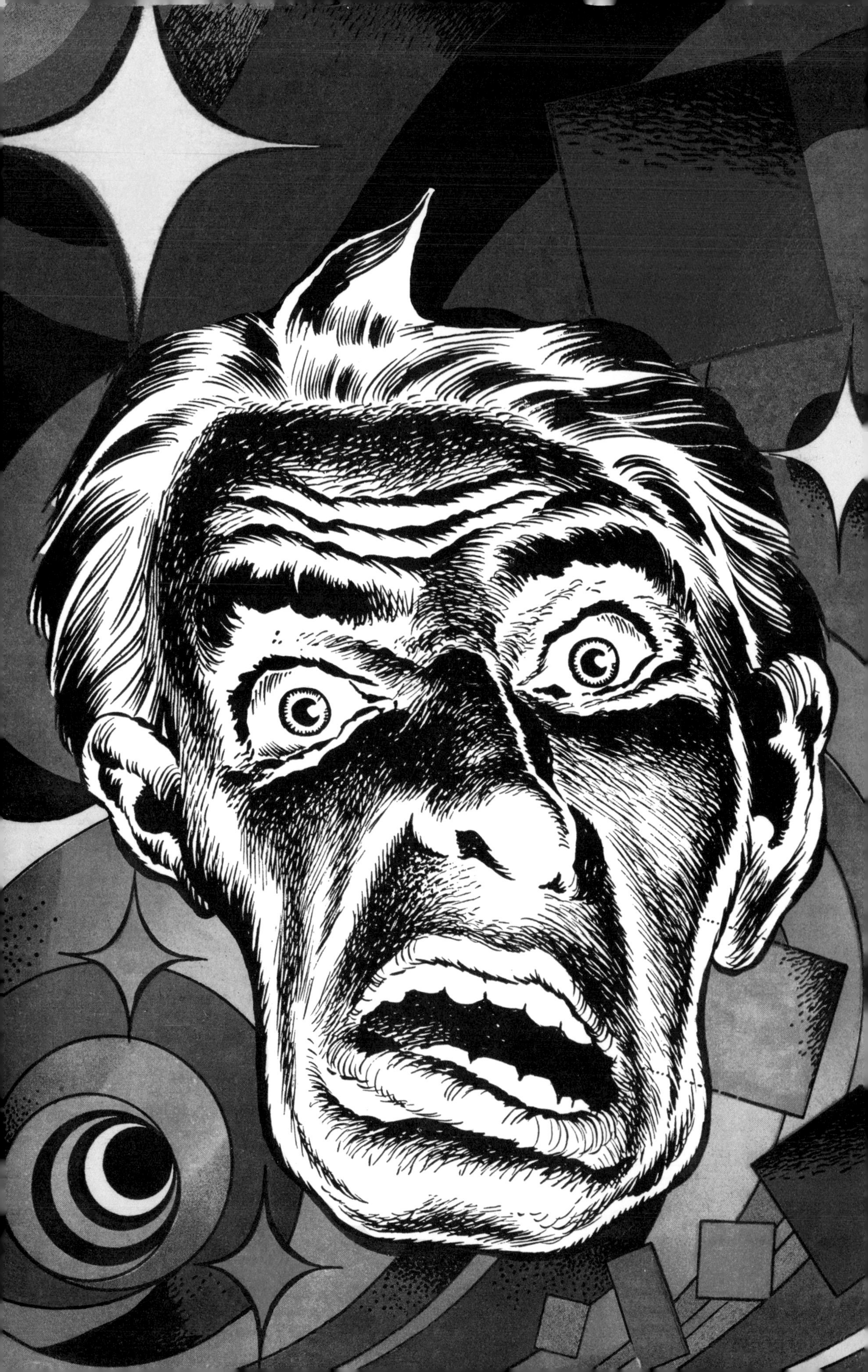